Criminal Justice in Europe

Criminal Justice in Europe
A Comparative Study

Edited by
PHIL FENNELL
CHRISTOPHER HARDING
NICO JÖRG
BERT SWART

CLARENDON PRESS · OXFORD

*This book has been printed digitally and produced in a standard specification
in order to ensure its continuing availability*

OXFORD
UNIVERSITY PRESS

Great Clarendon Street, Oxford OX2 6DP

Oxford University Press is a department of the University of Oxford.
It furthers the University's objective of excellence in research, scholarship,
and education by publishing worldwide in

Oxford New York

Auckland Bangkok Buenos Aires Cape Town Chennai
Dar es Salaam Delhi Hong Kong Istanbul Karachi Kolkata
Kuala Lumpur Madrid Melbourne Mexico City Mumbai Nairobi
São Paulo Shanghai Singapore Taipei Tokyo Toronto

with an associated company in Berlin

Oxford is a registered trade mark of Oxford University Press
in the UK and in certain other countries

Published in the United States
by Oxford University Press Inc., New York

ISBN 0-19-825807-0

To our colleague

Jane Morgan

who will be sadly missed

Acknowledgements

The editors of this book gratefully acknowledge the financial support of the Society of Public Teachers of Law, which assisted in the organization of meetings between co-authors of the papers collected here.

Contents

CONTRIBUTORS   ix

Introduction   xv
Phil Fennell, Bert Swart, Nico Jörg, and
Christopher Harding

1. Criminal Justice in the Netherlands   1
   Constantijn Kelk

2. The Evolution of Criminal Justice Policy in the UK   21
   Gavin Dingwall and Alan Davenport

3. Are Inquisitorial and Adversarial Systems Converging?   41
   Nico Jörg, Stewart Field, and Chrisje Brants

4. The European Convention on Human Rights and Criminal
   Justice in the Netherlands and the UK   57
   Bert Swart and James Young

5. Intergovernmental Co-operation in the Field of Criminal
   Law   87
   Christopher Harding and Bert Swart

6. The European Community and Criminal Law   107
   René Guldenmund, Christopher Harding, and Ann Sherlock

7. Discretion and Accountability in Prosecution: A
   Comparative Perspective on Keeping Crime out of Court   127
   Chrisje Brants and Stewart Field

8. Managing the Drug Problem: Tolerance or Prohibition?   149
   Jos Silvis and Katherine S. Williams

9. Diversion, Europeanization and the Mentally Disordered
   Offender   171
   Phil Fennell and Frans Koenraadt

10. Diversion in English and Dutch Juvenile Justice   199
    Loraine Gelsthorpe, Mike Nellis, Jeannette Bruins, and
    Annelies van Vliet

Contents

11. Prosecutors, Examining Judges, and Control of Police Investigations 227
    Stewart Field, Peter Alldridge, and Nico Jörg

12. Police Detention in the UK and in the Netherlands 251
    Alan Davenport and Peter Baauw

13. DNA Profiling and the Use of Expert Scientific Witnesses in Criminal Proceedings 265
    Peter Alldridge, Sanneke Berkhout-van Poelgeest, and Katherine S. Williams

14. Witness Evidence, Article 6 of the European Convention on Human Rights and the Principle of Open Justice 283
    Annemarieke Beijer, Cathy Cobley, and André Klip

15. Protection of and Compensation for Victims of Crime 301
    Jane Morgan, Frans Willem Winkel, and Katherine S. Williams

16. Sentencing Practice, Policy, and Discretion 319
    Constantijn Kelk, Laurence Koffman, and Jos Silvis

17. Prisoners' Rights in the Netherlands and England and Wales 341
    Gillian Douglas and Martin Moerings

18. The Transfer of Prisoners with Special Reference to the Netherlands and the UK 363
    Désirée Paridaens and Christopher Harding

19. Conclusion: Europeanization and Convergence: The Lessons of Comparative Study 379
    Christopher Harding, Bert Swart, Nico Jörg, and Phil Fennell

    GLOSSARY OF DUTCH TERMS 387

    Index 389

Contributors

PETER ALLDRIDGE graduated from University College London (1978). He became a tutorial fellow (1979–80), then lecturer and senior lecturer in Cardiff Law School. He has given a dissertation on coercion and legal responsibility. He has done recent research on blackmail.

PETER BAAUW studied law at Utrecht University (1968); he became senior lecturer in criminal law and criminal procedure at Utrecht University; he gave a dissertation on pre-trial detention (1978). He is a part-time criminal lawyer in practice (1980–); part-time judge at Utrecht district court (1985–) and Amsterdam Court of Appeals (1992).

SANNEKE BERKHOUT-VAN POELGEEST studied law at Amsterdam University (1977); she was a law clerk at the Amsterdam district court (1977–1982) and a lecturer in criminal law and criminal procedure at Amsterdam University (1982–1988) and at Utrecht University since 1988. Her recent research subject is human rights and investigatory restrictions on suspects detained on remand.

ANNEMARIEKE BEIJER studied law at Utrecht University (1986); she has been research associate (1988–92), lecturer in criminal law and criminal procedure at Utrecht University since 1992. A recent research subject was the intimidation of witnesses.

CHRISJE BRANTS studied journalism (Utrecht, 1969), law, and criminology at Amsterdam University (1978–82); she became a research fellow in criminology on corporate crime (1982–4, University of Amsterdam), and has been lecturer in criminal law and criminal procedure at Utrecht University since 1984; her dissertation was on the social construction of fraud (Amsterdam, 1991).

JEANNETTE BRUINS studied law at Utrecht University (1980); she became a law clerk at the Dutch Supreme Court (1981–1985), then lecturer in criminal law and criminal procedure at Utrecht University from 1985. She has done recent research on criminal law for juveniles.

CATHY COBLEY studied law at University College, Cardiff (1988); a former police officer, she has been lecturer in Criminal Law, Contract Law and the Law of Evidence at Cardiff Law School since 1988. Her recent research subjects include: child abuse and children as witnesses in criminal trials.

ALAN DAVENPORT studied law at the University of Hull (1989); he became tutor in the Department of Law at the University of Wales, Aberystwyth

(1992) and is now lecturer in law at the University of Northumbria at Newcastle. His research work has been in the field of police powers and human rights in criminal procedure; he is a reporter for the European Human Rights Reports.

GAVIN DINGWALL studied law at the University of Warwick (1992), and since 1992 has been a tutor, then lecturer in law at the University of Wales, Aberystwyth. He is currently undertaking research on diversionary policies within the criminal justice system.

GILLIAN DOUGLAS studied law at Manchester University and comparative criminal law and procedure and criminology at the London School of Economics. She taught criminal law and criminology at the University of Bristol (1987–9) and criminal law at Cardiff, where she is now a senior lecturer. She has obtained a research fellowship from the Council of Europe to undertake a comparative study of methods of the Local Review Committee handling parole applications at HM Prison, Bristol.

PHIL FENNELL is a senior lecturer in law at Cardiff University. He was a founder member of the Mental Health Act Commission (1983–9), and is currently a member of the Law Society's Mental Health and Disability Committee. He has written articles and books on mental health law, mentally disordered offenders, and psychiatric patients' rights. His current research is on treatment of psychiatric patients without consent.

STEWART FIELD studied law at Oxford and Criminology at Cambridge. His doctoral thesis, on the history of the Factory Inspectorate, was researched while a student at the Centre for Socio-Legal Studies (1981–4). A lecturer at Cardiff Law School since 1984, his research interests are in criminal justice process, regulatory crime and criminal law.

LORAINE GELSTHORPE is lecturer in criminology at the Institute of Criminology, University of Cambridge. She has published widely on issues relating to juvenile justice, women and criminal justice, and, more recently, discrimination and criminal justice. She is currently working on discriminatory aspects of decision-making in magistrates' courts and on theoretical developments in criminology since 1973.

RENÉ GULDENMUND studied European and international law at the University of Utrecht; he has been lecturer in human rights (1985–1994) and research and teaching associate in economic criminal law (since 1985) at the University of Utrecht. He has published a reference book on the enforcement of Community law in the Dutch legal order (1992). Since 1994 he has worked with the Ministry of Agriculture and Fisheries.

CHRISTOPHER HARDING studied law at the Universities of Oxford and Exeter (1973); he is now a reader in law at the University of Wales, Aberystwyth. He is the author of a number of books and articles in the field of criminal justice, European law, penal theory, and penal history, and most recently of a study of investigations and sanctions in the European Community.

NICO JÖRG studied law at Groningen University (1969); he was lecturer and senior lecturer in criminal law and criminal procedure at Utrecht University (1969–93). He has written a dissertation on rights for the military (Utrecht, 1979). He was visiting scholar at Yale Law School (1983–4) and at Berkeley School of Law (1987). Since 1993 he has been a judge at the Arnhem Court of Appeals. His publications include a comparative study on the criminal liability of corporations and directors in the USA and the Netherlands (1990).

CONSTANTIJN KELK studied law at Amsterdam University (1968). He was lecturer in criminal law and criminal procedure at Utrecht University (1969–79). His dissertation was on prisoners' rights (1978). He received the Modderman Award from Leyden University (1980). He has written books on Dutch criminal law and on detention law. Since 1980 he has been professor of criminal law, criminal procedure, and detention law at Utrecht University. He is a part-time judge of the Amsterdam Court of Appeals, and president of the board of supervisors of an Amsterdam house of detention.

ANDRÉ KLIP graduated from Utrecht University in 1989. He received the Willem Pompe Institute's prize for a student thesis (1990). He has been research and teaching associate in international criminal law (since 1990). His dissertation on 'the witness abroad in criminal matters in the law of the United States, Germany, and the Netherlands' (was published in 1994). He conducted research at Yale Law School (1992).

FRANS KOENRAADT studied psychology (1979) at Tilburg and Amsterdam. He has been lecturer in forensic psychiatry and psychology at Utrecht University since 1980. He is a forensic psychologist at the Pieter Baan Centre for Forensic Psychiatry in Utrecht, serves as a forensic psychological expert in Dutch courts, has co-edited several books in the area of law and mental health, and conducted research on the application of coercion in psychiatric hospitals. His current research is on parricide and on the history of forensic psychiatry and psychology.

LAURENCE KOFFMAN studied law at Keele University (1974), and later studied and taught criminology at Keele. He has been lecturer in law at the University of Wales, Aberystwyth since 1976. His publications include books on sentencing, policing, and the law of contract. He specializes in criminal law and his most recent research project is a Mid-Wales crime survey.

MARTIN MOERINGS graduated in sociology in Tilburg (1970) and in law in Utrecht (1988). His dissertation was on the social consequences of imprisonment. He is senior lecturer in criminology, penology, and criminal law at Utrecht University and chairman of the board of supervisors of an Amsterdam prison.

JANE MORGAN studied history at the University College of Wales, Aberystwyth, and was awarded a doctorate by the University of Leicester. Before returning to Aberystwyth in 1989, she was a researcher at the University of Oxford Institute of Criminology and was honorary lecturer in the Department of Law at Aberystwyth from 1990 to 1992. Her major works include a study of police and labour disputes in Britain and more recently of the way in which the legal system deals with child victims of crime.

MIKE NELLIS is a lecturer in probation studies at the University of Birmingham. He has previously worked as a social worker with young offenders and undertook a Ph.D. on the historical development of intermediate treatment at the Institute of Criminology, Cambridge.

DÉSIRÉE PARIDAENS studied law at the University of Utrecht (1984). She became a research associate, and later lecturer in international criminal law and comparative criminal law at Utrecht University. Her dissertation was on the conditions governing the execution of foreign criminal judgments (1994). Since 1993 she has been a part-time official of the International Legal Aid Division, Ministry of Justice.

ANN SHERLOCK studied law at University College Dublin (1980–5). She joined the Department of Law, University College of Wales, in 1985 as tutor, and has been lecturer in the Department since 1987. Her main teaching and research interests lie in the areas of constitutional law and European Community law.

JOS SILVIS studied criminology and law (1979) at the Erasmus University of Rotterdam. He became research associate at the Erasmus University (1980), and has been lecturer in criminal law at the University of Utrecht since 1981. A recent research project was 'Human rights and drug use in Europe' (1993). Since 1994 he has been a judge at Rotterdam district court; he has several editorial positions, is a member of the 'Comité scientifique of the European Group for the Research of Normativity' (France, 1991).

BERT SWART studied law at Nijmegen University and at the University of Poitiers (France). His dissertation was on the admission and expulsion of aliens in Dutch law (1978). Other books include *Dutch Extradition Law* (1986). He became a research associate, then associate professor at the University of Amsterdam. Since 1980 he has been professor of criminal law and criminal procedure at the University of Utrecht.

ANNELIES VAN VLIET studied criminology and law (1979, 1982) at Leyden University. She became lecturer in criminal law and criminal procedure at the Free University, Amsterdam (1981–4), and has been at Utrecht

University since 1985. She is a part-time judge at Amsterdam district court (1990–). Her recent research project was the rights of juveniles in juvenile justice institutions.

KATHERINE WILLIAMS studied law at the University of Wales, Aberystwyth, and at Cambridge University, and taught law at the University of Liverpool until 1990; since then she has been a lecturer at the University of Wales, Aberystwyth. She has published in the fields of criminology, criminal justice, civil liberties, and women's studies, including a textbook on criminology and other work on police accountability.

FRANS WILLEM WINKEL studied law at the Erasmus University of Rotterdam (1973) and psychology at the University of Amsterdam (1978). His dissertation was on police and crime prevention; effects and side effects of persuasive communication (1987, Free University of Amsterdam). He has been a senior lecturer in applied social psychology at the Free University since 1978. He is a member of the executive committee of the Dutch Association for Victim Assistance (LOS). His major research interests are in law and psychology studies and police studies.

JAMES YOUNG studied law at undergraduate and postgraduate level at the University of Oxford and is a lecturer at Cardiff Law School. He writes on private international law, constitutional law, and human rights law. His recent and continuing work includes a study of the European Convention on Human Rights in the United Kingdom.

Introduction

PHIL FENNELL, BERT SWART, NICO JÖRG, AND
CHRISTOPHER HARDING

This book is the product of a six-year association between the Willem
Pompe Institute for Criminal Law and Criminology at the University of
Utrecht and the Law Schools of the University of Wales at Aberystwyth
and Cardiff. It contains a number of comparative studies on various aspects of criminal justice in the Netherlands and in England and Wales. The
central themes of the book are convergence and Europeanization.

One of the fascinating aspects of comparative studies is that we each
view the information that we have gained about the respective legal systems through the lens of our own legal culture. It is a salutary experience
to see systems and procedures which have become reified in our minds
from a perspective which finds it hard to believe that things could be done
this way. By studying a different legal system and having discussions with
persons brought up in it we may not only acquire a better understanding
of that system but, at the same time, also of our own. What seemed strange
in the other system may appear to be not so strange at all, while familiar
and self-evident characteristics of our own system may become less obvious or even questionable. Comparative studies may teach us a number of
things. For instance, we may become aware that, behind different ways of
doing things, often the same goal is being pursued. On the other hand,
they may show that similar practices are sometimes based on radically
different assumptions or pursue quite different goals. Or they may warn us
that answers to problems that have been found within one system will,
despite their attractiveness at first sight, not always work within the framework of a different system. In the final analysis we are confronted with
different societal norms and values that are at the basis of the respective
legal systems.

Comparative studies of the criminal justice systems of the Netherlands
and England and Wales are, in all these respects, especially rewarding. For
on the one hand, being neighbouring countries, they share many cultural
traditions and values and they face roughly the same social problems. On
the other hand there are differences that seem to be of major importance.
The Netherlands has an inquisitorial system of justice, while that of England and Wales is accusatorial. While criminal justice in the Netherlands
has a reputation for being mild and tolerant to the extent that one may
wonder whether its reputation is well-deserved or largely a myth, criminal

justice in England and Wales is reputed to be considerably more harsh and punitive. Hence many interesting questions arise. To what extent are the different solutions adopted to confront the same problems directly related to the one jurisdiction having an inquisitorial and the other having an adversarial system of justice? Are adversarial systems of justice like that of England and Wales confronted with problems that do not arise in inquisitorial systems like that of the Netherlands, and vice versa? Does the fact that both countries have so much in common and face the same kind of social problems promote a development of convergence between accusatorial and inquisitorial systems of justice? How far can an adversarial or an inquisitorial system change without losing the distinguishing features which mark it out as adversarial or inquisitorial? Could there be a relationship between the mildness or severity of a penal climate and an inquisitorial or accusatorial system of justice, or is the question absurd? These are but some of the comparative issues that crop up in the various contributions to this book.

Closely linked to the issue of convergence of adversarial and inquisitorial systems of justice is that of Europeanization, the second main theme of the book. Being parts of Europe both the Netherlands and England and Wales are subject to a process of Europeanization that has already made far more headway than would have appeared possible twenty, or even ten, years ago. It is, moreover, a process that is not only irreversible but, as many contributions to the book show, affects national systems of criminal justice more deeply and in more varied ways than is commonly realized. A vision of some distant future emerges in which some sort of European system of criminal justice will have been established. We are faced with a possible future that may seem attractive to some but provoke feelings of distrust or rejection from others. For, instinctively, we all have a feeling that our own criminal justice system, somehow, is superior to others and that its autonomy should be jealously guarded.

Whatever the future may bring, Member States of the Council of Europe and those of the European Union must ensure that their criminal justice systems operate in accordance with the requirements of what may be termed European law. First, on the basis of the European Convention on Human Rights a distinct European rule of law is emerging that affects both adversarial and inquisitorial systems to an ever increasing extent. Secondly, despite the perception in the 1960s and 1970s that criminal law would not be affected by the Treaty of Rome, European Community law also has had a considerable impact and that impact, too, increases in scope and depth. Two powerful courts, the European Court of Human Rights and the Court of Justice of the European Communities are there to ensure compliance. Finally, within the Council of Europe, within the framework of political co-operation envisaged by the Treaty on European Union, and within other forums, notably that of Schengen, international co-operation in criminal matters is being developed and intensified to a point where harmonization of criminal policies is contemplated, and a first European law enforcement agency, that of Europol, is being created. There is hardly any area of criminal justice left that has not, in some way or another and to a greater or lesser extent, been touched by Europeanization. This development is of crucial importance to comparative studies. At the present time comparative studies of criminal justice systems in Europe inevitably have to become comparative studies of how Europeanization affects these systems and in what ways they respond to it. Inevitably too, in its own way Europeanization contributes to a process of convergence of national systems of justice. The various contributions to this book explore the different dimensions of Europeanization from a comparative angle.

The first three chapters of this book are of an introductory nature. In Chapter 1, Constantijn Kelk analyses the most important post-war trends in criminal policies in the Netherlands against the background of a shift from humanization to instrumentalism. In Chapter 2, Gavin Dingwall and Alan Davenport focus on developments in England and Wales during the same period and detect similar patterns. Both chapters provide the reader with essential information that serves as a background to the more specific comparative contributions. A third chapter, by Nico Jörg, Stewart Field, and Chrisje Brants examines whether and to what extent the inner dynamics of the criminal justice systems of both jurisdictions contribute to a process of convergence between adversarial and inquisitorial modes of procedure.

The following three chapters of the book deal with the theme of Europeanization in a general way. In Chapter 4, Bert Swart and James Young look at the reception of the European Convention on Human Rights in England and Wales and in the Netherlands. They examine the importance of its different domestic status in the two jurisdictions and its relevance to accusatorial and inquisitorial types of criminal procedure. This is followed by Chapter 5, in which Christopher Harding and Bert Swart explore developments in the field of European co-operation in criminal matters as well as their actual and potential implications for national autonomy. In Chapter 6 René Guldenmund, Christopher Harding, and Ann Sherlock discuss the third form of Europeanization: the enforcement of European Community law at a Community and a national level and the interplay between them. In their own way each of these chapters reveals the inexorable process of Europeanization in its attractive as well as menacing aspects to national systems of criminal justice.

The systematic development of diversion policies is a common feature of the criminal justice systems of England and Wales and the Netherlands. As is apparent from Chapters 7–10, diversion policies are interesting topics of comparative research. On the one hand, the reasons for diverting some categories of offenders, the ways in which this is being achieved, and the extent to which it is practised may differ considerably between the two jurisdictions while, on the other, the basic legal problems involved in diversion, control of administrative discretion, and freedom to choose for those who are candidates for diversion, may very well be the same. The European Convention on Human Rights poses the question of what legal safeguards should apply to decision-making within the framework of diversion. In Chapter 7, Chrisje Brants and Stewart Field discuss the role of law enforcement agencies in keeping crime out of court in general terms. They compare the various institutional incentives and restraints to which these agencies are subject and look at the issue of control of discretionary powers. This is followed by Chapter 8, in which Jos Silvis and Katherine Williams take a closer look at diversion within the context of drug offences. The main issues here are whether or not the different approaches in the Netherlands and in England and Wales are differences of form and presentation rather than substance, and whether they do, in fact, produce different results. In Chapter 9, Phil Fennell and Frans Koenraadt compare ways of dealing with mentally disturbed offenders within the criminal justice system and the different role of the criminal courts where extension of detention is concerned against the background of the European Convention on Human Rights. The uneasy relationship between benevolence and individual rights in juvenile criminal justice is the subject of Chapter 10, written by Loraine Gelsthorpe, Mike Nellis, Jeannette Bruins, and Annelies van Vliet.

Basic differences between adversarial and inquisitorial systems of justice are, of course, a fruitful area of comparative research. Are these differences as fundamental as they are believed to be? In what ways does the European Convention on Human Rights affect cherished traditions and practices that are typical for criminal procedure in common law or civil law systems? These are the questions discussed in Chapters 11–15. In Chapter 11, Stewart Field, Peter Alldridge, and Nico Jörg focus on the problem of ensuring the reliability and fairness of police investigations. They contrast two different attempts at solving that problem: the one imposing on the police an elaborate set of procedural rules to be enforced by the courts; and the other relying on bureaucratic monitoring and on institutional checks and incentives. In Chapter 12, Alan Davenport and Peter Baauw take the *Brogan* case as a starting point for comparing police custody in England and Wales and the Netherlands, and comment on the different impact of that decision in the two jurisdictions. Another issue crucial to fairness in criminal justice is that of expert evidence. Taking DNA tests as their example, in Chapter 13, Peter Alldridge, Sanneke Berkhout-van Poelgeest, and Katherine Williams look at the legal safeguards that apply to collecting and evaluating expert evidence, and at the significance of the law of evidence for accepting or not accepting specific forms of intrusive investigative measures. In Chapter 14, Annemarieke Beijer, Cathy Cobley, and André Klip discuss the right of the accused to confront witnesses against him. They explore tendencies in the Netherlands and in England and Wales to accept infringements of that right for the sake of protecting other interests, notably those of the witness. A mirror view of that problem is provided by Chapter 15, in which Jane Morgan, Frans Willem Winkel and Katherine Williams comment on efforts in England and Wales and in the Netherlands to improve the situations of victims of crime within the criminal justice system.

The last three substantive chapters of the book are devoted to imprisonment and the rights of prisoners. In Chapter 16, Constantijn Kelk, Laurence Koffman, and Jos Silvis contrast the sentencing system of England and Wales with that of the Netherlands, wondering whether a just deserts approach to punishment might bring sentencing practices in both jurisdictions closer together. The rights of prisoners and the impact of the case law of the European Court of Human Rights on prison regimes are discussed by Gillian Douglas and Martin Moerings in Chapter 17. Finally, in Chapter 18 Désirée Paridaens and Christopher Harding take a closer look at English and Dutch attitudes towards the transfer of prisoners from one country to another. The book concludes by considering the lessons of comparative study.

Utrecht/Wales
May 1993

1

Criminal Justice in the Netherlands

CONSTANTIJN KELK

THE IDEA OF RESOCIALIZATION AND THE REBUILDING OF SOCIETY
AFTER THE SECOND WORLD WAR

After the Second World War, the penal climate of the Netherlands underwent changes towards humanization. Although this was consistent with the
traditionally humane reputation (certainly when viewed from an international comparative perspective[1]) of existing penal culture, Dutch society as
a whole became tolerant and mild as a reaction to the extreme violence of
which humanity had shown itself capable during the war. The effects of
this development were not lost on penal law.

The country set about rebuilding a deeply hurt and severely damaged
society. One of the most important aspects for the development of penal
law at that time was the emergence of the so-called Utrecht School, which
is not to say, of course, that others were not influential too.[2]

The Utrecht School was made up of the legal scholar Pompe, the criminologist Kempe, the forensic psychiatrist Baan, and their pupils. Taking
their collective disciplines as a starting point, they sought to approach the
criminal offender as a human being, the central issue in criminal procedure
and punishment, especially imprisonment. The essential theme of their
work was an emphasis on the offender's own responsibility and on punishment as a means of making good the offence to society, after which rehabilitation could take place. They not only co-operated on an academic
level in teaching and research, but were also all involved in practical work;
as a substitute judge (Pompe), as a probation officer preparing reports on
offenders' social background (Kempe), as a practising psychiatrist in an
observation clinic (Baan). They were also all members of advisory bodies,
and they sat on many committees dealing with the offender's legal position.

One of the first innovations after the war was the reform of the Dutch
prison system. Many well-known and respectable Dutch citizens, who would
probably otherwise never have seen a prison from the inside, ended up
there during the war as victims of the Nazis, and what they saw in the

---

[1] John Howard praised Dutch houses of correction in his *State of the Prisons* (1777;
bicentennial edn., Abingdon; Professional Books 1977).
[2] Like Van Bemmelen and Vrij.

prisons shocked them so much that by 1947 a committee, of which Kempe was a member, had proposed drastic reforms, in which the principle of resocialization played an important part. The principle was included in the Prison Act of 1953.

Indeed, the very idea of resocialization suited a society in the process of being rebuilt. The representatives of the Utrecht School aspired to imbue society with a (cultural) mentality which would combine personal responsibility with the ideals of authentic community life. On the one hand, they wanted the restrictions of church authority to be relaxed; on the other, they were critical of the social power embodied in business and industry. Their ideal was a society based on general Christian morals.[3]

Resocialization as a basic idea underlying the Dutch prison system, and essentially extended by the Utrecht School to all penal law, fitted a generally tolerant society, as expressed in religion, in attitudes towards minority groups and sexuality (sexual reform), and also in a penal culture of which the main characteristic was a humane paternalism.[4]

This essentially Dutch penal culture was a contemporary interpretation of the combined theory of penal law that dominated Dutch legal thought in this field. Dutch penal law, as codified in the Criminal Code of 1886, is based not only on the ideas of Beccaria and the classical school of penal thought that followed him, but also on more modern penal philosophies. It refutes retribution as an absolute goal in itself, but maintains it as the basis of all punishment, and as a determinant of proportionality in relation to the offence. Within the limits of proportional retribution, actual punishment must be determined by specific aims (such as special deterrence, resocialization, general deterrence). In this connection, the probation service in the Netherlands has always played a very special part, very different from those of other countries. Originally it was a movement founded by private citizens in 1823, the aims of which were to improve the lot of prisoners by visiting them in prison and by providing material help and other support after they were freed. Later, when conditional release had been introduced (in 1915), the probation movement became involved in reporting to the courts about offenders' social backgrounds. This provided a guarantee of the offender's legal rights, while at the same time doing justice to the specific aims of punishment within the limits of retribution.

The practice of criminal justice is greatly affected by both the degree to which an offender is actually regarded as the weaker party in need of protection against the power of the state, and the way in which an offender is approached and treated by representatives of the state. A criminal justice

---

[3] Ido Weijers, *Terug naar het behouden huis* (Sua; Amsterdam 1991), 18–19.
[4] A. A. G. Peters, 'Authority in the Dutch Administration of Criminal Justice', in Yasuharu Hirabata (ed.), *Contemporary Problems in Criminal Justice: Essays in Honour of Professor Shigemitsu Dando* (Yuhikaku; Tokyo 1983), 149–90.

climate may be repressive or tolerant; the benign version of humane paternalism points to a certain tolerance. It is significant that the judiciary has always shown a dislike of imprisonment,[5] or at least a fair amount of scepticism. Indeed, Dutch penal law has been described as 'classical, with a bad conscience'.[6]

It must be said that the Utrecht School unwittingly saved the bureaucracy of the Ministry of Justice a lot of work: the concepts developed at Utrecht were admirable, but nevertheless not strong enough to resist the Ministry, where they were easily taken over and converted into the sort of criminal justice policies that are more worried about statistics than about quality.

WELFARE AND 'JURIDIFICATION'

In the 1960s and 1970s, the existing balances of power came under serious scrutiny and, like everywhere else, many democratization movements developed. In this heady atmosphere, 'repressive tolerance' and compelling paternalism were deemed unacceptable, to be replaced by new structures in which the right to co-determination by the weak within society or certain institutions was to be guaranteed. Citizens in many categories struggled to achieve a legal position of their own: workers, students, women, the poor, homosexuals. Even prisoners were given a legal right of complaint in 1977.

It was, of course, no coincidence that developments in the field of penal law also flourished for, to a large degree, they reflect existing power relationships. The injustice of penal law came under severe criticism. There were even two main streams of critical thought: one emphasizing individual and general welfare as an integral part of penal law; the other insisting that its essence lay in the protection of the individual by way of due process. L. H. C. Hulsman (Rotterdam) developed the welfare approach and, together with the association for penal reform, the Coornhert-Liga, he put great effort into initiating processes of depenalization and decriminalization. A criminal justice system in which the public prosecutor has the power to drop each individual case, and in which the judge has very wide margins of discretion with regard to sentencing, is by definition a soft target for abolitionism. Hulsman has always advocated solving conflicts between people by means, legal or otherwise, other than criminal law. His emphasis, it will be clear, is on conflict-solving.

---

[5] D. Downes, 'The Origins and Consequences of Dutch Penal Policy since 1945: A Preliminary Analysis', (1982) *British Journal of Criminology* 22, 325–57, noticed this in conversations with judges and public prosecutors. See also: Willem de Haan, *The Politics of Redress* (Unwin Hyman; London 1990), chap. 4.

[6] See G. E. Langemeijer, [1973] NJB 61–7.

The second approach, 'juridification' (which approximates to the term 'legalism' as used by some British and American writers), was initiated by A. A. G. Peters (Utrecht), who emphasized the legal character of penal law, seeing its strongest manifestation in the adversarial structure of criminal procedure in which contradictory interests may freely be expressed and solved in accordance with open-ended principles of law. These principles offer legal protection to the weaker individual against the state, and it is that protection that is shaped by criminal procedure. In this view, legal aid is an absolute imperative.

It will be clear that the welfare approach addressed matters of criminal policy as it was then, in a reductionist sense, while the 'juridification' approach sought structurally to reinforce the individual's legal position in criminal procedure and in prison. This provides a mixed bag of reductionism, both legally and in the practice of criminal justice: on the one hand improved welfare, on the other improved individual rights. The criminal justice system was influenced by both.

It seems to me that what we have here is the combination so characteristic of Dutch penal law, classically based on the rights of the individual, but modern in its emphasis on the offender as a human being, and his personal and social background.

There are, however, intrinsic limits to the official perspective, especially as far as 'juridification' is concerned,[7] within which penal law must function on a day-to-day basis. The primary function of penal law is to control crime and to maintain order in society, to which end officers of the law are afforded legal powers that allow them to act against and, if necessary, coerce citizens. This is the instrumentality of penal law. Beccaria's classical approach was the first to combine this with an inherent arsenal of legal principles and fundamental rights, in order to protect the individual against the arbitrary and unnecessary exercise of power. This is the legal protection that is inherent in penal law. Instrumentality and legal protection belong to each other and may, therefore, be regarded as two sides of the same coin.[8] It will also be clear that one must balance the other, and in that sense they form each other's boundaries. Legal protection has requirements that instrumentality must meet, and vice versa.

---

[7] However, the juridification approach still remains more securely rooted in criminal law itself than reductionist and abolitionist approaches. Abolitionism is predominantly utopian, and for that very reason theoretically weak. Like the ideas put forward by the Utrecht School, Hulsman's notions were easily incorporated into official policy where they underwent a fundamental change: e.g. settlement out of court (*transactie*), once thought of as a means of keeping offenders out of court, soon became part of a policy designed to streamline the criminal justice system and render it more efficient.

[8] R. Foqué and A. C. 't Hart, *Instrumentaliteit en rechtsbescherming* (Kluwer; Deventer 1990).

NEW REALISM AND NO NONSENSE

Meanwhile, in a short period of time there have been several developments that are of fundamental significance for the citizens of Holland. Organizations and corporations have increased rapidly, both in number and in scale; bureaucracy has extended its hold on state and other organizations; there has been the growth of technology, computerization, commercialization, internationalization; and a rapid increase in unemployment. While all these developments are, of course, interrelated, the net result has certainly been a depersonalized style of life and alienation between individuals. A lack of social attachments between people, and between people and social systems, is one of the reasons for the increase in many forms of crime that have occurred during the past decade.[9] This applies especially to (children of) members of minority groups, and to others who are unemployed and often addicted to drugs. Thinking in terms of 'us' and 'them' has become more prevalent, including between organizations, and even between ministries. In general, people seem to have become more egocentric.

The bastion that houses Justice has not remained unaffected by all this. There, too, people have come to think in terms of 'business', emphasizing 'output' and 'product-management', of being organized according to the requirements of efficiency agencies in order to be able to process certain predetermined numbers of cases. This quantitative approach has been stimulated by the growing tension between appreciable increases in crime (especially 'petty' crime with its exceedingly high nuisance value, but also traffic crime, vandalism, violence, and fraud); an overworked police force, public prosecution service, and judiciary; a prison service that is notoriously under-resourced; and a public that is rapidly losing patience.

Elsewhere, too, criminal justice systems show signs of what has been called 'new realism'.[10] This seems to have emerged from the fact that all attempts at rehabilitating criminals and resocializing prisoners—upon which the Dutch system has always laid great emphasis—have proved illusory: there have been no tangible or measurable results, and in these days of 'no nonsense' that is a shortcoming indeed. Partly because of these developments in the field of crime and criminal justice, many countries have increasingly fallen back on a harder, less humane approach, although there are shades of difference. In the United States we find the 'justice model',[11]

[9] See the theories of social control invoked by criminologist Riekent Jongman in Groningen (see his contribution to Cyrille Fijnaut and Pieter Spierenburg (eds.), *Scherp Toezicht* (Gouda Quint; Arnhem 1990), 31–45.
[10] C. Eliaerts, 'Het "nieuwe realisme" in het strafrecht en de criminele politiek' (1984) *Panopticon*, 8.
[11] See A. von Hirsch, *Doing Justice; the Choice of Punishment* (Hill and Wang; New York 1976).

in which punishment is meted out according to 'just deserts'. In the Netherlands we have a method, advocated by a previous Minister of Justice, that is known as 'swift and sure' and that involves a swift and sure penal reaction to the offence, without too much ceremony. It is logical that such ideas go hand-in-hand with a preference for more and heavier penalties. At the same time, this provides an answer to the demands that are increasingly made by society, although public opinion on the matter varies greatly according to a person's socio-cultural category.[12]

The justice model has had positive effects in the American context, in so far as its emphasis on proportionality between punishment and offence has led to the disappearance of the hated system of indeterminate sentences. But in the Dutch context, emphasis on the offence has the negative effect of causing the offender as a human being to be neglected, while retribution, supported this time by the principle of equality, returns in all its glory. These negative developments have been exacerbated recently in the fields of legal aid, probation, and juvenile protection, and by systematic reductions of procedural guarantees by numerous cuts in public spending that also affect the criminal justice system.

BUREAUCRACY AND CRIMINAL JUSTICE, AND THE DOWNFALL OF THE CLASSICAL VALUES OF PENAL LAW

We must conclude that an impersonal society is producing an increasingly impersonal system of penal law, whatever one wishes to call it: it is hardly surprising that, in an era of functionalism based on no-nonsense ideas, (criminal) law and the (criminal) justice system have become enamoured of legal notions that are easily translated in terms of ends and means.

All of this boils down to a process of *diminishing tolerance* in the traditional Dutch sense.[13] It can be seen in our attitude towards ethnic minorities, people on social security, and other weak groups in society. We take less care of the weak. And here the ambiguous nature of Dutch tolerance begins to tell. The weak side of tolerance, the side that fails to draw boundaries—for example, in family life and at school—seems to generate repression, and this in its turn puts excessive pressure on the strong side, the side that calls for tolerance towards the weak and the deviant fellow human being.

In criminal law this means that the traditionally good things about penitentiary law, the guarantees of criminal procedure and sentencing, the

---

[12] E. Rood-Pijpers, *Mensen over misdaad en straf* (thesis; Rotterdam 1988) with a summary in English: 'Crime and Punishment, the public's opinion'.

[13] See also Erhard Blankenburg and Freek Bruinsma, *Dutch Legal Culture* (Kluwer; Deventer 1991), 37.

things that form, as it were, the conscience of criminal law, are over-shadowed by identification with a purely instrumental way of thinking that, in the end, constitutes pure deterioration of fundamental values. Paradoxically 'juridification' is increasing, but not because of any deep-seated interest in the classical values of liberty, equality, and fraternity. On the contrary current tendencies towards 'juridification' entail rules and conditions that subordinate classical values to values and norms of economy and social control: not social control in the sense of mutual attachments and commitments between people, a caring society, but social control in the sense of supervision and one person watching another.

The rationality of means and ends, towards which the criminal justice system has gravitated, is increasingly based on the concept of 'policy'. In Dutch, the word 'policy' (*beleid*) was originally associated with wise choices, with the liberal state and the rule of law reluctant to interfere in affairs of the individual. But in the democratic state, in the state of relative prosperity that we have today, policy means *action*, rules and regulations, amenities provided by the state, with a corresponding and increasing number of obligations on the part of the citizen.[14] An enormous increase on the organizational level in society, and technology, have led people to aspire more than ever to an ideal of completeness. But—in that perspective—'priorities' are inevitable and so is the standardization of approaches to the problems that human beings face.

It is increasingly difficult to remain in touch with reality: policy-makers are distanced from the problems that require political approaches. Closely linked to this phenomenon is the process by which organizations, including the organizations that belong to the greater whole of the criminal justice system, are becoming increasingly independent. At present each part of that system seems to want to formulate its own policy within its own organizational context. The Public Prosecution Service, the judiciary, and the Ministry of Justice all have their own policy centres. At the same time, however, they feel the need for new structures of communication. The principle of equality figures large in all of this, albeit that it pertains most of all to bureaucratic equality: there are often guidelines, based on standard codes and standard categories. This process, whereby the organs of the criminal justice system are developing into more or less independent organizations, is greatly encouraged by efficiency operations, often with the aid of efficiency agencies.

It is obvious that over-emphasizing management has direct consequences for criminal justice work, especially if notions of management as such come to dominate the scene. In that case, the professional organization that is so essential for criminal justice will become subordinate to the

---

[14] Cf. Blankenburg and Bruinsma, 39 ff. on *beleid*, a typically Dutch concept.

formal organization that the system also represents. The efficiency of crime control, as a cold and self-evident aim of the 'justice business', will come to the fore in the guise of modern management, quite in keeping with that other phenomenon, new realism, that runs parallel with increasing instrumentalism and its orientation towards such amputated aims. And it is instrumentalism, increasingly a form of monomania, that fails to recognize the ambiguity of law.

THE PUBLIC PROSECUTION SERVICE

It was the Public Prosecution Service that played a very central and probably initiating role in these developments. To start with, the Prosecution Service was gradually accorded more powers, for example in the field of sanctions. In 1983, the new Act on Monetary Sanctions greatly increased the scope of transaction (settlement out of court), thereby endangering the adversarial nature of criminal procedure.[15] Under certain conditions, the prosecutor may offer to allow the offender to settle out of court by paying a certain sum (comparable to a fine); the amount of money involved may be very large. In such cases there is no finding of guilt during a trial, nor is an independent court in any way involved.

In practice, transaction forms a substantial part of the work of the Prosecution Service, confirming suspicions that this way of dealing with criminal offences greatly promotes the instrumentality of criminal law: in most cases transaction is conducted solely on the basis of guidelines by clerks of the court. Offenders are inclined to pay up without any fuss; there is no judicial control at all. If a clerk of the court were to attempt to find out about an offender's personal history or were to take an offender's background into consideration, he would run a considerable risk of not being able to meet relevant 'production' requirements, and therefore of damaging his career. Moreover, the Public Prosecution Service now dominates the simplified collection of administrative fines for non-serious traffic offences: the traffic officer imposes the fine, whereupon the offender can appeal to the prosecutor and, if he wishes—and after he has paid—, to a sub-district court. This is retrospective judicial control, still (just) within the limits of the requirements of Article 6 of the European Convention (according to the *Öztürk* judgment of the European Court of Human Rights in 1984).

Secondly, during recent decades, the Public Prosecution Service has increasingly manifested itself as an administrative organ. An administrative culture requires that controlling problems and finding swift solutions be given absolute priority. Guidelines may bring relief in difficult situations

---

[15] See n. 7, above, and the discussion in Chap. 7.

that require balanced reasoning (such as the decision to prosecute or to drop a case), while at first sight they seem to promote equality. It will be clear that guidelines have become increasingly popular. And so the Prosecution Service has willingly allowed itself to be 'streamlined'.

Outside the criminal justice system too, the Prosecution Service is to be found in the guise of 'administrator': for example, in tripartite consultations with the burgomaster and chief of police, especially if the concern is petty crime, for which 'administrative' measures of deterrence are indicated.

Finally, the guidelines for the Prosecution Service have also affected the judiciary and sentencing policy—and they are meant to in so far as they aim at promoting equality in sentencing. However, the Prosecution Service has gained in power to the detriment of the judiciary, so much so, in fact, that courts have come to examine the Prosecutor's actions in the light of principles of due procedure in order to maintain some sort of control over the Prosecution Service.

According to general criminal policy, the Prosecutor must not drop cases as often as he did in the past (especially if serious crime is concerned), when about 50 per cent of prosecutions for felonies were dropped.[16]

THE JUDICIARY

Obviously the judiciary as an independent protector of rights, guaranteeing a balanced weighing of the interests of the offender and others, is subject to great pressure in a system that is based increasingly on notions of management, means and ends, and production. Meanwhile, other criminal justice organizations can impose sanctions that are no longer the prerogative of the court, while social usefulness has become the driving force behind 'doing justice'. The latter is expressed, for example, in such new sanctions as community service orders (performing unpaid labour for the 'common good'), and in sanctions oriented towards restitution, such as confiscation of criminal gains and, in the future, reimbursement of the victim. Within the judiciary there is, as it were, a certain blurring of identities, especially in so far as courts consider themselves bound to follow the prosecution guidelines upon which the prosecutor's demand for sentence is based. This is 'tariff-justice'—in its most extreme form we find sentencing according to weight in drug cases (so-called kilo-justice)—and it has probably led to a decrease in the number of probation reports on the offender that courts request. It is also likely that this has been affected by the fact that the average age of judges has reduced enormously in a very

[16] The relationship between the Minister of Justice and the Public Prosecution Service is the subject of Chaps. 3, 7, and 11 in this book.

short time, not only in the sense that more young judges have joined the judiciary, but also in the sense that one can now become a judge at a much earlier age. But some personal experience of life is essential if one is to be a proper judge, and proper judges take an interest in the offender as a human being.

THE MINISTRY OF JUSTICE

It is the Ministry of Justice that has been most influential in affixing the stamp of instrumentalism to the criminal justice system, and it has gradually come to occupy a strong and central position of power in the system. This can be seen in several proposals on behalf of the Minister of Justice for amendments to criminal procedure, all aimed at further streamlining to the detriment of individual guarantees and rights; at present the Minister is advised by a Committee that was installed in 1988 and is looking into amendments to the Code of Criminal Procedure, because the Code is no longer effective in the control of crime. (Suggestions for 'streamlining' the Code include reducing rights of complaint and simplifying remand procedures.)

Unfortunately, the Supreme Court is not always prepared to protect the rights of the offender: several times the European Court of Human Rights has found that essential rights of the defendant have been infringed in Dutch procedure.[17] Proposed cuts in public spending on legal aid will be catastrophic for the position of the defendant, while increasingly bureaucratized and impersonal prison and probation services are the result of negative developments during the past decade.

The Prison Service

Over the years, it has become clear that the principle of resocialization entails highly idealized expectations with regard to actual rehabilitation in, and adaptation to, society in a psycho-social sense. The right of complaint, given to prisoners in 1977, is an important improvement from a point of view of resocialization (see Chap. 17). Prisoners both in prisons and remand centres may complain to a supervisory board if they consider that their rights have been infringed, or if they are subjected to disciplinary punishment by the director. This supervisory board is made up of independent citizens and there is one in every detention institution. The complaints committee comprises three members from the supervisory board;

---

[17] See e.g. *Kostovski*, European Court of Human Rights, 20 November 1989, Series A, 166; [1990] NJ 245.

it hears complaints in the presence of the complainant and the director. The complaints committee has the power to review the director's decision if it finds grounds for the complaint. A complainant may obtain legal aid, and both complainant and director may appeal against the complaints committee's decision to the Central Council for Criminal Justice in The Hague, which is an independent advisory board to the Minister of Justice. This not only offers a certain, albeit minimal, protection of rights within the compelling and repressive context of imprisonment; it also functions as a deterrent, encouraging the directors of detention institutions to take their decisions with due care. The value of this form of juridification depends on its essential factor: the adversarial nature of the procedure.

However, in 1982 the Junior Minister for Justice relinquished the resocialization ideal in its broadest sense: proceeding on the basis of realistic considerations, a report on the future of the prison service (*Taak en Toekomst van het Nederlandse gevangeniswezen*) put ministerial ambitions on a lower level. The danger of officially relinquishing such ideals, however, is that there is no incentive to aspire to them. This development should be regarded as the writing on the (prison) wall. At the same time, the traditional and much-praised humanitarianism of the Dutch prison system was threatened from several sides: cuts in public spending, leading to structured freedom of movement for detainees (i.e. less freedom of movement, fewer communal activities, especially during the weekends); a shortage of cells about which the Ministry became obsessional and which was given the highest priority; and, last but not least, the well nigh unstoppable march of management.

All of this has resulted in poorer quality prison regimes, in an increase in bigger prisons in which the opportunities for individualization are, by definition, fewer, and in structural changes to the organization of the prison system aimed at 'deconcentration' of detention institutions. On closer inspection, the latter refers mainly to a deconcentration of bureaucracy, and not to any real decentralization in the sense of the autonomous exercise of authority: central control imposes far-reaching conditions on local autonomy. When directors and prison staff feel badly treated, this has immediate repercussions for the position of the prisoner. His legal position—enforceable by means of the right of complaint—means less and less as structural conditions within the prison grow worse: for such conditions are simply an essential fact of life, providing the background for decisions by the director and for the examination of the reasonable and just nature of such decisions by complaints committees and appeal bodies. The same applies to the regulations and directives, in so far as they can easily be issued, amended, or withdrawn by the Ministry of Justice. The number of directives has multiplied many times in recent years. And so we see how one form of juridification (the protection of individual rights) can be smothered by another (centralized over-regulation). In other words, the former is very vulnerable.

Fortunately the Central Council takes the stand that changing structures within the prisons should not be allowed to affect the rights of prisoners too easily, and it refuses, with the exception of a very limited number of cases, to acknowledge the right of prison officers other than the director to impose disciplinary sanctions in the director's absence. This is an increasingly frequent occurrence as the director's management duties increase. The protection of prisoners' rights should be, and remain, part and parcel of the prison system, even if efficiency and security determine actual regimes. By its very nature, penitentiary law is predominantly instrumental; it must be, now that it governs whole institutions as part of a security system. This becomes painfully obvious if we consider how many drug addicts and hard-drug dealers are incarcerated in Dutch prisons: many prisons subject each prisoner to a total body search after every private visit; prisoners in so-called drug-free wings undergo urine tests; cells are inspected with depressing regularity. This has an increasingly negative influence on the climate in Dutch prisons as a whole, and there is not much that can be done about it from the perspective of prisoners' rights.

The Probation Service

The history of the probation service is full of ups and downs, but rarely have there been so many downs as during the past few years.

Increasing professionalization from the 1960s onwards has meant that there has been less and less scope for private initiative and voluntary work. An increasing number of professionally trained social workers in the probation service has meant a shift in emphasis towards, for example, non-material support. Moreover, during the 1970s the criminal justice framework within which the service operates was perceived as too restrictive, especially if it undermined the probation workers' position of trust towards the client. This was a thorn in the side of the Ministry of Justice for many years, and finally here, too, bureaucracy has taken hold. Bureaucratization is the only word for the reorganization of the probation service that was carried out in 1986. All probation work was organized into private foundations, responsible for any probation work in the district, including work within the prison walls in so far as it was concerned with the probation service. A co-ordinating organization is required to formulate annually a national policy plan, while the foundations are obliged to come up with their own annual policy plan that dovetails into the national plan. Everything must be approved by the Ministry of Justice. Probation work itself must meet strict requirements; producing a report for the courts, for example, is supposed to take a certain number of hours. The service is financed by the Ministry according to these standards.

While the probation service was attempting to adapt its activities to this strict framework, it was constantly hit by cuts in public spending. The significance of the probation service—an eminent and internationally unique part of the Dutch criminal justice system—depends entirely on its relatively autonomous and creative ideas on, and the performance of, probation duties, for these guarantee the best possible conditions for reporting to the courts and maintaining contact with clients.

In times of impersonal and routine justice, we cannot really do without influences that will guarantee some degree of individualization in sentencing if the position of the defendant in criminal procedure is to mean anything at all.

THE INCREASINGLY INSTRUMENTAL NATURE OF PENAL LAW

Changing policy concepts within the different organizations of the criminal justice system are partly responsible for the increasingly instrumental nature of penal law. But this intensivization is not only apparent in the field of criminal procedure and sanctions. It can also be traced in substantive law. Moreover, this also has repercussions on social control. The following is a brief outline of these developments.

Substantive Criminal Law

Important principles of substantive law have been put to one side several times in legislation—often with a view to controlling drug crime: the Opium Act, for example, contains a conspiracy provision (unknown in the Criminal Code, which requires that a crime must be in the process of being carried out in order to be a punishable offence).[18] Recently, the Criminal Code did change in the sense that conspiracy was introduced as a separate offence in many more cases; the idea is to allow the police to intervene at a much earlier stage than is currently possible if convictions are to follow, for previously they had to wait until the offence was in the process of being carried out, and by then it may be too late.

Another principle of penal law has always been that only one type of punishment may be imposed at once: either imprisonment or a fine. Now fines and imprisonment may be imposed together. It will also be made easier to prosecute and convict for receiving stolen goods, while those

---

[18] An attempt to commit an offence does not come within Dutch criminal law unless the person intending to commit the offence has actually started its execution, but is prevented from completing it solely because of factors external to his will. Preparatory actions that do not constitute a manifestation of the offence itself are not therefore governed by criminal law (e.g., buying an axe is not a manifestation of an attempt to murder, although it certainly betrays criminal intent).

suspected of this offence may be held on remand. These are offences in the social economic field.

In case law the Supreme Court has been decidedly lax in insisting on the traditional requirements for participation. Until recently there was no such thing as an accessory after the fact in Dutch law; there still is not in the Criminal Code, but this position has been recognized as punishable participation by the Supreme Court.

Provisions concerning the liability of persons for crimes committed by corporations, incorporated in such offences as being a member of a forbidden corporation, or ordering or actually directing an offence committed by a corporation, have also been interpreted in an increasingly broad and instrumentalist sense. Directing a corporate offence, for example, also includes failing to prevent actions by other officers of the corporation, if this means accepting the risk that criminal offences will be committed or continue to be committed within the corporation, although the offender was in a position to intervene and was reasonably obliged to do so. While social economic law requires an instrumental approach to a certain extent, such interpretations of provisions in the Criminal Code seriously undermine the principle of legality.

Criminal Procedure

There have been several amendments to legislation on criminal procedure that have resulted in fewer legal guarantees for the defendant. There is no longer any right of appeal against decisions on complaints against subpoenas by the prosecution, although the prosecutor may appeal if the complaint is upheld, a contravention of the principle of equality of arms. There are at present proposals for repairing procedural mistakes during a trial, changing the rules with regard to remand (fewer interventions by the court), and amendments to the preliminary judicial investigation by the investigating judge. On the other hand, the *Brogan* case has resulted in a Bill requiring earlier intervention by a member of the judiciary if a suspect is held for questioning by the police.

Here, too, the Supreme Court's case law shows a distinct lack of respect for individual rights in criminal procedure. A well-known lawyer, Ties Prakken, has compiled a *cronique scandaleuse* on the use of anonymous evidence (sometimes provided by informers or under-cover agents), on the lack of rules during police investigations, on the preliminary judicial investigation, and on illegally obtained evidence. We could add that provisions on searches of a suspect's body have now been so interpreted as to include searches *in* a suspect's body (the so-called 'rectum' decision of the Supreme Court). Unfortunately, it also looks as if cuts in public spending on legal aid by the Ministry of Justice will mean a decline in energetic and alert reactions to infringements of defendants' rights in court. The Public Prosecution Service, impersonal and smug as it has become, is unlikely to be very sorry about this, as is apparent from remarks by members of the service, that it is the lawyers who are guilty of unacceptable practice in attempting to use the rules of criminal procedure (for example, with regard to procedural mistakes) for the benefit of their clients.

Sanctions

The community service order has now officially been included in the system of sanctions, albeit under restrictive conditions, including the requirement that it may only be imposed in cases in which the court would not have imposed more than six months' imprisonment.

The Advisory Committee on Alternative Sanctions has advocated the community service order in other cases as well, and the introduction of a sanction called restriction of liberty that will cover a wide range of activities, such as compulsory enrolment in educational courses and projects. The idea is to impose such sanctions independently or in combination for offences for which no more than two years' imprisonment would have been imposed. In other words, the Committee advocates the restriction of liberty, including community service orders, for cases of more serious crime. Indeed, we already have conditional sentences that involve extramural projects for social skills and professional training, courses on alcohol and driving, treatment programmes for drug addicts, alcoholics, and even the incestuous, while all of these may be combined with each other, or with restitution or reimbursement of the victim. The Committee's proposals are derived from the existing situation. The basis of such sanctions that do not deprive a person of his liberty is what is officially regarded as their social usefulness, although one could add that they are also of some use to the individual.

But there are great dangers attached to extending the range and scope of such alternative sanctions, namely that the courts may impose them, not instead of imprisonment, but as independent sanctions, and thus also if imprisonment would not have been imposed anyway. They would then act as an extension of the current system of penalties, not as an alternative to it.

In a society in which there is an increasing demand for ever more severe penalties, even once by the Prime Minister, it is not entirely unlikely that the courts will be tempted to extend the system in this way, the more so now that they are inclined to underestimate the severity of alternative sanctions. I have the impression that some judges still think of alternative sanctions as a very mild form of (quasi) punishment. Research has shown that in reality offenders regard the community service order as quite severe. In complying with a community service order, the offender is in a dependent position: if the order is not carried out satisfactorily, the public prosecutor may request that the court make an order for imprisonment, against which it is assumed the offender can appeal. However, there are no regulations governing the position of the offender during the community service order, as regards the employer, the supervisor, and the probation service. He has no right of complaint against decisions concerning his compliance with the order, his behaviour, or his efforts. There have been calls for some form of legal protection in the light of the standard minimum rules for sanctions not involving the deprivation of liberty, as developed by the Council of Europe.

There is an even more remarkable neglect of any form of legal guarantee where the so-called Halt projects are concerned, projects that were designed specifically for young offenders (see Chap. 10). Their aim is to deter vandalism, and they include activities such as repairing and cleaning trams and bus shelters. Criticism that such swift and sure methods—in themselves possibly not unfavourable—lack any sort of individual guarantee is well founded. Offenders are always referred to a Halt project by the police and the matter usually ends with the police dropping the case if they consider that the offender has satisfactorily participated in the project. The Prosecution Service remains in the background. The Bill on revision of juvenile law legalizes this practice, that has grown phenomenally and is regarded as successful.

There are also proposals for including unpaid labour by juvenile offenders in the range of conditions for transaction by the prosecutor. Within juvenile law, the power of investigation and prosecution services in the imposition of sanctions is increasing, but there is no accompanying development in the field of legal protection for the offender. Any protection that there is with regard to the police exists mainly by reason of the fact that the police are hierarchically subordinate to the Prosecution Service, but this is something of an empty promise. Moreover, in practice juvenile and vice squads all over the country have developed their own local policies with regard to juveniles, including an inherent and wide range of semi-official sanctions.

It could be said that the juvenile police, balancing precariously between juvenile welfare and a consistent policy based on legal equality, are the traditional 'specialists' in the sense that they have always been creative in their attempts to individualize juvenile criminal law. But the latest tendency is to get rid of specific departments of juvenile police, despite advice to the contrary from the Council for Juvenile Policy.

Although there are dynamic developments in the field of sanctions with regard to both adults and juveniles, we should nevertheless ask ourselves in all seriousness whether these are not simply due to what happens to be in fashion, while the result may merely be an extension of the system of sanctions, with little or no regard for the legal position and rights of the individuals upon whom they are imposed.

There is one shining exception, namely the measure of detention at the government's pleasure or TBS (compulsory admission to an institution for mentally disturbed offenders—see Chap. 9). The measure may be imposed on mentally disturbed perpetrators of serious crimes that show that they are a danger to others. If the court considers them not normally accountable for their actions under criminal law, they may be detained at the government's pleasure for two years, after which the court may repeatedly extend the period for one or two years until such time as it considers that the danger posed to society no longer exists. These offenders have only recently been given the right to lodge an appeal against such extensions with a special chamber at the Court of Appeal. Within the TBS institutions there is a limited right of complaint, parallel to that in ordinary prisons. This right is to be extended in future. It is one of the few positive aspects of 'juridification' in recent years, and that in an area where psychiatry and law meet.

AN ENORMOUS INCREASE IN SOCIAL CONTROL

One of the more obvious effects of an increase in the rate of many forms of petty crime has been the rediscovery of social control and functional control as deterrents to all sorts of so-called petty crime in many social sectors.

For many years now, the policy at the Ministry of Justice has been as follows: petty crime should be tackled in a very different way from serious crime, namely if possible by means of so-called 'administrative deterrence'. The risk that this will lead to expansive networks of social control, with citizens supervising other citizens, is by no means simply a figment of the imagination. In so far as control is restricted to visual control, with the exclusive aim of preventing (petty) crime, there are few objections, but matters are different if measures of control are no longer merely visual, but by their very nature entail infringements of (fundamental) human rights, such as privacy or physical integrity. Obviously a society of hardening convictions and attitudes to crime and punishment is a fertile breeding ground for what Stanley Cohen has called 'the punitive city'.[19] I hasten to

---

[19] Stanley Cohen, 'The Punitive City: Notes on the Dispersal of Social Control', in (1979) 3 *Contemporary Crises* 349.

add that the climates of penal repression and social control are interdependent. In these 'no-nonsense' days it is probably no coincidence that society's call for more suppression of crime is matched by private initiatives of a repressive nature in other fields. I am reminded here of the Christian Democrat Employers' Federation, which advocated stricter measures (less pay) against employees laid off sick, in order to stem the rising number of working days lost through illness.

THE DANGEROUS SPIRIT OF INSTRUMENTALISM

The previous pages have painted a picture of a criminal justice system the organizations of which increasingly tend to predetermine their primary professional responsibilities in terms of policy: this applies to criminal investigation by the police, prosecution by the Prosecution Service, the trying and sentencing of offenders by the courts, and the execution of sanctions by the Ministry of Justice. Increasingly, such policies are formulated and informed by the official perspective of the relationship between means and ends and organizational efficiency: on the outside it all looks like a guarantee of equal treatment; on the inside there is predominantly bureaucracy and all the blurring and loss of identity that it entails. A quantitative approach to criminal justice reigns supreme, serving in the first place the interests of the Ministry of Justice, while individualization of penal law centred around the offender as a human being is being pushed ever further back. The spirit that has gradually come to dominate the criminal justice system seems to preclude interest in the individual offender, although that is what the system was all about in the first place.

This dominant spirit is one of efficient repression, paying lip service to individual rights as long as they are not enforced—for the latter is increasingly regarded as a spanner in the works of the justice machine.

It is the Ministry of Justice that expresses this spirit most in its policy memoranda, draft laws that propose reducing individual rights in criminal procedure and interference in the system in practice (for example the reorganization of juvenile protection and the probation service). But it should not be forgotten that there is support for these measures in certain sectors of public opinion where more and more severe penalties are advocated. In dealing with serious forms of crime, policy memoranda gratefully make use of almost automatic associations with organized crime, in order to promote (severe) penal repression as a cure for crime in general. This is not to say that there is no organized crime in the Netherlands; there is, but probably not to an excessive or even alarming degree compared with other countries.

One must always be aware of the risk that the quality of the criminal justice system can be reduced to an exceedingly low level through an excess of worry about a small sector of crime.

There is no reason penal law should lose credibility if the prosecution waives the right to prosecute in an increasing number of cases, for such waivers may be used wisely and communicatively (for example, if made conditional). Moreover, there are many creative opportunities in the use of conditional sentences, alternative sanctions and extra-mural execution of prison sentences, such as have recently been developed by the Advisory Committee on Alternative Sanctions. Nevertheless, the Ministry remains obsessed with extending the Prison Service as far as possible, which is what our punitive society seems to want.

Besides the desirability of a certain instrumentalism against the background of the principle that penal law should be the ultimate remedy, individual rights in criminal law and criminal procedure should always be given a very high priority, and at the same time the government's obsession with the criminal justice 'apparatus' must somehow be curbed. To start with, by its very nature the criminal justice system encompasses a wide range of ideals and social aims and it cannot, therefore, be compared to an industry or a business that is simply oriented towards obtaining measurable results, to which end it may be technically equipped. The 'rationality' of penal law cannot be determined unambiguously and it is not amenable to quantification. By definition, criminal policy can never get further than aspiring to a certain balance between crime and society, but where that balance lies depends partly on the crime that society is prepared to tolerate, therefore on the social threshold of tolerance. The state must not seek to control the phenomenon entirely, but to optimize deterrence. An eminent Dutch scholar once put it as follows: 'Every community of human beings has a certain amount of crime, has crime of a certain quality too. This is what makes that community human: man can usually choose between obeying or contravening the rules. His life does not consist of conditioned reflexes.'[20]

At the same time, penal law has an exemplary function towards other mechanisms of control, especially if the latter have punitive aspects. Indeed, penal law has ethics all of its own, closely linked to the necessary diffidence befitting a system that could impinge on the freedom and autonomy of the citizens of our democratic state. We must be aware of the drawbacks of greatly intensified social control, in order to prevent the dangers we are holding at bay at the front door from slipping in via the back. Here, too, it is government that should be providing the example: every form of control that is too far-reaching, too punitive, must be avoided, however

[20] Ch. J. Enschedé, in *Menswetenschappen* (Amsterdam; Uitgave Psychiatrisch Juridisch Gezelschap 1971) 5.

attractive such options may seem to be in preventing and controlling crime. Research has shown that citizens, for example small shopkeepers, are quite able to take quite a number of steps themselves in preventing crime in their own context. It is quite true, as has been said, that too much deterrence from above might lead ordinary people to forget how to take care of themselves.

While on the one hand penal law should not be reduced to just one of the many instruments for combating the social evil of crime, laid out for inspection in the light of its efficiency, on the other hand social control must not become a wildly expansive punitive alternative without the guarantees of protection for fundamental rights that are inherent in criminal law. If it does, society will harden even further until our reputation for tolerance is tarnished beyond repair.

Let us watch out for social control on the march! If its target consists in particular of certain marginalized groups in society, a dubious process of exclusion will have been set in motion among what used to be called the 'ethnic proletariat'. The cynic may even ask whether those concerned would not be better off in prison (for a while) with all its guarantees, than subjected to social measures that will be more permanent and more damaging. The idea of excluding and exiling categories of people who ask (too) much of a 'caring society' is more viable than ever. One only has to look at the negative attitude towards and treatment of AIDS patients. They, most of all, are the victims of deep-seated notions of *culpa in causa* (more chaste behaviour would have saved them from the disease) that blur the contours of their needs and the misery of their condition. Those seeking political asylum, and many others, encounter similar reactions. In that respect, internationalization of criminal law with its many effects on national matters—drug policy, for example—does not always imply improvement.

2

The Evolution of Criminal Justice Policy in the UK

GAVIN S. DINGWALL AND ALAN DAVENPORT

CRIMINAL JUSTICE POLICY AS A RESPONSE TO PENAL CRISIS

The United Kingdom today faces a problem of crime which could not possibly have been forecast at the end of the Second World War. Since then there has been a large increase in the number of crimes reported to the police. In 1950 approximately 500,000 crimes were reported. This figure rose to 1.6 million in 1970, 2.5 million in 1980 and 5.4 million in 1991.[1] In Table 2.1 the figures for 1992 reveal that the vast majority of crimes reported to the police are property offences. Of the 5 per cent of offences listed as being of a sexual or violent nature, roughly two-thirds involved minor wounding; homicide and serious wounding constituted only 0.3 per cent of recorded crime.[2] The criminal statistics show that the largest recent rises in reported crime have been for criminal damage and burglary.[3]

Such a rise in reported crime is clearly cause for concern; however, victim report surveys would suggest that criminal behaviour is more prevalent than the official statistics indicate. The British Crime Survey interviews a large sample across the United Kingdom in an attempt to gauge the true extent of crime. The latest survey suggests that in 1991 about fifteen million offences were actually committed.[4] Vandalism and theft from motor vehicles accounted for the majority of unreported crime according to the survey's results. The most common reason for not reporting an offence to the police was that the victim felt that it was too trivial to merit action, followed by the fact that the victim did not feel that the police would be in a position to do anything about the offence.

It is impossible to state to what extent this rise in reported crime represents an increase in actual crime. Studies in the United States have tentatively suggested that a rise in reported crime is roughly proportionate

---

[1] *Criminal Statistics, England and Wales,* 1970, 1980, 1992, HMSO. The 1992 figures are taken from 'Notifiable Offences 1992', *Home Office Statistical Bulletin,* 1993.

[2] 'Notifiable Offences 1992'.

[3] *Criminal Statistics, England and Wales,* HMSO, 1992.

[4] P. Mayhew and N. Aye Maung, *Surveying Crime: Findings from the 1992 British Crime Survey,* Home Office Research Findings, No. 2.

TABLE 2.1   Reported Crimes

Offence	% of Recorded Crime
Theft of/from Cars	29
Burglary	25
Other Theft	24
Criminal Damage	13
Sexual/Violent Crimes	5
Other Offences	4

Source: 'Notifiable Offences 1992', *Home Office Statistical Bulletin*, 1993.

to increases in actual crime.[5] This however fails to take account of a change of attitude, both public and private, towards reporting crime. The growing realization that certain types of criminal activity, such as domestic violence, were more common in society than previously thought has resulted in reforms designed to encourage victims to report offences. For example, many rape victims were deterred from reporting their ordeal to the authorities for fear of intimate details of their personal life being made public in court. Legislation has come into force supposedly to protect rape victims in the criminal trial by preserving their anonymity and only allowing questions of a personal nature where necessary.[6] In making the system more sympathetic to the needs of the victim it is unsurprising that more victims do now report offences, and this will be reflected in the Criminal Statistics. Similarly, the increased availability of telephones and cars has made it easier for people to report crimes.

Conversely, popular concern about rising crime may make individuals believe that the authorities will be unable to apprehend the criminal and therefore that it would be pointless to report the offence. This feeling that crime cannot be controlled effectively has led to the much publicized vigilante groups and private security forces that 'patrol' certain British towns and cities.

The Position after the Second World War

In common with the other countries involved, the social, political, and economic effects of the 1939–45 War were far-reaching in the United

[5] S. Field, *Trends in Crime and their Interpretation: A Study of Recorded Crime in Post-War England and Wales*, Home Office Research Study 119, 1990: 2.
[6] Sexual Offences (Amendment) Act 1976, s. 2(1): 'If at any trial any person is charged with a rape offence to which he pleads not guilty, then, except with the leave of the judge, no evidence and no question in cross-examination shall be adduced or asked at the trial, by or on behalf of any defendant at the trial, about any sexual experience of a complainant with a person other than the defendant.'

Kingdom. The sense of relief was tempered by a realization that the war had emphasized some deep social divisions which required solutions that challenged many traditionally-espoused political views. Popular support for this was reflected in the notable victory of the Labour party in the 1945 General Election.

It must be said, however, that the move towards social change had already been embraced by the wartime government (e.g. the celebrated Butler Education Act 1944 provided extensive state education for the first time). The role of the state had changed greatly. Instead of social provision being catered for in the family unit, or by charity, increasingly government saw such services coming within its ambit. Indeed it was in the immediate post-war period that most of the key elements of what today is termed the 'Welfare State' were introduced.

The Second World War had also tested the traditional assumptions of criminal justice. Before the war the average daily prison population in England and Wales had fluctuated between 10,000 and 11,000: however by 1945 it was just under 15,000, which represented an increase of almost 50 per cent in the space of five years.[7] Whilst the population at large may not have been aware of these challenges to the criminal justice system, the situation clearly caused considerable concern to the government and, given the reforming nature of the time, it is hardly surprising that far-reaching reform was to follow.

Earlier Reforming Legislation

In 1945 the vast majority of serious offenders were sentenced to imprisonment, often for crimes that today would be dealt with by alternative means such as probation or fines. This situation was exacerbated by the hostility shown by the legal establishment towards the penal reform movement.[8] The reticence of the judiciary in adopting alternative methods of sentencing is a problem inherent in British legal history owing to the conservative background and legal education of many sentencers.[9] This stance is heightened when the government of the time adopts particularly radical policies in the field of criminal justice.

The political climate at the time was demonstrated by the changes to the status quo contained in the Criminal Justice Act 1948. The Act's preamble stated that it was intended to 'reform existing methods and provide new

---

[7] Annual Reports of the Commissioner of Prisons for England and Wales, HMSO, 1920–38.

[8] The Magistrates Association was formed in 1921 by, amongst others, Margaret Fry, a descendant of the penal reformer, Elizabeth Fry, with the aim of challenging contemporary sentencing policy, but this organization only enjoyed a very small membership in 1945.

[9] See generally, J. A. G. Griffiths, *The Politics of the Judiciary* (4th edn., London; Fontana Press 1991).

methods of dealing with offenders' and the provisions therein represent a
serious attempt to redefine the penal process and demonstrate a liberal
ideology. An example of this is the abolition of penal servitude and hard
labour in prisons, and of corporal punishment as a judicial sentence.[10]

Alternatives to imprisonment were also contained in the Act. The use
of probation in the United Kingdom can actually be traced back to 1840
when the Recorder of Birmingham, Matthew Davenport Hill, started a
register of suitable supervisors for reforming juvenile delinquents.[11] It should
be said, however, that the use of probation orders was not wholeheartedly
embraced by the judiciary and section 3(1) of the 1948 Act was an attempt
to emphasize the procedure whilst reserving the courts' discretion in its
application. The section deemed that the court should look at the particular
circumstances of the case before it, having particular regard to the nature
of the offence and the offender's age, in determining whether to grant
such an order. This would suggest that Parliament intended probation to
be used primarily with young offenders, but research has shown that it is
often used with elderly offenders and those who generally appear worthy
of the support such a scheme offers.[12] Furthermore, the Act introduced
the concepts of absolute and conditional discharge, whereby if the court
deems it 'inexpedient' to punish the offender they may discharge him
absolutely or subject to the condition that he does not reoffend within a
given period.[13]

The Act also demonstrated a determination to encourage the use of
appropriate methods of dealing with juvenile offenders. Those under the
age of 18 years when the offence was committed could no longer face the
death penalty, which was still the mandatory sentence for murder.[14] Further
provisions restricted the use of imprisonment to those over the age of 21
unless the court was of the opinion that no other method of dealing with
a young offender was appropriate.[15] The Act introduced detention centres,
attendance centres, and separate remand centres for juvenile offenders.[16]

Concern with the position of the offender was also apparent in the pre-
trial process, through the extension of free legal advice to defendants of
limited financial means contained within the Legal Aid and Advice Act
1949. Until this time statutory provision for such legal advice was extremely
limited and available only for the most serious criminal charges, such as

[10] Criminal Justice Act 1948, s. 1.
[11] *Report of the Departmental Committee on the Treatment of Young Offenders* (1927),
Cmd. 2831, 10.
[12] R. Cross, *The English Sentencing System* (3rd edn., London; Butterworths 1981), 20.
[13] Criminal Justice Act 1948, s. 7(1).   [14] Ibid., s. 16.
[15] Ibid., s. 17(2). A court of summary jurisdiction could not sentence a person younger than
17 to imprisonment and a Court of Assize or Quarter Sessions could not sentence an offender
of less than 15 to imprisonment under s. 17(1).
[16] Ibid., s. 48.

murder.[17] The 1949 Act therefore had the effect of providing a defence solicitor to many accused persons who previously would have been seriously disadvantaged in the trial procedure, particularly given the lack of wide-spread state education for the needy before the Second World War. The administration of the Legal Aid Fund was entrusted to the Law Society, the professional body for solicitors in England and Wales, thereby strengthening its ambit.[18]

Further proof of a move towards a more humane penal policy came when the United Kingdom finally abolished the death penalty in the Murder (Abolition of the Death Penalty) Act 1965. As in other jurisdictions, capital punishment was, and is, a highly controversial subject. In many ways popular sentiments adopt either a retributive or a reformative stance depending upon the factual background to the death penalty's abolition, rather than a philosophical appraisal of its advantages and disadvantages.[19] Its abolition however is seen by Younger as highly symbolic:

The death penalty has for many years now been the last remnant of an old penal system, whose roots lie deep in a primitive past, where death was the only penalty prescribed for serious crimes of all kinds, and such alternatives as there were also involved various forms of physical barbarity.[20]

The Reorganization of Criminal Justice

During the 1950s the increasingly interventionist role of the Government became apparent in the sphere of criminal justice. The Prison Act 1952 contained a general provision that all powers and jurisdiction in relation to prisons and prisoners were to be vested in the Secretary of State, and the Prison Commissioners were to be appointed on his recommendation.[21] The Commissioners' function was to:

... visit all prisoners and examine the state of buildings, the conduct of officers, the treatment and conduct of prisoners and all other matters concerning the management of prisons.[22]

---

[17] See Criminal Appeal Act 1907, s. 10; Poor Prisoners' Defence Act 1930, ss. 1 and 2; Summary Jurisdiction (Appeals) Act 1933, s. 2.

[18] Legal Aid and Advice Act 1949, s. 9(1).

[19] Much has been written on capital punishment; an interesting collection of essays is contained in L. Blom-Cooper (ed.), *The Hanging Question: Essays on the Death Penalty* (London; Duckworth 1969).

[20] K. Younger, 'The Historical Perspective', in Blom-Cooper (ed.), *The Hanging Question*, note 19 above, 6.

[21] Prison Act 1952, ss. 1 and 2(2). Prison Commissioners were to be paid a salary under s. 2(3).

[22] Ibid., s. 4(2).

The requirement in section 5 of the Act for the Secretary of State to report annually to Parliament on all prisons demonstrated a growing political awareness that the lack of visibility of penal institutions led to a general ignorance of how such institutions functioned in reality, thus hindering effective reform. The 1952 Act further ameliorated the conditions of prisoners by banning corporal punishment in the vast majority of circumstances and also by formally allowing remission for good conduct.[23]

Centralization in the administration of criminal justice was seen to be beneficial, in that it increased control of the functions of criminal justice, thereby reducing the possibility of corruption. In the late 1950s there were several serious incidents which led to questions being asked over the propriety of police activity. First, the Chief Constable of the Cardiganshire force became subject to disciplinary proceedings after allegations that the force was run incompetently, and these proceedings resulted in the amalgamation of Cardiganshire with the Carmarthenshire force. In 1957 there were allegations of corruption involving three officers in the Brighton Borough Police, including the Chief Constable, which resulted in imprisonment for the two lower ranked officers and the dismissal of the Chief Constable by the Watch Committee even though he had been acquitted by the court. The Chief Constable's counterpart in Worcester was not to be so fortunate, however, when in the same year he was imprisoned for fraud. Finally, again in 1957, allegations of assault by two Scottish police officers on a juvenile became national news. By this time political tension was such that an investigation of the 'Thurso Boy' incident was set up under the Tribunals of Inquiry (Evidence) Act 1921. The inquiry found that the juvenile had been subject to an assault by the officers in question following his provocative behaviour; however, the tribunal concluded that there would have been insufficient evidence to obtain a prosecution under Scots law.[24]

The Police Act 1964 rationalized the number of separate police forces within the country, although it is interesting to note that the Act did not create one national police force, as had happened in most other countries, but rather elected to maintain forces on a regional model. It may be suggested that this pattern was adopted to avoid concern that the police were becoming unduly politicized although with the much higher degree of inter-force co-operation in recent years (see Chapter 5) the reality of national policing may now be a more politically acceptable position, especially with the increasingly international aspects of criminal activity becoming of paramount concern.[25]

---

[23] Ibid., ss. 18(1) and 25(1).

[24] See *The Allegation of Assault on John Waters* (London; HMSO, 1959), Cmnd. 718.

[25] See, generally, Laurence Lustgarten, *The Governance of Police* (London; Sweet and Maxwell 1986).

The Movement away from Imprisonment

Despite the important reforms in criminal justice, imprisonment was still seen as the fundamental method of punishment. In 1965 the average daily prison population in England and Wales was 29,580. While it is fair to say that the levels of recorded crime were increasing, not all countries experiencing such trends have witnessed corresponding increases in prison population. An example of this is provided by a comparative study by Biles, which demonstrated that in the period between 1960 and 1979 the recorded crime rose by 177 per cent in England and Wales and by a similar 180 per cent in Australia, whereas the prison population in England and Wales went up by an astonishing 45 per cent compared with a more modest 9 per cent in Australia.[26] It is not surprising therefore that attempts were made to reduce the prison population.

The Criminal Justice Act 1967 was prompted by this need; it introduced the suspended sentence and also made provision to release certain prisoners on licence. To this end it established a Parole Board to monitor the progress made by prisoners.[27] If the conduct of an inmate was satisfactory, the Parole Board could recommend his early release on licence to the Secretary of State provided the prisoner had served at least one year or one-third of his original sentence; if that sentence was for life the Secretary of State had to consult with the Lord Chief Justice and the trial judge, if available.[28]

At the same time, however, the prison system became more security-conscious following an increase in the number of escapes from custody. The figure had risen alarmingly from 864 escapes and attempted escapes in 1946 to 2,090 in 1964.[29] These escapees include such infamous criminals as Charles Wilson and Ronald Biggs, two of the 'Great Train Robbers', and George Blake, who had been found guilty of spying. Such notorious escapes demonstrated the pressures that the prison system was under and raised doubt as to its competence to perform even the function of containment. A committee was therefore established under the chairmanship of Earl Mountbatten to make recommendations on how security might be improved in penal institutions. The report was far reaching, but its main recommendation was to class prisoners into four categories depending on their perceived danger to security, and that each class of offender should be sent to an institution with corresponding levels of security.[30] In practice the report was only followed in parts. The Government opted to place

---

[26] David Biles, 'Crime and Imprisonment: A Two-Decade Comparison between England and Wales and Australia' (1983) 23 *British Journal of Criminology*, 167.
[27] Criminal Justice Act 1967, s. 59(1).   [28] Ibid., ss. 60(1) and 61(1).
[29] J. A. Sharpe, *Judicial Punishment in England* (London; Faber 1990), 112.
[30] *Report of the Inquiry into Prison Escapes and Security by Admiral of the Fleet, the Earl Mountbatten of Burma* (1966), Cmnd. 3175.

category A prisoners, those seen as the highest risk to security, in maximum security wings in a number of prisons, thereby 'dispersing' the most dangerous prisoners throughout the system rather than centralizing them in a specialist institution as recommended by Mountbatten. A further White Paper of 1969 recommended a strong central command structure for the prison system.[31]

Security therefore became of paramount importance for the prison system in the late 1960s. The ever-increasing prison population was causing strain both to the penal institutions and to the prison officers. It is not surprising, therefore, that the motives behind subsequent reform were twofold; first there was a genuine desire to find a way of dealing effectively with offenders given the rise in reported crime, but secondly there was a pragmatic desire to reduce the number of offenders who were sentenced to imprisonment in an attempt to relieve the strain on the system. It would also be desirable public policy for a government to be seen to be taking action, given the breaches of security, which received much adverse publicity.

The Criminal Justice Act 1972, like that of 1967, it is suggested, attempted to satisfy all these needs. Until this time the criminal justice system had been primarily concerned with the detection and subsequent treatment of offenders, and therefore had not concerned itself greatly with the position of the victims of crime. The legal system adopted a dual approach whereby an act of violence, for example, could be treated both as a crime, where the offender would be punished on behalf of the state, and as a tort, or civil wrong, which would entitle the victim to financial recompense for the same act. This process, however, was unduly complex and expensive with the frequent result that the victim was not likely to instigate private proceedings for damages. The 1972 Act introduced a provision whereby the criminal courts could impose a compensation order on the offender, rendering him liable to compensate the victim for any personal injury, loss, or damage suffered in consequence of the offence.[32] The compensation order would have priority over both the order for costs sustained in the trial and the payment of any fines due as a measure of punishment.[33]

In terms of reducing the prison population and treating the offender in the most effective manner, the Act further restricted the use of imprisonment to offenders only above the age of 21, unless the court considered that no other punishment was appropriate for a young offender.[34] However, it was in its novel methods of disposition that the Act was to have most importance. Community service was introduced as an alternative method of punishment.[35] This involved the offender undertaking unpaid

---

[31] *People in Prison in England and Wales* (1969), Cmnd. 4214.
[32] Criminal Justice Act 1972, s. 1.
[33] Ibid., s. 5.   [34] Ibid., s. 14(1).   [35] Ibid., s. 15.

work in the community, for example working in a hospital garden. Under section 15(2) of the Act it is a prerequisite that the offender consents to this course of action, a necessary condition to avoid allegations of forced labour under the European Convention on Human Rights. The 1972 Act also provided facilities for offenders who were in need of special help. Day training centres were established for offenders who 'can't cope with the complexities of present day life'.[36] A probation order could insist on attendance at such an institution.[37]

Attention was also being given to problems of intoxication in society. The Criminal Justice Act 1967 had actually reduced the types of drunkenness which constituted criminal offences.[38] A report by the Working Party on Habitual Drunken Offenders in March 1971 argued that the best method of treating such offenders would be in special 'detoxification units' attached to hospitals, where the individual would get help from medical practitioners and social workers. The 1972 Act empowered a police officer to take a drunken offender to such a treatment centre.[39]

A Growing Political Awareness of Criminal Justice

The steady rise in reported crime and the apparent impossibility of halting this trend has caused increasing concern to the general population. Indeed a survey undertaken by Kinsey in the early 1980s shows that crime is perceived to be an extremely serious problem among his sample of the population of Merseyside.[40] This anxiety was seized upon by the mass media as certain crimes were identified and the media developed scares by the over-reporting of each incident when that crime was committed. While these offences did occur, and indeed it is right that they are reported, the selective nature of press reports on criminal trials and the desire amongst the more popular end of the media to 'sensationalize' crime has the unfortunate result that the common perception of criminal activity is misguided.[41] Two criminal activities which provoked public concern were 'mugging', technically robbery, and hooliganism, often associated with disturbances at football matches. As both these types of offences were frequently carried out by juveniles, many felt that the increasingly liberal penal policy followed since the Second World War had led to less deterrence and therefore threatened the safety of society. This popular view, although simplistic,

---

[36] House of Commons, vol. 826, no. 15, col. 974.
[37] Criminal Justice Act 1972, s. 20(1).   [38] Criminal Justice Act 1967, s. 91.
[39] Criminal Justice Act 1972, s. 34(1).
[40] R. Kinsey, *The Merseyside Crime Survey* (Liverpool; Merseyside Metropolitan Council 1984).
[41] See, generally, J. Ditton and J. Duffy, 'Bias in the Newspaper Reporting of Crime News' (1983) 23 *British Journal of Criminology*, 159.

challenged not just liberal penal policy but the whole concept of 'welfarism' which Britain had espoused since the war. These sentiments were shared by the Conservative Party as it shifted politically to the right in the late 1970s. In the 1979 election campaign this was shown in the party's response to rising crime figures; it was necessary to deliver a 'short, sharp shock' to juvenile offenders.

After the Conservatives gained office, they did indeed reform the institutional regime for young offenders. Initially, a new, tougher regime was to be tested in two detention centres.[42] A report from the Home Office Young Offender Psychology Unit, however, suggested that the new regime had 'no discernible effect' on reconviction rates and was in fact not disliked by inmates.[43] Nevertheless the changes to the system that the Conservatives had envisaged were carried through in the Criminal Justice Act 1982. This Act provided a new framework for custodial sentences for offenders under the age of 21. Imprisonment and borstal were replaced by a new youth custody sentence and, for the most serious offences, custody for life.[44] The Act, however, required courts to justify the use of custody and also to obtain a social inquiry report detailing the offender's background before imposing a custodial sentence, although the failure to follow this requirement would not invalidate the sentence passed.[45]

The role of the police was also to change under the new ethos, first via the Police and Criminal Evidence Act 1984 and secondly with the establishment of the Crown Prosecution Service in 1986. The Police and Criminal Evidence Act 1984 (PACE) set out the powers available to the police, notably in the areas of searching suspects and the detention of individuals in the police station. Critics argue that the Act extended police powers to an extent that serious encroachments of human rights could occur.[46] This Act was extremely far reaching, especially in relation to the admissibility of certain types of evidence in criminal proceedings. As such it demonstrated a trend towards stronger state control of the criminal proceedings and a growing willingness to find solutions to what was a clearly perceived problem (see the discussion in Chapters 3 and 7).

Traditionally, the police in England and Wales had the dual function of investigating and prosecuting criminal offences. The Crown Prosecution Service was established in 1986 to separate these two functions—while the police maintained the right to charge defendants and gather evidence

[42] Sharpe, n. 29 above, 128.
[43] *Tougher Regimes in Detention Centres*, Home Office Young Offender Psychology Report 1984.
[44] Criminal Justice Act 1982, ss. 6 and 8.   [45] Ibid., ss. 2(2) and 2(8).
[46] See, generally, Michael Zander, *Police and Criminal Evidence Act 1984* (2nd edn., London; Sweet and Maxwell 1991).

relating to the offence, including the right to interview witnesses, the Crown Prosecution Service assesses the evidence and presents the case in court. The Crown Prosecution Service also has the power to drop or vary charges against the accused (see the further discussion in Chapters 7 and 11).

These measures, however, did little to stem the sense of penal crisis. By 1986 there were on average 46,900 people in prison per day in England and Wales. The gross expenditure on the prison service in England and Wales for the year 1985–6 was £786,500,000. After a decade in government the Conservatives had to redefine their penal policy, particularly as their earlier policy of expanding the prison building programme had been subject to much criticism.[47] It is also politically damaging to claim to be the party of 'law and order' and preside over a period when the reported crime rate has increased considerably.

This change of direction is demonstrated in the Criminal Justice Act 1991, which has considerable importance for the criminal justice system. Since the Second World War the legislature had tried to reduce the use of imprisonment as a punishment and had sought to offer alternative methods. The practice, however, showed that an ever-increasing number of people were being imprisoned despite parliamentary intent. What the 1991 Act attempted to do was to separate serious violent and sexual offences from other offences in the way that the courts treated offenders. A broad restriction was placed on the use of imprisonment; the court had to be satisfied that the offence was of such severity that no other sentence could be justified, except in the cases of offenders who had committed violent or sexual offences, where the criterion to be adopted was whether imprisonment was necessary 'to protect the public from serious harm'.[48] In short, imprisonment was to be used as a last resort or where containment was needed in order to reflect the seriousness of the offence or for public safety. The court further has to explain to the offender in open court why it is passing a custodial sentence,[49] as had been required in dealing with young offenders under the Criminal Justice Act 1982.

More use is also to be made of experts in the criminal process. The Act requires the court to obtain a pre-sentence report written by either a probation officer or a social worker which comments on the most suitable method of treatment for the individual in question.[50] However, if the case is triable only on indictment, this report can be bypassed if the court deems it unnecessary, and furthermore its decision is not invalidated if the court does not fulfil this general requirement.[51]

---

[47] A. Rutherford, 'Deeper into the Quagmire: Observations on the Latest Prison Building Programme', (1984) 23 *Howard Journal*, 129.

[48] Criminal Justice Act 1991, s. 1.   [49] Ibid., s. 1(4)(b).

[50] Ibid., s. 3(1).   [51] Ibid., ss. 3(2) and 3(4).

The 1991 Act also reforms the existing alternatives to imprisonment. The so-called 'community sentences' (namely probation orders, community service orders, combination orders, curfew orders, supervision orders, and attendance centre orders) are again subject to the restriction that they should only be used when the gravity of the offence demands it.[52] Additional requirements may be added to probation orders if the court sees fit; an example here would be restraining an individual who had committed public order offences at a football match from attending given matches for a specified period or requiring treatment for drug or alcohol addiction.[53] Section 12 of the Act provides for curfew orders, whereby offenders over the age of 16 are required to remain in a specified place for a specified period of time. The Act also allows for the electronic monitoring of offenders during curfew periods, a controversial measure which may well not be implemented.[54] Another concept introduced in the Act was the 'unit fine'; where the offender paid an amount calculated by taking into account both the severity of the offence and the offender's 'disposable weekly income'.[55] Although this made allowance for the offender's ability to pay, much popular dissatisfaction led to the Government abolishing unit fines in the Criminal Justice Act 1993.[56]

The distinction between the two classes of offender mentioned earlier in the Act, those found guilty of serious violent or sexual offences and other offenders, is now also important in relation to early release. Prisoners serving less than four years are to be released after half the sentence has expired, whereas for longer sentences the offender has to serve two-thirds of his sentence. Those serving discretionary life sentences for a violent or sexual offence, however, must serve the minimum period specified by the court before the Parole Board can direct their release.[57]

A further development, which represents a fundamental shift in penal policy, is that the Criminal Justice Act 1991 allows the contracting out to private management of certain prisons for remand prisoners.[58] While this is in keeping with governmental privatization policy, it is submitted that the primary motivation for this is to reduce overcrowding in certain prisons by providing more suitable accommodation for those awaiting trial. The recent adverse publicity given to privatizing parts of the criminal justice system following several escapes, and a death, of remand prisoners being escorted by Group 4 does not appear significantly to have altered government policy in this area.

[52] Ibid., s. 6(1).
[53] Ibid., s. 9(1); Sched. 1A of the Act lists some of the requirements that could be made.
[54] Ibid., s. 13(1).   [55] Ibid., s. 18(2)(b).
[56] Criminal Justice Act 1993, s. 65(1) and sch. 3.
[57] Criminal Justice Act 1991, s. 34(3).
[58] Ibid., s. 84; see, generally, Roger Matthews (ed.), *Privatizing Criminal Justice* (London; Sage 1989).

The General Evolution of Policy

The general liberalization of the criminal justice system following the Second World War was offset by a steady rise in both the reported crime figures and the use of imprisonment. This has made it difficult to assess the various policies put forward, as all in turn have failed to produce the beneficial effects their advocates had predicted. One has, therefore, to understand the frustration that successive governments have felt in trying to reform criminal justice policy. A prime example of this is the Criminal Justice Act 1991, where the Conservative government effectively conceded that the previous policy they had enacted had been unsuccessful in reducing reported crime; on the contrary it had increased substantially, and therefore the 1991 Act represents a fundamentally different penal policy from that which the same Conservative Party had advocated a decade earlier and had vigorously defended throughout the 1980s.

Remnants of the earlier philosophy survive, however. The Criminal Justice Act 1991, while adopting a different stance on the majority of offenders, contains special provisions relating to those who commit violent or sexual offences which retain the older philosophy. It should also be remembered that the policy contained in the Criminal Justice Act 1991 has to be viewed in tandem with specific pieces of legislation, such as the Dangerous Dogs Act 1991, which increase penalties in the attempt to combat specific threats to law and order at a given time. Therefore government action does not always follow a consistent path, but rather abandons general principles to concentrate on particular ways of dealing with particular problems. This has resulted in more and increasingly complex legislation being passed.

The Criminal Justice Act 1991 further attempts to structure sentencing practice to counter judicial resistance to reforms in penal policy. The insularity of the legal profession combined with the social background of its practitioners has the result of producing a judiciary with orthodox beliefs about the legal system and a deference to certain traditions, one of which is the discretion vested in the judiciary to determine an appropriate sentence in a given case. This privilege is guarded jealously. Clearly, when the judicial position runs counter to governmental policy, tensions result which hamper effective legal development. The conflicting nature of governmental criminal justice policy may even harden judicial attitudes in that the legislature seems uncertain of how to deal effectively with the rising problem of crime in society, and therefore the judiciary attempts to show some form of continuity in sentencing practice even where this may run counter to parliamentary intent.

This frustration would appear to be shared by contemporary academic criminology. A rising crime rate is increasingly seen to be inevitable. Again, this conclusion has resulted in a change in emphasis by commentators on both the left and right; those on the left maintain that reported crime will continue, whereas those on the new right, often termed the administrative criminologists, have reconciled themselves to a focus on containment alone. As Young puts it:

> Research grants come and research grants go and people are gainfully employed but crime remains, indeed it grows and nothing they do seems able to do anything about it.[59]

It is fair to say that the criminal justice system in England and Wales has evolved greatly since 1945. Greater use is made of alternative forms of punishment, there is a growing use of specialists in the criminal process, and archaic remnants such as the death penalty have been abolished. However, an initial reforming zeal would appear to have been replaced by an increasing frustration as the continual rise in reported crime makes penal policy appear ineffectual *per se*. Politicians realize that justice must not only be done but must be seen to be done. What recent legislation appears to be doing is trying to reconcile public concern with a realization that alternative forms of disposal to imprisonment would be beneficial. It may be that the primary motivation for such an initiative is economic rather than ideological. To what extent these objectives can be met remains to be seen.

EMERGENCY POWERS AND CRIMINAL JUSTICE IN THE UK

In the last twenty-five years there have been a number of developments in criminal justice policy which have been designed to combat the problem of terrorist activities, both in Northern Ireland and on the British mainland. The availability and use of extended detention powers are discussed in detail elsewhere in this volume;[60] here attention will focus more generally on the range of measures adopted in this context.

Internment

On 9 August 1971 the government of the day used Regulation 12(1) of the Special Powers Regulations as the legal basis for the introduction of a policy of internment.[61] This policy allowed for the arrest and detention of suspected terrorists without the need for a particular charge to be specified.

---

[59] J. Young, 'The Failure of Criminology: The Need for a Radical Realism', in R. Matthews and J. Young (eds.), *Confronting Crime* (London; Sage 1986), 29–30.
[60] See Chap. 12.
[61] The Special Powers Regs. were succeeded by the Detention of Terrorists (N. I.) Order 1972, Northern Ireland (Emergency Provisions) Act 1973, s. 10(5) and Sched. 1, and the Northern Ireland (Emergency Provisions) (Amendment) Act 1975, s. 9 and Sched. 1.

The detainee, who had the same rights and privileges as an ordinary re-mand prisoner, could be detained on the order of the Secretary of State, although such detention had to be reviewed on at least a yearly basis. This decision to intern was effectively unchallengeable in the courts and vested a large amount of discretionary power in the hands of an elected member of the executive. The courts were extremely reluctant to interfere with a decision to intern and preferred to leave accountability for such decisions to Parliament. This is in line with the courts' traditional approach to the use of such powers.[62] The consequences for the life of the individual of the exercise of this power were disastrous; he faced an indeterminate period of detention which did not result from a criminal conviction and could do very little about it. Arguably, the use of executive detention of this nature calls into question the existence of the 'rule of law' which is held out as a basic constitutional element of the British system. On the first day of the operation of this policy 342 people were detained,[63] and within six months, the powers were used against 2,357 people.[64] However, its use declined steadily and it was abandoned as a policy in 1975. It is worth noting, however, that the power to intern has been retained in section 34 of and Schedule 3 to the Northern Ireland (Emergency Provisions) Act 1991. While these provisions were not in force at the time of writing, their imple-mentation could be effected by means of a statutory instrument, providing of course that the prevailing political climate was conducive to such action.

The procedure by which the power to intern was introduced, and the scope and content of the power, are instructive as an illustration of the policy towards emergency powers in the period in question. The policy was instigated at a time of great public concern about terrorist activity and contained a series of measures which contradicted the traditional view of the legal system. First, detention was permitted at the order of the execut-ive rather than after conviction by the courts, by reviving a measure used during World War Two against aliens, but seldom against British citizens in non-war situations. Secondly, the maximum period of detention was not fixed at the outset, as the internment could continue indefinitely subject to an annual review. Thirdly, the exercise of the executive power, while theor-etically subject to the safeguard of judicial review, was not constrained by an effective legal control mechanism, thus subverting the doctrine of the separation of powers. There is no conclusive evidence to demonstrate that internment had a noticeable impact on terrorist activity.[65]

---

[62] See, e.g. *Liversidge* v. *Anderson* [1942] AC 206; *R.* v. *Secretary of State for the Home Department, ex parte Cheblak* [1991] 2 All ER 319.

[63] R. J. Spjut, 'Internment and Detention without Trial in Northern Ireland 1971–75: Min-isterial Policy and Practice', (1986) 49 *MLR* 712.

[64] M. Brake and C. Hale, *Public Order and Private Lives* (London; Routledge 1992), 61.

[65] Spjut, n. 57 above.

Trial without Jury

The second measure introduced was the system of 'Diplock Courts' which were mooted in the report of the Diplock Commission[66] and put on a statutory footing by the Northern Ireland (Emergency Provisions) Act 1973. The title of the Act indicates another feature of the policy in this area. The words 'emergency' and 'temporary' appear often in British anti-terrorist legislation because the introduction of the measures in question is justified as being necessary to combat a pressing short-term problem and they are to be repealed once the problem is solved. The length of time for which these measures have been in operation renders their use today to be at best an expression of hope.

The 'Diplock Court' system was introduced in an effort to combat the perceived problems of intimidation of jurors in terrorist trials and the possibility of perverse acquittals of suspects by mainly Protestant juries. The existence of the second problem has never conclusively been proved, but the potential for the first is undoubted and consideration of the position of jurors and victims of terrorist attacks provides some justification for the retention of the system. Under the system suspects accused of the offences listed in what is now Schedule 1 to the Northern Ireland (Emergency Provisions) Act 1991 are tried without a jury. This conflicts with a major principle of British law, that a man's guilt should be determined by a group of his peers. This system places a lot of pressure on judges and removes what many regard as a fundamental safeguard for the liberty of the individual. Whether or not this safeguard is merely symbolic is not so much the point as that its removal creates doubts as to the fairness of criminal procedures in the minds of those against whom such procedures are to be used. This can lead to a loss of confidence in the legal system, yet such confidence is exactly what is needed in 'emergency situations'. The accused's position as regards a jury trial is safeguarded by Schedule 1, which permits the Attorney-General to 'deschedule' a particular charge and so allow it to be tried in the traditional manner. Such descheduling occurs after a request to the Attorney-General. In 1990, 52 per cent of such applications were granted.[67] Again the measure has produced no discernible reduction in crime rates and the frequency of descheduling has led to calls for the system to be altered to create a position where scheduling must be applied for and the presumption towards it should be reduced.[68]

---

[66] *Report of the Commission to Consider Legal Procedures to Deal with Terrorist Activities in Northern Ireland* (1972), Cmnd. 5185.

[67] See J. Jackson and S. Doran, 'Diplock and the Presumption against Jury Trial: A Critique' [1992] *CrimLRev.* 755 at 763.

[68] Ibid.

Powers of Arrest

The third measure to be considered is the availability to the police of wide powers of arrest. This trend began with section 11 of the Northern Ireland (Emergency Provisions) Act 1973, which allowed the arrest of a suspected 'terrorist' without requiring the arresting officer to specify the nature of the suspected involvement with terrorism, or indeed any particular offence at all.

This power has gone through limited changes but survives now as section 14 of the Prevention of Terrorism (Temporary Provisions) Act 1989 (PTA). This section allows the police to make an arrest without a warrant if there are reasonable grounds for suspecting that one or more of the following conditions are satisfied:

(i) The arrestee is guilty of an offence under certain sections of the Act;[69]

(ii) The person 'is or has been concerned in the commission, preparation or instigation of acts of terrorism';[70]

(iii) The suspect is subject to an exclusion order[71] (see below).

The second condition is the most controversial. Under section 14(1) of the PTA the arresting officer does not have to specify a *particular* act of terrorism which he reasonably expects the arrestee to have been involved in, the only requirement is suspicion of involvement in *some* terrorist activity.[72]

This is a draconian power and again flies in the face of traditional legal procedure. No other arrest power under the law of the UK can be used without specification of the offence of which the arrestee is suspected. The PTA seems to permit the police to mount 'fishing expeditions' (to make arrests for the purpose of gathering information), a position previously considered to be unacceptable under British law. Further, it is a well-established principle of law in the UK that an arrested person should be told the reason for arrest.[73] This is seen as an essential safeguard for suspects' rights, since it precludes arbitrary arrest and allows the suspect to prepare a defence. However, the courts have held that a mere recitation of the arrest provision will satisfy this requirement.[74] It may be argued that, as long as section 14 remains in its present form, this safeguard is meaningless for those arrested under this power. The suspect has no knowledge of the offences for which the arrest is being made because the officer does not need such knowledge in order to effect a lawful arrest; this clearly affects the scope for defence. Furthermore, an objective of the safeguard

---

[69] PTA 1989, s. 14(1)(a).   [70] Ibid., s. 14(1)(b).
[71] Ibid., s. 14(1)(c).   [72] *Ex parte Lynch* [1980] NI 1.
[73] Ss. 28 and 29, Police and Criminal Evidence Act 1984.
[74] See *Lynch*, n. 72 above.

is to provide clarity, so that all parties concerned in the arrest know their respective positions: such clarity is not achieved by section 14(1)(b).

Here again, a wide power has been vested in an enforcement agency without any real control over its exercise, despite the existence of the concerns outlined above. This is a further instance of the policy of introducing a measure which is contrary to established legal principle at a time of great concern (the first PTA was rushed through Parliament in the wake of the Birmingham Pub Bombings in 1974), and describing it as a 'temporary' measure as a justification for its enactment. Since there has been a Prevention of Terrorism (Temporary Provisions) Act on the statute book since 1974, the word 'temporary' sounds increasingly hollow.

The Right to Silence

The fourth related area is that of restrictions on the right of silence. In 1988 the Home Secretary announced a number of restrictions on the right of suspects in Northern Ireland to remain silent.[75] These restrictions were introduced by way of delegated legislation, thus avoiding the full rigour of Parliamentary scrutiny necessary for primary legislation. A court is permitted to draw 'adverse inferences' from a suspect's failure to answer questions in a number of specified situations, two of which may be considered here. A suspect's failure to mention a 'relevant fact' during police interrogation may be subject to the drawing of an adverse inference.[76] In the light of the preceding discussion of section 14(1)(b), it is easy to understand the concern about this: what will be a relevant fact in the case of a person arrested under that section? Secondly, the accused who remains silent in court falls foul of this provision.

On the other hand, the introduction of this measure again illustrates the character of such emergency powers. A fundamental right of the accused has been restricted by executive action with little Parliamentary accountability, and its confinement to Northern Ireland ensured that the outcry against the measure would be far easier to deal with than if it had been a nationwide development. On the other hand, adverse inferences are not wholly alien to British legislation: section 62(10) of PACE allows such inferences to be drawn from a refusal to supply DNA samples (see Chapter 13). Two further points should be noted here: first, research has suggested that this measure has had little real impact[77] and, secondly, at the time this measure was introduced the Home Secretary indicated that the measure might be extended to the mainland,[78] though this remains to be seen.

---

[75] Criminal Evidence (Northern Ireland) Order 1988.   [76] Ibid., Art. 3.

[77] J. Jackson, 'Curtailing the Right of Silence: Lessons from Northern Ireland' [1991] *CrimLRev.* 404.

[78] *Independent*, 21 October 1988.

Exclusion

The final measure to be studied is the exclusion order. This is an executive order which prohibits entry into the United Kingdom or certain areas of it, usually the mainland or Northern Ireland.[79] The provisions for this are now contained in sections 4–8 of the PTA. Under these orders British citizens may be prohibited from entering parts of their own country, effectively confining them to certain areas of territory. This is a preventive power exercisable on similar grounds to the arrest power in section 14(1)(b). Until recently a challenge to the making of an order by way of judicial review was of little effective value[80] but in *Gallagher*[81] the Court of Appeal will, in the near future, be considering the legality of this measure in relation to European Community law.

It may be seen, therefore, that British criminal justice policy towards terrorists has a common core. Broad powers are given to the executive in the form of 'temporary' or 'emergency' provisions, and these are subject to little effective judicial control, despite the fact that they amount to radical changes in the criminal justice process and are rarely repealed.

[79] D. Bonner, 'Combatting Terrorism in Great Britain: The Role of Exclusion Orders' [1982] *Public Law*, 262.
[80] *R. v. Secretary of State for the Home Department, ex parte Stitt, The Times*, 3 February 1987.
[81] [1993] NLJ 355.

3

Are Inquisitorial and Adversarial Systems Converging?

NICO JÖRG, STEWART FIELD, AND CHRISJE BRANTS

INTRODUCTION: THE QUEST FOR THE TRUTH, THE FAIRNESS OF
CRIMINAL PROCEDURE, AND LEGITIMACY

It has been a long-standing habit among legal scholars to think in terms of families of law: civil law families on the continent of Europe, common law families in Great Britain and her former colonies. While differences *within* these systems are often regarded as incidental, those *between* them are seen as essential. From a comparative angle, the intriguing question arises whether the legal systems of continental and common law countries— usually portrayed as diametrically opposed—are gradually converging. If that is indeed the case, does this imply that both systems will eventually adopt so many of each other's characteristics as to become no more than variations on a theme—their differences no longer essential, our traditional frame of reference no longer appropriate?

It is also possible that the two systems are moving towards each other, but that convergence beyond a certain point is out of the question—for the simple reason that there is a critical limit at which each system would start to risk disintegration. This implies—and it may be especially true in the field of criminal justice—that these systems are the embodiment of such divergent norms and values in the field of criminal justice, in their turn reflecting profound societal values, that they can never be brought together entirely. And there is, of course, a third and more radical possibility. Perhaps due to the influence of shared European institutions (notably the European Community and Union Treaties and the Court of Justice in Luxembourg, and the European Convention on Human Rights and Fundamental Freedoms (ECHR) and the European Court of Human Rights in Strasbourg), one system will in the end come to dominate the other, thereby causing the latter to lose many of its salient and unique features.[1]

---

[1] Developments within the European Community and Union, and its different institutions especially, are usually referred to in terms of harmonization, which is indeed one of the goals of these institutions. Harmonization, interesting though it is, does not come within the scope of this chapter, for it is based on the assumption that each system will retain is own essential characteristics.

It is important to distinguish between these possibilities. Countries with different legal traditions (we shall use England and Wales on the one hand and the Netherlands on the other as examples) often face similar problems, but have traditionally resolved them in contrasting and sometimes seemingly incompatible ways—as even a cursory glance at the chapters in this book reveals. As knowledge of, and familiarity with, other systems increases, it is tempting to seek new solutions in the experiences of others. But the viability and acceptability of specific mechanisms and processes may often be related to their context—the norms and values of the system as a whole. To grasp these connections between the particular and the general, one needs a developed overview. Only then will we be able to draw conclusions about converging or permanently divergent systems, or about critical demarcation lines, domination, and points of no return.

Let us start with the classical distinction between adversarial and inquisitorial systems of criminal justice. The usual way of describing the former is as a contest between two equal parties, seeking to resolve a dispute before a passive and impartial judge, with a jury ('the people') pronouncing one version of events to be the truth. The inquisitorial system is described as the investigation of an event and the persons involved in that event by the state with a view to establishing the truth—the state doubly present in the 'fact-collecting' prosecutor on the one hand and, on the other, an impartial and independent judge actively involved in truth-finding. The adversarial system invokes images of peaceful medieval folk-gatherings under sacred oaks, disputes solved voluntarily and satisfactorily by means of oaths before the elders of the tribe. The connotation of inquisitorial proceedings is very much more terrible: the sinister red robes and pointed hats of an all-powerful Inquisition from which there is no escape, and the establishment of 'truth' by means of confessions, extracted, if necessary, under torture.

Both notions are, of course, quite ridiculous when applied to modern criminal justice, and even in their classical (i.e. ideal typical) forms, the aims of adversarial and inquisitorial justice are much closer than the classical models imply. Both systems have the finding of truth as a fundamental aim: the principle that the guilty should be punished and the innocent left alone. Yet whatever the system, it is surely fundamental that the truth—in so far as it can be established—should be established in what is regarded as a fair, and therefore socially legitimate, way. It is not here that the two systems differ, but in their fundamental assumptions as to the best way of going about things.

Within the adversarial culture, the most common and traditional assumption is that real equality of parties and the dialectical process of persuasion involved in courtroom procedure will somehow lead to truth emerging. Thus fairness of procedure and truth-finding are unproblematically related, and therefore there is no need to face issues of priority between the two. But this places inordinate faith in the notion that partisan manipulation of evidentiary materials, even under equality of arms, can put an independent judge in a position to determine truth—an assumption at best unproven, and at worst highly implausible. Add to this anxieties about the capacity of procedural rules to ensure equality of the parties, and the relationship between procedural fairness, truth, and legitimacy becomes more difficult.

An inquisitorial system assumes that the truth can be, and must be, discovered in an investigative procedure, and, because it may be in the interests of parties to conceal it, that the state is best equipped to carry out such investigations. This presupposes that the system is fair and legitimate, because it aims at a version of the truth that will be as nearly objective as possible. Therefore on the surface an unproblematic relationship again exists between the three ideas, albeit that in the classical view priority is given to truth finding. Determining the 'legal quality' of the truth is seen as best left to legal professionals. The legitimacy of the inquisitorial procedure in a democratic context requires an inordinate amount of faith in the integrity of the state and its capacity to pursue truth unprompted by partisan pressures of individual self-interest and untrammelled by equality of arms.

We would suggest that both sets of assumptions, if permanently hidden and therefore unchallenged, are equally dangerous. Truth-finding and fairness are the most important, distinct, aims of criminal justice. But they are also interrelated in the sense that they may clash and yet at the same time depend on each other for legitimacy.

Systems of (criminal) justice may differ in yet another way. Damaska has suggested in *Two Faces of Justice and State Authority*[2] that their overreaching goals may be regarded as conflict-solving or policy-implementing. He also notes that any modern system of criminal justice must be, to a great extent, policy-implementing. However, these goals too are interdependent, although differing in emphasis. In an adversarial system the visible solution of conflicts provides a vehicle for the state to implement policy, while in an inquisitorial system the implementation of policy may also serve as a vehicle for conflict-solving. Here again we would maintain that the legitimacy of the system depends on its ability to do both.

Bearing these remarks in mind, we now turn to examine the structural characteristics of the English and Dutch systems, which may be regarded as typical examples of adversarial and inquisitorial systems respectively. We will first try to formulate some general principles that are probably

---

[2] M. Damaska, *Two Faces of Justice and State Authority* (New Haven; Yale University Press 1986).

equally applicable to other examples of those criminal justice systems, but we also have to be realistic, limiting our excursions to England and Wales on the one hand, and the Netherlands on the other. In each case we shall be describing the classical model and following this with an account of modern developments. However, we must repeat that the classical model of these legal systems is a theoretical one, describing ideal types and not necessarily the functioning of the system in practice. Nevertheless, the implications of such basically ideological notions, and the structures of authority that both derive from and reinforce them, may be essential in determining the extent to which one type of system will be able to absorb elements of the other.

THE STATE: AUTHORITY, ACCOUNTABILITY, DOMINATING ASSUMPTIONS, AND AIMS

Damaska has emphasized the importance of hierarchical structures of authority to processes of state accountability within continental inquisitorial systems. The criminal justice system in the Netherlands conforms closely to this model of hierarchical/pyramidal organization, the underlying assumption being that the state is the benevolent and most powerful promoter and guarantor of public interest and can, moreover, be trusted to 'police' itself as long as authority is organized in a way that will allow it to do so. In essence that assumption is still based on the separation of powers doctrine of French revolutionary origin.

From an organizational point of view the situation in the Netherlands is close to the ideal type: the police are locally organized and accountable to the public prosecutors at the district courts as far as the investigation of crime is concerned. The public prosecutors are accountable to one of the five heads of the prosecution service, the *procureurs-generaal* at the five appeal courts. In their turn, the *procureurs-generaal* are accountable to the Minister of Justice who, at the end of this chain of accountability, must answer to Parliament. Ideally, both the police and the public prosecutor are impartially engaged in seeking the truth, not in winning a contest, even if it results in unsolved crimes.

The judiciary is equally pyramidally organized, with the Supreme Court as highest authority on points of law. Any case meriting prosecution must, ideally, be heard by the appropriate court. From a functional point of view the role of the judiciary is conceptually a relatively unimportant one, being adjudicative only and in no way legislative, although in court they are actively engaged in discovering 'the truth'. For, according to the ideology of inquisitorial justice, criminal procedure serves to uncover the substantive truth, thereby allowing state authority to proceed on the assumption that the outcome and consequences of a criminal trial are based on the truth. The state has a stake in this kind of justice, for it allows crime to become a subject through which central government can express its public-interest concerns.

Common law ways of thinking about accountability and state derive initially from a negative image of the state and a minimalist view of its functions. Forms of accountability are aimed primarily at the limitation and division of power. Authority is less clearly hierarchical, with a range of interdependent and yet independent authorities with few clear lines of subordination, each checking and restricting the power of the others. This objective is more crucial than efficient state promotion of the public interest.

Consequently, policing, prosecution, judging, sentencing, and penal administration are constructed as separate and localized spheres of decision-making, unlinked by a clear central thread of authority. One key aspect of this negative system of checks and balances is the rule of law, in which law-making by the higher judiciary is an openly acknowledged practice. But lack of central co-ordinated organization within the criminal justice system and the passive role of the judiciary render active truth-seeking by the state both difficult and, indeed, dangerous, there being no independent party available to intervene actively. According to the ideology of the adversarial process, criminal procedure therefore involves solving a conflict between equal parties and robbing it of its potentially destructive propensities by allowing those parties access to legal instruments and arbiters.

Modern tendencies have, however, mellowed and to some extent undermined both sytems. In the Netherlands, for example, the rationale of the French separation of powers doctrine still applies, but in practice it is being eroded. Boundaries between legislation and administration, and between legislation and adjudication, are fading. The judiciary has gained in importance, both quantitatively (with regard to the number of conflicts) and qualitatively (in the field of law-making). The police force has gained in autonomy, as a result of bureaucratization and specialization.

More important perhaps is the fact that, within the welfare state, the driving force behind criminal policy is more likely to be the protection of anonymous interests, such as public health, economic well-being, equal distribution of wealth, rather than the concrete interests of individuals, engendering a tendency to equate the public interest with the interests of the state, and to lose sight of individual conflict within the sphere of crime and justice (for example, between perpetrator and victim). Recently the victim's interests have re-emerged as a legitimate concern of criminal justice. Tightening controls on crime have meant the relaxation of written rules of criminal procedure which once carried strict procedural penalties. But the organizational fundamentals—the hierarchical ordering of criminal justice functions—remain unchanged. In the final evaluation of a case, the judiciary is therefore more likely to be assessing the substantive rather than formal fairness of the procedure.

Within the English system, the control of crime has become one of an increasing number of issues of public interest that come to be seen as requiring forceful and extensive state response. But despite the increasing desire for an effective instrument of social policy, clearer hierarchical organization of the criminal justice system as a whole has not emerged. There has been an expansion in the conception of legitimate techniques of police investigation (overt detention for questioning, wire-tapping). Police subordination to local democratic control is weakening, and although amalgamation of forces reduces the local flavour of policing, forces remain influenced by central government rather than coming under its authority (thus largely escaping parliamentary control).

As for legal and constitutional control of policing, moves toward hierarchically organized mechanisms of monitoring are hesitant or stillborn. Political contestation and public scandal create a demand for greater accountability, but the response is generally traditional: new procedural controls on the new investigative techniques. A partial qualification on this is the creation of the Crown Prosecution Service (CPS), a development of great potential importance. Itself a pyramidal-hierarchical authority, nevertheless it has not been accorded (nor has it sought) supremacy over the local police. Indeed, the relationship between police and prosecution service, who are mutually dependent on, and yet quite independent of, each other, is a modern example of old co-ordinate authority structures. Owing to the absence of a hierarchical relationship between the CPS and anybody else, the various stages in the criminal justice process still do not operate rationally co-ordinated policies. The role of central government is most visible in the increasing quantity of legislation on criminal justice matters, which is accompanied by greater reticence on the part of the judiciary in overt law-creation on criminal matters, although much continues to be done by way of creative exposition of the law.

Such general principles, goals, and developments are reflected at all stages of procedure. In the following we shall be looking at pre-trial procedure and the trial itself, and at the specific ways in which both are constructed to accommodate the idiosyncracies of the inquisitorial and adversarial systems to which they belong.

THE PRE-TRIAL PROCESS: THE (LACK OF) INTERPLAY BETWEEN DEFENCE, POLICE, AND JUDICIAL AUTHORITIES

Inquisitorial systems aim at the state actively discovering the truth, and the most salient feature of the pre-trial process in the Netherlands is probably the degree to which all parties co-operate in arriving at a pre-prepared version of it that is subsequently recorded in a case file or *dossier* as the basis for the coming trial. Professional investigators employed by the state—police, forensic psychiatrists, and scientists—are expected not only to do most of the work, but to do it in a detached and impartial way, an assumption that allows the defence to leave most matters of investigation to state-employed police officers or state-funded institutions. Public interest, not self-interest, is the key word here. The role of the defence is very much to safeguard the client's interests by seeing that these representatives of the state stick to the rules, which, though numerous, do not create equality of arms in the pre-trial stage. The defence may also suggest that certain aspects, favourable to the defendant, should be investigated. A prosecutor would be violating standards of professional ethics if he were to fail to take notice of evidence in the defendant's favour.

There are other built-in safeguards too. One is the *dossier* itself—reporting every step in the procedure—for it not only forms the basis for the trial, but also a coherent system of supervision and control, equally at the disposal of the prosecution and the defence. The other is the investigative judge, whose original role is to determine sufficiency of evidence and seek out truth using special investigative powers given to him for that purpose. The results of the judicial inquiry are included in the *dossier*.

Within the criminal justice system, however, essential relationships between parties and within state institutions are changing. Concerns about organized crime have resulted in increasing emphasis on secret undercover operations in criminal investigation—with all the dangers of entrapment, cover-ups, and inherently difficult verifiability and control. These developments leave a few traces in the *dossier*—or even no trace at all! As the police increasingly come to see themselves as a party opposing (organized) crime, doubts about their unambiguous commitment to truth-finding increase, and they lay themselves open to charges of partisanship.

At the same time (and linked to the foregoing), the other built-in guarantee that the *dossier* will be truthful is also under pressure. There are plans to cut back the truth-finding role and corresponding powers of the investigating judge (several countries with inquisitorial procedures have already done so), which will render the public prosecutor the sole functionary responsible for the collection of evidence, with the investigating judge merely authorizing the use of intrusive investigative techniques by others. This corresponds with the development of the prosecution service as rapidly becoming the central government organization where policy decisions are made on how to deal with crime, while undermining the quasi-judicial and impartial position of the prosecutor in safeguarding the due administration of substantive justice. The end result may well be a more adversarial relationship between defence and prosecution, as the possibly diminishing reliability of the *dossier* as a reflection of 'pre-trial truth' inevitably involves the defence more in truth-finding.

There is another reason why we must expect more active involvement by the defence in pre-trial decisions. In an ideal-typical inquisitorial system neither side has any right to let the case rest, or to bargain about its outcome or about the way in which it will be tried. The Dutch system has never been entirely inquisitorial in this sense (prosecutors have always been able to drop individual cases for reasons of public interest pertaining to the case). Moreover, modern tendencies have resulted in various ways of settling cases out of court with or without conditions like the payment of a legally fixed or negotiated sum of money. Consequently the incidence of negotiations between defence and prosecution is on the rise; while not called plea bargaining yet, the terminology has emerged in official documents.

In adversarial systems, each party is responsible for developing evidence to support its arguments. Investigation is motivated by self-interest rather than public interest. There is no investigating judge to seek out 'truth' and, despite official rhetoric about impartiality in prosecution, the concrete legal duties of police and prosecution lawyers do not extend to seeking out exculpatory evidence. Indeed what constitutes the truth is subject to negotiation by the parties. Extensive plea bargaining simply produces an agreed approximation of events on which to base conviction and sentence. It is rare for any judicial authority to challenge these agreed assertions.

Procedural regulation and structuring of the pre-trial process is traditionally limited. The system starts from a model of contest between equal and private parties and therefore the assumption that the state need merely provide an arena for the resolution of the conflict. The initial credibility of this model is maintained by resistance to the development of a state police and the use of terrible inquisitorial techniques of interrogation under detention, and to the development of an organized public party to the pre-trial process equipped with privileged powers. In the absence of these state institutions and powers, the suspect, with his right to refuse to testify or to co-operate, is in a position to maintain his interests without detailed pre-trial procedural rules.

Indeed, with both parties expected to develop separate and competing accounts rather than to work from a single case file, the building-up of a *dossier* with evidential significance is impossible in a system where the evidence that counts is oral evidence at trial.

In modern times the adversarial system has increasingly adopted the *instruments* of inquisitorial investigation: an organized police force and overt acceptance of police power to detain and interrogate in order to generate evidence against the suspect. This makes the traditional adversarial view of two equal, private parties difficult to sustain. To the inquisitorial eye this diminished status of the accused is immediately recognizable: the suspect as object of truth-finding in the hands of the state.

One response to this changed status of parties might have been to place a clear truth-finding duty on the police to seek out both exculpatory and inculpatory evidence. But such profound change has not yet occurred. Instead there is the development of a more detailed legal framework for the pre-trial process, both to obstruct the police's capacity to construct its case and to assist suspects in the development of theirs. From an inquisitorial viewpoint these procedural safeguards (which culminate in the Police and Criminal Evidence Act—PACE) look like a significant step towards inquisitorial policing, in that they seek to provide guarantees of reliability essential to truth-finding. But to the adversarial eye, in the absence of change in the fundamental functional duties of the police—which remains a duty of fairness but not to seek out all germane evidence—the changes are seen more in terms of equality of arms. Extended powers for the police necessitate extended rights for the defence.

This balancing process is shaped by the importance of crime control as a political objective and developed ideology. Hence the development of procedural control is uneven and uncertain, driven in one direction by public scandal over miscarriages of justice and in another by media and public concern over crime. Institutional developments such as legal aid and duty solicitors represent an alternative response. But these services are limited in reach and quality (especially access to computer data and forensic evidence). It has become clear that the equality of parties in the quest of the truth is only a theoretical one. If the defence cannot devote time and money to pre-trial investigation, the results of this failure will become clear during the later public hearing. It is for this reason that the system of the guilty plea has come under attack: defendants may accept guilt too readily as they cannot finance an effective defence, while they wish to avoid the risk of being sentenced more harshly after a full—but predictably unsuccessful—trial.

At the same time, the prominence of crime as a public issue, and thus a matter of legitimate state interest, has led to impatience with a concept of criminal justice rooted in a model of competitive contest. This has had contradictory manifestations. On the one hand there has been growing impatience with procedural impediments to police uncovering the 'facts' (limiting the right to silence), with defence obstruction of rational truth-finding (requiring more disclosure), and with some of the evidentiary technicalities (reform of the hearsay rule). On the other hand, worries about the partisan nature of policing have led to calls for the introduction of a pre-trial truth-finder such as the investigating judge. But fundamental change has not yet occurred; the system still relies on technical procedural rules at the trial to redress imbalances of institutional power that will remain for as long as funds preclude two detailed investigations of each incident.

THE TRIAL STAGE: ORAL CONTEST OR VERIFICATION OF THE *DOSSIER*?

An inquisitorial trial is a procedure between two essentially unequal parties. One may even argue that there is no party contest at all. The truth-finding process simply continues in court and is directed, and also conducted, by an actively (by interrogation) participating judge, assisted by the public prosecutor.

To a certain extent, compensation for such unequal distribution of power is to be found in the gradual reinforcement of the position of the accused as the procedure progresses towards its end, and especially in the requirement that a trial be conducted publicly and—to a certain extent—orally. Although this seems to emphasize the partisan role of the accused (and his defending counsel) at trial, the basic idea is not to provide 'equality of arms' between two parties, but to allow the defendant weapons of defence proportionate to the degree of coercion and intrusiveness of the procedure.

Generally the judges of an inquisitorial court—in the Netherlands only professionals—combine the task of guaranteeing that the trial is conducted in an orderly and fair manner, and of deciding on guilt or innocence, and the subsequent decisions. Compared with the pre-trial stage, there is little regulation, legal refinement, of the trial stage. There are few rules except those concerning the orderly course of events. The way an interrogation has to be conducted or issues brought up is all at the court's discretion.

In inquisitorial jurisdictions the public hearing is part of a continuum without climaxes. Because of the crucial importance of the *dossier* the public hearing is often much more a verification of its contents, the results of the pre-trial investigation, than the culmination of a contest. Hearsay evidence, being not regarded as fundamentally unreliable, is generally accepted. The same applies to expert written testimony. Why summon witnesses or experts if their statements or findings are laid down in clear and unambiguous reports? The principle of orality in the Dutch Code of Criminal Procedure of 1926 is a basic (and adversarial) requirement that was immediately undermined in the same year by the Supreme Court's acceptance of other (inquisitorial) considerations, to wit the admissibility of hearsay evidence.

All decision-making is subject to supervision, implying a complete retrial and a complete re-examination of the facts, even in the case of an acquittal. This is not regarded as a violation of the double jeopardy provision, but as a safeguard in the truth-finding process: two examining panels are more likely to arrive at the truth, if there is any doubt, than one.

Increasingly, the quest for the truth has to compete with other interests, such as the ethics of police investigation, the ethics of prosecution, an ethical attitude towards the defence. This may result in dismissals or acquittals contrary to the truth, yet in accordance with procedural ethics. But with the improved availability of legal assistance (for the indigent) within the setting of the trial, more is left to the initiative of the defence than was previously the case. For example, nowadays the court is less inclined to look for exculpatory evidence if not raised by the defence. Equally, if the defence does not object to the violation of (procedural) rules or regulations at the appropriate time, there is a fair chance that the objection, if raised later, will be overruled. In this sense the role of the judge is becoming increasingly passive.

Defence requests that witness testimony be challenged in court have increased, particularly in the context of expert and hearsay evidence. Defence fears have focused on the dangers of bias from experts and the difficulty of challenging reported hearsay statements. The criteria governing when the court may refuse such defence requests have been relaxed by statute, resulting in a great increase of litigation on the issue. Judicial reasoning in these cases results in a rapidly expanding framework of procedural regulations for the trial stage, aimed more at increasing procedural fairness than at truth-finding.

The rule that all criminal cases must be brought before a judge for trial has become the exception. Increasingly, police and prosecutor are adjucators, deciding on crime and punishment by means of extra-judicial settlements. There are—heavily disputed—proposals to introduce summary proceedings in which a confession will stop the judicial quest for the truth. The final word on what amounts to a guilty plea has yet to be spoken. Considerations of finance and manpower dictate that public trials be reserved for the most serious cases; those too serious to settle out of court, or in which no agreement can be reached, or in which incarceration seems the only adequate sanction. There are moves to restrict the almost unlimited possibilities of appeal, especially with a view to reducing the workload of the courts.

The adversarial process, on the other hand, is a party contest *par excellence*, each party attempting to defeat the other by presenting the most convincing evidence and undermining that presented by the other side. The assumption is that truth emerges indirectly from the *choc des opinions*.

The adversarial court is much more a referee than a judge deciding on issues of right or wrong. An adversarial judge is only active in his concern with adherence by both parties to the rules of the contest. These rules are meant to allow for and maintain equality between the parties, but also to shield the jury, which is the essential body of amateur adjudicators deciding on the strength of the mutual arguments, from wrongfully gained impressions from which it is difficult to dissociate oneself. No obligation exists on the judge to bring up possible defences if the defence rests in that respect.

The crucial stage in adversarial proceedings is the public hearing. Here the process culminates, more or less isolated from the pre-trial investigation. It is the oral screening of evidence for which the public hearing is designed and the oral performance of witnesses, the defence, and the prosecution that is decisive. With a few exceptions, evidence gathered during pre-trial investigations is of no value unless tested at a public hearing. Hence the rules against hearsay testimony, hence the need to interrogate experts in front of the jury, hence all rules on proper behaviour of the parties during the hearing.

Because of this model of regulated contest, the public hearing is so complicated, engulfed with rules, time-consuming, and hence costly, that it cannot be the standard model for all criminal trials. This coincides with the partisan nature of an adversarial trial, which not only allows the prosecution to refrain from starting proceedings, or to negotiate the boundaries of the contest, but also allows the defence the opportunity of starting negotiations—offering to plea bargain for example, resulting in the judge's involvement being restricted to sentencing.

In this system a confession is a crucial element, because it usually terminates the search for the truth. If a confession may put an end to the conflict, corroborative evidence becomes unnecessary, so that uncorroborated confessions suffice to terminate the contest regardless of their truthfulness. Where no public interest is involved, the truth becomes immaterial, and the necessity of having an adjucator able actively to elicit the truth disappears.

Yet plea-bargaining has come under attack from many (and competing) perspectives. Powerful voices (the Director of Public Prosecutions and the Bar) seek to make the system still more 'efficient' by increasing the number of guilty pleas. Proposals include greater judicial involvement in indicating sentences and regulating deals. This would represent a further recognition of the centrality of the pre-trial phase and a significant move towards judicial involvement in it. Others oppose any extension of plea-bargaining exactly because the pressure to co-operate is seen as a rejection of adversarial values and a sidestepping of adversarial arenas.

In the accusatorial system the rules on witness interrogation and the like, designed to facilitate the finding of the truth, often have the opposite effect. There is increasing criticism of the prohibition on hearsay evidence, and of other prohibitions relating to evidence not directly and primarily produced in court, but having a high value as to the truth. Witness interrogation and cross-examination are criticized as obscuring the truth more often than not, and at the expense of the—innocent—witness. It is to be expected that the increase of responsiveness of the criminal justice system to victims being cross-examined as witnesses will go at the expense of some traditional instruments thought to embody due fairness to the defendant.

The pure logic of the adversarial trial has been substantially qualified by duties of disclosure of evidence between parties. The extensive obligations placed on the prosecution may be seen as merely redressing inequality of arms in pre-trial accumulation of evidence, but the duties recently imposed upon the defence in relation to expert and alibi evidence are clearly prompted by fears that trial by ambush undermines truth-finding. In relation to expert evidence new proposals go further, suggesting a full-scale move to the inquisitorial tradition of neutral experts' reports with duty to report the truth. While these rules of evidence are being relaxed, other rules of evidence seem to become more strict. The exception to the hearsay prohibition, to wit the confession made at the police station, is seen as requiring an increasing number of safeguards in connection with its reliability.

The idea of the trial as a contest is reinforced by its very finality: rights of appeal are restricted. Indeed, under normal circumstances a new examination of the facts is regarded as double jeopardy. The number of appeal cases is further reduced by the high percentage of guilty pleas.

CONCLUSIONS

Our argument has been that fairness of procedure and the establishment of truth must be seen as distinct but related aspects of criminal justice which, at their most abstract, share no necessary relationship: they are neither necessarily complementary nor contradictory. The outcome of the relationship between partisan rights and truth-finding in a particular case depends on the effects of partisan intervention. Sometimes intervention by defence or prosecution will reveal truth; sometimes it will obscure it. The assumption that truth will *usually* surface of its own accord, if parties have been given a fair chance to challenge each other's version of it, is unproven. But if one places a responsibility upon the state for direct truth-finding, there is equally the potential for tension between the effective pursuit of truth and fairness of procedure. If there are distinctive values supporting both truth-finding and fairness of procedure, minimum standards for the pursuit of each must be established as explicit objectives.

In practice, at some level each system aspires to both the truth and a fair trial. Increasingly the Dutch legal system is acknowledging that there is a need to ensure that systems provide minimum standards of both truth-finding and procedural fairness (though truth-finding seems to remain the priority). English and Welsh acceptance of this aspiration may develop but is not so advanced: the traditional assumption that equality of arms itself leads (indirectly) to truth has an inhibiting effect on overt recognition of the tension between them. Furthermore, traditional Anglo-Saxon unease about the benevolence of the state may well play a part: if no real guarantee exists that the state has and always will have an interest in the truth (and in which truth?), then who knows what may be done in its pursuit?

However, changes are occurring in both systems, in the composition of the mixture between truth and procedural fairness, and these are reflected in piecemeal changes in the organization of criminal procedure. They seem to point more to convergence than to divergence. The more so since supranational considerations, deriving for example from the European Convention on Human Rights, are increasingly significant. In other words: inquisitorial procedure is increasingly influenced by the necessity of fairness in truth-finding at the trial stage, while there are some (less developed) indications that adversarial procedure is beginning to take on more direct truth-finding characteristics, or is at least beginning to avail itself of the instruments of truth-finding.

In their concurrent duty to uphold the rule of law as well as find the truth, Dutch courts are confronted with an increasing need to examine activities by prosecution service and police in the light of due process; as a result, judicial verdicts nowadays are more likely to confront issues of fairness, irrespective of the substantive truth. The clearest example is the exclusion of evidence gained by illegal entry of the home that may lead to acquittal although the reliability of that evidence, and therefore its capacity to reveal the truth, is beyond dispute.

On the other hand, the English adversarial system shows increasing concern about that very capacity. Thus far, the dominant response has been to attempt to work more seriously through the logic of the adversarial requirement of equality of arms. This represents a recognition that the state is not just another party to a private dispute and that equality of arms is not a balance in nature but must procedurally and institutionally be created. There are, however, pointers that go beyond this. They suggest some challenge to the assumption that equality of arms will, of itself, ensure that truth emerges and the possibility that a more direct approach to truth-finding will be adopted. Some of these involve qualification of the usual expectations of conflict between adversarial parties by imposing positive obligations of *co-operation* by disclosure of evidence. More of the same is being advocated. Other reforms have seen the state seeking to guarantee evidentiary quality (some aspects of PACE, the introduction of the CPS). This, too, may go further (the probable introduction of judicial supervision of plea-bargaining and maybe even investigation, the possible introduction of a corroboration requirement for confessions). Many such moves are opposed exactly because they are not true to adversarial assumptions.

All of this suggests gradual convergence. But the point at which convergence would begin to make it more sensible to see the systems as variations on a single theme—as we put the question in the opening paragraphs—would be when the UK placed active duties on the state to seek out and present all germane evidence or when the Netherlands abandoned such a duty. Neither, at the time of writing, seems likely.

The ideal mixture, of course, is optimal truth-finding and fundamental fairness. The ECHR has undeniably highlighted several fundamentally unfair aspects of Dutch procedure (especially in the field of hearsay evidence and the related problem of lack of orality at the trial stage), although there have been few complaints that such procedure failed to elicit the truth. However, equally undeniably, criminal procedure in the United Kingdom has been seriously discredited by a number of miscarriages of justice that show that, without equality of arms in investigation, the partisan assumptions of the adversarial process can make a nonsense of both truth and procedural safeguards. Indeed, such miscarriages prompt a need to at least question adversarial assumptions about protecting individual freedoms: are citizens really safer with negative rules and procedures constraining state officials rather than institutionalized positive expectations of them (most notably to seek out all exculpatory evidence)? Without such positive expectations, is there not always a risk of producing a moral climate where constraining rules and procedures come to be seen as obstructions to be circumvented?

We must not lose sight of the risk involved in adopting strategies and safeguards from each other's procedural styles. Each depends on its own historically developed institutions and the faith that different societies place in them. Continental systems function by virtue of society's faith in the fundamental commitment of state institutions to act in the interests of justice (in all senses of the word); they will continue to function legitimately only for so long as that trust is not abused and the safeguards provided by the division of power and subsequent hierarchical control continue to work. British society is disinclined to trust state institutions (and, in the sense that control is far less direct, is undoubtedly right not to do so). Here, direct participation of the people in truth-finding through the jury, and the right to establish one's own version of the truth directly, are the critical limits. But here, too, continuing faith in the system depends on the existence and actual functioning of adequate safeguards.

For safeguards to be adequate and effective they must be seen in the context of the surrounding assumptions, mechanisms, and procedures that make them work. What would it profit British suspects to give up the right to silence in exchange for a half-hearted version of the Dutch prosecutor, shorn of his traditional judicial attitude and his relationship to the *dossier*? And what would it benefit a Dutch suspect to gain a greater but still limited opportunity to question witnesses while losing the cultural commitment of the prosecutor to the active search for exculpatory evidence? Each system must seek its own balance of responsibilities for collecting and presenting relevant evidence, with institutional and procedural resources to match the weight of the respective duties.

It is in this field of safeguards, in the matter of forcing states to accept full responsibility for ensuring that their own systems produce optimal results, that European case law on human rights may have the greatest role to play. Relevant judgments reveal an important line of reasoning. The European Court of Human Rights does not insist on any one type of procedure, accepting each system in its own right, provided the end result is compatible with Articles 5 and 6 ECHR. A case in point is *Barberà* v. *Spain*,[3] in which the European Court held Spain to its own, inquisitorial guarantees. The component parts of the different procedures are not viewed in isolation: the Court is concerned with all interrelated aspects of criminal procedure, including appeals procedures. Its most crucial requirement is that the taking of evidence be adversarial, in the sense that persons charged with criminal offences are confronted with the evidence against them and given a real opportunity of challenging it, if possible in public. Undeniably, as far as this requirement is concerned, the Anglo-Saxon adversarial system is far better endowed than certain inquisitorial systems on the Continent. The Convention has nothing to say about the quest for the truth. It is too self-evident a goal of modern criminal justice to waste words on: a miscarriage of justice is never fair.[4]

[3] 6 December 1988, Series A No. 146.

[4] Since this was written, the Runciman Commission has reported (Royal Commission on Criminal Justice, HMSO, 1993, Cm 2236). It recommends a further dilution of classical adversarial principles with more elaborate pre-trial exchanges between parties, based more on written than on oral procedures and designed to define and indeed determine many of the key issues at trial. These exchanges would be built around more extensive duties of defence disclosure and more overt judicial involvement in plea negotiation. Conversely, the official Dutch commission charged with a review of the Code of Criminal Procedure (Commissie Moons) has now completed its work, and here many of the recommendations seem to favour the introduction of 'adversarial' themes (consensuality and bargaining for example as the basis for judicial decisions) but fail to introduce corresponding adversarial guarantees while undermining existing inquisitorial safeguards such as the role of the investigating magistrate. All of this suggests that while both systems are, essentially, still intact, there is a drift towards convergence that is based almost exclusively on a desire for 'more effective' criminal justice (whatever that might be) rather than on any awareness of the inherent structural possibilities and limitations within the systems themselves.

4

The European Convention on Human Rights and Criminal Justice in the Netherlands and the United Kingdom

BERT SWART AND JAMES YOUNG

INTRODUCTION

Both the Netherlands and the UK became parties to the European Convention at an early stage in its history, the UK in 1951 and the Netherlands in 1954. Both have accepted the right of aggrieved individuals to petition the European Commission of Human Rights and the compulsory jurisdiction of the European Court of Human Rights at the instigation of the Commission or another State Party to the Convention—the Netherlands in 1960 and the UK in 1966. However, the marked difference in approaches to the performance of their treaty obligations has made a considerable difference to the way in which the influence of the Convention has been felt in the two states. In the Netherlands the Convention is enforceable in the courts, whereas successive British governments have rejected proposals to make Convention rights domestically justiciable. Furthermore, the difference between the criminal justice systems in both countries has meant that challenges to national law and practice have been directed at different aspects of each system.

Differences between the two legal systems raise interesting questions of comparative law. First, what difference does it really make to the effective implementation of a human rights convention whether or not national courts of a Contracting Party are empowered to apply the convention directly? Secondly, can it be said that the Convention exerts a harmonizing influence on the criminal justice systems concerned? More specifically, the most tantalizing question here is whether the Convention contributes to a convergence between legal systems that belong to the common law tradition, like the UK, and those belonging to the civil law tradition, like the Netherlands. To these complex questions we shall try to provide elements of possible answers.

CONSTITUTIONAL STATUS OF THE CONVENTION

Absence of constitutional review of legislation is an established principle in both Dutch and British constitutional law. Although the Dutch Constitution contains provisions on basic rights of the individual, courts in the Netherlands are forbidden by the Constitution to pass judgment on the question whether an Act of Parliament is in conformity with the Constitution. This is a matter solely for the legislature. The UK, lacking a formal written constitution, does not even have a constitutional equivalent of a bill of rights or declaration of human rights. However, the two states differ markedly in their approach to international conventions.

The United Kingdom

The British Constitution adopts a dualist approach to international law, so that international conventions have no legal force in the UK unless implemented by Parliamentary legislation. At the time of the drafting and ratification of the Convention the official stance in the UK[1] was that national law was consonant with the Convention, and thus it was not necessary to incorporate it into British law. In the early years a variety of reasons were given for not accepting the right of individual petition. It might be abused by trouble-makers; the Convention should be applied to varying degrees in different British colonies, according to their level of political development; the state was the only proper subject of international law, and thus it was inappropriate to give to individuals direct rights under an international convention. There was also a deep, even xenophobic, conservatism, clearly expressed by the Labour Lord Chancellor, Lord Jowitt in 1950:

... we were not prepared to encourage our European friends to jeopardise our whole system of law, which we have laboriously built up over the centuries, in favour of some half-baked scheme to be administered by some unknown court.[2]

The UK's record of violations of the Convention has ruffled this complacency, although for some critics it has sometimes simply confirmed their view that the Convention is alien to the British approach to the protection of human rights. In any event, British governments have continued (not always enthusiastically) to renew the commitment to the right of individual petition and the jurisdiction of the Court. However, the Convention has still not been incorporated into domestic law and there is no constitutional

---

[1] Since the UK is a unitary state constitutional questions are not confined to England and Wales. While we discuss the European Convention primarily in relation to the criminal justice system in England and Wales, we refer to decisions of the Convention organs in Strasbourg affecting all parts of the United Kingdom.

[2] See Lester, 'Fundamental Rights: The UK Isolated?' [1984] *Public Law*, 46, 51.

protection of human rights in the form of a bill or declaration of human rights. There are a number of explanations for this, including an ingrained conservatism in matters of constitutional change. It is also apparent that the two main British political parties which have been in government since 1945 have not wished to restrict their freedom of action by giving power to the courts to rule on the validity of their legislation and administrative action, although there are now indications that the Labour Party is changing its view on this. This approach has been reinforced by the Labour Party's suspicion of the dominant political values of judges and among Conservatives a fear of politicization of the judiciary.

Political opposition to incorporation has been reinforced by the constitutional doctrine of Parliamentary sovereignty, according to which it is said not to be legally possible to entrench constitutional legislation or otherwise constrain the freedom of action of future Parliaments. According to this view the courts might be empowered to apply the Convention to review administrative action and even Parliamentary legislation enacted prior to the legislation conferring the power of review, but it would preclude its incorporation so as to permit judicial review of legislation. However, this objection to incorporation is open to question, as the scope and immutability of the traditional conception of Parliamentary sovereignty have been increasingly challenged, and membership of the European Union has put it under particular strain. In *Factortame* v. *Secretary of State for Transport*,[3] the House of Lords held that, as a result of the European Communities Act 1972, Community law prevails over Parliamentary legislation. The fact that an ordinary Act of Parliament may limit the legislative freedom of future Parliaments requires a modification of the traditional doctrine and thus further weakens constitutional objections against incorporation of the Convention, since it is far from clear that the breach in the doctrine may be confined within the context of Community law.

The fact that the Convention cannot be enforced in the courts of the UK affects its role in the continuing debates which have taken place since the early 1970s about fundamental aspects of the criminal justice system. In the course of these controversies over the extent of police powers of detention, search, and surveillance, the response to increasing terrorism, the reform of the penal system, and now, in the wake of the series of miscarriages of justice leading to the establishment of the Royal Commission, the criminal trial process itself, issues of human rights have been at the heart of the political and intellectual debate. However, in these public discussions the European Convention has not generally been used as the touchstone of individual liberties.

---

[3] [1991] 1 AC 603.

Perhaps because of the impossibility of direct enforcement of the Convention in UK courts, awareness of the Convention has been slow to develop amongst both academic and practising lawyers, and until recently it was only widely studied by international lawyers. Decisions of the European Court of Human Rights against other States Parties have not prompted widespread reaction among politicians or academic lawyers in the UK. However, as lawyers have been forced to focus their attention on law in the rest of western Europe, learning about the Convention is becoming an integral part of legal education. Reference to the Convention in reported cases has become more frequent, and the integration of knowledge of the Convention into the training of solicitors from 1993 will further increase awareness. Senior judges are increasingly participating in the debate about incorporating the Convention into English law and the influence it may have on the development of the law in the absence of incorporation.[4]

The Netherlands

Although there is no system of constitutional review in the Netherlands, the courts do have the power to apply human rights conventions and to set aside national legislation where it conflicts with these conventions. This explains why the debate on human rights and civil liberties in the Netherlands has increasingly become a debate on the meaning of human rights conventions. The European Convention is now to Dutch case law what the national constitution is to courts in countries like the United States or the Federal Republic of Germany. A situation that, of course, no one foresaw in the 1950s, it is the outcome of a slow development in which different factors have played a part.

In the 1950s and 1960s the Convention was of little practical significance to the administration of justice. It was commonly held that national standards of criminal justice were much higher than those laid down by the Convention. The Convention was seen as a guarantee against a recurrence of the times before 1945. Provisions of the Convention were rarely invoked in court. To argue in court that the Convention had been violated meant that one was short of better arguments.

Things were beginning to change at the end of the 1960s and during the 1970s. In the aftermath of the cultural revolution of the 1960s and the changed attitudes which this brought about towards authority, the criminal justice system came under strong attack. Its conservatism, paternalism,

---

[4] See e.g. H. Woolf, *Protection of the Public: A New Challenge* (London; Stevens & Sons 1989), 120–2; N. Browne-Wilkinson, 'The Infiltration of a Bill of Rights' [1992] *Public Law*, 397; J. Laws, 'Is the High Court the Guardian of Fundamental Constitutional Rights?' [1993] *Public Law*, 59; T. Bingham, 'The European Convention on Human Rights: Time to Incorporate' (1993) 109 *Law Quarterly Review*, 390.

and lack of efficiency were increasingly criticized. New generations of young lawyers engaged themselves in offering legal aid to impoverished and marginal groups in society. In academic circles the European Convention began to be studied, as well as the Warren court and its due process revolution. The Convention, however, was more important as a source of inspiration than for its immediate specific impact on the daily administration of criminal justice. Decisions of Dutch courts on the Convention remained rare and the number of individual complaints in Strasbourg low.

A third stage was reached at the end of the 1970s. In 1976 *Engel and others*, the first case against the Netherlands, reached the European Court, which held that the disciplinary sanctioning of a number of soldiers had contravened the Convention. The symbolic and psychological significance of its decision is especially important, as it made clear that even in the Netherlands human rights could be violated. At the same time the cultural climate had changed again. Rising crime rates and new forms of criminality such as drug crimes provoked new responses to criminality and a widespread desire to achieve stronger and more efficient law enforcement. It is especially hard to overestimate the influence of drug crimes on the development of criminal procedure in the Netherlands; it familiarized the criminal justice system with undercover agents, telephone tapping, and anonymous witnesses. In this new climate individual rights and liberties came under increasing pressure. Since the European Court had shown that the Convention had practical significance for the Netherlands, the Convention became the touchstone *par excellence* for those who criticized the swing from due process to crime control.

Nowadays the age of maturity has been reached. The developing case law of the European Court has made the tremendous importance of the Convention for criminal justice systems in Europe abundantly clear. The Convention is at the heart of every debate in the Netherlands on the quality of criminal justice. It is invoked in court proceedings on an almost daily basis. The road to Strasbourg has become familiar to defence lawyers.

THE CONVENTION IN THE COURTS

United Kingdom

Since the Convention cannot be directly enforced in the national courts the scope for its use in the courts is limited. It can only be taken into account in resolving textual ambiguities in legislation, developing the common law where it is unclear or undeveloped, or granting discretionary remedies. In these circumstances the courts may prefer the result which is consistent with the UK's international obligations. The limited scope which this gives for formal recognition of the Convention was authoritatively emphasized by the House of Lords in *Brind* v. *Secretary of State for the Home Department*.[5] Legislation gave the Home Secretary a broad power to prohibit the broadcasting of 'any matter or matter of any class', and contained no limitation on the exercise of the power other than that the prohibition should be in writing.[6] It was argued that it must be presumed that Parliament intended that the ministerial power should be exercised in accordance with the UK's international obligations and in particular the European Convention. The House of Lords rejected this contention, holding that since the language of the statute was quite unambiguous, the Convention could not be used to restrict the power granted under it. The clearly expressed words of Parliament must be respected, even if that were to lead to a breach of the UK's international obligations under the Convention.

Despite this judicial caution, reference to the Convention in judgments is quite frequent, and although its principal role is as a secondary justification for decisions, this does not mean that it does not influence the courts. Since British courts recognize that some human rights are principles of domestic law, in the absence of a codified statement, the Convention and Strasbourg case law can provide a ready-made definition of a right and its scope. A close interrelationship between English law and conventional definitions of rights is particularly apparent in the prisoners' rights cases, where the gradually evolving recognition of prisoners as bearers of legal rights, though initiated by judgments of the European Court of Human Rights, has been accompanied by domestic judicial activism. Two examples may illustrate this. In *Golder* v. *UK*[7] the Strasbourg Court upheld the right of a prisoner to consult a lawyer with a view to bringing legal proceedings regarding the conduct of a prison officer. Subsequently, the House of Lords upheld a prisoner's right of unimpeded access to the courts.[8] Lord Wilberforce referred approvingly to *Golder* and, echoing the judgment of the Strasbourg Court, invoked the presumption that a convicted prisoner retains his civil rights in prison. In *Campbell and Fell* v. *UK*,[9] the European Court held that certain prison disciplinary charges were 'criminal' for the purposes of the fair trial provisions of Article 6 of the Convention, so entitling the accused prisoner to legal assistance. In *Hone* v. *Maze Prison Board of Governors*[10] the House of Lords was concerned with the criteria to be applied under English law to determine the entitlement of a prisoner to legal representation in internal disciplinary

---

[5] [1991] 1 AC 696.
[6] Broadcasting Act 1981, s. 29(3), subsequently re-enacted with identical wording in the Broadcasting Act 1990, s. 10(3).
[7] 21 February 1975, Series A No. 18.　　[8] *Raymond* v. *Honey* [1983] 1 AC 1.
[9] 28 June 1984, Series A No. 80.　　[10] [1988] AC 379.

proceedings. Lord Goff quoted at some length from the judgment of the European Court of Human Rights and devoted considerable attention to demonstrating that the criteria developed by the English courts were consistent with the Convention.

The courts have not invariably held that domestic law is consistent with the Convention, and in such cases they may simply accept the conflict and apply national law. In *Malone* v. *Metropolitan Police Commissioner*[11] the judge expressed the view that the lack of legal regulation of telephone-tapping was clearly in breach of the privacy provisions of Article 8 of the Convention, but declared himself powerless to modify English law.

However, it is noticeable that while, in the past, reference to the Convention was usually prompted by a European Court of Human Rights judgment against the UK in the same field, its use is no longer so limited. Since in the British adversarial trial system the introduction of arguments based upon the Convention depends primarily, though not exclusively, on the initiative of counsel, this is evidence of the growing awareness of practising lawyers of the Convention and the possibility of initiating proceedings before the European Commission.

The Netherlands

A key role in the application of the European Convention in the Netherlands is played by the Dutch Supreme Court, notably its criminal division. Since leave to appeal is not required, almost any case in which a human rights issue has been raised may reach the court. Through the years the number of such cases has steadily risen from an average of three in the 1960s and early 1970s to an average of fifty during the last years. By its sheer volume this case law is impressive, touching on all aspects of criminal procedure in the Netherlands. Furthermore, in 9 per cent of these cases the Supreme Court has taken the view that the Convention has been violated. Whereas this record is quantitatively impressive, its substance is less so. The case law is characterized by its conservatism,[12] and the Court has been extremely cautious in interpreting and applying the Convention. The number of cases in which invocation of the Convention has been successful is misleading, since almost all of them concern the right to trial within a reasonable time. Other cases in which a violation of the Convention was found to have occurred are very rare indeed. It should also be noted that sometimes cases of great importance to the rights of the suspect have been decided without any reference to the Convention at all. Examples are the decision where the Supreme Court held that a suspect has no right

---

[11] [1979] Ch 344.
[12] See A. H. J. Swart, 'Rechten van de mens in de strafrechtspleging' (1989) 19 *Delikt en Delinkwent*, 554–72.

to the assistance of counsel during police interrogations and the first decision in which it held that statements of anonymous persons may be used
as evidence.[13]

The conservative approach of the Supreme Court is highlighted by comparison with that of the European Court of Human Rights. Where the two
courts differ in their interpretation of the Convention, it is the Dutch Court
which attaches more limited effects to the Convention than the European
Court. Cases in which the reverse is true are almost non-existent in the
context of criminal justice and the national court may be forced to change
course. Sometimes this may be because a judgment of the European Court
directly contradicts an earlier decision of the Supreme Court in the same
case, as in *Kostovski*[14] and *Abdoella*.[15] However, judgments of the European Court in cases against other states may have the same effect. For
instance, in 1983 the Supreme Court held that the suspect has no right
to be assisted by an interpreter during police interrogations since Article
6 is not concerned with these interrogations.[16] In *Kamasinski* v. *Austria*[17]
in 1989 the European Court later came to the opposite conclusion. A
further example is the judgment of the European Court in *Soering* v. *UK*[18]
which forced the Supreme Court to abandon its long-established case law,
according to which the European Convention could not confer a right not
to be extradited.

Regrettable as it may be, the conservative attitude of the Supreme Court
is easily understandable. The court is the highest judicial authority responsible for the administration of criminal justice, and in human rights matters
its main concern may be summarized as being not only to ensure that the
system works *fairly*, but that it *works*. There may appear to be a contradiction between this pragmatism and the relatively high number of cases
in which the Supreme Court has held that there has been a violation of the
right to a speedy trial, but the interest of the individual in having this right
respected coincides to some extent with the interest of the Court in preventing the court system in the Netherlands from becoming clogged. One
hidden fear underlies the Dutch case law: that the European Convention
will unduly disrupt the proper administration of justice.

The cautious approach of the Dutch Supreme Court is not unique. The
same phenomenon can be observed in the highest national courts of other
European states whose constitutional rules permit the direct application of
the European Convention. Indeed, the knowledge that a too narrow interpretation of the Convention can be corrected by the European Commission or the European Court of Human Rights may even induce national

[13] HR 22 November 1983, [1984] NJ 805, and 5 February 1980, [1980] NJ 319.
[14] 20 November 1989, Series A No. 166.
[15] 25 November 1992, Series A No. 248–A.   [16] HR 1 March 1983, [1983] NJ 517.
[17] 19 December 1989, Series A No. 168.   [18] 7 July 1989, Series A No. 161.

courts to favour a conservative interpretation where there is no relevant decision of the Strasbourg organs.

Both the UK and the Netherlands have recognized the right of individual petition and the jurisdiction of the European Court of Human Rights. As a consequence they both have had to face a critical appraisal of their criminal justice systems by the Strasbourg organs on a number of occasions.

As far as the European Court is concerned, in the area of criminal justice up to 1993, it had dealt with thirty-eight petitions against the UK, and had ruled in favour of the petitioners thirty-five times. Petitioners were successful against the Netherlands in eighteen out of nineteen cases before the Court. Since one judgment of the Court may concern several individual petitioners, a fairer impression of the Court's significance may be obtained by enumerating the number of decisions. For the UK this results in twenty-three cases and twenty 'convictions', and for the Netherlands ten cases and nine convictions. However, not all petitions that have been declared admissible by the European Commission are brought before the Court. Some have been submitted to the Committee of Ministers of the Council of Europe. Up to 1992 the Committee had dealt with twenty-one decisions, in eighteen of which the United Kingdom has been held to be in violation of the Convention. In the case of the Netherlands the numbers are two and one respectively.

The relevant areas touched upon by the European Court are a mixed bag, but many of the Court's judgments have been concerned with controversial issues of great importance for the administration of justice in the UK and the Netherlands. In discussing the case law of the Court and its impact in both countries we shall follow the provisions of the Convention.

Article 6: The Right to a Fair Hearing

Determination of a Criminal Charge
The first case decided by the European Court of Human Rights in proceedings against the Netherlands was *Engel and others*,[19] involving the disciplining of five soldiers for offences against military law. In its decision the Court held that disciplinary sanctions consisting of deprivation of liberty contravened the Convention, because not all the guarantees of Article 6 extending to the determination of criminal charges had been respected.

---

[19] 23 November 1976, Series A No. 22.

The Convention concept of a criminal charge was independent of any particular national classification. The case has had a lasting impact on military disciplinary law in the Netherlands, which was subject to a total revision in the 1989 Act on military disciplinary law. Among other things the Act created the possibility of an appeal to ordinary criminal courts against the imposition of disciplinary sanctions. Disciplinary sanctions depriving a person of his liberty had already been abolished while *Engel* was pending before the European Court.

In *Campbell and Fell* v. *UK*[20] the issue was whether prison disciplinary offences might be criminal charges under Article 6. The European Court, applying the *Engel* criteria, held that disciplinary proceedings involving offences, described under the prison regulations as 'especially grave', carrying serious penalties of loss of remission and privileges, and which could have been prosecuted as crimes in the courts, did involve criminal charges, and thus attracted the protection of Article 6 and, specifically in this case, the right to legal representation. This decision did result in an immediate change in the guidelines on the granting of legal representation, and ultimately an overhaul of the disciplinary system, with more serious disciplinary offences being abolished and replaced with a criminal offence triable in the ordinary criminal courts.

Another outstanding case involving this same question of the application of Article 6 was *Öztürk* v. *Federal Republic of Germany*.[21] The decision in this case that Article 6 applied to administrative offences has had a considerable impact on Dutch law. In 1985, the tax chamber of the Supreme Court held Article 6 to be applicable where fiscal fines might be imposed.[22] In line with the *Öztürk* decision the Act of 1989 on the administrative sanctioning of traffic regulations provides for an appeal to ordinary courts against the imposition of fines by administrative authorities. On the other hand, owing to the decision of the European Court in *le Compte* v. *Belgium*[23] Dutch case law now considers Article 6 to be applicable in disciplinary proceedings against practising lawyers and doctors because, the right to exercise those professions being at stake, civil rights and obligations are being determined in them. No similar immediate impact of this case law has been evident in the UK.

For the sake of completeness it might be pointed out that in *Monnell and Morris* v. *UK*[24] the European Court of Human Rights held that, although there was no requirement that a State Party should establish an appeal system, any appeal procedure 'constituted' part of the determination of the criminal charge, and thus was subject to the requirements of Article 6.

---

[20] 28 June 1984, Series A No. 80. [21] 27 May 1983, Series A No. 73.
[22] HR 19 June 1985, [1986] NJ 104.
[23] 23 June 1981, Series A No. 54. [24] 2 March 1987, Series A No. 115.

Access to Court

A number of cases against the UK under Article 6 have involved the right of prisoners to consult a lawyer with a view to taking legal proceedings. In *Golder*,[25] the first case against the UK to reach the European Court of Human Rights, the question was whether the restrictions on a convicted prisoner's access to a lawyer were contrary to Article 6. In a key decision for the development of prisoners' rights in the UK, the European Court held that preventing resort to legal advice impeded access to court required by Article 6 for the determination of civil rights and obligations. The immediate impact in the UK was not far-reaching. The British Government changed the regulations to permit access to a lawyer, provided that where the proposed proceedings were in connection with the prisoner's imprisonment, the prison internal complaints procedure had first been exhausted (the 'prior ventilation rule'). However, after this limited response there followed a stream of applications from prisoners concerning access to legal advice which resulted in further decisions against the UK in the European Court and the Committee of Ministers. The 'prior ventilation rule' was abolished following a friendly settlement in *Reid*[26] and was replaced by a rule requiring that the internal complaints procedure be used simultaneously with the commencement of legal proceedings. By the time that the European Court had ruled that this violated Article 6,[27] the rule had been abolished following a decision of the English High Court.

Independent and Impartial Tribunal

In a number of cases, starting with the decision in the case of *De Cubber* v. *Belgium*,[28] the European Court of Human Rights has emphasized the importance of judges not only being impartial, but also appearing to be so in the eyes of the accused. In *De Cubber* the trial judge had acted previously in the capacity of examining judge in the same case; in *Hauschildt* v. *Denmark*[29] he had among other things on numerous occasions decided on requests for release from pre-trial detention; in *Oberschlick* v. *Austria*[30] the trial judge had participated in the decision on a pre-trial request to order the prosecution of the accused. In each case the Court decided that the Convention had been violated.

In Dutch law a combination of judicial functions is not a rare occurrence. A juvenile judge may, for instance, have acted as an examining judge. The law starts from the presumption that judges who decide on pre-trial detention should preferably participate in the trial itself, and it is not impossible

---

[25] 21 February 1975, Series A No. 18.   [26] App. 9520/81.
[27] Series A, No. 80 (1984); (1985) 7 EHRR 165.
[28] 26 October 1984, Series A, 1986. See also *Pfeiffer and Plankl*, 25 February 1992, Series A No. 227 and *Nortier*, 24 August 1993, Series A No. 267.
[29] 24 May 1989, Series A No. 154.   [30] 23 May 1991, Series A No. 204.

that a trial judge has previously decided on the request of a victim to order the prosecution of a suspect or on the request of the accused to dismiss the case before it comes to court. The case law of the European Court of Human Rights disrupts existing practices in the Netherlands. In most cases they may be modified without legislative change, but in relation to juvenile justice, a bill has been introduced to change the Code of Criminal Procedure. There has been some debate on what the *Hauschildt* decision really implies for the situation in the Netherlands. The Dutch Supreme Court has refused to draw from it the consequence that a member of a Dutch court is always disqualified from participating in a public hearing if he has previously been involved in deciding on pre-trial detention.[31] The soundness of that view seems to be confirmed by the recent judgment of the European Court in *Sainte-Marie* v. *France*.[32]

Hearing within a Reasonable Time

Like the Dutch Supreme Court the European Court of Human Rights has on many occasions had the opportunity to decide the question whether a person had been tried within a reasonable time. It is the consistent practice of the European Court to examine whether in each and every stage of the criminal process the authorities have acted with deliberate speed. If that is not the case the Court will consider that the Convention has been violated, irrespective of the length of the delay. The approach of the Dutch Supreme Court is more global and therefore less strict, since it will usually consider whether the trial in its totality has taken too much time. Its case law shows that delays of less than two years have rarely been found to be unacceptable, while in the case of longer delays much depends on the circumstances in a given case.[33] In *Abdoella* v. *The Netherlands*[34] these differences came clearly to the fore. The case involved delays during appellate proceedings that did not, either taken in isolation or added together, amount to two years. Admitting that the proceedings in their totality were not unduly long, the Court nevertheless held that a breach of Article 6 had occurred since it regarded two periods of inactivity unacceptable. The case forces Dutch courts to study the European case law more thoroughly and to follow its leads more closely.

Whereas there have been numerous applications against the UK to the European Commission on the grounds of unreasonable delay in criminal proceedings, few of these have even been held to be admissible by the

---

[31] HR 26 February 1991, [1991] NJ 509.

[32] ECHR, 16 December 1992, Series A No. 253–A.

[33] To some extent this approach seems to have been influenced by *Marijnissen*, in which the European Commission and the Committee of Ministers found the Netherlands to have violated Art. 6 because of a delay in appellate proceedings amounting to a period of two years. See Committee of Ministers, 25 January 1985, DH(85) 4, 40 D. & R. 83–99.

[34] 25 November 1992, Series A No. 248–A; *Bunkate*, 26 May 1993, Series A No. 248–B.

Commission. In *Orchin*, the one decision against the UK, the Committee of Ministers held that a delay of five years between the applicant being charged and the decision to drop proceedings was unreasonable.[35] However, the delay in this case appears not to have been attributable to any basic flaw in the criminal justice system, but rather to a series of administrative errors. In other applications the Commission has been satisfied that the delays have been justified in the particular circumstances of the case. This is not to say that there has not been serious concern over delays in criminal proceedings in the UK, most recently culminating in successful judicial lobbying for an increase in the number of judges in England and Wales. The Prosecution of Offences Act 1985 includes provisions enabling the setting of time-limits on different stages of proceedings in England and Wales. (This is already a feature of the Scottish criminal justice system.) However, there is no publicly available evidence that this action has been prompted by European Court case law.

Equality of Arms

In its decision in *Borgers* v. *Belgium*[36] the European Court of Human Rights held that it is contrary to Article 6 to deny the accused an opportunity to comment on a 'conclusion' of an advocate-general before the Supreme Court. Belgian practice may be explained by the fact that an advocate-general at the Supreme Court is not considered to be a party to the proceedings, but rather an objective adviser to the court. As a consequence of the Court's judgment practice in the Netherlands will also have to change on this point.

Presumption of Innocence

The most important decision of the European Court of Human Rights on the significance of the presumption of innocence is that in the case of *Salabiaku* v. *France*.[37] It concerns presumptions of fact and of law in penal provisions. The Court considered such provisions to be acceptable on the condition that they are confined within reasonable limits which take into account the importance of what is at stake and maintain the rights of the defence. This decision has had consequences for Dutch fiscal law. If a person's tax liability is greater than may be deduced from his tax return, then a tax inspector may impose a fine, unless the taxpayer can demonstrate that he neither intended to misrepresent his tax liability nor did so through his own serious negligence. In 1988 the Dutch Supreme Court held that to impose this burden of proof on the taxpayer violates the presumption of innocence.[38]

---

[35] Committee of Ministers, DH(83) 14.
[37] 7 October 1988, Series A No. 141–A.
[36] 30 October 1991, Series A No. 214–B.
[38] HR 15 July 1988, [1988] BNB 270.

Legal Assistance

As we have seen, in *Campbell and Fell* the European Court of Human Rights held that prisoners were entitled to legal assistance because the disciplinary proceedings were characterized as criminal. One of the problems in the UK has been the extent to which legal aid should be available in appeal proceedings. Article 6(3)(c) only requires the granting of legal aid where justice requires it. In *Monnell and Morris* the European Court held that a State was not required to grant legal aid in appeal proceedings, simply because this had been available at the trial. In the UK, the formal principles for the grant of legal aid satisfy this criterion, by denying legal aid to cases where the appeal is unlikely to succeed. Generally then, complaints are unlikely to succeed. However, there have been a number of applications concerning appeals in Scotland, where the failure to grant legal aid has been held to offend against the principle of equality of arms. In *Granger* the Court held that the failure to provide legal aid in the course of a criminal appeal in Scotland was a breach of Article 6.[39] The defendant was refused legal aid on the ground of the lack of likely success of his appeal. However, during the course of the appeal the complexity of the issues involved became clear and, while the prosecution was represented by two lawyers, the defendant, who apparently had no legal training, was required to present his own appeal. The European Court's concern was not with the defendant's initial failure to obtain free legal aid in his appeal, but that he had no opportunity to reapply for it when the complexity of certain legal issues became apparent—issues which the appellant was not in a position to understand. An overhaul in the law on legal aid in Scotland was already in progress when Granger lodged his application with the Commission, but this did not apparently rectify some reluctance of appeal courts to review the decision to refuse legal aid to support appeals. The remedial action taken was to issue administrative instructions to the appropriate court authorities, explaining the circumstances in which the review of the decision to refuse legal aid is appropriate.

Disclosure of Evidence

The problem of disclosure of evidence by the prosecution to the defence is a particular problem in the context of an adversarial procedure and has been a disquieting feature of some of the recent miscarriages of justice.[40] In a system in which the prosecution is one party to a contest, there may

---

[39] 28 March 1990, Series A No. 174. Friendly settlements were reached in three further cases, *M* (App. 15861/89), *Higgins* (App. 14778/89), *R* (App. 1612/90).
[40] For a statement of the present rules on disclosure see *R.* v. *Judith Ward* (1992) 96 CrAppR 1.

be a conflict between the roles of the prosecution as contestant and as the agent of the state concerned with the securing of justice. In *Edwards* v. *UK*,[41] the prosecution had failed to disclose the existence of certain evidence at the trial. On appeal, the Court of Appeal considered that the jury would not have reached a different verdict if the undisclosed evidence had been available. One unsatisfactory aspect of the case was that the appellant's counsel decided not to seek either a cross-examination of certain witnesses or a disclosure of a confidential report into the conduct of the police, apparently because they believed that any request would be refused. The European Court emphasized that fairness under Article 6 requires that the prosecution disclose all material evidence for or against the accused. However, the Court rejected the argument that a new trial was necessary to consider all the evidence *de novo*. Following earlier judgments it held that the appeal proceedings should be considered in conjunction with the whole criminal proceedings to determine the fairness of the trial, and that a defect at the trial stage could be rectified at a later stage. Finally, the appeal proceedings could not be held to be unfair because of the failure of defence counsel to request cross-examination of witnesses or disclosure of a report. To this extent the adversarial nature of the proceedings, placing the onus on the appellant to raise material issues, was respected.

The Hearing of Witnesses

Traditionally, legal systems belonging to the civil law tradition have attached less weight to the right of the accused to interrogate witnesses than those belonging to the common law tradition. This fundamental difference is explained by the fact that, while in common law countries a trial is seen as a legal contest between two parties, in civil law countries it is perceived as an official inquiry by the court into the truth of a matter. This conception of fairness does not require that an accused be always afforded an opportunity to question a witness in court. In conformity with the civil law tradition, Dutch case law is characterized by a rather generous acceptance of hearsay evidence, even to the extent that statements of anonymous persons may be used as evidence. It is thought that the inability of the defence to question a witness can be compensated for by the care with which a court evaluates the available evidence.

Article 6(3) guarantees every accused the right to examine witnesses against him. Because the language of this guarantee is unconditional, the European Court's interpretation is crucial for civil law countries. Starting

---

[41] 16 December 1992, Series A No. 247–B. See also the rejection by the Commission of the petition of the 'Birmingham Six' complaining of the unfairness of the appeal proceedings in hearing new evidence: *Callaghan and others*, Commission Decision, 9 May 1989, 60 D. & R. 296.

with its judgment in *Unterpertinger* v. *Austria*,[42] the Court has frequently had to pronouce upon the examination of witnesses. In *Kostovski* v. *The Netherlands*, it condemned the Netherlands for having violated the Convention by declaring a person guilty of having committed a robbery on the sole basis of out-of-court statements by anonymous witnesses.[43] The European Court has never held that hearsay evidence in itself is inadmissible, but it has stressed that the accused must be given an adequate and proper opportunity to question a witness, either before or during the trial. It is this emphasis on the right to be confronted with a witness for the prosecution that is new for many European countries belonging to the civil law tradition, and they may even feel it to be a menace to their national systems.

Nevertheless, despite the unconditional language of paragraph (3), the European Court does not consider it to be without exception. In several cases it has made it clear that in some circumstances testimony of witnesses may be used without the defence having had an opportunity to question them. These circumstances seem to be how much other evidence is available and whether the prosecuting authorities have taken due care to provide the defence with an opportunity for questioning. Thus it has become hard to tell to what extent the defence may indeed effectively use its right to question witnesses. A further consequence is that the lack of clarity in the case law of the European Court provides national courts with an opportunity to play down the importance of the Court's judgments. This is what has happened in the Netherlands. Despite the forceful language which the European Court used to reject the practice of condemning persons on the basis of anonymous statements, the Dutch Supreme Court has interpreted that judgment to enable it to adhere largely to its own approach. A recent Act of 1993 reads more into the *Kostovski* judgment, but whether this is sufficient remains open to doubt.

While there is provision in the law of England and Wales for anonymous witnesses, this is more limited than in the Dutch system, and there is as yet no evidence that the Convention has had any impact on the formulation or application of the law.[44]

Assistance of Interpreters

Among other aspects of the right to a fair trial we should especially mention the right of the accused to be informed of the charge in a language which

[42] 24 November 1986, Series A No. 110. See also *Barberà*, 7 July 1989, Series A No. 146; *Bricmont*, 7 July 1989, Series A No. 158; *Windisch*, 27 September 1990, Series A No. 186; *Delta*, 19 December 1990, Series A No. 191–A; *Isgrò*, 19 February 1991, Series A No. 194–A; *Asch*, 26 April 1991, Series A No. 203; *Lüdi*, 15 June 1992, Series A No. 238; *Artner*, 28 August 1992, Series A No. 242–A.
[43] 20 November 1989, Series A No. 166. On statements of anonymous persons see also *Windisch* and *Lüdi*, above. See Chap. 14 for further discussion of the *Kostovski* judgment.
[44] See Chap. 14.

he understands and the right to have the free assistance of an interpreter. The European Court of Human Rights dealt with the first right in the cases of *Luedicke and Others* v. *Federal Republic of Germany*[45] and *Brozicek* v. *Italy*,[46] and with the second in *Kamasinski* v. *Austria*.[47] As far as the right to be informed is concerned, in 1974 the Dutch Supreme Court had already adopted the approach advocated by the European Court.[48] As has been seen earlier, in the matter of interpreters the European Court took a more liberal stand than the Supreme Court. Its decision in *Kaminski* has led to the preparation of a bill to improve legislation with respect to the assistance of interpreters.

Article 5: Deprivation of Liberty

While our discussion of Article 6 shows that the European Court of Human Rights' case law on the requirement of a fair trial has considerably more relevance to Dutch law than to British law, the reverse seems to be the case with Article 5, the habeas corpus provisions protecting freedom of the person.

The Lawfulness of Detention

The preliminary definitional problem of Article 5 has been what amounts to a deprivation of liberty. In the Netherlands this arose in the European Court's decision in *Engel*. In addition to the issue under Article 6, the question arose whether the disciplinary sanctions imposed involving various degrees of restrictions on freedom of movement were real deprivations of liberty or could simply be seen as 'different ways of performing military service', as was held by the Dutch Military Supreme Court. By the time of the decision of the European Court against the Netherlands the sanctions had already been abolished.

Article 5(1) lists the legal justifications for a deprivation of liberty. The European Court has passed judgment on whether measures taken in respect of convicted prisoners amounted to lawful detention after conviction by a competent court. In *Monnell and Morris*, in addition to holding the appeal to have been fair under Article 6, the European Court considered the English rule that, in order to discourage unmeritorious appeals, a period of imprisonment pending an appeal might not be treated as part of the prison sentence imposed at the trial. The Court found that this was a lawful deprivation of liberty since it was a legitimate part of the criminal justice process.

In the UK prisoners may be sentenced to life imprisonment where the

---

[45] 28 November 1978, Series A No. 29. [46] 19 December 1989, Series A No. 168.
[47] 19 December 1989, Series A No. 167. [48] HR 23 April 1974, [1974] NJ 272.

trial judge takes the view that, while it is not appropriate punishment simply for the offence, the offender's state of mind requires that the public be protected, until such time as it is safe to release the prisoner. In *Weeks* v. *UK*[49] the European Court of Human Rights took the view that the continued detention would cease to be lawful when it ceased to accord with the original reason for the sentence.

Article 5(1) provides that deprivation of liberty is justified if it is 'the lawful arrest or detention of a person effected for the purpose of bringing him before the competent legal authority on reasonable suspicion of having committed an offence'. Under anti-terrorism legislation police have the power to arrest persons whom they reasonably believe to be concerned in acts of terrorism. In *Ireland* v. *UK*[50] and *Brogan* v. *UK*[51] the European Court took the consistent view that complicity in acts of terrorism amounted to a criminal offence for the purposes of Article 5. However, in *Fox, Campbell and Hartley*,[52] the power of arrest was conferred on a police officer who 'believed' that a person was a terrorist. The Court accepted that the arrests were made on the basis of an honest belief, but held that, in the absence of evidence, they could not be satisfied that there was a reasonable suspicion. It is worth noting that this power of arrest had already been abolished after an official report criticized the power precisely because it conflicted with Article 5(1)(c).

Appearance before a Judge or Other Officer Authorized by Law

In *De Jong, Baljet and Van den Brink* v. *The Netherlands*[53] the European Court of Human Rights held that the *auditeur militair*, the military prosecutor charged with deciding upon detention, cannot be considered to be 'a judge or other officer authorized by law to exercise judicial power' within the meaning of Article 5, since he was not independent of the military authorities. The Court also considered the Article to have been violated in that the applicants were held in custody for six days or longer before they were brought before a judge. *De Jong* and similar cases have contributed to the abolition of a separate court system for members of the military in the Netherlands. By virtue of an Act of 1989, criminal cases against members of the armed forces are now dealt with by ordinary criminal courts, with a minority vote for the military member.

De Jong was a precursor of *Brogan*,[54] already mentioned in the context of paragraph (1), in which the power to detain for seven days persons suspected of involvement in terrorism without their being brought before

---

[49] 2 March 1987, Series A No. 114.   [50] 18 January 1978, Series A No. 25.
[51] 29 November 1988, Series A No. 145–B.   [52] 30 August 1990, Series A, 1990.
[53] 22 May 1984, Series A No. 77. See also *Van der Sluys, Zuiderveld, and Klappe*, 22 May 1985, Series A No. 78 and *Duinhof and Duijf*, 22 May 1985, Series A No. 79.
[54] *Brogan* and the other terrorist cases are discussed below more fully in Chap. 12.

a judicial authority was challenged. The European Court held that detention for periods of four days or longer without being brought before such an authority did not satisfy the requirement of promptness. The reaction of the UK was to seek to nullify the effect of the decision by entering a derogation under Article 15 on the basis that the terrorist threat is a 'public emergency threatening the life of the nation' and the measures are 'strictly required by the situation'. This derogation was upheld by the European Court in *Brannigan and McBride*.[55]

By contrast, *Brogan* is the most important European Court judgment on Article 5 for criminal procedure in the Netherlands. According to the Code of Criminal Procedure, arrest and police custody can last for a maximum of four days and fifteen hours before a suspect is brought before a judge. *Brogan* finally put an end to doubts about the conformity of that system with the Convention[56] and it is now clear that the period is too long. The consequences of *Brogan* for pre-trial detention and the way investigations are carried out are considerable. Thus, while the UK's response has been to avoid the consequences of *Brogan*, in the Netherlands a complicated Act has been adopted in 1994, aimed at bringing Dutch law more into harmony with the Convention.

Speedy Review of Lawfulness of Detention

The timely review of the lawfulness of detention has been a substantial problem in cases involving the UK where executive discretion has been chosen as the means of review. In *X* v. *UK*,[57] the Court held that in the procedures available to challenge the recall and continued detention of a mental patient, the courts did not have power sufficiently to consider the merits, while the Mental Health Review Tribunal had only an advisory role and did not have the power to order the detainee's release. The Court held that a detainee should be able to take proceedings before a court at reasonable intervals to test the continuing lawfulness of the detention. The British Government responded by legislation intended to satisfy the Court's judgment.[58]

In *Weeks* the arguments were much the same when applied to prisoners serving discretionary life sentences, and the Court came to the same conclusions as to lack of an adequate remedy. The Court further emphasized that the prisoner was entitled to adequate disclosure of the material on which the decision was based. In response, the British Government took the view that the facts of *Weeks* were unique, since it was unusually easy to distinguish the punitive element of the sentence from the public protection

---

[55] 26 May 1993 Series A No. 258.
[56] In a decision of 1966, the European Commission had found no discrepancies. See (1966) 9 *Yearbook*, 565.
[57] Discussed more fully in Chap. 9.   [58] See also Chap. 9.

element, and accordingly pardoned *Weeks*, but took no measures to amend the existing review procedures. This narrow interpretation was not accepted by the European Court in *Thynne, Wilson and Gunnell*,[59] where it became clear that the principle applied to all discretionary life sentences, and the Government accordingly introduced a legislative measure to take the discretionary power from the Home Secretary and give the prisoner the right to reviews every two years, and took administrative steps to improve a prisoner's access to information.

Given the marked reluctance of the British Government to respond to the Court's judgment in *Weeks*, it is not surprising that the law relating to the review of the cases of prisoners serving mandatory life sentences for murder has not been amended. However, perhaps surprisingly, the European Court unanimously held that such a prisoner is not entitled to a review of his detention.[60]

Among other things the decisions of the European Court in *Koendjbihari*[61] and *Keus*,[62] both cases against the Netherlands, are both concerned with procedures for the prolongation of measures imposed upon convicted persons suffering from a mental deficiency or mental illness. In *Koendjbihari* the Court held that a competent court had not decided 'speedily upon a request for prolongation'. In the meantime an Act had already revised procedural rules to bring them into better harmony with the Convention.

Article 8: Private Life, Home, and Correspondence

Criminalization of Private Conduct

In *Dudgeon* v. *UK*,[63] the European Court of Human Rights held that the criminalization of homosexuality in Northern Ireland was in breach of the Convention in so far as it extended to homosexual acts between consenting adults in private. This judgment resulted in a reform of the law, despite political opposition in Northern Ireland which had previously successfully defeated an attempt at reform.

Coercive Measures in Pre-trial Investigations

The European Court frequently scrutinizes coercive measures other than pre-trial detention. Its most important decisions are those in *Klass* v. *Federal Republic of Germany*,[64] *Malone* v. *UK*,[65] and *Kruslin* and *Huvig*, both against France.[66] The problem has generally been the lack of adequate

---

[59] 25 October 1990, Series A No. 190.
[60] *Wynne* v. *UK*, 18 July 1994. See further Chap. 17.
[61] 9 December 1988, Series A No. 185–B.
[62] 6 July 1988, Series A No. 185–C.   [63] 22 October 1981, Series A No. 45.
[64] 6 September 1978, Series A No. 28.   [65] 2 August 1984, Series A No. 82.
[66] 24 April 1990, Series A Nos. 176–A and 176–B.

regulation of the circumstances in which the investigative power may be exercised. In *Klass*, the European Court considered the German law relating to telephone tapping. Although the European Court held that there had been no breach in that case, it emphasized the need for 'adequate and effective guarantees against abuse'. English law contained no provision regulating surveillance by telephone-tapping, which was within the uncontrolled discretion of the executive. It was therefore clear that English law required reform in order to conform to the standards of the Convention. Aware of the issue, but heedless of the *Klass* judgment, the British Government did not introduce proposals for reform. However, only after *Malone* had unsuccessfully challenged the law in the British courts did the Government introduce the Interception of Communications Act 1985 and even here doubt has been expressed whether it complies completely with the Convention.[67]

While there have not been European Court judgments against the Netherlands, it is questionable, especially in the light of the *Kruslin* and *Huvig* cases, whether Dutch legislation on telephone-tapping is in conformity with all the Court's requirements. A bill is being prepared to improve the legislation in some respects.

Prisoners' Rights

The greatest number of admissible complaints to the European Commission against the UK concerns the rights of prisoners to freedom from restrictions on their right to send and receive letters.[68] The most important of these are *Golder* and *Silver*. These are discussed elsewhere,[69] but it should be emphasized that one of the reasons for the number of cases has been the reluctance of the British Government to recognize that the implications of the European Court's decisions are far wider than the narrow point at issue in each case, and required a radical revision of the underlying philosophy of the civil status of prisoners.

Other Aspects

Mention should be made of *X and Y v. The Netherlands*.[70] It disclosed a gap in the protection of victims of crimes, in that mentally-handicapped victims of sexual assault could not validly file a complaint with the public prosecutor, a complaint being a requirement to prosecute the alleged offender. The European Court held that, in order to be able to protect the

---

[67] See R. Churchill and J. Young, 'Compliance with Judgments of the European Court of Human Rights and Decisions of the Committee of Ministers in the UK' (1991) 62 *British Yearbook of International Law*, 283 at 321–6.

[68] Eight of the cases involving the UK before the European Court and 12 of the decisions of the Committee of Ministers have involved applications from prisoners, and many of these have been a consolidation of a number of different applications.

[69] See Chap. 17.   [70] 26 March 1985, Series A No. 91.

right to a private life, all victims of violent crimes should be able to raise such a complaint. Dutch law has accordingly been changed.

Article 3: Torture, Inhuman and Degrading Punishment

Police Methods

In *Ireland* v. *UK*, the European Court of Human Rights held that certain techniques of interrogating terrorist suspects had been 'inhuman and degrading'. Some of these were techniques which had been officially taught to members of the security forces, and the British Government ordered their use to be discontinued before the judgment of the Court. Others revealed an official tolerance of maltreatment, which the British Government took administrative steps to discourage, although the efficacy of these was open to doubt.

Corporal Punishment

In *Tyrer*,[71] the UK was held in breach of the Convention in respect of corporal punishment in the Isle of Man. The Isle of Man is self-governing in domestic matters, and the UK was reluctant to interfere. The Manx courts in practice discontinued corporal punishment, but only in March 1993 was a government Bill brought before the Manx Parliament to abolish it.

Extradition

In *Soering* v. *UK*,[72] the European Court held that the protection of the Convention might extend to extradition, and in particular that it was a breach of Article 3 for a prisoner to be extradited to the USA, where he might expect to spend a long period of time pending the carrying out of the death penalty. The remedy in the UK was simple, since the executive has a residual discretion to refuse extradition, and so Soering was not extradited until assurances had been given by the American authorities that he would not be executed.

For various reasons the criminal chamber of the Dutch Supreme Court has always been very reluctant to accept the possibility that the European Convention could stand in the way of fulfilling obligations arising out of extradition treaties. In the aftermath of *Soering*, the civil chamber of the Supreme Court held the surrender of an American soldier on the basis of the NATO Status of Forces Agreement to be contrary to the Sixth Protocol to the Convention, to which the Netherlands is a party, as long as the American authorities failed to give sufficient assurances that a death

---

[71] 25 April 1978, Series A No. 26.   [72] 7 July 1989, Series A No. 161.

sentence imposed by an American court would not be carried out.[73] The criminal chamber has also begun to follow the European Court.

Article 10: Freedom of Speech

Space prevents a full discussion of these cases. However, it should be noted that while the cases discussed so far have not touched upon substantive criminal offences, in two cases against the UK, *Handyside*[74] and the *Sunday Times*,[75] substantive provisions have been challenged in the European Court of Human Rights. In the first the Court held that conviction under obscenity law was not in breach of the Convention, being within the national discretion for the protection of morals. In the *Sunday Times*, English law enabled restraint of publication to prevent the commission of the criminal offence of contempt of court. The European Court held that the law was in breach of the Convention because it treated the protection of the administration of justice from prejudice as a public good to be weighed equally with freedom of expression, whereas freedom of expression should have been the paramount right to which contempt of court was a narrowly construed exception.

Concluding Remarks

Clearly the European Convention has had a considerable influence on the law of both the UK and the Netherlands. It is not merely an instrument to correct violations of human rights in individual cases. Rather, its significance for the structure of national systems of criminal justice is the most impressive aspect. Sometimes it does compel a Contracting Party to change its legislation in vital respects or to alter established practices that are deeply rooted in national conceptions of criminal justice and fairness.

This structural impact of the Convention on the administration of criminal justice has mainly been due to the existence of its advanced international supervisory mechanism. This is not only true for the UK where the Convention rights are not enforceable in the national courts, but also for the Netherlands where the individual has almost unlimited scope to rely upon the Convention as a source of enforceable rights. As we have seen, the Dutch courts have been rather cautious, even reluctant, in taking the initiative in interpreting the Convention as having consequences for the criminal justice system. Quite often they have looked upon the Convention as an outside influence that should not be permitted to disrupt existing practices too much. The European Court and Commission, on the

---

[73] HR 30 March 1990, [1991] NJ 249.
[74] 7 December 1976, Series A No. 24.   [75] 26 April 1979, Series A No. 30.

other hand, are, almost by definition, better able to take a dispassionate view. Consequently, it is they who have set standards which national authorities must follow.

The question then arises as to the ways and the extent to which each state is prepared to attach consequences to European Court judgments which are rendered against itself or which, although rendered against another party to the Convention, have direct or indirect implications for their own legal systems.

In the UK, since the guardian of the Convention in the UK is not the judiciary but the government, the attitude of the Executive is crucial.[76] The most obvious manifestation of this is in response to adverse Court judgments and decisions of the Committee of Ministers in Strasbourg. A study of the UK's response shows a patchy commitment to implementing decisions of the Court.[77] As regards terrorist legislation, the response has been to take advantage of the right under Article 15 to derogate from the Convention on the ground that the terrorist threat constitutes 'a public emergency threatening the life of the nation'.[78] In other cases the speed of the response has varied, and its adequacy has sometimes been questionable. Thus the legislation which now regulates telephone-tapping is at best minimal compliance. In cases involving prisoners' rights, implementation of the Strasbourg judgments has generally been prompt, but has been based on the narrowest interpretation of the judgment. One principle underlies all the prisoner cases, that prisoners should retain their civil rights except in so far as that is inconsistent with the maintenance of prison order. The failure to adopt a systematic approach to reform in the wake of the earlier Strasbourg judgments explains the volume of successful prisoner cases against the UK.

The response to the *Sunday Times* case is an interesting one because it demonstrates the reluctance of a British government to allow the European Convention to interfere with a cherished British institution. The response is thus an echo of the fears of Lord Jowitt quoted earlier. There is no doubt that the remedial legislation did not change the approach in the law of contempt from one of balancing two public goods (protecting the administration of justice and freedom of expression) to one giving primacy to freedom of expression. However, to have done this would have involved a major restatement of the principles of contempt of court in an unfamiliar form, and this kind of reform of an old-established area of the common law was simply not contemplated.

---

[76] For a discussion of the implications of the Convention for part of the criminal justice system in England and Wales, see Leigh, 'The influence of the European Convention on Human Rights on English Criminal Law and Procedure' (1993) 1 *European Journal of Criminal Law and Justice*, 3, at 18.

[77] Churchill and Young, above, n. 67.   [78] See Chap. 12.

It might be thought that the response to adverse judgments in Strasbourg truly reflects the extent of the implementation of the Convention, since these are often cases where the UK has been unwilling to compromise by reaching a friendly settlement—a point of principle has been involved. Yet, there is little evidence of the extent to which the executive acts to anticipate and eliminate inconsistencies between domestic law and the Convention. On at least one occasion the British government has wilfully ignored the implications of a judgment against another state. After the *Klass* judgment against Germany it was obvious that UK law on telephone-tapping would not bear the scrutiny of the European Court. In *Malone* an English judge publicly warned that this was the implication of *Klass*. However, the British Government procrastinated and only brought forward legislation after the Strasbourg Court had ruled against the UK.

Of course ministers insist that the European Convention is taken into account in the formulation of legislation and the implementation of policy. However, there is little evidence of a systematic approach to monitoring the implications of developments in Strasbourg and the relevance of the Convention to changes in the law. It is unusual, in the absence of an adverse report by the Commission of Human Rights or a judgment of the Court, for the Convention to shape political debate or bring about legislative change.[79] Indeed one commentator has suggested that, even where the Convention is the source of some reform, this is not publicly stated.[80] A possible example of this is *Hewitt and Harman* v. *UK*,[81] where the Committee of Ministers found in favour of the applicants' complaint that the security services had, in breach of Article 8, retained personal information obtained during telephone-tapping. The Security Service Act was passed in order to put the security service's operations on a statutory legal basis, with a complaints procedure. However, in the Government White Paper and the presentation of the Bill in Parliament, no government minister referred to any possible influence of the Convention.

There are, however, signs that government has become concerned with taking action to forestall successful petitions to Strasbourg. In 1987 the Cabinet Office circulated a memorandum to all government departments advising that they adopt as standard practice the consideration of the possible effects of the Convention, as interpreted in Strasbourg case law,

---

[79] One exception already referred to involved the repeal of the arrest provision which was under scrutiny in *Fox, Campbell & Hartley*, discussed above p. 74.

[80] C. Symmons, 'The Effect of the European Convention on Human Rights on the Preparation and Amendment of Legislation, Delegated Legislation and Administrative Rules in the UK', in M. Furmston, R. Kerridge and S. Sufrin (eds.), *The Effect on English Domestic Law of Membership of the European Communities and of Ratification of the European Convention on Human Rights* (The Hague; Nijhoff 1983), 387 at 390.

[81] Committee of Ministers Resolution, DH(90) 36.

on any proposed measures.[82] It is perhaps too early to tell whether this memorandum has made a marked difference, and in the context of the secretive nature of British government, it may remain difficult to determine.

Turning our attention to the Netherlands, we start with the role of the courts, for it is they who usually have to provide an immediate answer to the question of what consequences to attach to a judgment of the European Court of Human Rights, whether rendered against the Netherlands itself or against another country. Dutch case law does not provide a uniform picture. On the one hand there are areas of law in which the Dutch Supreme Court has a tendency to underestimate or even to downplay the importance of the European Court's case law. One example is provided by the Supreme Court's approach to the requirement that a person be tried within a reasonable time. Although the Supreme Court's case law in the matter is abundant, there have always been discrepancies between the Dutch court and the European Court. Such discrepancies led to *Abdoella*, in which the European Court corrected established case law in the Netherlands. Another example is that of the hearing of witnesses. In this case, while it would not be true to say that it has had no effect, it has not had the impact it deserves. The tendency to underestimate the significance of the European Court's case law in these areas is more or less a prolongation of the inclination to underestimate the significance of the Convention itself and is fed by the same sources.

On the other hand, it is fair to say that in other areas due and proper weight has been given to judgments of the European Court. Examples are the case law of the Dutch Supreme Court on the impartiality of a court and on the significance of the European Convention to extradition. Indeed, sometimes judgments of the European Court have served as a starting point for developments in Dutch case law on matters upon which the Court had not yet adjudicated. The prime example is the Dutch Supreme Court's case law on the imposition of fiscal fines. On the basis of the *Öztürk* judgment, concerned with administrative punishment of traffic violations, the Supreme Court held that the imposition of a fiscal fine on a taxpayer amounts to the determination of a criminal charge. It later found some provisions in Dutch tax law to be irreconcilable with the presumption of innocence.

As far as the legislature in the Netherlands is concerned, its awareness of the importance of the Convention and the case law of the European Court has increased considerably during the last ten years. Nowadays proposals for legislative change in the field of criminal law are almost always accompanied by a careful assessment of the relevance of the Convention

---

[82] This document is summarized in A. W. Bradley, 'Protecting Government Decisions from Legal Challenge', [1987] *Public Law*, 1 at 3.

to the matter. Moreover, to the credit of the Government one may observe that it does not matter in this respect whether the judgment of the European Court has been rendered in a case against the Netherlands or in a case involving another state. As a further comment we may add that the Government, too, is sometimes inclined to underestimate or down-play the importance of the European Court's case law in order better to promote its own goals.

Comparing the attitudes in both countries with respect to their preparedness to implement the case law of the European Court, the available evidence seems to suggest that practice in the UK shows more reluctance than that in the Netherlands. One difference between the two countries is striking. It is not uncommon for the Dutch courts to correct their interpretation of the Convention, or for the Government to propose new legislation under the influence of judgments of the European Court in cases in which the Netherlands was not a party (e.g. *Brogan* and *Soering*). On the other hand, we have not been able to find any example of similar responses in the UK to judgments of the Court against other countries. Part of the explanation for this difference might be that the decisions of the European Court simply have no relevance to the situation in the UK. This is certainly true with some of the cases under Article 6 which have posed particular problems for the civil law approach to evidence and the conduct of the trial. However, as we have seen with telephone-tapping and the failure to respond to the decision in *Klass* v. *Federal Republic of Germany*, this is not a complete explanation. Undoubtedly, the legal status of the Convention makes discussion of its relevance less rewarding in the UK, since the aggrieved individual's reliance on the Convention is likely to be marginal. In the Dutch courts, the question is not whether the Netherlands was in breach of the Convention, but whether a particular interpretation of the Convention by the European Court has implications for the Dutch legal order.

Inevitably the European Convention exerts a harmonizing influence on the various systems of criminal justice in Europe. It is true that the European Court has always stressed the fact that each national system has to be understood in its own individuality. The European Convention certainly does not require uniform justice in Europe. Owing to the Court's tendency to narrow the impact of its decisions to the cases it has to decide, to the avid reader of its case law it is often quite difficult to know whether more general consequences could be drawn from them. But it does not alter the fact that idiosyncracies of national systems have become especially vulnerable to criticism. The many cases involving the British prison system illustrate that point, but one may also think, for instance, of trials *in absentia* in Italy or of the features of the appeal system in Sweden. Moreover, cases like that of *Brogan*, *Soering*, and *Kruslin* simply set standards that must be obeyed by all Contracting Parties, irrespective of how their legal systems are structured.

It is our impression that, especially in matters of deprivation of liberty, the protection of privacy, home, and correspondence, and the freedom of speech, the European Court, on the basis of the various provisions of the Convention, has developed common standards which have become more specific and exacting over the years, thereby gradually diminishing the freedom of the States Parties to pursue their own solutions. To a considerable extent the same is true where the right to a fair trial is concerned, although the Court is confronted here with the fact that some parties to the Convention belong to the common law tradition and others to the civil law tradition. Our final remarks are therefore directed towards a closer look at the impact of the Court's case law in this area of criminal justice.

The most intriguing question within the framework of this book is whether the European Convention, as interpreted by the European Court, promotes a movement of convergence between common law and civil law systems in the context of the criminal trial, where the attitudes of the two systems were previously so different.[83] It has become apparent from our discussion of the European Court's case law that the judgments concerned with a fair trial under Article 6 are of considerably more importance to the Netherlands than to the UK. Is it true that civil law countries like the Netherlands are gradually being forced to relinquish their conception of what a fair trial consists of in favour of that prevalent in common law countries?

At the outset we may note that the language of Article 6 of the Convention has been influenced by the Constitution of the United States via earlier drafts of the International Covenant on Civil and Political Rights. This has a decidedly adversarial ring. On the other hand, the Convention operates within a predominantly civil law setting, since the large majority of the Contracting States belong to the civil law tradition. This dominance of the civil law tradition is reflected in the membership of the Commission and the Court. Furthermore, despite its language, Article 6 certainly does not simply impose on the Contracting Parties a pure common law model of a criminal trial. There is, for instance, no mention of a jury nor of cross-examination.

For its part the European Court has always refrained from explicitly choosing between the two legal traditions. On many occasions it has held that the Contracting Parties enjoy considerable freedom in the choice of the appropriate means to ensure that their judicial systems comply with the requirements of Article 6.[84] It has consistently refused to review national law and practice *in abstracto*, limiting itself to determining whether the

---

[83] See also Chap. 3.
[84] For the most recent authority in this respect, see *Hadjianastassiou*, 16 December 1992, Series A No. 252.

manner in which they were applied to or affected the applicant gave rise to a violation of Article 6.[85] A study of the case law confirms that the Court does not start from the presumption that the common law concept of a fair trial is superior to the civil law concept, or the latter superior to the former. What it has done in many decisions is to stress the fact that criminal proceedings should be adversarial. But that does not mean that its idea of adversarial proceedings necessarily corresponds in every respect with the notion as it is understood and realized in common law countries.

A closer study of the European Court's work reveals that one category of cases forming a majority is concerned with problems that are, from a theoretical point of view, of the same nature in common law and civil law systems of justice. This is most clearly demonstrated by comparing *Engel and Others* v. *The Netherlands* and *Campbell and Fell* v. *UK*, decisions on what kinds of procedures amount to determination of a criminal charge within the meaning of Article 6. Other examples in the case law are disclosure of evidence to the defence, a hearing within a reasonable time, free legal aid, the assistance of an interpreter. This is not to suggest that practical consequences of the Court's judgments are the same for all national systems of justice. The point is, rather, that these consequences have not much to do with the fact that a national system belongs to the common law or civil law tradition.

A second category of case is concerned with features of civil law systems which have no counterpart in common law systems. The problem here is a lack of role differentiation that seems to have its root in the civil law concept of criminal proceedings as an official inquiry into the truth of a matter. In a number of cases the European Court of Human Rights has ruled out or put in question the cumulation of judicial functions which is sometimes to be found in civil law systems. Examples of these are being an examining judge and a member of the trial court in *De Cubber, Pfeiffer* and *Plankl*, or that of deciding on pre-trial requests to order that the suspect be tried and being a member of the trial court in *Oberschlick*. Another example is provided by *Borgers*, where it was held that, although a *procureur-generaal* to a court of cassation acts more or less as an *amicus curiae*, this does not alter the fact that he still represents the prosecution.[86] In such ways civil law systems are forced to develop stronger adversarial elements. It is obvious, however, that these rulings do not strike at the basic characteristics of such systems.

Finally, there are cases in which basic differences between the two legal traditions are at stake. They concern the admissibility of hearsay evidence

---

[85] See e.g. *Thorgeirson*, 25 June 1992, Series A No. 239.

[86] Another example of role differentiation is provided by the Court's case law on Art. 5(3). According to the judgments in *Huber*, 23 October 1990, Series A No. 188, and *Brincat*, 26 November 1992, Series A No. 249–A, a public prosecutor in Switzerland or Italy cannot be considered to be an officer authorized by law to exercise judicial power.

and the questioning of witnesses against the accused. As has been seen, the European Court has emphasized the right of the accused to be able to question witnesses against the accused, to be given an adequate and proper opportunity to do so, preferably during the hearing. On the other hand, the Court does not consider this right to be without exception, and this raises the question whether the Court approaches the matter more from a common law or a civil law perspective.

A closer look at its case law reveals that the cases in which the Court accepted that out-of-court statements might be used as evidence without the accused having the opportunity to question them all concern witnesses who were, for one reason or another, unavailable through no fault of the prosecuting authorities. Since in the common law and civil law traditions unavailability may be an exception to the right of the defence to question witnesses, the Court's case law is consistent with the approach of both traditions.

However, the Court has also had to decide in cases in which the prosecution was (probably) able to produce the witness in court, but did not want to do so for reasons of policy. The most important example of these is the *Kostovski* case. In these cases in which the identity of the witnesses was kept secret from the trial court and the defence, the Court held that the impossibility for the defence to question the witness constituted a breach of Article 6.[87] However, the reasons adduced by the Court do not squarely rule out the possibility that, in other circumstances, it might accept the use of statements by a witness whom the prosecution does not wish to appear before the court.[88] Quite apart from the question of the differences between civil law countries, it is not possible to be sure whether the Court will be more inclined to follow a common law approach than a civil law approach.

While it is not yet possible to say whether the Court will really adopt a common law approach to the hearing of witnesses, its frequent emphasis on the importance of the defence having the opportunity to question witnesses as an essential element of fairness has significant implications for civil law systems. However reluctant they may be, as with the Netherlands, these systems are compelled to become more 'adversarial'.[89] To that extent we may indeed conclude that the case law of the European Court promotes some sort of convergence between the two legal traditions.

---

[87] See also *Windisch* and *Lüdi*, cited in n. 41, above.

[88] Cf. *Brandstetter*, 28 August 1991, Series A No. 211.

[89] For a more thorough discussion of the implications of the Court's case law on criminal procedure in the Netherlands, see A. H. J. Swart, 'Die Europäische Menschenrechtskonvention und das niederländische Strafprozeßrecht' (1993) 105 *Zeitschrift für die gesamte Strafrechtswissenschaft*, 48–76.

5

Intergovernmental Co-operation in the Field of Criminal Law

CHRISTOPHER HARDING AND BERT SWART

INTRODUCTION

Traditionally criminal law and its enforcement have been a part of the legal system jealously preserved within the area of sovereign competence of states, and moves towards co-operation and the pooling of resources and powers have met with both political and constitutional resistance. As McClean comments: 'In criminal matters . . . the traditional stance of states can only be described as one of non-co-operation . . . the general practice . . . remains coloured by the position that no country will enforce the penal law of a foreign state.'[1] This situation has arisen in part from the inevitable relation between the need for state security and the protection of other important national interests and the availability of criminal law as an obvious means of guaranteeing such interests; in part from the culturally specific character of some crime and the nationally specific thrust of much policy formulated to deal with crime problems. In contrast, for instance, to a field such as commercial law, where there have been cogent arguments and strong economic pressure for co-operation and harmonization at the international level, the internationalization of criminal law at a general level has remained to a large extent a speculative and utopian programme.[2]

But this general observation should be made with some qualification. To be sure, harmonization of substantive criminal law—except for very special topics—is likely to remain an uncertain subject for future action. But as regards some issues of procedure and enforcement, co-operative efforts have been made both bilaterally and (increasingly in regional contexts, in the latter half of the twentieth century) also on a multilateral basis. A classic example of bilateral co-operation is the extradition treaty,

---

[1] David McClean, 'Mutual Assistance in Criminal Matters: The Commonwealth Scheme', (1988) 37 *ICLQ* 177, at 178. Heike Jung has commented: 'traditionally criminal law and criminal justice are symbols of state sovereignty, so to speak its very core and centrepiece', in 'Criminal Justice: a European Perspective', [1993] *CrimLRev.* 237.

[2] See for instance the project undertaken by M. Cherif Bassiouni in *International Criminal Law: A Draft Criminal Code* (Alphen aan den Rijn; Sijthoff and Noordhoff 1980).

the device enabling the return of fugitive offenders to jurisdictions which are able and willing to put such persons on trial. In the course of time bilateral co-operation has extended to other aspects of criminal procedure, notably to facilitate the trial process, for instance by the provision of evidence, or the transfer of proceedings. Multilateral co-operation has also occurred in such contexts, as groups of like-minded countries have sought to establish a network of legal co-operation rather than rely on an increasing number of bilateral arrangements, which may be time-consuming to negotiate and result in a complex set of legal relations. Multilateral co-operation has also been prompted by an increasing international concern with the control of certain types of criminality which often transcend national boundaries—terrorism, drug trafficking, and money laundering being the contemporary illustrations which most readily come to mind. Here, the international dimension of the problem and the perceived need by governments for urgent and effective methods of control have led to multilateral treaties and other mechanisms of collaboration such that there has now emerged a body of rules and procedures which can fairly be described as a system of international criminal justice, which in turn has had an impact on the issue of legal protection and human rights at both the national and international levels.

If it is therefore possible to talk in terms of some internationalization of criminal procedure and enforcement of criminal law, it should also be possible to refer to a process of 'Europeanization' in this field. In between bilateral and global attempts to deal more effectively with crime problems, there have been a number of regional initiatives, prompted by obvious considerations of geographical contiguity, but also by a shared ideology which makes co-operation more feasible, the countries concerned having a sufficient consensus as regards the objectives of penal policy and the necessity for guarantees of legal protection. At a regional level, European countries (which has meant, until recently, for the most part west European states) have been especially vigorous in the business of multilateral co-operation. These efforts have occurred within a number of European institutional fora for collaboration. Foremost among these has been the Council of Europe, set up in 1949 with the aim of achieving 'a greater unity between its Members for the purpose of safeguarding and realizing the ideals and principles which are their common heritage and facilitating their economic and social progress'.[3] Two important points should be made about the Council of Europe's work in the field of crime: first, that it is essentially an inter-governmental body which promotes measures, most significantly in the form of international treaties, which are then accepted or not, as each Member State government decides; secondly, that the

---

[3] Art. 1, Statute of the Council of Europe.

emphasis on safeguarding and realizing ideals and principles implies a restraint on certain kinds of governmental activity. This can be seen most explicitly in Article 3 of the Council's Statute which stipulates as a condition of membership the acceptance of 'the principles of the rule of law and of the enjoyment of all persons . . . of human rights and fundamental freedoms'. This guarantee of democratic liberties therefore tempers the pursuit of some of the other objectives of the Council of Europe, including the way in which crime procedures are tackled. The clear manifestation of this concern with individual freedom is of course the Convention on Human Rights, the relevance of which to criminal questions was discussed in the previous chapter.

More recently, co-operation in the criminal law field has also developed in the context of the European Union. The impact of European Community law and policy on Member States' criminal law, in both a negative and a positive sense, is discussed more fully in Chapter 6, as is the protection of certain Community interests through national criminal proceedings, and the development of the Community's own system of investigations and sanctions, notably in the area of competition policy. What is provided for in Title VI of the Union Treaty, however, is something distinct, in that Article K talks in terms of 'co-operation in the fields of justice and home affairs'. The measures envisaged in Title VI are essentially of an intergovernmental character, co-ordinated within the European Community Council, which is seen as the appropriate institutional base for co-operation in these fields. The role of the Community in this respect is therefore comparable to that of the Council of Europe and so would be most appropriately discussed here under the heading of intergovernmental co-operation. As a matter of fact the Union Treaty forms the culmination of a development that started in the second half of the 1970s. Already, prior to its signing there had been a less formal alignment of policy through the so-called 'Trevi process'. Initiated in 1976, this comprised regular meetings of ministers of justice and home affairs to discuss issues relating to internal security and the investigation of crime. With the adoption of the Single European Act, envisaging a Community without inner frontiers, the work of the Trevi group became increasingly important. Finally, it should also be noted that within the framework of the European Political Co-operation the Member States have concluded a number of conventions on international co-operation in criminal matters.

It should also be borne in mind, however, that a number of European countries are at the same time party to global treaties providing for co-operation in the field of criminal law. Some of these instruments are the result of widely-based attempts by the international community to grapple with the issues of terrorism and drug-trafficking and embody a similar pattern of provision, first laid down in the 1970 Hague Convention on the

Unlawful Seizure of Aircraft.[4] What will commonly be found in such treaties is agreement to condemn the conduct in question (hijacking of aircraft, hostage-taking, or whatever) in strong terms as a matter of national criminal law; to maximize the possibility of jurisdiction being exercised over such offences by extending jurisdiction beyond the traditional grounds defined by reference to territorial and personal connection; and to accept an obligation to 'try or extradite' (*aut dedere aut judicare*) alleged offenders apprehended by States Parties. The most important conventions to note in this category are the 1970 Hague Convention; the 1971 Montreal Convention for the Suppression of Unlawful Acts Against the Safety of Civil Aviation;[5] the 1973 Convention on the Prevention and Punishment of Crimes Against Internationally Protected Persons;[6] the 1979 Convention Against the Taking of Hostages;[7] the 1980 Convention on the Physical Protection of Nuclear Material;[8] the 1988 IMO Convention for the Suppression of Unlawful Acts Against the Safety of Maritime Navigation;[9] and the 1988 UN Convention Against Illicit Traffic in Narcotic and Psychotropic Drugs.[10] Most European states are party to the Hague and Montreal Conventions, whereas adherence to the others listed above is variable, ranging from a high level of acceptance in the case of Scandinavian countries to a much more wary approach, as evidenced for instance by France. But even for those states which are party to such treaties, their legal obligation may not have much practical consequence (they may not often find themselves in the position either to try or to extradite hijackers, for example); or alternatively may be evaded in practice (such as the notorious expulsion of the alleged terrorist Abu Daoud from France in 1977 to avoid the obligation to take legal action against him[11]). Care should be taken, therefore, not to assume too wide an extent or activation of such treaty obligations.

COUNCIL OF EUROPE SPONSORED CO-OPERATION

A Network of Treaties and Recommendations

Legal co-operation within the Council of Europe may be embodied in measures taken in the wake of recommendations made by the Council's Committee of Ministers, or following adherence to multilateral 'European' Conventions promoted by the Council of Europe itself. The latter now span a period of almost forty years, ranging from the 1957 Paris Convention on Extradition[12] to the 1990 Convention on Laundering, Search, Seizure

---

[4] 10 ILM 133.   [5] 10 ILM 1151.   [6] 13 ILM 41.   [7] 18 ILM 1456.
[8] 18 ILM 1419.   [9] 27 ILM 668.   [10] 28 ILM 493.
[11] [1977] *Keesing's Contemporary Archives*, 28305–6.   [12] ETS 24.

and Confiscation of the Proceeds from Crime.[13] These two treaties also illustrate the main approach taken by European conventions in the field of criminal law, focusing on aspects of procedure rather than specific kinds of criminality.

There are a number of conventions on procedural questions. The Extradition Convention (in force 1960, twenty-one parties), with its two Protocols of 1975 and 1978,[14] provides for a collective network for extradition, on the basis of commonly agreed conditions, as between the parties. The 1959 Convention on Mutual Assistance in Criminal Matters[15] (in force 1962, nineteen parties) and its Protocol[16] (in force 1982, ten parties) provides for reciprocal assistance as regards such matters as the provision of evidence and extracts from judicial records and the serving of writs. Both these conventions are based on long-established state practice. Less widely adhered to are the Convention on the Supervision of Conditionally Sentenced or Conditionally Released Offenders of 1964[17] (in force 1975, seven parties), which allows for mutual co-operation as regards the supervision of offenders given suspended sentences or conditionally released from custody by one state but ordinarily resident in another, and the Convention on the Punishment of Road Traffic Offenders, of the same year[18] (in force 1972, four parties), which enables the transfer for prosecution of and enforcement of judgments against road traffic offenders from the state where the offence is committed to that where the offender is ordinarily resident. Similarly, the Convention on the International Validity of Criminal Judgments of 1970[19] (in force 1974, seven parties in 1992), concerning the enforcement of foreign criminal judgments and sentences, and the 1972 Convention on the Transfer of Proceedings in Criminal Matters[20] (in force 1978, seven parties), providing for the transfer of proceedings to the state where a suspected offender is ordinarily resident, already subject to criminal proceedings or serving a sentence of imprisonment, have both had a limited take-up. Generally, therefore, progress in relation to transfer of proceedings and enforcement of sentences has been tentative. On the other hand, the 1977 Convention on the Suppression of Terrorism[21] (in force 1978, twenty-one parties), imposing an obligation to extradite persons who have committed serious terrorist offences, overriding the traditional 'political offence' bar to extradition in such cases, was quickly adhered to (as is often the case with anti-terrorism treaties), although with significant reservations. Finally, there is the 1983 Convention on the Transfer of Sentenced Persons[22] (in force 1985, twenty parties in 1992), which provides for the transfer of convicted prisoners to their national state to complete

[13] 30 ILM 148. [14] ETS 86; ETS 98. [15] ETS 30. [16] ETS 99.
[17] ETS 51. [18] ETS 52.
[19] ETS 70. See also the discussion in Chap. 16, below. [20] ETS 73.
[21] ETS 90. [22] ETS 112. Discussed in detail in Chap. 16.

their sentence there. It may be seen that, broadly speaking, the principal purposes of this group of treaties are first to facilitate the prosecution and trial of offenders (by extradition, transfer of proceedings, and supply of evidence) and secondly to enhance the implementation of penal measures in both the custodial and non-custodial spheres.[23] It is also evident that the willingness of individual Council of Europe countries to be bound by these conventions is variable. This phenomenon raises interesting questions of comparative law, which will be addressed below in a closer examination of British and Dutch attitudes.

More recently, there has been a trend towards the adoption of treaties providing for a package of co-operative measures in relation to specific kinds of criminal conduct. Though not all of these treaties are yet in force, a number of headings of criminality have been covered in this way. Mention may be made of the 1978 Convention on the Control of the Acquisition and Possession of Firearms[24] (in force 1982, nine parties); the 1985 Convention on Offences Relating to Cultural Property;[25] the 1985 Convention on Spectator Violence and Misbehaviour at Sports Events[26] (in force 1985, twenty parties); the 1987 Convention on the Prevention of Torture and Inhuman or Degrading Treatment or Punishment (in force 1989, twenty parties);[27] the 1989 Convention on Insider Trading; [28] and the 1990 Convention on Laundering, mentioned above.

The main official process of measuring the implementation and impact of Council of Europe conventions in this field is the review procedure carried out by the Committee of Experts set up in 1981. This Committee may prepare recommendations for the Committee of Ministers to adopt (for instance, Recommendation R(83)12 concerning safe conduct for witnesses in connection with Article 12(1) of the Convention on Mutual Assistance in Criminal Matters). Although not legally binding, it may be considered that recommendations supply an expedient means for improving the operation of the conventions; the alternative approach—to draft protocols to the treaties—is undoubtedly time-consuming and still ultimately unpredictable, since there is no certainty that a State Party to a convention will also agree to be bound by later protocols.

In any assessment of the effectiveness of the European conventions in this field, account should be taken of the fact that some states may have a preference for other approaches to co-operation and that the multilateral treaty is just one of a number of options. In particular, the use of bilateral treaties, although theoretically more cumbersome and painstaking to negotiate, may in practice prove to be more feasible in both political

---

[23] See the review of progress in this area in (1987) *Netherlands Yearbook of International Law*, 298 ff.

[24] ETS 101.   [25] 25 ILM 44.   [26] 24 ILM 1566.

[27] 27 ILM 1152.   [28] 30 ILM 869.

and legal terms. In fact, this may be the only option in relations between non-like-minded states. The European convention system has on occasion been extended to Canada and the United States[29] (in which case the measures have a 'North Atlantic' character), but it is accepted that co-operation with third world countries is likely to require the negotiation of bilateral arrangements. Moreover, some states may be unwilling to submit to the collective assumptions and obligations inherent in the multilateral method, while wishing to engage in some forms of co-operation, or deal with particular countries. A method which lies somewhere between the bilateral and multilateral approach is to be seen in the 'scheme', as adopted by Commonwealth countries at Harare in 1986:[30] a model for mutual assistance in criminal matters, which is then available for states to adopt by means of implementing legislation, which may depart in some respects from the text of the 'scheme'. The principal perceived advantage of this approach (and equally, in the view of some states, a major weakness) is its flexibility, which enables states with, for instance, constitutional impediments or resource problems, to go part of the way. Whether such an approach will prove any more productive of actual co-operation than the multilateral treaty method remains to be seen, but it is suggestive that a state such as Canada, which is active in the field of criminal law co-operation, has a preference for bilateral treaties or, if such are not feasible, for 'administrative arrangements' of a specific and fixed-term nature and which are treated for domestic purposes as a treaty. As one commentator notes: 'The formalism of this approach may be regretted, but it is actual delivery of effective assistance which is crucial.'[31]

British and Dutch Approaches to International Co-operation within the Council of Europe

In their approach to interstate co-operation within a European framework the UK and the Netherlands show considerable differences. At the outset it may be noted that the UK has always stayed relatively aloof from participation in the drafting of Council of Europe conventions on co-operation in criminal matters while, on the other hand, the Netherlands has been actively engaged in the process. Moreover, until recently, the UK did not wish to become a party to these conventions, with the exception of the 1977 Convention on the Suppression of Terrorism and the 1983 Convention on the Transfer of Sentenced Persons. Recently, however, this attitude has changed. In 1991 the UK has ratified two of the major

---

[29] e.g., the 1983 Convention on the Transfer of Sentenced Persons.
[30] McClean (1988), n. 1 above. [31] Ibid., 190.

conventions: the 1957 Convention on Extradition and the 1959 Convention on Mutual Assistance in Criminal Matters. The Netherlands has become a party to all the major conventions. This includes the 1970 Convention on the International Validity of Criminal Judgments and the 1972 Convention on the Transfer of Criminal Proceedings, up to now the two most ambitious and daring conventions of the Council of Europe in the field of mutual co-operation.

These differences in approach may probably be explained by basic differences in philosophy relating to co-operation. Territoriality still appears to be the cornerstone of the British approach to co-operation: the state best qualified to try and to punish the offender is the state where the offence was committed. This implies a preference for extradition and mutual assistance, a relative indifference to transfer of the execution of criminal judgments and an outright dismissal or refusal of transfer of criminal proceedings as modes of co-operation. On the other hand, in civil law countries like the Netherlands, attachment to territoriality is traditionally less strong. It is, for instance, to some extent superseded by an equally traditional preference for bringing a person to trial and punishing him within the community to which he belongs, and this need not be the community in which he committed the offence. Accordingly, there is in the Dutch approach no a priori preference for some forms of co-operation over others. The idea is rather that, whatever forum is chosen to try a person and to punish him, that choice should best serve the proper administration of justice. This choice is determined by the interests of the co-operating states and those of the individual and the preferred choice is the one which best reconciles these interests. The various forms of international co-operation may, each in its own way, contribute to achieving this goal. Transfer of proceedings and transfer of the criminal judgments are, in this respect, tools as important as extradition and mutual assistance. The various modes of co-operation are interrelated instruments enabling states to be flexible in the interest of a proper administration of criminal justice.

A difference in philosophy is also revealed in the extent to which both countries are willing to transfer responsibility within the framework of co-operation. It is particularly relevant in relation to transfer of proceedings and transfer of the execution of judgments. In Dutch legislation the view is taken that these forms of co-operation should imply a willingness of the requesting state to transfer responsibility as much as possible. The requested state should enjoy an almost unfettered discretion in dealing with the case since it is that state on whose territory the offender is expected to remain after having stood trial or having undergone punishment. The requesting state should trust the requested state in its endeavour to find a proper solution to the offence, even if the requesting state would have opted for a different solution. A remarkable example of this philosophy can be found in the 1968 Benelux Convention on the Transfer of Execution of Criminal Judgments. The Convention enables the courts of the requesting state to declare a person guilty without imposing punishment. It is then left to the courts of the requested state to sentence him. As is apparent from the 1984 Repatriation of Prisoners Act the British approach is quite different. According to the Act punishment imposed elsewhere may only be altered if it is, by its nature or duration, compatible with British law (see Chapter 18). In this approach the responsibility for sentencing and for carrying out punishment remains to a larger degree the duty of the requesting state and there is less readiness to transfer responsibility to the requested state.

Such differences in philosophy explain why the UK has not ratified the 1970 Convention on the International Validity of Criminal Judgments and the 1972 Convention on Transfer of Proceedings, while it only wants to make use of the Convention on the Transfer of Sentenced Persons so as to allow for continued enforcement. As a matter of fact the British approach to the three conventions is shared by France and Germany, while, on the other hand, the Dutch approach is also that of the Scandinavian countries. This suggests that the important factor in explaining different philosophies is not so much whether a country belongs to the common law or the civil law tradition as its relative size and power. Perhaps smaller nations are more dependent on international co-operation in criminal matters and maybe experience has taught them that flexibility as well as a willingness to transfer responsibility are important conditions for fruitful co-operation.

Meanwhile the divergent attitudes in both countries towards co-operation are bound to influence the way they co-operate with one another. The case study in Chapter 18 provides a vivid example where the transfer of sentenced persons is concerned. Another important example is provided by extradition. Since 1988 the Netherlands has been prepared to extradite Dutch nationals to other states, but their extradition is seen as an option only. It is only natural for the UK frequently to apply for the extradition of Dutch nationals who have committed an offence in Britain. Nevertheless, to extradite nationals to other states in a specific case is far less of an obvious course for the Netherlands to take than for the UK. There will be cases in which the Netherlands would greatly prefer transfer of proceedings from Britain rather than extradition to Britain, an option that does not easily fit within the British approach to co-operation. Conversely it is also possible to conceive of cases in which the Netherlands would prefer transfer of proceedings to the UK in a criminal case involving a British national, rather than extradition by the UK. Since the UK has not ratified the 1972 Convention on Transfer of Proceedings this, however, is not an option.

Trevi

During a meeting in Rome in 1975 the Ministers of Home Affairs and Justice of the Community Member States decided to consult each other regularly on matters of internal security. Their group was called the Trevi group (*Terrorisme, Radicalisme, Extrémisme et Violence Internationale*). With the blessing of the 1976 European Council in Luxembourg two working groups were established. One concerned itself with the various aspects of (international) terrorism, the other with the organization, equipment, and training of police forces. Meetings were to be held every six months. A new impetus to Trevi was provided by the Single European Act, aiming at a Europe without inner frontiers. First, in 1986 a third working group was established within Trevi, concerned with various international crimes, notably traffic in narcotic drugs, armed robberies, and trade in weapons. Then, in 1988, a fourth group came into being, with the task of studying the specific consequences of the Single Act for co-operation in the field of criminal justice and home affairs. This working group was called Trevi 1992.

During the past seventeen years the Trevi group has dealt with an enormous variety of topics, all related to internal security and the investigation of crime, ranging from the creation of a secure communications network to the standardization of police equipment, from co-operation between security services to common measures to combat football hooliganism. The concerns of the Trevi ministers are as varied as police work itself. Owing to the rather secretive nature of the Trevi decision-making, however, there is no complete list available of proposals and decisions that have been made.[32] Meanwhile it is fair to say that the provisions in the Union Treaty on co-operation in the fields of justice and home affairs more or less codify and institutionalize an already existing situation.

Within and without the Trevi framework ideas of creating some form of European police force have circulated and have been debated, notably since the second half of the 1980s. The most important initiative in this respect was taken by the German Government during the 1991 European Council in Luxembourg. On the basis of these proposals the Council decided in favour of a Central European Investigation Office, to be established before 1994. It should start as a 'relay station for exchange of

---

[32] For an analysis of Trevi see *Practical Police Co-operation in the European Community* (London; HMSO 1990). On police co-operation generally: C. Fijnaut, 'The Internationalisation of Criminal Investigation in Western Europe', in C. Fijnaut and R. Hermans (eds.), *Police Co-operation in Europe* (Lochem, 1987), 32–56 and J. Benyon, P. Davies, and A. Willis, *Police Co-operation in Europe: A Preliminary Investigation* (Leicester; Centre for the Study of Public Order 1990).

information and experience'. In a second phase 'powers to act also within the Member States would be granted'. The idea has been adopted in the 1992 European Union Treaty, although with some modifications.

The Single European Act and Schengen: the Abolition of Frontier Controls

Turning to developments within the European Community, it may be noted that at the beginning of the 1980s two initiatives were taken to strengthen the process of European unification that have far-reaching implications for international co-operation in criminal matters. One led to the adoption of the Single European Act in 1986, the other to the Schengen Agreement of 1985[33] and the Schengen Convention of 1990.[34] Both initiatives are closely related.

Among other things the Single European Act represents an attempt by the Member States of the European Community to provide a new stimulus to the achievement of a truly common market. Article 8A of the Act defines this market as 'a space without internal frontiers in which the free circulation of goods, persons, services and capital is secured'. According to the Act this goal should be achieved at the beginning of 1993. At first sight the definition seems to imply a total abolition of border controls at the common borders of the Member States. Not all Member States, however, interpret the Act in that sense; notably the UK holds a different view with respect to control on the movement of persons. As a result of that disagreement, the abolition of border controls has not only not made much progress within the Community, but it has also been outflanked by an initiative taken by five Member States to abolish such controls as between themselves in preparation for future developments within the European Union. This initiative was taken first by Germany and France, and the Benelux countries then joined. The Agreement of Schengen (a small town in Luxembourg where the borders of Germany, France, and Luxembourg meet) sets the goal for the abolition of border controls at 1992 and creates obligations for the five contracting parties to develop compensatory measures in order to cope with the consequences of the abolition of controls. These compensatory measures are the substance of the Schengen Convention of 1990. Meanwhile Italy, Spain, Portugal, and Greece have acceded

---

[33] Agreement between the Governments of the States of the Benelux Economic Union, the Federal Republic of Germany and the French Republic on the Gradual Abolition of Checks at their Common Borders,. Schengen, 14 June 1985 (1985) 23 *European Yearbook*, Benelux, 17–31.

[34] Convention Applying the Schengen Agreement of 14 June 1985 between the Governments of the States of the Benelux Economic Union, the Federal Republic of Germany and the French Republic, on the Gradual Abolition of Checks at their Common Borders, Schengen, 19 June 1990 (1991) 30 ILM 84–117.

to the Schengen Agreement and the Schengen Convention. Of all the
Community States only the United Kingdom, Ireland, and Denmark stay
aloof. The Convention has not yet entered into force.

The Schengen Convention of 1990 is mainly concerned with compensatory measures in the fields of immigration law and criminal law. The largest part of the Convention, comprising more than fifty articles, is devoted
to police and security. It is supplemented by another part envisaging the
creation of a Schengen Information System. One of the most important
subjects dealt with within the framework of police and security is mutual
co-operation between police forces. The Convention creates a general
obligation for police authorities to lend assistance to each other upon
request, to the extent permitted by national law. This provision is supplemented by another, authorizing the authorities to provide information
without request. Three forms of operational co-operation have been regulated in considerable detail: cross-frontier pursuit, cross-frontier observation, and monitored delivery. Finally the Convention contains provisions
on technical co-operation and the stationing of liaison officers. All in all,
the chapter on police co-operation, however limited in scope it still may
be, nevertheless represents a unique innovative attempt to lay down rules
with respect to international co-operation between police authorities. The
same cannot be said of the chapters concerning mutual assistance between
judicial authorities, extradition, and transfer of the execution of criminal
judgments. They are mainly concerned with achieving equal standards of
co-operation between the Contracting Parties on the basis of the already
existing conventions of the Council of Europe. In between these chapters
is a separate chapter on the application of the *non bis in idem* principle,
for which the European Community Convention on the same subject has
provided a model.

Harmonization of legislation and policies with respect to drugs and firearms is dealt with in two other chapters. These topics were among the
most controversial during negotiations, as well as in the public debate at
that time. In both fields the outcome of the negotiations is basically an
agreement to disagree. National differences in legislation or policies are
accepted but rules have been adopted to cope with the consequences of
such differences. Finally there is the Schengen Information System, probably the most innovative part of the Schengen Convention. The System
consists of computerized information, which is made available to national
law enforcement authorities. The information relates to such categories of
persons as those wanted for arrest for extradition purposes, witnesses,
persons summoned to appear before judicial authorities in connection with
criminal proceedings, or persons who are to be notified of a sentence. The
system also contains information on objects sought for the purpose of
seizure of evidence in criminal proceedings.

The Schengen Convention represents the first cohesive attempt to develop common and comprehensive standards of co-operation in criminal matters.[35] It should also be noted that it pays much attention to the protection of personal data, and here again it is innovative. The importance of the Convention for future developments within Europe can, therefore, hardly be overestimated. In fact, the impact of Schengen on the measures to implement Article 8A of the Single European Act that are in the process of being prepared by the countries of the European Union is clearly visible. This is true not only of the 1990 Dublin Convention determining the state responsible for examining applications for asylum and the Draft Convention of the Member States of the European Union on the crossing of their external borders. It is also revealed in the intention to create a European Information System, closely modelled on the Schengen example.

The European Union Treaty: Co-operation in the Fields of Justice and Home Affairs

Title VI of the Union Treaty, signed in Maastricht in December 1991, provides for co-operation between the states of the European Union in certain areas, defined in Article K1 as being 'matters of common interest', which include:

(4) combating drug addiction;
(5) combating fraud on an international scale;
(7) judicial co-operation in criminal matters;
(9) police co-operation for the purposes of preventing and combating terrorism, unlawful drug trafficking and other serious forms of international crime . . .

What co-operation means more precisely in this context is laid down in Article K3, bearing in mind that Article K2 states that any action taken under Title VI will be in accordance with the European Convention on Human Rights and shall not affect the exercise of Member States' responsibilities with regard to 'the maintenance of law and order and the safeguarding of internal security'. (These limitations on action provided for in Article K2 pull in different directions, recognizing the very different interests of individuals and governments; this also provides a key to constraints on international co-operation generally, since both these interests tend to be invoked against such initiatives.)

---

[35] For a discussion of its provisions see e.g. David O'Keefe, 'The Schengen Convention: A Suitable Model for European Integration?' (1991) 11 *Yearbook of European Law*, 185–219, and A. H. J. Swart, 'Police and Security in the Schengen Agreement and the Schengen Convention', in H. Meijers (ed.), *Schengen, Internationalisation of Central Chapters of the Law on Aliens, Refugees, Privacy, Security and the Police* (Kluwer; W. E. J. Tjeenk Willink 1991), 96–109.

Article K3 lays down a general obligation of consultation for Member
States, who must inform and consult each other within the Council, with
a view to co-ordinating their action. To this end, there must be collaboration between relevant government departments and Article K4(1) provides for a Co-ordinating Committee to be set up to work with the Council
in this field. The Council itself is given a number of powers: to adopt joint
positions and promote co-operation, to adopt joint action and to draft
conventions which may be recommended to Member States for adoption.
However, the power to take such measures is carefully circumscribed. Such
action must be on the initiative of a Member State or States or the Commission; but the Commission may not initiate any Council action in relation to judicial co-operation in criminal matters, customs co-operation, or
police co-operation, thus excluding incursion from the 'centre' in those
areas. Joint positions and the promotion of co-operation must 'contribute
to the pursuit of the objectives of the Union'. But if this is a reference to
Article 8 of Title I of the Union Treaty, which lists the objectives of the
Union, it is not so much a helpful guideline as a circular cross-reference,
since the relevant part of Article 8 talks only of 'the development of close
co-operation on justice and home affairs'. Joint action is more rigorously
confined by reference to the principle of subsidiarity—that is to say, it is
enabled only so far as the objectives of the Union can be better attained
through joint rather than individual action on the part of Member States,
on account of the scale or effects of the action envisaged. As regards the
possibility of conventions being adopted, these may only be recommended;
it remains for each State to decide whether or not to adhere to any such
conventions.

It is impossible at this stage to predict the impact of such speculative
provisions. While it is clear that the Council may become a forum for the
exchange of information and a 'talking shop', through the obligation to
consult, it is far from certain what use would be made in practice of its
powers to promote or take action. It is possible to imagine constitutional
argument being used to block initiatives and action, by reference both to
the vague concept of 'objectives of the Union' and to the principle of
subsidiarity, both of which may prove to be fecund areas for judicial interpretation. In so far as the Council may wish to go into the business of
preparing conventions, it is difficult to see how its position will be any
more efficacious than that of the Council of Europe. What prospect is
there of Member States of the European Union becoming party to any
such instruments in any greater number than the Member States of the
Council of Europe, especially as membership of the two organizations
converges during the 1990s? Moreover, it should be asked: what is the
relationship of the Community—or, rather, the Union—to the Council of

Europe? Would the Community Council 'adopt' existing Council of Europe Conventions, or draft different or 'improved' versions? In fact, within the framework of European Political Co-operation six conventions have already been concluded by the Member States. Some are meant to be additions to Council of Europe instruments;[36] others seem to be for the most part watered-down versions of these instruments;[37] still others deal with subjects not covered by Council of Europe conventions or covered incompletely;[38] none have yet entered into force.

The underlying question must surely be to ask why much of this provision in Title VI is seen as necessary in practical terms when existing structures and mechanisms, encompassing a broader grouping of states, are already available within the Council of Europe. What is of perhaps more immediate practical importance in this context is Article 209a of the EC Treaty as amended by the Union Treaty, which obliges Member States to co-operate in the development of measures to deal with fraud against the Community and ensure assimilation of such measures to existing control of fraud at the national level. While this is perhaps little more than an explicit expression of the general obligation to facilitate the achievement of the Community's tasks under Article 5 of the Treaty, it should also be borne in mind that centrally co-ordinated co-operation in the context of fraud against the Community is not uncontroversial, as was seen in the recent challenge to Commission initiatives by the German Government in Case C–240–90 (see Chapter 6 below).

One of the most important and interesting aspects of the Union Treaty is that it declares police co-operation to be a matter of common interest and that it envisages in Article K1(9) the creation of a European Police Office (Europol). This marks the culmination of a development within the framework of European Political Co-operation that had started as early as the 1970s, referred to in the discussion of Trevi, above. In Title VI of the Treaty mention is made of a European Police Office (Europol), while a Declaration on Police Co-operation forms part of the Final Act to the Treaty. In the Declaration Europol is conceived as a body for the exchange

---

[36] Agreement on the Application of the European Convention on the Suppression of Terrorism between the Member States of the European Communities, Dublin, 4 December 1979, Cmnd 7823; Agreement on the Application between the Member States of the European Communities of the Council of European Convention on the Transfer of Sentenced Persons, Brussels, 25 May 1987, EC Doc CPE/1/x1; (1988) EC 32, Cm 488.

[37] Convention on Transfer of Proceedings, Brussels, 1990, and the Convention between the Member States of the European Communities on the Enforcement of Foreign Criminal Sentences, Brussels, 13 November 1991.

[38] Convention between the Member States of the European Communities on Double Jeopardy, Brussels, 25 May 1987, EC Doc CPE/ii/XI; (1988) EC 19, Cm 438; Convention between the Member States of the European Communities on the Simplification and Modernisation of Methods of Transmitting Extradition Requests, Donostia—San Sebastián, 20 May 1989.

of information and experience. In this respect Europol could fulfil the following functions:

- support for national criminal investigation and security authorities, in particular in the co-ordination of investigations and search operations;
- creation of databases;
- central analysis and assessment of information in order to take stock of the situation and identify investigative approaches;
- collection and analysis of national prevention programmes for forwarding to Member States and for drawing up Europe-wide prevention strategies;
- measures relating to further training, research, forensic matters and criminal records departments.

The Declaration makes no mention of power to act on the territory of Member States. It merely concludes by saying that, before the end of 1994, the Member States should consider whether the scope of co-operation should be extended. Negotiations are now taking place to create a statute for Europol on a treaty basis. Meanwhile the Member States have agreed to start with the building up of a provisional structure.

The Declaration on Police Co-operation hides the fact that the Member States have divergent views on the necessary shape for future police co-operation in Europe. It also raises four important and more or less inter-related questions that may be mentioned here. According to Article K1 of the Union Treaty police co-operation is envisaged for the purpose of preventing and combating terrorism, unlawful drug trafficking, and other serious forms of international crime. These crimes were already the concern of Trevi. Surprisingly, there is no mention of co-operation in relation to crimes directed against the financial and other interests of the European Community (especially fraud, see Chapter 6). It is not obvious why they should be excluded. Clearly Europol has been conceived as a form of inter-state co-operation, not different in structure from that which takes place within Interpol. Europol will not take its own decisions in criminal cases. It will have, as yet, no autonomous powers, many Member States opposing the idea. Indeed, a European police force endowed with its own power to act, an idea favoured by some Member States, would be something entirely new. Nevertheless, the question remains whether in actual practice Europol will remain only a clearing house for the exchange of information and experience, or whether possibly it will, sooner or later, acquire such momentum as to enable it to impose its views on Member States. Thirdly, Europol for the moment not being concerned with crimes against the European Community and having, as yet, no powers to act on its own authority, it comes as no surprise that it has not been proposed as part of the institutional structure of the European Community or the

Union. The approach is intergovernmental, not supranational. This is obviously explained by the fact that justice and home affairs are very sensitive areas in which any grant of powers to supranational bodies is viewed with apprehension.

Finally, Europol, along with the other forms of intergovernmental co-operation envisaged by the Union Treaty, inevitably gives rise to the question of harmonization in the field of criminal justice. To what extent do these new forms of co-operation generate a need for harmonization of substantive criminal law or rules of criminal procedure? That also is an issue of vital importance to the future of criminal justice in Europe.

CONCLUDING COMMENTS

There is little doubt that Europeanization is making headway now in the field of criminal justice and the provisions of the Union Treaty referred to above are at least an indication of the forces which are likely to shape future developments. In looking to the future it may be useful to comment on two possible lines of development: more intensive co-operation, and harmonization.

It is not unrealistic to foresee further developments in inter-state co-operation at the European level and the logical end of this process would include: an obligation of assistance, with little scope for discretion, and the disappearance of traditional exceptions, such as those based on military and fiscal considerations; the possibility of states extraditing their own nationals; the evolution of extradition into something like the rendition procedure used within the United States; comparable developments in the field of mutual assistance; and, as mutual trust and understanding grow, transfer of proceedings and the execution of sentences may become the rule rather than the exception. All of this would also imply a considerable simplification of procedure.

Attractive as this vision of the future may be in some respects, some critical comments are in order. The first set of comments concerns the individual person who is, as yet, merely the object of co-operation. To the extent national authorities increasingly co-operate in the interest of criminal justice, there is an increasing need to protect individual interests at an international level. This need takes two forms. First, increased international co-operation between authorities tends to disturb the fragile balance between prosecution and defence in a criminal case. In this respect the accused will have to acquire his own rights to co-operation, to the extent necessary for his defence (for instance, the right to compel the attendance of witnesses from abroad). The logical end here would be a situation in which national borders are no longer obstacles for the defence in a criminal case either. Secondly, international co-operation between authorities, important and legitimate as it may be, nevertheless is an exercise of power that needs to be controlled. At present, abuse of power or errors committed by national authorities in one state, almost never entail legal consequences in another state. Most courts in Europe are not prepared to attach consequences to illegal behaviour by officials other than those of their own country. The legal vacuum that is thus created should be addressed in some way.[39] For Dutch lawyers, at least, all this is a matter of some urgency: courts are faced with such issues quite regularly.

The other main point of critical concern relates to the possibility of harmonization. Inevitably, as co-operation develops, a stage is reached at which the question of harmonization becomes unavoidable. Should there be harmonization of substantive criminal law in order to deal with problems of double criminality? Should the powers of police and prosecuting authorities be harmonized so as to facilitate co-operation?[40] Harmonization is already a major strategy in the context of implementing Community obligations (see Chapter 6); outside the economic area, however, it appears as a more problematical objective. The experience of the Schengen negotiations is illuminating here. Harmonization of legislation on the possession of firearms has been impossible to achieve; the relevant parts of the Schengen Convention only deal with the consequences of having a number of different approaches. In relation to the control of drug use, there are important differences between the Schengen countries as regards their policies of criminal law enforcement, but the Schengen Convention simply agrees to accept such differences (see Chapter 8).

As has been argued by a number of writers[41] there is no virtue in uniformity of criminal law for its own sake. The content of national criminal law is often the product of long historical experience and particular national conceptions of justice and authority. To give just one example concerning freedom of speech: British legislation on the protection of official secrets would be wholly unacceptable in the Netherlands, while Dutch legislation making it a criminal offence to insult sections of the population on account of their race, sex, or sexual preference would meet the same reaction in the UK. In practice, the best way forward is to co-operate on the basis of mutual respect for deeply rooted differences in approach, as has happened

[39] See O'Keefe, and Swart, n. 35 above. Cf. also Heiner Busch, 'Europa: ein "Mekka der Kriminalität"?' (1990) 23 *Kritische Justiz*, 1–13.
[40] Cf. Reinhard Rupprecht, *Das Schengener Sicherheitssystem: Die neue Polizei* (1991), 555–60, advocating an all-embracing European criminal policy.
[41] L. B. Schwartz, 'The Model Penal Code: An Invitation to Law Reform' (1963) 49 *American Bar Association Journal*, 455, and Ch. J. Enschedé, *Model Penal Code for Europe*, Memorandum prepared at the request of the Legal Affairs Committee of the Council of Europe, 1971, published in 1991 as *Een uniform Europees strafrecht?* (Gouda Quint; Arnhem 1990).

in the case of the Schengen Convention. What is true for substantive criminal law would be equally applicable to questions of procedure.

However, harmonization may well be a worthwhile goal in some areas, and it may be argued that in that covered by the Convention on Human Rights it should be accepted as a matter of principle (see Chapter 4). But generally a minimum requirement of harmonization should be a careful study of how different national systems of justice operate and it may well prove necessary, on both political and moral grounds, to move ahead with a policy of 'optional harmonization' in many areas of criminal law and criminal justice. In a sense criminal justice is a 'service' not unlike the services of the EEC Treaty. Experience of the past decades has shown already that it is extremely difficult to harmonize national rules on the rendering of services, and this policy has been partly abandoned. To make harmonization, or even uniformity, a goal in itself on the assumption that uniformity increases effectiveness would probably lead to counterproductive results and rob national systems of criminal justice of much of their legitimacy in the eyes of the public.[42] The basic task that lies ahead is to achieve co-ordination between the national systems of criminal justice while at the same time taking into account that basically similar goals are often being pursued in different ways that reflect different national traditions, values and expectations.

A final point concerns the basic distinction which is conventionally drawn between the 'intergovernmental' and the 'supranational'. To be sure, it has some present validity in the context of this discussion. But will the distinction remain so tenable in the future? This point may be illustrated by the discussion on Europol. Some see Europol as a sort of European police force that, sooner or later, will have to be endowed with its own executive powers and its own competence to act on the territory of Member States, without authorization from national authorities: in short, a European FBI.[43] Others see Europol as an institutionalized form of co-operation between national police forces. This discussion raises many fundamental issues. How is a supranational European police force to be made subject to political and democratic control and how is it to be made accountable before national courts? Can a European police force exist without the creation of a European public prosecutor or even a European criminal court? And would these institutions not suppose harmonization of substantive criminal law and criminal procedure of the states concerned? Finally, what would

---

[42] On Dutch concerns in these matters see C. Frederik Rüter, 'Harmonie trotz Dissonanz, Gedanken zur Erhaltung eines funktionsfähigen Strafrechts im grenzenlosen Europa' (1993) 105 *Zeitschrift für die gesamte Strafrechtswissenschaft*, 30–47.

[43] Cf. the President of the German Bundeskriminalamt, Hans-Ludwig Sachert, 'Europol, Mehr Schlagkraft gegen das Verbrechen' [1992] *Kriminalistik*, 7–11.

be the relationship between these institutions and those concerned with implementing Community law at a European level?

The example shows that the intergovernmental road of Maastricht does not necessarily rule out the creation of supranational structures that, in their turn, may create an added pressure to harmonize criminal justice. There are serious dangers in this, especially if such developments were to be based on majority decision-making. In which case, perhaps the fears of the 'Euro-sceptics' are not without some foundation.

6

The European Community and Criminal Law

RENÉ GULDENMUND, CHRISTOPHER HARDING,
AND ANN SHERLOCK

INTRODUCTION

While in the case of a treaty such as the European Convention on Human Rights it was obvious from the outset that it would have an impact on the criminal law of the individual Contracting States, there was rather less appreciation until relatively recently that accession to the European Community would involve implications for the criminal law and procedure of the individual Member States. The subject matter of the three Communities—the European Coal and Steel Community (ECSC), the European Atomic Energy Community (Euratom), and the European Economic Community (EEC)—appears at face value to have little or nothing to do with the criminal law of the Member States.[1] Indeed, for some time conventional wisdom was that the criminal law of the Member States would remain unaffected by Community law. This was certainly the view of the British Government in 1971 when it set out the legal implications of membership of the European Community and stated that 'nothing in Community law would, for example, materially affect the general principles of our criminal law . . .'.[2] The thinking was that the Community operated only in the areas set out in the Treaty and there was no reference in the Treaties to matters of a criminal nature. Indeed, even as late as 1981 the European Court of Justice stated that:

In principle, criminal legislation and the rules of criminal procedure are matters for which the Member States are still responsible.[3]

---

[1] With the exception of Art. 194(1) Euratom, as noted by J. W. Bridge in 'The European Communities and the Criminal Law', [1976] *CrimLRev.* 88. For more recent discussion of the impact of the Community system on national criminal law, see Janet Dine, 'European Community Criminal Law?' [1993] *CrimLRev.* 246 and Hanna G. Sevenster, 'Criminal Law and EC Law' (1992) 29 *CML Rev.* 29.

[2] *Legal and Constitutional Implications of United Kingdom Membership of the European Communities*, Cmnd. 3301 (1971), para. 25.

[3] Case 203/80, *Criminal Proceedings against Guerrino Casati* [1981] ECR 2595, para. 27. Nor did the Commission dissent from this position—see, e.g., its *Eighth General Report on the Activities of the Community* (1974), para. 145: 'Criminal law as such is not a matter of Community competence but remains within the jurisdiction of the individual Member States.'

Yet, on closer examination, even these statements, which recognized the primary competence of the Member States in the area of criminal law, were not unqualified. During the 1970s the European Court of Justice had made it clear that, while the primary competence in criminal matters rested with the Member States, Community law set limits on what the Member States were free to do. Indeed, even the British Government's statement in 1971 recognized that some harmonization in this field would perhaps be necessary in order to avoid disparities between penalties for breaches of Community law as between the different Member States.[4]

More recently, the Treaty on European Union, concluded at Maastricht in 1991, has given the European Union competence to initiate policy in the field of home affairs and criminal law enforcement.[5] This system of co-operation is to form part of the Union but remains, as a pillar of that Union, outside the European Community. The provisions of the Union Treaty have already been discussed in Chapter 5 and, as was pointed out there, have to be seen essentially as intergovernmental mechanisms of co-operation. The action envisaged under these provisions is through the Council acting largely as an intergovernmental institution and not through the more supranational institutions available to the Union. For example, the Commission's competence even to initiate developments is very limited.[6] Thus, this development is more appropriately treated under the heading of intergovernmental co-operation than under that of the impact of Community law and policy on national criminal justice.

The impact which Community law has had on the Member States' criminal law has had two aspects. In the first instance, in certain situations Community law has required that particular parts of a Member State's criminal law should not be applied. In other situations, however, the obligation has been a positive one whereby the state is required to impose duties on individuals and other legal persons within its jurisdiction, duties which might have to be enforced by the state's criminal law. It is proposed to examine these negative and positive obligations in turn.

NEGATIVE OBLIGATIONS ON THE MEMBER STATES

The fact that it is no longer possible for Member States to determine their criminal law without reference to Community law became apparent as individuals began to resist the application of Member State criminal law

---

[4] Cmnd. 3301 (1971), para. 33.
[5] Art. K–K.9. These provisions entered into force on 1 November 1993.
[6] Art. K.2. For the role of the Parliament see Art. K.6. The Court is excluded from this area unless specifically given jurisdiction under particular conventions: see Art. K.3.

by relying on Community grounds. It is a basic doctrine of Community law that, in cases of conflict between Member State and Community law, the latter must prevail. The impact of Community law on the competence of Member States in the area of criminal law was increasingly obvious as individuals began to assert Community rights in the national courts to deflect or avoid the application of national law. In effect, Community law was, in such situations, being used as a shield against the application of national criminal law. For example, where the EC Treaty provides for the free movement of goods throughout the Community, that is, the dismantling of barriers to trade, individuals and companies gain the right freely to import and export goods subject only to exceptions set out in the Treaty which are restrictively interpreted by the European Court of Justice. Such rights have been held to be directly effective, which means that they may be relied on by legal persons before their own national courts and must be given effect to by those national courts. National courts are obliged to give precedence to Community law in cases of conflict with national law. Therefore, if the criminal law of one of the Member States prevents individuals or other legal persons from exercising a Community freedom then it is likely that that law is inconsistent with Community law and must not, therefore, be applied by the national court. Thus, for example, it was held to be contrary to free movement of goods provisions for British law to criminalize the import of sexually-explicit inflatable dolls into the UK, while a Belgian law imposing sanctions where imported whisky was not accompanied by a certificate of origin was held to be a restriction contrary to Community law. Member States do have some discretion to restrict these rights on grounds of important interests, including public health, public morality, and public policy. In such cases, it is essential that there is no discrimination on grounds of nationality and that the restrictions are proportionate to the aims being pursued.[7] In cases such as these, the defendants to criminal charges were seeking to use Community rights as a complete defence to the charges. By pointing to a Community right superior to national law they wished to establish that the Member States were no longer competent to prohibit or restrict their conduct on the particular matter and that the criminal law should not be applied in that situation.

In other situations with a Community dimension, where it is permissible for Member States to proscribe or to require certain conduct, their criminal jurisdiction may still be affected in that Community law may restrict the severity of the penalty which may be imposed. If a penalty is disproportionate to the offence in question it may be held to be an unjustified

---

[7] See e.g. Case 121/85, *Conegate* v. *HM Customs and Excise Commissioners* [1986] ECR 1007, where reliance on the ground of public morality was not permitted due to the element of discrimination on grounds of nationality; cf. Case 34/79, *R.* v. *Henn and Darby* [1979] ECR 3795.

restriction on the freedoms conferred by the Treaty.[8] For example, Article 48 gives to workers the right of free movement in the Community. This includes the right to go to another Member State and seek work there, to take up employment, and to reside there for the purposes of that employment. Community law has not, however, deprived Member States of the power to adopt measures in order to have an exact knowledge of the movement of population within their territories and allows the requirement of two formalities for the exercise of free movement namely, possession of a valid passport or identity card and obtaining a residence permit in the Member State in question. Member States are permitted to lay down penalties to secure compliance with these requirements[9] but any penalty must go no further than is necessary to secure compliance, and penalties which are disproportionate to the offence will be held to be inconsistent with Community law. Thus, for example, it has been held that the penalty of deportation for not obtaining a residence permit is totally out of proportion to the offence in question, negating as it does the right in the Treaty, and is therefore inconsistent with Community law.[10] The Court of Justice has stated on a number of occasions that:

the administrative measures or penalties must not go beyond what is strictly necessary, the control procedures must not be conceived in such a way as to restrict the freedom required by the Treaty and they must not be accompanied by a penalty which is so disproportionate to the gravity of the infringement that it becomes an obstacle to the exercise of that freedom.[11]

In more general criminal matters, states tend to have a fairly wide discretion in deporting aliens who have fallen foul of the criminal law.[12] However, when dealing with Community nationals a criminal conviction in itself is not a sufficient ground for deportation. In order for deportation of Community nationals to be permissible it must be shown that the circumstances which gave rise to the criminal conviction are evidence of personal conduct constituting a real and present threat to a fundamental interest of society.[13]

Thus, it was the claims of individuals trying to resist or limit the application of national criminal law to themselves which first began to highlight the effect which Community law had on the criminal laws of the Member States. Soon it became clear that the freedom of Member States to apply

---

[8] The principle of proportionality is considered further in another context later—see text accompanying n. 27.

[9] Directive 68/360 and Case 157/79, *R.* v. *Pieck* [1980] ECR 2171.

[10] Case 157/79, *R.* v. *Pieck* [1980] ECR 2171.

[11] Case 203/80, *Casati* [1981] ECR 2595, para. 27.

[12] e.g., in the UK under the Immigration Act 1971 the Home Secretary may deport a person who is not a British citizen if he considers it conducive to the public good to do so.

[13] Case 30/77, *R.* v. *Bouchereau* [1977] ECR 1999, para. 35. This is recognized in the United Kingdom's Immigration Rules 1990.

their criminal law and penalties was restricted by the need to ensure that Community rights were not infringed. Compliance with this obligation has been easily ensured as long as Member State courts have accepted the principle of the supremacy of Community law, which requires them to give effect to Community law over national law in the case of a conflict between the two. Although this enforcement was, and still is, carried out by the national courts of the Member States, under Article 177 of the EC Treaty those courts may refer questions to the Court of Justice for assistance regarding the scope and interpretation of Community law. In this way the Court of Justice was given an opportunity to expound upon the role of community law in the area of national criminal law.

However, the negative obligation of states not to enforce criminal law contravening Community law is only one aspect of the Community impact on the criminal law of the Member States. Community law not only confers rights on individuals; it also imposes obligations on them. It is the latter aspect which has given rise to positive obligations on states in respect of their criminal law and its enforcement. In order to understand how such positive obligations have come about, it is necessary to examine the way in which Community law imposes obligations on individuals and how those obligations are enforced.

INDIVIDUALS' DUTIES UNDER COMMUNITY LAW

Duties are imposed on individuals by Community law in a number of ways. Treaty Articles, and regulations which are directly applicable, may impose obligations directly on individuals without the need for intervening national measures. It is also possible for regulations to impose duties directly on individuals but also to impose a duty on the states to adopt measures to ensure compliance by individuals. Directives, on the other hand, always require action to be taken by the Member States to achieve goals set in the directive. A directive sets the objectives to be achieved and leaves the choice of implementing methods to the states, but this could include an obligation to be imposed on legal persons within that state. The choice of instrument used by the Community depends on the nature of the area being dealt with and kind of action which is required. In areas where the objective is to harmonize the differing laws of the states the directive is frequently regarded as the most appropriate instrument. In that case the obligations in question will reach the individual in the form of national legislation; in the case of regulations the obligation may come directly from Community law. However, in both cases one must ask how the obligation is actually enforced against the individual. Here we find two models of enforcement which are used in Community law, one which is something of an exception involving direct enforcement by the Community institutions and the other which is the conventional model involving a more indirect approach.

The first of these models of enforcement of Community law obligations against individuals is that which is used in relation to competition and might usefully be termed the 'direct model'. Articles 85 and 86 of the EC Treaty prohibit undertakings from entering into anti-competitive arrangements which have an effect on intra-Community trade. What is unusual in relation to competition law is that secondary legislation has set up machinery for direct enforcement by the Commission. The Commission is given primary responsibility for the development and enforcement of competition law and policy, with Regulation 17 of 1962 granting it quite draconian powers of enforcement. For example, the Commission has the right to request information from undertakings which is relevant to competition matters (Article 11). More draconian is the power to search premises and to take away papers and other relevant documents (Article 14). Failure to comply with requests for information or supplying false or incomplete information may lead to the imposition of penalties on the undertakings concerned. It is in this respect that competition law is radically different from other areas, for Regulation 17 sets up a comprehensive system of penalties which may be imposed on defaulting undertakings for substantive breaches of the competition rules or for failure to supply the Commission with requested information. Penalties which are deliberately described as administrative, as opposed to criminal, may involve a fine or a periodic penalty payment, which is imposed for as long as the breach continues. Thus the Commission has the power to deal directly with legal persons within the Member States without the intervention of any national body and, if necessary, has at its disposal Community penalties which it may impose subject only to review by the Court of First Instance and the Court of Justice. This model of enforcement has implications for the criminal law of the Member States once again in a negative sense. Quite obviously, it would not be permissible for national law to require action by individuals inconsistent with their Community duties. Furthermore, since the facts which disclose a breach of Community competition law may also involve a breach of national competition rules it is possible that an individual or company might find itself in the position of being dealt with by two separate sets of authorities, Community and national. This is not in itself objectionable under Community law, but each set of authorities is restricted in the penalties which it can impose by the rule against double jeopardy. Each must ensure that the person who may be subject to parallel proceedings must not be subjected to double penalties.[14] The implications of this

---

[14] Case 14/68, *Walt Wilhelm* v. *Bundeskartellamt* [1969] ECR 1.

enforcement model as regards the development of a Community 'criminal law' will be discussed later.

The other model of enforcement may be termed the conventional model, as it is the way in which most obligations are enforced against individuals. This model involves a division of labour between the Community and the Member States which recognizes the fact that in almost all cases the Community lacks a policing system to detect breaches of Community law by individuals and a system of sanctions to punish breaches. Therefore, while Community law may directly or indirectly impose an obligation on an individual[15] it is most frequently the Member States which are involved in the enforcement of Community law against individuals within their jurisdiction. This model of enforcement devolves the day-to-day implementation and enforcement of Community law on national bodies, and in most cases the individual or company within the state has little direct contact with the Community institutions. It requires the Member States to use national agencies to detect breaches of Community law, to make use of national criminal law to bring breaches to court, and to rely on any available penalties within the national criminal justice system to punish any breaches of the law. Thus, unlike the situations previously discussed, we can see that here there are positive obligations on the Member States in relation to their application of their national laws.

It is, of course, true that recourse to the criminal law is not necessary in all cases where individuals act in breach of Community law. As in national systems, less drastic responses may often prove as effective, or possibly more effective, than the application of the criminal law. For example, in many States certain conduct falling short of the desired standards may not give rise to criminal liability but to civil liability. Aggrieved individuals would have to seek a civil remedy such as damages for negligent conduct or the breach of a contractual duty, for example. The imposition of similar civil liability for breaches of Community law might also prove effective in certain circumstances. In other cases states may prefer to impose on wrongdoers an administrative or disciplinary sanction falling short of the full rigour of the criminal law. In certain cases, however, the use of the more drastic weapon of the criminal law may be necessary. The very process of deciding which acts should be criminalized and which should not often raises issues of great sensitivity within states and interference from 'outside' bodies is often unwelcome. Yet, it is precisely into this area that Community law has begun to move.

It may be useful to consider some examples of duties imposed on legal persons within the Member States which require a positive action on the part of the states to ensure compliance. One area which often catches the

---

[15] See the discussion at the beginning of this section.

news headlines is fraud in relation to the common agricultural policy.[16] The common agricultural policy involves the payment of various sums of money to producers and exporters of agricultural produce and the collection of levies from importers of agricultural produce into the Community. In order to enable Community produce to be competitive on the world market, export refunds are paid when produce leaves the Community while import levies are payable on produce entering the Community from third countries. These refunds and levies are part of a policy set at Community level and provision for their payment and collection is made in Community law, but the actual implementation of the law falls to the relevant Member State bodies. National bodies are responsible for assessing companies' entitlement to such payments or liability for levies, and for paying out or collecting the correct sums. As is well known the scope for fraud in relation to the common agricultural policy is very great; the responsibility for preventing fraud in this area falls on the Member States, with the Community institutions playing a supervisory or co-ordinating role.

The Community's rules on fishing illustrate the same division of responsibility. Among the Community's responses to the problem of over-fishing and the need for conservation has been the setting annually of total allowable catches (TAC) in relation to various species of fish. This TAC is divided among the Member States with each receiving a quota. Fishing vessels are required to cease fishing for species which are the subject of a quota when their Member State's quota is deemed to have been exhausted. Fishing regulations include various rules relating to the obligations of skippers of fishing vessels to keep records of catches and to declare these to the relevant Member State. There are also prohibitions on the use of nets with meshes below a certain size at particular periods. Similarly there are prohibitions on fishing for certain species during specified periods, and it is prohibited to sell undersized fish. These obligations are to be found in regulations which are directly applicable. The obligations, therefore, fall directly on the relevant individuals and companies without the need for the Member States to embody them in national legislation. But the detection and punishment of breaches is primarily a matter for the Member States.[17]

Unlike the competition model for enforcement, in these situations there is little scope for direct action by the Community institutions, the Community system lacking a general policing agency and system of sanctions.

---

[16] See generally John A. E. Vervaele, *Fraud Against the Community* (Deventer; Kluwer 1992), and Nikos Passas and David Nelken. 'The thin line between legitimate and criminal enterprises: subsidy fraud in the European Community' (1993) 19 *Crime Law and Social Change*, 223.

[17] For a discussion of implementation and enforcement in this area see Commission, *Report 1991 from the Commission to the Council and the European Parliament on the Common Fisheries Policy* (SEC(91) 2288 final), para. 1.2.3.2.

Therefore if these obligations are to be enforced at all against individuals the enforcement must be done by the Member States. It is this aspect which gives rise to positive obligations on Member States as to whether they are obliged to use their criminal law to support Community law. It is to this aspect that we now turn.

POSITIVE OBLIGATIONS ON MEMBER STATES

It is clear that, without the support of Member States' legal systems, including their criminal law, to enforce obligations against individuals and other legal persons, Community law could be seriously frustrated. Indeed, this is underlined by the fact that when Member States fail to give their full co-operation to the Community, Community law *is* very much weakened. This is certainly the case in relation to fraud in the agriculture sector[18] and also in relation to the enforcement of the fisheries policy.[19]

It is important to appreciate that enforcement does not involve just one single action, but rather a chain of events. The first link in the enforcement chain is that legislation must set out the required standards. Then there must be adequate policing to ensure that the legislation is complied with. This must be backed up by diligent investigation of suspected breaches and, if necessary, the initiation of enforcement action, whether criminal, disciplinary, or civil in nature. Where it is established that a breach has taken place, there must be the imposition of an effective sanction or, where civil liability is opted for, the award of an appropriate remedy to the injured party. Finally, the system must ensure that the sanction is properly executed. Thus, it must be emphasized that Member States do not fulfil their obligations in relation to the enforcement of Community law simply by enacting relevant legislation.

The full implications of this for Member States' competence in criminal law matters have not always been appreciated by the states or expounded by the institutions. The fact that it is not only permissible for States to take action in respect of such breaches but is in fact required of them to do so has become clearer only in very recent years. Indeed, as late as 1977 in *Amsterdam Bulb BV* v. *Produktschap voor Siergewassen*, the Court of Justice went no further than to talk in terms of it being permissible for Member States to provide penalties for the breach of Community law:

Although Article 5 of the EEC Treaty places Member States under a duty to take all appropriate measures, whether general or particular, to ensure fulfilment of the

---

[18] See the annual reports of the EC Court of Auditors including its famous report of 1985 (OJ 1985, C215).
[19] See Commission report, above, n. 17.

obligations resulting from action taken by the institutions of the Community, it allows the various Member States to choose the measures which they consider appropriate, including sanctions which may even be criminal in nature . . . in the absence of any provision in the Community rules providing for specific sanctions to be imposed on individuals for a failure to observe those rules, the Member States are competent to adopt such sanctions as appear to them to be appropriate.[20]

This was a very timid description of what Article 5 involves. That provision states:

Member States shall take all appropriate measures, whether general or particular, to ensure fulfilment of the obligations arising out of this Treaty or resulting from action taken by the institutions of the Community. They shall facilitate the achievement of the Community's tasks.

They shall abstain from any measure which could jeopardize the attainment of the objectives of the Treaty.

It is worth observing that in an earlier case in 1962, *High Authority* v. *The Netherlands*,[21] the Court had taken a more robust approach and referred to an obligation on Member States to adopt sanctions to be imposed on individuals for breaches of Community law. It stated:

the measures to be adopted by the Member States in order to fulfil their obligations . . . might have no effect in the absence of any checks on their implementation or *compulsory powers*. The taking of these measures is therefore the obvious and inevitable complement of the obligations imposed upon governments which are entirely responsible not only for providing for the attainment of the aims of Article 70 [of the ECSC Treaty] but also for ensuring their implementation.[22]

It should be noted that the remarks of the Court are stronger and more explicit in the Dutch text—the language of the case—than in the English. The Dutch text reads '*strafbepalingen*' (penal provisions) instead of 'compulsory powers'.[23] Thus the Court saw appropriate penal measures as 'the obvious and inevitable complement' to Member States' obligation to implement Community law.

The implications for criminal law matters of Article 5, which is directed

---

[20] [1977] ECR 137, paras. 32–3. The Court of Justice talked in these terms because this was the issue referred to it by the national court. The national judge wished to know whether it was *permissible* for Member States to provide penalties for the breach of Community law, not whether they were *obliged* to do so.

[21] Case 9/61, *High Authority* v. *The Netherlands* [1962] ECR 217.

[22] Ibid., 237. Emphasis added.

[23] The word '*strafbepalingen*' is used in Dutch Acts as a heading always to indicate a set of sections providing that certain conduct is an offence, which implies that the criminal law is applicable, and that the offence is either a crime or a misdemeanour, and further establishing the system of checks and investigative powers and the maximum criminal sanctions which can be imposed. (See, e.g., sections 55–62 of the *Visserijwet* 1963 (the Dutch Fisheries Act)).

at all organs of the Member States, legislative, executive, and judicial,[24] were clarified beyond doubt by the Court of Justice in 1989 when Greece was found to be in breach of Community law by reason of its failure to take any action to bring those responsible for a fraud against Community law to court and to ensure the imposition of a penalty.[25] In that case, underlining the significance of the obligation in Article 5 of ensuring the effectiveness of Community law, the Court of Justice clarified the standards to which the Member States must adhere in ensuring the enforcement of Community law.

A number of principles are highlighted in the Court's judgment. First, it is essential that enforcement is effective. This is to be measured by reference to the results achieved.[26] It requires, for example, that where a penalty is provided for it has a deterrent effect. Secondly, the Court emphasized the role of the principle of proportionality whereby any procedures and sanctions must be no more or no less than what is necessary in the particular case.[27] Finally, the Court stressed the 'assimilation' principle or principle of non-discrimination as between the treatment of breaches of Community law and breaches of national law. Indeed, the application of this principle to the enforcement of the law against fraud is expressly provided for in Article 209a of the EC Treaty as amended by the Treaty on European Union.[28]

The operation of these principles has implications for the three branches of government. The obligation of enforcement rests in the first instance with the legislature. Enforcement requires an initial choice as to the form of control to be used. As noted earlier, the criminal law is only one of the instruments available for enforcement. Other approaches involve the use of civil liability and administrative or disciplinary machinery. Unless it is specifically provided for in the Community legislation[29] the question whether the

---

[24] See Case 14/83, *Von Colson and Kamann* v. *Land Nordrhein-Westfalen* [1984] ECR 1891, para. 26, which emphasized that this was so, although not in the context of a criminal case. In *Von Colson* the Court primarily discussed the duty of the judiciary.

[25] Case 68/88, *Commission* v. *Greece* [1989] ECR 2979.

[26] *Von Colson and Kamann*, above, n. 24.

[27] See n. 8, above, and accompanying text. In the cases discussed there the sanctions were disproportionately severe; cases such as the Greek case illustrate the reverse, i.e. where the sanctions are not severe enough.

[28] It states: 'Member States shall take the same measures to counter fraud affecting the financial interests of the Community as they take to counter fraud affecting their own financial interests . . .'

[29] In some cases a specific penalty or consequence is provided for, e.g. Art. 85(2)—declaring void of an offending act; Art. 11 of Regulation 2241/87, OJ 1987, L207/1, as amended by Regulation 3483/88, OJ 1988, L306/2—requirement of penal or administrative action to deprive violators of the economic benefit of violation; Art. 7(4) of Regulation 3796/81, OJ 1981, L379/1—obligation to 'penalize' breaches of rules; Art. 3(3) of Regulation 2204/90, OJ 1990, L201/7—specific minimum penalty laid down; Art. 6 of Directive 76/207, OJ 1976, L39/40—the requirement that measures to obtain redress be provided for injured parties.

Member State is obliged to use its criminal law, as opposed to other forms
of control, is likely to be governed by the criteria of non-discrimination
and effectiveness. For example, if the use of disciplinary measures is standard procedure in purely domestic cases, then this may be permissible in
the case of a breach of Community law as long as this is an effective means
of dealing with the breach. Having decided on the form of control, national
laws must be in place to ensure that breaches of Community law are prohibited and sanctioned under the same conditions as similar breaches of
national law.[30] But the principle of non-discrimination between the treatment of breaches of Community and national law, the assimilation principle,
is only one element of the Court's guidance. Penalties provided for in
legislation must also be effective, proportionate, and dissuasive. As long as
these general principles are respected, the Member States have a discretion as to what penalty shall be provided for and how the offence will be
defined. For example, in Case C–326/88, *Anklagemyndigheden* v. *Hansen
& Son I/S*[31] the Court of Justice held that Denmark was entitled to make
a failure by employers to comply with a regulation on road transport a
strict liability offence and subject to a criminal sanction, as long as the
penalty provided for was similar to those imposed in cases of infringement
of provisions of national law of a similar nature and importance, and that
it was proportionate to the seriousness of the infringement in question.

The implications of Article 5 for the executive mean that that organ must
deal with breaches of Community law in an effective manner similar to the
treatment of breaches of the Member State law. In particular, infringements
of Community law must be proceeded against by the police, customs authorities, and other relevant agencies with the same diligence as offences
against national law, using the relevant national law and machinery. This
was the particular problem in the Greek case discussed earlier. Similarly,
where there is a discretion to prosecute, the Community interest must be
given appropriate regard.[32] Of course, the principle of non-discrimination
may not be allowed to operate in such a way as to frustrate the *effective*
enforcement of Community law, which should be seen as the primary
requirement of enforcement.

The duties imposed by Article 5 also require that the judiciary of each
state acts in a manner designed to ensure the enforcement of Community
law.[33] Thus, for example, frauds against the Community must be punished

---

[30] Obviously, a minimum requirement is for the state to ensure that all such laws are
validly enacted. For problems arising out of the failure to comply with constitutional requirements see the Irish case of *Meagher* v. *Minister for Agriculture and Food*, Johnson J., High
Court, unreported, 1 April 1993: *The Irish Times*, 2 April 1993.

[31] [1990] ECR 2911.

[32] e.g., in both Dutch and British law the prosecuting agencies, having regard to the general
interest, may decide whether to initiate a prosecution.

[33] As discussed earlier in *Von Colson and Kamann*, above, n. 24.

in a manner similar to the way in which an equivalent fraud against the national exchequer would be. This is clearly possible where national law has provided for a penalty. However, where it has failed to do so questions arise as to how far the judiciary may go in filling this lacuna. The *Kolpinghuis* case[34] made clear that a directive could not create obligations for individuals in the absence of implementing national law. However, the situation has not been dealt with expressly by the Court of Justice of an obligation arising under a regulation, which is directly applicable, for which no penalty is specified. Although such a measure may impose obligations directly on individuals, it would appear to run contrary to the principles of legality, in particular, the principle of non-retroactivity of criminal law, for a penalty to be imposed by a national court in this situation.

To the three principles discussed in the Greek case should be added a fourth—the principle of transparency, which was developed somewhat earlier in the *Amsterdam Bulb* case.[35] This principle acts as a constraint primarily on the legislature to ensure that national legislation does not conceal the Community nature and effects of a legal provision from the persons to whom it applies.[36] Certain recent directives expressly lay down this obligation.[37]

It is now necessary to evaluate the effectiveness with which Community law is enforced in relation to individuals.

EVALUATION OF THE ENFORCEMENT OF COMMUNITY LAW

It is clear that, where Member States are under an obligation not to apply their criminal law in particular situations, this is quite efficiently enforced. In such situations individuals benefit from the Community dimension and, as long as they are well advised concerning their Community rights, the issue will be brought to the attention of the national courts which must, in accordance with the doctrine of the supremacy of Community law, apply the Community provision and ignore the conflicting national provision. The doctrine of direct effect, allowing Community rights to be asserted and enforced in the national courts, draws the individual into policing the enforcement of Community law against Member States. It is a valuable complement to the machinery provided by the Treaty for the enforcement of Community law against Member States and this is true in relation to the

---

[34] [1987] ECR 3969.
[35] Case 50/76, *Amsterdam Bulb BV* v. *Produktschap voor Siergewassen* [1977] ECR 137.
[36] Ibid., para. 7.
[37] See e.g. Art. 29(2) of Directive 91/67, OJ 1991, L46: 'When Member States adopt the measures referred to in para. 1, they shall contain a reference to this Directive or shall be accompanied by such reference on the occasion of their official publication. The methods of making such a reference shall be laid down by the Member States.'

Member States' negative obligations in relation to criminal law as in any other area. This has been expressly noted by the Court of Justice, which has emphasized the importance of the role of individuals and other legal persons in ensuring Member State compliance with Community law. In the *Van Gend en Loos* case it stated that:

The vigilance of individuals concerned to protect their rights amounts to an effective supervision in addition to the supervision entrusted by Articles 169 and 170 to the diligence of the Commission and of the Member States.[38]

Cases such as these concern occasions where individuals benefit from Community law. However, in the case of positive obligations of the Member States in relation to criminal law, it is a situation where individuals are the recipients of obligations under Community law and are therefore unlikely to bring the matter to the attention of the national authorities.

Where Community obligations are imposed on individuals the difference between the two models of enforcement is obvious. Competition law is unusual in the direct contact between the Commission and the undertakings which takes place, and in the powers which the Commission has at its disposal. In all other cases, as noted, there is a division of responsibility between the Community and national authorities whereby the Community depends on the will and resources of the national authorities for the effective enforcement. This division of Member State and Community responsibility is sometimes pointed to as a weakness of the system in that it places responsibility for enforcement with the Member States, who may not feel the same direct interest in the successful enforcement as would the Community institutions.[39] In some cases Member States see no direct benefit in dealing with breaches of Community law and regard the process as merely penalizing their own undertakings as against those in other Member States. This lack of uniform enforcement will continue to represent an obstacle to real integration and the attainment of a single market as long as Member States take this view. However, this very problem may generate greater momentum in the Community to harmonize enforcement provisions.

It is clear, for example, that varying resources are allocated to the task of enforcement of Community law, which leads to uneven enforcement.[40] There is little information on the actual extent of variable enforcement

[38] Case 28/82, *Van Gend en Loos* v. *Nederlandse Administratie der Belastingen* [1963] ECR 1. See also Case 43/75, *Defrenne* v. *Sabena* [1976] ECR 455, where the Court also emphasized the importance of the role of the individual, especially since in that case the Commission had taken no action against the defaulting Member State over a lengthy period.

[39] See e.g., the annual reports of the Court of Auditors and the House of Lords Select Committee on the European Communities, *Fraud Against the Community*, for discussion of whether Member States perceive there being any direct interest in detecting and imposing sanctions on fraud against the Community.

[40] See the annual and special reports of the Court of Auditors.

over the whole field of Community activity, but to the extent to which information exists on this in relation to fraud it appears very clearly that staff and other resources are very unevenly allocated throughout the Community. Such uneven allocation of resources may indicate a genuine resource problem on the part of some of the Member States or it may indicate a less than enthusiastic approach to the enforcement of Community law. Even where the will to enforce Community law exists, there may still be uneven enforcement, since the system lacks uniformity in terms of definitions, evidential rules, procedures, and sanctions. Community law sets the course to be followed, but in order for Member States to take proceedings against breaches of Community standards it is necessary to use relevant national criminal law. Thus when Member States proceed against fraud against Community funds they must use their own national law and whatever offences exist within it which are relevant to the behaviour in question. For example, in the area of fraud, Community law, lacking a general system of offences and penalties, does not create an offence of fraud. This is left to the individual Member States and one finds a plethora of different offences among the Member States. One suggestion has been for a harmonized definition of 'fraud against the Community' with the same sanctions in each Member State.[41] This would deal with part of the problem, but the basic problem of the commitment of Member States to the enforcement of the law would remain. It would also leave untouched the problematic area of differing procedures and rules of evidence as between the Member States. And this is but one area, albeit very high-profile in the media, in which the criminal jurisdiction of the Member States needs to be engaged.

ALTERNATIVE APPROACHES ON ENFORCEMENT

It is because of such problems that other models of enforcement may seem attractive. Competition law and its machinery, which gives the Commission direct powers of enforcement, appears to solve some of the problems which arise in the conventional enforcement model. The Commission is well placed to receive information and is on the whole well informed as to what is going on in relation to competition matters. Its investigative and sanctioning powers put it in a strong position in this area compared with others where it is dependent on Member States for information and enforcement of the law. Of course, if undertakings refuse to pay the fines imposed by the Commission (so far a hypothetical problem), the jurisdiction of the national courts will have to be relied on, but even in such a case

---

[41] See Court of Auditors' Annual Report for 1986, OJ 1987, C336.

what is critically important is that the penalty does not lose its character of a Community penalty and there is uniformity in the system. Similarly, if undertakings refuse to allow the Commission to conduct an investigation the Commission must seek the support of the relevant local authorities and must respect the relevant national law on searches and investigations.[42] This is obviously a limitation on the Commission's powers but it is still in a relatively strong position as regards enforcement.

Yet, to suggest that this model of enforcement should be used in all areas would very clearly be impracticable. In the first place, it must be remembered that there were particular reasons why this model was adopted in the context of competition law. In particular, the widely differing stages of development of competition law among the Member States and the consequent absence of enforcement machinery in some of those states made it impossible to rely on national means of enforcement. Moreover, it is an indication of how jealously Member States have guarded their criminal jurisdiction from the Community institutions that Regulation 17, which sets out the machinery for the enforcement of competition law, expressly states that the fines provided for in Article 15 of the Regulation are not criminal in nature; but this is to use the term criminal in a formal rather than a material sense.[43] In practice such terminology does not detract from the seriousness of the breaches in question, nor does it mean that the Commission will not impose very harsh fines.[44] Furthermore, the practice of the Court of Justice is to purport to treat the breaches in a manner similar to the way in which criminal offences would be treated in the Member States in terms of the guarantees which are given to the accused.[45] Furthermore, the Court's approach in relation to extraterritorial jurisdiction goes a great distance in treating these breaches as criminal in nature.[46] The label given to these breaches and the penalties may therefore lack significance in practice. However, as long as Member States refuse to give to the Community any criminal jurisdiction so-called, it may be argued that there is the danger that if offences against Community law are dealt

---

[42] Case 46/87, *Hoechst* v. *Commission* [1989] ECR 2859.

[43] If the reasoning of the European Court of Human Rights were applied here it would conclude that these were criminal matters, at least in the more serious cases. See *Öztürk* v. *Germany*, ECHR, 1984, Series A No. 73; (1984) 6 EHRR 409.

[44] See e.g. *Polypropylene Cartel*, OJ 1986, L230/1—total fines: 57,850,000 ecu; *PVC Cartel*, OJ 1988, L74/21—total: 37 million ecu; *Soda Ash Cartel*, OJ 1991—total: 47 million ecu, although some individual fines were reduced on appeal; *Tetra Pak*, OJ 1991—total: 75 million ecu.

[45] See e.g. Case 374/87, *Orkem* v. *Commission* [1989] ECR 2859 on self-incrimination and the remarks of Advocate General Vesterdorf in Case T–7/89, *Re Polypropylene Cartel, Hercules Chemicals* v. *Commission* [1992] 4 CMLR 84.

[46] See e.g. Case 48/69 *ICI* v. *Commission* [1972] ECR 619, where the discussion on extraterritoriality by Advocate General Mayras is of interest although it was not expressly approved of by the Court.

with as administrative offences they will seem less serious than 'real' criminal offences. Thus it might be argued in relation to fraud that such a system would have disadvantages in separating two kinds of very similar behaviour, labelling frauds against national funds as criminal and frauds against Community funds as administrative offences. While it may be true that in practice such a difference might be less of substance and more of appearances it cannot be ignored totally in the effect it might have on perceptions of the seriousness of breaches of the law.

Of considerably greater practical importance, however, would be the resource implications of using the direct model of enforcement beyond the area of competition. The potential for breaches of Community law by individuals is enormous. In the area of environmental duties there are literally hundreds of possible breaches which could be perpetrated by individuals and companies. As we have already seen, the area of agricultural fraud alone provides huge scope for unscrupulous individuals and companies to make an illegal gain. The detection and punishment of these and other breaches would require resources far in excess of those currently enjoyed by the Commission. Indeed, the area of competition policy itself, with its efficient machinery, shows the pressures which exist on the Commission's resources. The use of informal administrative procedures such as 'comfort letters' to deal with individuals' cases is an attempt by the Commission to cope with the huge mountain of cases it receives. Furthermore, while the Commission has direct powers in competition it is not at all unhappy for the national courts to be involved where possible in the policing of the enforcement of the competition rules through individuals applying to the courts for national civil law remedies. It cannot be denied that, for practical reasons, the effective enforcement of Community law requires national bodies 'on the ground'. This approach has been taken on board by the Commission in a number of areas[47] and is not out of line with the principle of subsidiarity, stated for the first time in the Maastricht Treaty on European Union.[48] Moreover, on another level, the involvement of national bodies in the enforcement of Community law has the advantage of breaking down the idea that the two systems are separate and leads to greater integration of Community and Member State law.

Thus, while the conventional model of enforcement leaves a good deal to be desired in terms of effective enforcement, it remains the case that realistically the solution will have to be found in improving this system

[47] See e.g. *Eighth Annual Report to the European Parliament on the Commission's monitoring of the application of EC Law*, Annex C, para. 99.
[48] Art. 3b of the EC Treaty reads '. . . In areas which do not fall within its exclusive competence, the Community shall take action, in accordance with the principle of subsidiarity, only if and in so far as the objectives of the proposed action cannot be sufficiently achieved by the Member States and can therefore, by reason of the scale or effects of the proposed action, be better achieved by the Community . . .'.

rather than rejecting it entirely. Thus far, states, despite their rhetoric, have been slow to carry out such reform.[49]

One very obvious suggestion would be for the supervisory and co-ordinating roles of the Commission to be improved, so that it can monitor more effectively the ways in which Member States are carrying out their obligations. The increase in the number of actions brought by the Commission under Article 169 for breach of the general duty to enforce Community law is evidence that the Commission is sympathetic to this approach. Yet the Commission's ability to play such a co-ordinating or supervisory role will remain handicapped until it has adequate information about what is actually happening. Even where Member States are under an obligation to submit reports to the Commission the information which it receives is often incomplete and unreliable. There appear to be wide divergences in the quantity and quality of the information received by the Commission. This has been commented on very frequently by the Court of Auditors in relation to fraud against the Community. One of the aspects which makes the enforcement of the competition rules so effective is the amount of information received by the Commission. Such information is obtained by the Commission not only through its information-gathering and investigative powers, but most importantly by the voluntary action of the undertakings themselves, in whose interest it is to inform the Commission of their agreements in order to ensure that they do not leave themselves open to a penalty or the non-enforceability of their agreements. In addition to that channel of information, the Commission receives a good deal of information from competitors and other market participants who are anxious to ensure that undertakings do not obtain an unfair advantage by unlawful agreements. This flow of information ensures that the Commission is well placed to supervise and co-ordinate in the area, and to take enforcement action where necessary. Such volunteering of information and 'whistle-blowing' on competitors does not take place on the same scale in many other areas, and the Commission is often crippled into inaction by its ignorance of what is in fact going on. However, it is notable that an increasing amount of legislation embodies specific obligations on Member States to provide information to the Commission. And the active role which it has played in relation to the common fisheries policy may provide an indication of the potential of the Commission as an effective supervisory body. At the same time, however, there may be some national resistance to moves by the Commission to extend its supervisory role. Recently, Germany tried to challenge the Commission's prescription of exclusionary penalties (refusal of aid or subsidies), as a way of dealing with 'irregularities' in the field of agriculture.[50]

---

[49] For early and abortive attempts to harmonize enforcement, see *European Criminal Law* (Brussels, 1970).

[50] Case C–240/90, *Germany* v. *Commission*, not yet reported.

In certain other areas the role of interest groups has greatly assisted the Commission in its watchdog role in the Community. This is very much the case in environmental matters where interest groups have started to become a very useful source of 'on the ground' information for the Commission.[51] If environmental groups highlight the failure of the relevant national authorities to take action against offending companies, the Commission may then take proceedings against the Member State for its failure to ensure compliance with Community law in accordance with Article 5 or any more specific duties. Such overtures from interest groups are likely to play an important role in Community law enforcement in the future, and certainly need to be encouraged by the Commission as far as possible. Indeed approaches which capitalize on the role of individuals in general enforcement are likely to increase efficiency. Thus the imposition of civil liability in damages for breaches of Community law, as is being proposed in relation to damage caused by waste, may indicate an alternative effective approach to the criminal law for enforcement in certain cases. Consistently from the early years of the Community, both the Commission and the Court have recognized the importance and effectiveness of the role of initiatives by private parties in the enforcement of Community measures.[52] But the practical effectiveness of such initiatives in some areas remains to be tested, and depends heavily on the particular circumstances and context of the case.[53]

CONCLUSION

It is clear, therefore, that the Community system presents a hidden, or at least obscured, agenda of activity in the field of criminal law enforcement for a number of European countries. The practical impact of many Community policies has been both to circumscribe and to prescribe enforcement at the national level in order to ensure the implementation of Community programmes. Moreover, both Member State agencies and private individuals have been enlisted in this enterprise. But the Community impact is not limited to the emergence of Community-based defences and the spawning of new regulatory offences in the field of criminal litigation. It also has implications for national criminal justice policy, particularly as regards the allocation of resources and the relationship between national

---

[51] Some recognition of the importance of interest groups is found in the Draft Directive on Civil Liability for Damage caused by Waste, which requires in principle that interest groups be allowed to take action in the national courts to ensure that any environmental harm is remedied.

[52] Above, n. 36. See also Case C–6/90, *Francovich* v. *Italy* [1991] ECR I–5357; [1992] IRLR 84.

[53] Thus such initiatives appear to have been successful in relation to environmental issues, equal pay, and equal treatment.

and Community agencies. The outcome is axiomatic: the fact of an expanding body of criminal law, some of which is at the service of Community as distinct from national policies, inevitably complicates the operation of Member State systems of criminal law enforcement. Nor, on reflection, is this outcome surprising. With the hindsight of more than thirty years, it now appears naïve to have expected a complex legal order to operate at the level of individuals, as well as States, without drawing heavily upon the enforcement machinery which was available to Member States but, for political reasons, not transferable to the Community institutions. For the reasons given in the above discussion, delegated enforcement is likely to remain the norm; but it is not a straightforward solution and will continue to present a challenge to both national and Community institutions.

7

Discretion and Accountability in Prosecution: A Comparative Perspective on Keeping Crime out of Court

CHRISJE BRANTS AND STEWART FIELD

INTRODUCTION

The argument that offenders should only be brought before criminal courts as a last resort, and that diversion from prosecution is often a preferable response to crime, has only recently gained widespread official acceptance within the British criminal justice systems. Such views are of rather longer standing in Holland and this is reflected in the greater variety of diversionary mechanisms available there and the larger numbers of known offenders kept out of court. On the surface this might be seen as a straightforward reflection of the much-vaunted liberalism of the Dutch system, its greater concern about the negative effects of stigmatization, and greater scepticism about the deterrent effect of the public court appearance. While there is certainly something to this argument, any convincing explanation of the differences in diversionary practices must be rooted in more concrete analysis of contrasts in the institutions and legal culture underpinning respective criminal justice practices.

In the United Kingdom, the development of diversion has rested largely on encouraging the increased use of the traditional police caution, while the majority of criminal cases are processed through the courts. In Holland, in contrast, the majority of cases are not decided by the courts. There is extensive use of conditional diversion by the Public Prosecution Service and, in some cases, the police provides a state response to crime that is low-key and largely invisible. Conditional diversion involves the use of techniques whereby the decision not to prosecute is made conditional upon under-takings by the offender. The introduction of such techniques in England and Wales has until recently been rejected by the British Government. Comparative analysis offers an opportunity to examine the ways in which different attitudes to conditional diversion reflect very different institutional backgrounds and legal cultures. In particular, we shall highlight the important differences in both the formal role assigned to prosecutors and the very different cultural assumptions about how they approach that role.

Furthermore, we will show that institution and culture interact in mutually reinforcing ways.

In focusing on the causal relationship between culture, institution and diversionary practice, we have chosen not to examine in depth the arguments for and against the expansion of diversion in particular contexts. There may indeed be criminal offences where greater public stigma would be a good thing and extending diversion in these areas unjustified.[1] But there are strong arguments for believing that at least much trivial street crime could usefully be diverted.[2] If so, questions of how this is done in different countries become of central interest.

Before we go further, however, it is perhaps useful to define what we mean here by diversion, for, interestingly, the meaning changes according to the criminal justice culture of the country concerned. In Britain, the idea is primarily associated with keeping an offender out of court and therefore with almost anything that avoids sentencing by a judge: its main purpose is to avoid the stigma attached to public criminal proceedings. In the Netherlands, the concept of diversion orginally derived from the abolitionist movement that found such an eloquent spokesman in Louk Hulsman in the 1970s, and that advocated eventually abolishing the criminal justice system itself. Diversion was regarded as a step in the right (abolitionist) direction, but its goals were much broader than merely keeping offenders out of court. Indeed, the first idea was to keep them out of prison. The emphasis was on meaningful reaction to crime, i.e. meaningful for the parties concerned: the offender and the victim, and therefore also for society. This is a very utilitarian approach to punishment, that practically rules out the idea of retribution as a goal in itself. In this view, crime is not seen as inherently bad, but as the expression of social conflict, and punishment is only meaningful if it contributes to solving that conflict. In this context, reparation and mediation make more sense than imprisonment.

This notion of diversion does not necessarily exclude decisions by a (criminal) court; typical Dutch reactions to crime that are diversionary in the Dutch sense include community service orders imposed by a judge, or, recently, contracts between offender and victim regulating compensation for injury, financial or otherwise. At the same time, as we shall see, the Dutch criminal justice system itself has a number of principles in combination

[1] Obvious examples might be domestic violence and at least some forms of regulatory crime.

[2] What evidence there is in the UK suggests that cautions are no more, but no less, likely to be followed by reconvictions than public court appearances. See J. Mott, 'Police decisions for dealing with juvenile offenders' (1983) 23 *British Journal of Criminology*, 249. For contrasting positions on diversion see N. McKittrick and S. Eysenck, 'Diversion: A Big fix?' (1984) JPN 377 and 393; A. Sanders, 'The Limits to Diversion from Prosecution' (1989) 28 *British Journal of Criminology*, 513; A. Ashworth, 'Prosecution, Police and Public—A Guide to Good Gatekeeping?' (1984) 23 *Howard Journal of Criminal Justice*, 65.

with legal mechanisms that allow a great deal of crime to pass through the system without reaching court, while still sometimes providing some sort of 'sanction'. This is what the British think of as diversion, but it would not normally be called that in Holland: although it does serve to keep offenders out of prison, it lacks the ideological connotation with abolitionism and what is often thought of as a 'softy 1970s approach', that for the Dutch is so characteristic of diversion. Increasingly, the authorities have come to view such mechanisms as a way of streamlining the system and implementing criminal policy, and they are very much part of the normal state reaction to crime. Indeed, the first requirement is that they be meaningful for the criminal justice system itself and, contrary to any abolitionist goals, they actually help to keep the system going.[3]

In this respect, conditional diversion serves the same function as plea-bargaining in adversarial systems. Plea-bargaining is also a mechanism whereby criminal justice systems can seem to promise a better deal for suspects while making sure the system does not have to face the logistical consequences of a wholesale take-up of formal rights. Indeed, plea-bargaining raises many of the same issues: the drive to efficient processing of cases promotes invisible and informal settlement practices in which due process may be undermined.

These cross-cultural differences illustrate just how problematic comparisons of aspects of criminal justice systems may be. For while the 'normal' course of criminal justice in Britain would involve a court appearance, so that diversion refers to deflecting the offender away from the courts, in the Netherlands that sort of diversion is already part of the 'normal' course of criminal justice. For the purpose of this chapter, however, we shall take the British situation and the current debate on the introduction of different techniques of diversion as our starting point. We shall outline the Dutch system as it currently stands, looking especially at the, to British minds, almost incredible amount of discretionary power with which the public prosecutor is invested, for it is he (or she) who has the sole decision on whether or not to proceed with the prosecution, to drop the case or to 'settle out of court'. We shall also be examining the implications of the granting of such authority.

We may therefore restrict the concept of diversion for the purpose of this chapter to those forms that

1. do not involve decisions by an independent court,
2. are intended to keep offenders out of court (and therefore out of prison).

---

[3] See, on the distortion of Hulsman's ideas to provide a means of keeping the criminal justice system going, C. H. Brants and J. Silvis, 'Dutch Criminal Justice and a Challenge to Abolitionism', in: J. R. Blad *et al.* (eds.), *The Criminal Justice System as a Social Problem: An Abolitionist Perspective* (Rotterdam; Erasmus University 1987), 133–48.

Diversion from prosecution therefore means all decisions regarding the reaction to criminal offences by a duly-empowered authority within the criminal justice system, the purpose of which is to avoid court proceedings. Specifically excluded are decisions not to prosecute because of lack of evidence. This covers both the British situation in which, for the mainstream of offenders, there seem to be few ways of avoiding the trial stage, and the Dutch one in which there are several institutionalized ways of keeping even serious offenders out of court, yet still involving some sort of 'punishment' or at least some form of reaction on the part of the criminal justice authorities.

MECHANISMS FOR DIVERSION IN THE UNITED KINGDOM

In the United Kingdom there are a limited number of ways that the ordinary offender may be diverted from prosecution.[4] The most formal mechanism is the police caution. This is an official warning which, since 1985, may be cited in court as part of a criminal record and which will affect subsequent prosecution decisions. Cautions also form part of the official criminal statistics. In recent years there has been a significant increase in the use of formal cautions. In 1985 the Home Office issued new cautioning guidelines which made much of the advantages of diversion, primarily as a way of dealing with juveniles. In 1990, the Home Office issued further guidelines designed to encourage police forces to use cautioning more often for adult offenders.[5] Indeed, cautioning rates had already increased appreciably in the late 1980s. In 1985, 7 per cent of both 17–21-year-old males and men of 21 or over were cautioned for indictable offences. By 1990, the rates were 21 per cent for the younger group and 15 per cent for the older. Rates for women 21 or over started from a higher base (19 per cent in 1985) but showed similar rates of increase (to 33 per cent in 1990). The police may also informally caution. The only consequence of this is that a record may be kept which may influence later prosecutions. Home Office Guidelines state that informal cautions should only be given where the criteria for a formal caution are met but a formal caution is considered inappropriate.[6] Figures on this are not kept, so the figures quoted above are for the formal caution only.

---

[4] Questions of space preclude consideration of care orders in relation to minors and the mentally disordered; see P. Fennell, 'Diversion of Mentally Disordered offenders from Custody' (1991) *CrimLRev*. 323 and C. Harding and L. Koffman, *Sentencing and the Penal System* (London; Sweet and Maxwell 1988), at 266.
[5] Home Office Circular 59/1990, 16 July 1990, *The Cautioning of Offenders.*
[6] Ibid., Annex C.

In addition the Crown Prosecution Service (CPS) may discontinue proceedings after the police have charged, *inter alia* because prosecution would not be in the public interest.[7] However, the CPS lacks the effective power to discontinue regularly on such grounds because it is highly dependent on the police for the information which might suggest discontinuance. Crown Prosecutors are often loth to seek such information from other agencies, such as the Probation Service, and the police often do not perceive it as being in their interests to look for information that is mitigatory. The result is that only about 1–2 per cent of cases are discontinued on public interest grounds.[8] McConville *et al.*, in a study of over 1,000 cases in 1986–8, said that in their sample the CPS only ever dropped cases on public interest grounds, as opposed to evidential grounds, where (i) the defendant was already charged or sentenced for other more serious offences, or (ii) where the defendant elected for jury trial in minor cases such as shoplifting and the cost was regarded as prohibitive.[9]

All of this means that the United Kingdom has relatively high rates of conditional or absolute discharge after conviction in court because a range of relatively trivial cases get through.[10] Of all offenders in 1988, 15 per cent got conditional and 1 per cent absolute discharges. In 1990, 1 per cent of those convicted of indictable offences were given absolute discharges while 16 per cent were discharged conditionally. It should be noted that, geographically, caution rates tend to show an inverse relationship with conditional discharge rates.

THE BRITISH DEBATE ON EXPANDING DIVERSION: POTENTIAL AND CONSTRAINTS

Andrew Sanders has argued that the relatively slow and uncertain development of diversion by the police caution in the United Kingdom is the product of two obvious but contradictory impulses:

(a) the desire to avoid the stigma and labelling of criminal proceedings (recognized by Home Office circulars on cautioning)

---

[7] It should, of course, be borne in mind that the CPS does not take the initial decision on charge or caution.

[8] L. Gelsthorpe and H. Giller, 'More Justice for Juveniles: Does More Mean Better?' [1990] *CrimLRev.* 153 at 159–60; and S. Elliman, 'Independent Information for the Crown Prosecution Service', [1990] *NLJ* 812.

[9] M. McConville, A. Sanders and R. Leng, *The Case for the Prosecution* (London; Routledge 1991), at 163.

[10] Both forms of discharge may only be used where it is considered inexpedient to punish and a probation order is not appropriate. A conditional discharge is made subject to offenders not reoffending within a specified period of up to three years. If they do reoffend they may be sentenced for the original offence.

(b) the view widely held by police officers and magistrates that warnings are not enough to prevent offending and can therefore be used only for a small minority of trivial offences.[11]

Sanders sees a way of reconciling these two viewpoints by moving toward more diverse conditional diversion mechanisms such as exist on the Continent.[12] He stresses that the effect of the system is to avoid the stigma of a court appearance while not 'letting off' the offender in that conditions have to be fulfilled. He points to an experimental scheme in Cumbria as a possible model for expansion. The police selected juveniles who were then asked to offer to make reparation to the victim (apologies, compensation, or community work). If they agreed they were cautioned, not prosecuted. But the Home Office responded negatively to the scheme, in part because it feared that it made the police investigator prosecutor, judge, and sentencer.

Despite official rhetoric, a 1987–8 survey of police forces suggested that eighteen of forty-two were operating some form of 'caution plus' system whereby cautions would be given with conditions attached to them, such as attending an intermeditate treatment group and participating in reparation or mediation schemes. These schemes mainly existed on a localized basis: only three forces operated the system throughout the force area. Furthermore, they were almost exclusively applied to juveniles: only one force had a scheme for adults. The use of caution plus was squared with official rhetoric by some officers by insisting the decision to caution was made independently of the agreement to participate in treatment or reparation. Others accepted that the caution decision was affected by such an agreement.[13]

In interviews officers showed a growing interest in giving cautions teeth by use of such conditions.[14] More recently, the idea of developing conditional forms of diversion has surfaced again in official debate. In April 1990, the House of Commons Home Affairs Select Committee made radical

---

[11] A. Sanders, 'Diverting Offenders from Prosecution—Can we learn from Other Countries?' (1986) *Justice of the Peace*, 614. This attitude has been confirmed by interviews with officers, see R. Evans, 'Police Cautioning and the Young Adult Offender' [1991] *CrimLRev*. 598 at 601–2.

[12] A. Ashworth has also repeatedly argued for the adoption of various conditional diversion schemes. See 'Prosecution, Police and Public' and 'The Public Interest Element in Prosecutions' [1987] *CrimLRev*. 595 at 604.

[13] Circular 59/1990 specifically suggested when considering a caution that the police should consider the offender's 'attitude to the offence, including practical expressions of regret' (Annex B, para. 3). The scope for covert conditional diversion linked to reparation is surely apparent: R. Evans and C. Wilkinson, 'Variations in Police Cautioning Policy and Practice in England and Wales' in (1990) 29 *Howard Journal of Criminal Justice*, 155 at 169.

[14] C. Wilkinson and R. Evans, 'Police Cautioning of Juveniles' [1990] *CrimLRev*. 165 at 171.

proposals for an extension of the range of diversionary options available within the criminal justice system.[15]

The Committee was very keen to extend the level of diversion from prosecution and suggested, very much as Sanders had done, that one way of doing this would be to extend the range of available disposals. It argued that more offenders might be cautioned if some form of penalty were attached to the caution. The CPS recommended to it that a system of 'caution plus' should be introduced whereby an offender who consented could be dealt with by a caution and a form of penalty. Penalties envisaged were compensation for property broken or stolen or other forms of reparation.

As interesting as the proposal is the reaction to it. In evidence to the Committee, the National Association for the Care and Resettlement of Offenders, one of Britain's most prominent liberal penal pressure groups, welcomed the idea of increased diversion but expressed considerable concern at an 'alternative criminal system' which did not have the safeguards of due process. They were also concerned about the 'net-widening effect'. The Select Committee was not impressed by these worries and recommended the introduction of such a system. It felt the fact that the consent of the offender was required was a sufficient safeguard. Furthermore, the Committee felt the power to administer the system should remain exclusively with the police, and that the CPS should continue to deal only with prosecutions.

The Government rejected this proposal curtly: 'The police do not wish to become involved in sentencing, believing that this would be contrary to the basic principles of the criminal justice system . . . and the Government endorses this position.'[16] In July 1990, the Home Office issued cautioning guidelines to replace the 1985 version, which attempted to broaden the use of diversion by emphasizing that cautioning was suitable for age-groups other than juveniles. However, the Guidelines reflected the Government's rejection of the Select Committee's proposals, preferring to rely on encouraging the traditional police caution. The guidelines do stress that the effectiveness of cautions is likely to be enhanced if they are backed up by arrangements for referring offenders to welfare agencies for support and guidance. However, '[s]uch referrals should be on a voluntary basis but any agreement to be referred should not be made a condition of a caution'. It appears that conditional diversion has been dismissed for the immediate future.[17]

---

[15] Home Affairs Committee, Fourth Report, i. *The Crown Prosecution Service*, House of Commons Papers, Session 1989–90. Select Committees are non-executive cross-party committees of the legislature that 'shadow' and comment on matters within the responsibility of particular departments.

[16] Crown Prosecution Service, *The Government's Reply to the Fourth Report of the Home Affairs Committee* (HMSO, 1990).

[17] Since this was written, the Royal Commission on Criminal Justice has reported, recommending a system of conditional diversion.

MECHANISMS FOR DIVERSION IN THE NETHERLANDS

The Netherlands is one of the continental countries in which a great diversity of diversionary mechanisms exists, ranging from the police dropping the case unconditionally to (financial) settlements between the public prosecutor and the suspect in order to keep the case out of court. A system very like that proposed by the Select Committee, that could perhaps be regarded as one of 'punitive cautions', has existed in the Netherlands for decades as far as petty crime is concerned, and has been applicable to more serious crimes since 1983. Before examining the most important of these, however, we must briefly outline a few basic principles of the Dutch system, for they determine the way diversion works in practice.[18]

To start with, in Dutch criminal law the distinction between crimes or felonies (*misdrijven*) and misdemeanours (*overtredingen*) is of crucial importance to an understanding of diversion, for it governs the legal powers of police and public prosecutor with regard to decisions on non-prosecution. *Overtredingen* do not carry prison sentences, are usually dealt with directly by the police, and seldom reach a court. *Misdrijven* are punishable by fine or imprisonment (in the final event at the judge's discretion: there is no mandatory sentencing in Holland), but may in some cases also be dealt with directly by the prosecutor (or, more rarely, even by the police) and need not, therefore, come before a court.

The decision on whether or not to take a case further than the investigative stage, and to initiate court proceedings against a person suspected of a criminal offence, lies solely with the public prosecutor. This principle, so very characteristic of the Dutch system, is known as the monopoly of prosecution. The police, whose activities in the field of criminal investigation are directed by the prosecutor, have no powers of prosecution, but are there, among other things, to assist the prosecutor in his investigation of the offence, to deliver the necessary information, gather evidence, interview witnesses, etc. The prosecutor not only has a monopoly on the decision to prosecute: he/she is also free to decide how to use that monopoly. This is another principle of Dutch criminal law that governs the practice of diversion. It is known as the principle of expediency (or opportunity): prosecution must be expedient (or opportune). This requirement may lead a prosecutor to decide not to prosecute: in that case he may drop the case unconditionally (unconditional waiver); conditionally, e.g. on condition that the suspect makes reparation (conditional waiver); or he may enter into a financial settlement with the suspect which will guarantee non-prosecution in exchange for a certain sum of money: this is known as '*transactie*' (Article 74 of the Dutch Criminal Code).

---

[18] For a general review, see J. M. J. Chorus and H. T. Jeroen, *Introduction to Dutch Law for Foreigners* (Deventer; Kluwer 1993), Chap. 18.

The Police

The theory has it that the prosecutor has sole control of decisions regarding (non-)prosecution. In reality the police have a great deal of (negative) influence in the sense that information about the majority of offences never reaches the prosecutor's desk. We shall see further on just how much crime is processed out of the Dutch system on the way from the police to the courts. To start with, the police do not report everything that, strictly speaking and according to the law, they should. Every time the police learn about an offence but do not report it to the prosecutor, in theory this constitutes a 'police waiver' for which there is no legal basis.

Now, the system would obviously come to a standstill if the police did report everything, and in practice a great deal of crime comes to the attention of the police (either reported or otherwise discovered) and never reaches the prosecutor. This also applies to many categories of *misdrijven*, therefore to serious offences. The most obvious example in Holland is bicycle theft, which is reported routinely by citizens for insurance purposes and then forgotten (unless some form of traceable organized crime is involved). The same applies to many cases of burglary. These, of course, are cases in which there is no known offender, neither is one ever likely to be discovered. However, the police also drop cases in which the offender is known, for the simple reason that it is thought more sensible (although sometimes for different reasons) to keep some sorts of offenders away from the system entirely. In this connection, Leigh and Hall-Williams mention domestic disputes, cases involving the mentally disturbed and juveniles as likely to lead to 'police waiver'.[19]

But apart from the fact that the police exercise quite a bit of extra-legal discretion in what they actually report to the prosecutor, they also have legal powers of diversion. These powers are used on a very wide scale for petty crime and misdemeanours. Since 1958, the police have been legally empowered to offer a suspect '*transactie*' for *overtredingen* if they are discovered *in flagrante delicto* or are detected by technical means (the camera at the traffic lights, the video camera at the football match). Non-payment of the *transactie* sum will result first in an offer of *transactie* from the prosecutor (for a larger sum) and then, in theory, in a summons, although the prosecutor may also decide on a waiver at this stage. Most police *transacties* are for traffic offences. In 1988 an experiment was set up to allow police *transactie* for shoplifting in cases of adult first offenders (goods stolen valued at not more than f. 250). In 1989 the experiment was extended to include drunken driving (as long as no damage or injury was involved). Originally vandalism and simple assault were also included, but

[19] L. H. Leigh and J. E. Hall-Williams, *The Prosecution Process in Sweden, Denmark and the Netherlands* (Leamington Spa; James Hall 1981), at 46.

these cases proved too complicated. According to the government, the results are encouraging.

The Public Prosecutor[20]

In contrast to the police, the prosecutor is legally authorized to waive the right of prosecution for technical reasons (e.g. lack of evidence) or for policy reasons, vaguely described by the Code of Criminal Procedure as 'reasons deriving from the public interest'. Since the 1960s, (semi-)official policy has been to prosecute only if the public interest so demands (thereby reversing the legal system which is based on waiver only if the public interest so demands). Our field of interest lies in the policy waiver, for it is here that we find the greatest scope for discretionary decision-making. Policy waivers may be based on many factors: individual (age of the defendant, first offender, offence not so serious, etc.) or considerations of criminal policy. Policy matters are usually decided by the heads of prosecution (*'procureurs-generaal'*) and sometimes laid down in guidelines. The effects and legal implications of such guidelines are discussed below.

If the offence is serious, the waiver is likely to be accompanied by conditions which the offender must meet in order to keep the case out of court. These may involve paying compensation, or performing certain services (akin to the community service order). If the offender fails to meet these conditions, he will be summonsed. As we have already seen, a conditional waiver is an informal but widely used method of diversion that is, moreover, regulated by the same type of guidelines as apply to unconditional waivers. These guidelines, although not laws in any formal sense, nevertheless have legal status: they can be invoked by the citizen and scrutinized by the Supreme Court. Here we come up against yet another idiosyncracy of the Dutch system that we shall be examining more closely later: much of what goes on is not regulated by law, but by an informal system of guidelines and unwritten rules that sometimes, but not always, are eventually elevated to proper legal status.

This is less true of the system of *'transactie'*, for here at least the prosecutor is legally empowered to 'transact' for certain offences. Strictly speaking, *transactie* is just what the word says it is: a transaction between the public prosecutor and an offender. The offender buys off prosecution, but waives the right to trial by an independent court. The prosecutor waives

---

[20] The public prosecutor has a number of options when considering diversion. We have restricted ourselves here to the most common, i.e. waivers and *transactie*. Others, such as institutionalized community service orders administered by special agencies or the experimental contract between offender and victim, we have left out. Not only are they usually still in an experimental stage: in effect they constitute conditional waivers.

the right to prosecute, in exchange for payment of a certain sum (but not exceeding what the fine would have been), and sometimes the fulfilling of other conditions such as financial compensation for the victim (this option is rarely used, being already provided for by the informal conditional waiver system). Formally, *transactie* is not a penalty that is imposed, but a proposal by the prosecutor that is 'accepted' by the offender.

In a material sense however, and certainly according to the European Convention, *transactie* is a penalty: it replaces sanctions under criminal law, is implemented by the criminal justice authorities, and is intended to be both punitive and deterrent.[21] While in theory the offender is free to accept or refuse the offer of *transactie*, in practice there is a good deal of coercion involved. It is standard practice if the case comes to court to demand a higher fine than the negotiated sum would have been (and the offender is informed of this). Moreover, few people are willing to endure the trial process if they can avoid it.[22] Since 1983, *transactie* has been available for any offence which may incur a fine, except offences punishable by six years' imprisonment or more. Fines may now be imposed for all relevant offences.

Statistics

Before we look at the statistics of diversion in Holland, a word of warning is appropriate: like those the world over, Dutch crime statistics are notoriously unreliable, not only in the sense that they do not reflect 'real' amounts of crime, but also because categories may vary from one year to the next, or may not actually be what they seem. The following is therefore no more than an impression of the amount of non-prosecution for *serious offences* (*misdrijven*) that took place in Holland for the year 1989.

In that year, 1,135,952 *misdrijven* were registered by the police, i.e. either reported or discovered. The same year, 222,097 *misdrijven* were registered at the nineteen public prosecution offices.[23] These are offences

[21] It therefore meets the requirements set out by the European Court of Human Rights in the *Öztürk* judgment of 21 February 1984 (Series A No. 73) and is governed by Art. 6 ECHR.

[22] See, on the matter of coercion, the case of *De Weer*, where the European Court of Human Rights (27 February 1980) found that the complainant, a Belgian butcher, had not been free to decide whether or not to accept *transactie* offered by the Belgian prosecutor (the system is more or less the same, at least in social economic law, in Belgium), because the offer was accompanied by a threat that, failing *transactie*, the butcher's shop would be closed until the case had come to court. According to the European Court, Belgium was in contravention of Art. 6 ECHR with regard to the right to have one's case heard by an independent court. A waiver of that right is legal but not if the decision to do so is, in the words of the European Court, 'tainted by constraint'.

[23] See below for a description of the organization of the prosecution service.

of which the prosecution service has been notified by the police (but not necessarily exactly corresponding to those registered by the police in that year, for some will have carried over from previous years). However, comparison over a number of years reveals that fewer than a quarter of police-registered *misdrijven* are registered by the prosecution each year. What happens to the rest, and why, is not reported. Somehow, three-quarters has been 'diverted' along the way.

Together, the courts and the prosecutors dealt with 211,807 *misdrijven* in 1989, of which 36 per cent were prosecuted in court. In 48 per cent of the cases a waiver or *transactie* by the prosecution occurred and the case never came to court.[24]

Of the *misdrijven* dealt with by the prosecution (and therefore diverted from court proceedings)—a total of 98,305—31 per cent involved technical waivers, 36 per cent policy waivers and 33 per cent *transactie*. The average *transactie* sum was f. 389.[25] Of the policy waivers, 87 per cent were unconditional (although in 19 per cent of these the offenders were officially warned in writing and in 9 per cent in person), 8 per cent were conditional (statistics do not mention what conditions) and 4 per cent unknown.

It should be noted that these figures refer to 'ordinary crime' and, in many cases, to quite serious offences. They seem to confirm the stereotype of Holland as a country of mild penal climate, with a system of relatively high diversion rates (as is also borne out by one of the lowest incarceration rates in the world). By comparison, diversion rates in the UK are extremely low: for adult males we are talking about 15 per cent loss at the caution stage and maybe another 1–2 per cent lost because the prosecution has been discontinued on public interest grounds. In the Netherlands the official diversion rate for cases registered by the prosecution is at least 50 per cent. In reality the rate is much higher, because of the amount of crime that is 'lost' between the police station and the prosecutor's desk.[26]

---

[24] This is only 84% of all cases. The discrepancy is caused by a system known as '*voeging ad informandum*': additional information for consideration by the court. The prosecutor prosecutes and aims at proving one offence only, but adds others to which the same offender has confessed on the file; the court will take these into account when pronouncing sentence. This is also a form of diversion (of offences, not offenders) and serves to keep the system moving to everyone's advantage: the prosecutor and the court reduce their workload, the offender stands trial only once).

[25] In Utrecht the average was almost double (f. 747), caused, interestingly, by a high proportion of *transacties* for fraud.

[26] Not only do these statistics share the general characteristic of being extremely unreliable as to what actually goes on, it is also almost impossible to compare the figures, precisely because they do not reveal anything about the invisible parts of the system that exist in both countries. Perhaps all we can say is that on 'visibility ratings' the Dutch are more diversionary, and there is no reason to suppose that the invisible parts differ greatly in orientation. Although one could of course argue that more opportunities for official, visible diversion render unofficial, invisible diversion less necessary.

CONDITIONAL DIVERSION AND DUE PROCESS: EXTRA-LEGAL INFLUENCE IN
CAUTIONING PRACTICE IN ENGLAND AND WALES

What is striking in comparative terms is that such an accepted feature of the Dutch criminal justice system is so clearly out of bounds in Britain, despite the official policy of developing diversion. The starting point for analysis must be to look at the background to the fears expressed at an official level about the traditional structures of the criminal justice system. These anxieties focus on the problems of uncontrolled, invisible discretion. To understand why this is such a pervasive fear in the UK, one needs to mention some of the studies done on police cautioning. These have consistently revealed the influence of non-legal factors. Class, race, geographical location, and police value-judgement about character, quality of home background, and parental control have all been shown to influence the likelihood of caution.[27] In addition, studies by Steer (1970), Sanders (1988), and McConville *et al.* (1991) suggest that a significant proportion of people are cautioned where it is not clear that there is sufficient evidence to prosecute or where they have not really admitted the offence. Official Home Office guidelines require both these conditions to be satisfied before cautioning. Existing Home Office Circulars and individual Force Orders do not seem to control police capacity to caution or prosecute, with the police force acting on its own notion of institutional priorities and cultural stereotypes about real criminals.

All this has raised the obvious doubts: how to regulate police exercise of discretion where decisions have low visibility because they are taken in private and by large numbers of relatively low-ranking officers with very little contact with each other. In addition, the police have *de facto* been given very wide operational independence because the only checks on their discretion in cautioning are Home Office Guidelines, enforceable only through limited judicial review mechanisms.[28] No decision to prosecute or caution has ever successfully been challenged by these mechanisms. Hence there are many who would be very wary of extending invisible diversion decisions to the negotiation of penalties.

One response to these perceived difficulties has been to stress the need

---

[27] See T. Bennett, 'Social Distribution of Criminal Labels' (1979) 19 *British Journal of Criminology*, 134; C. J. Fisher and R. I. Mawby, 'Juvenile Delinquency and Police Discretion in an Inner City Area' (1982) 22 *British Journal of Criminology*, 63; S. F. Landau and N. Gad, 'Selecting Delinquents for Cautioning in the London Metropolitan Area' (1983) 23 *British Journal of Criminology*, 128; H. Giller and N. Tutt, 'Police Cautioning of Juveniles: the Continuing Practice of Diversity' [1987] *CrimLRev.* 367; R. Evans and T. Ferguson, 'Constructing the Case for Caution', Report to the Home Office Research and Planning Unit and Coventry Social Services Department (unpublished paper, 1991).

[28] See *R. v. Chief Constable of Kent, ex parte L.*, *R. v. DPP, ex parte B* (1991) 93 CrAppR 416, especially at 428, and *R. v. DPP, ex parte Langlands-Pearse*, Lexis CO/221/90.

to give the key role for decisions about diversion to the CPS rather than the police. Andrew Sanders has advocated such a view.[29] We will see that, in Holland, the central mechanisms for regulating the operation of diversion are internal mechanisms within the Prosecution Service and the quasi-legal status of guidelines produced by its heads, the five procurators-general. But, as presently constituted, the CPS is incapable of regulating diversionary practice by internal guidance. To change this position would mean very profound change in the constitutional relationship of police and prosecutor.

The Legal Position of the CPS

Until 1986, the police undertook the bulk of prosecution though they would often use lawyers (always in serious cases). However, the police were clearly in charge and there was no powerful independent body to scrutinize the decision to prosecute. One of the consequences of this was that, in a minority of cases, the police used to bring prosecutions where the evidence was clearly weak. The Government set up the CPS to reduce the proportion of cases pursued despite lack of sufficient evidence, improve preparation and presentation of cases in court, and thus use resources more effectively: therefore the CPS was established for reasons of cost-effectiveness and bureaucratic efficiency. There was no question of trying to remove the fundamental power of the police to set the priorities of the system. This is reflected in the concrete powers given to the two institutions.

The prime duty of the CPS is 'to take over the conduct of all criminal proceedings . . . instituted on behalf of a police force' (section 3(2) of the Prosecution of Offences Act). In addition there is a duty to give advice to police forces on all matters relating to criminal offences (section 3(2)(e)). Lastly, there is the absolute power where a charge has been brought by the police to 'discontinue proceedings' until the prosecution begins its evidence or until the completion of committal proceedings (section 23(4)).

Control still largely rests with the police. They take the initial decision to charge and usually the CPS only sees cases where charges have been instituted. The decision not to prosecute (and thus the decision to caution) rests entirely with the police. The duty to give advice (see section 3(2)(e) above) might give the CPS the ability to influence diversion, but only if the police choose to refer cases to them before charge. However, a recent study[30] found no evidence that the CPS was involved in routine decisions to caution or that police forces had any standard mechanisms for this to take place. Only eight police forces (out of a total of forty-three) said that they might seek CPS advice prior to making a prosecution decision. In

[29] A. Sanders, 'The Limits to Diversion From Prosecution' (1988) 28 *British Journal of Criminology*, 513 at 525–7.
[30] C. Wilkinson and R. Evans, 'Police Cautioning of Juveniles', n. 14 above.

addition, the study revealed that it was very rare for the CPS to be involved in the development of cautioning policy.[31]

It must also be stressed that the CPS is dependent on the files provided by the police. In order to make informed decisions about diversion the CPS needs information about the circumstances of the offence and offender. Armed with this information, the CPS could discontinue proceedings on the ground that they are not in the public interest. The Director of Public Prosecutions (the head of the CPS) has issued a code for prosecutors which suggests that in deciding to discontinue proceedings prosecutors should first ask if the evidence is such that there is a realistic prospect of conviction (the sufficiency of evidence criterion). Then they should ask if the public interest requires a prosecution. A number of things are borne in mind here, including whether the likely penalty will be nominal, whether the stigma is likely to cause irreparable harm to a young adult, whether the defendant is very old or infirm or suffering from mental illness, and the strain would make this worse.

To make decisions on this the CPS needs information from the police. But Andrew Sanders has made the point that police case files are not objective entities, but constructed and selected accounts that reflect the values and interests of those who construct them. Police officers know the case will be reviewed and can anticipate this in their file construction.[32] How serious or trivial an incident is or how morally culpable an offender is depends on how you tell the story. In some cases in McConville *et al.*'s sample this led to the construction of the circumstances as trivial. More often the file would construct the case in as serious a light as possible. For instance police files usually contain very little in the way of mitigating circumstances even when the police know them to exist. In contrast McConville *et al.* report that background information that justifies prosecution will normally be put on file.[33]

Generally, the police do not have the time or inclination to seek out mitigatory factors; seeing their role in a partisan way they are loth to spend time doing this. The CPS does not and cannot make them do so. Rank and file officers tend to have attitudes hostile to expansion in the use of cautioning for adult offenders.[34] This in turn reflects the relatively

---

[31] 25 force areas had no such CPS involvement, two had the CPS involved in working groups to discuss policy, five had regular meetings with the CPS on policy and three said that discussions were beginning to develop closer co-operation.

[32] A. Sanders, 'Constructing the Case for the Prosecution' (1987) 14(2) *Journal of Law and Society*, 229; M. McConville *et al.*, above, n. 19, at 126; L. Gelsthorpe and H. Giller, 'More Justice for Juveniles', n. 8 above.

[33] M. McConville *et al.*, n. 9, above, at 128. Some experiments have been conducted to involve the Probation Service in providing public interest information. Results suggest that this has a significant effect on discontinuance. See A. Brown, J. Scarabrook, and H. Matthews, 'Discontinuance of Criminal Proceedings in the Public Interest' (1992) 39 *Probation Journal*, 24.

[34] R. Evans, n. 11, above, at 601.

conservative ideologies about crime and punishment prevalent amongst police officers and the attendant stress on the importance of significant punishment in order to deter.[35] It is not surprising that the police files do not give the CPS too much opportunity to discontinue cases officers want prosecuted. The prosecutor is not legally in command of the police in the way that he or she is in Holland, and if the information is not in the file the prosecutor may never become aware of the circumstances that justify diversion, or may do so only after the trial has started. Note that the prosecutors do not simply get the whole file, and the files passed to them are often notoriously sketchy.

In addition very special institutional pressures operate within the CPS. It has been dogged since its inception by insufficient funds and insufficient manpower. In 1990 it was still short of 465 lawyers—23 per cent of its required complement. As a consequence there was significant sub-contracting out to inexperienced outside barristers.[36] Many of those in post were poorly qualified and had excessive case-loads. The service was under strong ideological pressure from the police, who portray them as unduly soft on criminals. There is often much-publicized chaos with late or inadequate preparation of cases. Not surprisingly an extensive survey based on analysis of nearly 1,000 files and interviews with police and prosecutors indicated that the dominant 'operational philosophy' of the CPS is one based on securing 'the smooth functioning of the prosecution process' rather than a distinctive professional ideology or set of values and principles about desired goals within the criminal justice system.[37]

In other words the limited role indicated by the terms of the legal powers of the CPS, has been 'internalized' within the organization. It does not see itself as an 'agenda setter'. McConville *et al.*, after a study in 1986–8 of over 1,000 cases, concluded that '[i]n reality prosecutors almost invariably defer to the police on question of policy and public interest on the basis that the close involvement of the police with the community makes them the best arbiters of local needs'.[38] In part this may be a product of the narrow bureaucratic pressures outlined above, but it may also reflect more deep-rooted questions of attitude and training. In England and Wales, lawyer-training leads more obviously to a role conceived in terms of checking sufficiency of evidence than to a broader role of agenda-setting.

If one takes the view that the police are inevitably prosecution-minded and partisan, they surely cannot be suitable people to be administering a

---

[35] N. Fielding and J. Fielding, 'Police Attitudes to Crime and Punishment: Certainties and Dilemmas' (1991) 31 *British Journal of Criminology*, 39. For Chief Constables' views see R. Reiner, *Chief Constables* (Oxford; Oxford University Press 1991), at 136–7.

[36] See *The Times*, 19 February 1990; *Guardian*, 1 and 16 February 1990.

[37] L. Gelsthorpe and H. Giller, n. 8, above, at 153.

[38] M. McConville *et al.*, n. 9, above.

non-criminal, negotiated penalty system. Only the CPS could do it and it does not at the moment have the powers to do so. It is not simply that it must make the decisions to caution or prosecute but that its legal and institutional relationship with the police must be such that it can demand information from the police (and indeed other agencies) and establish priorities. This would be a profound constitutional change which, Sanders argues, would remove the obvious due process worries about the police acting as investigator, prosecutor, judge, and sentencer. It would mean that far fewer and more highly-trained personnel would be taking the decisions. In addition, as trained lawyers, prosecutors would be more likely to stress the ideals of the rule of law and the avoidance of arbitrariness than police. This in turn would make it acceptable to introduce various forms of conditional diversion.

DIVERSION AND THE ROLE OF THE DUTCH PROSECUTOR

To what extent is Sanders's optimism borne out by the experience of operation of the Dutch system of diversion? If it is successful, is its success linked to institutional and cultural factors that could not be reproduced simply by changing the formal legal role of the Crown Prosecution Service? What implications does this have for grafting such an institution onto an adversarial system? And what of the doubts and concerns expressed by British writers with regard to the visibility and accountability of diversion?

Organization of the Dutch Public Prosecution Service

The Public Prosecution Service in the Netherlands is a hierarchical and bureaucratic organization, at the head of which stands the Minister of Justice. Under him come the five procurators-general, then the chief prosecutors in the nineteen districts of the district courts, then the prosecutors in each district.[39] The procurators-general formulate criminal policy in consultation with the Ministry and also produce guidelines for the prosecutors, including guidelines on waivers and *transactie* (this, among other things, in order to promote legal equality, the idea being that each type of offence should receive roughly the same treatment, in whatever district it has been committed).

The system however labours under a peculiar duality. Although it is hierarchical in the sense that the higher officials (including the Minister) can give orders to the lower, this rarely occurs directly, while guidelines

---

[39] The system is slightly more complicated, but this brief outline will serve to illustrate the essentially hierarchical nature of the Service.

from the top are not binding: the prosecutor at actual prosecution (district) level is free to make his own decisions on (non-)prosecution, based on his own assessment of the public interest. Now this, too, rarely occurs, for the simple reason that most prosecutors conform to 'the way things are done' and are moreover usually motivated in their decisions by other concerns (see below). But it is by no means impossible for a prosecutor fairly far down the hierarchical ladder to develop his own 'prosecution policies'.

Professional Roles

Research[40] has shown that public prosecutors at district level see themselves essentially as magistrates: impartial, making decisions on the basis of immanent legal values and basic principles of criminal law, and 'translating' these in each individual case into 'the public interest', while also guarding against disproportionate violation of the interests of the offender. This perception is highly valued within the profession: the prosecutor who earns himself the name of crime fighter at the expense of individual offenders is likely to find his esteem among colleagues diminished. Such professional attitudes are cultivated during training. The Public Prosecution Service is regarded as part of the judiciary, and the prosecutor is referred to as the 'standing magistrate' (because he stands in court); the judge is the 'sitting magistrate'. Public prosecutors and judges receive exactly the same professional training, lasting six years after they have graduated from a law school. During this time they become acquainted with all aspects of court proceedings (in theory and in practice). After the six years they opt either for the 'standing', or for the 'sitting' judiciary.

At the same time, however, although the prosecutors are magistrates, and independent in the sense that their decisions are autonomous (even if they go against the guidelines), they are also government employees, accountable to those higher up, who are expected to execute government policy and who, in extreme cases, may find themselves on the carpet or under pressure to conform. At the same time, public prosecutors need considerable managerial skills: they must manage the police in criminal investigations, and the workload on their desks; manage, too, to have their decisions to prosecute and the sentences they demand accepted by the court. These roles can run counter to magisterial considerations. For example, the fact that so much crime 'disappears' between the police station and the prosecutor's office is often the result of instructions from the prosecutors themselves. In an attempt to manage their workload they not only ask the police to select only those offences that have some chance of

---

[40] See H. G. van de Bunt, *Officieren van Justitie, verslag van een participerend observatieonderzoek* (Zwolle; Tjeenk Willink 1985); also C. H. and K. L. K. Brants, *De Sociale Constructie van Fraude* (Arnhem; Gouda Quint 1991).

being solved, they also set limits, per category of offences, for the amount of crime the police report for consideration by the prosecutor.[41]

And, finally, there are prosecutors who, for whatever reason (ranging from abstract notions of justice to personal ambition) and notwithstanding the hierarchical and managerial aspects of their job, seek to change criminal policy by sticking their necks out and not conforming to the way things are done. They may, for example, elect to prosecute offences that are usually diverted, as happened in the 1970s, when a small group of young, enthusiastic, and liberal prosecutors attempted, with no little success, to change official attitudes and policy towards fraud by systematically going for prosecution when, normally, diversion would have been indicated. Such prosecutors need the tenacity of a moral crusader, and this too is likely to interfere with magisterial values such as impartiality and consideration of the offender's interests, and with managerial performance (moral crusading seriously increases the workload, with regard both to the number of cases and to each case individually).

Moreover, the professional roles of government employee and manager are becoming ever more predominant. Increasingly, criminal justice is perceived at government level as a means of structuring and directing society in the desired direction, rather than of punishing individuals. As a result, criminal policy in general, as one of the main concerns of government, is the subject of an inordinate number of guidelines from the procurators-general. This leaves less and less time and scope for magisterial considerations or moral crusades at district level. Indeed, there is increasing discontent among ordinary prosecutors: a feeling that the minister and the heads of prosecution are not only out of touch with the reality of crime, but especially that their policies are guided by political expediency only (seeing crime as a political problem rather than a social issue) and not by any perception of, or real concern with, how the public prosecutor should deal justly and yet effectively with the case-load on his desk.

It will be clear that combining the ideal types of magistrate, government employee, manager, and (sometimes) moral crusader is no easy matter and causes personal and professional stress. It also influences decisions on (non-)prosecution, with the prosecutor caught in a cross-current of conflicting interests and professional roles. The existence of policy guidelines may only serve to make matters worse, by pressurizing the prosecutors at district level to take decisions they consider counter to other interests, while, with so many intangible factors at work, insight into and control of what goes on at the prosecutor's office are by no means self-evident.

---

[41] As far as the provision of information to, and co-operation with, the Prosecution Service by the police are concerned, these depend very much on informal contacts. A chief prosecutor would be very unwise to get on the wrong side of the chief of police in his district, for example, but his would also apply vice versa.

Control

In theory, the public prosecutor at district level enjoys a considerable amount of freedom of decision. However, means of control and supervision are subtle and indirect. At the top of the hierarchical pyramid, the Minister is politically answerable to Parliament for decisions within the criminal justice system. This is exceptional, but it does happen in spectacular cases (war criminals and, again, fraud). The heads of prosecution answer to the Minister, and so on down the line. In practice, despite the recent developments outlined above, prosecutors are not usually called to account this way. Criminal policy (including *transactie* and waiver policy) filters down from the top through guidelines, but even more through informal channels (such as seminars, conferences, etc., where policy is 'discussed', not imposed). And vice versa: policy often filters up from the bottom, the heads of prosecution being one step behind what is actually going on, or out of touch with 'reality'.

For the individual, faced with a decision by the prosecutor to prosecute or not, there are limited means of calling him to account. Anyone adversely affected by a prosecutor's decision to divert an offender from prosecution may have that decision reviewed by the Court of Appeal (a procedure based on Article 12 of the Code of Criminal Procedure). This is the only instance in which the law gives any other agency but the Prosecution Service itself the right to decide on (non)-prosecution. It is a complicated and little used procedure. Recently, the Supreme Court[42] has accepted that, because of general principles of fair trial and due procedure, an individual offender must be able to invoke guidelines and even standard practice to challenge a decision to prosecute.

But apart from such individual rights, the answer to the question 'who controls the prosecutor' must be, inconceivable as it may seem to British readers, 'nobody, really'. Although guidelines and policy plans are publicly accessible, the visibility of what actually goes on as far as decisions not to prosecute are concerned, is practically nil. This has meant that one of the traditional means of control of the criminal justice system—the fact that criminal trials are public, and therefore open to the media—is less and less effective, as more and more goes on behind the scenes. The system is based on confidence that the Prosecution Service will act in the public interest and on an (unwritten) code of professional conduct for individual prosecutors which, in itself, is based on an ideal-typical professional role.

This suggests similarities with the Anglo-American practice of plea-bargaining. Both operate in a semi-private nether-world of bargaining and tactical exchange; both lack developed mechanisms for public accountability;

---

[42] In judgments of 19 June 1990 [1991] NJ 119 and 5 May 1991 [1991] NJ 694.

both, if they are to be viewed as acceptable in their present form, require great faith in the integrity and competence of professional role-playing. The Dutch must trust the judicial impartiality of the prosecutor despite the evidence of bureaucratic pressures; the British must trust to the combative competence of defence lawyers to ensure suspects' interests are preserved in the bargaining process. Dutch faith in their prosecutor may be more durable because of the absence of publicized scandals.[43]

CONCLUSION

The system of public prosecution in the Netherlands is the result of historical development, and confidence and trust in the prosecution service are still based on the idea that, when it comes to the crunch, the prosecutor is part of the judiciary and not of the executive. The desire to promote the development of some version of Continental conditional diversion in England and Wales is understandable, but there is a need to be clear-eyed about the dangers of borrowing from other countries. Sanders and others rightly recognize the key difficulties in conditional diversion: problems of consistency, visibility, due process, and public accountability in decision-making. But there is also a need to recognize that the way these issues are addressed in other countries may not be replicable; indeed it may not be desirable to do so. Dutch regulation of the process of conditional diversion relies, unthinkingly and too heavily, on informal procedures and historically-developed checks and balances to prevent it going off the rails. At the end of the day, it only works as it does because society probably accepts (although no one knows for sure because the question never really arises as a public issue) that the prosecution service can be trusted to do what is best in the public interest. This derives from completely different institutional and cultural frames of reference, from attitudes and training rooted in the career judiciary system.

The Dutch system suggests, as British advocates of conditional diversion acknowledge, that conditional diversion would require a more dominant CPS with a monopoly of prosecution and access to public interest information from welfare agencies.[44] But more than this, there is the need for proper structures of accountability. If suspects are to be protected from arbitrary coercion, the Dutch experience suggests both strengths and weaknesses in faith in the image of prosecutors as judicial figures. Its strength

---

[43] For scepticism about the role of defence lawyers, see J. Baldwin and M. McConville, *Negotiated Justice* (London; Martin Robertson 1977); M. McConville *et al.*, n. 9, above, 165–170 and A. Sanders, 'Reforming the Prosecution System [1992] *Political Quarterly* 25 at 33–4.

[44] A. Sanders, n. 2, above, at 525–6.

may be the cultural commitment of prosecutors to the ideal, and its weakness a lack of public structures to monitor and check that the commitment is real.[45] To vest the same powers in prosecutors not brought up or trained within the career judiciary tradition would be inviting trouble. It might be possible adequately to structure and control the use of discretion in conditional diversion by publicly-declared criteria and review by the courts. But for this the Netherlands certainly provides no model.[46]

---

[45] A. Sanders, n. 11, above, at 617.

[46] Since this was written, two key shifts in British Government policy have taken place. In October 1993, the Home Secretary announced new plans to restrict cautioning, particularly of individuals who had previously been cautioned or where the offence was more serious. In 1994, this was encapsulated in new guidelines on cautioning: *The Cautioning of Offenders*, Home Office Circular 18/1994. If implemented rigorously by the police, these will reverse the upward trend in cautioning (see R. Evans (1994) 'Cautioning: Counting the Cost of Retrenchment' *CrimLRev*. 566). Suggestions for conditional diversion have also resurfaced. The Runciman Commission recommended, without much discussion, that the Scottish system of prosecutor fines be introduced in England and Wales and that conditions for cautions be looked at further (Report of the Royal Commission on Criminal Justice, HMSO, 1993, Cm 2263). The recent Home Office circular encourages police forces to monitor 'caution plus' systems with a view to making a decision on the future of such systems. In the Netherlands, the same need to maintain the political initiative over crime and to respond to media and public concerns over criminal justice that underlies British developments, seems to have prompted the former Dutch Minister of Justice to produce a policy plan geared towards a drastic increase in the number of prosecutions and a corresponding reduction of (conditional) waivers. However, the system is by no means equipped to cope with such measures, and by and large there has been no change in overall rates of prosecution. Moreover, the experiment with 'transactie' by the police for certain ordinary crimes is no longer an experiment and has become law, thereby increasing the number of future cases in which a 'sanction' is 'imposed', but reducing the number of visible prosecutions.

8

Managing the Drug Problem: Tolerance or Prohibition

JOS SILVIS AND KATHERINE S. WILLIAMS

THE HISTORICAL AND INTERNATIONAL BACKGROUND

The current drug policy of most states has a direct link to the early days of this century and earlier. It was at this time that the first steps were taken to bring drugs under (international) control.

As recently as the last century in Britain drugs, including opium (laudanum) and morphine, were freely available both for enjoyment and as the basis for many common remedies. Britain also had a large economic interest in the opium trade, especially to China. When, to protect their people, the Chinese authorities tried to block this trade, it led to war in 1841. Following this, the 'infant doping problem', and opium use by workers, the Quakers led a campaign which persuaded many British people that addiction to opium was a sign of moral depravity and that the drug was evil: the first step towards acceptance of regulation. Legal control began in 1868[1] when certain substances, notably opium, were placed under pharmaceutical control, but in practice they remained easy to obtain and the basis of many remedies until after the turn of the century. The first real control of drugs came in the First World War when, in 1916, the Home Office, through the Army Council, forbade the supply of certain drugs to any member of the armed forces unless administered by a doctor. In the same year Regulation 40B under the Defence of the Realm Act 1914 made it an offence for those in the medical and allied professions to possess cocaine or opium.

In the Netherlands drugs were also freely available, though a curious Act of 1865 limited to medical practitioners and pharmacists the sale of opiate products of less than 50 grams while everybody else was allowed to deal in larger amounts. Drug policy in both the Netherlands and Britain has some of its roots in their colonial past. Intervention in the drug market by the Dutch government in what is now the independent state of Indonesia was legitimated by the proclaimed goal of reducing consumption and production in order to protect the unfortunate addicted inhabitants of the

---

[1] Pharmacy Act 1868, s. 17.

colonies. This historical involvement in the struggle against drug misuse is one of the reasons the Dutch played an important role in the original international effort to universalize the repressive approach to narcotic drugs. In 1893 British concern about drug-taking in India was shown by the appointment of a Royal Commission[2] to review the use of opium and cannabis on the Indian sub-continent. The need for an international answer to the drug problem was first recognized in 1909 when a number of states, including the Netherlands and Britain, entered into the Shanghai Agreement. This was followed in 1912 by the Hague Convention, from which grew most modern international co-operation on dangerous drugs. The Hague Convention was not fully operational until the Versailles Peace Settlement required signatories to implement controls on narcotic drugs. The international regulation of drugs, initially given to the League of Nations, has now passed to the United Nations.

Since 1919 drugs treaties have had more participating countries than any other 'non-political' treaty. Following the Hague Convention, the Geneva Convention of 1924 (under pressure from Middle Eastern countries) was the first to include cannabis. Numerous treaties followed which were all consolidated into the Single Convention on Narcotic Drugs of 1961 (New York) which, along with the 1972 Protocol, is still the main legal document in the international co-operative effort against dangerous drugs. Both Britain and the Netherlands are party to this Convention and its 1972 Protocol. The Vienna Convention against Illicit Traffic in Narcotic Drugs and Psychotropic Substances of 1988 added the confiscation of funds and prevention of money laundering, and seeks to regulate equipment and substances used to manufacture controlled drugs. This last treaty had an extra significance as it was the first recognition in an international convention of the need to control psychotropic drugs, although on a national level both the Dutch and the British had already integrated the control of psychotropic drugs into their national legislation.

International agreements form the (largely accepted) external constraints within which a sovereign drugs policy can be developed. The treaties are strict in relation to the types of drugs needing to be regulated and the legislative control necessary in the participating states and have produced more or less harmonious legislation all over the world. But implementation and criminal justice policy decisions are left in the hands of each state, and these are often very different. If a state tried strictly to apply all its written law the courts would be unable to deal with the load and the police resources would be insufficient to cope. Clearly in order to prevent this every criminal justice system must set priorities. A country's formal legal

---

[2] *Report of the Indian Hemp Drugs Commission*, 1894–5 (Simla and Calcutta; Government Central Print Office 1897).

control thus gives little guidance to the way it deals with a particular problem. Studying what occurs on the streets may be equally misleading. For example, in Holland the possession of marijuana and hashish is forbidden, but in every large town one can find coffee-shops where consumers openly buy these products without fearing interference from the police. Even heroin and cocaine (also illegal) are fairly openly sold. An observer of the visible drug-trading and drug-taking may conclude that there is no real enforcement, but this would be too simplistic and misleading. To understand the situation it is necessary to study the written laws in a state, the criminal justice policies, the implementation of the laws by the law enforcement agencies, and the other methods of social control or support used to deal with the problem. While the present work will centre on the legal issues, all these aspects of the systems in Britain and the Netherlands will be considered and compared and the resultant effect on the problem in each of these states will be considered.

In both the Netherlands and Britain the police and prosecutors are allowed discretion in the implementation of their powers, but those in authority (ministries or Government) customarily set the parameters within which this discretion should be exercised by officers or prosecutors. In the Netherlands there are guidelines published, especially for prosecutors, setting out how to deal with particular situations. In Britain there are often policies set by senior police officers, Ministers or Government documents but individual officers or prosecutors can choose to ignore them. The guidelines nonetheless bridge the gap between law in the books and law in action and are especially important in the field of illegal drugs.

THE LAW

The Dutch *Opiumwet* (Opium Act) of 1928, as amended, remains the main official control of drugs, though it has been amended many times over the years, most notably in 1976, so that little of the original document is still in operation. It fulfils all the demands of the international conventions, setting out the punishments for possession, trade, cultivation, importation, and exportation, and a number of other acts and omissions in relation narcotic drugs (including cannabis products). Since 1976 the punishment for breach of the *Opiumwet* has depended on whether a drug is classified as list 1 or 2 (see Table 8.1). The most lenient penalties are used for list 2 drugs, basically cannabis products and some psychotropic substances. The low punishments for possession and trafficking in small amounts of cannabis reflect the compromise between the Government, which fears international condemnation if cannabis is not controlled, and those in favour of legalization of this drug. List 1 covers drugs like heroin and cocaine

TABLE 8.1:   Maximum Penalties for Drug Offences in the Netherlands

OFFENCE	LIST 1		LIST 2	
	Length of time in PRISON	FINE in 000's DFl	Length of time in PRISON	FINE in 000's DFl
POSSESSION				
Large Quantity, for trading	4 Years		2 Years	
Small Quantity	4 Years		1 Month	5
ILLICIT PRODUCTION				
Large Quantity	8 Years	100	2 Years	100
Small Quantity			1 Month	5
ILLICIT TRAFFICKING (Import/Export)				
Large Quantity	12 Years[2]	100[3]	4 Years	100
Small Quantity	1 Year	10	4 Years[4]	5

Source: Legislation—*Opiumwet* 1928, as amended[1]
1 Note that in the Netherlands judges have a wide discretion in sentencing, see Chap. 16 below.
2 For repeated offences the punishment may be 16 years.
3 If the volume of drugs exceeds f. 25,000 a fine of f. 1,000,000 may be imposed.
4 It is generally acknowledged that in relation to List 2 drugs the legislator should have distinguished between importation and exportation for own use and for other purposes. There is no rationale for higher punishment for importation or exportation of a small amount of cannabis (maximum 4 years) and a small amount of heroin or cocaine (maximum 1 year).

where breaches attract much harsher maximum penalties because, as indicated in the explanatory notes to the *Opiumwet*, the Government considers these to be an unacceptable risk. The *Opiumwet* also distinguishes between users, and dealers and traffickers. In 1985 the *Opiumwet* was changed to criminalize mere preparatory acts relating to serious drug offences (like importation), which makes it easier for the police to use their powers in a pro-active manner.

Doctors are permitted to prescribe any drug for those who are ill or injured. Addicts can only be given methadone; prescribing heroin is not allowed but is generally tolerated.

In Britain the Misuse of Drugs Act 1971, as amended, has offences relating to production, cultivation, supply, possession, and offences by occupiers of premises. For each of these, *mens rea* is an element in the commission of the offence.[3] Schedule 2 splits drugs into three categories

[3] The Netherlands distinguishes between intentional drug crimes and drug crimes by fault. For the last category *mens rea* is not demanded, but a defence of due diligence is allowed.

TABLE 8.2 Maximum Penalties for Drug Offences in
England and Wales

OFFENCE	CLASS A		CLASS B		CLASS C	
	Length of time in PRISON	FINE (£)	Length of time in PRISON	FINE (£)	Length of time in PRISON	FINE (£)
POSSESSION						
Indictment	7 Years	unlimited	5 Years	unlimited	2 Years	unlimited
Summary	6 Months	5,000	3 Months	500	3 Months	200
POSSESSION (with intention to supply)						
Indictment	Life	unlimited	14 Years	unlimited	5 Years	unlimited
Summary	6 Months	5,000	6 Months	5,000	3 Months	500
ILLICIT TRAFFICKING (supplying or offering to supply a controlled drug)						
Indictment	Life	unlimited	14 Years	unlimited	5 Years	unlimited
Summary	6 Months	5,000	6 Months	5,000	3 Months	500
ILLICIT PRODUCTION						
Indictment	Life	unlimited	14 Years	unlimited	5 Years	unlimited
Summary	6 Months	5,000	6 Months	5,000	3 Months	unlimited
ILLICIT CULTIVATION (of cannabis)						
Indictment	–	–	14 Years	unlimited	–	–
Summary	–	–	6 Months	5,000	–	–

Source: Legislation—Misuse of Drugs Act 1971, as amended Schedule 4

according to their perceived degree of dangerousness. The most serious offences involve class A drugs (opiates, heroin, cocaine, LSD, dipipanone, injectable amphetamines, and cannabinol). The next grade are class B drugs (oral amphetamines, herbal cannabis, cannabis resin, and dihydrocodeine), and finally class C drugs are the least dangerous (methaqualone and certain amphetamine-like drugs). The maximum punishments for each can be found in Table 8.2. There have been calls for changes in the law: in both 1979[4] and 1982[5] the Advisory Council on the Misuse of Drugs recommended that herbal cannabis and cannabis resin should be reclassified as class C drugs. To meet the objection that this would have led to their

[4] Advisory Council on the Misuse of Drugs, 1979, *A Review of the Classification of Controlled Drugs and of Penalties under Schedules 2 and 4 of the Misuse of Drugs Act 1971* (London; HMSO).
[5] Advisory Council on the Misuse of Drugs, 1982, *Report of the Expert Group on the Effects of Cannabis Use* (London; HMSO).

possession no longer being an arrestable offence, an influential report[6] suggested that class C drugs should become arrestable offences and that all present class C drugs should be reclassified as class D. This report also suggested that dealing for gain and social supply should be separate offences, and that the former should attract harsher penalties.

Practitioners in the medical and allied professions without criminal records may prescribe any drug for people (or animals) suffering from illness or injury. Only doctors specially licensed by the Home Office may prescribe cocaine, heroin, or dipipanone to addicts and those who prescribe irresponsibly may be disciplined. Doctors have to inform the Home Secretary of the personal details of patients who are being treated as addicts but the term 'registered addict' has no legal meaning. The Department of Health is responsible for providing facilities for the treatment of addicts, and there are now drug treatment clinics in most major towns.

The drug trafficking offences appear in the Customs and Excise Management Act 1979. The individual must be aware that the goods are prohibited but it does not matter if the exact nature of the substance is unknown.[7] Penalties for breach can be found in Table 8.3. Under the Drug Trafficking Offences Act 1986 confiscation orders are available to the Crown Court and people who assist traffickers to retain their assets now face a maximum penalty of 14 years imprisonment.

POLICY GUIDELINES FOR LAW IN ACTION

In the Netherlands

The *Opiumwet* crudely indicates the priorities in Dutch drug control but a clearer indication is obtained from policy statements. Until the 1970s the only drug which was in heavy use was cannabis and the authorities had taken a fairly permissive line towards that. As other forms of drug use arose in Holland the authorities seemed to allow this line to continue: a *laissez faire* attitude developed more through indecision than through adoption of a clear permissive approach.[8] In the 1970s it became evident to the authorities that greater law enforcement was necessary: a period of heavy law enforcement ensued, followed by the pursuit of a more integrated policy by the issue of guidelines.

According to the guidelines dealing in hard drugs needs to be controlled by firm action. This policy should be carried out by specialized agencies. It calls for prosecution of suspects, their pre-trial detention, and a demand

[6] Peter Crawford, 1991, *Drugs and the Law—a Report for Justice* (London; Justice).
[7] R. v. *Hussain* (1969) 53 CrAppR 448 and R. v. *Hennessey* (1978) 68 CrAppR 419.
[8] David Downes, *Contrasts in Tolerance: Post-War Penal Policy in the Netherlands and England and Wales* (Oxford; Clarendon Press 1988), at 127.

TABLE 8.3 Maximum Penalties for Trafficking in England and Wales

OFFENCE	CLASS A		CLASS B		CLASS C	
	Time in PRISON	FINE (£)	Time in PRISON	FINE (£)	Time in PRISON	FINE (£)
POSSESSION (importing or exporting drugs or fraudulent evasion of duty) Indictment Summary	Life 6 Months	unlimited 3 times the value of the goods or 5,000 whichever is the greater	14 Years 6 Months	unlimited 3 times the value of the goods or 5,000 whichever is the greater	5 Years 3 Months	unlimited 3 times the value of the goods or 5,000 whichever is the greater

Source: Legislation—Customs and Excise Management Act 1977, Schedule 1

for prison sentences (a minimum of three years for dealers, two years for couriers). Although this policy is largely adhered to, practice has gradually developed a slightly different sentencing system for traffickers. This is known as the 'Kilo-policy': the prosecution asks for one year per kilo of hard drugs, up to the maximum of twelve years. In such a system, the individual circumstances of each trafficker (such as 'how much he knew about his role in the illegal transport') are largely irrelevant.

In relation to cannabis the guidelines create a certain form of *de facto* decriminalization. There is a tacit policy of non-intervention in cannabis-dealing in small amounts in the controlled setting of youth centres by a so-called house-dealer. On top of this central policy each town or region often has tripartite discussions between the chief of police, the prosecutor, and the mayor. This recognizes the different interests of criminal justice and civil administration in drug control. In many areas these agreements have led to wider policies on non-intervention, accepting not only the house-dealer phenomenon but also cannabis-dealing in coffee-shops. In some cases the courts have acknowledged that coffee-shop dealers should not be prosecuted as long as they act according to a number of criteria, for instance: not selling to those under sixteen years; not promoting the business by advertisement; not selling in other than small amounts; not selling other illegal drugs (and not selling alcohol); not selling to foreigners; and not causing any public disturbance. If a disturbance occurs the police may step in to deal with it; if there is trouble on a regular basis the local government may take administrative action, including closing a shop or pub. The administrative court that may be addressed by the parties involved will not permit the closure of a shop or pub merely because soft drugs are sold there. Therefore although the *Opiumwet* makes possession a minor offence and dealing a serious one the selling of cannabis products has gained a pseudo-legal status in the Netherlands. Use of drugs as such is not punishable at all in the Netherlands.

On the question of possession merely for use, the guidelines bar the police from using their powers merely to detect possession of small quantities of cannabis. To avoid the need for a prosecution when a consumer is caught in possession of cannabis products, a *transactie* of 50 guilders (approximately £16) may be ordered.[9] The guidelines also give low priority to the detection of the possession of small quantities of hard drugs such as heroin or cocaine. Despite this, many drug-takers are prosecuted when they come into contact with the police for drug-related crimes (theft, including shoplifting, robbery, burglary, etc.). In these cases the prosecutors' guidelines explicitly recognize that a medical or socio-medical approach to users of hard drugs is preferable. To this end there is a strong network

---

[9] See Chap. 7 for a full discussion of *transactie*.

of treatment and support services in the Netherlands. Even with all these diversionary guidelines a large percentage of the prison population is addicted to drugs, showing a certain failure in the policy of dealing with drug dependants outside the prison system.

The final policy element is the recognition that the criminal law plays only a minor role in the Dutch war on drugs. Central government has accepted that criminal proceedings should not be allowed to cause individual drug users more harm than might occur through drug use itself. The resultant level of legal intervention, accompanied by a gradual process of controlled integration of drug taking, could lead to the removal of any stigma against drug users.[10] First, the Dutch try to teach individuals to be responsible for their choices rather than just warning them and thereby possibly glamourizing the drugs.[11] Secondly, treatment methods are not only aimed at ending addiction but also at improving the addict's physical and social well-being.[12] Thus aid agencies are very accessible, particularly the 'methadone bus', and treatment moves at the addict's pace allowing stabilization before any attempt at reduction. Dutch policy also aims to help addicts build a new life, meet new friends, finish education and training, and enter the job market, although underfunding here has been pinpointed as a main reason for relapse.[13] This element also involves treating the problems users and their families perceive they have rather than choosing what the agency or state considers best.[14] Thirdly, Dutch policy never prescribes heroin (only methadone) and take-home dosages are exceptional; all are consumed in the treatment centre, so preventing re-sale. Finally the Dutch have dealt with the health dangers in a practical and efficient manner; about 60–80 per cent of drug addicts in Amsterdam are being reached, facilitating needle distribution and reducing the danger from AIDS. Of those with AIDS in the Netherlands fewer than 10 per cent are drug users.[15] Finally all these policies have led some to believe that the drug problem is being contained or may even be decreasing,[16] and to claim that young people are no longer being attracted towards heroin use.[17] But there are recent claims from the managing director of the Jellinekcentre in Amsterdam that there is a new growth of young heroin users.

[10] Interdepartementale Stuurgroep Alcohol en Drugbeleid, *Drugbeleid in Beweging; Naar een Normalisering van de drugproblematiek (Drug Policy in Motion: Towards a Normalization of the Drug Problem)* (The Hague; Government Publishing Office 1985).

[11] E. L. Engelsman, 'Dutch Policy on the Management of Drug-Related Problems' (1989) 84 *British Journal of Addiction*, 211–18.

[12] Ibid.

[13] Govert F. Van de Wijngaart, 'A Social History of Drug Use in the Netherlands: Policy Outcomes and Implications' (1988) 18 *Journal of Drug Issues*, 481–95.

[14] Ibid.

[15] Govert F. Van de Wijngaart, 'Commentaries' (1989) 84 *British Journal of Addictions*, 990–2.

[16] Ibid.   [17] Downes, *Contrasts in Tolerance*, chap. 5.

In England and Wales

It is much more difficult to discern policy objectives in Britain. On the one hand the politicians state very clearly that they consider a hard line against traffickers is essential to win the fight against drugs. So, for example, the Home Affairs Committee 1985[18] recommended that more resources be made available for the enforcement of the law; that there should be stricter penalties imposed on traffickers of hard drugs; and that the armed forces should be used for surveillance operations against illicit importers. It is also clear that in recent years the expenditure on all anti-drug measures has been increased, more is spent on law enforcement, allowing the police and Customs and Excise larger budgets for this purpose. Although more resources are also available in the treatment, rehabilitation, welfare, and education areas,[19] the Government intends at the same time to take a hard law enforcement line, especially on trafficking. This intention is supported by all parties as was evident from the House of Commons debate on the Drug Trafficking Offences Act 1986. Street dealers, although not being quite so roundly condemned, probably also fall within this strict law enforcement policy. The judiciary has followed this lead. In *R.* v. *Aramah*[20] Lord Chief Justice Lane set out the evils of the drug trade and clearly stated that the courts should do everything in their power to pass deterrent sentences on those found guilty of drug trafficking, especially of class A drugs. Furthermore he stated that, because traffickers or couriers were often chosen because of their previous innocence, the personal circumstances and character of an offender were of less importance than in other cases, but confession and assistance to the police could be taken into account. The Court of Appeal suggested as appropriate sentences:

Class A

Importation—drugs worth £ 1 million or more.	12 to 14 years[21]
drugs worth £ 100,000 or more.	upwards of 7 years
appreciable quantities	at least 4 years

Class B (with particular reference to Cannabis)

Importation—large or massive amounts of drugs	10 years
20 kg or more	3 to 6 years
up to 20 kg.	18 months to 3 years

In the case of dealers in Britain it seems that lower sentences are likely, but the closer to the source of the drug the longer the sentence is likely

---

[18] Home Affairs Committee, *Fifth Report of The Home Affairs Committee: misuse of hard drugs (Interim Report)*, London; HMSO (House of Commons) 1985.

[19] Alan Wagstaff and Alan Maynard, *Economic Aspects of the Illicit Drug Market and Drug Enforcement Policies in the United Kingdom*, Home Office Research Study No. 95, London; HMSO 1988, 1.

[20] (1983) 76 CrAppR 190.

[21] The figure was raised to upwards of 14 years in *R.* v. *Bilinski* (1988) 86 CrAppR 146.

to be (this may reflect the fact that large quantities are often involved, the gain is likely to be greater, and the risk of being caught is lower). Although no one case sets out the tariff it seems likely that it would appear something like this:

Class A

Large-scale dealers	similar penalties as for importation[22]
Supplying to young persons	similar penalties as for importation[23]
Supplying small quantities	approximately 4 years[24] and seldom less than 3 years[25]

Class B (with particular reference to Cannabis)

Large-scale dealers 20 kg or more	similar penalties as for importation[26]
Manufacture or cultivation for sale	similar penalties as for importation[27]
Supplying small quantities	from 1 to 4 years[28]

This indicates a policy of strict law enforcement for importers and dealers, particularly large-scale dealers of all drugs.

It is more difficult to ascertain any central policy concerning users. In fact it is probably true to say that there is no policy, central or otherwise, but there are some operational practices which have grown up. Until the early 1970s Britain was known for its benign and essentially medical approach to users through its policy of heroin maintenance. Along with the very hard line on traffickers, it was hoped that this would both contain the demand for drugs to a minimum and remove the access to illicit drugs. From the early 1970s this approach was thought to have failed. Fear generated by the drug problem grew, the call for the intervention of law enforcement agencies became more prevalent and methadone was substituted for heroin in medical treatment. By the early 1980s the law enforcement agencies, particularly in large urban areas, were beginning to realize that they could not cope and would have to prioritize their intervention.[29] The police have now accepted a more permissive and less intrusive policy against drug users. There are local differences but most of the forty-three police forces now use the official caution for a first offence involving cannabis; a number may issue more than one caution, and some even caution small-time dealers in cannabis. For instance, a recent study found that a substantial minority of police officers in the Sussex force use their discretion to deal informally (either a warning or an informal caution) with simple cannabis offences (some even returned the drug to the offender but

---

[22] *R.* v. *Ashraf and Huq* (1981) 3 CrAppR (S) 287.

[23] *R.* v. *Macaulay* (1967) 52 CrAppR 230.

[24] *R.* v. *Gee* (1984) 6 CrAppR (S) 86 and *R.* v. *Guiney* [1985] CrimLRev. 751.

[25] *R.* v. *Aramah* (1983) 76 CrAppR 190.   [26] *R.* v. *Gilmore*, *The Times*, 21 May 1986.

[27] *R.* v. *Shaw* [1986] CrimLRev. 485.   [28] *R.* v. *Aramah* (1983) 76 CrAppR 190.

[29] Tony Judge, 'The Crisis in Drug Addiction' in B. Whitaker, *The Global Connection* (London; Wheatsheaf Books 1987).

most would confiscate or destroy it).[30] Sixteen forces caution for the first
use of hard drugs such as heroin, cocaine, and LSD. The Metropolitan and
Merseyside forces caution for any drugs use on the first, and in the case
of some substances even subsequent, offences. In most areas these decisions
have arisen not from careful analyses of the drugs problem but rather
as necessary to operational efficiency—there is therefore no policy. The
beginning of one may be on the horizon: at the Association of Chief Police
Officers (ACPO) Conference in 1993 senior police officers suggested the
adoption of an overall strategy on cautioning of people arrested for cannabis possession, and a substantial number of experienced drug squad
officers supported a policy of sale through licensed premises for both hard
and soft drugs.[31] Their support for such policies has resulted from a belief,
from a number of quarters, that it is one of the only ways of reducing both
drug-related and organized crime. This sort of support may permit real
policy changes to occur but in the interim some police forces, notably
Merseyside and parts of the Metropolitan force (Southwark), have taken
a rather more informed and real policy approach—on arresting for possession or drug-related crimes they make use of drug referral schemes which
give general advice and either help the user to live a reasonably useful and
healthy life with the habit or help them to do without the drug and build
a new drug-free life. These diversion schemes may be used at any stage of
the criminal justice process and have received some official recognition.[32]
Despite this change in attitude most of the convictions for drug offences
are for possession and nearly all relate to cannabis.[33]

Judicial approaches in cases of possession are much more difficult to
generalize. As with trafficking and supplying, courts tend to treat those in
possession of soft drugs (particularly cannabis) more leniently than other
users. Most cannabis users can expect a fine, with a custodial sentence
being reserved for persistent offenders. Generalization about hard drug
users is more difficult: much depends on the personal circumstances and
the willingness to be treated, but imprisonment cannot be ruled out even
for a first offence.[34]

What is lacking, compared with the Netherlands, is any systematic and
integrated multi-agency approach to the drug problem. As seen above, the
law enforcement element lacks policy. In the treatment area there has

[30] Andrew Frazer and Michael George, 'Cautions for Cannabis' (1991) *Policing*, 88. The
researchers also discovered that 20% of police approve of the decriminalization of cannabis
possession, whereas only about 8–12% of the general population would so approve.
[31] *Guardian*, Friday 14 May 1993.
[32] Home Office Green Paper, *Punishment, Custody and the Community* (London; HMSO
1988) and in the Criminal Justice Act 1991.
[33] Institute for the Study of Drug Dependence, 'Drug Misuse in Britain', in *National Audit
of Drug Misuse Statistics* (London; ISDD 1991).
[34] R. v. *Aramah* (1983) 76 CrAppR 190.

often been a policy but it has been driven by a response to the individual pathology rather than considerations of social or public health requirements.[35] Yet drug dependency clinics and other agencies are plentiful, particularly in large urban areas. Doctors in these clinics and some general practitioners are licensed to prescribe heroin and cocaine but most, although they may begin with this type of support, usually substitute methadone and then try to reduce doses or detoxify the addict. To back this up there are a number of rehabilitation houses and other agencies designed to help rebuild the addict's life but, from the mid-1970s, gross underfunding of this type of help has contributed to a heavy relapse rate by addicts. The Institute for the Study of Drug Dependence has initiated a number of family referral schemes for juveniles arrested for drug offences or drug-related offences which allow the users' parents to obtain help to facilitate reintegration into society.

Unfortunately the law enforcement and treatment elements of the system do not have an integrated policy. There are some encouraging local initiatives. In Merseyside a co-ordinated approach has tried to move away from prosecution towards harm reduction (trying not to allow law enforcement to increase the problems of the addict). The early assessment seems favourable: at the least there has been no unexpected increase in either drug offences or drug-related crime. Some doctors have also taken the initiative in prescribing heroin in place of the more normal methadone. One such is Dr John Marks in Widnes, whose action has been supported by the Cheshire Police as it has virtually removed heroin from the streets and drug-related crime has been reduced. Most such initiatives operate between police and drug dependency clinics, not between these agencies and the courts, where more mutual understanding would be helpful.[36]

Despite the lack of policy, some claim that the drugs problem in Britain is proportionate to that in Holland (taking account of the number of addicts per 1,000 population) and therefore perhaps the British lack of system is no less effective.[37]

COMMENT

The Netherlands has a drug policy and any enforcement, or lack thereof, arises out of a decision, usually emanating from the prosecutors. In Britain there is no real policy. Enforcement decisions have arisen because the

---

[35] Griffith Edwards, 'What Drives British Drug Policies?' (1989) 84 *British Journal of Addiction*, 219–26.
[36] Andrew Johns and Michael Gossop, 'Drug Use, Crime and the Attitudes of Magistrates' (1990) 30 *Medical Science Law*, 263.
[37] David Downes, *Contrasts in Tolerance* (Oxford; Clarendon Press 1988).

police, overloaded by strict law enforcement, have had to limit their intervention and their motivation has been driven by operational needs. However, despite the strong statements by British politicians, the final outcome in law enforcement is not vastly different in the two states. What is perhaps very different is the view society has of drug-taking and the way in which in the Netherlands the police work with other agencies towards a co-ordinated policy. In the Netherlands the low level of intervention has been accompanied by a gradual process of controlled integration of the drug user into society and a normalization of drug-taking. A comprehensive normalization policy would perhaps need to see the drug problem as related to all drug addictions—including illicit drugs, alcohol, tobacco, and any prescribed drugs such as tranquillizers—and have a co-ordinated treatment policy for all these. Partly due to the lack of any honest central policy to tackle the drug user problem, in Britain there is no such co-ordinated approach even for the illicit drug problem. Elements may exist in various regions but, without co-ordinating them, it seems impossible to achieve any real change. The Netherlands is certainly ahead of Britain in the beneficial provision of policy directives covering the whole area of drugs. Despite the welcome recent work of the Research and Planning Unit[38] in Britain (even if it is limited to economic questions mainly pertaining to law enforcement to the exclusion of treatment) the real difference may be more deep-rooted and cultural. The present discussions, initiated by the Drug Policy Foundation and the European Movement for the Normalization of Drug Policy, and aimed at harmonizing the European approach to the drug problem, may be doomed to failure unless they take account of this factor. Simple copy-cat use of policies from other countries may not be adequate.

CONSEQUENCES OF A CRIMINAL JUSTICE APPROACH

Both countries take a hard line on drug trafficking, and this has a number of consequences, some positive and others negative. A strong law enforcement programme against suppliers, as in Britain, may reduce availability of drugs, which usually leads to a price increase. Such a result is most likely if the probability of being caught is increased; less effect is felt by increasing the penalties or seizing assets. Care also has to be taken not to affect the supply of one drug only to facilitate a larger market in another.[39] Moreover, the increase in street price may lead to an increase in drug-related offences to pay for the habit: greater efficiency in catching traffickers and higher sentences have led to more professional, organized trade which

---

[38] Wagstaff and Maynard, *Economic Aspects of the Illicit Drug Market.*   [39] Ibid.

increasingly uses violence and/or corruption of enforcement agencies to protect itself. It also leads to the use of relatively innocent couriers for the most risky elements of the operation, so that even when imports are seized this rarely affects those most culpable in the operation. There are other social costs such as the cost of the enforcement system, the diversion of police and customs officers away from other tasks, overloading of the criminal justice system: most important is the constant pressure to increase the powers of the law enforcement agencies. The police use informants and infiltration methods which can lead them to use or request powers which lessen the constitutional guarantees in law and therefore have a negative effect on all criminal cases. The idea that due process frustrates crime control in the fight against drugs is a misleading but very strong notion. It is misleading because a criminal justice system that allows due process to slip is more prone to miscarriages of justice. In both countries there are instances of such lowering of the guarantees to the individual. Some arise out of the very operation used in drug control. For example in the Netherlands, to carry out a search an officer normally needs objective individualized grounds for suspicion, but in cases of drugs the courts have decided that it is sufficient to be present at a place where it is known that drugs are sold and used.[40]

In Britain and the Netherlands the elements which might most undermine the criminal justice system are the need to rely on undercover agents and the use of anonymous informants. British courts have refused to exclude evidence of undercover agents even when it is obtained by entrapment,[41] the only controls exist in unenforceable Home Office circulars. Furthermore although the officer in an undercover job often commits a crime for which he/she could be punished such actions are very rare. Similarly in the Netherlands the Supreme Court has permitted similar actions although setting some, minor controls.[42] Anonymous witnesses are rare: in Britain, because it is an adversarial system, they anyway appear in person for questioning and so more normally informants are not used as witnesses and are thus never identified. In Holland anonymous sources are more likely to remain unknown as it is possible for the court to question such witnesses: to an extent this has been condoned under the case law of the ECHR.[43] Both these practices interfere with rights of defendants. Another threat to human rights is the use of supergrasses, known informants who by giving information on other people hope to gain either a reduction in sentence or, in a few cases, even immunity for themselves. Another problem particular to Britain which affects users rather than

---

[40] *Ruimte*, HR 14 January 1975, [1975] NJ 207.
[41] *R. v. Sang* [1980] AC 402. [42] HR 4 December 1979, [1980] NJ 356.
[43] See *Brandstetter* v. *Austria*, ECHR Series A, No. 211, judgment of 28 August 1991, Apps. 11170/84, 12876/87 and 13468/87.

dealers arises because there are no rules concerning the interviewing of suspects under the influence of, or withdrawing from, a drug. Clearly to interview suspects who are incapacitated in this way can lead to unreliable testimony which may be withdrawn at a later stage. It also brings the criminal justice system into disrepute and could be avoided by barring the interrogation of anyone intoxicated by any drug, legal or illegal, and by the application of medication to addicts to stabilize their habit before questioning. In cases of doubt the police surgeon, trained in drug problems, should be called and in metropolitan areas there is a case for specialist surgeons.[44]

In both states investigative work is used to discover most of the big dealers and this involves the use of intrusive investigative measures. For example, in the Netherlands more than 50 per cent of telephone taps relate to drugs. Rather than being used to solve a specific crime these serve to gain information on future activities. To an investigation this is logical, dealers are unlikely to discuss old transactions, but generally such intrusive measures are only condoned because of suspicion arising out of a crime which has already been committed. It may be difficult to limit such measures to drugs cases, raising the problem of how to guarantee the necessary safeguards under the ECHR.[45]

The fight against illegal drugs is leading to a gradual retreat from norms of due process. This may be a very high price to pay. Given the relative ineffectiveness of the anti-drug campaigns it is essential that the evils of law enforcement should be balanced against the evils of drug-taking. Each state needs to consider at every stage whether the likely gains are worth the sacrifice of general rights and whether there are other, less socially damaging, means to control the drug problem.

EUROPEAN DRUG POLICY

There are many multilateral and bilateral initiatives in Europe which have a direct impact on drug policy. Most important in this respect are the Schengen Agreement of 1985 and Convention of 1990, the Maastricht Treaty on European Union, and the activities of the Council of Europe.

The Netherlands and Britain are closely involved in the process of Europeanization and this has a direct impact on their respective drug policies. Clearly as EC Member States both Britain and the Netherlands will be bound by the provisions of Maastricht, but Schengen is less widely applicable. Of the EC Member States, Britain, together with Ireland and

---

[44] Crawford, *Drugs and the Law* (1991), see n. 6.
[45] *Kruslin* v. *France*, Series A No. 176–A, judgment of 24 April 1990, App. 11801/85 (1990) 12 EHRR 547.

Denmark, has remained outside the Schengen Agreements, whilst all other EC Member States have made moves to join. Therefore the Netherlands, as a member of the Schengen Convention, is more affected by the European initiative. Each of these European initiatives will be considered in order.

The main function of the Schengen Agreement of 1985 and Convention of 1990 is the removal of internal border controls for economic reasons, but additional measures were considered necessary in matters like police and criminal justice operation, systematic registration of individuals, immigration and visa policy, asylum, control of fire-arms, drug policy, and drug legislation.

In the area of drugs the Schengen Agreement/Convention is directed at harmonization of legislation and policy (Article 19 of Schengen 1985).[46] The negotiations concerning this area were very complex, but basically the Netherlands was seen as being out of line with the strict drugs enforcement in all other states and faced strong pressure to alter its policies. Eventually the compromise set out in Chapter 6 of the Schengen Convention of 1990 was adopted. This deals specifically with narcotic drugs (it makes no distinction between hard and soft drugs) and leaves each state to decide the policy within its own territory but allows collective responsibility for the effects of that policy for other Schengen countries. To deal with the latter part a permanent working group has been set up to examine common problems relating to the combating of offences involving narcotic drugs and to draw up proposals to improve the practical and technical aspects of co-operation between the contracting parties. The Schengen Convention of 1990 stresses that a permissive approach in one Schengen state must not endanger a more repressive approach in another Schengen state, and requires each state to combat illegal import and export of drugs to the territory of other parties. This clearly indicates pressure on the Netherlands to bring its drug policy in line with the German and French standards. So although in Article 71 the Schengen Agreement formally acknowledges that drug policy remains a matter of national autonomy, it is going to be very difficult for the Netherlands to resist pressure to conform. Britain, as it is not a member of Schengen, is free of such pressures.

Drug policy is clearly also an important matter within the EC although the Community's formal competence in this domain is very limited. The protection of health is not an explicit aim of the Treaty of Rome but general initiatives, based on Article 235, can be adopted and, furthermore, Article 100A(3) of the Single European Act 1986 states that the Commission will presume a high level of health protection when proposing actions

---

[46] Art. 19 merely refers to legislation, but it was clear from the negotiations that harmonization of policy was the central goal, see P. L. Bot and A. J. van Doorn, 'Nederlands drugsbeleid blijft overeind' (1990) 139 *Algemeen Politieblad*, 253–8.

directed at a single market. One of the central aims of the EC is the free movement of people and goods, and this clearly has important consequences for health policy in the Member States. In some of the health initiatives that have been launched within the European Community the relevance of substance-use has been recognized. In 1977 and 1978 the Ministers of Health gave priority to:

- economic aspects of health policy,
- campaigns against smoking, illegal drug use, and poor food habits,
- reciprocal support in case of disasters or epidemic diseases.

Since 1984 the health ministers have met regularly to talk about matters such as drug use, cancer, AIDS, ecological matters, economic developments in health services, and about the free movement of people in Europe. Recently the linking of drugs with AIDS has brought the drug issue into the centre of European health policy. Although the Commission and the European Council have paid considerable attention to the matter of illicit drug use, this has drawn much more attention within the European Parliament.[47]

October 1990 heralded a change because the European Community, as a regional organization, became a signatory to the Convention on Illicit Trade in Drugs and Psychotropic Substances. According to Article 27(2) of this Convention, regional organizations for economic integration may indicate the reach of their competence in the regulation of substances which are often used for the illicit production of narcotic drugs or psychotropic substances. This opened the door to a more active involvement in drug control within the Community.

This change is evidenced in the Treaty on European Union, where the matter of drug use is referred to more than once: Article 129 of the EC Treaty (as added by the Treaty on European Union) sees primary prevention of 'drug addiction' as a matter of health policy; whilst Article K(1) deals with the free movement of people in Europe in the context of co-operation in justice and home affairs, and includes the fight against drugs as a matter of communal interest in so far as it is not already covered by co-operation in the areas of criminal justice, customs co-operation, and policy co-operation (Europol). With regard to earlier European Community policy the latter seems to entail a shift from health promotion to law enforcement. If that is the case then the matter of human rights will have increased relevance in the European drug policy context. Despite these incursions into areas which were previously perceived as the domain of each state, drug policy within the European Community will, for the time

---

[47] See resolutions of March 1980 (OJ C85 of 8 April 1980), May 1982 (OJ C149 of 14 June 1992) and September 1985 (OJ C262 of 14 October 1985).

being, remain a matter of intergovernmental co-operation, not of Community competence. In consequence drugs policy remains a matter of national autonomy, but there is pressure to harmonize and this is likely to increase. Due to the geographic position the pressure is more acutely felt on the Continent than in Britain.

The above changes in policy did not suddenly emerge, and their roots can probably be traced to the decision to set up, and the work of, CELAD (Comité Européen de Lutte Anti-Drogues/European Committee to Combat Drugs). CELAD was set up on 1 December 1989 and is made up of national co-ordinators, appointed by each Community Member State and by the European Commission. Soon afterwards the European Council commissioned the Group to take all necessary steps to ensure the vital co-ordination of Member States' actions in the main areas of the fight against the drugs scourge, namely prevention, health and social policy with regard to drug addicts, the suppression of drug-trafficking, and international action. In doing this CELAD takes into account resolutions of the European Parliament and seeks co-operation with the United Nations and the Pompidou Group,[48] and is represented on working groups which include the DEA (the US Federal Drugs Enforcement Administration), Trevi,[49]

---

[48] SEe P–PG (91) Inf. 1, 'A Brief Description of the Activities of the Pompidou Group and its Establishment Within the Framework of Europe', Council of Europe, Strasbourg, 9 September 1991. In resolution (80)2 the work of the Pompidou Group was taken over by the Co-operation Group to Combat Drug Abuse and Illicit Trafficking in Drugs. The Group has adopted a multi-disciplinary approach to provide a basis for co-ordination of action at European level. The work of the Pompidou Group was generally confidential but some publications were forthcoming: *Symposium on drug misusers in criminal proceedings: a difficult balance between punishment and treatment* (October 1986); *Multi-city study of drug misuse in Amsterdam, Dublin, Hamburg, London, Paris, Rome and Stokholm* (1987); *Symposium on methods of reaching young people particularly at risk* (May 1987); *Symposium on the criminal justice system and social rehabilitation measures for drug misusers* (December 1987); *Symposium on women and drugs* (April 1988); *Symposium on the role of primary care services in the treatment of drug misuse* (October 1990); *Study on basic criminal law concepts of Pompidou Group member countries on the prevention of drug trafficking and abuse*(April 1991); *Study and synopsis of basic criminal law concepts of Pompidou group member countries on the prevention of drug trafficking and its abuse.*

[49] Trevi (a French acronym for *Terrorisme, Radicalisme, Extrémisme et Violence Internationale*) is a political planning group set up in Rome in 1977 and made up of Ministers of the Interior and Justice drawn from European Community States (see Chap. 5). During the preparation of European Conventions (such as the Schengen Agreement and Community agreements) co-operation exists with Trevi on matters concerning internal security. Trevi has four working groups: I, II, III and Trevi 92. Within Trevi 92 the consequences of the elimination of the internal borders within Europe have been subject of study and initiative. In Dublin the Ministers accepted a 'Programme of Action' (June 1990) which began the setting-up of 'national drugs intelligence units' and the 'European Drugs Intelligence Unit'. It has been an issue of debate whether further police co-operation in Europe should be linked with Interpol structures or whether such operation should be independent from Interpol. In England (governmental paper: 'Practical Police Co-operation in the European Community') there was official support for an integration of EDIU in Interpol, but the idea to place a Europol within the General Secretariat of Interpol in Lyon was not accepted in the end.

HONLEA[50] and Interpol.[51] CELAD proposes that the Community and its Member States endeavour to establish close co-operation with the United States of America and other third-party countries on all aspects of the fight against drugs and therefore welcomed meeting with the USA, Canada, Japan, Sweden, and Australia in June 1990. CELAD has concentrated its efforts on drawing up a 'European programme to fight against drugs', which was presented to the European Council meeting in Rome on 14 and 15 December 1990. On that occasion, the Council asked the competent bodies to make sure that the programme was rapidly implemented, with special emphasis on the reduction of the demand for drugs. To achieve this objective CELAD recommends that information and statistics should be centralized and that the actions of the Member States and the Commission should complement each other. To this end guidelines are proposed on how to prevent drug-taking through dissemination of information; development of social and health services for drug addicts; organization of social and professional intervention; and the prevention of AIDS. CELAD also recommends harmonization of legislation in order to facilitate free movement of persons, which is a central European aim. On the other hand CELAD did propose to repress the trade in illicit drugs and psychotropic substances by reinforcing external border controls, intensifying co-operation inside European borders, fighting against the illicit production of drugs, taking measures against the laundering of the money acquired through the illicit trade in drugs, strengthening the judiciary and legal systems, and improving the collection of statistical information.[52] Clearly all of these are moving towards strict enforcement of drug control legislation.

Since the drug policy of the Netherlands is clearly different from that of other European countries and the practical application in Britain has, in certain respects, been moving towards the Dutch model, European harmonization will put pressure on both systems to alter their policies. In practice this will be far more marked in the Netherlands, where it could imply a retreat from pragmatism to more repressive action and less experimentalism.

---

[50] HONLEA is a co-operation of the Heads of National Drug Law Enforcement Agencies. Inter-regional and regional HONLEA meetings take place regularly with secretarial support from the Division of Narcotic Drugs. The emphasis of activities is on drug trafficking.

[51] Interpol has a central role in exchanging information between national police organizations. Its information infrastructure is constantly being used by its European members. Within EUSEC, the European Secretariat, the information exchange is analysed systematically, as well as the functioning of the European Contact Officers System (ECOS).

[52] The issue of combating money laundering had already been the focus of the Vienna Convention of 1988 on illicit drug-trafficking. Also the convening of a financial action task force by the Heads of State or Government of seven major nations and the President of the Commission of the European Communities in Paris in 1989 may be mentioned in this context. In the same context the Council of Europe Convention on laundering, search, seizure, and confiscation of the proceeds from crime may be referred to (Council of Europe, No. 141, Strasbourg, 8 November 1990).

Such a drugs policy is likely to take the shape of a war on drugs, such as that in the United States. Taking the USA as an example, the results of such a policy could be an increase in the number of addicts, an increase in violence in urban areas due to increased violent interaction in the drug market, police corruption, a deterioration in both the health and social situation of addicts. If these are the likely results of a war on drugs it is clear that such a solution is not suggested as a practical solution to the problem but rather as an outward manifestation of moral indignation at the use of, and traffic in, drugs. It has seemed to many, especially in European cities, that this is a high price to pay for moral purity. They fear a recourse to a war on drugs because they will have to deal with the consequences of such a moral crusade. To show their fear of such an outcome these cities have drawn up the Frankfurter Resolution, which asks for harm reduction to be adopted as the main target of any drugs policy, and they take the example of the Netherlands as the approach to be embraced. Unfortunately those in power have not given much credence to harm reduction policy. It seems likely that in time the Netherlands will be forced to retreat from its practical harm reduction strategies and to increase strict law-enforcement policies. Britain, because of its physical separation from the Continent and its refusal to accept Schengen, may be slightly less controlled by these European harmonization procedures and may there-fore be able to progress with practical policies of harm reduction such as those presently practised in the Netherlands and those recommended by the recent ACPO conference.[53]

CONCLUSION

Drugs are harmful. Drugs may damage an individual psychologically or physically and can even lead to death, usually as the result of an overdose. However, most drug-related deaths and much of the physical damage caused by drugs result from the impurities which are 'cut' into them to increase the profits (a direct result of criminalization). Users may become physic-ally or psychologically dependent, and the means of administration may cause damage, especially needle-sharing. Serious social consequences arise from general public health considerations, from family break-up, from child neglect, from accidents caused by drug use (including road accidents), from foetal damage, and from the loss or reduction of the economic use-fulness of the individual. Other social ills such as drug-related crime are largely a result of its criminalization. It may be necessary to try to separate those genuinely in need of, and more likely to respond to, treatment from

---

[53] See *Guardian*, Friday 14 May 1993.

those who are primarily law-breakers (for whom drug-taking is just another form of criminality).[54] Furthermore drug use and crime are, to an extent, interrelated and sometimes arise from a common cause: therefore in trying to tackle the drug problem the problem of crime is also addressed. Thus the social setting which most frequently produces opiate use also spawns many other social ills, including crime. It may be that more might therefore be achieved through urban renewal and the creation of real jobs than through either treatment or law enforcement. Drug use is not always problematic. There are probably a large number of recreational drugs users, who cause no problems either for their environment or for their own health.[55] The policies now emerging in Europe do not seem to take account of these factors.

Drug policy as it is described here has long historical roots and is not primarily developed on the basis of the analysis of current drug problems and of the capacities and characteristics of the services and organizations involved. In Europe the Netherlands has a reputation for tolerance and pragmatism in drug matters. Neighbouring countries following more repressive paths fear spill-over effects of this tolerance owing to the removal of border controls. This situation results in political pressure on the Netherlands to shift policies in a more repressive direction. The British drug policy has been much less controversial in the European context, despite the fact that Britain has developed certain harm reduction policies, most notably heroin prescription that, due to the attitude of neighbouring countries, was not even permitted in the Netherlands. Both the Netherlands and Britain have favoured a medical approach towards hard drug users and a repressive approach to traffickers in hard drugs. In soft drugs the pseudo-legal acceptance of small-scale dealing in the Netherlands is different from anything in this field in Britain. Europe as a region and the EC in particular is becoming increasingly involved in formulating drug policies which are intended to be harmonized throughout the Community. It is thus of significance for both the Netherlands and Britain that European policy-making has been driven by different objectives: the European tendency is moralistic and thus pursues repression whatever the costs. This is likely to have a direct impact on the drug policy in the Netherlands, whilst in Britain more autonomy may be possible. Perhaps Britain can profit from this freedom and consider some of the Dutch policies (though these will need to be altered to fit in with British culture), along with harm reduction ideas of its own. Britain could then possibly lead the way in reducing the harmful effects of drug use.

[54] Richard Hammersley, 'Drug Addiction and Crime' (1988) 83 *British Journal of Addiction*, 445–6.

[55] Peter Cohen, *Cocaine Use in Amsterdam in Non Deviant Subcultures* (Amsterdam; 1989).

9

Diversion, Europeanization and the Mentally Disordered Offender

PHIL FENNELL AND FRANS KOENRAADT

INTRODUCTION

In recent years diversion policies for mentally disordered offenders have
been adopted with particular fervour in England and Wales. They rest on
three principles: (1) that special safeguards are necessary governing questioning of mentally disordered suspects in the police station and their
confession evidence, since they may be especially liable to make false
admissions;[1] (2) that mentally disordered suspects and offenders should be
diverted away from the penal system and into the health and social care
system; (3) that, once in the psychiatric system, patients are entitled to be
cared for in the least restrictive setting commensurate with the need to
protect the public.[2] However, the gulf between policy and practice remains
wide because, although a legal framework for diversion has existed since
1959 and since 1984 for the protection of vulnerable suspects in the police
station, it was not until 1990 that Circular 66/90 on the Diversion of
Mentally Disordered Offenders from Custody was issued following renewed
expressions of concern about the high numbers of mentally disordered
prison inmates and the increasing numbers of suicides in prisons.[3]

In the Netherlands, which has a reputation as a model for humanitarian
forensic psychiatric practice, the demand for forensic psychiatric assessment
has decreased in recent years, reflecting concerns to limit the psychiatrization of criminal justice, lack of faith in the efficacy of psychiatric treatment, and an increasing belief that the TBS regime for dangerous mentally

With thanks to Nico Jörg, Bert Swart, and Johan Legemaate for their help concerning the
legal position in the Netherlands

[1] See *R.* v. *Ward* (1993) 96 CrAppR 1; *R.* v. *Raghip, The Times,* 9 December 1991; and *R.*
v. *McKenzie, Independent,* 28 July 1992—where convictions based on confession evidence of
mentally-vulnerable defendants were quashed.
[2] The principle of the least restrictive alternative was frequently mentioned in the debates
leading to the Mental Health Act 1983, and its importance was re-emphasized in the *Review
of Health and Social Services for Mentally Disturbed Offenders and Others Requiring Similar
Services* (Chairman Dr John Reed), HMSO 1992, Cm 2088.
[3] *The Report of a Review by Her Majesty's Chief Inspector of Prisons of Suicide and Self
Harm in Prison Service Establishments* (The Tumim Report), 1990, Cm 1383.

disordered patients offers insufficient protection of the public. In response to this concern, forensic psychiatric hospitals have become increasingly closed institutions through the renewal of old buildings and the installation of electronic security systems.

A key issue for both systems has been the provision of safeguards for the rights of offenders who become detained patients, and we shall see a strong influence from the European Convention on Human Rights (ECHR) in enhancing their entitlement to active participation in the judicial determination of the duration of their psychiatric detention.

In the Police Station

The Police and Criminal Evidence Act (PACE) 1984 and PACE Code of Practice C provide for the special treatment of suspects appearing to be mentally disordered, mentally handicapped, or mentally incapable of understanding the significance of questions, a recognition of the fact that they may be particularly prone in certain circumstances to provide information which is unreliable, misleading, or self-incriminating. The custody officer must immediately call in the forensic medical examiner (formerly known as the police surgeon) or, in an urgent case, send the person to hospital or call in the nearest available doctor.[4] A mentally disordered person may not be interviewed or asked to sign a statement without an 'appropriate adult' attending unless the criteria are met for a superintendent or other senior officer to authorize an urgent interview.[5]

There is evidence to show that the number of occasions on which appropriate adults are summoned to the police station is very low by comparison with the numbers of suspects known to be vulnerable by reason of mental disorder.[6] An appropriate adult may be a relative or guardian of the suspect, a person experienced in dealing with the mentally disordered or handicapped, such as a social worker, or some other responsible adult who is not a police employee.[7] The role has three aspects: (1) to advise the person being questioned; (2) to observe whether or not the interview is being conducted properly and fairly; and (3) to facilitate communication

[4] PACE, Code C, para. 9.2.
[5] PACE, Code C, para 11.14. For the exceptions, see para. 11.14 and Annex C.
[6] Barry Irvine and Ian MacKenzie, *Police Interrogation* (1989) (London; Police Foundation), 70–3; Keith Bottomley, *The Impact of PACE on Policing in a Northern Force* (1991); G. Gudjonsson, I. Clare, S. Rutter, and J. Peane, *Persons at risk during interviews in police custody: the identification of vulnerabilities*, Royal Commission on Criminal Justice, research study No. 12 (London; HMSO 1993).
[7] Ibid., para. 1.7 (b).

with the person being interviewed.[8] It is difficult to achieve a balance between these elements, and there is a danger that, in facilitating communication, an untrained appropriate adult will unwittingly lean towards acting as the agent of the interviewing police officer.

Admissibility of Confession Evidence

Section 77 of PACE states that where the case against a mentally handicapped defendant depends wholly or substantially on a confession by him and the judge is satisfied: (a) that he is mentally handicapped; and (b) that the confession was not made in the presence of an independent person, the judge must warn the jury that there is a special need for caution before convicting the accused in reliance on the confession. In practice, however, this is a 'fall back' provision, which 'serves a very limited, supporting role for those confessions which are allowed to proceed for the jury's consideration',[9] and does not rule out the possibility that the confession of a mentally disordered person may be excluded under sections 76 and 78, as having been unfairly obtained.[10]

In *R. v. McKenzie*[11] the appellant was a compulsive confessor of below-average intelligence, who had admitted to a number of murders which it later transpired he could not have committed. Lord Taylor CJ, delivering the judgment of the Court of Appeal, said that where:

(1) the prosecution case depended wholly upon confessions;
(2) the defendant suffered from a significant degree of mental handicap; and
(3) the confessions were unconvincing to a point where a jury properly directed could not convict upon them,

then the judge, assuming he had not excluded the confession earlier, should withdraw the case from the jury. In *R. v. Ward*[12] the Court of Appeal found that admissions made by the appellant, who had been suffering from a severe personality disorder, could not be relied upon as being true and her conviction was overturned as unsafe and unsatisfactory.[13]

In the Netherlands there are no special rules governing the interrogation of mentally disordered suspects as such, but there is a special title of the Code of Criminal Procedure devoted to assuring the assistance of responsible persons, once the court has decided that a defendant is unable

---

[8] PACE, Code C, para. 11.16.
[9] V. Bevan and K. Lidstone, *The Investigation of Crime: A Guide to Police Powers* (London; Butterworths 1991), 414.
[10] As happened in *R. v. Moss* (1990) 91 CrAppR 371.
[11] *Independent*, 28 July 1992.   [12] *Independent*, 5 June 1992.
[13] For the position where the suspect is suffering from psychotic illness, see *R. v. Miller* [1986] 1 WLR 1191.

to look after his own interests by reason of insanity.[14] The court may give a declaratory verdict to that effect at any stage of the criminal process, including pre-trial, and if this is done various safeguards from the Code of Criminal Procedure regarding juvenile offenders apply, such as the compulsory assistance of parents, other relatives, or guardians. However, these provisions are seldom used.

Equally there are no special rules on the admissibility of confessions by mentally vulnerable suspects. The general rule is that the interrogator should refrain from obtaining answers which cannot be said to be given voluntarily. The defence is not entitled to have a confession ruled out simply because it was given by a mentally disordered suspect, but if the confession is shown to be involuntary, it may be excluded from evidence.

More important limits on police behaviour in the interrogation of mentally disordered suspects are imposed by the institutional incentives and impediments described by Field, Alldridge, and Jörg elsewhere in this book. The evidentiary centrality of the *dossier* in Dutch criminal procedure, which encompasses screening of its contents by the public prosecutor, by the investigating judge (in serious cases), and finally by the trial court, inspires the police to present a professional impression of the manner in which they have interrogated suspects who are vulnerable by reason of mental disorder. Particularly if the offence is serious, more attention will be paid to detail, as a result of which the mentally disordered offender has to convince the police that he is the real perpetrator. Only then will the police close the file and send it to the prosecutor, who must in turn be convinced before charges will be brought. So although there are few formal rules, it is hard to envisage a Dutch judge placing reliance on a confession such as that in *McKenzie*. Presuming such vigilance on the part of the police, prosecutors and the judiciary, and in the absence of a jury in the Dutch system, a provision analogous to section 77 of PACE would be otiose.

DIVERSION FROM CUSTODY

Diversion policies for mentally disordered offenders aim to promote the welfare of the offender while at the same time protecting society through preventive therapeutic detention. They create a tension between the welfare entitlements of the offender to be looked after in a setting which is appropriate to an ill person and his interest in not being detained on grounds of public protection for longer than any sentence of imprisonment which he could have received for his offence. In examining any diversion

---

[14] CCP Art. 509.

policy we must be aware of the dangers inherent in any psychiatrization of criminal justice, namely that policies of preventive detention may be dressed in therapeutic garb, and sight may be lost of the principle that the duration of detention should be in proportion to the severity of the offence. Instead of a determinate sentence, the authority to detain a mentally disordered offender sentenced to hospital may be renewed at specified intervals and detention is therefore for an indeterminate period. The offender may be released after a short time if the goals of therapy have been achieved, even if the offence is serious. On the other hand a trivial offender who has not responded to treatment may be detained for many years. The public defence element in the goals of diversion poses most clearly the question of the legal safeguards which are needed to ensure that continued psychiatric detention is really necessary. Before considering the tension between psychiatrization and the rights of psychiatric detainees, we must describe the legal mechanisms for diversion.

(A) Pre-Trial

England and Wales

In England and Wales, diversion is promoted by Home Office Circular 66/90, which has two principal goals. The first is the diversion of petty offenders with a mental disorder away from the criminal justice system by asking the police and prosecutors not to prosecute such cases where this is not required by the public interest. Treatment as an in-patient or an out-patient may take place informally or under civil powers of detention or guardianship. There are significant obstacles to the success of this policy. Psychiatric hospitals cannot be obliged to admit anyone and, because they are contracting in size and being closed pursuant to government community care policies, they are more selective about the patients they will accept.

The Code for Crown Prosecutors states that where there is evidence that an accused or person under examination was suffering from a mental disorder at the time the offence was committed, prosecution will not be appropriate unless it is overridden by the wider public interest. The principal criterion is the gravity of the offence, but other relevant considerations include the circumstances of any previous offences, the nature of the person's condition, the likelihood of his further offending, and the availability of suitable alternatives to prosecution.[15] The Code also advises the discontinuance of prosecutions where the probability that the ordeal of criminal proceedings will have adverse effects on the defendant's mental health outweighs the considerations in favour of prosecution.

The second goal of Circular 66/90 is that where cases are prosecuted,

---

[15] Code for Crown Prosecutors, para. 8 (v) (a).

mentally disordered offenders should be given a therapeutic rather than a penal sentence. Section 4 of the Criminal Justice Act 1991, passed since the Circular was issued, places a duty on a court, before passing a custodial sentence on a defendant who appears to be mentally disordered, to obtain and consider a medical report from a doctor with experience in the diagnosis and treatment of mental disorder. The duty is not absolute in that the court need not obtain a medical report if it considers it unnecessary to do so.

The Mental Health Act 1983 introduced two new powers allowing courts to remand unsentenced defendants for assessment or for treatment. Although their use has gradually increased, these have been used very infrequently. The power to remand to hospital for treatment was used only thirty-eight times in 1989–90, and the remand for assessment 283 times. This contrasts with over 5,000 psychiatric reports carried out in prisons in the same period.

The Netherlands

In the Netherlands diversion from the entire criminal justice system may take place when a person is arrested by the police, who may, instead of initiating a criminal procedure by informing the public prosecutor, choose to arrange a civil commitment, particularly if the person has a history of previous admissions to psychiatric hospital. Once the matter has reached the prosecutor, there are no prosecutorial guidelines for the non-prosecution of mentally disordered offenders, and the appropriate disposal will be a matter for the court. Forensic mental health assessments may be carried out on an out-patient (the majority of cases) or in-patient basis in a psychiatric hospital,[16] or in the Pieter Baan Centre (the observation hospital of the Ministry of Justice). In most court districts the district psychiatric service is involved in arranging forensic mental health reports if the examining judge needs one, by a psychiatrist, a psychologist, or both. In 1991 in the court district of Amsterdam 324 reports were presented to the courts (105 by a psychiatrist, 107 by a psychologist, 106 by both a psychiatrist and a psychologist and 6 by a neurologist).[17]

Although there has in the past been a certain reluctance on the part of psychiatric institutions to carry out forensic assessments for the criminal justice system,[18] recently they have been more prepared to admit forensic psychiatric patients and make forensic psychiatric reports, and special wards for these patients have been constructed in some Dutch mental hospitals.

---

[16] ex Arts. 196–8 WvSv (CCP).

[17] *Jaarverslagen 1991 Bureau Psychiatrisch/Psychologisch Adviseurs en Districtpsychiatrische Diensten*, 's-Gravenhage; Ministerie van Justitie 1992.

[18] P. D. Barneveld, *De bereidheid van psychiatrische instellingen tot observatie en rapportage in het kader van een gerechtelijk vooronderzoek*, 's-Gravenhage; Ministerie van Justitie 1983.

The Pieter Baan Centre is a criminal justice institution where defendants who are suspected of serious crimes can be subject to intensive psychiatric and psychological observation and assessment over a seven-week period using a multidisciplinary approach.[19] The Centre has a total capacity of thirty-two beds. It is equipped for forensic behavioural evaluation, but has hardly any facilities for treatment. The voluminous multidisciplinary reports end with a conclusion concerning the degree of the offender's responsibility and with a recommendation whether mental health intervention or treatment are necessary in order to prevent recidivism. Simple diagnosis in terms of psychiatric classificatory systems is not enough; the links between the possible mental disorder and the commission of the crime have to be explained.[20]

In the Netherlands, as a consequence of Montesquieu's '*séparation des pouvoirs*', the assessment and treatment of mentally ill offenders are strictly separated and take place in different institutions. This contrasts with the United Kingdom, where an offender may be assessed in an institution prior to sentence, and then sentenced to be detained and treated in that same institution. In the United Kingdom the majority of court reports are made by psychiatrists and, whilst reports from psychologists are not unknown, they are much less frequent than in the Netherlands. A further point of contrast is that in the Netherlands if a criminal court is going to sentence a patient to a psychiatric disposal, the person's mental disorder must have had an effect on his responsibility for his criminal act. In England and Wales this is not a legal prerequisite of a psychiatric sentence, as long as the court has before it reports that the offender is suffering from mental disorder.

(B) The Relevance of the Mental State of the Defendant at the Trial—Unfitness to Plead

The Netherlands

In the Netherlands the fact that a defendant is mentally incapacitated will not prevent the court from discussing the most appropriate course of action. All defendants have the duty to stand trial. Article 16 of the Code of Criminal Procedure provides that, where a defendant is mentally disordered to the extent that he does not understand the meaning of his prosecution, the court may order a break in the prosecution and take any necessary measures. A pre-trial detention order may stay in force. However, Article 16 is rarely used because, among other reasons, the Supreme Court

---

[19] A. W. M. Mooij, F., Koenraadt, and J. M. J. Lommen-van Alphen (eds.), *Considering the Accused* (Amsterdam; Swets & Zeitlinger 1991).
[20] Ibid.

reserves this provision for the most serious cases of mental illness (*krankzinnigheid*).[21]

England and Wales

In England and Wales, a defendant is unfit to plead if he is unable to plead to the indictment, and is unable to understand the proceedings so as to be able to challenge jurors, to understand and give evidence, and to make a proper defence.[22] In recent years few defendants have been found unfit to plead.[23] This was because, as with the plea of insanity, the automatic consequence was that the defendant would be subject to a hospital order with restrictions on discharge without limit of time. Under the old law, the defendant could be returned to court to face trial if, at a later date, his psychiatrist advised that he was fit to do so, but this did not happen often.

The Criminal Procedure (Insanity and Unfitness to Plead) Act 1991 provides for 'a trial of the facts' to take place where a defendant is found to be unfit to plead. A jury is required to determine whether it is satisfied that the defendant did the act or made the omission charged against him as an offence. It remains to be seen whether the effect of this change will be completely to remove any mental element as a fact that must be proved, but the intention is that the defendant's mental state at the time of the act or omission should be irrelevant. If the jury is satisfied that the defendant did the act or made the omission charged, it must make a finding to that effect; if it is not so satisfied, it will be obliged to return a verdict of acquittal. The defendant must always be represented in a trial of the facts, whether by someone chosen by him, by a lawyer appointed by the court, or by the Official Solicitor who has the task of representing incapacitated people in legal proceedings.[24] Since the 1991 Act came into force, the Crown Court judge has discretion to impose a range of different therapeutic disposals, and may even discharge the defendant absolutely, except in a murder case, where the sentence for the offence is fixed by law and there must be a restriction order without limit of time.[25]

These changes in the law were prompted by injustices in cases where, because of defendants' unfitness to plead, they were subject to potentially

---

[21] HR 5 February 1980, [1980] NJ 104 (the *Menten* case).

[22] *R. v. Pritchard* (1836) 7 C & P 303.

[23] D. H. Grubin, 'Unfit to plead in England and Wales 1976–1988: A Survey' [1991] *British Journal of Psychiatry*, 540.

[24] Home Office Circular 93/91 on the Criminal Procedure (Insanity and Unfitness to Plead) Act 1991, para. 13.

[25] Criminal Procedure (Insanity) Act 1964, s. 5, as amended by the Criminal Procedure (Insanity and Unfitness to Plead) Act 1991, s. 3 and Sched. 1. For a full discussion of the 1991 Act see S. White, 'The Criminal Procedure (Insanity and Unfitness to Plead) Act 1991' [1991] *CrimLRev.* 4–14 and P. Fennell (1992) 55 *MLR* 547–55.

indefinite commitment to hospital without the adequacy of the prosecution case being tested, whether or not the offence was serious.

(C) The Relevance of the Mental State of the Defendant to Sentencing

The Netherlands

In the Netherlands the Criminal Code distinguishes between two categories of mentally disordered offender. On the one hand are persons who are disturbed to such an extent that their offences cannot be 'imputed' to them because of mental deficiency or mental illness.[26] They ought never to be convicted and may, if dangerous to themselves, to other persons, or to property, be committed by a criminal court to a psychiatric hospital for a period of one year, renewable for further periods of one year.[27] Once committed to hospital, such patients 'leave' the criminal justice system altogether. They are then subject to the same legal regime as civilly committed patients, the only exception being that, if leave from the institution is to be granted, the advice of the prosecutor must be obtained beforehand.

On the other hand, if it is necessary for the protection of the public, the court may direct that a mentally disordered offender be placed at the Government's disposal. This is called a *Terbeschikkingstelling* (TBS) measure. There are two general types of disposal open to a Dutch criminal court, *straffen* (punishments) and *maatregelen* (measures). *Straffen* require responsibility since they involve inflicting intentional punishment on the offender. *Maatregelen* do not require responsibility, as punishment is not a goal, but often it exists as a by-product, as in the case of confiscation of illegal profits. TBS is the only measure which cannot be imposed on an offender with full responsibility.

The conditions for imposing an in-patient TBS are that:

(a) the offence is punishable with at least four years' imprisonment, or is on a list of specified serious offences;[28]

(b) the TBS is necessary for the protection of other persons, the public or property;[29] and

(c) there must be a recent (within the past year) forensic mental health report written by both a psychiatrist and another mental health expert (who in most cases is a psychologist), demonstrating defective development or impairment of the person's mental faculties at the time when the offence was committed.

---

[26] Criminal Code, Art. 39.

[27] The new Act on formal admissions to psychiatric hospital (BOPZ) came into force in January 1994, Art. 19 providing that once the person has been detained for five years continuously, renewal takes place at two-yearly intervals. Civil commitments lasting for longer than five years are very rare.

[28] Criminal Code, Art. 37a, s. 1(1).   [29] Ibid., s. 1(2).

In-patient TBS orders require detention in a specialist TBS hospital. This measure is imposed approximately a hundred times a year. In February 1993 the total number of persons subject to an in-patient TBS order was 606, and thirty-nine were subject to an out-patient order. If the offence cannot be imputed to the defendant and the conditions for imposing a TBS are met, the court has a choice between commitment to psychiatric hospital or a TBS measure. If the offender's mental disorder is such that the offence cannot be imputed to him, he will be sentenced to an immediate TBS. If his responsibility was diminished at the time of the offence, then a TBS measure may be imposed in conjunction with a prison sentence. If this happens, the offender serves the prison sentence first, and the TBS measure is suspended until that term expires. This option is often used for patients with personality disorders. A Dutch visitor to forensic mental hospitals abroad will often find the large number of schizophrenics in such hospitals striking, whereas in Dutch TBS hospitals the majority of patients are psychopaths or patients with personality disorders. This may be because the psychotic patients tend to be treated in the general psychiatric hospitals rather than in TBS clinics. However, in recent years the percentage of TBS patients suffering from psychosis has shown a dramatic increase. About one third of the TBS population consists of sex offenders who have committed rape, sexual assaults, or molestation of children.

The system has important consequences. Offenders subject to TBS measures do not leave the criminal justice system. The criminal court that imposed the TBS also decides on extension of periods of detention. In so doing, it has to observe a number of provisions of the Criminal Code and the Code of Criminal Procedure. The internal rights of TBS patients are considerably more developed than those of offenders who enter the system of general mental institutions, although a Bill on psychiatric patients' rights is currently under discussion.

An Act of 1986 (The TBS Act 1986), which came into force in 1988, made important changes to the TBS system. One of its principal goals was to give effect to the principle of proportionality between offence and sanction by limiting TBS to serious crimes. This reflected a trend which was already under way. In 1971, 43 per cent of TBS detainees had been convicted of crimes against property, whereas in 1983 the equivalent was only 4 per cent. In 1971 39 per cent of the TBS population had committed offences involving physical aggression, whereas in 1988 91 per cent had committed such offences.

England and Wales

The English arrangements for sentencing mentally disordered offenders to detention in hospital do not share the necessary focus of the Dutch system on the state of mind of the offender at the time of committing the offence. Unless the charge is murder, whatever the mental condition of the offender at the time of the offence, a hospital order may be imposed as long as the court has before it reports to the effect that he is mentally disordered at the time of sentence for an offence punishable with imprisonment. Restrictions on discharge may be imposed by a Crown Court if it is considered necessary to protect the public from serious harm. However, there are two defences where the mental state of the offender at the time of the offence is relevant; the insanity defence, and the defence of diminished responsibility to a murder charge.

The insanity defence may be pleaded in any criminal case. If successful in a trial of a less serious offence in a magistrates' court, it entitles the defendant to an acquittal. If successful in the Crown Court, it entitles the defendant to a special verdict of not guilty by reason of insanity. At the time of committing the act, the accused must have had such a defect of reason from disease of the mind that he did not know either the nature and quality of his act, or that it was wrong.[30] Medical evidence is needed from two doctors, one of whom must have psychiatric expertise. The defence has been little used in recent years,[31] partly because 'it requires the defendant to be very mad indeed not to know the nature of his act or, if he did know what he was doing, not to know that it would attract the unfavourable attentions of the police'.[32] A second reason for its infrequent use was that until the coming into force of the Criminal Procedure (Insanity and Unfitness to Plead) Act 1991 the automatic consequence of a special verdict in the Crown Court was that the defendant was made subject to a restriction order[33] without limit of time, raising the possibility of indefinite detention. Since the 1991 Act came into force, the Crown Court judge has discretion to impose a range of different therapeutic disposals, and may even discharge the defendant absolutely, unless the offence is murder, where a restriction order without limit of time is mandatory.[34]

The plea of diminished responsibility is available only in murder cases. The accused must be suffering from such abnormality of mind as substantially impaired his mental responsibility for his acts or omissions in doing or being a party to the killing.[35] It is for the jury to decide on the balance of probabilities whether the defence has been established, but the court will accept pleas of guilty to manslaughter except in cases where medical

---

[30] *McNaghten's Case* (1843) 10 Clark and Finnelly 200, 201.

[31] See R. D. Mackay, 'Fact and Fiction about the Insanity Defence' [1990] *CrimLRev.* 247–55.

[32] Butler Committee Report, para. 18.37.

[33] The Mental Health Act 1983, ss. 37 and 41.

[34] Criminal Procedure (Insanity) Act 1964, s. 5, as amended by the Criminal Procedure (Insanity and Unfitness to Plead) Act 1991, s. 3 and Sched. 1.

[35] Homicide Act 1957, s. 2.

opinion is divided or is open to challenge.[36] The result of a successful plea
of diminished responsibility is that the defendant is convicted of manslaughter. This means that, instead of being bound to impose a life sentence, the judge has sentencing discretion, and could impose a hospital
order with or without restrictions. Sometimes a charge of murder will be
dropped in exchange for a plea of guilty to manslaughter on grounds of
diminished responsibility, although the judge may insist on a murder trial
taking place.

Turning to sentencing options, less serious offenders may be subject to
probation with a condition of in-patient or out-patient psychiatric treatment.[37] The effects of the order must be explained to the offender, whose
consent is necessary before an order may be made. The annual figures
since 1985 show between 850 and 890 probation orders with a condition of
non-residential psychiatric treatment, between 130 and 170 with a condition of residential psychiatric treatment.[38]

A Crown Court or a Magistrates' Court may impose a hospital order in
the case of a defendant convicted of any offence punishable by imprisonment (unless the offence is murder). The court must be satisfied, on the
evidence of two doctors,[39] that the patient is suffering from mental illness,
severe mental impairment, mental impairment, or psychopathic disorder
which makes detention in hospital for medical treatment appropriate. Unless
a hospital is willing to take a patient, no hospital order may be made, but
courts are empowered to request the Regional Health Authority responsible for the patient to give information about hospitals where the patient
could be accommodated.[40] Since 1984 the annual number of hospital orders has ranged between approximately 650 and 750.

A Crown Court may attach restrictions to a hospital order where it is
satisfied that such an order is necessary for the protection of the public
from 'serious harm'.[41] At least one doctor must have given oral evidence
in court.[42] The effect of a restriction order is that the patient may not be
granted leave of absence, transferred to another hospital, or discharged

---

[36] *R.* v. *Cox* (1968) 52 CrAppR 130; *R.* v. *Vinagre* (1979) 69 CrAppR 104.
[37] Powers of the Criminal Courts Act 1973, s. 3.
[38] Home Office, *Probation Statistics England and Wales 1990*, Home Office; London, April
1992, table 2.10.
[39] One of whom must be recognized under s. 12 of the 1983 Act as having special experience in the diagnosis and treatment of mental disorder.
[40] Mental Health Act 1983, ss. 37(4) and 39. In its Third Biennial Report (1989, London,
HMSO, at 36), the Mental Health Act Commission recorded its disappointment at 'the
limited use' made by the courts of the power under s. 39.
[41] Ibid., s. 41. In *R.* v. *Birch* ([1989] *CrimLRev.* 757) Mustill LJ stated that the term 'serious
harm' need not be confined to personal injury, but that the potential harm must be serious
and a high probability of the recurrence of minor offences will no longer be sufficient to
justify a restriction order.
[42] Ibid., s. 41(2).

(except by a Mental Health Review Tribunal), without the permission of the Home Secretary, a Government minister.[43] During 1990, 133 restriction orders were made in England and Wales. Since 1987, between eighty and ninety patients have been admitted per year to top security special hospitals pursuant to restriction orders.

With psychiatric probation orders, hospital orders, and restriction orders it is not a legal prerequisite that there be a connection between the offender's mental disorder and the offence, although in practice such a connection often exists.

(D) Extending Detention

The Netherlands

TBS placements last for two years in the first instance, renewable for one or two years on an application by the public prosecutor. The director of the hospital may discharge the patient subject to conditions but only with the approval of the Minister of Justice, who may at any time terminate an in-patient or an out-patient TBS measure.[44] If the measure is to be extended, the prosecutor must apply to the court in question not more than two months and not less than one month before the expiry of the current measure. The 1986 Act introduced a 'maximum' term of four years, which is only extendable if a violent crime is involved endangering other people and/or if the extension is necessary for reasons of public safety.[45] In practice TBS detention frequently exceeds the maximum of four years, because the majority of measures are imposed for serious offences like murder, manslaughter, rape, and sexual assault. The average duration of a TBS is five years, except for detainees who have committed a sexual offence, whose average time in detention is eight and a half to nine years.

When an extension results in a total period of detention exceeding six years or a multiple of six years, the new law requires that the court have before it a recent report by a psychiatrist and a psychologist, who may not be affiliated to the institution where the patient is detained.[46] The new law also introduced equality between the psychiatrist and the other forensic expert (usually a psychologist) in place of the previous hierarchical relationship in which the psychiatrist was dominant. This contrasts sharply with the United Kingdom where the psychiatric profession has a near monopoly of forensic reporting work.

In the *Keus* case, a TBS patient complained that the court considering the extension of the measure did not reach a decision until the current measure had expired, and that his detention was therefore a breach of

---

[43] Ibid., s. 41(3)(c).   [44] Criminal Code, Art. 38h–38i.
[45] Criminal Code, Art. 38e.   [46] Code of Criminal Procedure, Art. 509o.

Article 5(1) because it had no express basis in domestic law.[47] Keus's complaint eventually reached the ECHR, but by the time the Court delivered judgment, the TBS Act 1986 had already been brought into force. It transferred the provisions on the prolongation of TBS from the Criminal Code to the Code of Criminal Procedure, where they became Articles 509o–509x. Article 509q now expressly provides that, as long as an extension application has been made by the prosecutor within the time period specified above, the original order remains in force even if the court has not reached a decision on prolongation before the orginal order expires. Article 509t provides that the court must decide on the prolongation request within two months after the expiry of the original order, although, if the court is considering refusing the extension, that period may be five months. If the court does not reach a decision within these time limits, it must be presumed now that the offender is entitled to release, the consequence which the Hoge Raad would not accept in *Keus*. The prosecutor's application must be supported by a report from the clinic on the physical and mental health of the patient, and a reasoned declaration, which should come from the doctor treating the patient, as to the desirability of extending the measure. A decision whether or not to order extension of a TBS measure is subject to appeal by the public prosecutor and the offender. One of the five Courts of Appeal, the Arnhem court, is empowered to hear those cases. The decision-making panel consists of two expert 'counsel' who are psychiatrists or psychologists as well as five judges.[48]

In 1992 TBS hospitals recommended extension of TBS orders in 389 cases. By May 1993 the courts had decided 341 of these applications. In twenty-seven cases the hospital recommended ending the TBS, and this was followed in twenty-six cases. In 314 cases extension for one or two years was proposed, and in twenty-eight of these the court decided to end the TBS order.[49] There is considerable debate about so-called 'contrary release', where the court decides to discharge against the advice of the therapists in the TBS hospital.[50] Hospital staff use a higher threshold for granting leave than do the judges, and there is a tendency for TBS institutions to avoid taking responsibility for discharging patients themselves, by recommending prolongation and leaving the decision to the court, which

[47] HR, 14 June 1974, [1974] NJ 436.
[48] K. J. M. van de Loo, 'Over de rol van de psycholoog in de penitentiaire kamer van het Arnhemse gerechtshof', in F. Koenraadt and S. Steenstra (eds.), *Forensische Psychologie* (Arnhem; Gouda Quint, 43–51); N. W. de Smit, 'The Role of the Psychiatrist in the Penitentiary Appeal Court in the Netherlands' (1983) 6 *International Journal of Law and Psychiatry*, 473–80.
[49] Jaarcijfers TBS 1992, 's-Gravenhage, Ministerie van Justitie, June 1993.
[50] T. R. Drost, 'De rechter weet het beter' (1990) 3 *Sancties* 142–53; J. L. van Emmerik, 'De rechter weet het beter' (1990) 5 *Sancties* 268–76; T. R. Drost, 'Beter weten, Tien opmerkingen bij van Emmerik's commentaar' (1990) 5 *Sancties* 277–81; T. R. Drost, *Wikken en Wegen* (Groningen; Wolters Noordhoff 1991).

will face public outcry if it terminates the measure contrary to advice and the patient subsequently reoffends. This phenomenon can also be observed in the English system, but in a different way. The patient's psychiatrist may encourage the patient to apply for discharge to a Mental Health Review Tribunal and submit a report supporting discharge, rather than take direct responsibility, but this seems to happen more rarely nowadays than was the case previously. Where the patient is restricted and only the Home Office has the power of discharge, applications to the tribunal may also be encouraged by the patient's doctor.

England and Wales

An English hospital order lasts for six months in the first instance, renewable for six months, and thereafter at annual intervals. The patient's psychiatrist may discharge him at any time. As is the case with civilly committed patients, the detention is renewed by an administrative procedure whereby the patient's psychiatrist furnishes a report to the hospital managers stating that the conditions justifying detention are still met. The managers may decide to discharge the patient, but they rarely do. The patient may ask the managers for discharge at any time and, in such a case, the Code of Practice on the Mental Health Act says that they should grant him an opportunity to be heard. He can also appeal against detention to a Mental Health Review Tribunal.

Restriction orders may be imposed by the sentencing court for a finite period or without limit of time.[51] Here the patient's psychiatrist has no power of discharge. He must first seek the permission of the Home Secretary. If the patient is discharged subject to conditions, for example of residence or acceptance of medical treatment, the Home Secretary retains a right of recall until the expiry of the restriction order.[52] If the restriction order was imposed without limit of time by the sentencing court, there is no need to renew the detention, although medical reports must be sent to the Home Office at annual intervals. If the restriction order was time-limited by the sentencing court, once it expires the patient is treated as if detained under a hospital order without restrictions.

Where the risk of a restricted patient reoffending is considered particularly difficult to assess, the case for transfer or discharge is considered by the Advisory Board on Restricted Patients, which advises the Home Secretary.[53] The patient does not appear in person before the full Board, but is visited by a Board member who prepares a written report of the visit which is distributed to the other members prior to the meeting, and offers

---

[51] Ibid., s. 41(1).   [52] Ibid., s. 42(3).

[53] The Board has eight members: two lawyers (one of them, a judge, is chairman); two experienced forensic psychiatrists; two senior social work representatives; and two members with special experience of the criminal justice system.

his views in the light of discussion with the patient and others responsible for his case. The Board is an extra-statutory body. Its task is to advise the Home Secretary on the exercise of his discretion. It has no power to take decisions on its own, and for that reason has been held not to be amenable to judicial review.[54] If a patient appeals against detention to a Mental Health Review Tribunal and the tribunal decides to discharge, the Home Secretary has no power to override that decision.

Some interesting comparative points arise here. In the Netherlands the courts have the first and final say in the decision to extend psychiatric detention. The criminal court which sentenced the offender makes the decision about extension of TBS; if the patient is sentenced to detention in a general psychiatric hospital, decisions about duration of detention are taken by civil courts. In England and Wales, once the court has sentenced an offender to detention in hospital, it has no further involvement in decisions to extend the detention. If the patient is subject to a hospital order, the decision to extend is taken administratively by the hospital managers on the recommendation of the patient's psychiatrist. If the patient is subject to a restriction order, there is no need to renew the detention. It is authorized as long as the restrictions are in force, although the Home Secretary may at any time discharge the patient absolutely or conditionally. Restricted patients are rarely absolutely discharged. The sentencing court decides how long the restrictions should last, and then responsibility is transferred to the Home Office, an administrative department of state, which retains significant power and influence over these patients. In the Netherlands, with its emphasis on the separation of powers and judicial control of deprivation of liberty, such an arrangement would be unthinkable.

(E) The Treatment of Personality-Disordered Offenders

A significant issue in both systems is the treatment of patients with personality disorders, and the English legal category of psychopathic disorder, which means a persistent disorder or disability of mind (whether or not including significant impairment of intelligence) which results in abnormally aggressive or seriously irresponsible conduct. In England and Wales such offenders may be dealt with in one of a number of ways. A psychopathically disordered offender may be sentenced to a hospital order, if 'medical treatment' (which is broadly defined to include nursing and care

---

[54] *R. v. Secretary of State for the Home Department, ex parte Powell* (unreported), QBD, 21 December 1978, reproduced in L. Gostin and E. Rassaby, *Representing the Mentally Ill and Handicapped* (London; MIND/LAG, Quatermaine 1980). The court held that in consequence of its status the Board is not subject to a duty to act judicially or fairly.

habilitation and rehabilitation) 'is likely to alleviate or prevent deterioration in his condition'.

In the Dutch system, personality-disordered patients may be subject to imprisonment followed by a TBS measure. A serious discussion between the academic community and the judiciary in the Netherlands centres on the combination of a long prison sentence (more than five years) and TBS. As diminished, or lack of, responsibility is a precondition of a TBS measure, according to the academics, the fundamental culpability principle would prevent the punishing of a mentally disordered offender more severely than is merited by his level of responsibility. The classic case is that of the *Zwarte Ruiter* (Black Horseman).[55] Professor Pompe strongly criticized the ruling of the Supreme Court, which allowed a combination of fifteen years' imprisonment plus TBS for a violent escapist, mentally disordered offender. The court accepted the long prison sentence because of the lack of security in the carrying out of TBS measures at the time. It seems to be accepted now that it is not permitted to take into account external factors, independent from the defendant, in determining the length of the prison sentence. Nevertheless, debate continues whether internal or personal factors, such as the level of perversion in executing the offence, may increase the prison term beyond the level of mental responsibility, as was demonstrated in the recent case of the kidnapping and murder of the president of the AH supermarket chain.

In England and Wales, a personality-disordered patient might be admitted direct to hospital under a hospital order with or without restrictions if he is 'treatable', or he might be given a prison sentence. The nearest English equivalent to the prison plus TBS possibility is the discretionary life sentence. The criteria established by case law for the imposition of a discretionary life sentence where the courts have discretion to do so are: (a) that the offence is serious enough to require a very long sentence; (b) that the offender is mentally unstable and, if at liberty, would probably reoffend and present a grave danger to the public; and (c) that the offender will remain unstable and a potential danger for a long and uncertain period of time.[56] In such cases, the judge imposes a minimum period which must expire before the prisoner is entitled to have his case referred to the Parole Board. It is important to note that, unlike in the Netherlands, where at the end of the punitive period of the sentence the prisoner is transferred to the TBS institution, in England and Wales, the prisoner remains in prison.

In *Thynne Wilson and Gunnell* v. *United Kingdom*[57] the ECHR held that, once the punitive element of the sentence has been served, because continued detention was justified on the grounds of dangerousness and

---

[55] HR 10 September 1957, [1958] NJ 5.
[56] See now the Criminal Justice Act 1991, s. 2.   [57] (1991) 13 EHRR 666.

mental instability which might change with the passage of time, Article 5(4) required that detention should be reviewed by a court at reasonable intervals. Section 34 of the English Criminal Justice Act 1991 introduces such a right of review at intervals of two years. The hearings before the Discretionary Lifer Panels of the Parole Board rely very much on psychiatric evidence, and with the burden of proof on the prisoner to satisfy the Board that it is no longer necessary for the protection of the public that he should be confined. Legal aid is available for representation of prisoners who have insufficient means to pay, and the prisoner may present independent psychiatric evidence. This development undoubtedly improves the ability of the prisoner to challenge continued detention by the introduction of these hearings, and represents a move towards juridification, but it also increases psychiatrization, because of the centrality of the evaluation by the psychiatrist of likely future dangerousness. Moreover it is at least arguable that this burden of proof contravenes Article 5(4) of the Convention.

(F) Transfer of Sentenced Prisoners to Hospitals

In both systems there are significant numbers of mentally disturbed prisoners, with estimates suggesting that as many as 25 per cent might benefit from psychiatric help. While demand for psychiatric treatment has increased, the ability and willingness of general psychiatric hospitals, with their open door and community based philosophies, to receive such people as patients has not.

Article 47 of the *Gevangenismaatregel* (GevM) allows for the temporary transfer of a prisoner who becomes insane to a general mental hospital, and Articles 13 of the Criminal Code and 120 of the GevM authorize the transfer of a mentally-disturbed prisoner to a TBS clinic. In the latter case, the power is vested in the Minister of Justice, acting on experts' reports, and subject to review on appeal by the transferred prisoner to the Arnhem Court of Appeal. In such cases the extension rules for TBS do not apply, the legal basis for detention being the sentence of imprisonment, and the Minister of Justice retains the power to return the patient to prison during the currency of the sentence. In the case of a combination of prison sentence and TBS, as discussed above, transfer under Article 120 of the GevM may be used to bring about adequate psychiatric treatment before the full prison term has been served. For that reason later TBS extensions may be rather limited in number and duration, and much of the practical significance of the debate referred to above between Dutch academics and judges thereby reduced.

It must be remembered that a transfer from prison to hospital has important consequences for legal status. It may mean that detention is prolonged beyond the end of the sentence which the prisoner was serving. Moreover, in both the Netherlands and the United Kingdom, the substantive legal entitlements of prisoners under prison rules are better than those of psychiatric patients. At the time of writing, Bills on the rights of psychiatric patients and TBS detainees are being discussed in the Dutch legislature.

In England and Wales a mentally disordered prisoner may be transferred to hospital.[58] Since 1983, the number of sentenced prisoners transferred shows a steady increase from ninety-one in that year to 156 in September 1990. In 1991, following a government initiative, the number of prisoners transferred went up to 470, but Home Office estimates showed that there were at least 1,000 prisoners requiring hospital treatment. Grounds' research suggests that transfer may be motivated as much by a desire to protect the public as it is by a wish to ensure that the patient receives the care which he needs, with many transfers taking place close to what would have been the prisoner's release date.[59] The Code of Practice on the Mental Health Act, brought into effect since Grounds' research was carried out, states that 'the transfer of a prisoner to hospital under the Act should not be delayed until close to his release date. A transfer in such circumstances may well be seen by the prisoner as being primarily intended to extend his detention and result in an unco-operative attitude towards treatment.'[60]

THE SYSTEM OF PSYCHIATRIC INSTITUTIONS IN ENGLAND AND
WALES AND THE NETHERLANDS

The Netherlands

As noted above, offender patients who are subject to a TBS measure must be detained in a TBS hospital. In the Netherlands the average population of a forensic mental hospital is eighty-five. In February 1993 the total capacity in TBS hospitals was 541 beds. There are three state hospitals; a selection and crisis intervention hospital for thirty TBS patients, and two longer-stay hospitals with a capacity of ninety and 104 patients respectively. There are three private TBS clinics, two with a capacity of seventy-five and one with eighty-five beds. There are two special hospitals within

---

[58] Mental Health Act 1983, s. 47.
[59] A Grounds, 'Transfers of Sentenced Prisoners to Hospital' [1990] *CrimLRev.* 545–51.
[60] *Department of Health and the Welsh Office, Mental Health Act 1983 Code of Practice*, para. 3.13. In this context the figures showing ethnic origin of prisoners transferred are a cause for concern, since they show that 21% of those transferred under s. 47 in 1987 and 17% in 1988 were Afro-Caribbeans.

the general mental health system, one with a capacity of twenty-eight to which non-offender patients as well as TBS patients are admitted, and the other a forensic psychiatric hospital with fifty-five beds. The small population per institution is a necessary condition for using a socio-therapeutic approach, instead of the more custodial approach found in many other forensic mental health systems. In Dutch forensic mental hospitals one patient to a room is a common practice, as in the prison system. Dormitories are no longer used.[61] Those who are detained in the general psychiatric system may be looked after in a locked ward or a general ward. The TBS hospitals vary as to their degree of security, with a state clinic providing maximum security (S. van Mesdag). Some TBS hospitals, acting in cooperation with probation and out-patient services, have created half-way houses and day hospitals for out-patients.

England and Wales

In England and Wales, there is a three-tiered system of hospital provision for offender patients. At the secure end are three special hospitals for patients with dangerous or violent propensities—Broadmoor, Rampton, and Ashworth—which provide about 1,700 secure beds. There are approximately 1,800 patients detained in hospitals who are subject to restriction orders, and about two-thirds of these are in special hospitals.[62] The second level was introduced following the recommendations of the Butler Committee in the mid-1970s.[63] It consists of regional secure units, less secure than a special, but not as open as a local psychiatric, hospital. They serve the dual function of providing both an intermediate level of security and a base for a local forensic psychiatric service. Although the Butler Committee recommended 2,000 beds in regional secure units, as yet only about 600 currently exist. The Reed Committee, which reported in November 1991, has recommended a revised target of 1,500 medium secure beds, or twenty per million of population.[64] The third tier consists of local psychiatric hospitals. The level at which a patient enters the system depends on his dangerousness.

The level of provision in local hospitals and the community is not known,

[61] D. Downes, *Contrasts in Tolerance, Post-War Penal Policy in the Netherlands and England and Wales* (Oxford; Clarendon Press 1988).
[62] Home Office Memorandum Restricted Patients Detained in the Special Hospitals: Information for the Special Hospitals Service Authority 1990: *1* 114, Chadwick Healey Microfiche 90: 421, para. 1.2.
[63] *Report of the Committee on Mentally Abnormal Offenders*, Cmnd 6244 (London; HMSO 1975).
[64] *Department of Health and Home Office Review of Health and Social Services for Mentally Disordered Offenders* (1991).

but the system is often described as an inverted pyramid with most of the provision at the secure end. This has implications for patients who may be kept in conditions of greater security for years longer than is necessary because of an absence of less secure provision.

Comparison of the Dutch and English systems shows that they both operate on the basis that patients who are being considered for discharge should be granted gradual increase of freedoms by movement to less secure units or hospitals, and thence into the community under supervision. Both face similar problems in terms of the lack of facilities for offender patients who do not require treatment in conditions of security. However, anyone who has visited the institutions of the two systems cannot fail to be struck by the contrast between the large, prison-like, special hospitals in England, and the smaller, more therapeutically-oriented, institutions in the Netherlands. English regional secure units are the nearest equivalent to Dutch TBS clinics, which is hardly surprising, given the fact that in the 1970s and 1980s the English have looked to the Dutch system for models of forensic service delivery. Recently, in an effort to move away from the overly custodial culture of special hospitals, the Special Hospital Services Authority has called for the construction of another three special hospitals, so that there would be six maximum security establishments with a greater geographical spread and a much smaller bed complement.

LEGAL SAFEGUARDS FOR PATIENTS

In the mid-1970s the British mental health charity MIND (the National Association of Mental Health), directed its activities towards protecting patients' rights and made several applications to the European Commission on Human Rights. These cases were based on Articles 3, 5 and 6 of the Convention. Swart and Young have already commented upon the contrast between the monist approach to the Convention adopted by the courts of the Netherlands, which apply the rulings of the Strasbourg Court directly, and the dualist approach of the United Kingdom.[65] The Court of Human Rights has contributed significantly to the juridification of the psychiatric system in both countries. This final section deals with what Kelk and Legemaate call the 'external rights'[66] of patients, focusing on review of the lawfulness of detention. Constraints of space prevent consideration of the

---

[65] Chap. 4 above. Nevertheless, the ruling in *Megyeri* v. *Germany* (1992) 11 BMLR 110, has been brought to the attention of the Lord Chancellor to emphasize that cuts in legal aid for psychiatric patients would contravene the Convention.

[66] C. Kelk and J. Legemaate, *Legal Protection in Psychiatry: A Comparative Perspective*, Willem Pompe Instituut; University of Utrecht; 1990.

internal rights of patients, relating to their treatment in the institutional system.

(A) Review of the Lawfulness of Detention

The Netherlands

(i) *Review of Commitment to a General Psychiatric Hospital*

The most influential case on the rights of detained psychiatric patients is undoubtedly the judgment of the Court of Human Rights in *Winterwerp* v. *The Netherlands*.[67] Winterwerp had made repeated requests to a prosecutor for his release, but the prosecutor, believing them to be without prospect of success, did not refer these to a court. The Dutch government had argued that Article 5(4) did not compel a court to hear an individual whose mental condition was established to be such that he was incapable of presenting relevant statements to the court. The ECHR ruled that 'it was essential that the person concerned should have access to a court and the opportunity to be heard either in person, or, where necessary, through some form of representation, failing which he will not have been afforded the fundamental guarantees of procedure applied in matters of deprivation of liberty.'[68] The court went on to say that 'special procedural safeguards may prove called for in order to protect the interests of patients who, on account of their mental disabilities, are not fully capable of acting for themselves'.[69] The court also held that the prosecutor's actions in withholding the request from the District Court effectively denied the right to court proceedings under Article 5(4).

Although the applicable legislation, the Mentally Ill Persons Act 1884, empowered but did not bind the court to hear the patient, in a judgment of 2 December 1983, the Hoge Raad held that, in the light of Article 5 of the Convention, these provisions should be interpreted as conferring on the patient the right to be heard, entailing the right to be assisted by a lawyer and the right to demand the presence of an expert to counter the arguments of the hospital board.[70]

In *Van der Leer* v. *The Netherlands*,[71] the applicant had not been informed of the fact that she had been detained, contrary to Article 5(2), and this had impaired her ability to seek speedy review as was her entitlement under Article 5(4). There was an effective delay of five months between the time when she sought review by a court, and the time when a hearing was actually convened. Even if a patient does not apply for review, the detention must be extended by a court, and the patient has the right to be heard and represented at that hearing.

---

[67] (1979–80) 2 EHRR 387.   [68] Para. 60 of the judgment.
[69] Ibid.   [70] [1984] NJ 164.   [71] (1990) 7 BMLR 105.

(ii) *Review of TBS*

Whereas in England and Wales the principal modes of review of the lawfulness of continued psychiatric detention take place following an application by the patient, in the Netherlands an important opportunity for review by a court takes place if and when the authorities seek to extend the detention. Case law also gives the patient a right to challenge the decision by application to the court, but here the burden of proof is on him to justify release. In *Keus* v. *The Netherlands*,[72] the ECHR said that 'relying on Article 5(4), which is directly applicable in the Netherlands, and on the fundamental adversarial principle,[73] [the applicant] could have pleaded that, in the light of the improvement of his mental state, public order no longer required the continuation of his placement. It appears from Dutch case law that the court would undoubtedly have ordered the applicants' immediate release if they had accepted his arguments.'[74] In extension proceedings, the formal burden is on the authorities to justify the continuation of the measure. It is also possible for the patient to apply to the Minister of Justice for release, but the European Commission and Court of Human Rights have held that, being himself part of the executive, the Minister lacks the essential independence of the executive and the parties to the case to be considered a competent court for the purposes of Article 5(4).[75]

In *Koendjbiharie* v. *The Netherlands*[76] the European Court upheld a complaint that a four-month gap between the lodging of the application to extend the TBS and the communication of the decision on the application to the complainant was unacceptably long, and breached the requirement of speedy review in Article 5(4). The commission had held that it also meant that the detention of the applicant was contrary to Article 5(1) because it was not in accordance with a procedure prescribed by law, but the Court did not find it necessary to consider this aspect.[77] The applicable domestic law allowed a maximum of three months in exceptional cases and the Court could find no good reason why a delay of four months had occurred. The Court noted that the Court of Appeal had taken a month after the hearing to supply the complainant with its decision, and thought that this was also too long.

By the time judgment was delivered in these cases, the new law on

---

[72] (1991) 13 EHRR 109 (Commission), and 700 (court).

[73] The 'fundamental adversarial principle' in Dutch law means the right of the parties to be heard.

[74] App. 12228/86, *Keus* v. *The Netherlands* (1991) 13 EHRR 109 (Commission), 700 (Court), at 718 (para. 28 of the judgment).

[75] App. 11487/85, *Koendjbiharie* v. *The Netherlands* (1991) 13 EHRR 118, 13 EHRR 820 para. 72, pp. 835–6.

[76] App. 11487/85, *Koendjbiharie* v. *The Netherlands* (1991) 13 EHRR 118, 13 EHRR 820.

[77] Judge Bernhardt dissented on this point, agreeing with the Commission that there had been a breach of Art. 5(1) and (4).

extension of TBS (discussed above) had already come into force. One problem raised by the *Koendjbiharie* case is solved by a requirement in Article 509s of the Code of Criminal Procedure that the offender must be heard before the court makes a decision on the prosecutor's application to extend a TBS.

England and Wales

The most significant case in terms of its impact on English law was *X* v. *United Kingdom*,[78] based on Article 5 of the Convention. Prior to the ruling the Home Secretary had the final word on detention, discharge, and the decision to recall restricted patients. The ECHR held that a patient detained on grounds of unsoundness of mind must be given the opportunity, at regular intervals, to call into question the lawfulness of his detention, 'lawfulness' including both formal legality and the existence of sufficient substantive justification for the detention. The court or tribunal undertaking this review must have the power to direct discharge.

Review of the lawfulness of detention under English law is carried out by Mental Health Review Tribunals (MHRTs), exercising a statutory jurisdiction, and by the High Court through judicial review and habeas corpus. MHRTs look at the evidence justifying continued detention at the time of the hearing and decide whether the continued detention of the patient is still justified. It is not part of their task to review the formal legality of the initial admission, which is for the courts through judicial review and habeas corpus.[79] The tribunals have always had the power to direct the discharge of unrestricted patients. Each tribunal consists of a lawyer president, a psychiatrist, and a 'lay member'. The psychiatrist has the task of examining the patient prior to the hearing, and reports to the other tribunal members, which places him in an influential position as witness and member of the adjudicating panel. The formal burden of proof is on the patient to satisfy the tribunal that he is *not* mentally disordered or that detention is *not* necessary for his health or safety or for the protection of others. Under the Mental Health Act 1959, tribunals did not have the power to discharge restricted patients, their function then being to advise the Home Secretary, who was free to reject their advice.

Following the *X* judgment, the Mental Health Act 1983 conferred a new power on the tribunals to direct the discharge of restriction order patients, introducing a requirement that such tribunals be chaired by a judge with criminal court experience. It also entitles offender patients to apply more frequently for review of their detention by a tribunal, and provides for automatic review if a patient has not made an application. The hospital

---

[78] (1981) 1 BMLR 98.
[79] *R.* v. *Hallstrom, ex parte W* [1985] 3 All ER 775 (CA), (1985) 2 BMLR 73.

managers have a duty to do everything practicable to ensure that all detained patients know what provisions of the legislation they are detained under and of their rights to challenge detention. Provision for automatic review has been introduced if a patient has not himself applied for a tribunal hearing within the past three years. However, the formal burden of proof in tribunal proceedings remains on the patient to satisfy the tribunal of his entitlement to discharge. It may be questioned whether this complies with the requirements of Article 5(4), in that the tribunal is not obliged to discharge even if it is not satisfied that the person is mentally disordered, as long as it is not satisfied that he is not disordered. Moreover, continued detention does not require dangerousness. It may be justified in the interests of the patient's own physical or mental health.

The European Commission and Court of Human Rights have repeatedly emphasized the need for effective legal representation as part of the 'special procedural guarantees' required in mental health cases.[80] In 1982, as a result of *Collins* v. *United Kingdom*,[81] the British government extended legal aid to applicants to MHRTs where the applicant has insufficient means to pay for his own lawyer. Legal aid also covers funding for the patient to commission his own psychiatric report. The Law Society operates a panel for MHRT advocates, who must have undergone special training in this work. The official panel list of specialist advocates is circulated to psychiatric hospitals, to serve as a guide to patients in choosing their representative.

The right under Article 5(4) to speedy review was raised in *Barclay Maguire* v. *United Kingdom*,[82] where there was a delay of eighteen weeks between application and hearing. The United Kingdom Government reached a settlement with the Commission, with thirteen weeks as a reasonable target figure.[83] Since the 1983 Act there has been a dramatic increase in the tribunal case load, and this has led to increased delays. In 1986 the Council on Tribunals, a body which oversees the functioning of the tribunal system, reported a case where the hearing did not take place until over a year after the patient's original application.[84] Since then every report has criticized tribunal delays,[85] but there has not been any British application to the European Commission on this point since *Barclay*

---

[80] See e.g. *Winterwerp* v. *The Netherlands* (1982) 4 EHRR 288, paras. 60–1, 101–2, and more recently in *Megyeri* v. *Germany* (63/1991/315/386), judgment of 12 May 1992 (1992) 11 BMLR 110.

[81] App. 9729/82. Collins argued that the failure to grant him legal aid for this MHRT hearing was a breach of Art. 5(4). The case was declared admissible by the Commission, but withdrawn when the English law was changed.

[82] App. 9117/80, admissibility decision of 9 December 1981.

[83] *Van der Leer* v. *The Netherlands* (1990) 12 EHRR 567.

[84] *Annual Report of the Council on Tribunals 1985–6* (1986), HMSO, paras. 4.27–4.30.

[85] *Annual Report of the Council on Tribunals 1990–1* (1991), HC 97, 39–41.

Maguire, because a threat of recourse to Strasbourg will often expedite a hearing.

Despite the enhancements in the 1983 Act of the rights of restricted patients, a number of questions remain regarding the Home Secretary's widely-drawn power to recall a conditionally-discharged restricted patient to hospital,[86] a power which can be used in an arbitrary way to achieve the goal of preventive detention.

Once a restricted patient has been conditionally discharged, he may be recalled to hospital by the Home Secretary at any time even if, since discharge, he has received a sentence of imprisonment. The prison sentence does not cancel out his liability to psychiatric detention. So when the offender has finished the prison sentence, there is nothing in English law to stop the Home Secretary from recalling him to hospital. This happened in the case of *K*. Shortly after his conditional discharge after more than ten years in hospital under restrictions following a manslaughter conviction, K was convicted of two assaults on women, and was sentenced to six years' imprisonment. Just before his release date from prison, the Home Secretary issued a warrant recalling him to a special hospital.[87]

K applied for judicial review of the Home Secretary's decision, contending that the recall warrant was issued unlawfully, because the Secretary of State had not sought medical reports before recall, and in fact the most recent medical evidence was that he was not suffering from mental disorder.[88] Both the High Court and the Court of Appeal rejected the application, ruling that there was no need for the Home Secretary to consider doctors' opinions prior to the issue of a recall warrant. The argument for K was based primarily on the assertion of the United Kingdom Government in *X* v. *United Kingdom* that it was implicit in the wording of the recall power that:

unless the Home Secretary on the medical evidence available to him decides that the candidate for recall falls within the statutory definition, no power of recall can arise.[89]

In *X* the European Court recognized the legitimacy of recall without psychiatric evidence if the patient is in the community and evidence comes to light which justifies recall as a matter of emergency. However, it is harder to justify when the patient has been sitting in a prison cell for a period of years with psychiatrists at hand who could furnish the necessary reports. K argued that the English statute must be construed in the light of Article 5 of the European Convention because psychiatric detention cannot be lawful in the absence of objective evidence that the person

---

[86] Ibid., s. 42(3).   [87] *Per* Parker LJ.
[88] *R.* v. *Home Secretary, ex parte K* [1990] 1 All ER 703, [1990] 1 WLR 168.
[89] (1982) 4 EHRR 188.

detained is of unsound mind, and that no such evidence had been available to the Home Secretary at the time when he issued the warrant.[90] The Court of Appeal rejected this argument on the basis that the wording of the English provision was clear, and there was no requirement that the Secretary of State must act on medical evidence of mental disorder. The court applied the principle laid down in *R. v. Secretary of State for the Home Department, ex parte Brind*[91] that where the words of an English statute are plain and unambiguous it is not open to the English courts to look to the Convention for assistance in their interpretation.

K's appeal was dismissed. He has since applied to the European Commission on Human Rights. The Court of Human Rights has repeatedly stressed that national authorities have a certain margin of appreciation as to what is mental disorder of a nature warranting confinement, but has also maintained a commitment to the principle in *Winterwerp* that, except in emergencies, objective evidence of mental disorder is required.[92] K's application, was declared admissible by the Commission on 8 July 1993.[93]

An important contrast between the two systems is that, while in the Netherlands detention of an offender under a TBS or under the civil law is extended only by the court after judicial proceedings, in England and Wales the extension procedure is essentially administrative, and the patient can challenge the decision to extend after it has been made, rather than participate in making it. In the case of non-restricted patients, the hospital managers extend the detention on the application of the patient's psychiatrist. With restricted patients, the detention need not be renewed while the restriction order is in force, and it may be imposed without limit of time.

In both jurisdictions review of psychiatric detention has traditionally been conducted in a strongly inquisitorial style where the main role played by the patient was at worst as a piece of evidence to be examined by the medical profession, or at best as a key witness. The influence of *Winterwerp* and *X v. United Kingdom* has been to introduce entitlements for patients to more active participation in the hearings, and to provide them with a measure of equality of arms through legal aid.

CONCLUSION

The English and Dutch systems are very different in terms of the sheer numbers of patients being looked after, and the relative sizes of prison population. This may explain the ability of the Dutch system to develop

---

[90] *R. v. Home Secretary, ex parte K* (1990) 6 BMLR 1.   [91] [1990] 1 All ER 720.
[92] Most recently re-affirmed in *Herczegfalvy v. Austria* Series A No. 242–B, judgment of 24 September 1992.
[93] App. 17821/91, *Kay v. United Kingdom*, Decision of 7 July 1993.

through small institutions, in contrast to the large special hospitals in England and Wales. However, there are strong similarities in the problems faced by each: both have significant numbers of mentally disturbed prisoners; both have difficulty bridging the divide between the specialist forensic institutions and the general psychiatric hospitals.

An important aspect of comparative work is ensuring that we are comparing like with like. A superficial analysis would suggest that TBS is the equivalent of an English restriction order. Closer examination reveals that the Dutch TBS system combines functions performed in England by two different legal arrangements. Where TBS is used to admit a dangerously psychotic patient direct to a TBS clinic, it is indeed rather like the English restriction order. The key difference is that in the Netherlands the court decides whether the measure should be extended. In the English system a restriction order may be time-limited by the sentencing court but, where it is not, it extends potentially indefinitely and the Home Office exerts significant control over patients' detention. Where TBS is used following a prison sentence, the nearest English parallel is the situation of discretionary lifers.

In both countries there is a tension between two tendencies. On the one hand there is pressure towards the psychiatrization of criminal justice, as seen in the strong and almost unquestioned popularity of diversion schemes in England and Wales at present. On the other there is the movement towards juridification of psychiatry, imposing limits upon its power by vesting procedural and substantive rights in detained patients, a movement which has drawn particular inspiration from the ECHR. In England and Wales, the juridification brought about by the 1983 legislation, although significant, still leaves extensive discretionary power with the Home Secretary, and the burden of proof is on patients seeking discharge, rather than on the authorities, to justify prolonged detention. The Convention brings a certain measure of juridification, but at the same time permits significant psychiatrization of criminal justice. The key questions now concern the margin of appreciation left to Member States in determining the existence of mental disorder of a nature or degree warranting detention.

10

Diversion in English and Dutch Juvenile Justice

LORAINE GELSTHORPE, MIKE NELLIS, JEANNETTE BRUINS,
AND ANNELIES VAN VLIET

INTRODUCTION

Diversion has been a dominant thrust in juvenile justice policy for the past twenty-five years in England and Wales as well as in the Netherlands. In England, we can see the concept of diversion in embryonic form in the nineteenth-century debates about the establishment of separate institutions and courts for juvenile offenders.[1] The 'child savers' sought to promote the welfare of children by diverting them from the heavy-handed criminal courts, the more formal court procedures, and contaminating gaols. At the same time, reformers sought to divert 'pre-delinquents' from a career of crime, by inculcating 'appropriate' moral and religious values in children.[2] The concept of diversion employed in twentieth-century debates is no less complicated, though ironically, the aim in the past twenty-five years has been to keep juveniles out of the earlier systems of justice and welfare specially created for their reception.

What is common to both England and Wales and the Netherlands is that developments in diversion owe much to the impetus given by the USA in drawing attention to the idea that the existing juvenile justice systems were not effective in changing juveniles' behaviour. Moreover, the systems themselves seemed to be promoting an inescapable paternalism which circumvented legal protections to be afforded to young people.

To set the scene, we should note that in both the English and Dutch juvenile justice systems we can recognize elements of broadly similar theoretical models. That is, a 'welfare' model on the one hand, and a 'justice' model on the other. In essence, the welfare model symbolizes 'protection, help, and treatment' whilst the justice model emphasizes proportionality between crime and punishment and is akin to 'just deserts' principles currently espoused in contemporary penal debates. Indeed, it

[1] A. Morris and M. McIsaac, *Juvenile Justice?* (London; Heinemann 1978).
[2] Ibid.; J. Carlebach, *Caring for Children in Trouble* (London; Routledge and Kegan Paul 1970).

might be argued that the 'justice' model of juvenile justice was born out of criticisms of the extended 'resocialization' treatment programmes and indeterminate sentences associated with welfare policies and practices. With increasing recognition that juveniles will generally 'grow out of' delinquency if allowed to do so, some of the debates in this area have focused on the desirability of always choosing the least restrictive alternative. It is official policy in the Netherlands, for example, to give the least drastic reaction possible, though the more serious an offence the more formal and drastic the reaction should be.[3] There is a similar, if perhaps less explicit, commitment to this sort of approach in England—made manifest in the most recent Home Office Circular on cautioning,[4] Crown Prosecution Service guidelines[5] and in the White Paper which led to the 1991 Criminal Justice Act.[6] But neither juvenile justice system is characterized purely by 'welfare' or 'justice' principles. Indeed, in reviewing developments there is evidence of an uneasy amalgam of these principles at times. Moreover, there is now suggestion not only that juvenile justice is characterized by 'corporatism',[7] but that it is largely dominated by administrative concerns of effectiveness, efficiency, and economy. We can also see a specific 'crime-control' focus in developments. Some of these points will be elaborated upon below.

Broadly speaking, there are three forms of diversion identifiable: (a) diversion from crime—this is mainly associated with policies of crime prevention either directed at reducing opportunities for the commission of offences or targeted on particular crime-prone groups (such as juveniles) who participate in certain offences (for example, offences connected with motor vehicles); (b)diversion from court—here, those who act as gate-keepers into the court system are given the opportunity to discontinue proceedings (entirely or conditionally) and either do nothing or substitute some kind of intervention; and (c) diversion from institutions—in this, community-based programmes or training projects are promoted as an alternative to penal institutions for those who would otherwise be removed from the community because of their offending behaviour. This chapter is largely concerned with the second of these since, as Brants and Field[8] have suggested, diversion from court is the predominant form of diversion in England and Wales and in the Netherlands.

[3] Uitgangspunten voor het beleid ten aanzien van strafrechtelijk minderjarigen, vastgesteld in de vergadering van procureurs-generaal, 26 February 1986.
[4] Home Office Circular 59/1990, *The Cautioning of Offenders*, and Circular 18/1994, *The Cautioning of Offenders*, London; Home Office.
[5] Crown Prosecution Service, *Code for Crown Prosecutors*, London; Crown Prosecution Service 1992.
[6] Home Office, *Crime, Justice and Protecting the Public, The Government's Proposals for legislation*, Cm. 965, London; Home Office 1990.
[7] J. Pratt, 'Corporatism: The Third Model of Juvenile Justice', (1989) 29 *British Journal of Criminology*, 236–54.
[8] See Chap. 7 of this book.

We can see that there has been in the past and that there still is a popular belief that general moral education programmes conducted in schools could inculcate appropriate moral attitudes in children and young people so that they would resist being drawn into crime. Alternatively, it is believed that young people commit crimes because of boredom through lack of leisure facilities or because youthful 'high spirits', when acted out in an urban environment, are likely to lead to conflict with the police.

As a consequence, it is believed that the provision of directed adventurous activities which channel the energies of young people could therefore divert them from criminal activity. In England, and this is also true for the Netherlands, this kind of philosophy has made appearances in wide-ranging social and educational policy as well as in child-care policy which specifically addresses the needs of juvenile offenders. Criminal justice policy has reflected these ideas to an extent, but has never given statutory recognition to them—such recognition emerges much more in relation to diversion from court and custody. Diversion from crime, then, has included many forms of prevention—activity leisure groups run by social workers, the universal provision of youth facilities, behaviour modification, and other treatment programmes, counselling and a wide range of 'social crime prevention' schemes which often focus on 'at risk' groups (for example, children who live in high rise flats, large-scale council housing estates and so on); but also more 'mechanical' forms of intervention—greater surveillance in shops[9] and public transport, the introduction of 'vandal-proof' building materials and the physical security of buildings, for example. Indeed, 'situational crime prevention' of this sort has recently found favour in national and local crime prevention strategies alike.[10]

In Holland, diversion from crime has included a variety of different forms of prevention, essentially based on opportunity theory and social control theory.[11] Paradoxically, however, this does not mean diversion from judicial responses to crime. Rather, judicial responses have shifted from traditional concepts of punishment and so on to 'alternative' responses and community-based programmes which involve confronting the young offender with the consequences of his or her offending behaviour and encouraging a more responsible attitude to the community at the same time. (For example, there are special community-based programmes directed at vandals and shoplifters.) Clearly, such an approach is not unknown in the English system, but formal responses of this nature tend to come at a later stage in the system when the young offender is perhaps

---

[9] One initiative in West Amsterdam involves surveillance of the shopping centre carried out by juveniles themselves. It is thought that this might encourage a sense of shared responsibility.

[10] R. Clarke, *Situational Crime Prevention* (New York; Harrow and Heston 1992).

[11] J. Junger-Tas, 'Recent trends in juvenile delinquency and juvenile justice', in *The Future of the Juvenile Justice System* (Acco; Leuven/Amersfoort 1991), 1–8.

subject to a supervision order. The supervision order might involve some sort of community-based programme designed to encourage the young offender to realize the consequences of criminal actions.

What follows then is a description of the two juvenile justice systems, but a description which serves to point to a number of unresolved issues and emerging legal problems relating to legal values enshrined in the European Convention on Human Rights, especially Article 6(1) and (2) which is concerned first with entitlement to a fair and public hearing where criminal charges are laid, and secondly, with the need to presume innocence until the person is proven guilty.

The use of diversionary programmes becomes problematic if they involve action being taken without proper recourse to the law and to an impartial body (magistrates or a judge). The presumption of innocence prescription can also be under pressure where young offenders are encouraged to participate in diversionary schemes as an alternative to a judicial response without having first been proven guilty.

Given the direction that juvenile justice has taken in the English and Dutch juvenile justice systems in recent years it is not clear that these rules are strictly adhered to. Indeed, there are good grounds to be concerned about possible contraventions. We return to this point in the conclusion of the chapter.

DIVERSION FROM COURT IN ENGLAND AND WALES: THE FRAMEWORK FOR DIVERTING CHILDREN AND YOUNG PEOPLE

Turning now to the main form of diversion in England and Wales, we should note that the framework for diverting childen and young people is one which includes both legal and purely advisory dimensions. Generally speaking, a young offender reported to the police (who has reached the age of criminal responsibility—ten years) will first be considered for diversion in what is known as a 'juvenile liaison office' within the police organization. If the offence is a 'trivial' offence there may be 'no further action' or the juvenile may be given an 'instant' caution in the presence of his or her parents or guardian (that is, one given by a senior officer within hours of the commission of the offence). If the offence is a little more serious, juvenile liaison police officers will normally meet with or at least consult representatives from other agencies (such as education, social services, probation) to decide whether or not the young offender should be cautioned or recommended for prosecution (though the police retain the power of discretion). There has been guidance in the form of circulars from the Home Office to the police on the appropriate use of cautions: the first of these was Home Office Circular 14/1985, which was replaced by Home

Office Circular 59/1990. Before a caution can be given three conditions must be met: (i) there must be sufficient evidence of the offender's guilt to give a realistic prospect of conviction, (ii) the offender must admit the offence, and (iii) the juvenile offender's parents or guardian must give consent to the young person being cautioned.

Some police service areas in England and Wales have introduced 'caution plus' schemes which involve voluntary participation in schemes designed to keep youngsters out of further trouble or in reparation schemes. These may involve voluntary attendance at a series of meetings designed to focus on relationships between young people and those in positions of authority, for example, though the nature and content of such meetings varies considerably. This is an important development and one which may have been subject to far too little scrutiny. There are no legal cases to suggest abuse of due process here, but neither has there been research to take into account 'consumer views' on the matter.

If the juvenile liaison panel decides that prosecution is warranted the case will proceed to the Crown Prosecution Service. Here, juvenile specialists will examine the case for prosecution. Crown Prosecutors use a 'code of practice' as guidance in their decision-making; they look at evidential sufficiency and at 'public interest' criteria (which include the staleness of the offence, the seriousness of the offence, the age of the offender, the likely penalty if the case were to proceed to court, and so on). If the case does proceed to court, rather than being referred back to the police with the suggestion that no further action be taken, or that the police caution the young offender, the Crown Prosecution Service may at any stage prior to a plea being taken decide to withdraw or discontinue the case. The court then has sole responsibility for deciding upon sentence, though it may request agencies such as the Probation and Social Services to produce pre-sentence reports.

DIVERSION FROM COURT: POLICY AND PRACTICE

Various strategies to divert young people from court have been in practice since the 1950s, though it is only since 1969 that cautioning has gained prominence.[12] In essence, diversion from court has usually, but not exclusively, meant police cautioning—it is based on the idea that the juvenile court experience is a potentially harmful and negative one and should, therefore, be reserved for the more serious and persistent offenders. Thus

---

[12] A. Morris and H. Giller, *Understanding Juvenile Justice* (London; Croom Helm 1987); J. Ditchfield, *Police Cautioning in England and Wales*, Home Office Research Study No. 37 (London; Home Office 1976).

it is argued that the juvenile court should be a last resort after other less formal strategies have been tried and failed. Diversion here is a protection from the consequences of a court appearance and, indeed, there is some research evidence to show that court intervention may exacerbate delinquent behaviour.[13] The 1969 Children and Young Persons Act which perhaps marked the ascendency of a diversionary (and, importantly, a welfarist perspective) in regard to juvenile offenders[14] fully endorsed the idea that court was to be a last resort. The diversionary intent was most evident in a number of sections which were never actually implemented because of a change in government and because of a groundswell in opposition to some of the ideas contained within the Act. It is worth commenting on one of the sections never implemented: section 5 made consultation between the police and social services a statutory requirement prior to the decision to prosecute any child or young person. The incoming Conservative Government decided not to implement the Act in full and so section 5 was never brought into effect (successive Labour and Conservative Governments showed no inclination to implement the section either). However, the failure to provide a statutory requirement for consultation did not stop many agencies implementing the section voluntarily, and although the voluntary nature of consultation led to wide variation in practice between different police force areas and unreliable and variable responses from social services agencies, it is undeniable that the 1969 Act gave impetus to the philosophy of diversion, and specifically to the practice of cautioning. Endorsement came in other subsequent Government documents and White Papers too,[15] despite a swing away from a 'welfarist' perspective towards 'justice' or 'crime control' thinking,[16] or to a 'just deserts' model which the government has recently brought into play throughout the whole of the criminal justice system in the Criminal Justice Act 1991.[17]

---

[13] D. Farrington, 'The effects of public labelling' (1977) 17 *British Journal of Criminology*, 112–25.

[14] A. Morris and H. Giller, *Understanding Juvenile Justice*; A. Rutherford *Growing Out of Crime: The New Era* (2nd edn., 1992) (Winchester; Waterside Press 1987); L. Gelsthorpe and A. Morris, 'Juvenile Justice 1945–92', in R. Morgan, R. Reiner and M. Maguire (eds.), *Oxford Handbook of Criminology* (Oxford; Oxford University Press 1993).

[15] See e.g. Home Office, *Young Offenders* (1980), Cmnd. 8045, London, HMSO; Home Office, *Cautioning by the Police: A Consultative Document* (1984), London, Home Office, and most recently a further Home Office Circular (1990a), Circular 59/1990, *The Cautioning of Offenders*, London; Home Office.

[16] A. Morris and H. Giller, *Understanding Juvenile Justice* (1987); L. Gelsthorpe and A. Morris, 'Juvenile Justice 1945–1992' (1993).

[17] As stated, the philosophy underlying the Criminal Justice Act of 1991 is outlined in the preceding Government White Paper: *Crime, Justice and Protecting the Public* (London; Home Office 1990). In addition to the outline of 'just deserts' thinking it contains some reference to the managerial/social control model described by A. Peters, 'Main currents in Criminal Law Theory', in J. van Dijk, C. Haffmans, F. Ryter, J. Schutte, S. Stolwijk, *Criminal Law in Action: An Overview of Current Issues in Western Societies* (Arnhem; Gouda Quint 1986).

There is no doubt that there has been an enormous expansion in terms of police cautioning. The decade of the 1970s marked its first growth period: in 1970 35 per cent of known juvenile offenders were cautioned for indictable offences and by 1979 this had increased to 50 per cent. This trend continued throughout the 1980s and into 1990 when the rates were 69 per cent for 14–16-year-old boys and 90 per cent for 10–13-year-old boys (the rates for girls were even higher).[18] But the practice of diversion has its disadvantages too. Probably the best-documented feature is the tendency to bring more juveniles into the juvenile justice system than would otherwise have been the case: the so called 'net-widening' effect. Rather than operating as real diversion, the cautioning procedure was said to be 'widening the net', labelling more and more young people as delinquent.[19] Other concerns included differential policies and procedures over England and Wales—which makes for inconsistent justice—or what some commentators have termed as 'justice by geography';[20] prejudicial decision-making (research studies suggest that black and Asian youngsters are less likely to be cautioned than those who are white;[21] and other kinds of 'subjective' decision-making. Landau (1981) and Landau and Nathan (1983), for example,[22] found that the type of offence and previous record were both of primary importance in the decision to charge directly or to refer through diversionary systems. But superimposed on these were the age, family background, and race of the offender. Other researchers have pointed to the relevance of class and parental attitudes.[23]

Some of these difficulties have been negated to an extent, especially with Home Office guidance on the criteria for cautioning introduced in 1985.

---

[18] Home Office, *Criminal Statistics England and Wales*, London; HMSO 1991.

[19] Ditchfield, *Police Cautioning in England and Wales* (1976); D. Farrington and T. Bennett, 'Police cautioning of juveniles in London' (1981) 21 *British Journal of Criminology*, 123–35; A. Morris and H. Giller, *Understanding Juvenile Justice* (1987).

[20] N. Richardson, *Justice by Geography III: Legislation, Demography and Decision-Making*, Manchester; Social Information Systems (1989); H. Giller and N. Tutt, 'Police cautioning of juveniles: the continuing practice of diversity', [1987] *CrimLRev*. 367–74.

[21] NACRO, *Some Facts and Findings about Black People in the Criminal Justice System*, (1989); *Reducing the Use of Custody for Young Offenders* (1992a), Young Offenders Committee Policy Paper 1; and *Diverting Young Offenders From Prosecution* (1992), Young Offenders Committee Policy Paper 2, London, National Association for the Care and Resettlement of Offenders; Commission for Racial Equality, *Cautions v. Prosecutions: Ethnic Monitoring of Juveniles by Seven Police Forces*, London; Commission for Racial Equality 1992.

[22] S. Landau, 'Juveniles and the Police' (1981) 21 *British Journal of Criminology*, 27–46; S. Landau and G. Nathan, 'Selecting Delinquents for Cautioning in the London Metropolitan Area' (1983) 23 *British Journal of Criminology*, 128–49.

[23] D. Farrington and T. Bennett, 'Police Cautioning of Juveniles in London' (1981); C. Fisher and R. Mawby, 'Juvenile Delinquency and Police Discretion in an Inner City Area' (1982) 22 *British Journal of Criminology*, 63–75. C. Wilkinson and R. Evans provide an overview of some of the problems associated with police cautioning (especially concerning the different ways in which police services have interpreted policy), 'Police Cautioning of Juveniles: The Impact of Home Office Circular 14/1985' [1990] *CrimLRev*. 165–76.

Indeed, in 1990 Bottoms *et al.*[24] were able to report that 'net-widening effects' of diversionary strategies appeared to have disappeared. But other difficulties such as those in relation to race may have persisted[25] and there are still differences in the rate of cautioning across the country.[26]

There are also criticisms of the role of the Crown Prosecution Service. Not only may it be argued that the crown prosecutors depend too heavily on police evidence, without reviewing cases independently,[27] but there are suggestions that crown prosecutors merely endorse the sometimes rather 'subjective' excercise of discretion.[28] That is, that there may be a certain amount of 'moral accounting' occurring—which involves prosecutors in assessing the 'moral character' of juveniles and the timeliness or otherwise of prosecution, as opposed to strict evidential and public interest criteria. In any case, Andrew Ashworth (1987)[29] has already outlined some of the difficulties in interpreting 'the public interest' in a clear and consistent fashion.

Diversion from the court has essentially involved setting up 'gatekeeping' procedures to ensure that young people do not enter any stage of the criminal justice process inappropriately. The support of other agencies has been enlisted so that there is a shared philosophy and co-operation with regard to young offenders in the criminal justice system. However, research suggests that the system does not always work according to plan. Indeed, whilst there has been an enormous increase in the number of children and young people diverted from court over the past two or three decades, there are more than lingering suspicions that the exercise of discretion leads to inconsistency and perceived unfairness. This being said, alternative suggestions (for tighter criteria to be drawn up, for example) may lead to a highly inflexible and insensitive system of decision-making.

It is clear from the description of the framework of policy and practice that the Government aims to divert as many young people as possible away from courts, even if attempts to divert young people from crime seem a little faint-hearted to those critics who would like to see more resources

---

[24] A. Bottoms, P. Brown, B. McWilliams, W. McWilliams and M. Nellis, *Intermediate Treatment and Juvenile Justice: Key Findings and Implications from a National Survey of Intermediate Treatment Policy and Practice* (London; HMSO 1990).

[25] It is difficult to provide empirical evidence of this, but there are strong suspicions—not least from recent evidence which points to discrimination in sentencing—see B. Hudson, 'Discrimination and Disparity: The Influence of Race on Sentencing' (1989) 16 *New Community* 23–34, and R. Hood, *A Question of Judgement, Race and Sentencing*, London, Commission for Racial Equality (1992), for example. This is clearly an area in which there ought to be further research.

[26] Wilkinson and Evans, 'Police Cautioning'.

[27] M. McConville, A. Sanders and R. Leng, *The Case for the Prosecution: Police Suspects and the Construction of Criminality* (London; Routledge 1991).

[28] L. Gelsthorpe and H. Giller, 'More Justice for Juveniles: Does More Mean Better?' [1990] *CrimLRev.* 153–64.

[29] A. Ashworth, 'The "Public Interest" Element in Prosecution' [1987] *CrimLRev.* 229–320.

offered in this sphere and to those who would like to see more vigorous efforts to keep young people out of custody.[30]

Given that cautioning is the central component of diversion policies, it is important to understand recent developments which have been designed to bring a measure of standardization to the system.

CAUTIONING AND CIRCULARS 59/90 AND 18/94

The current framework for the cautioning of offenders is provided by Home Office Circular 59/90 and its replacement, Circular 18/94. Circular 59/90 itself was in part a response to research into the operation of the previous Circular 14/85, which had identified five basic problem areas.[31] First, the meaning of parts of the 1985 circular was unclear, leading to inconsistency in deciding which crimes to caution and which to designate as no further action. Secondly, the circular had failed to promote consistency across police forces. Thirdly, police monitoring practices were poor, leading to criticisms of variations in practice, and concerns that cautioning was operating in a racially discriminatory way. Fourthly, there was cause for concern where cautions were repeatedly used without offers of support or assistance to the offender. Finally, there was no justification for the sharp decline in cautioning which occurred at the age of 17 (then the upper age limit for the juvenile court[32]), 16-year-olds being four times more likely to be cautioned than 17-year-olds.

Circular 59/90 contained no clear and unequivocal philosophy of diversion from court. Considerations of the welfare of the young person and administrative or public interest considerations of efficiency were conflated in the statement of purpose of formal cautioning, which was defined as a means of: (a) dealing quickly and simply with the less serious offenders; (b) diverting them from the criminal courts; and (c) reducing their chances of reoffending.

The two most novel aspects of Circular 59/90 were its indication that cautioning could, and should, be used for older age groups, not just juveniles, and its inclusion of national standards for cautioning. The national standards replaced the Attorney-General's guidelines on the criteria for prosecution, and represented an attempt to ensure consistency of practice by offering guidance on the circumstances where prosecution should not

[30] NACRO, *Reducing the Use of Custody for Young Offenders*, and *Diverting Young Offenders from Prosecution* (1992); J. Pitts, *The Politics of Juvenile Crime* (London; Sage 1988); A. Rutherford, *Growing Out of Crime: The New Era* (1992).
[31] R. Evans and C. Wilkinson, 'Variations in Police Cautioning Policy in England and Wales' (1990) 29 *Howard Journal of Criminal Justice*, 155–76.
[32] Under the Criminal Justice Act 1991 the Juvenile Court was renamed the 'Youth Court' and it now deals with offenders between the ages of 10 and 17 years inclusive.

be seen as necessary, and, where it was not, on which alternative to use—caution, informal warning, or no further action. At the same time, Chief Constables were invited to draw up their own policy statements, based on the national guidelines, which left scope for continuing diversity in practice, given some of the ambivalences in the circular, which as will be seen particularly affected monitoring and multiple cautioning.

Although primarily addressed to the police, Circular 59/90 endorsed multi-agency approaches at the level of both policy-making and decision-making in the belief that participation by other agencies would improve the quality and consistency of cautioning decisions.[33] Those parts of the country which had not yet developed multi-agency juvenile liaison panels, consisting of representatives of education, social services, the youth service, and the probation service, were invited to do so.[34] For the most trivial offences, the circular conceded that an informal warning or even an instant caution (which do not require the panel to meet) might be appropriate.

In general, the Circular promoted a higher standard of monitoring the effectiveness of cautioning policies, but it left scope for local variation. It drew on comments from the Commission for Racial Equality in its insistence that there must be 'fair and equal treatment irrespective of ethnic origin',[35] but although decisions of the panels were to be recorded, ethnic monitoring was not made mandatory, but was left to the Chief Constable's discretion. The same was true of the recording of informal action (as opposed to cautions), making it difficult to assess the extent of non-prosecution.

A frequent point of criticism of practice under the 1985 circular was multiple-cautioning, on the ground that it undermined the credibility of the police and the criminal law if the same offenders are cautioned time and time again. Although Circular 59/90 noted that there was widespread agreement that the courts should be a last resort,[36] it expressed ambivalence about multiple cautioning, pointing out on the one hand that it was appropriate for some offenders if the nature and circumstances of the latest offence warranted it, and on the other noted the possibility that the credibility of the police and the law may be weakened.

It is acknowledged in the circular that one of the ways in which strategies of multiple-cautioning had been developed was by linking a caution with reparation to, or mediation with, the victim. Previously, cautions themselves had sometimes been made contingent on the satisfactory completion

---

[33] Home Office Circular 59/90, para. 10. Research has not entirely borne this out, see J. Macmillan, 'Social Information and Decision-Making in Juvenile Liaison Panels', in T. Booth (ed.), *Juvenile Justice in the New Europe*, Social Services Monographs, Research in Practice (1991), Community Care and the Joint Unit for Social Services Research, University of Sheffield; S. Uglow, A. Dart, A. Bottomley and C. Hale, 'Cautioning Juveniles: Multi-Agency Impotence' [1992] *CrimLRev*. 632–41; R Evans, 'Evaluating Young Adult Diversion Schemes in the Metropolitan Police District', [1993] *CrimLRev*. 490.
[34] Home Office Circular 59/90, para. 12.   [35] Ibid., para. 17.   [36] Ibid., para. 7.

of some reparative task, or the payment of compensation. This was a variant of the 'caution with penalties' approach that had in fact been encouraged by the Parliamentary Select Committee on the Crown Prosecution Service. Circular 59/90 emphatically rejected this view, insisting that 'only the courts may impose such requirements'.[37] Consistent with the requirements of the Victims' Charter,[38] the views of victims were to be ascertained prior to a prosecution decision, but their consent to cautioning was not deemed to be essential. On the offender's side, 'a practical demonstration of regret such as apologizing to the victim and/or offering to put matters right as far as he is able',[39] was at least indicative of the appropriateness of a caution, so long as it was offered voluntarily. However, the police were warned against becoming involved in the negotiation of compensation or reparation.[40] Similarly, referral to support or assistance agencies such as drug or alcohol projects was to be voluntary, and a refusal to participate was not to count against a caution. Decision-making in this area, however, has remained largely invisible.

The cases of *R. v. Constable of the Kent County Constabulary, ex parte L (a minor)* and *R. v. Director of Public Prosecutions, ex parte B (a minor)*[41] raise the question of the extent to which the cautioning circular (in this case 14/85) and the Code for Crown Prosecutors may form the basis of an application for judicial review where the police or the Crown Prosecution Service have proceeded with a prosecution instead of cautioning the offender. Watkins LJ, delivering the judgment of the court, held that 'if judicial review lies in relation to current criminal proceedings, it lies against the Crown Prosecution Service as the body with the last and decisive word'. Although judicial review was available, it would only lie where it could be demonstrated that the decision had been made without regard to, or clearly contrary to, a settled policy which had been formulated in the public interest, such as the policy of cautioning juveniles. In L's case, although he had admitted his guilt, apologized to the victim, and the victim's parents had agreed to a caution, the offence, which involved violence to the person, had been viewed as too serious. In B's case, she did not admit her guilt, which is a precondition for a caution. Both applications were dismissed. Watkins LJ said that it was likely to be a rare case where a defendant would be able to show that a decision was fatally flawed. The circulars require the weighing of different factors in the decision to prosecute or caution, and as long as those factors have been weighed, the relative importance attached to each is unlikely to be challenged successfully

---

[37] Home Office Circular, App. B, note 1C.
[38] Home Office, *Victims' Charter: A Statement of the Rights of Victims of Crime*, London, Home Office (1990).
[39] Home Office Circular 59/90, App. B, note 3F.
[40] Ibid., App. B, note 4C.   [41] [1993] 1 All ER 756.

unless it can be shown that the decision was one which no reasonable prosecutor in the circumstances could have arrived at.

Just as a decision to prosecute rather than to caution may lead to objections, so too can avoidance of prosecution lead to objections or criticisms of neglect of due process. As the National Association for the Care and Resettlement of Offenders has pointed out, in some cases the 'penalties' exacted through 'cautioning plus' schemes may exceed the disposal which a court would have been likely to impose had the young person been prosecuted.[42] The extent to which these are truly 'voluntary' activities has also been questioned.

Circular 18/94 does not fundamentally alter the framework set out in the earlier circular (59/90), but it replaces it with the intention of reminding police force areas yet again to seek greater consistency in the rate of cautioning and to promote the better recording of cautions. The circular also includes more detailed National Standards. A key issue in the circular is perhaps that it aims to discourage the use of cautions in 'inappropriate cases', for example for offences which are triable on indictment only. The cautioning of such offenders was not condoned in earlier guidance, but the new circular describes that statistical research shows that cautions had been given for very serious offences and that this should be avoided in the future. The circular also includes a note to guard against multiple cautioning—since the Government believes that this brings the disposal into disrepute. To some extent we might read the circular as intending a reversal of any 'presumption in favour of a caution', but it is not clear that this is the case. In any case, previous circulars do not unequivocally reflect a presumption of this sort. The chief impact of the circular might be to draw attention to the 'seriousness' of the offence. This reflects Government suspicions that cautions have perhaps been given to too many too readily, and the new 'sharp' guidelines and national standards clearly reflect its law and order rhetoric. Thus a main aim of the new circular might be to 'put a brake on cautioning'.

Crucially, the circular does offer further guidance with regard to the role of victims in the decision-making process—though once again stressing that whilst efforts should be made to find out the victim's view about the offence, which may have a bearing on how serious the offence is judged to be, this should not be regarded as conclusive. Interestingly, the circular suggests that the offender's name and address should be disclosed wherever the victim wishes to institute civil proceedings to recover property/repair damage and so on. The circular also calls for any 'caution plus' schemes (involving a caution and reparation or mediation with the victim, or other short schemes of activities) to be carefully monitored and evaluated.

---

[42] NACRO, *Diverting Young Offenders from Prosecution* (1992).

The response to such schemes was rather guarded in the 59/90 Circular, the 18/94 Circular is not overwhelming in its support, but does fully acknowledge that different police force areas may be experimenting in this way.

In many senses, discussion about diversion from court cannot be divorced from wider discussions about the direction of criminal justice in England and Wales. Thus it is important to make reference to these wider discussions in our concluding comments. In the late 1980s the government initiated a major overhaul of the criminal justice system, part of which was premised on the successful, albeit incomplete, revolution that had occured in juvenile justice during that decade.[43] In the ensuing debate, a variety of juvenile justice interest groups pressed for the implementation of measures that had still not been attained—the end of juvenile remands to prison department custody, the abolition of penal custody for sentenced juveniles,[44] the placing of cautioning on a statutory footing, and the raising of the age of prosecutability from 10 to 14.[45] Interestingly, these pressure groups could draw no support from international statements on such issues; this is a point to which we return in our concluding comments on the English/ Dutch juvenile justice systems.

Neither statutory cautioning nor the raising of the age of prosecutability then, nor complete abolition of custody for under-seventeens, was achieved (although custody for 14-year-old boys was successfully abolished and a campaign to achieve the same for 15-year-old boys and girls gained serious momentum). Following a spate of suicides among remanded youngsters (including some juveniles) the government did, however, agree—resources permitting—and phased over a four year period, to end the remanding of juveniles to prison department establishments. This was to be achieved through greater use of secure accommodation (ostensibly caring, rather than punitive, establishments, run by local authorities rather than the Home Office) and by the provision of bail support schemes at the pre-trial or presentence stage.

The Criminal Justice Act (CJA) 1991 was the culmination of the government's reform process. It was implemented on 1 October 1992 and, as yet, it is too early to say what its effects have been although it has been criticized strongly by police and magistrates. The Act, as indicated above,

[43] R. Allen, 'Out of Jail: The Reduction of Penal Custody for Male Juveniles 1981–1988' (1989) 30 *Howard Journal of Criminal Justice*, 30–52.

[44] NACRO, *Reducing the Use of Custody for Young Offenders* (1992).

[45] The thrust of all these demands was diversionary in a literal sense, although that particular terminology was no longer used consistently even by the protagonists, and figured hardly at all in official discourse.

was largely based on an earlier White Paper, 'Crime, Justice and Protecting the Public',[46] whose stated aims, overall, were to reduce crime, reduce the use of imprisonment, introduce a just deserts model of sentencing, and introduce concepts of efficiency, economy, and effectiveness into the administration of criminal justice policy. Because of their disproportionate involvement in crime, and their disproportionate numbers within the prison system, the White Paper focused particularly, though not exclusively, on young adults, and in doing so it proposed changes to the criminal justice system which effectively blurred the traditional distinctions between juveniles and young adults. (The term 'juvenile' having, in English, connotations of greater immaturity than 'youth', with widespread public support, the Act raised the upper age limit from 17 to 18.[47]) This was in fact more than a change of nomenclature because the Children Act 1989 had already transferred the civil functions of the juvenile court to a family court; the new youth court was thus a purely criminal court (albeit one which retained the formal obligation to have regard to the welfare of the child). It was in principle able to deal with all juveniles between 10 and 18, although given the high rates of diversion from court among under-14-year-olds, it was anticipated that 75 per cent of its workload would consist of 16–17 year-olds.[48]

Despite appearances, this was not simply a case of bringing 17 year-olds in to an erstwhile juvenile jurisdiction; a number of adult penalties were transferred down, too (attendance centre for thirty-six hours, community service orders of 240 hours, probation orders, and a range of potentially intrusive requirements including curfew orders) and applied to 16-year-olds as well as 17-year-olds.[49] Although a strong emphasis remained on keeping them out of custody, the range of community penalties available for 16-year-olds was increased and substantially toughened.[50] Concern that

---

[46] Home Office, *Crime, Justice and Protecting the Public* (1990b), Cm 965.

[47] C. Ball, 'Young Offenders and the Youth Court' [1992] *CrimLRev.* 277–87.

[48] Home Office, 1990, para 8.30.

[49] A less cynical interpretation is that the change is designed to implement the principles embodied in the United Nations Minimum Standard Rules for the Administration of Juvenile Justice and the United Nations Convention on the Rights of the Child. These provide that a child—that is defined as a person of below 18 years—shall be entitled to be dealt with under a jurisdiction separate from that for adults and should be subject to a range of penalties and dispositions that take into account his or her welfare and are different from those available for older offenders (United Nations Standard Minimum Rules for the Administration of Juvenile Justice (The Beijing Rules), approved on 6 September 1985 by the Seventh Congress and adopted by the General Assembly on 29 November 1985; United Nations (1989) Convention on the Rights of the Child, Geneva's Defence for Children International and the United Nations Children's Fund).

[50] This provides clear evidence of what T. Jefferson and J. Shapland have described as the 'subordination of welfare' within the England and Wales juvenile justice system; 'Justice, pénale, criminologie et production de l'ordre: les tendances de la recherche et de la politique criminelle depuis 1980 en Grande Bretagne' (1991) 2 *Déviance et société*, 187–221.

such measures are properly targeted has intensified as a result[51] and it is worth noting that, after almost a decade of decline, rates of custody for juveniles increased between 1990 and 1991, from 1,700 to 1,887.[52]

For the first time, however, it has become possible to deal with 17-year-olds using the same mechanisms for diversion from court that have been available for juveniles. Some resistance to this by the police was anticipated because of the stereotype, also shared by some of the general public, that 17-year-olds (and young adults generally) would be more experienced, more 'street-wise' offenders, unresponsive to lenient measures. Interestingly, Evans's research has undermined this to some extent. He found in a small sample of 17–20-year-olds that 'half of the males and two-thirds of the females had no criminal histories as juveniles and 80 per cent of both sex groups had no citable cautions at the time of sentence'.[53] He suggested that a strict application of the new national standards, and careful oversight of police practice by the Crown Prosecution Service, would significantly reduce the number of young adults who are currently prosecuted.

The history of juvenile justice in England and Wales has largely been a history of unintended consequences and, despite the availability of increasingly sophisticated monitoring procedures, it is by no means a foregone conclusion that the CJA 1991 will work as the policy-makers intend. However, it seems highly unlikely that high rates of diversion from prosecution that have been achieved with under-14-years-olds, and the high rates of diversion achieved with young women generally, will be significantly reversed. Given the fact that so few under-14-year-olds are prosecuted, it may well be that resistance to raising the age of prosecutability will be worn down and that the age of criminal responsibility will be brought more into line with other age limits in Europe. There is even the possibility, if the numbers become low enough for young men (they are already low for girls) that penal custody for 15-year-olds will be abolished. In both cases there are European precedents for such developments.

The situation with young men aged 16–17 is more problematic. Whatever statistics may suggest to the contrary, they are easily associated with an image of serious crime. It may prove difficult to abolish custody for this age group, even if numbers can be lowered, particularly in those parts of the country whose use of custody is above the national average. As respects cautioning the same applies, and there is a possibility that those areas with low cautioning rates will yet be brought up to the standards of the best, and that 17-year-olds will benefit from this process. The process will be helped by the fact that diversion from prosecution seems no longer to be associated with any particular philosophy in England and Wales, and

[51] C. Ball, 'Young Offenders and the Youth Court' [1992] *CrimLRev.* 277–87.
[52] Home Office, *Criminal Statistics England and Wales* (1991).
[53] R. Evans, 'Cautioning and the Young Adult Offender' (1991), 603.

has come to be regarded as good practice, whether one subscribes to a welfare (help the children) model, a developmental (growing out of crime) model, a just deserts (offence seriousness and proportionality) model, or merely an administrative (cost-effectiveness) model.

DIVERSION IN THE NETHERLANDS: THE FRAMEWORK FOR
DIVERTING CHILDREN AND YOUNG PEOPLE

As Brants and Field[54] have described, the Netherlands is one of the continental countries in which a great diversity of diversion mechanisms exists. The police can drop a case unconditionally (no further action) or might give a fine, although this is only possible for a certain number of misdemeanours (*overtredingen*). This is the so-called '*transactie*' by the police. The case will not come to court unless the offender fails to pay the fine, whereupon a higher fine will be demanded by the public prosecutor in court. It is purely a matter of efficiency to deal with the large bulk of misdemeanours in this way. This legal power (Article 74c of the Criminal Code) is given to the police to deal with offenders who have reached the age of 16.

The police power to drop a case unconditionally is used particularly frequently in cases involving delinquent juveniles between 12 and 18 years old. Depending on the attitude and circumstances of the offender and the gravity of the offence, the police may send the juvenile home or bring the juvenile and perhaps his parents into contact with an agency specializing in social and truancy problems. No conditions, apart from attendance at a Halt project (discussed below), may be attached to a decision to dismiss a case, and no legal consequences attach to such a decision.

The decision whether or not to take a case further and to initiate court proceedings against an adult suspected of a criminal offence lies solely with the public prosecutor. In juvenile criminal law the monopoly on the decision to prosecute has been restricted by a requirement that if a public prosecutor wishes to dismiss a case conditionally, he/she must ask the permission of the juvenile judge. The conditions may include the absence of reoffending during a fixed period, reparation for damage caused, or fulfilment of an alternative sanction (see below). Under Article 74 of the Criminal Code, the public prosecutor also needs the permission of the juvenile judge when he/she wishes to settle the case with the suspect and guarantee non-prosecution in return for payment of a sum of money (*transactie*—discussed in detail in Chap. 7). The maximum amount of a

---

[54] See Chap. 7.

transactie for a juvenile is f. 500 (£150), the same as the maximum fine which a juvenile judge may impose. In the Bill to Revise Juvenile Criminal Law, recently passed, the maximum is f. 5,000 (£1,500), and the public prosecutor can impose an alternative sanction as a condition for a dismissal.

The legal basis on which the juvenile judge might divert a juvenile offender from (pre-trial) custody is by suspension of the order for pre-trial detention. This suspension of pre-trial detention is also legally possible in adult criminal procedure. Juvenile criminal law does not create more diversion from trial instruments for the juvenile judge. As we shall see below, the juvenile judge has, however, the opportunity to impose an 'alternative sanction' instead of a juvenile detention order, which means diversion from custody.

Thus there is some legal basis for diversion from court and custody in juvenile criminal law. We will see below an important difference between what has been settled in law and developments in policy and practice.

DIVERSION IN THE NETHERLANDS: DEVELOPMENTS IN POLICY AND PRACTICE

The fundamental attitude of the authorities (police and public prosecutors) which deal with young offenders is pragmatic. The purpose of the exercise is seen more often as finding the most effective solution for the individual juvenile, rather than applying the law. This tendency, which originated in the 1960s, is frequently characterized by opponents as a soft approach, and is currently under pressure from government and from public opinion. The authorities are more and more called upon to give offenders a short, sharp shock, an approach advocated by the government and sometimes described as 'the justice approach'. The Royal Commission on juvenile criminal law, which put forward a blueprint for revising legislation,[55] stressed the changing position of juveniles and youth in society. The lowering of the age of majority from 21 to 18,[56] the development of a children's rights movement and in general the greater self-awareness of youth gave this Commission the justification for emphasizing the responsibility of juveniles and youth for their own (criminal) behaviour. The Bill to Revise the Juvenile Criminal Law has adopted most of the Commission's suggestions. Thus the Bill stresses the idea of responsibility and would institute a less protective and less welfare-orientated criminal procedure for juveniles with consequences for diversion mechanisms too.

[55] Commissie Anneveldt, *Sanctierecht voor Jeugdigen*, 's-Gravenhage; Staatsuitgeverij (1982).
[56] The Bill to lower the age of majority to 18 was put to the Second Chamber in 1978, but only passed in 1987 and brought into force in 1988.

As already seen above, the police have broad discretion in handling criminal cases, and determine the input of cases to the public prosecutor. The development of selection policies with regard to juvenile criminal cases has become well known and in some police departments this is seen as a very effective way of dealing with juvenile delinquency. Doing nothing, dismissing the case, except for a discussion at the police station and a meeting with the parents will keep most juveniles from committing offences. The police have the informal power to report only the more serious cases to the Public Prosecution Service. In order to promote more national equality in this field the procurators-general have established guidelines for the police regarding the exercise of their informal discretionary powers in criminal cases against juveniles, distinguishing between the more serious cases and comparatively trivial cases. The use of violence and the extent of the cost of damage caused are criteria for the category of 'serious' cases, which will always be reported. Recidivism in serious or less serious cases is also a criterion for formal reporting to the Public Prosecution Service. To some extent, largely depending on the impact and philosophy of the juvenile police department, the police will give some sort of support to the juvenile. This can consist of having discussions with the parents and the juvenile, in an effort to find a school or training, or some other institution for youth welfare, which can give support and help on a voluntary basis. When serious family problems are detected, especially when younger children of about 12 to 14 years are involved, the police will provide a social report to the Child Welfare Council.

The exercise of discretionary powers by the police in juvenile criminal cases is largely accepted and does not meet with criticism. Only the fact of inequality between different districts in the country appears to be criticized.

In about 1981 a new phenomenon emerged in juvenile police practice in combination with the increased attention given to the prevention of crime in political debates and from the government. Confronted by a serious problem of vandalism, municipal authorities, acting in close co-operation with the police and the public prosecutor, introduced a project whereby the young offenders (vandals) would clear up any mess they had caused. Offenders who were apprehended had a choice between being reported and prosecuted, or spending some Saturdays repairing the damage they had caused, or completing another similar repairing or cleaning task of about twenty hours. Until the introduction of these so-called Halt projects,[57] vandals—and especially first offenders—were mostly dismissed by the police, with no action being taken against them. Classifying vandalism as 'trivial cases', however, was alleged to be a poor policy from an educational

---

[57] Halt means in Dutch *Het Alternatief* (the alternative).

point of view. Research which suggested that these schemes were effective (for example, less recidivism when a Halt project was executed) gave the government the necessary evidence to justify continuing financial support.[58] This research led to the extension of Halt projects to include shoplifting as well as vandalism. A Halt project is a diversion mechanism which is unique in the Dutch criminal justice system because it is only possible in juvenile criminal cases, not in those involving adults.

Interestingly, it is the connotation of pedagogic and educational values which underlies this police diversion mechanism, giving the Bill to Revise the Juvenile Criminal Law some clear ideological principles upon which to base changes in the law. The Bill introduces the 'conditional dismissal by the police' into the Criminal Code by giving the offender the opportunity to complete a project of up to a maximum of twenty hours. When the juvenile has completed the project to the satisfaction of the police, this will be reported to the public prosecutor and the right to prosecute is consequently no longer open. The government takes the view that the legal position of the suspect/offender does not merit discussion, because of the lenient treatment of the juvenile at this stage in the juvenile justice system. Nevertheless, we must consider the adverse legal position of the juvenile. Although the juvenile can reject the proposed project, the genuineness of the required consent of the young offender to the project is perhaps doubtful. Moreover, the juvenile will not be acting under legal advice. If the required project is refused or not carried out properly, the police are bound to send the official report about the crime to the prosecutor. Before 1980, however, most of these juveniles would have had their offences of vandalism dismissed by the police and would have escaped with nothing more than a reprimand.

Dismissal by the public prosecutor is based on the 'expediency' or 'opportunity' principle. In juvenile cases the condition will not only be an amount of money: the public prosecutor has the power to impose an alternative sanction as an additional condition of dismissal. The case will not be dismissed unless the alternative sanction has been carried out satisfactorily. The alternative sanction may include community service or an element of training to improve the juvenile's social skills. In the Guidelines for Experiments with Alternative Sanctions[59] the aims of the work projects are described as follows: 'to carry out within a fixed period of time, certain well described tasks, useful to the community and of an educational character,

---

[58] M. Kruissink and C. Verwers, *Halt: een alternatieve aanpak van vandalisme, Eindrapport van een evaluatie-onderzoek naar Halt-projecten*, WODC/Gouda Quint, 's-Gravenhage/Arnhem (1989).

[59] 'Raamwerkvan uitgangspunten en richtlijnen voor experimenten met alternatieve sancties voor jeugdigen', (1983) 5 *Justitiele Verkenningen*, 43–57.

218   *L. Gelsthorpe, M. Nellis, J. Bruins, Annelies van Vliet*

preferably during leisure time. The educative impact might be increased if the nature or content of the activities to be developed is related to the committed crime and/or damage done to society or to the individual.'

Training projects have to a certain extent the same features as the English intermediate treatment programmes (which served as a model). The aims of the training projects are described in the Guidelines as 'to undertake, within a fixed period of time, some form of training, to take courses, or other educational activities, aimed at improving social and/or practical skills needed to face life's stresses'.

The main objective of the introduction of alternative sanctions, whether implemented by the public prosecutor or by the juvenile judge (see below), is to promote a more educative juvenile justice system. Ideally, the public prosecutor is supposed to be able to give more substantial content to the conditional dismissal in giving the opportunity of an alternative sanction.

This method of dealing with juvenile offenders diverts them from court, and is faster, less stigmatizing, and more effective than a traditional punishment[60] imposed by a judge. Nevertheless, there are also negative aspects to the scheme which focus more on the juridical position of the suspect. Firstly, the prosecutor may impose a sanction which is more severe than that which a juvenile judge might have imposed had the case come to court. Secondly, diversion from court means diversion from legal safeguards, including representation by a lawyer.

In the Guidelines for Experiments with Alternative Sanctions the duration of the alternative sanction suggested by the public prosecutor could be a minimum of four and a maximum of 150 hours. Research has shown that the average number of hours is about sixty, whether imposed by the public prosecutor or the juvenile judge.[61] In the Bill to Revise the Juvenile Criminal Law the maximum duration of work or training projects which can be imposed by the public prosecutor is forty hours. In the Bill the legal settlement is based on the regulation of *transactie* by the public prosecutor by extending the conditions to include community service orders, work to repair damage caused, or attendance at a training project. The legal position of the juvenile suspect is reinforced by giving compulsory legal advice.

An alternative sanction by a juvenile judge is diversion in the sense that, although the juvenile is not diverted from the juvenile court system, he or she is diverted from detention. The juvenile judge may impose an alternative sanction at two stages in the process: pre-trial and during the trial. When the judge is considering pre-trial detention (which lasts a maximum

[60] Traditional punishments are fines of up to a maximum of f. 500 (approximately £150) and detention of up to a maximum of 6 months.
[61] P. van der Laan, *Experimenteren met alternatieve sancties voor jeugdigen, Een onderzoek naar de invoering en resultaten van alternatieven in het jeugstrafrecht* (Arnhem; Gouda Quint 1991).

of 100 days) he or she may order a so-called *Kwartaal-cursus* (quarterly course), which means that the juvenile has to attend a three-month project for five days a week during working hours.

The main objective of the development of alternative sanctions has been to promote a more educative criminal justice system—reflecting a development in modern society and the aim of reforming the juvenile offender; a welfare orientation rather than one based on classical legalist notions.

THE DUTCH SYSTEM: A FINAL COMMENT

As can be seen, Dutch diversionary mechanisms include a variety of formal and informal responses. Formal responses are formulated by the government and are directly based on the criminal law. Informal responses, as we understand it, are those which stem directly from the agencies who deal with young delinquents—such as the police, the public prosecutor, assistance bureaux, and child welfare institutions. Halt projects are an example of an informal response to a specific kind of delinquency—involving co-operation between the police, the public prosecutor, and municipal authorities. The Bill intends to bring the Halt project and other similar alternative sanctions within a formal, legal framework.

There is support for informal action in Recommendation (87) 20 of the Committee of Ministers of the Council of Europe on social reactions to juvenile delinquency which, under the heading of 'Diversion—Mediation' encourages 'the development of diversion and mediation procedures at public prosecutor level or at police level, in countries where the police has prosecuting functions, in order to prevent minors from entering into the criminal justice system and suffering the consequences'.[62] There is a useful supplementary recommendation which aims to 'ensure that in such procedures the consent of the minor to the measures on which the diversion is conditional and, if necessary, the co-operation of his family are secured'. In other words, appropriate attention should be paid to the rights and interests of the minor as well as to those of the victim. The Recommendation endorses reference to procedural rights in Article 6 of the ECHR. All too clearly, then, it can be seen from the above description of developments that diversion and mediation can come into conflict with procedural rights.

Recent research on juvenile crime shows some data on diversion and sentencing. About one-third of all recorded juvenile offenders are dealt with by the police through dismissals and diversion. Of the total of 'prosecutable' juveniles, 70 per cent are dealt with by the public prosecutor by

---

[62] Committee of Ministers of the Council of Europe, Recommendation No. R. (87) 20.

conditional or unconditional dismissal and 30 per cent are convicted and sentenced by the juvenile judge. Alternative sanctions increased from about 300 in 1983 to about 2,800 in 1990. More than a quarter are imposed by the prosecutor as a condition of a dismissal.[63] In the preamble to the Recommendation mentioned above it can be seen that the Committee of Ministers is 'convinced that the penal system for minors should continue to be characterized by its objective of education and social integration and that it should as far as possible abolish imprisonment for minors'. A decrease in custodial sentences was expected to be the consequence of the introduction of alternative sanctions. However, despite the increase in the use of alternative sanctions, there has not been a corresponding decrease in the use of custodial sanctions.[64] The number of unconditional custodial sentences has stabilized during the last three years.[65] Between 1980 and 1990 the amount of recorded juvenile crime diminished. Property offences were about 80 per cent of the total. Violent offences increased by 38 per cent during the period of the research, and amount to about 6 per cent of the total. The overall increase in the total number of juveniles sentenced can be questioned in the light of the fall in the amount of recorded juvenile crime. All in all, the introduction of alternative sanctions has not succeeded in achieving diversion, but on the contrary may have resulted in net-widening.

DIVERSION AND HUMAN RIGHTS

The European Convention on Human Rights is of importance in the Netherlands as in England and Wales. As Swart and Young[66] indicated, in the Netherlands the Convention is directly applicable as part of Dutch law, and the judge has to apply international law in cases of conflict with national law. When it comes to an alternative sanction imposed by the police or the public prosecutor, however, the case never gets to court, which calls into question the application of Article 6, which requires observance of the right to a fair trial and an impartial judge. The Convention applies to juveniles as well as to adults. Apart from the European Convention, international standard minimum rules are also applicable in this context.

Traditionally, an important distinction between prosecution systems in Europe has been between those based on the legality principle, and those

[63] J. Junger-Tas, M. Kruissink and P. van der Laan, *Ontwikkeling van de Jeugdcriminaliteit en de justitiele jeugdbescherming: periode 1980–1990*, Gouda Quint/WODC, Onderzoek en Beleid, Nr. 119 (1992).
[64] Ibid.   [65] Ibid.   [66] See Chap. 4.

based on the 'opportunity' or 'expediency' principle. The former requires that all cases in which there is sufficient evidence are prosecuted in the courts. The argument in favour of this system is that it can prevent potential abuses of official power, and ensures equality of treatment before the law. The opportunity principle, which operates in England and Wales and in the Netherlands (as well as in France), means that the prosecutor has the opportunity to bring a case to court, but is not obliged to do so. The advantage claimed for this system is that it better expresses the demands of modern penal philosophy and, more pragmatically, it avoids the courts having to deal with all kinds of violations, including very minor ones. Avoidance of prosecution, however, can lead to criticisms of a neglect of due process. Such criticisms have been applied, for example, to 'caution plus' schemes in the United Kingdom and to Halt projects in the Netherlands.

As has already been noted, in some cases, the 'penalties' exacted through 'caution plus' schemes may exceed the disposal which a court would have been likely to use if the young person had been prosecuted. The Dutch National Ombudsman has decided that cautioning (a reprimanding speech) by the public prosecutor is not allowed, because a caution is a form of infliction of sorrow, and thus fulfils the definition of punishment.[67] The *trias politica* requires a separation between administrative, judicial, and legislative power. Punishments should be imposed by the court. Since a caution does not interfere very much in a person's life, the objections of the Ombudsman are perhaps over-stated, but we must be careful because therein lies a slippery slope. Halt projects represent a much greater interference because they entail restrictions on liberty. They are imposed by non-judicial Halt bureaux following referral by the police. The public prosecutor has little to do with the matter, and the judge nothing at all. In the Bill there is a slight improvement, since the public prosecutors have to give approval to a designated police officer before he or she can impose a Halt project on an offender. However, this may well develop into a mere formality. A lawyer need not be present, and it is considered to be sufficient if the police officer informs the juvenile of his or her rights. It is difficult to be confident that the police will offer all the arguments for and against diversion and going to trial. There should be a lawyer to give independent advice. Moreover, there should be some possibility of appeal and a procedure to deal with any grievances that arise during a project, a necessity also stressed by international rules.[68]

---

[67] Nationale Ombudsman, *Rapport* 90/R847, 20 December 1990.

[68] United Nations Standard Minimum Rules for the Administration of Juvenile Justice (Beijing Rules), General Assembly Resolution 40/33, 29 November 1985; United Nations Standard Minimum Rules for Non-Custodial Measures (Tokyo Rules), General Assembly Resolution 45/110, 14 December 1990.

In support of Halt projects the proponents of the Bill refer to a Recommendation of the Committee of Ministers of the Council of Europe (Recommendation No. R (87) 20). This does indeed recommend the development of diversion and mediation procedures at public prosecutor level or at police level, but only in so far as the police have prosecutorial functions, which is not the case in the Netherlands. Therefore, if the permission of the prosecutor becomes a mere formality, this will not be enough to meet the requirements of the Recommendation. If the public prosecutor wishes to impose an alternative sanction, the Bill provides that a lawyer must be appointed, which is an improvement on the present protection for the rights of the juvenile. There will be a lawyer only where the duration of a project is for more than twenty hours.

The exent to which the activities are truly voluntary has also been questioned. Of course the consent of the juvenile is needed before an alternative can be imposed. But, as it is, he or she has to decide without the help of a lawyer. It is doubtful whether the juvenile will be able to weigh appropriately the pros and cons of diversion and going to trial without such help. Den Hartog,[69] basing her comments on several European judgments,[70] finds a number of requirements for a waiver of the exercise of the rights of Article 6 to be valid; (a) the offender must act of his or her own free will; (b) he or she should be informed sufficiently and clearly of the situation; (c) he or she must be mentally competent; (d) any form of constraint must be absent; (e) he or she must be given a sufficient amount of time to come to a decision; (f) the waiver must be established in an unequivocal manner. As for requirement (d), it may not be easy to avoid any form of constraint, but the offender must be aware of pros and cons and then make his or her own decision.

In the case of procedural rights a waiver requires minimum guarantees commensurate with its importance. In the *Pfeifer* case, a legal question was put to Pfeifer in the absence of a lawyer, and as a layperson she was not able to appreciate its full implications. The European Court held that there had been a breach of Article 6(1).[71]

Since a juvenile, confronted with the question whether or not to have his or her case decided by an impartial judge, will be a layperson, he/she needs the help of a lawyer. When he/she goes to court, the judge will have to decide on his/her guilt according to rules of evidence. Until then the offender is entitled to the presumption of innocence (see Article 6(2)

[69] J. den Hartog, *Artikel 6 EVRM: grenzen aan het streven de straf eerder op de daad te doen volgen*, Antwerpen–Apeldoorn, Maklu Uitgevers (1992).
[70] See e.g. ECHR, 27 February 1980, Series A No. 35, 54 (*Deweer*); ECHR, 12 February 1985, Series A No. 89, 28 (*Colozza*); ECHR, 6 December 1988, Series A No. 176, 82 (*Barberà*); ECHR, 23 May 1991, Series A No. 204, 51 (*Oberschlick*).
[71] ECHR, 25 February 1992, Series A No. 227, 37 (*Pfeifer*).

ECHR). Moreover, the punishability of the offender may then be challenged in court. When the police or the public prosecutor impose an alternative sanction, these matters will not be scrutinized in the same way.

The United Nations Standard Minimum Rules for Non-Custodial Measures (the so-called 'Tokyo Rules')[72] do not give the police powers to impose non-custodial measures. Public prosecutors have such powers, but only for minor offences, and the consent of the offender is required.

The United Nations Standard Minimum Rules for the Administration of Juvenile Justice (the 'Beijing Rules') stress (in the Commentary) the point that the consent should not be unchallengeable, since it might sometimes be given out of sheer desperation on the part of the juvenile. Care should be taken to minimize the potential for coercion and intimidation at all levels in the diversion process. Provision should be made for an objective appraisal by a competent authority. Moreover, any disposal in relation to a juvenile offender should be in proportion to the nature and circumstances of the offence, and the character and antecedents of the offender. Responses geared towards the welfare of the juvenile may exceed what is appropriate and therefore infringe his or her fundamental rights. Here, too, proportionality should be safeguarded. That means that the imposition of a rather severe alternative sanction for a minor offence for no other reason than that it is educative for the juvenile should not be allowed.

The United Nations Convention on the Rights of the Child came into force in September 1990. In September 1992, 123 states had ratified it, including the United Kingdom (on 16 December 1991), but not the Netherlands. The Netherlands did propose a Bill for approval in September 1992, and that is now under discussion. Article 40 of the Convention deals with the administration of juvenile justice. It suggests that States Parties seek to promote measures for dealing with children without resorting to judicial proceedings, providing that human rights and legal safeguards are fully respected. The Dutch Government states in the commentary on the Bill for approval that Dutch juvenile criminal law is and will be in accordance with the requirements of the Convention. But there is scope for doubt about the accuracy of this statement.

It follows that diversion in both the United Kingdom and the Netherlands entails diversion away from legal safeguards. The Dutch government just sits and waits, because there has as yet been no decision on the matter by the European Court. There is a tendency to interpret international provisions narrowly, thus minimizing both the guarantees and the costs. But it may be argued that it is time for a judgment of the European Court on Dutch practice.

---

[72] Adopted at the Eighth United Nations Congress on the Causes of Crime and the Treatment of Offenders, Havana, Cuba, 27 Aug.–7 Sept. 1990.

DIVERSION IN ENGLAND AND WALES AND THE NETHERLANDS:
TOWARDS AN INTEGRATED ANALYSIS

In the past decade the United Nations has produced the Beijing Rules on Standards of Administration of Juvenile Justice (1985), the Convention on the Rights of the Child (1989), and, more recently, the Riyadh Rules on the Prevention of Juvenile Delinquency (1990),[73] but the UN rules are curiously coy about making definitive statements on some key areas of delinquency policy. For example, age is widely recognized to be a key and enduring variable in delinquent behaviour—with the peak age of delinquency being between 16 and 18 throughout Europe and the USA—yet the UN has not provided any concrete age limits, and instead refers to the 'economic, social, political, cultural, and legal systems of member states'. This makes for a wide variety of ages coming under the definition of juvenile, ranging from 7 years to 18 years or above.[74] England and Wales, with an age of criminal responsibility at 10, is second only to the Republic of Ireland and Switzerland,[75] whose age of criminal responsibility remains at 7. In the Netherlands the age of prosecutability is 12; an age chosen because it signifies a new phase in a child's life with a move to secondary education. Whilst some pressure groups in England and Wales press for the age of prosecution to be raised to 14,[76] some juvenile justice interest groups in the Netherlands argue for the lowering of this age to 10. In this sense then, any suggestions of Europeanization of justice are limited. There are good reasons to adopt a consistent age of criminal responsibility (for example, the evidence from child development studies suggests that children do not have sophisticated understanding of concepts of crime until a certain age) and yet there is no consistent view on this.

The upper age limit for specifically 'juvenile' justice is 18 in the Netherlands (though there is scope to prosecute 16 and 17-year-olds as adults— depending on the seriousness of the offence). In England and Wales the cut-off age limit of the newly named 'youth court' is now 18.[77] But in neither the Dutch nor the English and Welsh system does the inclusion of eighteen-year-olds in 'juvenile' or 'youth' justice necessarily mean an

[73] United Nations Standard Minimum Rules for the Administration of Juvenile Justice (Beijing Rules); United Nations Convention on the Rights of the Child; United Nations Guiding Principles for the Prevention of Delinquency (The Riyadh Rules).
[74] F. Dunkel 'Legal Differences in Juvenile Criminology in Europe', in Booth (ed.), *Juvenile Justice.*
[75] Though in Switzerland only educational measures (as opposed to criminal) are imposed up to the age of 14.
[76] Following the public outcry concerning the alleged murder of 2-year-old James Bulger in an English city it would have to be acknowledged that this is a remote possibility.
[77] C. Ball, 'Young Offenders and the Youth Court', 277–87.

extension of diversionary principles. Rather, as we can see from the description of each system, this phenomenon emphasizes dual thinking—diversion on the one hand, but tougher and longer penalties for 16 and 17-year-olds especially.

It is also possible to suggest that, while the court has long since been seen as a 'last resort' for dealing with juvenile offenders, the idea of juveniles being seen as 'more responsible' for their actions is not one which is easily dismissed. Such ideas are enshrined in the move towards 'just deserts' thinking which is evident in both countries. In the English/Welsh system this sort of thinking becomes clear in the periodic attacks on the effectiveness of cautioning and other diversion tactics. In the Netherlands it can be seen that there is perhaps little hesitation now in bringing offenders to court to impose 'alternative' sanctions; in some senses this development echoes the 'net-widening' effect of diversion strategies widely debated in England and Wales in the 1970s.

In England and Wales diversion from court can be decided by the police, juvenile liaison panels, or the Crown Prosecution Service. Diversion here includes the possibility of taking no further action, reporting matters to Social Services, or issuing formal cautions (including 'instant' and 'caution plus' cautions). In the Netherlands, the police have corresponding powers to take no further action or to report juvenile offending to the Child Welfare Council. Diversion from court can also be decided by the police in proposing a so-called Halt project for the juvenile.

Interestingly, while the idea of a juvenile liaison panel to consider the desirability of prosecution has been officially endorsed in England and Wales, formal tripartite meetings between public prosecutor, child welfare council, and juvenile judge in the Netherlands are to be phased out. The Bill to Revise the Juvenile Criminal Law does not provide scope for these three-way meetings to continue; there is only official endorsement for communication between the public prosecutor and the Child Welfare Council.

In conclusion it is worth noting that the whole area of diversion decision-making in England and Wales is governed by policy circulars which are essentially resistant to legal enforceability as the *L* and *B* cases show, whereas in the Netherlands there is now a law which will put diversion decision-making on a statutory footing.

Examination of the different juvenile justice systems in this way is necessarily brief and selective. However, even the most cursory exploration of the different legal frameworks, decision-making procedures, policy, and practice suggests that the Europeanization of juvenile criminal justice remains a distant phenomenon. Indeed, the exploration of the differences here serves to highlight a number of disturbing issues in relation to due

226   *L. Gelsthorpe, M. Nellis, J. Bruins, Annelies van Vliet*

process, possible contravention of certain legal values embodied in Article 6 of the European Convention on Human Rights, and differences between official juvenile justice policy and practice. What emerges is a picture of a 'tidy' theoretical legal world and of an 'untidy' reality of social practice.

11

Prosecutors, Examining Judges, and Control of Police Investigations

STEWART FIELD, PETER ALLDRIDGE, AND NICO JÖRG

RULES AND COURTS: CONTROLLING THE INTERROGATION PROCESS

At present, in both countries 'interrogation is *the* investigative strategy of the police'.[1] Accordingly, in our discussion of the role of rules and courts in the control of investigation we concentrate on the procedural framework for interrogation.

(i) The Netherlands

Suspects arrested and interrogated by the Dutch police have more limited rights than their English or Welsh counterparts. They have no right to have a lawyer present during police interrogation: a duty defence counsel will be informed that the suspect is held in police custody, but questioning may continue in his/her absence. The police can hold the suspect for six hours for interrogation; for seventy-two hours in the interest of the investigation without prosecutorial consent, and for another seventy-two hours with the consent of the Prosecutor. The only record of the interview(s) is a police statement usually signed by the defendant. Interviews are not tape-recorded nor taken down verbatim. Thus arrested Dutch suspects are faced with a police force with very broad discretionary control over the circumstances of custody and questioning. In some ways the picture resembles the situation in England and Wales before the Police and Criminal Evidence Act 1984 (PACE). Then, a number of observation studies of police interrogation concluded that a variety of inducements and threats were routinely offered to get confessions.[2]

Though no empirical studies appear to have been done in the Netherlands

We are very grateful to Joanne Mortimer for her assistance in the preparation of the final text of this essay.

[1] M. McConville, A. Sanders and R. Leng, *The Case for the Prosecution* (London; Routledge 1991), 57; J Naeyé, *Heterdaad* (doctoral thesis V.U.); Lochem; van den Brink 1989, 231.

[2] B. Irving, *Police Interrogation: The Psychological Approach*, Royal Commission on Criminal Procedure Research Studies Nos. 1 & 2 (London; HMSO, 1980).

on police tactics in interrogation,[3] there are regular complaints about un-acceptable inducements to confess. Suspects usually make or are alleged to make admissions or damaging statements in the first seventy-two hours. In the 1970s, research indicated that 90 per cent of suspects denied the charge on arrest but after four days of police detention 90 per cent had confessed.[4] Defence lawyers claim that psychological pressures will often be used to achieve this.[5] Article 29 of the Dutch Code of Criminal Procedure forbids the use of any interrogation tactics which are likely to produce involuntary confessions. If a confession is ruled involuntary it will be inadmissible because illegally-obtained evidence is excluded. In the 1970s the Dutch adopted the exclusionary rule in respect of improperly obtained evidence and applied it to the 'fruits of the poison tree'. But while the consequences of breach are certain, the standard determining what is a breach remains vague. What is an involuntary statement? What is likely to produce one?

The received academic view in the Netherlands is that it is unfair to deceive a suspect or to promise freedom in exchange for a confession.[6] But the burden of proving involuntariness is on the defence. In most cases this is an insurmountable burden because the only witnesses are the inter-rogating officers. This produces an intractable problem familiar in British policing. Threats or inducements may or may not have been used to get the admissions. The police report of the interrogation is not likely to reveal this. If there is significant evidence to support defence claims of unaccept-able inducement the prosecutor may drop the case if he is not convinced that there is sufficient alternative evidence to put before the court. But if he decides to proceed, Dutch prosecutors cannot exclude the statement from the file even if they think it was obtained illegally. Whether it actu-ally constitutes admissible evidence would be for the trial judge to decide. In general, cases go forward with damaging statements from the accused on file, with little concrete evidence of how they were obtained.

The Dutch then have strict exclusionary rules but the framework of procedural rules determining how interrogation is to be conducted is rather limited. In England and Wales the problems associated with unregulated interrogation gave much of the impetus to PACE. Yet there are only

[3] The exception to this is Naeyé, *Heterdaad*, who hired actors to post bills contrary to a city ordinance. Thereafter they merely refused (perfectly legally) to state their names. They then observed police reaction.

[4] A. Rosett, 'Trial and Discretion in Dutch Criminal Justice', (1972) 19 *UCLA Law Re-view* 353 at 363; unpublished research by C. N. Peyster, cited by R. L. Bergsma, 'Het J. C. B., tussentijdse balans' (1971) 1 *Delikt en Delinkwent* 408–17, 414. L. C. M. Tigges and A. C. Berghuis, *Voorlopige hechtenis: toepassing schorsing en zaken van lange duur* (WODC–Ministerie van Justitie, 1981).

[5] L. H. Leigh and J. E. Hall Williams, *The Prosecution Process in Denmark, Sweden and The Netherlands* (Leamington Spa; James Hall 1981), 51.

[6] W. P. J. Pompe, 'Het bewijs in strafzaken' (1959), reprinted in *Vijf opstellen van Willem Pompe* (Zwolle; Tjeenk Willink, 1974) 39; J. Remmelink, 'Het verhoor in strafzaken', 1966 *RM Themis*, 331–8.

limited signs of reform in the Netherlands.[7] In part this may be because there are alternative checks on the strength of the prosecution case (see below). But it may also be that confessions made in police custody but retracted shortly afterwards are given less probative weight in the Dutch system. This is also hard to prove without detailed empirical analysis of case files and no such studies have been done. But there are some pointers.

First, in law an uncorroborated confession alone cannot form the evidential basis for a conviction. It is true that the rules governing the kind of evidence that can act as supporting evidence are relatively lax. For example, if there is a confession in a murder case, evidence of a dead body is sufficient corroboration. However, it is not just a question of the technical minimum requirements; the court has to be convinced that the probative weight of evidence reaches the standard of proof. It is said that a confession has to be detailed and coherent before it will lead to conviction where the supporting evidence is as inconclusive as a body. If confessions are less detailed and the defence can point to circumstances associated with false admissions, judges are sceptical. The depressed, the immature, the addicted, the wounded, are known to be vulnerable. In more serious cases,[8] suspects must be re-interviewed by an examining judge, usually with the suspect's lawyer present, and this provides an early opportunity to deny that the confession was made or to allege the offering of threats or inducements. When this happens what the suspect says in these less coercive circumstances is regarded as important. Furthermore, quite regularly the trial judge will refer a case back for interrogation by the examining judge if the defence is that the statements to the police are contradictory or unclear.[9]

It should also be remembered that, within the Dutch legal system, convictions and acquittals may be reviewed *de novo*[10] by one of the five courts of appeal. This offers a mechanism for encouraging a consistent view of the weight of factual evidence that can be regarded as discharging the burden of proof. A jury system only operated in the Netherlands between 1811 and 1813: all first instance cases are now decided by professional judges and they tend to look to their court of appeal for a standard. This means that the way in which the courts of first instance reason in rejecting claims of coerced confessions is regularly tested by the courts of appeal and the ultimate legal standard is set by the Supreme Court.[11]

---

[7] A proposal to require that lawyers be present during police interrogation was defeated in Parliament. There has been some suggestion that records of interviews be taken down verbatim and there has been some increase in tape-recording.

[8] That is, those in which the prosecution request that the investigating judge order pre-trial detention.

[9] Art. 316 CCP.

[10] This is appeal by way of full rehearing, and includes re-examination of witnesses and even the examination of new ones. Sentences may be reduced or increased.

[11] The standard is set in HR 22 January 1980, [1980] NJ 203. If the (trial/appeals) court uses the confession as evidence despite defence allegations of coercion, the court has a duty to give reasons for rejecting the defence claim.

(ii) England and Wales

In contrast, in England and Wales since 1984, stronger attempts have been made to use detailed legal rules on interrogation to prevent the police using inducements and threats to get confessions. The origins of this concern may be rooted in the great probative significance accorded to confession evidence. Not only can an uncorroborated confession sustain a conviction, but the weight given in practice to disputed confessions is a matter for individual juries or magistrates. Not surprisingly, some juries place great weight on them. Within a tradition based on orality in the presentation of evidence, a court of appeal which does not hear witnesses is reluctant to interfere with first instance assessment. This may very well be regarded as one of the least desirable consequences of the respect given to the verdict of the jury. This means that suspects will quite regularly be convicted largely or exclusively on the basis of confessions to the police.[12]

If confessions are often decisive pieces of evidence the need to control how they are obtained becomes crucial. Before PACE, investigating officers had wide. discretion to control the interrogation environment. As in the Netherlands today the limits of permissible persuasive tactics were vague[13] and it was hard to know what tactics had actually been used to obtain confessions in the absence of credible witnesses and reliable interview records. Legal advisers were seldom present because even when requested (and this was rare) the police routinely refused access and were able to do so because there were very vague exceptions[14] to the right to see a solicitor. Amongst other things this meant there was normally no independent witness to what went on in the interview. As in the Netherlands now, exchanges between suspect and police were not recorded. The only product of the interview was a statement, usually written by the police and signed by the suspect. As these statements would not reveal any inducement or threat offered, the prospects of a challenge to a confession were uncertain. Most suspects hate uncertainty more than anything[15] and there were pressures to make them think twice before calling police officers liars at trial[16]— and officers almost always denied offering inducements. For most it made

---

[12] Baldwin and McConville's study suggested about 20 per cent of cases would be fatally weakened by the loss of the confession evidence: 'The Role of Interrogation in Crime Discovery and Conviction' (1982) 22 *British Journal of Criminology*, 165.

[13] By the 1980s the law was that confessions would be excluded if they were not given of the defendant's 'own free will': *R. v. Rennie* [1982] 1 All ER 385.

[14] *Judges Rules* [1964] 1 All ER 327, Preamble, para. (c).

[15] M. Zander, *Cases and Materials on the English Legal System* (6th edn.) (London; Weidenfeld 1992), 281–4.

[16] If a suspect does challenge the character of a prosecution witness, this puts his/her character (credibility) in issue, and allows previous convictions which are relevant to his/her credit to be adduced before the judge: see J. McEwan, *Evidence and the Adversarial Process* (Oxford; Blackwell 1992), 158–63.

more sense to take the discount on sentence[17] for an early guilty plea and, in their eyes, minimize the chance of the prison sentence. In contrast, in the Netherlands there is no equivalent to the guilty plea and the evidence of the police may be challenged without penal consequences, so withdrawal of confessions or allegations of police duplicity carry no adverse consequence.

As a result, the problem of the induced confession led to the development of a much more detailed framework of rules to govern police interrogation. Furthermore the courts have adopted a prominent role in their enforcement by excluding at trial confessions obtained after serious and substantial breach of key parts of the legal framework.[18] PACE has become an attempt to use procedural rules and courts to control police interrogation practice by tightening the definitions, thereby reducing police discretion and enabling the courts to find out what is going on.[19]

Codes made under PACE require that contemporaneous notes or tape-recordings be made of interviews with suspects in police stations or other premises (including cars), unless this is impracticable.[20] The Codes also set out in detail the limits of permissible bargaining. Officers may only indicate what effect co-operation will have on bail or charges or the ongoing investigation if it is in response to a clear request for information from the suspect. Otherwise inducements or threats are prohibited.[21] Furthermore PACE gives a right to immediate consultation with a solicitor, subject only to relatively narrowly drawn exceptions.[22]

These reforms have had a real, albeit variable, impact on interrogation practice. PACE has probably made outright fabrication of evidence and the use of sustained psychological pressure in questioning more difficult.[23] Once the tape is on the officer must be careful to comply with the Codes. PACE has probably reduced the incidence of ill-treatment in police stations.[24]

---

[17] A. Ashworth, *Sentencing and Criminal Justice* (London; Weidenfeld and Nicolson 1992), 130. The discount is one-quarter to one-third.

[18] Though the criteria for exclusion remain vague in key respects.

[19] The Royal Commission that preceded PACE tended to see the internal scrutiny of the application of the Codes of Practice by the police as the key reform, but failure of senior police scrutiny and the willingness of the courts to use the Codes of Practice as a guide to exclusion of evidence have made the Act more characteristic of the typical Anglo-Saxon, *ex post facto*, approach. This has led to rules written as guides for policemen being construed by courts as statutes dealing with admissibility.

[20] Revised Code C, *Questioning, Detention and Treatment of Persons by Police Officers*, April 1990, para. 11, reprinted in V. Bevan and K. Lidstone, *The Investigation of Crime* (London; Butterworth 1991), 600–2.

[21] Code C, para. 11.3.   [22] See s. 58(1) PACE.

[23] This is certainly the view of officers. See M. Maguire, L. Noaks, R. Hobbs, and N. Brearley, *Assessing Investigative Performance* (Cardiff; Social Research Unit, University of Wales 1992), 25.

[24] M. Maguire and C. Corbett concluded that complaints of such treatment were now relatively rare: *A Study of the Police Complaints System* (London; HMSO 1991).

But British experience suggests that, as a strategy for protecting suspects, reliance on courts and detailed rules have very real limitations. The problem has been that the police have successfully adjusted their practices to minimize their impact on police institutional goals—getting confessions from suspects they think are guilty. The courts have often been stringent in excluding confessions from 'interviews' which have not been properly recorded or from which lawyers have been wrongfully excluded. But the rules are avoided by the use of 'informal chats'.[25] The police have argued with some success before the courts that these are not interviews if their purpose is only to explain suspects' legal positions or if the exchange is initiated by them.[26] Alternatively, the police may simply deny the conversation has taken place. The result: continued off-the-record bargaining. The Home Office has responded by defining 'interview' and demanding that a note in writing be made of any comments 'volunteered' by the accused even outside the context of an interview.[27] But there is no requirement that the whole exchange be recorded and a smart detective will simply ensure that what is recorded cannot be construed as an interview. This process has undermined attempts to regulate bargaining tactics because the police offer inducements outside the formal interview which are not recorded. Thus the earlier problems of assessing reliability and pressures to confess have re-emerged in modified form.

Similar problems have beset the attempt to get solicitors present during interviews. Certainly, the courts have been fairly tough in interpreting the relevant PACE provisions[28] with the result that about 20 per cent of suspects have legal advice before charge, and rates are higher for more serious charges. Around 13 per cent have a solicitor present during interview. But again empirical evidence suggests the weakness of procedural rules, even

---

[25] These exchanges may take place at the suspect's home just after arrest, during the subsequent search of premises, in the police car on the way to the station, in the cells, or in the interview room before the formal interviewing is deemed to have started. D. Dixon, K. Bottomley, C. Coleman, H. Gill, and D. Wall, 'Safeguarding the Rights of Suspects in Custody' (1990) 1 *Policing and Society*, 115; McConville, Sanders and Leng, *The Case for the Prosecution*, 56–65; M. McConville, 'Video-taping Interrogations: Police Behaviour On and Off Camera' [1992] *CrimLRev.* 532; A. Sanders, L. Bridges, A. Mulvaney, and G. Crozier, *Advice and Assistance at Police Stations and the 24 Hour Duty Solicitor Scheme*, Lord Chancellor's Department, 1989; M. Maguire and C. Norris, *The Conduct and Supervision of Criminal Investigations*, Royal Commission on Criminal Justice Research Study No. 5 (HMSO, 1992), chap. 5(4).

[26] A comparable situation exists in the Netherlands. There is a strict requirement that a suspect should be informed of the right to remain silent. This caution should precede a formal interrogation, but the Supreme Court has ruled that 'chats' and 'unsolicited outbursts' do not fall within the rule: HR 29 September 1981, [1982] NJ 258.

[27] Revised Code C, para. 11.13 and Note of Guidance 11A.

[28] Confessions will often be excluded because of wrongful denial of access: *R.* v. *Samuel* [1988] 2 All ER 135. But see *R.* v. *Allardice* (1988) 87 CrAppR 380, *R.* v. *Dunford* (1990) 91 . CrAppR 150.

when they are detailed and rigorously enforced at trial.[29] The police usually comply with the terms of the Act by getting the suspect's signature on
the custody record declining a solicitor but frequently use a variety of
ploys to do so. Rights are read out incompletely or incomprehensibly, and
stress is placed upon the delay involved in waiting for a solicitor, the
triviality of the offence, the possibility of a solicitor later, or of early bail.
If a detained suspect exercises his/her right to a solicitor the investigators
spend time persuading suspects to let them start before the solicitor arrives.[30]
Thus for the vast majority of interviews even now there is no solicitor
present to act as independent witness or to give legal advice.

There is some suggestion, particularly from the police, that one key
effect of PACE has been ideological rather than instrumental. Emphasis
by detectives upon 'crime management' as an investigative technique has
increased. This involves greater stress on forward planning, rational use of
criminal intelligence, and the systematic collection of evidence in advance
of arrest, and accordingly less stress on obtaining confessions. But the
evidence on this is, at best, ambivalent. The most recent study of CID
culture concluded that most detectives had not 'internalized' the values of
PACE.[31] Instead, they have generally sought to limit the impact of the *ex
post facto* enforcement of the rules and to preserve their capacity to bargain with suspects.[32] Rules and courts seem to offer some, but limited,
potential for protecting suspects.

MONITORING THE INVESTIGATIVE PROCESS: THE NETHERLANDS

Although the procedural framework governing police investigation in the
Netherlands is less elaborate than in England and Wales, the police there
are subject to much greater day-to-day judicial monitoring of the way they
investigate. This is mainly done by the prosecutor but the investigating
judge plays a key part in many of the most serious cases. The primary
purpose of judicial involvement is not to enforce systems of sanctions
against the police for procedural rule-breaking but to monitor and guarantee the evidentiary quality of the official written *dossier* of evidence that
is the basis of any decision at trial. Dutch trials have developed from a new
independent, *tabula rasa*, search for the truth into what is now typically
much more a process of verification of the written results of the pre-trial
investigation stage. The *dossier* is the official account of this investigation.

---

[29] A. Sanders and L. Bridges, 'Police Malpractice and Access to Legal Advice' [1990]
CrimLRev. 494; Sanders *et al.*, *Advice and Assistance at Police Stations*, chap. 4; D. Dixon
et al., 'Safeguarding Rights', 121–3.
[30] Sanders and Bridges, 'Police Malpractice', at 501.
[31] M. Maguire and C. Norris, *Criminal Investigations*, chap. 5(3)(ii).
[32] See Dixon *et al.*, 'Safeguarding Rights'.

It is not just an internal unofficial document, as case files are in England and Wales, but an official and legally competent basis for prosecution and (where appropriate) conviction. Judges at trial usually expect to be able to make judgments solely on the basis of its contents. Witnesses are rarely called to give testimony.[33] Judges expect all relevant exculpatory and inculpatory evidence to be already in the file. They tend to object to the introduction of 'surprise' evidence during trial and will refer the case back to the investigating judge (rather than conduct interrogation themselves) if attempts are made to use such matter.

A *dossier* has four possible elements:

(1) the police file: this consists of a formal account of arrest, search and seizure, police detention, witnesses' statements, the appearance of counsel, (various) statements of the accused, police evidence from the scene of the crime, summary of the results of wire-tapping, and (where applicable),

(2) the file of the investigating judge (*Rechter-Commissaris*, henceforth RC): a statement of the accused, and of witnesses interrogated by the investigating judge on request by the prosecutor or defence counsel; forensic expert evidence; social and psychiatric reports; results of wire-tapping and an inventory of seized objects.

(3) the pre-trial detention file: a formal account of all decisions taken on such detention, together with statements by the defendant before the examining judge and possibly before the court in chambers when further extended detention is requested,

(4) a file of pre-trial proceedings: wire-tapping orders, seizure of property orders, record of appeal against pre-trial detention orders, and/or decisions on requests to discontinue the prosecution.

Trial judges make decisions largely on the basis of these reports. Only if witness or expert testimony is seriously contested will such persons be called to give oral evidence at trial. Furthermore, in most cases there will only be the police file because there will be no formal *instruction*,[34] pre-trial detention, or proceedings.

SHAPING THE FILE

To the sceptical British observer this may well appear to produce a real structural weakness at the heart of the system. Given the importance of the *dossier* it is absolutely vital that the police file is reliable. The process by which police files in England and Wales can be constructed to conceal police malpractice or the weakness of cases has been well documented.

[33] This may have to change as a result of the European Convention on Human Rights. See, *inter alia, Saj'di* v. *France*, 20 December 1993, A—261c, (1994) N.J. 358.

[34] *Instruction* is a formal pre-trial investigation by the RC.

Those who monitor police-work from such materials are rendered impotent by this construction process.[35] Does the same process occur in the Netherlands? It is true that the Dutch police, like the French, are under 'a duty to prepare an investigative record that is complete and formally correct, available to the defence as well as the prosecution, and able to withstand a searching examination'.[36] But how can one be sure that files are as complete and thorough and balanced as inquisitorial theory requires? If the file is constructed in a partisan way, the consequences are even more serious than in the British systems, where the evidence is more likely to be subject to testing examination at trial.

One answer is that the roles and relationships surrounding the building up of the *dossier* are structurally very different in Holland. First, the responsibility of the prosecutor for the case file is of very different significance in an inquisitorial context.[37] Secondly, apart from the crucial police-prosecutor relationship, defence counsel, investigating judge, and the trial judge(s) all may play a part in shaping the *dossier*. Thus the construction of the *dossier* is subject to a number of effective influences other than that of the police. At different times, the prosecutor, defence counsel, and judge will all be looking at it for evidence of weakness with the prospect of further investigation by police or examining judge. It is institutional incentives to thoroughness in the investigation of both inculpatory and exculpatory evidence that are the strength of the system.[38] The intersecting relationships involved and their effect on the *dossier* should by no means be assumed to work in the same way as the equivalent relationships in England and Wales.

Dutch prosecutors are under pressure to use their power within the system to ensure that the *dossier* is thorough and complete as a statement of germane evidence pointing to both conviction and acquittal. If they do not do so, they run the risk of being discomforted at trial. Once the police file is provisionally closed and handed to the prosecutor the complete file that will be the basis of the prosecution must be made available to defence counsel.[39] If defence counsel, having heard the client's

---

[35] McConville, Sanders and Leng, *The Case for the Prosecution*; A. Sanders 'Constructing the Case for the Prosecution' (1987) 14 JLS 229.

[36] J. H. Langbein and E. Weinreb, 'Continental Criminal Procedure: Myth and Reality' (1977) 87 *Yale LJ* 1549 at 1553–4.

[37] Even though, as in England and Wales, it is based upon police reports.

[38] Occasionally one may find in a *dossier* a copy of a letter from the RC to a local police branch asking for reasons why a mandatory procedure has not been followed. Such letters are very embarrassing to the police.

[39] In *Jespers*, the European Commission of Human Rights argued that although the ECHR did not expressly guarantee a right of access to the prosecution file, such a right could be inferred from Art. 6(3)(b). This extended to information about the offence with which the defendant was accused, credibility of witnesses, etc.: *Jespers* v. *Belgium* (1982) 27 D. & R. 61. The principle of full disclosure is regarded as being of great importance in the Netherlands. The ECHR is, of course, incorporated into Dutch law and therefore binding on Dutch courts (see Swart and Young, Chap. 4, above).

account, see ambiguity that can be resolved by inquiry, they should (and routinely do) ask the prosecutor for this to be investigated or referred to an investigating judge. Prosecutors have strong incentives to treat such requests seriously because at trial, if such a request has been refused and the defence can show the existence of unexplained, ambiguous, or incomplete information on the file, the court will postpone the trial for the information to be sought.

Such postponements can be embarrassing for the prosecutor for a number of reasons. If a prosecutor regularly gets cases referred back on the basis that supplementary investigation is required because the police case has been swallowed unsceptically or reasonable defence requests ignored, he or she will suffer two kinds of stigma. The first is the stigma of those who do not display proper judicial impartiality. The training and cultural outlook of prosecutors is that of a judicial rather than executive figure. Dutch prosecutors are selected and trained in the career judiciary system typical of the continental European tradition. Prosecutors and judges (including examining magistrates) undergo the same selection and training process for at least four years after graduation. Those brought up in the adversarial tradition are often sceptical of this notion of prosecutor as judicial functionary. But the most recent substantial study of the way Dutch prosecutors see themselves and their role suggests that the idea cannot just be dismissed as 'a resort to fiction'.[40] On the basis of a twelve months period of observation, Van de Bunt has argued that the idea of the Dutch prosecutor as judicial figure has taken root in their professional self-image.[41] Ordinary prosecutors, he argues, are:

... keen to present themselves as magistrates; according to their own statements, they do not see themselves as one of the contending parties, but as dignitaries of the court, engaged in an impartial weighing of the different interests involved, just like any judge who passes right judgments.[42]

Certainly, Van de Bunt sees tensions in the prosecutor's role as independent magistrate, who is nevertheless expected to implement the prosecution policy of the Ministry of Justice.[43] But ultimately, he sees them as an organization of magistrates stubbornly unwilling to accept bureaucratic threats to their judicial independence. Prosecutors are expected to resist

[40] The words of Goldstein and Marcus, who argue that Continental prosecutors do not see themselves as 'truly judicial' but merely accept enough of the myth to prevent themselves adopting what they regard as the partisan stance of the American prosecutor. A. Goldstein and M. Marcus, 'The Myth of Judicial Supervision in three "Inquisitorial" Systems: France, Italy and Germany' (1977) 87 *Yale LJ* 240 at 248.
[41] H. G. Van de Bunt, *Officieren van Justitie: verslag van een participerend observatie-onderzoek* (doctoral thesis, University of Utrecht, 1985), at 398.
[42] Ibid., at 399.
[43] A tension expressed in the Continental maxim: 'la plume est serve mais la parole est libre'.

pressures from the bureaucracy above to make them into obedient admin-
istrators, by balancing the public interest in crime control with the public
interest in due process. Prosecutors should not pursue conviction at any
cost. Though one can certainly find prime examples of the Dutch prosecutor as crime fighter, in general, to be thought heavily-oriented to crime
control is a threat to one's self-image and career prospects within the
prosecution service and possibly as court judge.

Regular referral back for re-investigation also brings the stigma of bureaucratic inefficiency, because it wastes court time. This is important for
two reasons. First, there is the right, laid down by Article 6 of the ECHR,
to a speedy trial. Any referral back will carry a delay of at least three to
four months. In cases where the prosecution is to blame for the delay,
violation of this right may lead to discharge or lesser sentences. Secondly,
delay has other, rather idiosyncratic, consequences. Local public prosecutors' offices always complain that an insufficient number of judges are
available to do criminal work. But how many criminal judges are allocated
depends on the number of cases *decided*, not the number pending. Incomplete files waste time and fewer decisions can be made. So the number of
judges allocated to criminal cases will be reduced and waiting times length-
ened. Because prosecutors must drop cases in which there is excessive
delay[44] this means they are placed under greater pressure to weed out
cases or prepare them properly the first time around.

These institutional incentives emphasize the basic task for the prosecutor, to ensure that all germane evidence is in the file so that the trial judge
can make decisions largely based on it. As a result, although there are no
detailed empirical studies of the way prosecutors respond to weakness in
the file, one can say that it is by no means uncommon for the prosecutor
to direct the police to pursue lines of inquiry favourable to the accused
(often at the request of defence counsel).

If Dutch prosecutors feel strong pressures to ensure that both inculpatory and exculpatory evidence is reflected in the *dossier*, how do they
make sure the police feel this too? It should be remembered that members
of the Dutch Prosecution Service, largely by virtue of its monopoly of
prosecutions, are primary agenda-setters within the criminal justice system
in a way that the Crown Prosecution Service is not.[45] The Dutch police
work within a legal structure that places them under the jurisdiction of the
prosecutor in the investigation of offences. It is part of the job of the

---

[44] See HR 2 June, 9 June 1992, [1992] NJ 731, 732. The Netherlands has a rather poor
record before European institutions in relation to the undue delay provisions. See, most
recently, ECHR, 25 November 1992, *Abdoella* v. *Netherlands* [1993] NJ 24. Generally a
delay of two years between the moment of official activity and the moment of trial needs
explanation; similarly any delay of eighteen months between court appearances.
[45] See Brants and Field, Chap. 7, above.

prosecutor to control the police.[46] Prosecutors can and do issue general investigative guidelines to the police. They can direct the police to pursue particular lines of inquiry and seek particular pieces of evidence in individual cases. Though there are no direct mechanisms for enforcing these directives, prosecutors have available the very simple expedients of refusing to prosecute and/or publicly denouncing police action if the quality of their investigative work fails to satisfy. Sometimes, the prosecutor will act in a judicial capacity and set the accused free if it turns out that there is distorted or fabricated evidence on the case file.[47] Individual officers guilty of misconduct may be reported to one of the five *procureurs-generaal*, who may bring in the internal investigative police.[48] (Procedures have been altered in 1994.) Not often but regularly prosecutors will start criminal proceedings against police officers under their jurisdiction.[49]

Defence counsel also have a key role the significance of which is sometimes not appreciated by those brought up in an adversarial tradition.[50] As well as pointing out absences and ambiguities in the file, they should monitor police distortion of evidence (for example, police pressure on witnesses). However, if they become dissatisfied with the integrity of the police file, they will not themselves re-investigate or re-interview, as might be expected of defence solicitors in England and Wales. Rather, they would ask the examining judge to start an *instruction* or petition the trial judge to order further investigation, including re-interviewing of relevant witnesses. If defence counsel continue at trial to assert that the police reports contain factual inaccuracies crucial to the issue of guilt, no more than prima-facie evidence of this is required for further inquiry to be ordered. Since it will worsen the backlog this will not make the police popular with the court or the prosecutor.[51]

This is not to say there are no points of weakness in the system.[52] A number of problems have arisen which have limited defence counsel's ability to influence the construction of the file. Some restrictions have already been touched upon: the police will deny defence lawyers access to

[46] Leigh and Hall Williams, *The Prosecution Process*, at 45; Art. 148 CCP.
[47] For example, see NRC 9 Feb. 1993, 3.
[48] *Rijksrecherche* = the police of the police. The *procureurs-generaal* are the heads of the prosecution office at the level of the Courts of Appeal.
[49] On the Dutch prosecutor generally see also L. H. C. Hulsman and J. F. Nijboer, 'Criminal Law and Criminal Procedure: The Dutch Criminal Justice System from a Comparative Perspective', in J. M. J. Chorus, P. H. M. Gerver, E. H. Hondius, A. K. Koekkoek (eds.), *Introduction to Dutch Law for Foreigners* (2nd edn., Deventer; Kluwer 1993), chap. 16.
[50] Goldstein and Marcus, 'The Myth of Judicial Supervision', 264.
[51] Reasoning by trial courts to deny defence requests can ultimately be tested before the Supreme Court.
[52] See, for recent criticism, W. A. Wagenaar, H. F. M. Crombag and P. J. Van Koppen, *Dubieuze Zaken: De Psychologie van Strafrechtelijk Bewijs* (Amsterdam; Contact 1992); *idem*, *Anchored Narratives: The Psychology of Criminal Evidence* (Wheatsheaf; Harvester 1993).

a suspect during police interrogation. But furthermore, the Supreme Court has decided that defence lawyers have no right to be present during police interrogation of witnesses. The police can, and routinely do, deny counsel access—even where the interrogation has been ordered by the investigating judge as part of the *instruction* process. It is thought that an RC could order the police to invite counsel to attend.[53]

There are also problems for defence lawyers in attending interrogations conducted by investigating judges. Though there are statutory criteria which normally entitle the defence lawyer to be present, the exceptions to the principle are very vague, giving great discretion to the investigating judge.[54] Sometimes this exception is abused, particularly where the investigating judge is trying to preserve the anonymity of the witness. Even when a witness will not be called upon to testify at trial, the investigating judge may still proceed to interrogate them in the absence of defence counsel if there are reasons for interrogating without delay. All of this means that defence counsel have no effective opportunity to challenge the witness's account, either at trial or during the initial interrogation. This makes it much harder for them to play their key role of pointing up weaknesses in the file.

This acquires greater importance in the light of Dutch attitudes towards hearsay evidence. The Supreme Court, contrary to Parliament's intention when passing the CCP, has ruled that such evidence is to be accepted. The consequences are enormous. Not only is a hearsay statement during trial legally accepted as evidentiary material,[55] but also a police *proces-verbaal* in which a hearsay witness makes a statement. In theory this witness may be called to testify, but even so the reliability of the original speaker is never tested.[56] This went so far as to allow a guilty verdict to be based solely on statements in the *dossier* by anonymous witnesses, added as part of a *proces-verbaal* of a police officer or the investigating judge. The practice was condemned in the ECHR ruling in *Kostovski* v. *the Netherlands*[57] but the Dutch Supreme Court has placed only minimal controls on it.[58]

Despite the difficulties, it is these intersecting relationships between police, prosecutor, defence counsel, investigating judge, and trial judge which form the institutional background to the system. They are intended

[53] C. F. Ryter and C. H. Haffmans, 'De raadsman op zijn retour' (1984) 33 AA 491 *et seq.*
[54] Art. 186 CCP. Where the witness could, if necessary, be called to testify at trial, RCs may legally deny access if they consider it contrary to 'the interests of the ongoing investigation'.
[55] At the time of writing, the Supreme Court is said to consider restricting the acceptability of hearsay evidence. This would lead to more evidence being given by witnesses in person, and greater emphasis on traditional adversarial courtroom techniques.
[56] Art. 342 states that a witness statement is a statement of 'facts and circumstances that witness has noticed or experienced personally'. The Court simply reasoned that a hearsay witness states the personal experience of what another person said: HR 20 December 1926, [1927] NJ 85.
[57] A 166, 20 Nov. 1989, [1990] NJ 245.   [58] See Chap. 14 below.

to create entrenched bureaucratic imperatives toward thoroughness in investigation that put the court in a position to assess the facts in a fair and impartial way. The incentives are to direct the prosecutors' efforts to presenting the court with a *dossier* that is complete, ready for trial, and satisfies the ECHR test of fairness.[59]

MONITORING THE SERIOUS CASE: THE INTERVENTION OF THE EXAMINING
MAGISTRATE IN THE NETHERLANDS

The examining judge is a common institution in continental systems but unknown in the English and Welsh. In the Netherlands, the *Rechter-Commissaris* plays a rather more limited role than the French *juge d'instruction*. His/her involvement depends greatly on the seriousness of the case. Under the Code of Criminal Procedure, no offence compels *instruction*.[60] Of the 85,600 cases that actually reached court in 1989, about 71,700 were petty crimes heard by the *enkelvoudige kamer* (single judge) with a maximum possible sentence of six months in prison.[61] Hardly any involved a *Rechter-Commissaris*. On the other hand, almost all the 8,300 more serious cases heard by the *meervoudige kamer* (three judges) would have had some involvement by an investigating judge. In most of these cases his involvement would not go beyond authorizing the use of certain coercive powers. Several such powers are exercised in practice only with RC approval. The main ones are extended pre-trial detention (ten days)[63], wire-tapping, search and seizure of evidence from homes, and opening of mail. In this context RCs play a more passive, quasi-judicial role which may be seen as an extended version of what lay magistrates do in England and Wales.

Actual criminal *instruction*, in which the examining magistrate gets personally involved in the investigation process and questions witnesses and the defendant, only takes place in about 3 per cent of the cases that go to court.[62] These are the most serious cases. Usually *instruction* results from

[59] As professionals working without a jury in a system without plea-bargaining judges share the ideal of being very efficient: e.g. thorough *dossiers* enable two murder cases to be tried in a day.
[60] This contrasts vividly with the situation in France where all *crimes*, as opposed to lesser offences, must go to *instruction*.
[61] Centraal Bureau voor de Statistiek, hoofdafdeling Statistieken van rechtsbescherming en veiligheid.
[62] *Herziening van het gerechtelijk vooronderzoek: Een rapport van de Commissie Herijking Wetboek van Strafvordering*, Arnhem, Gouda Quint, 1990, as to which see *Herziening van het gerechtelijk vooronderzoek*, special isssue of (1991) 21 DD No. 6; A. E. Harteveld, *De rechter-commissaris in strafzaken: enkele oriënterende beschouwingen*, Arnhem, Gouda Quint, 1990 (diss.); C. Fijnaut and E. Kolthoff (eds.), *Afschaffing of herziening van het gerechtelijk vooronderzoek*, Arnhem, Gouda Quint, 1991 (SMP deel 5). Contrast 10 per cent in France, J. Monahan 'Sanctioning Injustice' [1991] *NLJ* 679.
[63] Generally offences carrying a maximum penalty of 4 years' imprisonment or more.

a request from prosecutors. They receive the case *dossier* after it has been provisionally closed by the police. On reviewing it, they may decide to drop the case, to charge, to order further police investigation, or to request a preliminary judicial inquiry. The defence will often ask the prosecutor to request an *instruction* if dissatisfied with the investigation. If a suspect is in pre-trial detention the RC may initiate *instruction* without a request from the prosecutor. If defence suggestions are rejected by the prosecutor or the examining judge, the defence can ask the trial judge to remit the case for further RC investigation. Hence the suspect or defence counsel has various opportunities to seek further investigation. Again it should be remembered that there is no expectation that defence counsel himself should pursue inquiries to develop evidence. Whether the decision is being made by prosecutors, RCs, or the trial judge the question for *instruction* is the same: does the file currently represent a full and legally competent basis for the trial judge(s) to decide on guilt or innocence. If not, could further investigation, armed with the additional coercive powers (to summon witnesses etc.) available to the RC, resolve the ambiguity or contradiction?

Where *instruction* takes place, the function of the investigating judge is not to produce a personal report or to draw any conclusions, but rather to commission and collect information to be placed on the file.[64] First, the RC examines the police file. Then he normally interviews or re-interviews witnesses and/or suspects[65] and sometimes commissions experts' reports (often psychiatric) or interviews experts. When witnesses or suspects are questioned, the RC produces a summary of their account which they are asked to check and, having modified it as appropriate, sign as accurate.

Apart from this, the RC's role is limited.[66] He does not draw conclusions or make decisions about guilt. The information that is produced is supposed to provide a dispassionate factual basis for judgement by another person rather than a judgment itself.[67] Even when the investigating judge is officially involved, most investigation is actually done by the police under overall prosecutor supervision. This is because even when an investigating judge has been allotted the case his/her investigation does not exclude continuing work by the police which is not under his/her direction.[68] The police, with the support of the prosecutor, can and do continue to pursue

[64] Contrast the role of the French *juge d'instruction*, who decides whether the evidence is sufficient for a case to go to trial.

[65] Often the police will already have interviewed witnesses once. The advantage that RCs have over the police is that they are empowered to subpoena witnesses and demand witness depositions.

[66] Occasionally they will officially visit the scene of the crime and report on their findings. And, except for emergencies, they will normally be present during a search of the home.

[67] Rosett, 'Trial and Discretion', 368.

[68] This is a key contrast with the French *juge d'instruction*, who takes overall responsibility for supervising the police investigation in cases under *instruction*: Code of Criminal Procedure, Art. 81.

their own investigation, going to the investigating judge only for stronger coercive powers. The RC is empowered to direct the police to investigate particular matters but the case remains the prosecutor's responsibility.

The intervention of the investigating judge does provide certain opportunities for the defence. Suspects may argue at the earliest possible stage that their confessions are false and were obtained by inducements or threats. When interviewed by the investigating judge, they are entitled to have their lawyer present, and conditions and conduct of the interview tend to be non-coercive and informal.[69] This gives suspects and witnesses a better chance to give their accounts clearly and positively and to resist police construction of events during initial interrogation. Even if there is evidence that a confession to the police was obtained by inducements or threats, it is not struck from the file by the RC, because it would be for the trial judges to decide whether to exclude the evidence and, if not, to decide what credence, if any, to place upon it. The RC might informally warn the prosecutor of the need to seek further evidence, but it would not be for him/her to determine guilt, innocence, or truth. If the suspect also confessed in front of the RC any subsequent claim of police misconduct or any other factor[70] going to the admissibility or weight as evidence of the confession would not be likely to be believed at trial.

The RC, like the prosecutor, is under significant institutional pressure to investigate defence claims and to pursue relevant exculpatory evidence. If he rejects a defence suggestion that evidence be sought, the defence may raise the issue again at trial and, if the trial judges consider that the investigation might have yielded germane evidence, the case will be sent to the RC to conduct the investigation. Clearly the defence account has to be relevant and have some plausibility, but the Supreme Court has ruled that if the defence claims that evidence has been obtained illegally, it does not have to provide proof of this to be entitled to further investigation.[71] And the embarrassment of repeated referral back for further investigation should not be underestimated. RCs want to be seen to be efficient in their processing of cases and judicial in their decision-making. This provides a strong motive for them to show distance and impartiality in their day-to-day dealings with police and prosecutor. Once an *instruction* has been started it is not unusual for an RC to order further investigations to check defence stories or allegations at the suggestion of the defence. The police may interrogate witnesses supporting defence alibis, but if the reliability and testimony of a specific witness is crucial, the RC will do the interview him- or herself.

Reform of the role of the examining magistrate is being considered in

[69] Leigh and Hall Williams, *The Prosecution Process*, 67–8.
[70] e.g., the fact of having been under the influence of drugs.
[71] HR 28 June 1983, [1983] NJ 798.

Holland. Academics and practising lawyers, from the bench, prosecution service, and the Bar, have expressed doubts as to the performance of RCs. Some claim RCs are too passive. Equally, some Dutch scholars and practitioners argue that the RC's involvement in investigation should be restricted and the RC take on a less pro-active judicial role. Their argument is that constitutionally it should be the state that investigates. Official proposals[72] do not go this far. It is now proposed that the RC's power be restricted to authorizing certain investigative action by others on request by the prosecutor, who would then become responsible for the exercise of these powers. The only investigative role remaining to the RC would be the questioning of witnesses. This power would only be exercisable on the request of the prosecutor, the trial court, or (for the first time) the defence.

PROSECUTORS AND MONITORING IN ENGLAND AND WALES

Until recently in England and Wales bureaucratic monitoring had tended to be seen as something operating exclusively through police hierachies.[73] The role of the custody officer in the context of detention and interrogation, review of detention by senior officers, and stop and search by sergeants, and the structuring of career incentives within a hierarchical organization, represent different facets of such processes. But inevitably the values that inform this monitoring are the values of the police themselves.[74] The creation of the Crown Prosecution Service might be said to be a step toward monitoring by external sources, but criminal justice relationships in England and Wales are very different from those in the Netherlands. The CPS is not in a clearly hierarchical relationship with the police and does not see itself as a police superior.[75] The prosecution file is not intended to be an objective official basis for judgment on guilt or innocence. It is an unofficial aid to the prosecution's oral presentation of its case. Furthermore, because of the strongly competitive nature of the defence–prosecutor relationship, defence lawyers are much less prepared to reveal the defence case and to suggest new exculpatory avenues of inquiry or witnesses to the prosecution. They like this kind of thing to come as an unwelcome surprise to the opposition. This fact, combined with the absence of investigating judges, means that the CPS is heavily dependent on the information it gets from

---

[72] See Report of the Commissie Herijking, note 63 above.

[73] (Sir Cyril Phillips, Chairman) *Royal Commission on Criminal Procedure*, HMSO, Cmnd. 8092(1), at 110–11.

[74] D. McBarnet, 'The Royal Commission and the Judges' Rules' (1981) *BJLS* 109; *eadem*, 'Legal Form and Legal Mystification: An Analytical Postscript on the Scottish Criminal Justice Act, the Royal Commission on Criminal Procedure and the Politics of Law and Order' (1982) 10 *IJSL* 410.

[75] See Brants and Field, Chap. 7.

the police who construct the case *against* the suspect. Prosecution know-ledge of the case is thus necessarily incomplete. There is a duty placed upon the prosecutor to disclose evidence germane to the defence. This has been reconsidered recently by the Court of Appeal in *R.* v. *Ward* and by the European Court of Human Rights in *Edwards* v. *United Kingdom*.[76] *Edwards* emphasized that it was a requirement of fairness under Article 6(1) that all material evidence for or against the accused be disclosed to the defence. *Ward* tightened procedures for allowing non-disclosure of germane evidence on grounds of public interest immunity.[77] But neither case challenges the fundamental assumption of the adversarial process, that prosecution obligations do not involve a duty to *seek out* exculpatory evidence. To these structural factors, one must add the logistical problems of late and sketchy files and the fact that prosecutors are not trained as judges but as lawyers with adversarial skills. From all this it should be clear that the duty and capacity of the CPS to monitor and supervise police investigation is rather limited when compared with the Dutch Prosecution Service.

JUDICIAL MONITORING OR RUBBER-STAMPING?

Some commentators from adversarial jurisdictions have expressed reser-vations about the effectiveness of the inquisitorial judicial monitoring proc-ess. One fear has already been discussed: the danger of the coerced confession, given the looser framework of procedural rules governing in-terrogation. But this can be seen as part of a broader scepticism. The main lines of this were set out in the 1970s by Goldstein and Marcus. They concluded that in reality judicial monitoring did not amount to much and that it left the police with much more autonomy in investigation than was true of the adversarial process. In particular they argued the following:

(i) examining magistrates are involved in only a small minority of cases and their role is more limited than the rhetoric of judicial control of investigations would suggest. This leaves the more dominant role to the prosecutor and 'the resort to the fiction' that they can act as judicial figures;[78]

(ii) in the ordinary case 'most investigative work has been completed by the police before the other officials enter the picture';

---

[76] *R.* v. *Ward*, (1993) I.W.L.R. 619; *Edwards* v. *United Kingdom* (1993) EHRR 417; see Stewart Field and James Young, 'Disclosure, Appeals and Procedural Traditions', (1994) *CrimLRev*. 264.

[77] The key unresolved question is whether the very existence of a public interest immunity in criminal cases is itself contrary to the Convention. The Court did not express a clear view on this in *Edwards* (but see the Dissenting Opinion of Judge Pettiti).

[78] Goldstein and Marcus, 'The Myth of Judicial Supervision', 247.

(iii) prosecutors are generally passive and reactive, relying mainly on the evidence the police provide and the conclusions they draw. They were said to leave it 'largely to the police to develop the facts to be entered in the *dossier*;[79] and

(iv) prosecutors are said rarely to question officers or witnesses to see whether police practices have been conducted lawfully. The 'overwhelming presumption is that official action has been regular and lawful'.[80] The implication is that prosecutorial supervision does not produce stringent control on police malpractice.

Some of the descriptive elements of this analysis are certainly true of the Dutch system. Our account above emphasizes that the role of the examining judge *is* limited only to the most serious cases. Even when they do get involved they do not control or supervise police investigations. On the other hand some elements betray an inability to discard adversarial assumptions: Van de Bunt confirms that the value-systems of the Dutch prosecutor *are* profoundly influenced by his institutional role, selection, and training. Goldstein and Marcus cannot seem to credit this. But the main difficulty with Goldstein and Marcus' account is the way they deduce that monitoring is not effective from the fact that prosecutors or investigating judges do not themselves investigate or keep in routine, close, daily contact with the police over the development of individual cases, verifying the legality of procedures. In one sense this assumption is not surprising to the British reader. This is because one tends to assume that it means that the prosecutor becomes completely dependent on the police for information about the relevant incident.[81] Defence lawyers in Holland themselves say that one cannot get to grips with supervising the police if this is based on written materials which they themselves supply.[82] But how far is this the case in the Netherlands?

Certainly, in routine cases there is very little prosecutorial involvement with the case as it develops. Apart from the statutory requirement that the defendant be brought before the prosecutor if a pre-trial detention order is requested, it is extremely rare, even in the most important cases, for the prosecutor to have any significant face-to-face contact with the suspect. He does not interrogate a suspect or visit scenes of crime. Furthermore, the extent to which the prosecutor is involved as cases develop and assist in the development of investigative strategy varies between the trivial and the serious case. The prosecutor generally becomes involved in the more serious or complex cases only because the police require coercive powers for which the consent of the prosecutor is necessary, or they want

---

[79] Ibid., 249.   [80] Ibid., 262–3.
[81] McConville, Sanders and Leng, *The Case for the Prosecution*, 201.
[82] Leigh and Hall Williams, *The Prosecution Process*, 59–60.

legal advice on requirements as to further evidence. Usually, the police will try to conduct investigations in a way that does not require the formal exercise of such powers.[83] Officers will not involve prosecutors until they believe their investigations are complete. Then the file will be closed (provisionally) and sent to the prosecutor. This ability to do the basic job of investigation without involving prosecutors does mean that, in many routine cases, any scrutiny effectively occurs after most of the investigation has been completed. Often the investigation is effectively over inside seventy-two hours, before the prosecutor is aware of its existence. It is rare for prosecutors, on review of the police file in a routine case, to ask for more evidence.[84] Concerned to deal with a high volume of work, they aim to make decisions as much as possible on the basis of the available data on file rather than seek new information if this is hard to obtain. There are only a limited number of prosecutors (around 250 nationally) and they cannot devote a great deal of time to individual cases unless the offences alleged are serious.[85]

But the success or failure of the Dutch monitoring system is not dependent on close day-to-day contact with the investigators as the evidence develops.[86] As should be evident from the account above, the two key elements are (i) a diversity of effective influences on the file, and (ii) the structure of institutional incentives to balance and thoroughness in its development. Here one cannot look in isolation at the respective roles of the police, prosecutor, investigating judge, trial judge, or defence counsel. They must be seen as interactive. Goldstein and Marcus in particular fail to appreciate the significance of the defence counsel–prosecutor relationship. They complain of the inactivity of defence counsel in the inquisitorial system in not investigating in preparation for trial: '[e]ven if his client should suggest someone who he thinks will offer testimony favourable to the defence, he often passes the name onto the prosecutor or judge without even troubling first to interview the witness himself.'[87] But this is not the job of defence counsel within the system: all the assumptions are that re-investigation is done by the police at the behest of the prosecutor and the expense of the state. This does not mean that defence counsel's role is not vital. The drawing of ambiguity or impropriety to the attention of the prosecutor is a key element in the structure of incentives toward thoroughness

---

[83] Ibid., 46. The Supreme Court allows the absence of explicit refusal by the person concerned to be treated as consent to some intrusive investigations (notably search).

[84] However, quite regularly there will be correspondence between the prosecutor's office and the police concerning irregularities in form-filling, e.g. wrong boxes having been ticked or signatures of officers missing or errors in dating.

[85] Van de Bunt, *Officieren van Justitie*, chap. 6.

[86] As Goldstein and Marcus, 'The Myth of Judicial Supervision', have assumed in relation to the French system.

[87] Ibid., 264.

in investigation. If a case appears unproblematic on the basis of the police file, the prosecutor will rarely look beneath the surface unless defence counsel has indicated there is something down there. If defence counsel is incompetent or lazy the system will not work.[88] But once prosecutors are alerted to difficulties they are often decisive in response. If the submitted completed file reveals a case that is complex or evidence that is ambiguous or unconvincing in the light of comments from defence counsel, then, unless the case is serious, the prosecutor may well simply drop it or settle it rather than seek to direct the police to strengthen it.[89] It should be remembered that, unlike England and Wales, in the Netherlands it is quite routine to drop cases in such circumstances. About 50 per cent of cases are dropped or *transactied* by the prosecutor.[90] About a third of these will be technical waivers (including those generated by lack of evidence).

Similar considerations apply to evidence of malpractice by officers. There is considerable disagreement about the extent to which routine requests for coercive powers are used by the prosecutor as a real opportunity to scrutinize closely police tactics and procedures.[91] It is also said that officers do their best to avoid malpractice appearing on file. It is, for example, said that commonly sources of information are concealed. But defence counsel, who have a right of access to the file, have a responsibility to point out any impropriety of which they are aware to the prosecutor. If the police play tricks with a prosecutor and this produces embarrassment for him or her before an investigating judge or court in chambers, or worse still the trial court itself, then the prosecutor, apart from reporting the officer to his/her disciplinary superiors, will look at future information from that officer with greater scepticism. This will make the officer's job more onerous as, in the end, it is the prosecutor's decision to charge, and a waiver would mean the officer having worked hard to no avail. The police need to retain prosecutors' confidence and there are limits to their credulity. In the end much of the system depends on the development of a relationship of mutual trust between police, prosecutor, and court in the context of institutional incentives very different from those in the adversarial system.

CONCLUSION

The Dutch system places great faith in the importance of balanced thoroughness in pre-trial investigation and the centrality of monitoring by judicial figures, because the role of the trial is completely different. We have seen that one of the consequences of such faith is a more restricted

---

[88] But of course this is equally true of the adversarial system in England and Wales.
[89] Van de Bunt, *Officieren van Justitie*, 401.   [90] Brants and Field, Chap. 7, above.
[91] See Leigh and Hall Williams, *The Prosecution Process*, at 59–60.

regime of procedural rights for the suspect interrogated by the police. Worries expressed from within the adversarial tradition typically tend to revolve around two issues. The first is the danger of confessions coerced by the police in view of the looser framework of rules. This includes no access to a defence lawyer during interrogation and limited recording duties on the police. A central question is posed: to what extent does the initial encounter with the police, rather than the interventions of prosecutors and investigating judges, exercise a determining influence on subsequent events? If the key events take place during police custody then the suspect in the Netherlands gets the worst of both worlds: adversarial rights for defence lawyer intervention restricted, but not yet access to the judicial monitors. But if the system works in the way theory demands, the combined interventions of defence counsel, prosecutor, and examining judge should mean that redirection and re-examination of the inquiry can be properly triggered. Inquiries will be thorough in the pursuit of both exculpatory and inculpatory evidence, even when a confession has been obtained by the police. The impact of the coerced confession on the course of an investigation should then be more limited than is presently the case in England and Wales. Almost all recent British miscarriages have involved disputed confessions or damaging admissions,[92] and it may be that the Dutch system is no better designed to prevent these. But in most of the British miscarriages, it was not just that weakness in the case could not be discovered because it was not apparent how the admissions were obtained. Rather, when the whole of the evidence on the face of the record was looked at coolly, it had obvious inconsistencies and weaknesses. What would surely have prevented them would have been a less pressured and partisan mind sifting the evidence on the face of the files with the power to follow up inconsistency and seek alternative views.[93] In the theory of the Dutch system powerful figures are given strong structural incentives to see that this is done.

Certainly there is a need for caution in assessing the reality of the Dutch system, largely because, as we have pointed out at various places, there is a lack of detailed empirical work into many aspects of the way the key relationships work. In the absence of this evidence conclusions are necessarily preliminary. But it may be that the absence of such studies is in part due to the notable lack of the prominent miscarriages of justice that have made British empirical work a matter of pressing urgency. Furthermore, Leigh and Hall Williams stated that in interviews with Dutch defence

---

[92] Birmingham Six (see C. Mullin, *Error of Judgement*, revised edn., Dublin; Poolberg 1990), Guildford Four (see R. Kee, *Trial and Error*, revised edn., Harmondsworth; Penguin 1989), Tottenham Three (see D. Rose, *A Climate of Fear*, London; Bloomsbury 1992).

[93] This was explicitly the conclusion of the *Confait* inquiry by Sir Henry Fisher ('Report of an Inquiry into the *Confait* case', HMSO, 1977), para. 2.30.

lawyers, they found a high degree of confidence that, even though abuses of power occur, the right result is usually reached in the end. They were told, for example, that although the police may adopt a set against an individual, this is infrequent and usually resolved during the investigation. It seems unlikely that British defence lawyers have the same degree of confidence.

In England and Wales there appear to be structural problems: *inter alia*, the resources of defence counsel do not match those of the police against whom they are matched, and consequently they cannot adequately play the very extensive competitive role expected of them under an adversarial system. Attempts to redress this imbalance by detailed controls on the police codified in rules and enforced in the courtroom have had an effect in controlling grosser abuses. But police ability to avoid and limit the impact of the rules has preserved much of the power of covert bargaining with suspects. In the end predominant reliance on rules and *post hoc* enforcement is a strategy made dangerous by powerful repeat players with a belief in the illegitimacy of the rules and an interest in avoiding them. But if there is a step toward judicial monitoring in England and Wales it is vital to recognize the profound differences in the way the structure of institutional incentives is set up within inquisitorial systems. Judicial monitoring by prosecutors outside the context of a career judiciary and without the cultural assumptions thus inculcated is difficult to achieve. But if prosecutorial review is to be office- and file-based, it is equally vital that attention must be given to ensuring that actors other than the police have the opportunity to shape that file.

12

Police Detention in the UK and in the Netherlands

ALAN DAVENPORT AND PETER BAAUW

THE BRITISH LAW

Detention of Suspected Terrorists

The United Kingdom has two different sets of procedural rules for detention, those applicable to suspects arrested under the Police and Criminal Evidence 1984 (hereafter PACE) and those pertaining to people detained under the Prevention of Terrorism (Temporary Provisions) Act 1989 (hereafter PTA). This second statute, being specifically concerned with anti-terrorist measures, has no direct parallel in the Netherlands and is the successor of legislation which came about because of events some twenty years ago.

An earlier Prevention of Terrorism Act was brought into force in 1974 in an attempt to combat the activities of the Irish Republican Army (IRA), which at the time was conducting a campaign of bombings on the British mainland. On 21 November 1974, bombs went off in Birmingham, resulting in the loss of twenty-one lives and injuries to 162 people.[1] The PTA 1974 was introduced into Parliament on 25 November and became law on 29 November, a remarkably swift passage through the legislature. The Act extended police powers in a number of areas and the then Home Secretary conceded that the measures contained therein were '. . . unprecedented in peacetime', but nevertheless '. . . fully justified' given the circumstances at the time.[2] The legislation was to remain in force for a period of six months[3] as it was intended to be a short-term emergency law, the existence of which would, it was hoped, cease to be necessary within a very short period of time.[4] The need for the very existence of the anti-terrorist legislation has consistently been questioned[5] but it has survived, subject to

[1] C. Mullin, *Error of Judgement* (Dublin; Poolberg Press 1990), 7.
[2] HC Deb., Vol. 882, col. 35, 25 November 1974, Mr Jenkins.
[3] PTA 1975, s. 12(1).
[4] For a fuller account of the background to the legislation, see C. Walker, *The Prevention of Terrorism in British Law* (Manchester; Manchester University Press, 2nd edn.), chap. 4.
[5] See C. Scorer, S. Spencer, and P. Hewitt, *The New Prevention of Terrorism Act: The Case for Repeal* (London; NCCL 1989).

some amendments, and its latest incarnation can be found as the PTA 1989, which adopts the definition of 'terrorism' as '... the use of violence for political ends'.[6] The Netherlands has no obvious counterpart to this legislation as it has not had domestic problems with terrorism on the same scale as the United Kingdom (see Chapter 2).

Three main issues cause concern in the area of detention and questioning of suspected terrorists, namely the treatment of such suspects, the length of detention permitted at law, and the method by which decisions to extend detention are taken. The European Convention on Human Rights (ECHR) has been invoked in all three areas, and its effect will be considered in some detail. The rights which are alleged to have been violated are those contained in Articles 3 and 5 of the ECHR and are of fundamental importance. It is interesting therefore to examine the approach of the Convention institutions to the complaints which they have received and the reaction of the British Government to the decisions of those institutions.

There has been persistent concern about the treatment suspected terrorists receive whilst in police detention in Northern Ireland.[7] During the early 1970s, attention was focused on the use of the 'five techniques', which included sensory deprivation and long periods of standing in a painful position. The Irish Government was sufficiently concerned to bring an inter-state case against the United Kingdom alleging a violation of Article 3 of the Convention which prohibits torture and 'inhuman and degrading treatment'. The importance of Article 3 is evidenced by its inclusion in the list of Articles from which *no* derogation is permitted.[8] The European Commission on Human Rights considered that the techniques amounted to torture, whilst the Court took the view that, although not torture, they did amount to 'inhuman and degrading treatment' and their use was therefore inconsistent with the United Kingdom's obligations under the ECHR.[9] The Government had already discontinued the use of the techniques by the time of the judgment, perhaps in anticipation of an adverse finding, but the publicity surrounding the case was sufficient to bring the situation to the attention of a larger number of people than would otherwise have been informed of it.

---

[6] PTA 1989, s. 20(1).

[7] See, *inter alia*, P. Taylor, *Beating the Terrorists?* (London; Penguin 1980); D. Walsh, *The Use and Abuse of Emergency Legislation in Northern Ireland* (London; Cobden Trust 1983). The cases of the 'Guildford Four' and the 'Birmingham Six' highlight the concerns: see, *inter alia*, G. Conlon, *Proved Innocent* (London; Penguin 1990); P. Hill, *Stolen Years* (London; Corgi 1990); R. Kee, *Trial and Error* (London; Penguin 1986); G. McKee and R. Franey, *Time Bomb* (London; Bloomsbury Press 1988), and C. Mullin, note 1, above. More recently, see Haldane Society of Socialist Lawyers, *Upholding the Law? Criminal Justice under the 'Emergency Powers' in the 1990s* Haldane Society, 1992).

[8] Art. 15(2) ECHR.

[9] *Ireland v. United Kingdom*, judgment of 18 Jan. 1978, (1979–80) 2 EHRR 25.

The length of time for which a suspect may be detained under the PTA is far greater than that permitted under PACE. Under the PTA 1984, an arrested person could be detained for an initial period of forty-eight hours.[10] The detention could then be extended by a further five days upon the Home Secretary's approval.[11] This meant that a suspect could be held in custody for a maximum of seven days before being charged and brought before a court.

Article 5(3) of the ECHR states that an arrested person '. . . shall be brought *promptly* before a judge or other officer authorized by law to exercise judicial power . . .' (emphasis added). In the case of *Brogan* v. *United Kingdom*[12] the Court was asked to determine whether section 12 of the PTA 1984 met with the required standard of 'promptness'.

Brogan and three others had been detained for periods ranging from four days and six hours to six days and sixteen and a half hours before being released without charge. They complained that their detentions violated Article 5(3) because they had not come before a court 'promptly'. The Government contested the claim. It referred to the particular difficulties faced by the police when dealing with terrorists in Northern Ireland, arguing that terrorism posed a threat to the peace in the United Kingdom and that extended detention was 'an indispensable part of the effort to combat that threat'.[13] This could be said to be especially true, given that terrorists were trained in anti-interrogation techniques.

The Government also defended the fact that the decision to extend detention lay in the hands of the executive, an issue also raised in this case. It claimed that judicial control of detention was impractical because of the sensitive nature of the information involved in such cases. It was said that any judicial hearing could not involve the detainee or his legal adviser and would have to be held in secret for security reasons. A further justification was that ministerial scrutiny of the detention adequately protected suspects' rights.[14] The Court concluded that Article 5(3) had indeed been violated. The term 'promptness' in Article 5(3) was to be interpreted narrowly in order to protect the rights of the individual. Judicial scrutiny of the lawfulness of a subject's detention was an essential safeguard of his liberty. Even the shortest period of non-scrutinized detention in this case, four days and six hours, failed to satisfy the requirements of the Convention. The right to liberty protected by Article 5 was of fundamental importance and the Court would not tolerate arbitrary interference with that right. As regards the point made about terrorism, the Court said:

---

[10] PTA 1984, s. 12(4).   [11] Ibid., s. 12(5).
[12] Judgment of 29 Nov. 1988, (1989) 11 EHRR 117.
[13] Ibid., 132.   [14] Ibid., 133.

254   *Alan Davenport and Peter Baauw*

The undoubted fact that the arrest and detention of the applicants were inspired by the legitimate aim of protecting the community as a whole from terrorism is not on its own sufficient to ensure compliance with the specific requirements of Article 5(3).[15]

The Government responded to this judgment by taking two measures. First, on 23 December 1988, the Government introduced a derogation from its obligations under Article 5 of the Convention in respect of the PTA. The derogation was entered under Article 15 of the Convention and cited the situation in Northern Ireland as a justification for this. The derogation had *not* received prior approval from Parliament and its introduction was entirely at the wish of the executive.

The British derogation was challenged in the case of *Brannigan and McBride* v. *United Kingdom*.[16] This case again involved lengthy detentions and one of the applicants' arguments was that the derogation was invalid in that it did *not* meet the conditions laid down in Article 15. Article 15(1) states:

In time of war or other public emergency threatening the life of the nation any High Contracting Party may take measures derogating from its obligations under this Convention to the extent strictly required by the exigencies of the situation, provided that such measures are not inconsistent with its other obligations under international law.

The applicants argued that the derogation's terms were too wide and that the decision to extend detention *could* have been taken by a judge. The Commission however, recognized that a public emergency did exist and said that the question of who makes the decision to extend detention came within the 'margin of appreciation' accorded to each state in fulfilling its treaty obligations; as such the Commission would not interfere with the present arrangements. The derogation was therefore found to be lawful under the Convention, and this was subsequently confirmed by the Court of Human Rights in its judgment of 26 May 1993.

The second measure adopted by the United Kingdom Government was to re-enact the offending provision as section 14 of the PTA 1989. This section retains the same length of detention and the same arrangements for its extension, but there has been one significant change in the new Act with the introduction of a system of earlier reviews of detention. The first review is to be conducted as soon as is practicable after the suspect has been detained and the detention must be reviewed at regular intervals, which must not exceed twelve hours.[17] The reviews must be carried out by an

---

[15] Ibid., 136.
[16] Apps. 14553-4/89. Decision of the Commission, 3 December 1991, ECHR judgment, 26 May 1993, Series A No. 258-B (1994) 17 EHRR 539.
[17] PTA 1989, Sched. 3, para. 1.

officer unconnected with the case, who must be an inspector or officer of higher rank for the first twenty-four hours, and a superintendent thereafter.[18] The British Government contends that this provides an additional safeguard for the suspect, as there is now an independent check on the lawfulness of his detention at frequent intervals, although the role of the reviewing officer ends after the application for extended detention has been made.[19]

The introduction of this review may be seen as an attempt to comply with the spirit of Article 5 of the Convention. However, the review still falls short of the requirements of that Article. The police officer conducting the review could not be said to be an '. . . officer authorized by law to exercise judicial power' in the decision-making process. Although the officer must be independent of the particular case, it is difficult to perceive him playing an effective control role. The situation in Northern Ireland is such that many would consider that it may be very difficult for a police officer to be completely detached from an investigation into alleged acts of terrorism. Moreover, the Court of Human Rights in *Brincat* v. *Italy*[20] stated that only the 'objective' appearances at the time of the decision on detention are material. If it appears at that time that the 'officer authorized to exercise judicial power' may intervene later in the proceedings as a representative of the prosecuting authority, there is then a risk that his impartiality may arouse objectively-justified doubts. The lack of effective judicial scrutiny of detentions under this Act remains a cause for concern even in the light of the *Brannigan* case.

In *Brannigan*, the British Government set great store by the fact that detention is scrutinized by a Minister after forty-eight hours and that this provides a safeguard for the accused. While the PTA does not provide any guidance to the Home Secretary as to *how* this decision is to be made, there are, as the Human Rights Court noted, other safeguards after forty-eight hours, in the form of habeas corpus and the right to consult a solicitor.

Detention of Non-terrorist Suspects

The procedures adopted under PACE are very different from those described above. When an arrestee is brought to a designated police station[21] the custody officer,[22] who must be an officer completely independent of the case, must decide whether or not that person should be charged with an offence.[23] If no charge is to be preferred at that point, the custody officer may authorize the detention of the suspect if he reasonably believes that such detention 'is necessary to secure or preserve evidence relating to

---

[18] Ibid., para. 4.   [19] Ibid., para. 3.
[20] Judgment of 26 November 1992, Series A No. 249, 7. See also *Huber* v. *Switzerland*, judgment of 23 October 1990, Series A No. 188.
[21] s. 35, PACE.   [22] s. 36, PACE.   [23] s. 37(1), PACE.

an offence for which he is under arrest or obtain such evidence by questioning him'.[24] If the decision is to detain the suspect without charge then the regime controlling it is regulated in detail by the Act.[25]

The first review of detention must take place within six hours of the initial decision to detain[26] and must be conducted by the 'review officer', an officer of the rank of inspector or above who is unconnected with the suspect's case.[27]

Such reviews must be recorded on the custody record. The purpose of reviews is to ensure that the detention lasts only for as long as is necessary. The review officer must make subsequent reviews at least every nine hours after the first review has been conducted.[28] The maximum detention time available under this review system is twenty-four hours.[29] If the police wish to extend the suspect's detention beyond the twenty-four-hour period then a separate procedure must be followed. A further twelve hours' detention may be authorized by a superintendent or officer of higher rank if three conditions are satisfied, namely:

(i) 'the detention of that person without charge is necessary to secure or preserve evidence relating to an offence for which he is under arrest or to obtain such evidence by questioning him',

(ii) 'an offence for which he is under arrest is a serious arrestable offence',

(iii) 'the investigation is being conducted expeditiously and diligently'.[30]

The important difference between this review and those carried out under Schedule 3 of the PTA is the requirement that the suspect arrested under PACE must be suspected of having committed a 'serious arrestable offence'[31] before extended detention can be considered, whereas under the PTA the person does not have to be suspected of any particular offence. The necessity for suspicion of a serious arrestable offence indicates that the legislature intended extended detention to be available only in exceptional cases. Again, the authorization for such an extension and the reasons for it must be recorded.[32]

Upon the expiry of this twelve-hour period, the power of the police to authorize extended detention ceases and further extensions must be granted by a court.[33] So, under PACE a suspect may only be detained for a maximum of thirty-six hours without charge before he is brought before a court, which will decide on further detention. This would seem in accordance with Article 5(4) of the ECHR. Under the PTA, detention prior to an appearance before a court can last up to seven days.

---

[24] s. 37(2), PACE.   [25] ss. 40–2, PACE.   [26] s. 40(3)(a), PACE.
[27] s. 40(4)(b), PACE.   [28] s. 40(3)(b) and (c), PACE.   [29] s. 41, PACE.
[30] s. 42(1), PACE.   [31] s. 116, PACE.   [32] s. 42(5)(b), PACE.
[33] s. 43, PACE.

Comparison of the manner in which decisions on extended detention taken by the Home Secretary under the PTA and a magistrates' court under PACE are regulated by the law highlights the distinctions between the two statutes. After a person has been held under the PTA for forty-eight hours, upon application by the police the Home Secretary is empowered to extend the detention of a person arrested under that statute by up to a further five days.[34] As noted above, the PTA does not specify the manner in which this discretion should be exercised and no application has ever been refused.[35] The lack of such guidance as to the exercise of the discretion renders its susceptibility to judicial review difficult, although there remains the possibility of habeas corpus. In contrast the magistrates' powers under PACE are regulated in far more detail. A person appearing before the court in an application for extended detention has the right to be legally represented[36] and the magistrates' discretion to authorize further detention is controlled by the same three conditions applicable to the superintendent's decision after twenty-four hours. The magistrates have the power to extend detention by thirty-six hours and may authorize a further twenty-four-hour period at the end of this initial extension, again subject to the three conditions.[37] At the end of this period the suspect must be charged or released. So, a suspect arrested under PACE faces a maximum of ninety-six hours in detention without charge (compare the Dutch law in this respect), and this only after a senior officer's authorization and two court appearances, a far more regulated system than that pertaining under the PTA, where seven days' detention is permitted at the discretion of a member of the executive. It would seem therefore that PACE follows the ECHR far more closely than the PTA and its approach is to be preferred.[38]

POLICE DETENTION IN THE NETHERLANDS

The Code of Criminal Procedure (CCP)

Police custody in the Netherlands has always been a problematic issue. Following the first national Code of Criminal Procedure (1838) the practice was developed whereby, during police investigations, suspects were

---

[34] s. 14(5)(b), PACE.   [35] Walker, n. 4 above, 178.
[36] s. 43(3), PACE.   [37] s. 44(3), PACE.
[38] See, further, A. M. Berkhout-van Poelgeest, P. Jones and L. Koffman, 'Police Detention in the Netherlands and in the UK' (1990) 21 *Cambrian Law Review*, 48. This article deals specifically with the situation facing persons arrested and detained under PACE as opposed to the PTA. For information on the impact of PACE see, *inter alia*, K. Bottomley, C. Coleman, D. Dixon, M. Gill, and D. Wall, *The Impact of PACE: Policing in a Northern Force* (Kingston upon Hull; Centre for Criminology and Criminal Justice, University of Hull 1991).

held in police custody: there was no legal basis for this practice. When, in 1926, the second Code of Criminal Procedure came into effect, this established conventional procedure was legalized. On the one hand, the new Code established a distinction as to whether or not a suspect was caught red-handed, and, on the other hand, it specified a distinction based upon the seriousness of the offence.

In the case of suspects caught red-handed (Article 53 of the CCP) they can be arrested and detained, for interrogation, for a period of six hours; this can be extended to fifteen hours by virtue of the period midnight–09.00 a.m., which is excluded from the six-hour rule. In all other instances (Article 54 of the CCP) suspects can only be arrested and detained if the offence if one for which detention on remand is permitted; in general, this refers to offences for which a term of imprisonment of at least four years is possible. In this latter case, the initial detention can be extended on the warrant of a police officer who also has the function of assistant District Attorney—i.e., an officer of middle or senior rank. Such an extension lasts for two days and may be extended for a further two days if the District Attorney personally orders it (Articles 57 and 58 of the CCP). As grounds for extending the first forty-eight hours of police custody, the law specifies, without elaboration, 'the requirements of the investigation' or 'urgent necessity'.

Any eventual further extension of detention requires the affirmative intervention of a judge. It is usually the examining magistrate who, finding the suspect's detention to be based upon a prima facie case involving an offence for which detention on remand is permitted (Article 67 of the CCP), orders such detention; at this moment police custody becomes detention on remand. The examining magistrate performs this function by testing both the lawfulness and the expediency of the detention. Until recently, such a measure could be imposed for six days and then extended for a further six; it can now be imposed for one period of ten days only. The law stipulates specific grounds, such as a serious danger of failing to appear to answer the charges or substantial reasons of societal security (Article 67a of the CCP). Further, pre-trial detention may be ordered by the court in chambers for up to three periods of thirty days. Any decision on detention on remand requires a provisional charge, which only serves to enable the court to decide on the lawfulness of the detention.

This regulation implies, therefore, that a suspect must be brought before a judge no later than after a preliminary period of police custody lasting a maximum of four days and fifteen hours. This period can, incidentally, be extended in those cases where, at the end of the period, the suspect is charged with an alleged new offence. The most serious excesses of this abuse of power were dealt with by a ministerial circular in 1978.[39]

---

[39] Circular: *Aansluitende inverzekeringstellingen*, 3 January 1978.

The European Convention on Human Rights (ECHR)

When, in 1954, the European Convention on Human Rights became operative in the Netherlands, no-one could have expected that it would ever have such far-reaching consequences for the established practices of police custody. This could occur because the Convention contains a variety of clauses which are 'self-executing' according to Articles 93 and 94 of the Constitution of the Netherlands. Therefore, individuals could invoke provisions of the Convention before Dutch courts. During the parliamentary ratification procedures for the Convention it was specified by the Government that the Convention was only of declarative significance: the Convention constituted only those rights which were already self-evidently anchored in the Dutch legal system. In short, the Convention would have no effects worthy of mention upon the national legal system. It is for this reason that, during the ratification procedures, neither police custody nor detention on remand was perceived as a problem or brought into discussion. The relevant clauses were, thus, accepted without any form of derogatory condition.

Thus, since ratification, it is automatically the case that each suspect, after arrest, *'should be brought promptly before a judge or another officer authorized by law to exercise judicial power'* (Article 5(3) of the ECHR). What should be precisely understood under the term *'promptly'* would be a question subjected to more refined interpretation by the authorities in Strasbourg. One should realize in this context that the direct applicability of Convention obligations implies that the interpretations given by the European Commission and the European Court will be followed.[40] This can be the case in issues where the complaint is directed against the Netherlands, and also where the issues involve other Treaty states whereby a particular interpretation is given which is directly relevant to judicial practice in the Netherlands.

'Promptly'

In 1966—twelve years after the ratification and implementation of the ECHR—the European Commission had to adjudicate two complaints, lodged against the Netherlands, concerning the 'promptness' of being brought before a judge. In the first case, the Commission determined that a period of four days between arrest and appearance before an investigating judge was in agreement with the specifications of Article 5(3) of the ECHR. In the deliberations it was reported that: neither that paragraph nor any other provision in the Convention confers on the detained person the right to be interrogated within a particular period of time.[41] The complaint in

---

[40] In this context see the judgment from the Supreme Court (HR, 1 February 1991, [1991] NJ 413) pursuant to the consequences of the *Kostovski* judgment.

[41] App. 2621/65, (1966) 9 Yearbook 474 ff.

the second case was also declared inadmissible. The Commission considered that the parties to the Convention, with respect to the interpretation and application of Article 5(3) relating to the demand for 'promptness', possess 'a certain margin of appreciation'. In addition, the Commission considered, on the basis of a comparative judicial orientation, that the legal regulations in the Netherlands were 'consistent with the general tendency of other Member States of the Council of Europe'.[42]

In reaction to other complaints, too, directed against other Convention states, the Commission did not come to any decision with regard to an interpretation of Article 5(3) which had any consequences for the period of police custody customary in the Netherlands. In two cases against Belgium, for example, a period of five days was considered acceptable.[43] However, according to the Commission, a period of seven and eleven days is incompatible with the demand for 'promptness'.[44]

The European Court, too, has commented in judgments about the demand for 'promptness'. The first such comments relate to diverse complaints concerning the duration of pre-trial detention which were made by military personnel against the Netherlands.[45] The Court specified in advance that the demand for 'promptness' could not be handled in the abstract, but, rather, 'must be assessed in each case according to its special features'. However, periods which varied from six to twelve months, wherein the complainants were held in pre-trial detention, could not be considered as 'consistent with the required promptness'.[46] A later condemnatory judgment against Sweden also relates to a period (fifteen days) which is significantly longer than the period of a maximum of four days and fifteen hours permitted by the Dutch CCP.[47]

In its *Brogan* judgment[48] of 1988 the Court of Human Rights considered it unnecessary to determine whether or not, in an 'ordinary criminal case', a period of, for example, four days was reconcilable with Article 5(3). Four days and six hours is in any case too long, even given 'the special features of the case' (the case in question concerned an investigation into terrorist offences). Hereby a Strasbourg judgment was given which, dealing with the concept 'promptly', rejected a period shorter than the maximum permitted four days and fifteen hours in the Dutch legal system. Apparently, the Dutch period is, thus, too long. The possibility of regarding the public

[42] App. 2894/66, (1966) 9 Yearbook 364 ff.
[43] Decision, 19 July 1972 (1973) 4 Coll. Dec. 47; Decision 8 July 1974 (1974) 46 Coll. Dec. 62.
[44] Report, 11 October 1982, Series B No. 62 (1987), 31 (*de Jong*), and Report, 15 July 1983, Series A No. 83 (1984), 18 (*Skoogström*).
[45] The relevant military law has since been repealed.
[46] Judgments of 22 May 1984; *De Jong, Baljet and Van der Brink*, Series A No. 77; *Van der Sluijs, Zuiderveld and Klappe*, Series A No. 78; *Duinhof and Duijf*, Series A No. 79.
[47] Judgment of 26 October 1984; *McGoff*, Series A No. 83. [48] See n. 12 above.

prosecutor as 'the other officer authorized by law to exercise judicial power' has been ruled out by the *Brincat* judgment.

The Uniformity of Justice

Since the foundation of the Kingdom of the Netherlands in 1815 a system of uniformity of justice has been maintained. However, this system was abruptly disturbed as regards preventive detention by the judgment in *Brogan*. Legions of lawyers have contested the lawfulness of their clients' custody by the police, and the different judges and various courts have given the most variable grounds and diverse decisions as to why one suspect should be released and the other should remain in police custody.[49]

In order to retrieve the uniformity of justice and the principle of legal certainty in the Dutch system, three routes are available:

(a) *A decision by the Supreme Court of the Netherlands*: such decisions are in practice accepted and followed by the lower courts, but, given the duration of the necessary procedures (first an appeal, then the Court of Cassation), this route does not offer any relief in the short term.

(b) *An amendment of the Code of Criminal Procedure*: the same objection holds in this case: preparation of a new bill and the subsequent parliamentary procedure require years rather than months.

(c) *An official policy instrument*: given the fact that the Ministry of Justice is an official, hierarchically-organized apparatus it is possible to issue directives from above. In this specific case, it was the five *procureurs-generaal* at the courts of appeal who, in March 1989, formulated a regulation which the public prosecutor should follow in the district courts. It was stipulated that each suspect, on the third day of police custody, should be brought before the investigating judge. This regulation has been the common practice since it was issued.

Dutch Arithmetic

In the meantime, the Ministerial Commission charged with recalibrating the Code of Criminal Procedure was asked to produce speedy advice. In March 1989, the Commission produced a report which included a recommendation for a change in the law.[50] The majority of the Commission proposed that, in the future, the decision concerning the extension of a

---

[49] See, for a survey, A. M. Berkhout-van Poelgeest *et al.*, n. 38 above.
[50] Report of the Commissie Herijking, Wetboek van Strafvordering: *Inverzekeringstelling in het licht van art. 5 EVRM* 's-Gravenhage 1989.

suspect's custody should be taken by the investigating judge rather than the public prosecutor. In order to compensate for the earlier appearance before this judge, namely on the second day of custody, the extension period would be changed to three days (i.e., total custody for five days). A minority of the Commission was of the opinion that the first period of custody should also consist of three days (so, total custody for six days). The subsequently submitted bill contained yet another variant: after two days, the investigating judge should be able to order an extension of four days (again, a total of six days).

Given the major objections of the Ministry of Justice, which saw its authority being curtailed, a new departmental working group was instituted in December 1989. The report of this group, in April 1990, proposed thirteen (!) different variants and chose, finally, an extremely public prosecutor-friendly model: the first term of three days could be extended by another term of three days, but it would be the public prosecutor rather than the investigating judge who would be responsible for the extension (a total of six days' custody). In this model, the position of the investigating judge was drastically curtailed: the suspect would be brought before him on the second day, but he would only be able to assess the lawfulness of the current police custody which, the following day, could be extended by the public prosecutor. As habeas corpus judge, as provided for in Article 15 of the Dutch Constitution and Article 5(4) of the Convention, the investigating judge would only be left with the function of performing a marginal judicial review. A complete judicial examination would, with this model, only occur on the sixth day when the investigating judge would determine whether or not detention on remand should be ordered.

Under pressure from the Ministry of Justice the proposed model from the departmental working group was incorporated, by means of a memorandum of amendment, in the then existing proposed Bill.

But this does not constitute the last word on the issue. Recent decisions of the European Commission, handling cases brought against the Netherlands with respect to the current duration of police custody, have rejected disputed periods of three days or three days and nineteen hours as not admissible for complaint.[51] From this latter decision the Commission has clearly stipulated that the fatal moment must lie between the three days and nineteen hours which it has stipulated as acceptable and the four days and six hours which the European Court regarded as unacceptable in the *Brogan* case. On the basis of these findings, the Ministry of Justice has once again prepared two amendments to the existing bill and submitted them to the Council of State (*Raad van State*) for advice. In the new law

---

[51] App. 18090/91, *T.* v. *The Netherlands*, 4 July 1991; App. 19139/91, *J. C.* v. *The Netherlands*, 30 March 1992. See also E. Myjer in 1992 *NJCM Bulletin* 560 *et seq.*

which comes into force in October 1994 the habeas corpus check by the investigating judge will be shifted from the second to the third day of police custody. In this manner the proposal will remain within the 'safe' margin which the Commission has accepted and thus it will also block access to the European Court.

CONCLUSION

At first glance it seems remarkable that *Brogan*, which related to the United Kingdom, has led to far fewer developments in that country than is the case in the Netherlands. But on closer inspection, it is less surprising, bearing in mind the British treatment of the Convention (see Chapter 4). Precisely through the direct application of particular Convention obligations and their interpretation by the Strasbourg authorities, the *Brogan* case has resulted, in the Dutch legal system, in substantial activity in the area of judicial decisions, policy, and legislation. After more than four years of drafting this process will be completed in the near future. The United Kingdom on the other hand has used the situation in Northern Ireland as a justification for a derogation from its obligations under the Convention—a position which has now been accepted by the Court of Human Rights. While non-terrorist suspects in the United Kingdom are protected by PACE, which restricts detention without judicial scrutiny to thirty-six hours, well within the Convention limits of 'promptness', suspected terrorists are still governed by a system of detention which is subject to severe criticism and which may continue to be tested before the Convention institutions for a long time to come.

It is, however, disappointing that the Dutch legislature is apparently busy seeking to place a policy-favourable 'spin' on the *Brogan* decision. While the Court of Human Rights sought to improve the legal position of suspects—even terrorist suspects—with respect to the duration of police custody, it would appear that their position is more likely to be worsened by the current proposed Bill. The maximum duration of police custody, for example, will be extended from four to six days, something which constitutes a worsening of the position for suspects who thereafter are *not* subjected to detention on remand. In addition, appearance before an investigating judge on the second day will be reduced to the constitutional guarantee for an examination of the lawfulness of the detention, something which appears to satisfy the habeas corpus requirements of the Constitution and Article 5(4) of the Convention, but does not meet the right to an unrestricted judicial review of all factors and relevant interests, as intended in Article 5(3) and (1)(c), of the expediency of that detention.

Given that the previously mentioned recent decisions of the European

Commission concerning the Netherlands deal with cases whereby the investigating judge could perform a complete judicial review, it would appear that even after the implementation of the proposed Bill the issue of police detention in the Netherlands will still not be finished in relation to appeals to the Strasbourg authorities.

13

DNA Profiling and the Use of Expert Scientific Witnesses in Criminal Proceedings

PETER ALLDRIDGE, SANNEKE BERKHOUT-VAN POELGEEST,
AND KATHERINE WILLIAMS

INTRODUCTION

One of the areas of comparison between adversarial and inquisitorial systems of criminal justice is fact-finding.[1] The adversarial system relies upon oral evidence at trial, with cross-examination as the primary formal test of veracity. Facts are proven dialectically through a dramatic contest between two inconsistent narrative accounts of (often common) data.[2] The inquisitorial system involves the court in the preparation of evidence, leaves fewer questions to the trial itself, and presents itself as a search for truth rather than a contest of divergent accounts. The adversarial method of fact-finding is not in general well directed towards ascertaining the truth of the matter. The problems were well summarized by Goodpaster:[3]

In such a system, the truth might emerge if the mutual and misleading distortions of two equally matched and similarly purposed adversaries annihilated each other, like a collision of particles in a cyclotron, leaving historical fact behind as a trace particle. This cherished belief is, however, just a hopeful supposition . . . There is no empirical evidence indicating that contests of advocates deliver truth in this manner.

But if the problem with the adversarial system is that it is not well directed towards discovering truth, the problem with the much more explicit search for truth undertaken in the inquisitorial system is the simple epistemological one that truth often cannot be known, and that searching for it should take second place to the provision of mechanisms which generate acceptable resolutions to disputes.

We are grateful to Celia Wells and Stewart Field for their comments upon an earlier draft of this chapter.

[1] Mirjan Damaska, 'Presentation of Evidence and Factfinding Precision' (1975) 123 U. Pa. LR 1083.

[2] Gary Goodpaster, 'On the Theory of the American Adversarial Trial' (1987) 78 J. Crim. L. & Crimin. 118.

[3] Ibid. at 124.

The methods of science[4] were not developed for the resolution of disputes at all. They are methods directed towards finding truth. Consequently internal conflicts are bound to arise when the criminal justice system deals with scientific evidence, and these conflicts might be expected to be greatest where the role of the court is least pro-active, that is, in the adversarial system.[5] There are all sorts of reasons why it might be particularly difficult for a tribunal of fact, particularly if entirely untrained, to choose between (wholly or partly) mutually contradictory testimony of scientific experts. If the role played by science in criminal law is simply that of a neutral supplier of information then there is everything to be said for the methods of scientific inquiry[6] to be employed within a system of court-appointed experts.[7] But there are other considerations, both as to the particular role played by scientific evidence and as to the rights of the accused.

Difficulties in receiving scientific evidence arise in the most acute form when the science is furthest removed from the experience of the factfinder. The human rights of accused persons are endangered throughout the criminal process, but are raised very clearly when access is required to the body of the defendant, or when the prosecution proposes to lead evidence having the oracular status of science. All these questions fall for consideration when DNA-profiling evidence is in issue.

This chapter will consider expert scientific evidence in general, and DNA-profiling evidence in particular, in the following areas:

- procedural regulation of laboratories by exclusionary rules of evidence;
- the nature of DNA profiles;
- the nature of expert testimony and means of challenge to it;
- human rights and scientific evidence;
- paying for forensic scientists;
- means of obtaining body samples;
- a brief consideration of the possible development of DNA databanks.

It will use the particular example of DNA profiling to consider the general problems which arise out of the use of scientific evidence and expert witnesses, together with the more specific human rights issues posed by the use of DNA in criminal cases. Besides considering how these issues are presently resolved in the laws of England and Wales and of the Netherlands, it will examine the impact of the ECHR and its case law in this area.

---

[4] T. Kuhn, *The Structure of Scientific Revolutions* (2nd edn., Chicago; University of Chicago Press 1970).

[5] See also Paul Roberts and Chris Willmore, Royal Commission on Criminal Justice Research Study no. 11, *The Role of Forensic Science Evidence in Criminal Proceedings* (London; HMSO 1993), 107–19.

[6] Peter Brett, 'The Implications of Science for the Law' (1972) 18 McGill LJ 170.

[7] J. R. Spencer, 'The Neutral Expert: An Implausible Bogey' [1991] *CrimLRev.* 106.

SYSTEMS OF EVIDENCE: FREE AND CONTROLLED PROOF

In England and Wales admissibility of evidence is determined by the tribunal of law (in the Crown Court, the judge; in a magistrates' court, the magistrate) and its weight assessed by the tribunal of fact (a jury or, in less serious cases, a magistrate). In the Netherlands there is no jury. The judge must be satisfied of guilt. In both systems the judge or juror may decide as he sees fit on the facts presented to the court. He does not have to believe the evidence of the expert witness nor does he necessarily have to accept scientific 'proof' as being true (though Dutch judges must and English juries must not explain their decisions).

The system of evidence in England and Wales is 'free' in the sense that almost any relevant evidence is *prima facie* admissible and that the tribunal of fact (the magistrate or jury) can place whatever value it chooses on any information—there are no rules giving priority to particular types of evidence and conviction may in general (and subject to specific exceptions) result from one piece of evidence alone.[8] The Dutch system adopts a system of controlled legal evidence. The judge must be satisfied (*overtuigd*) by *legal means of evidence*.[9] Generally more than one type of evidence is required. For example, the defendant may not be convicted solely on his own evidence or that of one witness.[10] This does not mean however that each type of evidence has to relate to all the allegations made. For instance, a corpse might constitute supporting evidence together with an admission in a case of murder.[11] The requirements that there be legal means of evidence and that the judge be satisfied are cumulative.[12]

Conversely the problem for systems of free evidence is that the tribunal of fact may be misled by evidence which is relevant and prejudicial into granting it greater probative value than is logically justifiable.[13]

---

[8] L. Jonathan Cohen, 'Freedom of Proof', in William Twining (ed.), *Facts in Law* (ARSP; Wiesbaden 1983), 1.

[9] 'Wettige bewijsmiddelen'—Code of Criminal Procedure (Wetboek van Strafvordering 1926), Art. 338. Art. 339 sets out exhaustively the legal means of proof as: statement of the defendant at the trial; statement of witnesses at the trial; statement of an expert at the trial; written evidence, which must be read aloud at the trial; observations of the judge at the trial.

[10] Arts. 341.4 and 342.2 CCP, respectively.

[11] That is, the concept of supporting evidence is far wider than the English law concept of corroboration which, when it applies, requires that the corroborating evidence connect *that* defendant to *that* crime. See Law Commission No. 202, *Corroboration of Evidence in Criminal Trials* (1991, Cm 1620).

[12] e.g., the defendant may not be found guilty only on his/her own testimony (Art. 341.4 CCP) nor may guilt be attributed on the evidence of one witness alone (Art. 342.2 CCP).

[13] The connection between the system of evidence (controlled/free) and the system of procedure (inquisitorial/accusatorial), if any, is unclear. It might have been thought that a system with trained fact-finders would fit more easily with a system of free proof, and a system of amateur fact-finders would require controls.

PROCEDURAL REGULATION OF LABORATORIES BY
EXCLUSIONARY RULES OF EVIDENCE

Under a system of free evidence, evidence is either relevant[14] evidence, prima facie admissible, or it is not. There are no rules which render particular classes of scientific evidence inadmissible. And there is no real control over the standards to be met in forensic laboratories in England and Wales. This is something under consideration by the Royal Commission, and regulation will be necessary to introduce any exclusionary rules of evidence and to comply with the Council of Europe recommendations.[15]

In England and Wales, in the absence of specified procedures, in principle errors in carrying out tests affect the weight of the evidence, not its admissibility. The only challenges that can currently be made to the admissibility of relevant scientific evidence are, under section 78 of PACE 1984, to have such evidence ruled inadmissible as an exercise of discretion on the ground that to admit it would have 'an adverse effect on the fairness of the proceedings' or to ask the court to use its general discretion to exclude evidence when its prejudicial effects outweigh its probative value.[16] However, in the absence of established procedural rules it is difficult for the defence to claim that the tests have been carried out improperly.

Any other challenge would not be as to admissibility but as to weight. The theory is that it is for the tribunal of fact to decide the value of the evidence. The defence can attempt to discredit prosecution claims as to the weight to be given to evidence by cross-examination or by use of its own expert witnesses. The criminal procedure of England and Wales still rests upon the oral tradition, but cross-examination is ill-suited to revealing errors in the performance of scientific tests. By that stage, the evidence-in-chief will already have been given, making it too late to rule it inadmissible: reliance then has to be placed on a direction to the jury to ignore the evidence or to its giving it little credence.

One general solution within the adversarial system is to lay down specific procedures for the conduct of any of the standard forensic science tests, place the burden upon the prosecution of proving beyond reasonable doubt that those procedures were carried out in the particular case, and make discharge of that burden a precondition to admission of the evidence.[17]

---

[14] The standard definition of relevance is as follows: The word relevant means that any two facts to which it is applied are so related to each other that according to the common course of events one either taken by itself or in conjunction with other facts proves or renders probable the past, present or future existence or non-existence of the other. James Fitzjames Stephen, *Digest of the Law of Evidence* (5th edn., London; Macmillan 1899).

[15] Council of Europe Committee of Ministers Recommendation No. R. (92) 1 (1992). Principle 6 calls for accreditation of laboratories.

[16] Colin Tapper, *Cross on Evidence* (7th edn., London; Butterworths 1990), 370 *et seq.*

[17] See Peter Alldridge, 'Admitting Novel Scientific Evidence—DNA as a Test Case' [1992] *CrimLRev.* 687.

This could be done by a committee of experts and lawyers which could assess, and in effect license, novel scientific techniques for gaining evidence before such evidence may be given to the court. The committee would work on an inquisitorial basis and determine whether a particular area of knowledge was sufficiently reliable to be used in evidence. It could also be used to license experts and laboratories.[18]

In the Netherlands there are no special legal procedures for forensic tests in general, but in the case of drunken driving there is supplementary legislation[19] which describes in detail the manner in which the tests have to be carried out (breath, urine, or blood test) and the methods that have to be employed. Where it appears that the rules have not been followed, the trial judge must exclude the results:[20] errors go to admissibility not to weight. Under the new legislation in force since September 1992[21] only approved laboratories can carry out DNA tests and only experts working in or connected with these laboratories will be able to give expert evidence.[22] Supplementary legislation[23] sets out methods and standards of performance. It may be expected that judges will handle DNA evidence in the same way as results of tests in cases of drunken driving: if the rules have not been followed the results will not be used.

THE NATURE OF DNA PROFILES

DNA contains the genetic code of the individual from whom it is taken. It is hereditary and is responsible for many attributes of the individual.[24] DNA is present in the nucleus of every living cell (except red blood cells) of the body so that any trace of blood (white cells contain DNA), semen, or hair root (not hair or nails) found at the scene of the crime may help to ascertain who was present because a DNA profile of the material may be matched with those of suspects. Despite these positive characteristics there are strong grounds for exercising caution. Despite the hopes of some to the contrary, DNA profiling evidence is not the same as a unique calling card left at the scene of the crime. In particular, using DNA profiles raises

---

[18] Council of Europe Committee of Ministers Recommendation No. R. (92) 1 (1992). Principle 6 calls for accreditation of laboratories.
[19] To Art. 33a, Road Traffic Act.   [20] HR, 22 September 1992, [1993] NJ 84.
[21] 8 November 1993, Stb. 1953, 596.
[22] Art. 195a and d CCP. The test will only be able to be carried out in a laboratory approved by Sterlab/Sterin, the Dutch institution for licensing laboratories. Such a licence will be given for a period of two years at most.
[23] Royal Decree of 4 July 1994, Stb. 1994, 522.
[24] Identical twins have the same DNA. Furthermore DNA may mutate during a person's lifetime. Though this is rare, it may affect the use of DNA in criminal cases. Alec Jeffreys, Nicola Royale Victoria Wilson and Zilla Wong, 'Spontaneous Mutation Rates to New Length Alleles at Tandem Repetitive Hypervariable Loci in Human DNA' (1988) 332 *Nature*, 278.

questions in three crucial respects: the reliability of the conduct of the tests;[25] their interpretation; and the implications for human rights.

Proper use of DNA samples requires that expertise in molecular biology, population genetics, and statistics be brought to bear.[26] The production of the profiles requires biochemical expertise. The hazards of testing include: possible mixing of samples before the tests are carried out; mishandling causing contamination either at the time the sample is collected or later in the laboratory; contamination with bacterial, viral, other human, or non-human DNA at the scene of the crime. A small sample can complicate the test and make further verification impossible;[27] and the test itself may be carried out incorrectly.[28] After the biochemical part of the testing has been done the question will arise whether there is a 'match' between the DNA profile of the accused and that of the sample. This is not without problems. Practice hitherto[29] has been to set an arbitrary threshold of similarity and to treat as irrelevant anything falling short and as compelling anything satisfying the criteria. It has been powerfully argued that:[30]

Common sense rebels against the notion that samples differing by 2.99 standard deviations 'match' and that samples differing by 3.01 sd do not 'match'. The problem in fact is the whole idea of a 'match'.

The interpretation of the data sometimes requires expertise in population genetics. Fragments from two people may be the same or similar, especially within a community which has inter-bred extensively. Such circumstances increase the chances of two profiles being similar, thus rendering the probability that the DNA profile could originate otherwise than with the accused.[31]

EXPERT EVIDENCE AND CHALLENGES TO IT

DNA profiles will always require expert interpretation to the court. In both jurisdictions expert evidence has long been available to the courts on

---

[25] See, generally, National Research Council, *DNA Technology in Forensic Science* (Washington, DC; National Academy Press 1992).

[26] Bernard Robertson and G. A. Vignaux, 'Expert Evidence: Law Practice and Probability' (1992) 12 *Oxford Journal of Legal Studies*, 392.

[27] In the Netherlands this problem may soon be addressed by the proposed Art. 195a(2) presently before Parliament: if the sample is too small for an independent test then the accused will be able to choose the expert who is to carry out the tests. Tweede Kamer No. 22447: addition to the CCP concerning DNA testing in criminal cases.

[28] On all these problems see National Research Council, *DNA Technology in Forensic Science* (Washington, DC; National Academy Press 1992), 89–90.

[29] Ibid., 53–4.

[30] Bernard Robertson and G. A. Vignaux, 'Why the NRC Report on DNA is Wrong' (1992) 142 *NLJ* 1619.

[31] See R. C. Lewontin and Daniel L. Hartl, 'Population Genetics in Forensic DNA Typing' (1991) *Science* 1745; John J. Walsh, 'The Population Genetics of Forensic DNA Typing: "Could it have been Someone Else?"' (1992) 34 *Crim L Q* 469.

matters of scientific knowledge. The formal significance is that an expert witness is permitted to give opinion evidence whereas a non-expert is not, and that the rule against hearsay is obviated because the expert is regarded as the embodiment of a field of learning.

The question that arises is whether and how it is possible to challenge the evidence of an expert, and in particular an expert giving inculpatory DNA evidence. The defence may want to challenge each of the three stages in the provision of the evidence. A small-scale research study for the Royal Commission on Criminal Justice[32] found that of thirteen respondent defence lawyers whose expert evaluations differed from those of the prosecution, six disputed statistical calculations, three disputed whether matches had been obtained and two were concerned over the possibility of contamination, while two were not convinced by the whole process of DNA profiling.

HUMAN RIGHTS AND SCIENTIFIC EVIDENCE

Certain types of evidence have a particular potential for misleading the tribunal of fact. Examples include confessions and eye-witness evidence. In consequence the case has been made for more rigorous controls in those areas. Attention is now directed to scientific evidence. Defendants have turned for protection to the European Convention on Human Rights (ECHR). Article 6(1) of the Convention provides that when faced with a criminal charge everyone has a right to a fair and public hearing by an independent and impartial tribunal. Article 6(3) goes on to list certain minimum rights to be afforded to all defendants.[33]

It is essential to a fair trial that the suspect have the opportunity to challenge the reliability of the results of scientific testing. Although in both countries the expert witness is, in theory, independent of the state, most are employed and remunerated by it.[34] But the Dutch expert witness is neutral and court-appointed,[35] whilst the expert in England and Wales is retained as a witness *for*[36] the prosecution.[37] This follows from the obligation

[32] Beverley Steventon, *The Ability to Challenge DNA Evidence*, Royal Commission on Criminal Justice Research Study No. 9 (London; HMSO 1993), 22–3.
[33] These include: adequate time and facilities to prepare a defence (Art. 6(3)(b)); rights to legal representation paid for, if necessary, by the state (Art. 6(3)(c)); to obtain the attendance of and examine witnesses as well as examining the witnesses provided by the state (Art. 6(3)(d)). See, generally, Chap. 14 below.
[34] Some amelioration of the position was achieved in the United Kingdom by the introduction of the Forensic Science Service with autonomy from the Home Office and power to work for defendants. None the less, since this service is the one which is always employed by the prosecution, it is rarely invoked by the defence. And see First Report from the Home Affairs Committee, *The Forensic Science Service* (Cm 699, 1989).
[35] J. R. Spencer, 'The Neutral Expert: An Implausible Bogey' [1991] *CrimLRev.* 106.
[36] This is the crux. The idea of being a witness *for* a particular side is anathema to the civil lawyer.
[37] The formal significance of being called by one side is that hostile questions cannot in the first instance be asked by the side calling the witness.

upon parties to adversarial proceedings to bring evidence favouring their account to the court's attention. It affects the way evidence is constructed, given, and challenged.[38]

The Dutch Code also allows a general request for an expert (to be employed by the pre-trial judge)[39] and gives the defendant the right to employ his/her own expert (as a second expert who has the right to be present during the *expertise*) and the right to a counter-expert. Another possibility for the defendant is to take an expert with him/her to the trial.[40] The European Court in *Bönisch*[41] and *Brandstetter*[42] decided that the demands of the Convention are satisfied as long as the court permits a counter-expert to be heard (where the defence asks for one), even if only as a witness, and does not give priority to the court expert.

Under the case law of the Dutch Supreme Court there is no general right to a counter-expert (or expert for the defence), but the case law of the ECHR has been influential. A well-founded defence request for a counter-expertise may only be refused[43] if the evidence to be gained is to be based to a decisive extent on other than the first expertise.[44] If a counter-expert contests the scientific method which has been used or the inferences made by the court's expert, the court is allowed to use the court expert's expertise but it has to state reasons[45] why it nevertheless uses this piece of evidence.[46] The Dutch proposal accepts the importance of counter-experts. Article 195b of the Bill will give the accused the right to have a counter-expert, and, if only a small amount of material is available for testing, the accused (if the only suspect) can choose the expert to carry out the test. This would ensure that in Holland DNA profiling complied with the Convention. In England and Wales there are at present no formal restrictions, other than those rules which apply to all witnesses, upon the defence right to call alternative experts and to cross-examine prosecution experts. Whatever may be wrong with this,[47] it is clearly in accordance with the Convention.

---

[38] In adversarial proceedings considerable freedom is given as to the questions which may be put to 'hostile' witnesses.

[39] Arts. 227 and 151(2) CCP.   [40] Arts. 280(6) and 296 CCP.

[41] *Bönisch* v. *Austria*, ECHR, Series A No. 92, judgment of 6 May 1985, App. 8658/79, (1987) 9 EHRR 191.

[42] *Brandstetter* v. *Austria*, ECHR, Series A No. 211, judgment of 28 August 1991, Apps. 11170/84, 12876/87 and 13468/87 (1993) 15 EHRR 378.

[43] HR, 6 March 1990, [1990] NJ 467; HR, 28 April 1992, [1992] NJ 644; HR, 26 May 1992, [1992] NJ 679; HR, 18 February 1992, [1993] NJ 28.

[44] HR, 25 February 1992, [1992] NJ 555.

[45] A Dutch finding of guilt has to be 'reasoned', which means that being convinced that the evidence suffices is not enough. The court has generally a duty to respond—by stating reasons—to all defences.

[46] HR, 28 February 1989, [1989] NJ 748.

[47] See also Roberts and Willmore, *The Role of Forensic Science Evidence* (1993).

PAYING THE FORENSIC SCIENTIST

The present position in the Netherlands is that the defendant pays for any expert and then claims back such money from the court. Under Article 234(3) of the CCP the costs will be reimbursed if the evidence is helpful in ascertaining the facts of the case.[48] This procedure still means that the defendant takes a gamble, not knowing whether a refund will be forthcoming,[49] but where the defence has insufficient funds advance payment may be possible. The first draft of the new Dutch legislation would have given the suspect a right to employ his or her own expert and this, read in conjunction with Article 234(3) of the CCP, would have obliged the state to fund such experts and the right to challenge would clearly have been 'practical and effective'. The text has now been changed so as to require a (small) contribution from the suspect.[50]

In England and Wales the case is somewhat different. A client's need for legal aid is carefully assessed and special expenditure is controlled so that if the state considers that a certain type of expenditure is unnecessary it will not be permitted.[51] In the exploratory study for the Royal Commission[52] it was found that applications for legal aid to supply defence experts to challenge DNA evidence are almost always successful. It is rare for a defence expert actually to give evidence in a DNA case. Far more commonly they assist in the preparation of cross-examination or advise during cross-examination of the prosecution witnesses.

If the defence is unable to afford to pay expert witnesses, this right to call counter-experts is effectively denied and becomes a right limited to the wealthier. To guarantee the right requires the state to pay for such witnesses. Article 6(3)(b)[53] of the Convention and the cases under it, when read together, suggest that the accused has a right to call expert witnesses and that if there are insufficient funds to pay for that, the state should pay for the costs of such a witness. The European Court decisions in this area seem to place such a positive duty on the state when it is necessary for a fair trial.[54]

OBTAINING BODY SAMPLES

In order to use DNA profiling it is necessary to obtain certain types of body material. The sample may be obtained by chance. In the case where

---

[48] Art. 591 CCP.   [49] Art. 16 on tariffs in criminal cases.
[50] Art. 195b. The costs are about f. 5,000, towards which the defence has to pay f. 250.
[51] For a full discussion of legal aid see John Clegg and Stephen Dawson, *Profitable Legal Aid* (London; Fourmat Publishing 1991).
[52] Steventon, *The Ability to Challenge DNA Evidence*, 33–4.
[53] '... adequate ... facilities for the preparation of his defence'.
[54] *Airey* v. *Ireland*, ECHR, Series A No. 37, paras. 24–6, judgment of 9 October 1979, 2 EHRR 305. *Artico* v. *Italy*, ECHR, Series A No. 37, para. 33, judgment of 13 May 1980, (1981) 3 EHRR 1.

the sample is obtained without coercion (for example, by taking a hair follicle from the defendant's clothing) the sample is lawfully obtained both in the Netherlands and in England and Wales.[55]

The crucial juridical question in the Netherlands is whether it is permissible to use body samples for DNA testing which have been obtained by chance. This question has not yet been fully resolved in the Netherlands. Two lines of reasoning are possible. The first is that the DNA test as such forms no separate interference with the right to the integrity of the body, so if the body material has been obtained lawfully, there is also the right to perform a DNA test on such material. This line is based on the view that there is no legal consideration specific to DNA testing.[56]

The second line of reasoning is based on the view that all persons have the right to decide what happens to their own body tissue.[57] This method of reasoning is especially strong in health law. It is based on the view that there is a need for greater protection of body tissue, as a consequence of the evolution of science.[58] According to this view DNA testing as such is an interference with the right to integrity of the body, resulting from prior interference, caused by the taking of body materials against the suspect's will.[59] Consequently there has to be a specific consent from the suspect in order to perform a DNA test on his body tissue, even if this material was legally obtained. The solution for criminal investigations is to create a special power to perform DNA testing against the suspect's will, allied to the investigation power to obtain body tissue against his/her will.

According to the Dutch Supreme Court the taking of body tissue from the suspect for the purpose of DNA testing is not permitted under the existing law.[60] This judgment can be interpreted in the two different ways described above. At present, there is no case law of the Supreme Court on the specific question: is there a need for specific consent if the legally obtained body tissue of the suspect will be subjected to a DNA test? The Amsterdam Court of Appeal has held that it is enough if the suspect gave his/her consent to the performance of tests in general (in a case in which the body tissue was legally obtained). Specific consent for DNA testing was, in the opinion of the court, not necessary. Under the new legislation the mandatory taking of body samples and the use of these samples for

---

[55] Technically, the defendant might have a proprietary right in the follicle, but the seizure provisions of PACE confer power upon the police to override it.

[56] By analogy, if the police lawfully seize a car in the Netherlands, they may also search it.

[57] *Zelfbeschikkingsrecht* is protected by Art. 11 of the Dutch Constitution.

[58] See, e.g., J. K. M. Gevers, 'Rechtsbescherming na de dood', in *Grenzen aan de zorg, zorgen aan de Grens, liber amicorum voor Prof. Dr. H. J. J. Leenen*, Alphen aan den Rijn (1990), 170–9.

[59] See the comment of the Dutch section of the Commission of Jurists for Human Rights (NJCM): NJCM Bulletin 1992, 410–54, especially 433–41.

[60] HR, 2 July 1990, [1990] NJ 751.

DNA testing will be regulated: there will be investigation powers to do so. Therefore since 1 September 1994 it is lawful[61] to perform a DNA test on body samples which have been obtained by chance.

No jurisdiction permits a suspect to refuse to co-operate without adverse consequences. The options to be considered are:

(i) obtaining the sample by coercion, using force if necessary; or
(ii) creating a separate offence of refusal to co-operate; or
(iii) allowing adverse inferences to be drawn from refusal to co-operate.

Obtaining the Sample by Coercion

The most drastic solution is that of forced testing. In the law of England and Wales[62] a distinction is made between intimate and other body samples. A non-intimate sample can, under appropriate circumstances, be taken without consent.[63] An accused cannot be forced to donate an intimate body sample such as a sample of body fluid.[64] Under Part IV of the Criminal Justice and Public Order Bill, some DNA-yielding samples, including cheek-scrapings, are to be reclassified as non-intimate.

Until 1 September 1994, when the new law entered into force, it was not allowed in the Netherlands to obtain a sample by force.[65] Body samples for DNA testing could only be taken if the suspect agreed to it or, if requested so, in order to prove his/her innocence.[66] The new law legalizes both mandatory DNA testing and the taking of samples (by force if necessary) for DNA profiles.[67] This is similar to fingerprint evidence where both countries permit the use of force, if necessary.

Does the use of force run counter to the ECHR? The use of force to obtain DNA samples must be considered in the light of Articles 3 and 8[68]

---

[61] According to prior case law on *voortgezette toepassing van bevoegheden* (HR, 2 December 1935, [1936] NJ 250) which permits the subsequent use of evidence gained in good faith by chance or by the lawful use of a different investigative power.

[62] Compare in this respect the law of Scotland where coercive testing is permitted: Law Commission of Scotland Report No. 120, *Evidence: Blood Tests DNA and Related Problems* (Edinburgh; HMSO 1989). In Northern Ireland what operates is a more repressive version of the position in England and Wales. By Sched. 14 of the Criminal Justice Act 1988 and para. 53 of the Police and Criminal Evidence (Northern Ireland) Order 1989 a mouth swab is a non-intimate sample and therefore force can be used to obtain it.

[63] PACE, s. 63(3).   [64] PACE, s. 62.   [65] HR, 2 July 1990, [1991] NJ 170.

[66] Such a request for expert evidence cannot be turned down by a court without good reason: HR, 2 July 1990, [1990] 1 NJ 751.

[67] Tweede Kamer No. 22447: addition to the CCP concerning DNA testing in criminal cases.

[68] Art. 5 ECHR might also be important if the individual is being detained merely to provide a body sample. In *X* v. *Austria* (Commission Decision of 13 December 1979, App. 8278/78) deprivation of liberty for a short period was said to contravene Art. 5 but was justified if under a court order. So, to obtain evidence, minor infringements of liberty may be justified.

of the ECHR. Of these, Article 3 covers extreme interferences with the physical or psychological integrity of the person.[69] In practice contravention of Article 3 is unlikely partly because the authorities would stop before that point was reached but also because most people would submit.[70] Breach of Article 8 is more likely. Clearly the non-consensual taking of a blood sample is an interference with private life contrary to Article 8(1).[71] It will only be permitted if it is 'in accordance with the law' and 'necessary in a democratic society . . . for the prevention of crime and for the protection of other rights'.[72] According to *Kruslin*[73] to be 'in accordance with the law' the power must be clearly set out in law; its consequences accessible to the person; and it must be compatible with the rule of law.[74] As indicated in *Kruslin*[75] and *Malone*[76] the last requirement is the most useful control because, to be compatible with the rule of law, there must be some practical and meaningful control incorporated into the domestic law which will protect against arbitrary interferences or misuse of discretionary powers. The checks required in any law depend on the severity of any interference with human rights. In the draft Dutch law there will be safeguards of this sort built into the system so that the decision to take a sample by force will be taken by a judge, the investigating judge, but only if the test is necessary to establish the facts and there is good reason to suspect the individual, a

[69] *Ireland* v. *United Kingdom*, ECHR, Series B No. 23–I, 388, report of the Commission of 25 January 1976, App. 5310/71; *Ireland* v. *United Kingdom*, ECHR, Series A No. 25, para. 167, judgment of 18 January 1978, App. 5310/71.
[70] Though the mere threat may itself conflict with Art. 3, see *Campbell and Cosans* v. *United Kingdom*, ECHR, Series A No. 48, para. 26, judgment of 25 February 1982, (1982) 4 EHRR 293. The significance of the breach being of Art. 3 in addition to Art. 8 is that no derogation from the rights conferred by it can be justified under Art. 3.
[71] Even minimum physical interference with a person against his/her will contravenes this article: *X* v. *Netherlands*, Commission Decision of 4 December 1978, App. 8239/78. Although, in a paternity suit, it was interference to order that a person be brought by force for a blood test it was, none the less, considered reasonable: *X* v. *Austria*, Commission Decision of 13 December 1979, App. 8278/78, 154. A psychiatric examination of an accused person is also an 'interference': *X* v. *Federal Republic of Germany*, Commission Decision of 7 May 1981, adopted on 14 December 1981, App. 8334/78.
[72] To be 'necessary' it need not be indispensable or absolutely necessary, but it must be more than useful, desirable or reasonable. There must be a 'pressing social need', the interference must be 'proportionate to the legitimate aim pursued'. See e.g. *Handyside* v. *United Kingdom*, ECHR, Series A No. 24, especially paras. 48 and 49, judgment of 7 December 1976, App. 5493/72, 1 EHRR 737, where a conviction for publication of obscene material did not contravene Art. 10 as it was necessary for the protection of morals; and *X* v. *Austria*, Commission Decision of 13 December 1979, App. 8278/78, in which a forced blood test was said to be lawful as it was relatively harmless and necessary to protect another individual's rights under a paternity suit. There must be safeguards against abuse: *Malone* v. *United Kingdom*, ECHR, Series A No. 82, para. 56, judgment of 2 August 1984, App. 8691/79, (1985) 7 EHRR 14.
[73] *Kruslin* v. *France*, ECHR, Series A No. 176–A, judgment of 24 April 1990, App. 11801/85, (1990) 12 EHRR 547.
[74] At para. 27.   [75] At para. 30.
[76] *Malone* v. *United Kingdom*, ECHR, Series A No. 82, judgment of 2 August 1984, App. 8691/79, (1985) 7 EHRR 14 at paras. 67–8.

probable cause (*ernstige bezwaren*) in relation to a very serious crime.[77] Even then the suspect has a right of appeal. Any sample must be taken by a doctor.[78] There will also be a control on where, how, and by whom the test can be performed. Safeguards such as those in the Dutch law[79] are necessary to protect the rights of the individual.

The Council of Europe Recommendation does not forbid the use of coercion in relation to the taking of DNA samples for analysis, but states that

... the introduction and use of these techniques should take full account of and not contravene such fundamental principle as the inherent dignity of the individual and respect for the human body, the rights of the defence and the principle of proportionality in the carrying out of criminal justice.

The Dutch proposal is thought to conform.

Alternatives to Coercion: (1) Separate Offences

The word 'necessary' in the Convention implies the unavailability of less drastic measures. This may not be the case. There are two other solutions which are less intrusive into human rights. First, it might be possible to make a separate crime of refusal to undergo a blood test. This is a pragmatic solution where the punishment is relatively slight, such as drunk driving.[80] But in cases where DNA profiling is being used the defendant may stand charged of a very serious crime—typically rape or homicide[81]— and it would clearly be inappropriate to allow equivalent penalties for refusal to supply samples.

Alternatives to Coercion: (2) Adverse Inferences

The other possibility is to allow adverse inferences to be drawn from refusal to supply samples. In England and Wales, if the suspect, without good cause, refuses to comply with a request in proper form to give an intimate body sample, the court can draw such inferences as it sees proper from the refusal. This means that refusal to supply a sample is capable of amounting to evidence of guilt. Failure to supply samples when an appropriate request is made may also be used to corroborate other evidence.[82] The safeguards

---

[77] Defined in Arts. 195d(1) and 2 CCP.
[78] See Art. 195d(1) and (2) CCP.　　　[79] Above, n. 67.
[80] In England and Wales, Road Traffic Act 1988, s. 7. In the Netherlands, Art. 33a Road Traffic Act (*Wegenverkeerswet*, of 13 September 1935, Stb. 554).
[81] In the survey of forensic scientists for the Royal Commission about 80 per cent of DNA cases were rape, attempted rape, or other sexual offences, and about 10 per cent were homicides. Steventon, *The Ability to Challenge DNA Evidence*, 2.
[82] PACE, s. 62(10).

278   *Peter Alldridge, Sanneke Berkhout-van Poelgeest*

against abuse are: that the suspect may only be asked to provide an intimate body sample if there are reasonable grounds for suspecting that he has been involved in a serious arrestable offence;[83] that a police officer of at least the rank of superintendent must authorize the request; and that the suspect must be informed of the authorization and the grounds for giving it.

Why is it that the possibility has not been canvassed in the Netherlands of allowing adverse inferences to be drawn? The answer lies in the Dutch system of controlled evidence, which makes it necessary to search for actual proof of guilt (*materiele waarheidsvinding*). The argument here is that refusal to co-operate may arise for any number of reasons and is therefore no proof positive—refusal to undergo a blood test therefore cannot be used as evidence of guilt.[84] Evidence as to how the defendant behaved after the alleged offence is regarded as irrelevant. The opposing argument from free evidence is that the following line of reasoning is, in general, a legitimate one, and shows refusal to be logically relevant.

> Major Premiss: the fact that a suspect refuses to give a sample makes it more probable than before the request that s/he is guilty.
> Minor Premiss: the suspect, when asked for a sample, and after having had explained to him/her the consequences of refusal, does not allow a sample to be taken.
> Conclusion: therefore it is more probable than before the refusal was considered that this suspect committed the offence.[85]

There may be other reasons for the refusal. There may be suspects who are deeply distrustful of DNA tests, or phobic about personal intrusions. But none of these are reasons within a system of free evidence for excluding the *possibility* of drawing adverse inferences, by treating the refusal as irrelevant. It is the Netherlands' system of controlled evidence which forecloses the possibility of drawing adverse inferences and drives the Dutch system towards the position of compelling the production of samples. The introduction of compulsory samples under the 1994 Criminal Justice and Public Order Bill arises not from such doctrinal necessity, but from political opportunism.

DATABASES

The final area to be considered is the question whether DNA profiles of either convicted or suspected persons should be stored on a data bank[86]

---

[83] Defined in PACE, s. 116.
[84] HR, 31 March 1987, [1987] NJ 868; HR, 8 November 1988, [1989] NJ 657.
[85] On the use of inference in a system of free evidence see Terence Anderson and William Twining, *Analysis of Evidence* (London; Weidenfeld 1991), 66–7.
[86] Generally, see National Research Council, *DNA Technology in Forensic Science* (Washington, DC; National Academy Press 1992), 111–43.

for possible use in future cases. Clearly both the storage and use of such data implies an interference with the right to privacy guaranteed in Article 8[87] and could therefore only be justified if they are both 'in accordance with the law' and 'necessary'. In a Council of Europe recommendation on the use of DNA evidence[88] the general exigencies of the Data Protection Convention and the recommendations on data protection, particularly that regulating the use of personal data in the police sector, are rehearsed. Under the Council of Europe Convention on the Protection of Individuals with Regard to Automatic Processing of Data, if data are held in automatic data banks special care must be taken in their storage.[89]

It is possible to store and search through profiles by computer. The attraction of computerized databases is easily understood: information can be held on unsolved cases and be cross-referenced with those from new offences to see if the crimes are connected; profiles of individuals can be tested against those from the scene of a crime, and information can be exchanged between jurisdictions. Databases of DNA profiles from convicted sex offenders have been accepted or are being discussed in some US states.[90]

In England and Wales if a suspect is cleared of an offence or if no prosecution is brought then section 64 of PACE requires the destruction of all intimate and non-intimate body samples collected pursuant to sections 62 and 63. But the section does not require the destruction of the DNA profile[91] once it has been obtained, nor is there anything which would prevent its use for purposes not directly related to the particular crime under investigation. If the individual is convicted there appears to be no protection at all. Better protection is afforded to fingerprint evidence under the amendments made to section 64 of PACE in 1988.[92]

The Metropolitan Police Laboratory has a computerized DNA database which holds information on unsolved cases, on individuals waiting for trial, and on people already convicted. At the moment, the information is obtained from casework and the British Government has stated that it is exploring the possibility of developing a DNA databank.[93] In the Netherlands, samples found at the scene of the crime will be kept as long as there is no suspect. If there is a suspect, the samples must be destroyed as soon as they are no longer necessary for the investigation. But there is also to

---

[87] App. 8371/78, *McFelly* v. *UK*. See also Apps. 8022, 8025, 8027/77, *McVeigh, O'Neill and Evans* v. *UK*, report adopted by the Commission on 18 March 1981, pursuant to Art. 31 of the Convention, 25 D. & R. 15.

[88] Council of Europe Committee of Ministers Recommendation No. R(92) 1 (1992).

[89] Council of Europe Recommendation No. R. (92) 1 refers to both the Data Protection Convention and Recommendation R(87) 15.

[90] National Research Council, *DNA Technology in Forensic Science*, 124.

[91] The DNA profile can be stored as a series of numbers.

[92] Criminal Justice Act 1988, s. 148.

[93] Governmental reply to the First Report from the Home Affairs Committee, *The Forensic Science Service* (Cm 699, 1989), at para. 21.

be a databank of profiles,[94] which will be subject to the same regulations as those which deal with fingerprints. Stored profiles will only be removed from the databank if the person is shown to have been wrongly suspected. The profile must be removed if there has not been a conviction, or the suspect dies, or after thirty years. There is to be no regulation for the storage of unknown (anonymous) samples, the argument being that when the person is unknown there can be no-one whose rights require protection.[95] In short, there is some legal protection against the misuse of personal information in the Netherlands but it is not very strong.[96]

There is a number of different bases on which a DNA profile database could be compiled:[97]

(i) non-selectively: DNA profiles of all the inhabitants of a particular geographical area (either national or local) might help to eliminate the innocent from all enquiries but it would be prohibitively expensive and could not be said to be 'necessary' under the Convention.

(ii) *ad hoc*: a bank of profiles collected as part of all future investigations (whether there is a conviction or not) might be possible, but would generate a random sample.

(iii) selectively: all people convicted in the future, or all those convicted of a serious offence, should have DNA profiles taken and recorded, or all those convicted of violent and/or sexual offences, whether these arose in the past or the future.

The last is the one whose adoption is most probable in England and Wales.

DNA profiles contain genetic information concerning the individual. Although we are not at present able to read all this information, the person's race, colour, and other genetic details may be revealed in a profile and we need to prepare for a time when we can interpret it, because the uses to which such information could be put raise crucial questions concerning human rights.[98] If certain types of profiles appear more frequently in those who commit particular types of crimes this could lead to pressure to impose very intrusive punishments (such as their being permanently removed from society). Such punishments may be invoked even in the absence of clear understanding of the connection between the profile and

---

[94] Royal Decree of 4 July 1994, note 23 above.

[95] Tweede Kamer, 1992–1993, 22447, No. 6, p. 5.

[96] Hence the reservation by the Dutch representative in respect of principle 8 of the Council of Europe recommendation, which permits retention of information only where the individual concerned has been convicted of serious offences against the life, integrity or security of persons.

[97] National Research Council, *DNA Technology in Forensic Science*, 119–22.

[98] Even if not damaging, some of this information is very personal and therefore private, so ought to be protected, but such information, in the wrong hands, might also affect a person's insurance risk, employment prospects, and other aspects of his/her life.

the pattern of behaviour. This type of mistake was made, with appalling results, at the beginning of this century.[99] Storage of samples may lead to unwelcome research on general features of 'criminals'.

Dangers remain. Any proposal for databanks would have to be viewed in the context of the European Union and other inter-state commitments. In the European context extra care must be taken as more and more frequently police authorities will be working together and passing information over international boundaries. Article K.1(9) of Maastricht provides for greater co-operation in the field of justice, including police co-operation, for the purposes of preventing and combating serious forms of international crime.[100] In certain international crimes, there may be resort to the use of DNA samples as part of the evidence. In these cases DNA data-banks will be of international use and importance. Under the provisions of Maastricht it may be that the information contained in DNA databanks will be shared between the forces in a number of different states. The data protection implications of this are immense. At the moment there is no real detail concerning the way in which the provision might be implemented. Of more immediate interest is the Schengen agreement of 1985, presently operative in the Benelux States but in which other States in the European Union have shown an interest.[101] In the 1990 Convention that applies the agreement there is provision for the transfer of data between states;[102] for a new information system, the Schengen Information System;[103] and for the protection of data.[104] The protection is to be based upon the Council of Europe Convention for the Protection of Individuals with regard to the Automatic Processing of Data and the Council of Ministers Recommendation Regulating the Use of Personal Data in the Police Sector. Although in certain respects the 1990 Convention goes beyond each of these the protections may fail because the Contracting Parties are not required to harmonize their data protection laws. Clearly Schengen poses problems for the transfer of any personal data[105] but these are magnified when the data are as personal as that contained in a DNA database.

---

[99] For a discussion of the types of treatment considered and used see David Garland, *Punishment and Welfare* (Aldershot; Gower 1985) or Katherine S. Williams, *Criminology* (London; Blackstone 1991), s. 10.1.7.

[100] For further details see Chap. 5, above.

[101] Britain is the only EC State not to have shown any interest in this agreement.

[102] Arts. 38, 39, 46, 48 and 91. Some of these, such as Art. 46, allow the transfer of any information that may be of interest. These provisions are a serious threat to data protection.

[103] Art 94 limits the sorts of data that can be held on the SHS, it includes any particular objective and permanent physical features that may cover DNA profiles.

[104] Arts. 117, 126, 127 and 128.

[105] For further details concerning this see L. F. M. Verhey, 'Privacy Aspects of the Convention Applying the Schengen Agreements', in H. Meijers *et al.*, *Schengen: Internationalisation of Central Chapters of the Law on Aliens, Refugees, Privacy, Security and the Police*, Kluwer Law and Taxation Publishers (1991).

For this reason there is a strong case for saying that all DNA samples should be destroyed as soon as the DNA profile is obtained and that the information on that profile should only be used for purposes directly related to the particular crime under investigation. Such provisions would protect individuals against serious human rights violations.

CONCLUSION

Despite initial enthusiasm DNA profiling is not a flawless investigative and probative tool. There are problems over quality assurance, interpretation of the test, independent scrutiny, and rights of the defence to gain access to the evidence. All these difficulties should at least generate accepted methods and standards of testing and quality controls.

The reliability of DNA profiling in criminal cases has not been challenged frontally in the courts of either country. In England and Wales there is at present no appellate case law, but challenges are expected imminently. In a Dutch case[106] when the defence tried to question the *general* reliability of DNA testing the *Hoge Raad* rejected the challenge on the ground that the defence were not claiming unreliability in that particular case. In each system, therefore, much remains unresolved. The new Dutch law introduces more detailed formal safeguards. In England and Wales the Royal Commission on Criminal Justice considered this issue and suggested a number of measures to ensure that such evidence is carefully obtained, tested and presented and that the rights of defence are preserved.[107] In both jurisdictions clearer formal controls will doubtless soon be in place.

---

[106] HR, 18 February 1992, [1993] NJ 28.
[107] See the Report of the Royal Commission on Criminal Justice (London; HMSO 1993), chap. 9.

14

Witness Evidence, Article 6 of the European Convention on Human Rights and the Principle of Open Justice

ANNEMARIEKE BEIJER, CATHY COBLEY, AND ANDRÉ KLIP

INTRODUCTION

In any democratic society the principle that criminal procedures are carried out in public is considered to be of vital importance. Article 6 of the European Convention on Human Rights provides that 'in the determination . . . of any criminal charge against him, everyone is entitled to a fair and public hearing within a reasonable time by an independent and impartial tribunal established by law . . .' and that 'everyone charged with a criminal offence has the following minimum rights: . . . to examine or have examined witnesses against him and to obtain the attendance and examination of witnesses on his behalf under the same conditions as witnesses against him.' Article 6 aims to protect litigants against the administration of justice in secret with no public scrutiny:

By rendering the administration of justice visible, publicity contributes to the aim of Article 6—namely a fair trial, the guarantee of which is one of the fundamental principles of any democratic society, within the meaning of the Convention.[1]

But publicity is only one aspect of the principle of open justice. A second element is that all the evidence is to be presented in open court, in the presence of the defendant and the judge, where it is subject to challenge. This means a witness is generally required to give his evidence orally in open court where he can be examined.

However, a public trial is often traumatic for all involved and may even endanger the safety, not only of the suspect but also the witnesses, who play a central role in any criminal trial—as Bentham commented 'witnesses are the eyes and ears of justice'. It has long been recognized that, without the co-operation of witnesses, legal systems would simply cease to function. However, some witnesses are more vulnerable than others. For example, a witness who has been frightened by the defendant or his associates will

---

[1] See e.g. *Axen*, ECHR 8 December 1983, Series A No. 72.

be reluctant to testify at a public trial. Both the English and Dutch criminal justice systems are familiar with the problem of witness intimidation and have recognized that such witnesses require some form of protection. Since 1980, the Dutch legal system has dealt with the problem by granting the witness partial or complete anonymity, but the English courts have been more reluctant to take such drastic steps.

Also, in recent years, much concern has been expressed over the position of children as witnesses in criminal trials and in England and Wales some child witnesses are now allowed to give evidence via a live video link.[2]

Mainly due to trans-national crime, more and more problems of practical significance arise if the witness resides outside the jurisdiction where the case is being tried. The witness cannot generally be forced to travel and testify and the presence of the defence at a hearing abroad is hard to realize.

One question is whether the measures taken to protect intimidated and child witnesses and various restrictions on the taking of statements from witnesses abroad infringe Article 6 of the European Convention and the principle of open justice.

In ensuring that justice is done, the courts face the difficult task of balancing the perceived needs of the witness against the right of the accused to a fair and public trial. As the Lord Chief Justice has commented:

> The learned judge has the duty ... of endeavouring to see that justice is done. Those are high sounding words. What it really means is, he has got to see that the system operates fairly; fairly not only to the defendants but also to the prosecution and also to the witnesses. Sometimes he has to make a decision as to where the balance of fairness lies ...[3]

The differing approaches adopted to the balancing exercise by England and Wales and the Netherlands illustrate significant differences between the two legal systems and their understanding of the principle of open justice and Article 6. This chapter explores the differing approaches of the two legal systems by comparing the way vulnerable witnesses are heard and how evidence is taken from witnesses outside the jurisdiction.

THE HEARING OF WITNESSES

England and Wales

In England and Wales, in accordance with the common law traditions of open justice and the primacy of oral evidence, the criminal trial takes the form of an adversarial contest and generally consists of a 'day in court'

---

[2] S. 32 Criminal Justice Act 1988.   [3] *R.* v. *X, Y, Z* (1990) 91 CrAppR 36 at 40.

when both sides present oral evidence in one continual presentation, the question of guilt or innocence being determined by the trier of fact—in more serious cases, the jury. For witnesses, this means that they are expected to appear in person in open court, to take the oath or affirm, to identify themselves, to give their evidence orally to the court in the presence of the accused, and to be examined by the opposing party. An important assumption underlying the trial procedure is that the oral testimony of live witnesses in open court is superior to any other type of evidence.

It is undoubtedly true that there are certain advantages associated with oral evidence—there can be no doubt about what the witness said, he will be available for clarification and examination, and the court will be able to see and hear him, thereby being able to assess his credibility. Wigmore argues that the requirement of open testimony produces:

In the witness' mind a disinclination to falsify; first, by stimulating the instinctive responsibility to public opinion, symbolised in the audience, and ready to scorn a demonstrated liar; and next, by inducing the fear of exposure of subsequent falsities through disclosure by informed persons who may chance to be present or to hear of the testimony from others present.[4]

But there are also distinct disadvantages. The trial inevitably takes place some considerable time after the events giving rise to the criminal charge and the witness is usually suffering from a considerable amount of stress associated with giving evidence and facing examination. As Spencer and Flin point out:

If there are two scientific facts about the psychology of human memory which are clear beyond any doubt, one is that the memory of an event fades gradually with time and the other is that stress beyond a certain level can impair the power of recall.[5]

Therefore, it has been argued that the trust placed in oral evidence is unwarranted and that more weight should be accorded to written evidence. Whatever the merits of such arguments, they have had comparatively little effect on the trial procedure in England and Wales. The main reason for this is the legal system's stubborn adherence to the rule against hearsay evidence. This generally prevents a witness's previous statement, whether written or oral, being used in court and thereby ensures that the witness will be available to face cross-examination. Although certain common law and statutory exceptions do exist, the hearsay rule provides a major obstacle for those seeking to introduce anything other than the direct oral evidence of witnesses at the trial.

The common law exceptions are of limited value in the majority of

---

[4] J. H. Wigmore, *Evidence* (Boston, Mass.; Chadbourn Revision 1976), vi. 435–6.
[5] J. Spencer and R. Flin, *The Evidence of Children* (London; Blackstone Press 1990), 220.

cases.[6] Statutory exceptions to the hearsay rule may be of more use in this respect. In many cases the witness will have made a statement containing the relevant evidence some time between the event in question and the trial. If there is no wish to examine the witness, both parties will usually agree to the admission of the statement in place of oral evidence and no controversy arises. More controversial is the situation where there is dis-agreement between the parties, yet the statement is admitted and the defendant is denied his right to cross-examine the witness. The scope for the admission of documentary evidence in such circumstances has expanded over the last few decades, culminating in the provisions of sections 23–6 of the Criminal Justice Act 1988. In essence, a witness statement may be admissible in place of oral testimony if, *inter alia*, the witness is dead or unfit to attend as a witness, he is outside the UK and it is not reasonably practicable to secure his attendance, or he made the statement to a police-man or some other person charged with the duty of investigating offences or charging offenders but he does not give oral evidence through fear or because he is kept out of the way. However, the statement will only be admitted with the leave of the court and this will only be granted if the court is of the opinion that the statement ought to be admitted in the interests of justice. The admissibility of such statements ultimately depends on the discretion of the trial judge. The most obvious feature that gives rise to concern is the lack of opportunity to examine the witness. This, combined with the primacy of oral evidence in English trials, severely restricts the potential use of such provisions.

The Netherlands

The Dutch inquisitorial trial can be described as an official inquiry into the defendant's guilt. The primary purpose of the Dutch criminal process there-fore is to seek the truth based on all the relevant, material evidence avail-able to the court. In contrast to the English system, the Dutch system does not have a rule against hearsay evidence. In 1926, the Supreme Court decided that hearsay would be admissible.[7] This means that out-of-court declarations can be used as evidence regardless of whether the witness is available to be called. In practice the significance of the investigation at the trial has therefore been reduced as the question of guilt or innocence can be decided on out-of-court declarations and written documents result-ing from preliminary investigations. Immediate contact between the court

---

[6] As Lord Ackner commented on the use of the doctrine of *res gestae*: 'I would strongly deprecate any attempt in criminal prosecutions to use the doctrine as a device to avoid calling, when he is available, the maker of the statement' *R.* v. *Andrews* [1978] 1 All ER 513 at 521.

[7] HR, 20 December 1926, [1927] NJ 85.

and the sources of information is no longer necessary. Written declarations can be used as evidence, even if they emanate from a person who could have been called. As long as the judges of fact observe caution in evaluating the statements, the use of hearsay evidence is permitted. In most cases a Dutch trial is therefore more of a verification of the results of the prior stages than an active inquiry by the judge who examines all witnesses himself.

Instead of relying on live testimony given at trial, Dutch courts base their judgments in a large majority of cases mainly on the *dossier*, which contains the results of the pre-trial investigation.[8]

Dutch criminal proceedings are to a large extent shaped as an official inquiry rather than a contest between two parties who are responsible for bringing out the evidence. This is illustrated by the rules governing the right of the defence to call witnesses. The Dutch Code grants a defendant the right to request the hearing of a witness at the trial.[9] Normally the court will allow a request to hear a witness: however, the court has the power to refuse to call a witness if there is no reason to believe that this will harm the defence.[10] If there is no apparent reason to call a witness, the court will refuse the defendant's or prosecutor's request. For example, according to the Supreme Court, the lower courts have the discretion to refuse to call a witness if he has been heard by an examining magistrate or the police and his appearance is not necessary to establish the facts.

The witness's statement can be used at the trial even if the defendant was not present when the statement was taken. For example, a doctor was recently convicted of sexually abusing numerous of his young and confined patients.[11] The victims were heard by the investigating judge, in the presence of defence counsel during the preliminary investigation. However, one of the victims, whose statement was used as evidence, was heard only by the police. This witness was experiencing emotional problems caused by the abuse. For this reason she refused to answer the summons before the investigating judge or appear in court. So the defendant did not get the opportunity to question her. The defendant in this case has lodged an application with the European Commission in which he complains his right to examine opposing witnesses was violated.

From the witness's point of view the Dutch practice has many advantages. In most cases a witness does not have to appear in court, which means he does not have to travel or spend many hours in a waiting room, and victims of violent crimes such as rape or robbery are spared the trauma of being compelled to testify in the presence of the accused. But it can be argued that the court's refusal to call a witness at the request of the

---

[8] See Chap. 11.   [9] Art. 263 CCP.
[10] Art. 280(4) CCP.   [11] HR, 1 October 1991, [1992] NJ 197.

defendant is a serious infringement of the principle of open justice because the witness is not heard in open court and the defendant is not given the opportunity to probe openly the veracity of the witness's statement.

THE EUROPEAN CONVENTION ON HUMAN RIGHTS AND
THE RIGHT TO EXAMINE WITNESSES

In the opinion of the European Court of Human Rights Article 6 requires in principle that all evidence must be produced in the presence of the accused at a public hearing with a view to adversarial argument.[12] 'In principle' means that there is room for exceptions. Article 6 is not violated when the accused's counsel is present at the hearing of the witness instead of the accused himself or when the accused does not ask for the hearing of the witness. The European Commission accepts that in exceptional circumstances a trial court may hear witnesses in the absence of the defendant and the Commission has found fear of reprisal a sufficiently exceptional circumstance.[13]

Another aspect of the principle is that the trial courts should be able to observe the witness's demeanour under questioning and to form their own impression of their reliability.[14]

Article 6 also guarantees the defendant the right to question the witness. According to the European Court 'the accused should be given an adequate and proper opportunity to challenge and question a witness against him, either at the time the witness was making his statement or at some later stage in the proceedings'.[15] The defendant may waive this right.

The Court does not consider the use of statements obtained at the pretrial stage in itself inconsistent with Article 6, provided that the rights of the defendant have been respected.[16] The Court in principle accepts hearsay evidence. Deficiencies at the trial stage can be compensated for by procedural safeguards during the investigation stage.[17] 'The Court's task is to ascertain whether the proceedings considered as a whole, including the way in which evidence was taken, were fair.'[18]

The circumstances of the case may prevent an accused from using his right to question the witness. In *Asch*[19] the Court accepted that a witness who, after her first statement, relied on her testimonial privilege was never questioned by the defence. The Court observed that 'it would clearly have

---

[12] *Delta*, 19 December 1990, Series A No. 191, para. 36 and *Windisch*, 27 September 1990, Series A No. 186, para. 26.

[13] *Kurup v. Denmark*, 10 July 1985, 42 D. & R. 287.

[14] European Court in *Kostovski*, para. 43 and *Windisch*, para. 29.

[15] *Kostovski*, 20 November 1989, Series A No. 166, para. 41.   [16] *Delta*, para. 36.

[17] *Barberà, Messegué and Jabardo*, 6 December 1988, Series A No. 146, para. 84.

[18] *Asch*, 26 April 1991, Series A No. 203, para. 26.   [19] Para. 28.

been preferable if it had been possible to hear her in person', but the Court considered the fact that the statement was corroborated by other evidence as a decisive factor.[20] This distinguishes *Asch* from *Unterpertinger*,[21] in which an uncorroborated statement could not be used.

It is important to note that the Court's cases on the questioning of witnesses are often cases in which, for some reason, it is impossible to question the witness (*Unterpertinger, Kostovski, Windisch, Asch*). The *Artner* case clarifies that, before reaching the conclusion that it is impossible to hear the witness, it must be 'proved that the authorities had not been negligent in their efforts to find the persons concerned'. Thus when the authorities are not responsible for the failure to ensure the presence of the witness, earlier statements may be used.

In short, the case law of the European Court of Human Rights makes clear that Article 6 does not guarantee the accused an unlimited right to a direct examination of a witness. In principle, hearsay evidence may be accepted, depending on the specific circumstances of the case.[22]

THE PROTECTION OF WITNESSES

The Problem of Witness Intimidation

Like most other western legal systems, both the Dutch and English systems are familiar with the intimidation of witnesses. Witness intimidation may take many forms—threats range from ominous looks or gestures to direct verbal and physical confrontation. The threatening of witnesses is often found in the area of organized crime. In fact, witness intimidation is considered to be a characteristic aspect of this type of crime[23]—in order to maintain a smooth-running organization, potential witnesses have to be silenced. However, the problem is not limited to this area, individual suspects are just as capable of intimidating witnesses.

In many instances, a witness who fears reprisals may well be reluctant to give evidence in open court. In England and Wales, in accordance with the oral tradition, such witnesses will usually be compellable—i.e. they may be forced to give evidence. In deciding whether to compel a reluctant witness, the prosecuting authorities will take into account, *inter alia*, the

[20] The same reasoning in *Artner*, 28 August 1992, Series A No. 242.
[21] 24 November 1986, Series A No. 110.
[22] Craig Osborn 'Hearsay and the European Court of Human Rights', [1993] *CrimLRev.* 255–67 overlooks this emphasis of the court on the circumstances. By taking only one aspect of Art. 6, he concludes that the use of hearsay evidence infringes the Convention. 'The Court's task is to ascertain whether the proceedings as a whole, including the way in which evidence was taken, were fair.
[23] Michael H. Graham, *Witness Intimidation* (Westport, Conn.; Quorum Books 1985), 5.

gravity of the charge and the possibility of intimidation. Once it has been decided that a witness should be called to give evidence, refusal to do so will result in the witness being held in contempt of court.[24] Those who intimidate witnesses will, of course, themselves be held in contempt of court—as Lord Denning stated:

... there can be no greater contempt than to intimidate a witness before he gives his evidence or to victimise him afterwards for having given it.[25]

In the Netherlands reluctant witnesses risk being taken into custody for a maximum period of thirty days.[26] In practice, courts rarely take these measures. Witnesses are only taken into custody if their appearance is absolutely necessary to establish the truth, and if the court expects this measure to have the desired effect.

The Protection of Witnesses in England and Wales

In Camera Hearings

In England and Wales derogations from the principle of open justice have traditionally been strictly limited, both in allowing the defendant an adequate opportunity to question a witness and in revealing the identity of the witness. Although trials are usually held in public, a defendant cannot insist on a public trial as of right. Certain statutory provisions enable a court to sit in camera.[27] In addition to statutory powers, courts have an inherent power to hold a trial wholly or partly in camera or to take such other measures as may be deemed necessary, but only if it is considered necessary in the interests of justice.

In *Attorney General* v. *Leveller Magazine*,[28] the identity of a prosecution witness was kept secret from the public in the interests of national security. In the House of Lords, Lord Scarman observed that the practice of allowing the witness to remain anonymous was a substitute for sitting in private and that the device was an acceptable extension of the common law power of a court to control its proceedings by sitting in private.

Hiding the Identity from the Defendant

Thus the identity of a witness may be withheld from the public if it is 'necessary to serve the ends of justice', but more difficult considerations arise if the identity of the witness is to be withheld from the defendant himself, thereby severely restricting his ability effectively to examine the

---

[24] *The Times*, 7 November 1986, reports the jailing of a rape victim for a day for failing to comply with a witness order.

[25] *Attorney-General* v. *Butterworths* [1963] 1 QB 696 at 719.   [26] Art. 289 CCP.

[27] e.g. s. 8 Official Secrets Act 1920 and Children and Young Persons Act 1933, s. 37.

[28] [1979] AC 440.

witness. The English courts have recently had to face this question in the case of *R. v. Brindle.*[29] At a trial for murder, an application was made by the prosecution for three prosecution witnesses to be granted total anonymity. The anonymity extended extraordinarily to the defence having no knowledge of the identity of the witnesses. The witnesses were examined by the judge, when all expressed fear and indicated that they would refuse to give evidence in open court, preferring to be held in contempt of court. The judge concluded that the fears of the witnesses were genuine—stressing that 'genuine fear' as opposed to 'justified fear' was sufficient because it was the state of mind of the witness which was vital—and ordered that they be granted the protection of anonymity.

The measures adopted allowed the public and the defendant to hear the entire proceedings, although they could not see the witnesses due to the positioning of screens. Thus, it was argued, the principle of open justice was largely honoured. The prosecution had argued that, should the application for anonymity be refused, they would apply to have the witness's statements admitted in place of oral testimony under the provisions contained in sections 23–6 of the Criminal Justice Act 1988. The judge alluded to the possibility of the statements being admitted in this way and concluded that that would result in the defendant being placed in a far worse position. Therefore, it seems, the judge chose the 'lesser of two evils' in granting the anonymity requested.

The defendants were acquitted, but the judge's ruling had caused some concern, particularly amongst the media, who were severely restricted in what they could publish as a result of the ruling. It was claimed that the ruling went 'beyond creeping censorship and strikes at the root of open justice', thereby setting a dangerous precedent for future criminal trials. The order is currently being challenged in the Court of Appeal.[30] If the court confirms the order made by the trial judge, many more witnesses may seek such protection in future and it is inevitable that questions will be raised in relation to Article 6.

The Protection of Witnesses in The Netherlands

In Camera Hearings

The Dutch Code allows cases to be heard in camera in order to protect witnesses. After a request made by the public prosecutor, the defence, or a witness, the court can decide to conduct the entire trial, or part of it,

---

[29] Unreported, Central Criminal Court, 28 April 1992.
[30] The challenge is made by a Court Reporter under s. 159 Criminal Justice Act 1988 whereby a 'person aggrieved' may challenge orders made by the Crown Court that interfere with the principle of open justice.

behind closed doors.[31] The law demands that there be 'an important reason' for doing so. In deciding which reasons are important enough to grant a party's request, the Dutch courts use Article 6 as a guideline.[32] Dutch lower courts seem to accept a witness's fear of reprisals as an important reason to close the court-room doors.[33] If the court fears that the witness will not make a truthful statement if he has to testify in public, it is regarded to be in the interests of justice to conduct the trial in camera. So the courts do not consider the closing of the court-room doors to be a violation of Article 6. Undercover agents who fear that testifying in open court will endanger their safety are sometimes also permitted to testify behind closed doors.[34] One of the consequences of such a policy is that the investigation tactics that have been used in a particular case are kept from the public.

Hearing by the Court in the Absence of the Defendant

If the court feels that the witness will be intimidated by the presence of the *defendant*, the latter will be excluded from the court-room. After the witness has testified, the defendant will be permitted back into the court-room and he will be informed of the contents of the witness's statement.[35] This is not an in camera hearing; the public, press, and defence counsel attend the questioning of the witness.

Granting the Witness Anonymity

In some cases *partial* anonymity will offer the witness sufficient protection. The defendant is given the opportunity to question the witness directly, but the witness does not have to state his name or address.

But on occasion even partial anonymity or hearing the case in camera will not be sufficient to allay the fears of an intimidated witness. In such cases a frightened witness may be granted *full* anonymity.[36] The investigating judge may question the witness during the preliminary investigation without the public prosecutor, the accused, or his counsel being present. In most cases the defence will be given an opportunity to submit written questions, but the judge is at liberty to decide not to ask some of these questions in order to preserve the anonymity of the witness.[37] In some

---

[31] Art. 273 CCP.
[32] U. Van de Pol, *Openbaar terecht* (Arnhem; Gouda Quint 1986), 168.
[33] The Supreme Court has not yet decided this issue.
[34] See e.g. HR, 17 September 1984 [1985] NJ 763.   [35] Art. 292 CCP.
[36] A recent study of 600 cases where a preliminary judicial investigation had been conducted found that in 12 cases (2%) witnesses were heard anonymously. Those witnesses were most frequently involved in drug cases, cases where violence was used, or burglary. Van der Werff and M. W. Bol, *Het gerechtelijk vooronderzoek in Woord en daad (WODC onderzoek)* (Arnhem; Gouda Quint 1991), 46.
[37] e.g. questions such as 'what kind of relationship do you have with the accused?' can be highly relevant to the defence, but the answers can easily identify the witness.

cases a witness is heard by way of telecommunication. The judge examines the witness, and the defence and public prosecutor are placed in a separate room where they can listen to the interview and question the witness by means of telecommunication. The magistrate is allowed to bar questions that may reveal the witness's identity. This method is, of course, preferable to a written questioning because the witness is at least subjected to a form of direct examination. At the trial stage the court weighs the evidence; it decides whether or not the anonymous statements are trustworthy, although the court has never examined the witness itself.

In 1980 the Dutch Supreme Court accepted the use of anonymous statements as evidence.[38] The court adopted the same formula as it did in 1926 when it accepted hearsay evidence.[39] According to the Supreme Court the use of such statements does not violate the existing law, providing the trial court 'observed caution in evaluating the statements'. This reflects a great confidence in the ability of the judge carefully to weigh the evidence.

In 1983 it became clear that the Supreme Court also accepts anonymous statements made to the police as evidence.[40] In such cases the police—who cannot be expected to have 'judicial impartiality'—are the only ones who question the witness.

The use of anonymous statements clearly weakens the position of the defendant—he is unable to challenge the credibility of the witness or contest his statements—and it must be considered whether this affects the right of the defendant to a fair and public trial as accorded by Article 6. The issue has been considered by the Dutch Supreme Court in the case of *Kostovski*. Kostovski was arrested after two anonymous witnesses made a statement to the police naming him as one of three men responsible for a bank raid. The police report demonstrates that the witnesses had not been eye-witnesses to the crime, but does not indicate how they received their information. After Kostovski's arrest, the investigating judge interviewed one of the witnesses in the presence of the police but in the absence of the public prosecutor and Kostovski's counsel. The investigating judge did not know the identity of the witness, but respected his wish to remain anonymous because he considered the fear of reprisals to be well founded.

Kostovski's lawyer submitted fourteen written questions to the witness through an examining magistrate, but only two of these questions were answered. The second anonymous witness was examined only by the police. The evidence against Kostovski consisted solely of the two anonymous statements. One of the police officers and the investigating judge were heard in court and they declared that the witnesses were 'reliable'. The

---

[38] HR, 5 February 1980, [1980] NJ 319. See also HR, 4 May 1981, [1982] NJ 268.
[39] HR, 28 November 1983, [1984] NJ 476.
[40] See e.g. HR, 28 November 1983, [1984] NJ 476.

court did not allow the defence to put certain questions concerning the reliability of the witnesses and their sources of information.[41]

The District Court used the statements as evidence because it was convinced that the statements were reliable and because the statements strengthened and partly complemented each other. Kostovski and his co-accused were convicted. The Supreme Court dismissed an appeal by the defendant, ruling that Article 6 had not been violated.[42] The European Court did not share this view, concluding unanimously that Article 6 had been violated.[43]

THE EUROPEAN COURT ON ANONYMOUS WITNESSES

The judgment of the European Court of Human Rights indicates that the use of statements obtained at the pre-trial stage is not in itself inconsistent with Article 6, provided the rights of the defence have been respected.[44] These rights generally require that an accused should be given an adequate and proper opportunity to challenge and question a witness against him.[45]

Kostovski was not given such an opportunity. Although the defence was able to submit written questions to one of the witnesses, the 'nature and scope of the questions was considerably restricted' in order to preserve the anonymity of the witness. According to the Court the submission of written questions cannot replace the right to examine a witness directly, as to determine the truthfulness of the witness's testimony it is important to be able to observe the demeanour of the witness.[46]

Another difficulty faced by Kostovski was the anonymity of the witness—if the defence is unaware of the identity of the person it seeks to question, it may be deprived of the very particulars enabling it to demonstrate that he or she is prejudiced, hostile or unreliable.

In paragraph 43 of its judgment the European Court also criticized the fact that the trial court had not seen and heard the witness itself:

Furthermore, each of the trial courts was precluded by the absence of the said anonymous persons from observing their demeanour under questioning and thus forming its own impression of their reliability. The courts admittedly heard evidence on the latter point ... and no doubt—as is required by Netherlands law ... they observed caution in evaluating the statements in question, but this can scarcely be regarded as a substitute for direct observation.

[41] Art. 288 CCP empowers the court to prevent a question put by the accused, his counsel, or the public prosecutor being answered.
[42] HR, 25 September 1984, [1984] NJ 134.
[43] *Kostovski*, 23 May 1989, Series A No. 166.
[44] *Barberà, Messegué and Jabardo*, 6 December 1988, Series A No. 146.
[45] *Unterpertinger*, 24 November 1986, Series A No. 110.
[46] See also *Windisch* v. *Austria*, 27 September 1990, Series A No. 186.

The Court also commented on the way in which the witnesses were questioned during the pre-trial investigation:

It is true that one of the anonymous persons was heard by examining magistrates. However, the Court is bound to observe that—in addition to the fact that neither the applicant nor his counsel was present at the interviews—the examining magistrates themselves were unaware of the person's identity, a situation which cannot have been without implications for the testing of his/her reliability. As for the other anonymous person, he was not heard by an examining magistrate at all, but only by the police. In these circumstances it cannot be said that the handicaps under which the defence laboured were counterbalanced by the procedures followed by the judicial authorities.

The European Court concluded that Article 6 had been violated because the Government had accepted that the conviction was based 'to a decisive extent' on anonymous statements.

In *Lüdi* v. *Switzerland*[47] the European Court again concluded that Article 6 had been violated because neither Lüdi nor his counsel had at any time during the proceedings had an opportunity to question the witness, an undercover agent. The Court distinguished *Lüdi* from *Kostovski* and *Windisch*.[48] In *Lüdi* the anonymous witness was a sworn police officer whose function was known to the investigating judge. Moreover, the applicant knew the agent, if not by his real identity, at least by his physical appearance, as a result of having met him on five occasions. According to the Court it should have been possible to give the defence an opportunity to question the witness in a way which took into account the interest of the police in preserving the anonymity of their agent, so that they could protect him and also make use of him again in the future.

Dutch Reaction to the *Kostovski* Judgment

The *Kostovski* judgment leaves some room for interpretation because it seems that even if it is impossible for a witness to be questioned, this may be counterbalanced by procedures followed by the judicial authorities. It is, however, clear that the European Court does not categorically forbid the use of anonymous statements. Inspired by the European Court's decision in *Kostovski*, the Dutch Supreme Court has ruled that anonymous statements can, in principle, only be used as evidence provided that certain conditions are met;[49]

  (i) the statement has been made before a judge who knows the identity of the witness; and

[47] *Lüdi* v. *Switzerland*, 15 June 1992, Series A No. 238.
[48] *Windisch* v. *Austria*, 27 September 1990, Series A No. 186.
[49] Judgment of 2 July 1990, [1990] NJ 692.

(ii) the judge has expressed his opinion about the reliability of the witness in an official report; and

(iii) the defence has been given the opportunity to examine the witness; in practice this means that the defence is given the opportunity to submit written questions or to examine the witness by means of telecommunication.

It is, however, still possible to use anonymous statements that do not satisfy these conditions, as long as corroborating evidence is available. The Supreme Court decides on a case-by-case basis whether these statements can be used as evidence. The CCP does not as yet contain express provisions on anonymous statements. In 1993 an Act was adopted making the use of anonymous statements legitimate, subject to certain conditions.[50] Courts are only allowed to use anonymous statements if the defendant is charged with a serious offence (which means one prison sentence of four years or more can be imposed), and a conviction may not be based exclusively on anonymous statements. As a rule, witnesses will be questioned by an investigating judge and the use of anonymous statements made before the police will be severely restricted.

The Dutch government believes that the legislation is in accordance with the case law on Article 6. This belief is based mainly on the most puzzling paragraph of the *Kostovski* judgment—paragraph 43. According to the Dutch Government this paragraph indicates that an investigation by a judge who is informed about the identity of the witness is sufficient to counterbalance the disadvantages to the defence, even if the defence does not get an opportunity to question the witness directly. Others consider the right to examine a witness to be a right of the *defence* which cannot be 'taken over' by a judge, however impartial the judge may be.[51] According to this view, the disadvantages for a defendant who does not get an opportunity fully to question a witness can hardly ever be counterbalanced.

THE PROTECTION OF CHILD WITNESSES

England and Wales

Recent reforms in relation to children as witnesses in criminal trials in England and Wales reinforce the system's view of the importance of effective cross examination. It has long been accepted that traditional court procedures are unsuitable for children who are required to give evidence in court. Certain child witnesses are now allowed to give evidence via a live video link, thereby removing the child from the court-room itself but

---

[50] Act of 1 February 1993, s. 603.
[51] See e.g. A. H. J. Swart, 'Anonieme getuigen', *Ars Aequi* (1990), 320.

retaining the accused's right to cross-examine the child at the trial itself.[52] The derogation from the principle of open justice is considered minimal in that the child, although not actually present in the court-room, can be seen and heard by all those present. But it is argued that the child witness should not be expected to play any part in the trial itself. It has been recommended that the child's evidence should be video-recorded.[53] The accused should then be allowed to examine the child at a preliminary hearing and, at the eventual trial, the initial recorded interview should be shown at the point where the child would now give evidence in chief, and the video recording of the preliminary hearing should be shown at the time when cross-examination would usually follow.

The Criminal Justice Act 1991 partly implements the recommendations. A video recording of an interview may be given in evidence, with the leave of the court (as an exception to the hearsay rule), but the recording will only be admitted if the child will be available for examination at the trial. Such examination may take place via a live video link, but the fact remains that the right to examine a witness at trial is considered fundamental— even in the case of a child witness.

The Netherlands

In contrast, child witnesses are rarely expected to give oral evidence at a trial in the Netherlands. To protect children from a face-to-face confrontation with the defendant and the trauma of having to testify in court, children are mostly heard only during the pre-trial investigation. They are usually examined by child psychologists, whose reports can be used as evidence in court. However, problems have arisen in recent years, as the child psychologists have been accused on several occasions of having used wrongful interrogation methods, for example, asking leading questions.

Recent experiments with video-recording the questioning of the child— in the absence of the defence—have been called a success. This method has the advantage that the court and the defence can criticize the way the interview has been conducted. Special policemen are also now being trained to examine the child witness in place of the child psychologists.[54]

THE RIGHT TO EXAMINE WITNESSES ABROAD

The requirements of Article 6 also have consequences for witnesses who do not reside in the country in which a criminal trial is taking place. Such

---

[52] Criminal Justice Act 1988, s. 2.
[53] Home Office, *Report of the Advisory Group on Video Evidence* (London; HMSO 1990).
[54] M. S. Groenhuysen, 'Audio-visuele registratie van verhoren van jeugdige getuigen' [1992] *Delikt en Delinkwent*, 3.

witnesses are not obliged to travel to another country and, if their evidence is taken abroad, the defendant will frequently not be present.

The European Commission on Human Rights accepts in some cases the questioning of witnesses abroad as an exception to the principle that all the evidence must be produced in the presence of the accused at a public hearing. In *Asch*, the European Court accepted that 'it may prove impossible in certain cases' and the Commission has recently regarded the refusal of a witness abroad to be confronted with the accused as such an impossibility.[55] The Commission's decision implies that all possibilities, that is the instruments of mutual assistance in criminal matters, should be explored, before the hearing of the witness in the presence of the accused can be seen as impossible.

In England and Wales the Criminal Justice (International Co-operation) Act 1990 provides for the issue of letters of request, but the Act does not of itself render the evidence thereby obtained admissible—the oral tradition and associated problems of hearsay evidence remain. The court retains a discretion whether or not to admit the evidence under sections 23–6 of the Criminal Justice Act 1988 and the 1990 Act specifically provides that the court shall have regard to whether it was possible to challenge the statement by questioning the person who made it and whether the local law allowed the parties to the criminal proceedings to be legally represented when the evidence was being taken. However, the Criminal Justice Act 1988, section 32, allows for the possibility of a witness in a foreign country giving evidence via a live television link.

In the Netherlands, there is no special legislation concerning witnesses abroad. As a consequence, courts deal with the specific problems of witnesses abroad in the same way as they deal with witnesses in general. The Dutch Supreme Court does not object to using statements of witnesses abroad, even if the defence did not have an opportunity to question the witness. Even in situations in which the accused has a right to be present,[56] statements of witnesses taken in the absence of the accused can be used.[57] In most cases, the accused will be given an opportunity to submit questions, which will be asked by a foreign authority or by a Dutch judge.[58] If the defence wants to hear a witness abroad, it will often find a very reluctant court in its way. Depending on the stage of the proceedings the court may deny such a request when it thinks that it does not interfere with the interests of the accused,[59] or if it is not obvious that the hearing is necessary.[60] If the court does order the summoning of a witness abroad, it may

---

[55] *Loopmans* v. *Belgium*, App. 14440/88, 10 September 1991.
[56] See the mutual legal assistance treaties of the Netherlands with the United States and with Germany.
[57] HR, 14 September 1988, [1988] NJ 301.   [58] HR, 12 May 1992, [1992] NJ 660.
[59] Art. 280(3) CCP.   [60] Art. 315 CCP.

change its mind at a later stage when it considers the summons 'without merit' or 'superfluous'.[61] In cases where the statements of witnesses abroad have been used, Dutch case law reverses the order given by the European human rights case law. Instead of trying to come as close as possible to the 'normal' situation and inviting the witness to come to the court-room in the Netherlands, it regards the hearing of the witness abroad as priority.[62] In this respect Dutch practice is not in accordance with the requirements of Article 6. The fact that the witness resides abroad as such cannot be seen as an impossibility in the sense of the *Asch* judgment. Various mutual assistance treaties give the Dutch authorities the opportunity to hear the witness in the presence of the accused. In some recent decisions, the Supreme Court has required efforts to be made to reach the witness abroad.[63] These decisions appear to indicate a hopeful development.

CONCLUSION

In England and Wales, the defendant generally has a right to confront and examine an identified witness in open court. However, in the Netherlands more reliance is placed on written testimony; the right of the defendant to examine a child witness, an intimidated witness, or a witness abroad is frequently restricted to the submission of written questions. These differences cannot be attributed solely to the legal systems' interpretation of, and compliance with, the provisions of Article 6. It is argued that the fundamental difference lies in the historical development of the systems and the distinction between the adversarial and inquisitorial mode of trial and the way in which the truth is established (see Chapter 3).

In the common law system, the trial is the focal point of the whole procedure and the decision-makers come unprepared to the trial. As a result, those who prepare the trial—the parties—have to present the evidence to the decision-maker. This explains why live testimony and oral communications are preferred.[64] In England and Wales the principle of open justice, the strong oral tradition, and rule against hearsay are themselves generally sufficient to ensure compliance with Article 6, and measures taken to protect witnesses are comparatively limited. However, in the Netherlands, the procedure is hierarchical and sequential. At each successive stage the *dossier* is taken as the starting point. The Dutch system relies on the skill and

[61] HR, 13 March 1979, [1979] NJ 268.
[62] This may be caused by the fact that it often concerns witnesses against the defendant, which were heard during the investigative stage of the proceedings: see, e.g. European Commission, *T v. Netherlands*, App. 13143/87, 9 November 1989.
[63] HR, 2 June 1992, [1993] NJ 119; HR, 29 September 1992, [1993] NJ 222.
[64] Mirjan Damaška, *Two Faces of Justice and State Authority* (New Haven, Conn.; Yale University Press 1986), 65 *et seq.*

competence of the professional judge to decide on the basis of cold files. An important question is whether the caution of the judge in evaluating the statements can be regarded as a proper substitute for the examination of a witness at the trial.

It seems that both legal systems are currently struggling to find a suitable balance between the rights of the accused as encapsulated in Article 6 and the need to ensure that justice is done. Although the two systems have many differences, the central issue is the same. According to the European Court's case law all the evidence must normally be produced in the presence of the accused at a public trial with a view to adversarial argument. The problems encountered with witnesses illustrate how far each system will be prepared to deviate from this requirement. In England and Wales, the right to examine a witness is generally considered fundamental and will be retained wherever possible. But in the Netherlands, the right to examine the witness can be restricted to the submission of written questions, and is sometimes denied completely, as in the *Kostovski* case or in the case of witnesses abroad. After the decision of the European Court in *Kostovski* the Dutch Supreme Court has somewhat restricted the use of anonymous statements and some recent decisions of the Supreme Court on witnesses abroad also show more respect for European case law.

15

Protection of and Compensation for Victims of Crime

JANE MORGAN, FRANS WILLEM WINKEL, AND
KATHERINE S. WILLIAMS

INTRODUCTION

Traditionally, the victim has not occupied a prominent position in the criminal justice system in either the Netherlands or England and Wales. But since the 1970s there has been a growing interest in both Europe and North America in victims of crime. During this period the nature of victimization and its extent has received widespread publicity. A great deal is now known about the effects of crime on victims, the needs that may arise from victimization, and the reaction of various agencies to those needs. Strategies to help victims have been developed. In November 1985, the United Nations General Assembly adopted a charter of victim rights—the Declaration on the Basic Principles of Justice for Victims of Crime and Abuse of Power—and 157 governments declared their commitment to providing equitable treatment, access to justice, reparation, and services for victims of crime.[1] In the USA victimologists have followed a largely rights-based strategy—encouraging the passing of state and federal legislation to allow victims greater participation at all levels of the criminal justice process.[2] In Europe, by contrast, the major preoccupation has been with improvements in services to victims rather than with either victims' rights or radical legislation on their behalf. The Council of Europe has taken a number of steps to encourage measures to improve the plight of crime victims: the European Convention on the Compensation of Victims of Violent Crime 1983; the Recommendation on the Position of the Victim in the Framework of Criminal Law and Procedure 1985[3] and recommendations

---

With thanks to Nico Jörg for his help concerning the legal position in the Netherlands.

[1] Report of the Seventh UN Congress on the Prevention of Crime and Treatment of Offenders, Milan, 26 August–6 September 1985. See also R. W. Schaaf, 'New International Instruments in Crime Prevention and Criminal Justice' (1986) 14 *International Journal of Legal Information*, 176–82.

[2] David Miers, 'The Responsibilities and the Rights of Victims of Crime' [1992] *MLR* 483.

[3] Council of Europe Recommendation No. R(85)11 of the Committee of Ministers to Member States.

on the establishment of services to assist victims.[4] Another example of this welfare-based ideology can be found in the European Forum for Victim Services (both Britain and the Netherlands are members), which produces a handbook outlining the provision for victims in the twelve Member States and which studies new initiatives in the provision of services.

Britain and the Netherlands have been in the van of the 'victims movement' in Europe and in both countries developments have been along similar lines: the extension of services to deal with issues which have caused most concern for victims—how to obtain financial compensation for their injuries; how to obtain welfare services; and better treatment of victims by the police and courts. In the UK in 1990 a victim's charter was produced by the government which claimed to be a statement of the legitimate expectation of victims of crime.[5]

Neither strategy is ideal: a rights-based ideology broadly guarantees to the victim a certain legally-enforceable position, whereas a welfare ideology either tries to alter the working practices of professionals or provides for certain discretionary facilities for which victims can apply. Although a system based on rights ensures legal standards it depends upon cases being brought to enforce those rights, thus depending on people having both time and money to litigate. Without legal aid it fails to address the needs of the poor, the largest group of victims. A welfare-based ideology can have far-reaching effects by persuading the professionals to consider the interests of victims at all points of the process: but that depends on the goodwill of the practitioners and cannot be enforced in a court of law.

Whichever system is chosen, a major problem from the point of view of criminal lawyers resides in restructuring criminal justice to meet the needs of victims. In a rights-based ideology every increase in victims' rights necessarily interferes either with the rights of defendants or with considerations of public interest, or both. Some suggest that in the American experience defendants' rights have been excessively eroded, as if they were already guilty.[6] If so, this is unacceptable: enhancing victims' rights must not be at the expense of defendants. A welfare ideology poses similar problems, even if these are less severe. For example, the traditional criminal justice system is concerned almost exclusively with the relationship between the state and the offender, while the welfare of the victim often calls for compensation. Compensation of the victim by the offender is designed to increase the importance of the relationship between the victim and the

---

[4] Before this only the United Kingdom, the Netherlands, and the Federal Republic of Germany had been involved in major new initiatives.

[5] Home Office, *Victim's Charter: A Statement of the Needs and Rights of Victims of Crime* (London; HMSO 1990).

[6] T. P. O'Neil, 'The Good, the Bad and the Burger Court: Victim's Rights and a New Model of Criminal Review' (1984) 75 *Journal of Criminal Law and Criminology*, 363.

offender; a state-funded compensation scheme for victims is designed to strengthen the link between the victim and the state. This creates a structural strain.[7] Should compensation be left to the civil courts? Should the demands of state punishment be subordinated to those of compensation for the victim? Can compensation ever be a real part of the system of punishment when the central part of the equation is the harm done to society? Most of these questions remain unanswered in currently available systems, which have tended to make provision for compensation whilst ignoring the competing factors. This is unsatisfactory: the issues need to be debated and the law framed to reflect the outcome of that debate.

This chapter will focus on the experience of both the Netherlands and the United Kingdom. It will discuss both the rights and the services enjoyed by victims at each stage of the criminal justice system. Finally it will consider what changes might be appropriate and appraise the dangers inherent in provision for victims.

PROVISION OF WELFARE SERVICES

In both countries the voluntary sector has been most prominent in the provision of specialist, non-financial assistance for victims.[8] In Britain, help for specific groups of victims has been developed by voluntary organizations such as rape crisis centres for victims of rape and sexual assault, and women's refuges for victims of domestic violence. There is a wide range of agencies which do, or could, help victims of crime but one organization, Victim Support (founded in 1974), exists specifically to give practical support and emotional help to all victims of crime.[9] Referrals to Victim Support come from the police[10] and therefore miss unreported crimes,[11] and depend upon the co-operation of the local force. Reliant largely upon the work of unpaid volunteers, the schemes seek to provide a sympathetic, listening ear for the fears, distress, and anger which many victims need to express. The Government has provided funding for Victim Support schemes[12] and

---

[7] Peter Duffy, 'The "Victim Movement" and Legal Reform', in Mike Maguire and John Pointing (eds.), *Victims of Crime: A New Deal?* (Milton Keynes; Open University Press 1988), 147–55.

[8] R. I. Mawby and M. L. Gill, *Crime Victims: Needs, Services and the Voluntary Sector* (London; Tavistock Publications 1987).

[9] For a discussion of its background, see P. Rock, *Helping Victims of Crime: The Home Office and the Rise of Victim Support in England and Wales* (Oxford; Clarendon Press 1990).

[10] See M. Maguire and C. Corbett, *The Effects of Crime and the Work of Victims Support Schemes* (Aldershot; Gower 1986).

[11] Many crimes remain unreported: the British Crime Survey estimates that only one in four crimes committed are reported to the police.

[12] In 1991 funding approached £4 million: Home Office, *Crime, Justice and Protecting the Public*, Cm 965, London, HMSO, 1990. See also C. G. Barclay (ed.), *A Digest of Information on the Criminal Justice System* (London; Home Office Research and Stats. Dept. 1991).

there is also local, official, and voluntary support. Although finances are tight the rapid development of Victim Support in England and Wales during the 1980s augurs well. Annually they offer help to nearly 600,000 victims. The organization is constantly endeavouring to improve the service to victims and to ensure that all victims are offered help.

In the Netherlands, too, there are a variety of organizations, which mostly address specific categories, such as *Vereniging tegen Kindermishandeling* and *Bureaus Vertrouwensartsen* (child abuse), and *Tegen Haar Wil* (rape). The largest organization, the Dutch Association for Victim Assistance (DAVA),[13] offers assistance to victims in general. It was founded in 1984 and was influenced by the British Victim Support scheme. Its main finance comes from central government (mainly the Ministry of Justice), with some backing from both local government and the community at large.[14] The 1990 Annual Report indicates that over 60,000 victims were assisted and, despite regional differences,[15] it is a general policy to ensure that all local centres at least provide support, information, and some practical help to victims.

In both countries victim assistance is provided by organizations which are now largely government-funded. This has led to a requirement towards greater professionalism, better record keeping, and the handling of more complex cases (such as victims of extreme violence, rape, and counselling of families whose relatives have been killed). This type of work requires careful training and long and expensive follow-up facilities.[16] All of this is moving the organizations away from the community which they serve. Both countries are experiencing the difficulties inherent in these trends, neither has fully resolved these problems.

VICTIMS' TREATMENT BY POLICE, PROSECUTORS, AND COURTS

During the 1980s the insensitive way in which victims were treated in the British criminal justice system became the subject of much criticism. There was a growing recognition that an unsympathetic response by the police and the legal system may result in what has been termed 'secondary victimization'.[17] The NAVSS report, *The Victim in Court*, emphasized the

---

[13] Vereniging Landelijke Organisatie Slachtofferhulp (LOS).

[14] The organization which co-ordinates fundraising was established in 1990: Fonds Hulp aan Slachtoffers or HAS-fonds.

[15] For information concerning some of these see: *Rapport van de Commissie Doelgroepen* (Utrecht; Landelijke Organisatie Slachtofferhulp 1992).

[16] Claire Corbett and Mike Maguire, 'The Value and Limitations of Victim Support Schemes', in Maguire and Pointing (eds.), *Victims of Crime*.

[17] J. Shapland, J. Willmore, and P. Duff, *Victims in the Criminal Justice System* (Aldershot; Gower 1985).

anxieties experienced by victims, not only about their appearance in court, but also during the period leading up to the trial; the report stressed the need to improve procedures, to modify court buildings to take account of victims, and to provide information and support to victims both before and during trial.[18] This emphasis is also reflected in the resolution of the Council of Europe and the UN Declaration of Basic Principles of Justice for Victims of Crime, both of which appeared in 1985.[19]

In both jurisdictions public and political attention on the plight of crime victims in their respective criminal justice procedures was first stimulated by publicity about the treatment of rape victims by the police and later by that of children. In the case of rape, attention was drawn to the problem in England and Wales after a television programme in 1983,[20] whilst in Holland similar interest arose in 1978. In both jurisdictions public outcry then led to official statements concerning how to obtain evidence from victims while causing as little trauma as possible and ensuring that victims obtain help and assistance from other agencies.[21] In each country specific measures were taken to implement these recommendations.

Both countries have also been active in providing a response to allegations of child abuse. The number of reports to the police have increased dramatically since the mid–1980s and the taboo which formerly existed in discussing these subjects is now disappearing. Both jurisdictions have developed guidelines explaining how agencies should respond; in England and Wales police are encouraged to undertake investigation jointly with social workers,[22] and criminal justice considerations, such as the arrest and prosecution of the alleged abuser, are secondary.[23] In both jurisdictions client-centred interview rooms, equipped with extensive video facilities, are provided.[24]

The advances made in these areas led to a generally successful plea for

---

[18] National Association of Victims Support Schemes, *The Victim in Court: Report of a Working Party* (London; NAVSS 1988).

[19] See Schaaf, 'New International Instruments' (1986).

[20] This showed a male detective in the Thames Valley Police interviewing a rape victim in a particularly unsympathetic manner.

[21] In Britain the authority came from Home Office Circular 25/1983 and Home Office Circular 69/1986. For a detailed account of the response to rape victims see L. J. F. Smith, *Concerns About Rape*, Home Office Research Study No. 106, London, HMSO (1989). In the Netherlands the De Beaufort Commission reported to the Ministries of Justice and of Internal Affairs in December 1981 (*Rapport van de Werkgroep Angifte Sexuele Geweldsmisdrijven*, 's-Gravenhage, Ministerie van Justitie en Ministerie van Binnenlandse Zaken) on the basis of which 24 victim-oriented recommendations were issued.

[22] Home Office, *The Investigation of Child Sexual Abuse*, Circular 52/1988.

[23] S. Conroy, N. G. Fielding, and J. Tunstill, *Investigating Child Sexual Abuse: A Study of a Joint Initiative*, London, Police Foundation (1990). Metropolitan Police and Bexley Social Services, *Child Sexual Abuse: Joint Investigative Programme: Final Report*, London; HMSO 1987.

[24] Both jurisdictions have also addressed the problem of court apprearances: see Chap. 12.

more positive action on behalf of crime victims as a whole. In England and Wales, Home Office circulars to the police during the 1980s emphasized the importance of various good practices, such as keeping victims informed,[25] and the Home Office drew the attention of courts to the needs of victims such as provision of separate waiting areas. Finally, the publication of the Victims Charter in 1990 gives no legally binding rights but informs victims what ought to happen and sets out the help available to them.[26] In the Netherlands similar progress was made following a report of the Vaillant Commission (Commission on Judicial Policy and the Victim).[27] Again circulars designed to address crucial issues were used to improve the treatment of victims by officials.[28]

In both systems the worst treatment of victims arises from bureaucratic incompetence: files disappearing; failure to answer letters; delay; failure to notify court dates, court decisions, and appeals. Recent research in both England and Wales,[29] and the Netherlands,[30] confirms this. The emphasis has thus been on changing, through guidelines and orders, the experience of the victim at the police or prosecution stage rather than at the trial. The effect of this approach has been to address what the state sees as the needs of victims rather than what victims actually need. At all events, very little has been done to alter the experience of victims in court. This is particularly marked in the UK where the adversarial system places the rights of the defendant to the fore and makes it difficult to alter the position of victims without undermining these rights. It is only in the evidence of children that any real inroads have been made towards protecting the victim from the unpleasant experience of a court appearance,[31] in particular through the use of properly obtained[32] early videotapes as the evidence-in-chief of a child witness.[33] All other victims are really at the command of the prosecutor

---

[25] Home Office Circulars 20/1988, 7/1989.   [26] Home Office, *Victim's Charter*, 1990.

[27] Available in Basisdocumentatie LOS, Vereniging Landelijke Organisatie Slachtofferhulp, Utrecht, January 1992.

[28] The circulars are discussed by L. Penders, 'Guidelines for Police and Prosecutors: An Interest of Victims; a Matter of Justice', in *Guidelines for Victim Support in Europe* (proceedings of the Eerbeek Conference of Victim Support Workers), Utrecht; Vereniging LOS 1989, 75–87.

[29] T. Newburn and S. Merry, *Keeping in Touch: Police–Victim Communication in Two Areas*, Home Office Research Study No. 116, London; HMSO 1990, at 38.

[30] For more details see F. W. Winkel, 'Responses to Criminal Victimisation: Evaluating the Impact of a Police Assistance Program and some Social-Psychological Correlates' (1989) 12 *Police Studies*, 2, 59–73; F. W. Winkel, 'Police Communication Programmes Aimed at Burglary Victims: A Review of Studies and an Experimental Evaluation' (1991) 1 *Journal of Community and Applied Social Psychology*, 6.

[31] See Chap. 12.

[32] Home Office and Department of Health, *Code of Practice: Video Recorded Interviews with Child Witnesses for Criminal Proceedings* (1992).

[33] See D. Birch, 'The Criminal Justice Act 1991: Children's Evidence' [1992] *CrimLRev.* 262–76; J. Temkin, 'Child Sexual Abuse and Criminal Justice—1' [1990] *NLJ* 352–5. And J. Temkin, 'Child Sexual Abuse—2' [1990] *NLJ* 410–11.

who decides whether they will give evidence and at the command of prosecution and defence lawyers as to how that evidence is given. This questioning may amount to a second victimization, especially in cases involving sexual attacks,[34] and thus undo much of the good work done earlier.

The experience in many continental systems is very different. In the Netherlands it is now quite normal for the public prosecutor, after receiving the file on a serious crime from the police, to have an informal meeting with the victim. This is particularly common in sex offences. If a detailed statement by the victim is a precondition for a conviction (as is common in sex offences), and if that statement will be debated by the defence, the victim will be re-interviewed by the investigating judge.[35] The aim is to keep the victim from the witness stand. Finally, in court victims' statements are often presented in full without interruption and, if questioning is necessary, questions which violate the integrity of the victim in the witness box may be denied. It is thought that this rule enhances the awareness of both the bench and the legal profession about how victim-witnesses should be treated.[36] Such procedures protect the interests of the victim but they may well interfere with the defendant's rights to a fair hearing as guaranteed under Article 6 of the ECHR.[37] To reduce this risk the interview by the examining judge, though informal, can be tough, especially if there is any doubt whether he/she has been victimized. Defence counsel may attend the interview and suggest questions.

Clearly at the court stage the situation of victims within the two systems is different but the underlying ideology in both is similar—neither has given the victim any rights. Most of the changes which have occurred at all stages of proceedings are the result of guidelines and orders. The aim is to make professionals aware of the problems faced by victims and persuade them to alter their practice accordingly. The difficulty is that such change is slow, depends on the changes being possible within the self-image of the profession and has to be accommodated without altering the fundamental principles on which professional decisions and actions are based.[38]

MEDIATION AND THE VICTIM'S POWER TO INSTIGATE PROCEEDINGS

In both countries there has been experimentation with using mediators to effect reconciliations, including agreed recompense, between offenders and

---

[34] For evidential aspects of this question see Chap. 14.   [35] See Chap. 14.
[36] E. Leuw, De behandeling van verkrachtingszaken voor de rechtbank, [1985] TvCr 129–51, 212–34.
[37] See Chaps. 4 and 14.
[38] M. Maguire and J. Shapland, 'The "Victims Movement" in Europe', in A. J. Lurigio, G. S. Wesley, and R. C. Davis (eds.), *Victims of Crime: Problems, Policies and Programs* (San Mateo, Calif.; Sage 1990).

victims. But in Britain, although 40 per cent of victims of violence were willing to participate in mediation, the Government decided in 1990 not to extend the project.[39] In the Netherlands a similar *dading* experiment of 1989–90 was tried. Negotiations were started in 47 per cent of the selected cases, which led to the continuance and extension of the scheme.[40] Such schemes do, of course, carry dangers: agreed recompense may satisfy the private wrong but takes no cognizance of the public aspect of offensive behaviour, and can lead to pressure on victims. The procedures are thus dubious in legal theory.

More generally the dominance of the welfare approach ensures that, in both Britain and the Netherlands, the powers of victims within the criminal justice system are very limited. Victims tend only to appear in the system as witnesses, and then mainly on the decision of the prosecution or defence lawyers.[41] The only small exceptions are in the area of private prosecutions and the questioning of state decisions not to prosecute: even these are heavily circumscribed.

In England and Wales under the Prosecution of Offences Act 1985 most prosecutions are carried out by the CPS,[42] but section 6(1) permits individuals to pursue private prosecutions when the police have not instigated proceedings. There is formally very little restriction on the right of any individual to bring a criminal prosecution and, once a private prosecutor has obtained a committal for trial, the police can be compelled to produce all statements and exhibits in their possession which may be relevant to the case.[43] However, by section 6(2) the Director of Public Prosecutions (DPP) can take over any proceedings begun by someone else. Such action may be taken in order to ensure its more efficient conduct in the public interest but it also permits the DPP to discontinue the action if this is thought to be in the best interests of the public. The DPP thereby effectively has the power to prevent any prosecution, giving the state control over all prosecutions which have any public interest element. Furthermore, apart from the limited action of judicial review of any administrative

---

[39] For a full account of reparation and mediation schemes see M. Wright and B. Galaway (eds.), *Mediation and Criminal Justice* (London; Sage 1989). See also M. Maguire, 'Victims' rights: Slowly Redressing the Balance', and J. Gretton, 'Can Victim–Offender Mediation Change the Face of Criminal Justice?', in J. Gretton and T. Harrison (eds.), *Crime U.K. 1988* (London; Policy Journals 1988), at 72–4 and 75–86. For Government reaction see Government White Paper, *Crime, Justice and Protecting the Public*, Cm 965, London, HMSO (1990), at paras. 4.25–4.26.

[40] See *Dading in plaats van strafrecht*, Verslag van de begeleidingsgroep voor het experiment met Strafrechtelijke Dading, Amsterdam, Humanitas (1991); and Heikelien Verrijn Stuart, *Dading tussen civielrecht en strafrecht* (1992) 4 *Nemesis* 21–4.

[41] For the procedural details see Art. 280 CCP and for a discussion see Chap. 14, above.

[42] See also Chaps. 7 and 11.

[43] Criminal Procedure (Attendance of Witnesses) Act 1965. See also *R. v. Pawsey* [1989] *CrimLRev*. 152.

decision[44] there is no effective scrutiny of decisions of either the police or the prosecutors. Beyond this there is the limit of costs. No legal aid is available for a private prosecution. An award to cover expenses incurred by the private prosecutor and those of witnesses may be possible out of central funds but there is no guarantee of repayment. Effectively for most people this means that unless the police and CPS choose to prosecute their case there will be no action taken. The decision about whether to charge an individual and, if so, what charge to place is taken on legal and policy grounds. Both the new cautioning guidelines and the DPP's Code for Crown Prosecutors instruct agencies that the victim's view should be an important, though not overriding, factor in the decision.[45] As there is no real scrutiny of the process it is difficult to ascertain the extent to which this occurs. The power of the victim is therefore minimal at this stage of the British criminal justice system.

In the Netherlands victims cannot start criminal proceedings; only the prosecutor has this power. The prosecutor's decision is based on both the legal rules involved and regulatory guidelines (including policy). One element considered is the role of the victim: his contribution to the offence; or the degree of suffering inflicted. However, by Article 12 of the CCP 'anyone concerned' may complain to the Court of Appeal against a decision of the prosecutor not to prosecute. In cases where there is a policy reason for the non-prosecution the review will be marginal; in all other instances, for example where non-prosecution is based on legal or evidential grounds, the court assesses the validity of the decision in the light of the facts and the law. This is a qualitative assessment which involves a full consideration of the merits of the decision. If the complaint is upheld the case must be prosecuted. Since a change of the code in 1984 victims have certain rights in the preparation and presentation of their case before the Court of Appeal. To provide some balance the alleged perpetrator may be summoned to comment on the complaint. Interestingly even if there has been a *transactie*[46] in respect of the case and the defendant has already complied with its terms the Court of Appeal may still order a prosecution (of course the *transactie* is repaid).[47]

Thus, although in the British system the victim enjoys a stronger legal right to prosecute, the Dutch victim is in practice given greater powers, since appeals against decisions of the state not to prosecute are given a public airing and the victim is awarded legal representation to make this

[44] Judicial review is generally not concerned with the merits of the decision but rather with its 'validity' or the limits of the power under which it is exercised.

[45] Home Office Circular 59/1990. See also D. Westwood, 'The Effects of Home Office Guidelines on the Cautioning of Offenders' [1991] *CrimLRev*. 591–7.

[46] See Chap. 7, above.

[47] The possibility of complaining is only lost if more than three months have elapsed since the alleged perpetrator complied with the *transactie*.

right real and enforceable. In practice the Dutch system affords the ordinary victim greater protection and is free of charge, whilst its public scrutiny provision acts as a check against arbitrary decisions. Discretionary decisions which are not scrutinized always lay the system open to allegations of corruption over subjective decision-making. The only way to prevent this would be a system of formal rules (both states have guidelines, though not rules, for these decisions; in the Netherlands these guidelines can be invoked in court) along with review and appeal of decisions (this is less evident in the British system). However, it way well be that the victims' interests might be better addressed by provision of further information and an opportunity to take an active part in the decision to prosecute rather than by a check on the discretion whether to prosecute.

DAMAGES AND COMPENSATION PAID BY OFFENDERS

In the Netherlands compensation may form part of the decision not to prosecute, it may be informal[48] or formal.[49] It may be conditional on a *transactie*[50] or form part of a conditional sentence. Furthermore under the Code of Criminal Procedure (CCP) victims may join their claim for loss, damages, and personal injury (both physical and emotional) to the criminal trial (*voeging*) in a *partie civile* procedure. It is the latter procedure which will be discussed here.[51] The claim may be submitted orally or in writing but all evidence must be documented.

In order to make *partie civile* claims more attractive a new Act[52] was passed which provides that:

- under the old law the District Court was limited to awarding a maximum of f. 1500 (serious offences) whilst the magistrate's court was limited to f. 600 (non-indictable offences). The Act abandons these maxima and substitutes a qualitative test: whether civil liability and the level of damages can easily be assessed. Failure of a claim due to its complicated nature would not preclude a civil action.
- the claim can be split, the simple part to be joined to the criminal proceedings whilst the more complex element will be heard in the civil courts;

---

[48] *Voorwaardelijk sepot*, a condition imposed by the public prosecutor.
[49] Art. 244(3) CCP.   [50] Art. 74 Criminal Code: see Chap. 7, above.
[51] Arts 332–7 CCP, 56, 44 RO.
[52] TK 21345 (23 December 1992) s. 1993, 29. The Act came into force on 1 April 1993 in two judicial districts, Den Bosch and Dordrecht (s. 1993, 71), and will come into force for the rest of the Netherlands in 1995.

– joinder to take place as soon as the police file is registered, facilitating early access to the prosecution files and allowing the defence time to prepare this part of the case. There is no need to appear in court: a written claim suffices.

Certain limiting aspects of the present system would remain: victims are not permitted to call any witnesses but can question any called by either prosecution or defence; and, above all, execution of the decision remains the responsibility of the victim, which is the main disadvantage with the present system (victims have to rely on civil distraint procedures which are slow and relatively ineffective). Both civil execution of the orders and *partie civile* are only useful if victims are either well informed about legal procedures, or at least not intimidated by them.

In order to reduce the effects of these shortcomings the Act also introduces a judicial compensation order *(schadevergoedingsmaatregel)* making compensation a new criminal sanction of the court. At the discretion of the court compensation would then be possible instead of, or along with, a fine. As it is a sentence of the court, execution will be performed by the public prosecutor. This provision is not to be reliant on joinder of the victim who will not need to appear in court. Of course compensation cannot exceed actual loss and a lesser amount might well be in order, as it is a sentence of the court not a civil law payment for damages. If compensation is not paid the prosecutor can seize assets or can incarcerate the offender for a maximum of six months (custody does not interfere with the obligation to pay the compensation). This provision is likely to be welcomed by victims in the Netherlands.

The Act has two very different effects: the reforms to the joinder procedure increase victims' legal rights but leave severe practical problems concerning the execution of these rights; whilst the new compensation orders leave victims' rights unaltered but assist the victim to obtain payment.

In England and Wales it has never been possible to have a *partie civile*, but where an offence has caused loss, damage, or personal injury, a court is required to consider whether the offender should pay compensation to the victim. Such compensation may cover material loss as well as that for pain and suffering etc. Compensation orders were first introduced in 1972[53] as an addition to the appropriate sentence. Since 1982[54] a compensation order may be the only sentence for the offence, or it may be made in addition to any other sentence (including a probation order or discharge). The 1982 Criminal Justice Act also provides that, where a court considers both a compensation order and a fine appropriate but the offender's means are not adequate to pay both in full, the court is required to give preference to the ordering of compensation. Finally, to encourage the use of

[53] Criminal Justice Act 1972.   [54] Criminal Justice Act 1982 s. 67.

312   *Jane Morgan, Frans Willem Winkel, and Katherine S. Williams*

these orders the Criminal Justice Act 1988 obliges courts to give reasons for not ordering compensation for injury, loss, or damage. Major barriers to victims obtaining compensation still remain: insufficient details of the victim's loss still hamper many courts,[55] especially as victims have no right of audience; even when compensation orders are made, enforcement is not straightforward (though it is carried out by the state)—it has been estimated that between a fifth and a quarter of compensation orders are not paid in full and delay in payment is common. Nevertheless, victims approve of offenders paying compensation, even if orders do not cover all their losses and payments come in halting and uneven dribs and drabs of instalments. Dissatisfaction arises largely if awards are derisory and if courts do not inform victims about the amount of the award, the reasons for non-payment, and the means being taken for enforcement.[56]

Compensation as a sentence of the court is welcomed by most victims, but there are practical difficulties—it can never embrace all victims as it depends on the conviction of the offender and is therefore hampered by low clear-up rates, particularly in property offences. It also presents lawyers with more basic problems—one of the central roles of the criminal justice system is often seen as matching the punishment demanded by society for the wrong done to it with the offender who performed that wrong. It is unclear how far the system should try to address the wrong done to this particular victim especially in so direct a way as compensation.

STATE COMPENSATION FOR VICTIMS

In both the UK and the Netherlands, financial aid in the form of compensation is available for victims of crime through state compensation schemes, whilst the European Convention on Compensation for Victims of Violent Crime (1983) sets out the minimum which Member States should provide.

In the UK the CICB was established in 1964 and put on a statutory footing by the 1988 Criminal Justice Act.[57] It administers an *ex gratia* scheme to compensate those who suffer personal injuries directly attributable to a crime of violence. Since 1988 family violence has been included. Victims' claims are not dependent on either prosecution or conviction, nor even on the discovery of a possible offender. Awards of compensation cannot be made for injuries assessed at less than a specified figure (currently £1,000)

---

[55] T. Newburn and S. Merry, *Keeping in Touch: Police–Victim Communication in Two Areas*, Home Office Research Study No. 116, London; HMSO 1990, 28.
[56] Maguire and Shapland, 'The "Victims Movement" in Europe'.
[57] For a fuller account see D. Miers, 'The Criminal Justice Act—the Compensation Provisions' [1989] *CrimLRev.* 32–42.

but substantial sums are awarded for more serious injury.[58] There is a three-year limitation period on making a claim after the incident but this may be waived at the Board's discretion, particularly in relation to claims made by or on behalf of child victims.[59]

In the Netherlands, two funds offer substantial amounts of money to compensate victims: the Criminal Injuries Compensation Fund established in 1975, in cases of damages due to intentional violent crimes; and the Road Accident Victims Compensation Fund. The latter was established in 1965 to consider making payments when damage is caused by a road traffic incident not covered by insurance.

Anyone who has suffered serious physical or psychological harm as the result of a violent crime perpetrated with intent may apply for an *ex gratia* payment from the Criminal Injuries Compensation Fund. Claims can be made for both non-material injury (such as pain, fear, or distress) and for material damage resulting from the injury. Injuries are considered serious if they entail immediate danger to life; if they disable a person for at least six weeks; lead to disability to perform daily tasks; or entail permanent medical consequences. Assessment of claims is very slow, as much as two years, causing dissatisfaction with the scheme[60] though in the Netherlands in violent cases this should no longer be a problem following a recent Act aimed at speeding up the process.[61]

At first sight state provision of compensation in both jurisdictions appears to address some needs of the victim, although doubts remain. Compensation is set by the level of harm done to the victim after taking account of the amount the victim may have contributed to that victimization.[62] It is paid to all victims regardless of need. It is not means tested nor is there any assessment of the support necessary to any particular victim. Can it therefore be said to meet the real needs of victims? Is it rather a means of reducing the injustice felt by victims? Looked at very cynically in cases where there is no prosecution it could be seen as a way of reducing any attacks which may be made on control agencies for their low clear-up rates. Having said this it is one of the few measures whereby the interests of victims can be addressed without any consequent effects for the lessening of the rights of the offender.

---

[58] Prior to 1989 the ceiling was £550. For statistical information see Barclay, *A Digest of Information*, at 13.

[59] For further details see Criminal Injuries Compensation Board, *Twenty-Sixth Annual Report for the Year ended 31 March 1990*, 31 March 1990, Cm 1365, 43.

[60] Delays are so long that victim support organizations are not recommending it to victims, see Maguire and Shapland, 'The "Victims Movement" in Europe', at 215.

[61] Act of 17 March 1993, S1993, 167 (Bill No. II 22464). This will not include road accidents.

[62] It could be argued that this condition may easily result in secondary victimization: P. de Beer, 'De schadevergoedingsstraf: twee mogelijke nadelen (1988) 18 *Delikt en Delinkwent*, 205–19, but this is the way courts assess civil claims for damages.

CONCLUSION

Despite the development of victim provision, there have been a number of criticisms. Victimologists generally feel that not enough has been done to help victims of crime in the legal process while criminal lawyers express a number of reservations about the impact on defence rights.

In both countries the officials making decisions at each stage are now instructed that the views and interests of the victim are important and must be taken into account. Victimologists argue that more needs to be done[63] in both the service provision for victims and in the victims' relationship with the criminal justice system.[64] Nils Christie has asserted that the state has stolen the conflict between the two parties, offender and victim, and that the victim is effectively excluded.[65] Some therefore assert that the victim should be accorded a place in decision-making at the pre-trial, trial, and sentencing stages of the system; that the victim should have separate legal representation in criminal proceedings, and that compensation and reparation should form the basis of sentencing.[66] Shapland, while not going this far, sees little problem in introducing more 'civil' functions into criminal courts, and advocates more victim participation—at least in the sense of consultation—throughout the process of arrest, trial, and prosecution.[67] All these developments would need major changes in the legal relationship between the state and the citizen.

The most commonly mooted suggestions are for increased rights to: decide whether to prosecute and for what charge; decide whether to release on bail; appear at trial and have the opportunity to challenge the defence; put a victim impact statement before the court at the sentencing stage; be permitted to indicate which sentence the victim considers most appropriate; and appeal lenient sentences. To allow real and effective enjoyment of many of these rights it would be necessary to permit the victim legal representation and the right to legal aid. Furthermore, it might be necessary to permit the victim to appeal any decisions taken and have the issues debated in open court. All of this involves considerable alteration to the very nature of the criminal justice system. It moves the focus away from the moral wrong done to society (and the state) and society's

---

[63] E. Fattah, 'Victims and Victimology: The Facts and Rhetoric' (1989) 1 *International Review of Victimology*, 57.

[64] John Pointing and Mike Maguire, 'Introduction: The Discovery of the Crime Victim' (1988), in Maguire and Pointing (eds.), *Victims of Crime*, at 12–13.

[65] N. Christie, 'Conflicts as Property' (1977) 17 *British Journal of Criminology*, 1–11.

[66] R. C. Davis, F. Kumeuther and E. Connick, 'Expanding the Victim's Role in the Criminal Court Dispositional Process' [1984] *Journal of Criminal Law and Criminology*, 2; P. S. Hudson, 'The Crime Victim and the Criminal Justice System' (1984) 11 *Pepperdine Law Review*.

[67] Joanna Shapland, 'Fiefs and Peasants: Accomplishing Change for Victims in the Criminal Justice System', in Maguire and Pointing (eds.), *Victims of Crime*, 193–4.

interest in punishment, towards a more directly reparative model involving a conflict between two parties. Furthermore, it might well have serious implications for defence rights guaranteed under Article 6 ECHR.[68]

Consider, for example, rights at the sentencing stage. Although there is virtually a right to a compensation payment in Britain, the victims still have to present their claim through the police and the CPS; they cannot address the court directly. If direct audience was permitted the offender would need the opportunity to disprove the claim, particularly as there may be contributory factors which would reduce any claim. To date the court has avoided such problems by only allowing cases which are clear; if the victim is given any extended rights of audience it may prove difficult to continue this practice.[69] Still greater problems would arise if the victim were permitted to address the court more widely on the most appropriate sentence or to present a victim impact statement.[70] Most victims will lack knowledge of either the options available to the court or the wider policy considerations which must be considered in sentencing,[71] which is supposed to reflect the moral wrong suffered by violation of societal rules and the personal responsibility and moral guilt of the offender. Any large increase in victims' rights in sentencing might destroy this relationship; interfere with the objective decision of sentencers; and blur the difference between civil wrong and crime.[72] Such far-reaching consequences would require a complete reconsideration of the whole area of criminal law, sanctions, and the moral right to enforce them. This may be excessive since the American experience indicates that few victims use the right to make a statement.[73]

Both Ashworth[74] and Duff[75] point out that attempts to improve the legal position of the victim have been piecemeal and lack logical coherence. These difficulties arise even with a welfare model. There are clear difficulties in defining state compensation and identifying the theoretical basis for its introduction.[76] Should compensation be forthcoming if the offender does

---

[68] Under the ECHR a *partie civile* enjoys the rights of Art. 6 (*Moreira de Azevedo* v. *Portugal*, 1990, Series A No. 189; *Tomasi* v. *France*, 27 August 1992, Series A No. 241-A). This is in accordance with the well-established case of *Le Compte, Van Leuven and De Meyere* v. *Belgium* (23 June 1981, Series A No. 43).

[69] D. Miers, *Compensation for Criminal Injuries* (London; Butterworths 1990), 272–5.

[70] For the position in the USA see Deborah Kelly, 'Victim Participation in the Criminal Justice System', *Victims of Crime*, in A. J. Lurigio *et al.*, or D. Hellerstein, 'The Victim Impact Statement: Reform or Reprisal?' (1989) 27 *Am. Jo. Crim. L.* 391.

[71] Andrew Ashworth, 'Punishment and Compensation: Victims, Offenders and the State' (1986) 6 *Oxford Journal of Legal Studies*, 86–122.

[72] Keisel, 'Crime and Punishment' (1984) 70 *American Bar Association Journal*, 25.

[73] E. Villmoare and V. V. Neto, 'Victim Appearances at Sentencing Under California's Victims' Bill of Rights', *Research in Brief* (August 1987), 1–5, referred to in Robert Elias, 'Which Victim Movement?' in Lurigio *et al.*, *Victims of Crime*.

[74] Ashworth, 'Punishment and Compensation', 122.

[75] Duff, 'The "Victim Movement" and Legal Reform'.   [76] Ibid.

not have the mental capacity necessary for conviction? Does violent crime include dangerous machinery in factories? What should be the standard of proof required—'balance of probabilities' or 'beyond reasonable doubt'? What is implied is a need for clarity about reasons before altering the law, as well as careful assessment of the practical and theoretical effects of such changes.

One of the main reasons for change is said to be to give more weight to victims' interests. Traditionally criminal justice systems have ignored victims' interests whilst using victims to obtain convictions. A number of changes have occurred which appear to redress the balance, but it is necessary to consider in whose interests these alterations have worked and are intended to work. For example, increasing the possibility of reparation and compensation at the pre-trial stage may help some victims to accept their victimization and give them some compensation. But it may be that both the state and the defendant have much more to gain; the defendant avoids a criminal conviction, the state saves money whilst still appearing to follow a retributive ideal. None the less, compensation paid by the offender to the victim after conviction may reduce the victim's feelings of vengeance and dissatisfaction and may also increase the willingness of victims to report offences; it may increase the offender's feeling of responsibility for his/her actions, which may be the first step towards rehabilitation; and it may reduce the need for the use of expensive sentencing options such as custody. The results of each small alteration are so wide that clarity about which are essential and which only by-products is desirable. But such clarity is elusive. For example, it is possible to argue that the American system of victims' rights does little to benefit victims,[77] and is a smokescreen for other alterations in the system. In the absence of clarity about effects it can be argued that the victim is being manipulated by the state; that there is no, or little, real benefit for the victim; and that both victim and the general public are being bought off in order to meet state and governmental interests.

Furthermore, there has been a more sinister side to increased interest in victims—it has been linked with calls for increased responsibilities on the part of victims to prevent their own victimization. Of course crime prevention, and especially teaching individuals to be law-abiding, has always been the responsibility of every individual and of society, it is one of the functions of education, at home, in school, and in all social relationships, but this is only a general responsibility: the new responsibilities go further than this. It is suggested that they should alter their lifestyles and secure their possessions, and so curtail their freedom. Such calls arise largely out of victim surveys which have shown certain types of behaviour are likely to

---

[77] Robert Elias, 'Which Victim Movement?' in Lurigio *et al.*, *Victims of Crime*, 242–6.

heighten the risk of victimization (going out frequently at night, using public transport, high levels of alcohol consumption).[78] Care must be taken as this tends to ignore other types of victimization, such as that arising out of commerce and public agencies.[79] If information concerning lifestyles is offered as advice on how to avoid victimization it might be seen as being useful, but in some countries it has had rather more far-reaching effects. In Britain the CICB may reduce or deny compensation where it deems that the victim has taken part in improper conduct, it assesses the 'innocence' of the victim. All insurance companies take this further by requiring certain types of behaviour before any payment is made.[80] Associated with the victim-blaming has been a call for victims to join with others in their community to perform local 'policing' functions.

Although none of this is mooted as replacing public control of crime (by police and other public agencies of control), it does move attention away from the failures of contemporary criminal justice and place some blame on the victim and the community. It also might work to alter the police function. In Britain one can already see the police reacting to this possibility: due to limited resources police cannot respond to all calls. They therefore prioritize both types of offences and offences within each offence category. Therefore they have reduced their active role in dealing with the less serious property offences, so releasing them to deal with crimes which more clearly demand a public response (violence or large-scale property offences).

The clear indication would be that potential victims should take relatively more responsibility to protect themselves against minor transgressions. There are a number of problems associated with this. First, where the community tries to act there will always be the free-loaders who enjoy the increased protection provided by their neighbours but who refuse to contribute to the cost. Secondly, there is a danger of vigilantes who may, in an effort to prevent crime, actually commit offences themselves. Finally, it is questionable whether private methods of prevention actually stop crime or merely displace it to other targets.[81] If the latter, pushing responsibility onto victims solves nothing except making the control agencies appear more efficient while not actually increasing law abiding behaviour. Any

---

[78] See M. Gottfredson, *Victims of Crime: The Dimensions of Risk*, Home Office Research Study 81, London; HMSO 1984, ch. 2.

[79] D. Miers, 'Positivist Victimology: A Critique' (1990) 1 *International Review of Victimology*, 3–22 and 219–30; C. Wells, 'The Decline and Rise of English Murder: Corporate Crime and Individual Responsibility' [1988] *CrimLRev.* 788–801; M. Levi and S. Pithouse, 'Victims of Fraud', in D. Downes (ed.), *Unravelling Criminal Justice* (London; Macmillan 1992).

[80] As most individuals tend to provide too low a level of crime prevention, so far as society is concerned this strategy could be very distressing for victims: see S. Field and T. Hope, *Economics and the Market in Crime*, RPU Research Bulletin, London; HMSO 1989, 40–4.

[81] T. Bennett, *Evaluating Neighbourhood Watch* (London; Gower 1990).

shift of responsibility away from the state needs to be more carefully considered: are the motives economic or genuinely the greater protection of the individual's property and person? A basic axiom should be that any responsibility of community and/or victims must not be permitted to reduce that of the state: the responsibility of the state to secure the safety of its citizens is fundamental.

If victims are to be represented, through rights or otherwise, in the criminal justice system, it is desirable that this should not be done at the expense either of the state's responsibility to its citizens or of the rights of defendants. Such ends are not easy to achieve. Concern for victims necessarily interferes with the public interest elements of criminal prosecutions. Its accommodation requires a wholesale consideration of the intentions underlying the criminal law and the criminal justice system. Only then can the victim be integrated with integrity.

16

Sentencing Practice, Policy, and Discretion

CONSTANTIJN KELK, LAURENCE KOFFMAN, AND JOS SILVIS

INTRODUCTION

The penal culture, and more specifically the sentencing culture, of the Netherlands is in many respects different from that of England and Wales. The English system has a tradition of deterrent sentencing whereas, in the Netherlands, humanitarian concerns[1] combined with a greater awareness of the destructive effects of imprisonment have resulted in differentiated and relatively lenient sentencing.[2] In the Netherlands the idea that punishment ought to be a last resort, an *ultimum remedium*, is still a widely shared notion, despite the remarkable increase in very long prison sentences.

Obviously in close connection with the Dutch perspective on sentencing there has been a tradition of paying attention to the psychological situation of the offender in relation to the crime. Dutch sentencers cannot escape exposure to the psychiatric and behavioural analysis of prosecuted persons, since an elaborate presentation of professional expertise on these matters is a common feature of serious cases dealt with in court. Therefore it is possible to suggest that there might have developed a significant difference in empathy with and insight into the psychology of offenders between Dutch sentencers and their English counterparts.

Differences in tradition and culture influence the way in which discretionary powers in sentencing are exercised. But there are new developments which sometimes escape the traditional approaches: for instance, in drug cases there is a tendency in the Netherlands to give long prison sentences on the merits of the case without much consideration for personal characteristics of the offender.

It is important to have an idea of traditional differences between sentencing in the Netherlands and in England and Wales so as to understand

---

[1] See, for the humanitarian concerns in Dutch sentencing, J. A. Janse de Jonge, 'Rechtsgelijkheid: nog een lange weg', (1983) D en D 544–68; J. A. Janse de Jonge, 'Om de persoon van de dader: opmerkingen over straftoemeting, voorlichting en rechtsgelijkheid (I)', (1987) D en D, 454–67 and (II) (1987) D en D 567–83; J. A. Janse de Jonge, 'Om de persoon van de dader. Over straftheorieen en voorlichting door de reclassering' (diss.), Pompe reeks deel 4, Gouda Quint, Arnhem/Willem Pompe Instituut, Utrecht (1991).

[2] For a historical perspective of Dutch penal theory on this issue see J. A. Janse de Jonge, *Om de persoon van de dader* (Arnhem; Gouda Quint 1991).

the effects of Europeanization, including case law from the European Court of Human Rights, and of the tendency to develop sentencing guidelines in the countries under consideration. In the Netherlands the importance of the European Convention for the Protection of Human Rights and Fundamental Freedoms (ECHR) is considerable in the area of criminal procedure, and in relation to the treatment of prisoners. However, the issue of sentencing has not as yet been subjected to the same critical human rights perspective, even though a future linkage is possible.

In England and Wales there has been growing dissatisfaction with the use of certain sentences, especially long periods of imprisonment, when they are disproportionate to the gravity of the offence actually committed. When one considers the various aims of punishment, such as public protection, general or individual deterrence, and treatment of the offender, it is obvious that the pursuit of one or other of these objectives could lead to the use of disproportionate sentences to achieve some utilitarian goal: for example, a not-so-serious offence could be dealt with very harshly so as to deter would-be offenders.[3] However, there are other approaches to punishment which stress the need for justice and proportionality. In a sense this justice approach can be identified as part of a more general concern with human rights; in turn, this can be seen as reflecting the impact of internationalization. It is now thought to be objectionable that an offender should receive a long sentence simply to allow the opportunity to 'reform' or 'treat' him. Similarly, disproportionate sentences are not acceptable if their aim is simply that of general deterrence. Incarceration of those who are perceived (correctly or incorrectly) as a danger to the public is a more contentious area of sentencing and social policy, and there is less consensus on this issue.

The question may be raised whether the development of guidelines on sentencing is part of an international development, which might even have the characteristics of a movement. In the European context, in 1974 a subcommittee of the European Committee on Crime Problems published a report on sentencing, which was followed in 1987 by a colloquium of the Council of Europe on 'Disparities in Sentencing: Causes and Solutions', which led in 1988 to the creation of a Select Committee of Experts on Sentencing with the following task:

To examine, in the light of the conclusions of the Colloquium, the results of empirical research relating to sentencing, the drawing up of general sentencing principles which would enable the development of a coherent and consistent sentencing policy in Europe with the co-operation of the judiciary taking into account the freedom of appreciation of the judge and to study the legal education and the dissemination

---

[3] For a discussion of this see C. Harding and L. Koffman, *Sentencing and the Penal System* (London; Sweet and Maxwell 1988), 185–7, and 360–8.

and exchange of information among judges and other concerned persons. The committee should make recommendations relating to these matters.

Of course this development by itself does not imply a movement for restricting the exercise of discretion in sentencing. But there are also clear indications in the penological literature of strong support for proportionality in sentencing and the development of sentencing guidelines.[4] Moreover, in practice there has developed, in some jurisdictions, an increasing adherence to sentencing guidelines or presumptive sentences. Traditionally, sentencing has been an area in which judges have enjoyed considerable freedom, and this is well illustrated by the English system where (until very recently) there were few restraints on the exercise of sentencers' discretion. But today many countries are introducing (or considering) statutory frameworks for sentencing.[5] In particular, the sentencing 'guidelines' movement had been closely associated with the United States of America, where at the federal level, as well as at state level, such legislation has been introduced,[6] especially in order to restrict the use of indeterminate sentences. Sometimes this guidelines approach takes the form of a detailed numerical sentencing 'grid' (such as the Minnesota system), but other countries have also shown interest in enacting non-numerical statutory sentencing principles. There is currently a growing interest in Europe in this type of legislation, as evidenced by the recent Swedish statute.[7] The appeal of this type

[4] See for the background and practice in the United States: Dean J. Champion, *The US Sentencing Guidelines: Implications for Criminal Justice* (New York; Praeger 1991). M. Tonry, 'The Politics and Processes of Sentencing Commissions', in (1991) 37 *Crime and Delinquency*, 307–29; A. W. Alschuler, 'The Failure of Sentencing Guidelines: A Plea for Less Aggregation', (1991) 58 *University of Chicago Law Review*, 901–51. For England: Ralph J. Henman, *Sentencing Principles and Magistrates' Sentencing Behaviour* (Aldershot; Gower 1990); Barbara Hudson, *A Critique of the Justice Model of Correction* (London; Macmillan Education 1987); For Scandinavia: J. Andenaes, 'The Choice of the Sanction: A Scandinavian Perspective', in M. Tonry and F. E. Zimring (eds.) *Reform and Punishment, Essays on Criminal Sentencing* (Chicago; University of Chicago Press 1983); I. Antilla, 'The Ideology of Crime Control in Scandinavia: Current Trends', in *Selected Issues in Criminal Justice*, Helsinki, HEUNI (1985), 66–77; 'New Perspectives on Justice in the Criminal Justice System,' in *New Trends in Criminal Policy*, Bonn, International Penal and Penitentiary Foundation (1984), 11–19; 'Punishment versus Treatment—Is There a Third Alternative' in *Abstracts on Criminology and Penology*, 12 JRG, no. 3, 1972, 287–90. See for recent Dutch developments in this field several editions of *Trema* 1992 and 1993; [1992] Justitiële Verkenningen; Van de Bunt *et al.* (eds.), *Richtlijnen Openbaar Ministerie*, Ars Aequi (1993).
[5] See the Research Report of the Canadian Sentencing Commission, entitled *Issues Relating to Sentencing Guidelines: An Evaluation of United States Experiences and their Relevance for Canada* (Ottawa; Canadian Department of Justice 1988).
[6] See A. von Hirsch, K. Knapp and M. Tonry, *The Sentencing Commission and its Guidelines* (Boston; North Eastern University Press 1987). Also Dean J. Champion (ed.), *The U. S. Sentencing Guidelines* (New York; Praeger 1991). For a critical view see A. W. Alschuler, 'The Failure of Sentencing Commissions' [1991] *NLJ* 829–30.
[7] For a useful discussion, see Andrew von Hirsch, 'Guiding Principles for Sentencing: The Proposed Swedish Law' [1987] *CrimLRev.* 746; and A. von Hirsch and N. Jareborg, 'Swedish Sentencing Statute Enacted' [1989] *CrimLRev.* 275.

of statutory guidance is that it can stipulate which of the potentially conflicting penal objectives is to have primacy in sentencing policy and this, in turn, can promote a coherent body of sentencing law.

On a theoretical level there is also a movement away from the rehabilitation ideal; this is closely linked with the criticism of indeterminate sentencing in the USA during the 1960s and 1970s. In a political climate in favour of reducing the cost of public services there is a clear interest in favouring the theoretical perspective of neo-retributionism, even though in the long run this may increase social costs as a consequence of neglected social problems.

What has prompted the international tendency to stress proportionality in relation to the seriousness of offences in sentencing? In England and Wales there is a growing disillusionment with the idea that the sentencer's task is primarily to pass a sentence which reflects the requirements of the individual case. Too often this approach has led to disparity of sentences, with judges seeming to pursue their own personal sentencing philosophies with little regard for principle or consistency. It is again part of a general human rights movement that like cases should be treated alike in terms of the sentences imposed by the courts. It could be argued that in England, for instance, sentencing disparity and inconsistency has been dealt with by the Court of Appeal, especially in its guidance to the lower courts on both sentencing principle and policy. Yet there are many weaknesses in relying solely on the appellate process to produce consistency in sentencing practice by developing a detailed body of case law and guideline judgments. These are well illustrated by the many shortcomings of the Court of Appeal in England and Wales. In the past, there was little guidance on policy matters; indeed the guidance was sometimes unrealistic and even counter-productive.[8] The Court did not always follow its own guidance and the case law which emerged was too often muddled and lacking in penological expertise.

In the Netherlands there are several reasons for this renewal of interest in judicial discretion and sentencing, which, although linked, may nevertheless be viewed separately. To start with, a wide margin of judicial discretion is incongruous with a penal policy of increasing instrumentalism.[9] Sentencing by the courts could disrupt the planning of penal policy, and

---

[8] For a notorious example, see *R.* v. *McCann* (1980) 71 CrAppR 381, discussed at [1980] *CrimLRev.* 375.

[9] See on instrumentalism in penal law: R. Foqué and A. C. 't Hart, *Instrumentaliteit en rechtsbescherming, grondslagen van een strafrechtelijke waardendiscussie* (Arnhem; Gouda Quint 1990). A report by the Scientific Council for Government Policy (Wetenschappelijke Raad voor het Regeringsbeleid), *Rechtshandhaving*, The Hague (1988), shows clearly how instrumentalism has come to overshadow the idea of due process. A gradual shift in emphasis away from the magisterial role of the public prosecutor is another pointer: see H. G. Van de Bunt, *Officieren van Justitie* (Tjeenk Willink, Zwolle 1985).

Melai, not without reason, has referred to it as 'the libido' of current penal culture.[10] Secondly there is the pervasive process of computerization, which not only includes a tendency to collect computerized data, but also an inclination to process reality in a way that allows it to be filed away in computerized form. Thirdly, internationalization, a process in which European unification looms largely, has taken its toll in the sphere of sentencing. The Dutch worry that, in a Europe without borders, no one country can permit itself the luxury of being out of step in the punishment line. The result has been a tendency to impose more severe sentences. To put it in a more popular and somewhat demagogic way: the Dutch do not want to be 'the cheap island' of crime. But leaving such pressure aside, it must still be said that internationalization has created a need for comparisons between simple schemes of sentencing.[11]

Moreover, penal practice confronts countries with each other's sentencing policies in so-called *exequatur* procedures, by means of which foreign sentences can be transferred and executed in other countries. Contrary to German and Swiss practice, Dutch courts deciding on *exequatur* have the power to amend foreign sentences, although they rarely seem to do so.[12]

Although some writers argue that individualized sentencing enables the judge to choose a sentence that reflects the offender's culpability and that the guidelines movement is too concerned with aggregations of cases,[13] it is difficult to resist the conclusion that many countries are now interested in sentencing reform because of the serious shortcomings of the traditional approach. However, it will be obvious from the sections which follow that the trend towards internationalization does not lead individual countries inexorably in one direction only. It will be appreciated that there are diverging, but equally valid, interpretations of what is meant by a 'justice' approach to sentencing and punishment.

Notwithstanding this important caveat, the international movement has a number of identifiable beliefs: greater proportionality and consistency in sentencing; the use of moderate and short prison sentences, except where

---

[10] See Melai's commentary on HR, 13 Sept. 1988 [1989] NJ 285.

[11] In 1988, the Council of Europe installed a Select Committee of Experts on Sentencing, with a view to developing 'a coherent and consistent sentencing policy in Europe': see L. Frijda, 'Eventuele Straatsburgse aanbevelingen over straftoemeting', in (1992) 15 *Trema, Gelijkheid van straffen*, 77–135.

[12] HR, 19 June 1990 [1991] NJ 188 (commentary by A. H. J. Swart). In four of the first five *exequatur* cases that came before the Supreme Court (all concerning drugs), the same punishment was imposed as abroad, although the Netherlands emphatically defended the right to amend foreign sentences: see *Report concerning international co-operation in criminal matters between the member states of the Council of Europe NYbIL* [1988] 298–308, also cited by Leijten in [1991] NJ 190.

[13] For a sceptical view of the 'guidelines' approach, see D. A. Thomas, 'The Justice Model of Sentencing: Its Implications for the English Sentencing System' in *The Future of Sentencing* (1982) (Univ. of Cambridge, Occasional Papers No. 8).

longer sentences are clearly required for public protection; the development and increased use of non-custodial and community penalties; stricter legislative guidance for sentencers, together with better judicial training and information.

DISCRETION AND PUNISHMENT: THE DUTCH SYSTEM

One of the most salient features of Dutch criminal law is the amount of discretion courts have in sentencing. While this has been a matter of debate ever since the Criminal Code came into force in 1886, of late it has become a veritable hot issue, and it is unlikely that penal practice will escape its effects.

The developments, mentioned in the introduction, in the field of instrumentalization, computerization and internationalization, could drastically change the nature of sentencing. Already some are calling for equality of punishment.[14] Considering the lack of reliable empirical research on the issue, inequality is all too easily assumed.[15] The idea of equality upon which criticism of inequality in sentencing is based seems to be synonymous with uniformity. Indeed, we can all see that sentencing is not uniform per crime, not even in cases that are dealt with by the same court during the same trial. However, it is much more complicated to examine the practice of sentencing against a more complex concept of equality that leaves room for differentiation according to relevant criteria. Historically, the court's discretion to vary punishment according to the circumstances of the case was a hard-won victory in the face of the strict uniformity that, as the fruit of the enlightenment, was meant to replace arbitrary justice as meted out by the old regime.

Indeed, legal security, promised to the French citizen as a direct result of the Revolution, required legally fixed penalties according to the type of crime.[16] This effectively cut short any arbitrary tendencies the judge, as a servant of government, might have. This idea was soon reversed around

---

[14] It was not without reason that the editors of *Trema*, professional journal for the judiciary, published a special edition in March 1992, under the title: 'Gelijkheid van straffen' (Equality of Punishment), (1992) XV *Trema* 44–140.

[15] A study by A. C. Berghuis showing huge differences in sentencing in different district courts was found to be so full of methodological holes that it is impossible to draw any conclusions from it: see 'De harde en de zachte hand van een statistische analyse van verschillen in sanctiebeleid', in *Trema*, 'Gelijkheid van straffen', 84–93, and the reaction by L. F. D. ter Kuile, 'Straffen', in XV *Trema*, no. 5, 187. On the methodology of such research, e.g. H. I. Sagel-Grande, 'Straftoemeting sociologisch beschouwd', in [1974] D en D 409–18. Also P. van Duyne, *Beslissen in eenvoud* (Arnhem; Gouda Quint 1983).

[16] Recently 't Hart has reminded us of this in his commentary on HR, 22 October 1991, [1992] NJ 282. He refers to a strict principle of legality as envisaged by Beccaria.

1800, as the enormous injustices to which such a system must, of necessity, lead became apparent; for many reasons, not all thefts are the same and neither are all murders. At the turn of the century, newly-gained criminological insights intensified this notion, as modern thought in penal law and criminal justice inserted behavioural and sociological ideas into thinking about people as subjects of law. This also affected the system of punishment and led, for example, to the introduction in 1924 of involuntary treatment for the mentally ill in the Netherlands.

Since the introduction of the Criminal Code in 1886, the culture of sentencing in the Netherlands has always significantly reflected a great deal of faith in an independent judiciary, given wide margins of discretion in order to be able to do justice to the seriousness of the crime and the conditions in which it was committed, as well as to the perpetrator as a person and the personal background against which he/she came to commit a crime. In addition to the classical foundation of punishment—retribution, and its classical goal—general deterrence, growing importance was attached to special deterrence and resocialization. Faith in the judiciary meant that Dutch criminal justice had a specifically paternalistic flavour. After the terrors of the Second World War, a new dimension has been added in which the principles of civilized society and elementary human rights must be respected.[17] And it is these human rights that, increasingly and in ever more detail, have come to dominate criminal procedure, mainly through the European Convention on Human Rights and the Convention on Political Rights and Freedoms.[18]

The legal margins of judicial sentencing have remained wide. It should be noted, however, that a large number of penal sanctions can now be imposed in fields other than that of criminal law, and by bodies other than criminal courts.[19] Such systems of sanctions usually leave less room for discretion than is allowed a criminal court in sentencing. The imposition of sanctions by bodies other than a court is not only found outside criminal law. Within it, the police[20] and the public prosecutor nowadays have considerable powers in this field; as well as dropping a case (conditionally), the scope of the system of settlement out of court (*transactie*) has been greatly enlarged since the 1983 Act,[21] while a recent Act has introduced an

---

[17] A development that is also reflected in the change from 'défense sociale nouvelle'.

[18] The direct influence of the European Convention on Sentencing is limited. See E. A. Alkema, 'Een strafmaathof en het EVRM' in xv 3 *Trema*, Gelijkheid van Straffen, 106–111.

[19] e.g. the municipal social services, the inland revenue service, etc. According to the European Convention, whether a sanction constitutes a penal sanction is decided by the nature of the behaviour, in connection with the severity, nature, and purpose of the sanction.

[20] By the Act of 31 March 1983, s. 153. See Art. 74 of the Penal Code, giving the police powers to settle a case out of court (*transactie*) and AMVB Besluit Politietransactie and the *Besluit transactie Rijksdienst voor het wegverkeer*, 2 July 1987, s. 332, amended by decree of 3 July 1989, s. 260.

[21] *Wet Vermogenssancties*, Act of March 31st 1983, s. 153.

administrative fine for simple traffic offences.[22] The main characteristic of settlements with the police, and with the public prosecutor, is that they are of a singular and predetermined uniformity. However, there is still inequality as far as the question of punishment or not is concerned. In ordinary criminal cases, the court is bound by a legal sentencing framework, with a maximum penalty applicable for each type of offence. Dutch criminal law has a general minimum for all offences; one day in prison or a five guilder fine.

There is also always the possibility, applicable to all offences, of a conviction without the imposition of any penalty, known as judicial pardon. Where there is a conviction, the court can therefore choose between a judicial pardon or a penalty within the wide margin of the general minima and maxima applicable to the particular offence. In cases of theft (Article 310 of the Criminal Code), the legal maximum is four years' imprisonment or a fine of f. 25,000.[23] In the case of murder (Article 289 of the Criminal Code), the general minimum of one day remains applicable, but there is also the possibility of a life sentence. It will be clear that the margins are very wide. There are three sets of circumstances in which the law allows penalties to be increased by one-third.[24] The maximum fine for corporations is not the legal maximum for the offence concerned, but the next highest maximum.[25] A combination of penalties is subject to legal restrictions, as are community service orders and conditional sentences, while 'extra' penalties such as impounding, the removal of certain rights, and publication of the sentence are only applicable in a limited number of cases.

This, in a nutshell, is the Dutch system of sentencing. In passing sentence the court must observe a number of procedural rules that, to a certain extent, restrict judicial freedom. An important rule in this connection is that any penalty imposed must be motivated. In many—but not all—cases, reasoning of sentences goes no further than the statement that the sentence corresponds with the seriousness of the offence, the circumstances in which it was committed, and the offender's personality. The Supreme Court sometimes requires further reasoning of sentences, depending on whether the offender raised a defence aimed at a reduced sentence, and on whether a more severe sentence was passed on appeal. In general, the Supreme Court seems to require that lower courts reason their sentences more elaborately than used to be the case, but nonetheless the wide discretion for the lower

---

[22] *Wet administratiefrechtelijke handhaving verkeersvoorschriften*, Act of 3 July 1989, s. 330, amended, by Act of 29 August 1990, s. 434.

[23] This is a fine of the fourth category: Art. 23 of the Criminal Code distinguishes between six categories of fines, with maxima of f. 500, 5,000, 10,000 25,000, 100,000 and one million.

[24] Recidivism (Arts. 421–3 Criminal Code); concurring offences (Arts. 55–63a Criminal Code) and offences committed in an official capacity (Art. 44 Criminal Code).

[25] Art. 23(7), Criminal Code; only if suitable punishment would otherwise be impossible.

courts remains characteristic.[26] Since a legislative change in 1983, the court must provide separate reasoning in imposing a prison sentence, explaining why this type of sanction has been chosen and, if the sentence is more severe than that demanded by the prosecutor, why this court considers a more severe sentence appropriate. The court must also give its special reasons for not imposing any penalty at all (always possible if the offence is trifling), or for not accepting an offender's offer to comply with a community service order.[27] The idea is to limit prison sentences as much as possible, although it is doubtful whether this actually works in practice.

If a case is heard on appeal (and in Dutch law there is always a right of appeal for both defendant and prosecution, entailing a full new hearing), the appeal court has the same margin of discretion in sentencing as the first court. However, if it is the defendant who has appealed and the appeal court wishes to impose a more severe sentence, it can only do so unanimously (Article 424 of the Code of Criminal Procedure), a special form of legal protection in the field of sentencing. The same applies to being found guilty on appeal while acquitted at first instance.

All in all, it will be clear that the legal framework within which sentencing in the Netherlands takes place, despite (tightening) requirements of judicial reasoning of sentence, still leaves the courts a great deal of leeway in choosing the type of sentence they deem most appropriate, as well as determining its severity; in short, the margins of judicial discretion in sentencing are very wide.

Undeniably, such judicial freedom is of great value in the light of the tendency to individualization that underlay the principles of modern thought at the beginning of the century, and in the light of new incentives for humanization of criminal law that occurred after the Second World War; in this respect it promotes justice in criminal law. But justice entails more than simply doing justice to the circumstances and needs of an individual case; it also implies legal security and equality. Indeed, judges would agree, and the courts have long been wont to compare the case in hand with other cases, and in discussing sentence have gradually developed 'tariffs'. Over the years there have also been attempts to reconcile the very different ideas and principles that underlie justice in sentencing. An important notion was that the personality of a judge and the social dynamics of court decision-making greatly influence the sentencing process and that it is not always easy to find a rational starting point.[28]

[26] L. Frijda, n. 11.
[27] Some of these requirements, now law, had already been introduced by the Supreme Court some years ago: see G. Knigge, *Beslissen en motiveeren, De arts. 348, 350, 358 and 359, Wetboek van strafvordering*, Alphen aan de Rijn (1980).
[28] This personal element, that is not limited to sentencing decisions, is well illuminated by J. Hogarth's well-known study, *Sentencing as a Human Process* (Toronto; University of Toronto Press 1971).

Hulsman has designed a system of references for sentencing, in which certain principles, norms, and values are ordered according to a hierarchical principle; the idea is to provide courts with a guideline for sentencing decisions. The system is based on a preference for non-custodial sentences and aims at influencing behaviour.[29] Others have sought to impose stricter requirements of reasoning, while recognizing the necessity of substantive rules of sentencing.[30] And there are some who have sought to develop models of factors implicit in the circumstances and effects of the offence that would serve as sentencing models.[31] Enschedé, for example, advocated a sentencing handbook that would also serve as a starting-point for the prosecution in demanding sentence.[32] The relative value of a tendency to rationalization and equality has been stressed by criminologists and others, who emphasize such factors as social inequality that inevitably lead to selectivity in decisions on prosecution, and also play a part in sentencing. Without resorting to such notions as conscious class-justice—something that Jongman, who has conducted much research into problems of selectivity,[33] never did—it must be recognized that an offender's social position can play an important role. Nowadays this is especially important for the unemployed,[34] young offenders from ethnic minority groups,[35] and drug users.

However, this is not the inequality to which those who call for greater equality in sentencing are referring. They mean (in)equality in sentencing policy between different criminal courts, or between different (panels of) judges at the same court.[36] This is the equality that has received all the attention during the past two decades, both from the judiciary and from the (heads of the) Public Prosecution Service. It is also the equality that figures most in academic research. Gradually an ideal of equality has been developed by means of which the margins of judicial discretion can be filled in. This ideal has been considerably reinforced by an enormous increase in numbers of criminal cases, requiring ever more judges, and increasingly giving rise to questions of equality in sentencing. However, in our opinion

---

[29] L. H. C. Hulsman, 'Straftoemeting, een preadvies', in *Straf,* Anthos (1969), 61 *et seq.*

[30] H. W. R. Beeling, 'Motivering door de rechter van de strafmaat', in [1973] NJB 125 *et seq.*

[31] See C. P. Chr. Oomen in [1978] D en D 314–30.

[32] Ch. J. Enschede, 'Een nieuw handboek', [1975] D en D 1–6.

[33] See publications by R. W. Jongman c. s. in [1976] and [1977] TvC. His ideas and research have been criticized by F. W. M. van Straelen and C. van be Werff, [1977] TvC 3.

[34] J. Strikwerda, H. Timmerman, R. W. Jongman, 'Werkloosheid en opgelegde gevangenisstraffen' [1983] TvC 201–8.

[35] H. Timmerman, J. J. Bosman and R. W. Jongman, 'Minderheden voor de rechter' [1986] TvC 57–72.

[36] Terminology here is crucial, especially the term 'policy' that plays a central part in the debate. It should be noted that the Dutch word for policy, *'beleid'*, can mean two things: policy in the English sense (formalized and recognizable patterns of decision-making) and prudence, decision-making after rational consideration of the case in hand.

the spirit of our (computerized) age also plays an important part, oriented as it is towards quantity rather than quality, with its corresponding and pervasive tendencies towards registration and information that have their own optical norms of conveniently arranged data. Of course, no one would dispute the injustice of sentencing that was completely dependent on the personality of the judge, and of course consensus exists on the necessity of treating equal cases as equally as possible, given the exorbitant context of criminal law and its consequences for the lives of ordinary people. The questions then arise: what are equal cases, what is equal treatment, and how unequal must a case be to warrant unequal treatment? Everyone recognizes these questions, but the problem is that there are many different answers, and that such answers cannot be objectively tested. For that reason, we should stop trying to find uniform answers and concentrate on *pluriformity*. This is closely linked to the fact that more or less equal circumstances may seem to exist at first sight, while there may still be other actual or individual circumstances that affect the subjective experience of punishment, and therefore the severity of a penalty in individual cases.

Within the intense culture of directives that has taken hold of society at almost every level, those that govern the policy of the prosecution service in demanding sentence are meant to provide a *starting point* from which the prosecutor may deviate in individual cases.[37] Nevertheless, in reality they can still lead to routine and petrification in sentencing, because there will be a tendency to remain within the directives as far as severity of the penalty is concerned, although the type of penalty may vary. For example, in cases of drunken driving, courts are inclined to create variable-package sentences of equal weight considering characteristics of the offender's situation: meaning a longer prison sentence or higher fine than the directive suggests, because there are too many objections to revoking the offender's licence for any length of time. We are not suggesting that a certain level of punishment is not indicated for certain types of offences committed in comparable circumstances. Such levels will largely be based on accepted practice. However, this severity scale is not the only determinant. There must also be scope for the special normative aspects of a case; a penalty may be excessively severe in some circumstances, if the offender has already been 'punished' (been injured for example) or if there is a deplorable family background, or serious illness. In such cases the best remedy, with most behavioural effect, could well be a fine or a community service order, rather than a custodial sentence. Such special normative aspects could result in *moderation* of what is, at first sight and according to the

---

[37] Meanwhile, prosecution directives have been recognized by the Supreme Court as a form of (pseudo) law. See HR, 19 June 1990, [1991] NJ 119: directive on the public prosecutor and inland revenue service must be regarded as 'law' as meant by Art. 99 RO.

directives, a justified penalty in the given circumstances. Moderation could mean a less severe sentence, or a different type of penalty. In the traditional terminology of criminal law, this means the following: retribution, the essence and legal basis of all punishment, may very well justify a certain sentence, but different purposes of punishment, principles of humanity, and subjective experience may all serve to undermine retribution. A blameworthy transgression of the rules may remain (partially) unrevenged because punishment 'as a sanction is subject to the purpose of the sanction, namely the maintenance of legal order, and to the purpose of legal order itself, namely the promotion of public well-being'.[38]

This also explains why Dutch criminal law is not dominated by an absolute theory of retribution, but by a combined theory (the legal basis of punishment is retribution, but punishment is also determined by a number of different purposes). In the light of this theoretical background, any form of 'mechanical' sentencing that is more or less automatically linked to 'objective' factors should be refuted. The most rigid version of that American school of thought from the 1970s, 'just deserts' within the framework of the so-called 'justice model', tends towards just such 'mechanical sentencing'.[39] However, fixed penalties were of some significance in providing legal protection for individuals in the United States, for they put an end to the notorious practice of indeterminate sentencing. As well as the way in which penalties are imposed, the way in which sentencing guidelines are developed is also important; in the United States, federal guidelines are produced by a sentencing commission, on which judges form a minority. Politicians have the last word about the guidelines. Their application requires extremely complicated, almost mathematical, calculations, sometimes based on a system of points for certain factors. One cannot escape the conclusion that all of this—partly because of prosecutorial discretion—could lead to new forms of inequality: 'overreaching uniformity'.[40] There is some doubt whether the guidelines have indeed led to greater equality in the criminal justice system in the United States.[41] At the same time it must be said that, with the increase of guidelines, probation activities have decreased. Preoccupation with the seriousness of the crime

---

[38] W. P. J. Pompe, *Handboek van het Nederlandse strafrecht* (Tjeenk Willink, Zwolle, 3rd edn., 1950), 10–11.

[39] See for a theoretical explanation, Andrew von Hirsch, *Doing Justice, the Choice of Punishments, Report of the Committee for the Study of Incarceration* (New York; Hill and Wang 1976). This report still contains niceties of distinction as far as personal factors pertaining to the offender are concerned, but these have become increasingly less important as the success of the 'justice model' has increased.

[40] J. A. W. Lensing, 'Richtlijnen voor de straftoemeting. Kunnen wij iets leren van de US Sentencing Guidelines?' xv 6 *Trema*, 207 at 216.

[41] G. W. Heany, 'The Reality of Guidelines Sentencing: No End to Disparity?' (1991) 28 AmCrimLRev. 161–232; Clarke, McKenna and Cuneo, 'The Sentencing Guidelines: What a Mess', in (1991) 55/4 CA Fed. Prob. 45–8.

apparently goes hand-in-hand with a loss of interest in the offender as a person.

Considering the desirability of pluriformity in criminal justice, guidelines for the prosecution rather than for the courts, as in the United States, are by far the more preferable option. Because of the hierarchical structure of the Dutch Prosecution Service, prosecution in the Netherlands could be under suspicion of being easily influenced politically. But in this respect there are certainly counteractive forces within the prosecution, rooted in the traditional culture of the prosecution being part of the independent magistracy. This however cannot rule out all vulnerability to direct political pressure. For this reason, any further restriction of judicial freedom would potentially upset the system of checks and balances, and therefore constitute a fundamental risk to current legal order. We are not maintaining that there are no inequalities in sentencing and we would welcome more and better information for the judiciary on this point.[42] Indeed, equality is an important source of legitimacy in criminal justice. Nevertheless, the strictly individual nature of a criminal case should have a meaning of its own besides that of equality of judicial decisions, and legitimation of that meaning should be found in the reasoning of sentences.[43] In itself, computerization offers many possibilities for processing a broader reasoning into sentences, although in practice the standard formula seems to offer an all too easy way out.

Substantive reasoning of sentences affords some insight into the plausibility of the sentence itself. In a penal climate that is governed by a combined theory of punishment, formal, or even 'optical', equality is less important than the weight of conviction carried by the fact that the penalty imposed is (relatively) 'correct' in the light of the actual case and the offender's personality—all, of course, within certain margins.[44] It is this sort of equality that should reach maturity in an accusatorial system, a procedure in which both sides are heard, in which witnesses and experts are examined, and which will result in a reasoned sentence that is appreciated as such. This point of view is also to be found in other European countries, from which we may deduce that internationalization need not lead in one direction only. In countries such as Austria and Denmark, these ideas have even filtered through into international co-operation in criminal matters.[45] There, the purpose of executing a sentence is to achieve the best possible result in an individual case. This means that the purpose of transferring the execution of sentence is to promote the due administration of justice. In that case it may be necessary to adapt a sentence that has

---

[42] Such information is a must if judges are to do their work properly.
[43] L. Frijda, n. 11, 101.
[44] J. A. Janse de Jonge, 'Rechtsgelijkheid: nog een lange weg', [1983] D en D 544–68.
[45] See commentary by A. H. J. Swart on HR, 26 June 1990, [1991] NJ 188.

been imposed elsewhere to local circumstances. The future of the con-victed person lies in the state where the sentence will be executed, and the courts of that state are best equipped to decide on the penalty with an eye to the future. This is confirmed by the explanatory report to Article 44 of the European Convention on the International Validity of Criminal Judgments, where it refers to 'tendances d'individualiser la sanction' and to 'la pratique et la politique criminelle de l'Etat requis' as justifications for judicial freedom in adapting sentences.[46]

In our view, practically intensifying procedural guarantees is more essen-tial than intensifying guidelines, in order to arrive at acceptable standards of equality and inequality in criminal cases, while still leaving the matter in the hands of an independent judiciary.

SENTENCING POLICY AND PRACTICE IN ENGLAND AND WALES

Although pre-sentence (formerly 'social enquiry') reports are of consider-able assistance to sentencers,[47] the ultimate choice of either type or length of sentence is still a matter for the judge or magistrate in England and Wales. Sentencing is seen as a judicial function father than a matter for penal 'experts'. The position of judges as sentencers is particularly assured today in view of the increasing recognition of proportionality and justice as the main objectives of sentencing, rather than ideas of rehabilitation and treatment of the offender. The fact that judges have frequently been strong proponents of the efficacy of deterrence is perhaps a cause for some concern, especially when there is little empirical support for their faith in long sentences for this purpose. But although the position of judges as sentencers is secure, there is still some discontent with the way in which they are trained for this sentencing role. In England and Wales judges are generally recruited from amongst successful barristers who may have little experience of criminal procedure and sentencing. The traditional judicial reply has been that no such specialist knowledge is required and that such matters can be learnt with practice.[48]

This argument, which was never truly convincing, is clearly outmoded today. The sentence of the court should not be a matter for the individual preference, philosophy, or caprice of the judge. It should be part of a principled approach to sentencing and punishment. Amongst the various pieces of information that the judge is presented with, he must decide

---

[46] Ibid.

[47] For discussion, see Harding and Koffman, above, n. 3, 66–75 (and also 2nd edn., forth-coming).

[48] On the question whether specialist training is appropriate for judges, see Patrick Devlin, *The Judge* (Oxford; Oxford University Press 1979), 37–40.

which aspects of the offence and which circumstances of the offender should be most influential when deciding on the sentence. This should not be an isolated decision, but rather one which forms part of a coherent sentencing policy. It has been a frequent criticism of sentencing in England and Wales, in the past, that like cases have not always been treated alike and that judges have often pursued their own individual philosophies or theories of sentencing. Other recurring criticisms have been that the training period for new judges on sentencing matters is insufficient,[49] and that the guidance given by the Court of Appeal is not always effectively communicated to the lower courts. However, the gradual extension of the role of the Judicial Studies Board has led to some improvements in both training and the provision of information.

The English sentencing system has traditionally permitted judges a wide discretion in passing sentence. It is rare that the sentence for an offence is fixed by law (murder being the notable exception), and so there is no such thing as a 'correct' sentence. Apart from statutory provisions such as those stating the maximum penalty for an offence, or providing separate rules for dealing with specific types of offender (like the young or the mentally disordered), the sentencer traditionally enjoyed considerable freedom in his choice of sentence. The task of providing guidance or controlling this wide discretion was a matter for the Court of Appeal. On matters relating to principles of sentencing—such as the appropriate use of concurrent as opposed to consecutive sentences—it is unobjectionable that an appeal court should provide such guidance. But the distinctive feature of the English system has been the central involvement of the Court of Appeal in formulating sentencing policy. It might be thought that sentencing and penal policy would be closely synchronized and compatible but that has not been the tradition in this country. Penal policy has been a matter for the executive and, occasionally, Parliament. However, the formulation of sentencing policy has been traditionally regarded as the concern of the Court of Appeal.[50]

It could be argued that there was originally no particular constitutional justification for the Court of Appeal's influence on sentencing policy, but that it developed in the absence of any other body assuming responsibility for it. However, it became accepted that there was an important constitutional principle involved, namely that the Court of Appeal's role was defensible on the basis that it helps to ensure the independence of the judiciary and prevents the manipulation of sentencing policy by politicians for short-term pragmatic ends. As constitutional theory in England and

---

[49] For an account of the training given to newly-appointed part-time judges, see Clare Dyer's article in the *Guardian*, 14 February 1990.

[50] For an interesting discussion, see A. Ashworth, 'Judicial Independence and Sentencing Reform', *The Future of Sentencing* (University of Cambridge, Occasional Papers No. 8, 1982).

Wales concerning a separation of powers is suitably ill-defined, it is difficult to accept that there are any valid legal objections to curtailing judicial independence in relation to sentencing policy.[51] Moreover, there are strong practical reasons for doing precisely this, as the lack of harmony between Home Office policy and the sentencing policy pursued by the courts hampers the development of a coherent approach to sentencing for this country. Indeed, it is easy to sympathize with the views of one eminent critic of our sentencing system, who concluded 'that the time has surely come to dismantle the barriers between penal policy and sentencing policy—both should equally be the concern of the government'.[52]

Some people are uneasy about the prospects of such a fusion and argue that sentencing policy will be at the mercy of economic expediency, public outrage at certain types of crime, and sudden shifts in penal philosophy. This concern must be taken seriously and it is comforting to think of the judiciary ensuring consistency, moderation, and impartiality in sentencing matters. But this view does tend to presuppose that judges are not swayed by public outcry, media-induced panic, and fluctuating attitudes to punishment—and there is little evidence to support this assumption, as shown by the punitive response of judges in the past to 'mugging' offences and football 'hooliganism'.[53] More crucially, the independence of the judiciary in relation to sentencing policy, and its resentment of any encroachment on this, can have undesirable and counter-productive results. For example, in 1981, senior judges threatened to respond to the Home Office's proposed policy of extending the parole scheme by passing longer sentences; this would have nullified the government's aim to enable the supervised early release of many prisoners and reduce the serious overcrowding in British prisons. In the event, the Home Secretary backed down from such a confrontation—a vivid illustration of the traditional importance of the judiciary in matters of sentencing policy.

A related and further example of the government's fear of 'trespassing' on the judiciary's sentencing territory is its unwillingness (until recently) to restrict judicial discretion by legislative means, in order to promote shorter prison sentences and non-custodial alternatives. For many years the government attempted to persuade sentencers to adopt such a policy, but it stopped short of any coherent legislation on the subject. The Court of Appeal did take the initiative in *Begum Bibi*[54] (and successive cases), and also in *Clarke*,[55] by attempting to indicate to the lower courts the type of offences which should receive more lenient treatment, but without any appreciable success.

As an effective means of influencing the sentencing practices of the

---

[51] Ibid., 46 *et seq.*   [52] Ibid.
[53] See Harding and Koffman, above, n. 3, 366–7.   [54] (1980) 71 CrAppR 36.
[55] [1982] 1 WLR 1090.

lower courts, Court of Appeal guidance has its limitations. For example, in *Bibi*, the court concentrated on the type of offence which was or was not to attract leniency from the courts, without addressing the vital problem of how to punish the persistent, but non-violent, offender. Also, it was not perhaps made sufficiently clear to the lower courts that the cases chosen in the *Bibi* initiative were intended to represent a detailed and coherent set of guidelines: that is, a new policy. The guidance itself was piecemeal and did not go far enough in its intended direction.[56] A criticism often levelled at the Court of Appeal is that it is not particularly well informed as to the sentencing practices of the lower courts; in other words, it is not an expert sentencing body or council.[57]

Despite successive pleas for shorter sentences, the parlous state of over-crowded British prisons, and the creation of a number of alternatives to the custodial sentence, the policy of persuasion and piecemeal legislation was not a success. It became increasingly apparent that more direct legislative intervention into sentencing policy and practice was required. We have noted (above) the theoretical and traditional objections to such a course of action, but a number of circumstances have combined to override them. A major one has been the depressing fact that the prison population for England and Wales is consistently higher than those of most, if not all, other western European countries.[58] This is not necessarily a reflection of the crime rate in England and Wales, but rather of the sentencing policies of the courts. There has been a tendency to incarcerate the persistent non-violent offender almost as if he were a danger to the public. There is a tradition of long sentences of imprisonment, for a variety of offenders, in what can be characterized as a judicial 'culture' or ethos which believed in the efficacy of deterrence regardless of a paucity of evidence to support this belief. Despite the deplorable conditions in British prisons (which resulted in serious rioting in 1990), and a series of highly critical official reports and studies,[59] there is nonetheless a judicial and public tolerance of prison overcrowding and degrading conditions.

Thus there was little doubt that the traditional approach to sentencing policy was failing to produce the required changes; sentencing policy became too important to be left to the judges. Perhaps fortuitously for the government, this need to curb sentencers' discretion has coincided with an international and European movement towards introducing statutory sentencing

---

[56] See *McCann* (1980) 71 CrAppR 381, discussed at [1980] *CrimLRev*. 375.

[57] For a discussion of these issues, see A. Ashworth, 'Reducing the Prison Population in the 1980s: The Need for Sentencing Reform', *A Prison System for the 1980s and Beyond* (London; NACRO 1982).

[58] See Vivian Stern, *Bricks of Shame, Britain's Prisons* (Harmondsworth; Penguin 1987), chap. 3. Also see successive Council of Europe figures on prison populations.

[59] Culminating in the Woolf Report: *Prison Disturbances April 1990* (1991), Cm 1456, HMSO.

principles. Under such schemes, there is still an important role for the courts—it is in no sense sentencing by numbers or by computer—but judicial discretion is to be exercised within a consistent and coherent framework. For example, as part of its revision of penal legislation in the 1970s, Finland introduced statutory sentencing principles. In 1988, Sweden enacted a sentencing statute which lays down general principles to be followed by the courts when passing sentence, with the emphasis very clearly on proportionality of sentence.[60]

In 1990 the British Government published its own plans for a radical reform of sentencing practice in its White Paper entitled 'Crime, Justice and Protecting the Public'.[61] Unlike so many previous sentencing reforms in this country, it was not concerned with piecemeal reform: it had a more specific aim of putting forward a clearly-defined set of principles. The White Paper stated that the reforms were aimed at 'getting a coherent framework for the use of financial, community, and custodial punishments, decisions on releasing long-term prisoners on parole, and the arrangements for supervising offenders in the community'.[62] Of particular significance is the fact that the government so clearly espoused the notion of just deserts or proportionality rather than the traditional reliance on deterrent principles. It stated:

The government's aim is to ensure that convicted criminals in England and Wales are punished justly and suitably according to the seriousness of their offences; in other words that they get their just desserts [*sic*]. No government should try to influence the decisions of the courts in individual cases. The independence of the judiciary is rightly regarded as a cornerstone of our liberties. But sentencing principles and sentencing practice are matters of legitimate concern to government ... Punishment in proportion to the seriousness of the crime has long been accepted as one of the many objectives in sentencing. It should be the principal focus for sentencing decisions.[63]

The White Paper, therefore, proposed a new legislative framework for sentencing in England and Wales based on the proportionality approach and it observed that other jurisdictions were currently following the same path.[64] In an important admission that a central tenet of traditional sentencing philosophy was misconceived, the report explicity rejected a deterrent approach as the correct method of deciding on the type and length of sentence.[65] In turn, the Criminal Justice Act 1991[66] was passed to give effect to the Government's reform proposals: the severity of the sentence

---

[60] See A. von Hirsch and N. Jareborg, 'Sweden's Sentencing Statute Enacted' [1989] *CrimLRev.* 275.
[61] February 1990, Cm 965, HMSO.   [62] Ibid., paras. 1–1. 15, 4.
[63] Ibid., paras. 2.1–2.2, 5.   [64] Ibid., para. 2.3., 5.   [65] Ibid., para. 2.8, 6.
[66] For a useful guide to this legislation, see M. Wasik and R. Taylor, *Criminal Justice Act 1991* (2nd edn. London; Blackstone Press 1993).

in an individual case should reflect primarily the seriousness of the offence committed and not other aims such as rehabilitation or crime prevention.

To this end, restrictions are imposed on the passing of custodial sentences. Section 1(2) states that a court is not to impose a custodial sentence unless it is of the opinion that the offence[67] was so serious that only such a sentence can be justified; or, in cases of violent or sexual offences, that only such a sentence would be adequate for the purposes of public protection. This subsection shows that, although proportionality is now to be the guiding sentencing principle, courts may in limited circumstances impose a sentence to incapacitate an offender from whom the public requires protection.

Where a court passes a custodial sentence, it now has to state in open court that one or both of the above reasons applies to the case and why it is of that opinion.[68] Section 2(2) provides that where a custodial sentence is imposed it shall be:

(a) for such a term as in the opinion of the court is commensurate with the seriousness of the offence, or the combination of the offence and one or more offences associated with it; or

(b) where the offence is a violent or sexual one, for such longer term as in the opinion of the court is necessary for public protection.[69]

Thus the length of a prison sentence is now, primarily, to reflect the seriousness of the offence which has been committed. Similarly, section 6(2)(b) of the 1991 Act provides that restrictions on liberty imposed by a community sentence are to be 'commensurate with the seriousness of the offence, or the combination of the offence and one or more offences associated with it'. Also, in relation to the fixing of fines, section 18(2) states that 'the amount of any fine fixed by a court shall be such as, in the opinion of the court, reflects the seriousness of the offence'.

The 1991 Act is a major piece of legislation and this is not the place for a detailed description or evaluation of its provisions. What needs to be stressed is the important departure of this statute from previous sentencing enactments. It attempts to give sentencers a clear indication of priority when choosing between the potentially conflicting and disparate aims of sentencing. Formerly, in the name of sentencing discretion, such choice had been left to the individual sentencer with only minimal (and frequently inconsistent) guidance from the Court of Appeal. The new legislation does

---

[67] Or 'the combination of the offence and one or more offences associated with it' (as amended by the 1993 Criminal Justice Act).

[68] S. 1(4), Criminal Justice Act 1991.

[69] To this extent the Act permits a prison sentence which is more severe than that which would otherwise be imposed according to the 'just deserts' principle. This departure from the basic principle is permitted only in relation to violent or sexual offences, and in order to protect the public.

not do away with the need for sentencing discretion, but it creates a much more coherent and principled framework for its exercise.

Whether the Act will be successful in achieving its intended goals is a matter for serious debate and it has divided some of the most expert writers on the sentencing system.[70] It is a matter for concern that the government responded so precipitately to criticism of some of the new provisions by amending them, within twelve months, in the Criminal Justice Act 1993. In view of the exhaustive consultation which preceded the 1991 Act, it was surely premature to start tinkering with such a carefully constructed piece of legislation. It remains to be seen how committed sentencers will be to the central philosophy of the 1991 Act.[71]

CONCLUSION

Although it might be thought at first sight that the impact of Europeanization on the sentencing system of England and Wales has been relatively slight, it would be unwise to dismiss its importance in relation to sentencing policy and practice. The repeated appearance of England and Wales at the top of the European 'league table' for the use of imprisonment, and the unfavourable comparison with European neighbours in terms of prison conditions, have served to add urgency to the need to reform our sentencing system. Even an insular body like the British judiciary can hardly have been unaware of these facts. The British government has been painfully aware of them and, perhaps belatedly, has decided to tackle these problems. Whether the Criminal Justice Act 1991 (as amended by the 1993 Act) will prove the correct or most effective means of doing so remains open to debate.

The international movement in favour of a justice or proportionality approach to sentencing has also been noted. There is a growing intolerance of prolonged incarceration to achieve other penal objectives, such as deterrence or treatment. England and Wales share with other European countries a growing willingness to promote and use community-based alternatives to imprisonment. Thus the impact of Europeanization on national sentencing policy may not be easy to measure in exact terms, but it should not be underestimated. It should not be forgotten, however, that

[70] In a recent article, David Thomas, a leading authority on the sentencing system, concluded that 'urgent action is needed to remedy the deficiencies of the Criminal Justice Act 1991': see *Guardian*, 30 March 1993. The Criminal Justice Act 1993 came into force during August and September 1993.

[71] See A. Ashworth and B. Gibson, 'The Criminal Justice Act 1993: Altering the sentencing Framework', [1994] *CrimLRev.*, 101. The authors describe the amendments to the 1991 Act as 'one of the most remarkable volte-faces in the history of penal policy in England and Wales' (see 101).

there are varying, and equally valid, interpretations of what is meant by a 'justice' approach to sentencing. Not all countries accept that the way forward lies in the adoption of stricter sentencing guidelines and the restriction of judicial discretion.

17

Prisoners' Rights in the Netherlands and England and Wales

GILLIAN DOUGLAS AND MARTIN MOERINGS

INTRODUCTION

In this chapter, we compare the protection of prisoners' rights in the Netherlands and England and Wales.[1] We outline the current position in the two jurisdictions, and then consider the extent of European influence upon the recognition of the rights prisoners seek to enjoy. We regard the isolation of prisoners from the outside world, and their consequent powerlessness, as the key features of imprisonment, and therefore focus on whether, and if so how, prisoners may seek to uphold their rights to social contacts, and to challenge internal disciplinary findings against them.

Not only are the two systems significantly different in their attitude towards, and the consequent treatment of, prisoners, but they also differ radically in the extent to which they look, or are forced to look, to European and international influences in deciding whether to grant enforceable rights to prisoners. The case law of the two countries plays a part in this difference. While the European Convention on Human Rights is incorporated into Dutch law, and must therefore be taken into account by domestic courts and authorities when considering whether rights have been infringed, this is not the position in the United Kingdom. There, courts may try to rule on the law so as to be compatible with the Convention, but cannot change the law to achieve this. Public authorities may, but are quite likely not to, consider the possible ramifications of a breach of the Convention when reaching decisions or drafting policies affecting human rights.

We start by describing the prison system in the two jurisdictions to clarify the problems which exist and how far the rights of prisoners can be used to address these.

---

[1] England and Wales form one legal jurisdiction, and have one prison system. Scotland and Northern Ireland are separate legal jurisdictions and have their own separate prison systems. Discussion in this chapter is confined to England and Wales.

The Population

There are 10,000 prisoners in the Netherlands in 1994. The prison population has more than doubled in the last ten years. This is due to tougher
penalties being given for certain types of crimes, especially drug trafficking, and means that judges are not sending offenders to prison more
frequently, but for longer periods. About 40 per cent of prisoners are
on remand, mostly in houses of detention, though some have to be held
in police stations due to shortage of places elsewhere in the system. The
average length of imprisonment is about two months, although sentences
for drug trafficking and serious crimes of violence are longer, usually two
years or more.

The prison rate is about 70 per 100,000 population. The Dutch prison
population used to be one of the lowest in the world, but the Netherlands
may lose this favourable position if the Government continues to build
new prisons to house the growing number of offenders sentenced to longer
prison terms. The Dutch system can prevent overcrowding by the so-called
'walking sentence', whereby less serious offenders sentenced to imprisonment for, say, up to two months, wait at home until required to report to
the prison. They may indeed have to wait for several months before they
can serve their sentence.

Prisons are rather small, most providing space for 100–250 inmates. The
vast majority of prisoners are male. There are only about 250 female
prisoners (although this number has doubled in the last fifteen years).
Approximately one-third of prisoners are users of hard drugs at the time
they enter the prison system, sentenced for trafficking or drug-related
crimes. The percentage in some houses of detention is even higher, especially in Amsterdam, Rotterdam, and the Hague. It is estimated that the
proportion of such users in houses of detention in these cities is at least
around 60 per cent. The population is very heterogeneous as far as nationality and ethnicity are concerned, with approximately fifty nationalities
being found in the prisons. About half of all prisoners are foreign and/or
members of another (non-Dutch) ethnic group.

The Prison System

The most important principles underpinning the prison system are contained
in the Principles Act for the Prison System (Beginselenwet Gevangeniswezen)
of 1953.

(i) The sentence must be served in association. Work, leisure activities, sport, daily exercise, and religious services take place in the

company of fellow inmates. During the night, prisoners remain in their own cells. But in houses of detention and in some high security prisons, they spend most of the day time in their cells as well. Hitherto, each prisoner has had his or her own cell, but this is likely to change, at least for prisoners serving short sentences.

(ii) Prisons are placed into various categories. For example, they are divided into those for short-term and long-term prisoners; for men and women; and for adults and juveniles. As far as security is concerned, they are divided into closed, semi-open, and open prisons.

(iii) The regime of the prison is directed to the resocialization of the prisoner. Previously, the authorities were optimistic about the possibilities of training and educating prisoners so that they could participate in society as ordinary, careful citizens after their release. But in the 1980s, the Minister of Justice[2] had to accept that resocialization thus described appeared impossible. He made a more down-to-earth statement: imprisonment should limit and reduce the damage to the prisoner as far as possible and must be carried out humanely. The aim of resocialization was not dropped, but re-interpreted as preparing prisoners for their release. This can also imply making them aware of the social problems they may face after release, such as unemployment, stigmatization, complicated social relationships etc.

Imprisonment as Punishment

These criteria must be placed within the context that individuals who commit crimes are sent to prison *as* punishment and not *for* punishment. It is the deprivation of liberty which is the punishment and, this apart, prisoners should retain as many rights as possible. This philosophy is reflected in the Dutch Constitution. Article 15(4) prescribes that the basic rights of prisoners can only be limited to the extent that the assertion of these rights is incompatible with the deprivation of liberty. This is in accordance with the judgment of the European Court of Human Rights in the *Golder* case, which explicitly rejected the theory that a prison sentence in itself involves a number of obvious limitations that exceed the mere physical deprivation of liberty.[3] This principle is very important and seems far-reaching, but in the daily reality of prison life, the assertion of rights often seems incompatible with the deprivation of liberty: social contacts for the prisoner and his/her family are limited; the prisoner may have to

---

[2] *Nota Taak en Toekomst van het Nederlandse Gevangeniswezen*, Ministerie van Justitie, 's-Gravenhage (1982).

[3] C. Kelk, 'The Netherlands' in D. van Zyl Smit and F. Dunkel (eds.), *Imprisonment Today and Tomorrow: International Perspectives on Prisoners' Rights and Prison Conditions* (Deventer; Kluwer Law and Taxation 1991), 391.

supply urine samples in certain circumstances; there is no normal salary for prison work, and so on.

The principle that deprivation of liberty is the punishment is clearly violated in institutions with a so-called 'special level of security'. Since 1990, such prisons have been used for prisoners who are alleged to have attempted to escape and to have used violence in such attempts. Inmates stay in small wings with a maximum of five other prisoners. They do not remain in the same wing for more than six months and can be transferred to another institution with the same regime without notice. The regime in such prisons will be stricter still if the Ministry of Justice accepts the recommendations of the Hoekstra Commission,[4] which proposed, *inter alia*, that outside space used for prisoners' exercise be wired over. This was prompted by some sensational escapes using helicopters.

Prisoners' Rights and Complaints Procedures

A formal right of complaint was introduced into the Principles Act in 1977 for those held in prisons and houses of detention. A complaint may be made when a disciplinary punishment is imposed; when a prisoner is refused permission to receive or send letters and when visitors are not admitted; and when a right derived from the rules prevailing in the institution is infringed by or on the authority of the governor. This is the most important, and vaguest, ground for complaint.

Each prison has a Complaints Committee which is part of the Board of Supervision, made up of representatives of different social fields, such as a lawyer, judge, university professor, housewife. Members are appointed by the Minister of Justice on the recommendation of the Board itself. The Complaints Committee can change or review the governor's decision after hearing both sides. In simple complaints, the chairman can handle the case by him/herself. The complainant may be assisted by a professional lawyer or by anyone else whom he trusts, including a fellow prisoner. After a decision by the Committee, the prisoner and the governor have a right of appeal to the Appeal Committee of the Central Council for the Enforcement of Criminal Law (also appointed by the Minister of Justice).

Disciplinary Penalties and Complaints

When a prisoner commits an act (e.g. fighting, use of drugs) which the governor considers incompatible with good order and discipline, he can impose a disciplinary penalty. There is no list of disciplinary offences.

---

[4] Commissie Hoekstra, *Rapport van de Evaluatiecommissie Beveiligingsbeleid Gevangeniswezen*, The Hague; Ministerie van Justitie (1992). See also J. Henley, 'Hard line on soft cells', *Guardian*, 27 April 1993.

Penalties include solitary confinement for up to two weeks in a strip cell; isolation in the prisoner's own cell for up to two weeks; a fine of up to two weeks' pocket money (about £15) or a reprimand.

The Complaints Committee can alter the disciplinary punishment awarded by the governor on the basis either that procedural requirements were not properly followed (e.g. the prisoner was not given a hearing); or that the decision 'should be considered unreasonable or unfair, all relevant interests and circumstances considered' (Principles Act, section 57). If the Committee rules in favour of the inmate but the penalty has already been carried out, compensation may be awarded after consultation with the governor. For example, an extra visit, extra time for exercise, or financial compensation may be offered.

When order or safety within the prison is affected, the governor may impose a 'safety measure' as an alternative to a disciplinary penalty. A penalty presupposes guilt while a safety measure need not, but it is not always clear why a governor has imposed a penalty in one case and a safety measure in another. The complaints committees are reluctant to pass judgment on the validity of this choice, confining themselves to ensuring that the correct procedures have been followed, which entail a hearing for the inmate where a penalty is imposed, and consultations with staff for a safety measure. For the prisoner, it makes little difference, since solitary confinement can be imposed as a safety measure as well as a penalty. The disadvantage however is that, where a safety measure is given, isolation may be extended for another two weeks.

Social Contacts Outside and Complaints

To underline the special importance attached to social contacts, infringement of the right to visits and correspondence is a special ground for complaint (see above). An inmate may see visitors for at least half an hour a week in houses of detention, usually in a room with other prisoners under the supervision of prison officers. The governor decides who may be admitted as a visitor, if necessary on condition that a body-search is carried out. In long-term prisons, inmates are allowed to meet their partners without supervision once a month, offering the opportunity for sexual contact.

Prisoners can send and receive as many letters as they like. In exceptional cases, such as to prevent crimes or escapes, the governor can impose limitations. Letters may be checked for their content, although in open and semi-open prisons they may only be checked for drugs, in the presence of the prisoner. In recent years, telephone calls have become a popular way of communicating with outside. In a closed prison, the prisoner may call for at least five minutes per week; in more open conditions, the opportunities are greater, and in many prisons telephone cards are available.

In the context of preparing inmates for their release, visits *to* relatives and partners are very important. In open prisons, it is part of the regime for inmates to spend their weekends at home. In closed prisons, leave can be awarded under certain circumstances.

Infringement of Rights and Complaints

A prisoner is allowed to complain about the infringement, by or on the authority of the governor, of a right derived from the rules prevailing in the institution. Rules may be laid down in, for example, international treaties (e.g. the right to humane treatment), the Constitution (right of privacy), national laws (right of resocialization), rules drawn up by the Ministry of Justice, internal rules made by the governor, or even unwritten customs within the particular institution. But many rules are so vague that it is almost impossible to derive a right from them. As Kelk points out, many rights are formulated very cautiously or conditionally, for example, a prisoner has the right to *state* which spiritual adviser or chaplain attached to the prison he or she would like to contact.[5] If the governor does not permit the prisoner to meet the chaplain of his or her choice, it is difficult to say that such refusal has violated the prisoner's right. Nonetheless, the Appeal Committee has given a broad interpretation to 'infringement of a right'. A very important criterion for the Committee is the *care* taken by the governor in reaching the decision. For example, in this particular context, did the governor give the prisoner an opportunity to explain the reasons for his or her choice, and did the governor take account of the prisoner's interests?

The Complaints Committee can revise a decision of the governor where, according to section 57(1)(b) of the Principles Act, it 'should be deemed unreasonable or unjust weighing all interests at stake, and all the circumstances'. For a complaint to be admissible it must relate to a decision taken by or on the authority of the governor. This is widely interpreted as well. For example, if an officer injured an aggressive prisoner and transferred him to an isolation cell, and the governor supported the officer's report of the incident, such support would be viewed as a positive decision of the governor.

Complaints about inadequate provision of medical care or facilities are admissible, since these are the responsibility of the governor. However, clinical decisions about medical treatment are outside the governor's jurisdiction, and hence a complaint about these is not admissible, as can be demonstrated by reference to the way drug users are dealt with.

[5] Kelk, 'The Netherlands', 412.

Drug Use and Prisoners' Rights

In most houses of detention, methadone is supplied to drug-dependent prisoners for a period of about ten days. This is considered as medical treatment and therefore is within the competence of the medical officer. The policy is not the same in each institution. If, say, a prisoner who received methadone in one institution is denied it in another to which he is moved, a complaint would not be admissible. By contrast, some houses of detention have developed 'drug-free units' which offer treatment facilities (but no methadone) with the assistance of specialized organizations from outside, which operate in the prison. These are wings for twelve to twenty-four prisoners. Prisoners can only join such units having signed a contract accepting that their urine will be tested for drugs and that their bodies and clothes will be searched after visits. A prisoner who is not placed in a unit can complain about this, since it is the governor who determines placements.

Role of International Law

The Complaints Committee, Appeal Committee, and the civil courts and national ombudsman may all base their rulings on international obligations contained in treaties. For example, when an inmate appealed to the Appeal Committee of the Central Council for the Enforcement of Criminal Law about limited visiting facilities in a house of detention, the Appeal Committee dismissed the appeal on the basis that the limitations were not in violation of Article 17 of the International Covenant on Civil and Political Rights (right to privacy). In another case, it ruled that limited time for visits was not in breach of Article 8 of the European Convention on Human Rights, which guarantees a person's right to respect for his private or family life.[6] In other cases, prisoners have been more successful. For example it has been held by the Appeal Committee that refusing permission to consult one's own doctor is a breach of Article 8, as is the examination by a governor of the criminal record of a prisoner without his consent.

As a result of this application of international treaty provisions by domestic bodies in the Netherlands, prisoners seldom need to take their complaints to the European Commission, in contrast to the position in the United Kingdom. From 1987 to 1992, only one inmate had lodged such a complaint.[7]

Prisoners may not complain under the internal procedures about a decision taken by the Ministry of Justice, nor about the validity of regulations. In such cases, proceedings in the civil courts may be used as an

---

[6] C. Kelk, *Kort begrip van het detentierecht*, Ars Aequi Libri, Nijmegen (1993), 110.
[7] *Asma v. The Netherlands*, 14 April 1989.

alternative, as where female prisoners, paid lower wages than male inmates, successfully brought an action against the prison authorities. Similarly, a prisoners' association refused facilities for a meeting inside a prison took proceedings in the courts, relying, *inter alia*, upon Article 11 of the European Convention on Human Rights. The Supreme Court recognized that prisoners have a right to freedom of association, but also ruled that a governor may refuse the facilities to implement this right when order and safety within the institution are endangered.[8]

ENGLAND AND WALES

The Prison Population

The number of prisoners in England and Wales[9] was around 46,000 in 1992. This figure has held roughly steady for the past five years, although it is now predicted to rise due to harsher sentencing and bail policies introduced by the Government in response to political pressure from its supporters.[10] The prison rate for England and Wales was 96 per 100,000 population in 1989, and the United Kingdom as a whole had a higher prison population, both in absolute numbers and in relation to overall population, than any other member state of the Council of Europe. About 20 per cent of prisoners are awaiting trial or sentence, but many of these are held in police or court cells because places in prison cannot be found for them.[11] The average length of sentence for adult male indictable offenders was 16·9 months in 1990. The bulk of prisoners are sentenced by the Crown Court, and the average length of sentence for such prisoners was 20·5 months, compared with 2·6 months for prisoners sentenced in the magistrates' courts. At the other extreme, nearly 3,000 prisoners are serving life sentences in England and Wales. The size of prisons varies quite widely, with some holding around 200 inmates, and others containing over 1,000. While the system as a whole was only 1 per cent overcrowded in 1992, overcrowding is very much a problem of local prisons, which were 30 per cent overcrowded, with eleven of these holding over 50 per cent more prisoners than they officially had space for. Exactly the same proportion of prisoners are women as in the Netherlands—3·5 per cent, and here too, there was a rapid increase in numbers from about 1977 to 1987. However, a far lower proportion of prisoners are from the ethnic minority groups, with a significant difference between male and female prisoners. While 16 per cent of male prisoners were known to be from the ethnic minorities in

---

[8] HR 25 June 1982, [1983] AB 37.
[9] All statistics are taken from NACRO Briefing Papers 1991/1992, NACRO, London.
[10] See *Guardian*, 6, 7 and 13 October 1993.
[11] The number declined from 1,440 on 16 Dec. 1991 to 287 on 31 Dec. 1992.

1990, 28 per cent of female prisoners were from these ethnic groups. The higher proportion is due to the numbers serving sentences for drug trafficking. One third of the women are drug couriers from abroad, and 9 per cent of women prisoners are drugs offenders, compared with 4 per cent of men. About 2,000–3,000 inmates are reported as having some degree of drug dependence by medical officers at the time of their reception into prison.[12]

The Prison System

Prisons and prisoners are governed by the Prison Act 1952, the Prison Rules made as delegated legislation under the authority of this Act, and by internal standing orders and circular instructions—directions on detailed policy and implementation of policy issued by the Prison Service. The constitutional position of the Prison Service changed on 1 April 1993, when it became a Government Agency rather than a department of the Home Office.[13] The effect is to render government ministers only indirectly accountable for the actions of the Prison Service, which is headed by a chief executive (who is still, however, known as its Director-General). The running of some prisons has also been put out to tender by private security firms.[14] However, the position of prisoners is not *directly* affected by these changes. There are general provisions concerning accommodation, exercise, work, education, and leisure facilities in the Act and Rules, but these are not guaranteed to prisoners who, as we discuss below, have limited methods of seeking to enforce them. It remains far from uncommon for prisoners in local prisons to spend virtually all of their time locked together in their cells, with no work available, and limited opportunities for association. In 1992, over 9,000 prisoners were held two to a cell designed for one, and over 1,000 were held three to such a cell. The Woolf Inquiry recommended that the Dutch requirement of single cell occupancy should be domestic policy,[15] and while the trend in the Netherlands might be towards considering the possibility of dormitory or two-person accommodation, the aim in England and Wales is to move the other way.

Prisons are divided into various categories, depending upon their function and security classification. Remand centres hold persons remanded for trial or sentence. Local prisons, situated in the cities, take remand prisoners, those serving short sentences, and those who have been sentenced and

---

[12] Woolf Report, para. 12.339.

[13] See the draft Framework Document for the Prison Service, 1992.

[14] The power to contract out, or 'market test' the running of prisons is contained in the Criminal Justice Act 1991, s. 84. The first prison to be privately run was The Wolds Remand Prison, Humberside. For a valuable discussion of this issue, see S. Livingstone and T. Owen, *Prison Law: Text and Materials* (Oxford; Oxford University Press 1993), 24–8.

[15] Para. 11.90. The White Paper, *Custody, Care and Justice: The Way Ahead for the Prison Service in England and Wales,* Cm 1647 (1991) accepts that prisoners should not usually be required to share cells: para. 6.11.

are awaiting allocation to other prisons. Prisoners serving longer sentences will be sent to training prisons. Prisons and prisoners are also given a security classification, basically divided into four categories, with Category A—highest security risk—down to D, who are suitable for open conditions. Those requiring Category A security are not all concentrated in one or two very high security institutions, but are sent to a number of training prisons designated as 'dispersal prisons', where Category B prisoners are also kept. Security precautions are heightened in these prisons to cater for the Category A inmates, thus subjecting prisoners who are not deemed dangerous to a level of unnecessary security.[16]

Rule 1 of the Prison Rules states that

The purpose of the training and treatment of convicted prisoners shall be to encourage and assist them to lead a good and useful life.

As in the Netherlands, it has been recognized that this is no more than an aspiration. It has been supplemented by a 'statement of purpose' or 'mission statement'. This states that

Her Majesty's Prison Service serves the public by keeping in custody those committed by the courts.
  Our duty is to look after them with humanity and to help them lead law abiding and useful lives in custody and after release.

The Woolf Inquiry shifted attention away from resocialization to viewing the prison system as an aspect of the criminal justice system. It therefore suggested that the Prison Service should be regarded as having a special responsibility for maintaining law, order, and justice in society, to be furthered by co-ordinating its activities with other sections of the criminal justice system. It further argued that, as a part of a criminal *justice* system, the prison system must stress the importance of treating the prisoner with justice. Deterrence from (or encouragement against) reoffending became merely the third of Woolf's suggested objectives for the Prison Service.[17]

Imprisonment as Punishment

The guiding principle concerning the recognition of prisoners' rights in English law was set out by Lord Wilberforce in *Raymond* v. *Honey*:[18]

---

[16] This is a policy which has long been criticized—see Vivien Stern (2nd edn., London; Penguin 1989), 214–6.
[17] Woolf Report, 240–2. The White Paper accepted this order of priority—see Chap. 1, but the Home Secretary reversed it at the Conservative Party Conference in October 1993, leading to an unprecedented public disagreement between him and Lord Woolf, by then a judge in the House of Lords, on penal policy. See the *Guardian*, 13 October 1993.
[18] [1983] 1 AC 1. The principle was accepted by the Government in its White Paper (above), Introduction, para. 16, in the context of the Citizen's Charter, Cm 1599 (1991).

Under English law a convicted prisoner, in spite of his imprisonment, retains all civil rights which are not taken away expressly or by necessary implication.

However, even if one identifies a 'right' vesting in the prisoner, it is not always obvious how that right may be vindicated, and the English courts have not been generous to prisoners in accepting that they may need such vindication.[19]

Prisoners' Rights and Complaints Procedures

The complaints procedure[20] lays down a hierarchical structure whereby the prisoner approaches the wing, landing, or personal officer first, on an informal basis, and then complains higher up within the service, to the governor, board of visitors, and Prison Service headquarters. The board[21] is a group of people, appointed by, but independent of, the Prison Service, whose role is to act as watchdog of what goes on in prisons, and which may be approached by prisoners with specific or general grievances about what is happening to them. Although it is made clear to the prisoner that he or she may also write to someone outside the prison to complain, this hierarchical procedure could have the effect of delaying a resolution of the grievance. Woolf recommended that boards should not expect prisoners to have gone to the governor first before approaching them, as no fetter should be placed on their becoming involved in a case. Woolf also proposed[22] the creation of an independent 'complaints adjudicator' to sit at the top of the grievance procedure hierarchy. This person would not be able to receive complaints at an earlier stage, contradicting the point Woolf made in relation to the importance of boards not being fettered from taking action.[23] It is regrettable that the Government regarded this model as the way forward in its White Paper and later Consultation Paper.[24] As an alternative administrative remedial mechanism, the Parliamentary Commissioner for Administration—the Ombudsman—has jurisdiction to entertain complaints of 'maladministration' from prisoners, but a lack of power to enforce his recommendations renders them of little impact.[25]

---

[19] See A. J. Fowles, *Prisoners' Rights in England and the United States* (Aldershot; Avebury 1989), 41.

[20] Introduced in 1990 after a Report of the Chief Inspector, *A Review of Prisoners' Complaints* (Home Office 1987), and an internal Prison Department working group review.

[21] See Justice, Howard League and NACRO, *Boards of Visitors of Penal Institutions* (Chichester; Barry Rose 1975); Justice, *Justice in Prison* (London; Justice 1983).

[22] *Woolf Report*, paras. 14.342–14.362.

[23] *Woolf Report*, paras. 14.352, 14.356.

[24] *Custody, Care and Justice: The Way Ahead for the Prison Service in England and Wales*, Cm 1647 (1991), para. 8.10; HM Prison Service, *An Independent Complaints Adjudicator for Prisons*, March 1992. Now known as the Prisons Ombudsman and operational from the end of 1994.

[25] See G. Douglas, 'Dealing with Prisoners' Grievances' (1984) 24 *Brit. J. Criminol.* 150.

(Prisoners may also complain to their MPs, who can sometimes help them obtain redress.)

It was therefore important to persuade the courts to accept jurisdiction over what happens in prison, to enable prisoners to find an independent and effective channel of complaint. Although prisoners were given the right to litigate by statute in 1948, they were not permitted to consult a solicitor in respect of any legal proceedings they wished to commence, without the leave of the Home Secretary. This rule was declared contrary to Article 6 of the European Convention in the *Golder* case on the basis that this Article guarantees a right of access to the courts, which could not be exercised if a person was denied access to legal advice in order to decide whether to take legal proceedings.

While prisoners continued to take cases to Strasbourg after *Golder*, they also made greater use of the English courts to obtain a ruling on unimpeded access, which was finally conceded in *Raymond* v. *Honey* and *R.* v. *Secretary of State for the Home Department, ex parte Anderson.*[26]

Even if the courts now accept their jurisdiction over prisoners' complaints, they have consistently held[27] that the Prison Rules do not confer on a prisoner a cause of action for breach of statutory duty in tort. The only ways a prisoner may challenge in court what happens to him or her during imprisonment are through a claim in tort alleging negligence, or by seeking judicial review of the decision about which he or she is complaining. The English courts could never take the kind of action seen in the United States, where entire prison systems have been declared unconstitutional and, more significantly, the court itself has supervised reform to make the system comply with the Constitution.[28]

Complaints about the Disciplinary System

The disciplinary system involves a detailed set of regulations, laying down twenty-two offences.[29] These range from offences which could also be charged in the criminal courts, such as assault; to offences 'related to infringements of the institutional life of a prison',[30] such as being disrespectful to an officer; to catch-all offences designed to mop up any other behaviour which could conceivably, or inconceivably, be construed as detrimental to the running of the prison—especially the charge of 'in any way

---

[26] [1984] QB 778.
[27] *Arbon* v. *Anderson* [1943] 1 KB 154; *Hague* v. *Deputy Governor of Parkhurst Prison, Weldon* v. *Home Office* [1991] 3 All ER 733.
[28] See Fowles, *Prisoners' Rights*, chap. 7.
[29] Prison Rules 1964, SI 1964 No. 388, r.47, as amended by the Prison (Amendment) Rules 1989, SI 1989 No. 330.
[30] Woolf, para. 14.374.

[offending] against good order and discipline'.[31] Contrary to the Dutch approach, which, as we outlined above, contains no list of specific offences, such comprehensive provisions are regarded as highly undesirable, and Woolf agreed with guidance by Prison Service headquarters, which advised governors to lay specific charges wherever possible instead.[32]

Punishments for disciplinary offences range from adding up to twenty-eight days to the sentence, under the Criminal Justice Act 1991, section 42, to forfeiture of privileges, exclusion from associated work, or loss of pay, to cellular confinement for up to three days.[33]

Disciplinary charges are dealt with by the prison governor or, if grave, dealt with as offences and tried by the courts.[34] It had long been argued that the previous system whereby boards of visitors heard serious disciplinary charges undermined their watchdog role, and the Prior Committee which reviewed the prison disciplinary system recommended that they should lose this function.[35] Prisoners dissatisfied with the adjudication or penalty awarded in disciplinary proceedings can 'appeal' by using the normal internal complaints procedure described above. However, Woolf envisaged using the proposed 'complaints adjudicator' as a final point of appeal from governors' adjudications, thus reintroducing the confusion of function between grievance mechanism and disciplinary body which underlay the original criticism levelled at the role of boards of visitors.[36] The Government accepted this proposal.[37]

Prisoners dissatisfied with internal avenues of appeal have had a measure of success by resorting to the courts.[38] It was first accepted[39] that the decisions of boards of visitors were amenable to judicial review and could therefore be quashed if arrived at in breach of the rules of natural justice. The next step was to determine whether the mass of disciplinary hearings conducted by the governor are similarly challengeable. Megaw and Waller L JJ, in *ex parte St Germain*, had considered that a distinction could be drawn between the board and the governor, the latter being more like a

---

[31] Among the charges the Prior Committee on the Prison Disciplinary System found had been made under this provision were 'putting too many toys into model snowmen in workshop' (Cmnd 9641, Vol. 2, App. 4, Annex B, 37), 'playing a ball game', 'standing at cell door talking', and 'causing officer to lose count of roll check' (Vol. 2, App. 20, 154).

[32] Woolf Report, para. 14.375.

[33] While the board of visitors retains its disciplinary role, it can sanction up to 120 days' loss of remission, and up to 56 days' cellular confinement.

[34] From 1 April 1992.   [35] At para. 5.53.

[36] Woolf, however, considered that, by the final appeal stage, there is little difference as far as the prisoner is concerned, between a disciplinary mechanism and a grievance mechanism: see para. 14.424.

[37] White Paper, para. 8.8.; Woolf Report, paras. 14.398–14.435; see also R. Morgan and H. Jones, 'Prison Discipline: The Case for Implementing *Woolf*' (1991) 31 Brit. J. Criminol. 280.

[38] See the discussion by G. Treverton-Jones, *Imprisonment: The Legal Status and Rights of Prisoners* (London; Sweet and Maxwell 1989), chap. 7.

[39] R. v. *Hull Prison Board of Visitors, ex parte St Germain* [1979] 1 All ER 701.

military commander or head teacher of a school. The issue was resolved by the House of Lords in *Leech* v. *Deputy Governor of Parkhurst Prison*.[40] Lord Bridge pointed out that the prison authorities had been compelled to turn the arguments presented in *ex parte St Germain* on their heads. There, they had argued that the functions of boards and governors in adjudicating on disciplinary offences, were indistinguishable and:

that the last defensible bastion to prevent a disastrous intrusion by the courts into the management of prisons could only be held by refusing jurisdiction to review boards of visitors' decisions . . .

Now, they were arguing that:

the system of internal prison discipline, having survived and even benefited from judicial review of decisions of boards of visitors, would nevertheless be totally undermined if the court once crossed the threshold of the governor's province beyond which it could not stop short of accepting responsibility for every facet of prison management.[41]

The courts also accepted[42] that a board of visitors hearing a disciplinary charge had a discretion to permit a prisoner to be legally represented, which should certainly be exercised in the prisoner's favour in the most serious cases. However, Woolf argued that, under the proposed system whereby governors would hear the minor infractions, prisoners should have no *right* of legal representation, considering that, first, boards of visitors would be able to advise and assist a prisoner in such hearings, and secondly, that '*at the discretion of the Governor*'[43] the prisoner should be allowed to bring another prisoner, a lawyer, or (unbelievably) a prison officer.

As in the Netherlands, there is a danger that 'informal' penalties can be used as an alternative to the procedural safeguards provided for disciplinary offences. Prisoners regarded as disruptive may be transferred to other prisons, allocated to 'special units',[44] or placed in segregation under rule 43 of the Prison Rules. The governor may only order this for three days, but the board of visitors (or Secretary of State) may authorize segregation for up to one month, which can be renewed. The prisoner can appeal through the usual channels. Woolf recommended that boards should not involve themselves in such decisions, for the same reason as relates to discipline— that it compromises their independence. However, the Government rejected

---

[40] [1988] AC 533 (see G. Richardson, 'The House of Lords and Prison Discipline' [1988] PL 183).
[41] At 565A–B.
[42] *R.* v. *Secretary of State for the Home Department and others, ex parte Tarrant and another* [1985] QB 251.
[43] Para 14.430, emphasis added. The discretion could also be exercised by the area manager or the complaints adjudicator.
[44] Report of the Control Review Committee, 1989.

this criticism, and sees boards continuing to fulfil this task on the basis that the board is 'best placed to satisfy itself that it is necessary for segregation to continue'.[45]

Complaints about Social Contacts

As regards contact with the outside world, conditions have improved considerably during the last few years. Convicted prisoners may receive two visits every four weeks, lasting at least half an hour at the weekend, and an hour during the week. Unconvicted prisoners may receive daily visits of at least fifteen minutes or, alternatively, three one-hour visits a week. Visitors on low incomes can receive financial help with travel costs. But all visits are supervised, and take place within the sight, though not the hearing, of a prison officer. The routine censorship of mail has stopped, except in dispersal prisons, following the recommendation of the Woolf Inquiry, though governors retain the discretion to read any prisoner's mail for security reasons.[46] Incoming mail is searched for contraband, especially drugs. Cardphones are now available in all prisons. Eligibility for home leave, lasting either two or five days, depends upon the prisoner's security classification and the length of sentence being served. The minimum sentence is eighteen months, for those in open prisons, and three years for those in category B prisons. Leave can be taken once the prisoner has become eligible for early release. Women prisoners at Holloway Prison can enjoy day-long visits from their children, and this experiment may be extended to other prisons (initially for women only). Liberalization of all these facilities has resulted largely from the Woolf Inquiry, with its stress on the importance of family ties, notwithstanding the lip service paid to these by the Prison Service in the past. Most are privileges, rather than enforceable rights.[47] Prisoners have been unable to secure entitlement, either through internal procedures or by using the courts.

The European Convention on Human Rights

The gradual improvements made to the ability of prisoners to enforce entitlements have been due, in no small measure, to their taking their grievances to Strasbourg and invoking the European Convention on Human Rights. Thus, in relation to discipline, while the English courts were finally

[45] White Paper, para. 8.15.
[46] Rule 33(3) of the Prison Rules 1964 was declared *ultra vires* by the Court of Appeal in *R. v. Home Secretary, ex parte Leech*, *The Times*, 20 May 1993 in so far as it applied to reading and stopping confidential correspondence with legal advisers on wider grounds than simply to ascertain that such correspondence was genuine.
[47] Indeed, the Director-General of the Prison Service stressed the 'privilege' status of home leave in announcing a review of the scheme in the wake of complaints about violent prisoners being granted such leave—*Guardian*, 14 August 1993.

accepting their jurisdiction to review procedures to ensure fairness, so too was the European Court finding that the former powers to deprive prisoners of *all* their remission when charged with very grave disciplinary offences, with no legal representation allowed, was a breach of Article 6 which requires a fair and public hearing by an independent and impartial tribunal in respect of any criminal charges.[48]

In relation to controls over prisoners' correspondence, the European Court also found that the restrictions broke Article 8, which guarantees a person's right to respect for his private or family life. Until the *Silver* case,[49] a convicted prisoner was *entitled*, under the Prison Rules and Standing Order 5 (which was unpublished), to send and receive only one letter a week except in special circumstances, and letters were censored.[50] The contents of letters were subject to detailed restriction: most importantly, a prisoner could not complain about treatment or conditions in prison, unless these complaints had been raised internally first.[51] In *Silver*, the European Court, upholding the view of the Commission, held that several of these restrictions were not 'in accordance with the law' nor 'necessary in a democratic society' and infringed a prisoner's right to respect for his or her private and family life under Article 8.[52]

The other area where the European Convention has had an impact is in relation to executive release on parole or licence. The argument that prisoners enjoy privileges, not rights, has been put forward most strongly in relation to such release. Under the old system, replaced in October 1992 by the Criminal Justice Act 1991, a prisoner could obtain remission of half his or her sentence if serving twelve months or less, and one-third if serving more. Such remission could be forfeited for misconduct under the disciplinary rules but, as Treverton-Jones argues,[53] the prisoner would definitely receive remission *unless* it were forfeited, so that, even if regarded as a privilege, the doctrine of legitimate expectation effectively equated it with a right. This view was shared by both the English courts and the European Court.[54] However, the other form of executive release, through parole (or licence, in the case of prisoners sentenced to life imprisonment), was not accepted as reviewable[55] until the European Convention organs forced an important statutory change and they seem also to have prompted a change of attitude in the courts.

---

[48] *Campbell and Fell* (1985) 7 EHRR 165.   [49] (1983) 5 EHRR 347.
[50] Prison Rules 1964, rr. 34(3), (6)–(8), r. 33(1)(3).   [51] See below.
[52] For the continuing need of prisoners to challenge the Prison Service approach to censorship, see *Campbell,* v. *UK, The Times,* 1 April 1992. The ECHR held that the Scottish prison authorities were in breach of Art. 8 in their regular reading of prisoners' correspondence with solicitors, and in their opening of correspondence with the European Commission of Human Rights.
[53] *Imprisonment*, 148.
[54] In *ex parte St Germain*, Waller LJ at 464 and in *Campbell and Fell*.
[55] *Payne,* v. *Lord Harris of Greenwich* [1981] 1 WLR 754; *Re Findlay* [1985] AC 318.

Weeks v. *UK*[56] concerned a prisoner sentenced at the age of 17 to life imprisonment for the robbery of a pet shop armed with a starting pistol loaded with a blank cartridge. He had been released on licence and then recalled after being charged with offences committed whilst on release. The European Court held that a prisoner recalled to prison while on licensed release was entitled, under Article 5(4), to take proceedings whereby the lawfulness of his detention could speedily be decided upon by a court. Although the Parole Board was accepted as being an independent body akin to a court, it was held that the Board's decisions on parole were either advisory only or, where binding on the Home Secretary as in recall cases, procedurally inadequate, because the prisoner was not entitled to full disclosure of the material on which the Board reached its decision. Notwithstanding the Court's ruling, the Government did not change the system. However, in *Thynne, Wilson and Gunnell* v. *UK*,[57] it was again made clear that the requirements of Article 5(4) apply to discretionary life-sentenced prisoners, detained because of their perceived dangerousness beyond the 'tariff' (retributive) part of their sentence. Once that part has expired, continued detention in prison can be justified only by reference to dangerousness and, since this must change over time, the prisoner must be entitled to regular review of his or her continued detention.

In the light of this ruling, new legislation altered the position concerning discretionary life-sentenced prisoners. Section 34 of the Criminal Justice Act 1991[58] applies to persons sentenced to a discretionary life sentence for violent or sexual offences, where the trial judge orders that the section is to apply and specifies the tariff part of the life sentence. Once the tariff has been reached, the prisoner may require the Home Secretary to refer his or her case to the Parole Board. If the Board is satisfied that it is no longer necessary for the protection of the public that the prisoner be confined, it may direct release, with which the Home Secretary must comply. The prisoner is entitled to legally-aided representation, disclosure of evidence, and a reasoned decision. This system is compatible with the European Court's ruling. The problem is that a judge is not *required* to order that section 34 applies to the discretionary life sentence he or she has just passed, and prisoners not so certified could in theory remain outside the procedural protections given.[59] Nor does the section apply to *mandatory* life-sentenced

---

[56] (1988) 10 EHRR 293. See G. Richardson, 'Discretionary Life Sentences and the European Convention on Human Rights' [1991] PL 34.

[57] Series A No. 190 (1990).

[58] See M. Wasik and R. Taylor, *Blackstone's Guide to the Criminal Justice Act 1991* (London; Blackstone 1991).

[59] P. Ashworth, 'Release of discretionary lifers' [1991] NLJ 1085. But see 'Practice Note: Imposition of Discretionary Life Sentences', [1993] 1 All ER 747, where the Lord Chief Justice directed that s. 34 should be used except 'in the very exceptional case where the judge considers that the offence is so serious that detention for life is justified by the seriousness of the offence alone, irrespective of the risk to the public. In such a case, the judge should state this in open court when passing sentence'.

prisoners. The rationale for this distinction is that, in a mandatory life sentence, the *whole* of the sentence reflects the retributive aim, but a tariff period is set for such cases as well, and it is difficult to justify treating prisoners differently depending upon whether their life sentence was imposed by law, or at judicial discretion. Indeed, it could be argued that it is precisely where sentence is fixed by law that a prisoner should know what tariff has been set, because there are no determinate sentences with which to compare the individual case.[60]

It seems likely that, despite some hiccups, the European Convention will force the government to make further changes in opening up the system to effective challenge. Although the European Commission dismissed a complaint in 1988 of a prisoner serving a mandatory life sentence for murder, distinguishing the *Weeks* decision on the ground critized above,[61] more recently it ruled a similar complaint admissible. It rejected the argument that a prisoner might be required to be detained to maintain public confidence in the criminal justice system and that only the Home Secretary, as an elected person, could judge such confidence. The case was referred to the European Court, which interestingly rejected the complaint unanimously,[62] at the same time as the English courts have begun to voice strong criticism of the current system for mandatory lifers.[63]

But outside these areas of prison life, both the domestic courts and the European Convention organs have had little to say. In particular, complaints about the physical conditions in which a prisoner is being held have not succeeded. The House of Lords in *Hague and Weldon* held that a prisoner may not allege wrongful imprisonment if confined unlawfully to a more restricted regime, such as segregation under rule 43 (removal from association for the maintenance of good order or discipline). Lord Jauncey, with whom the other Lords agreed, argued that a prisoner's:

whole life is regulated by the regime. He has no freedom to do what he wants, when he wants. His liberty to do anything is governed by the prison regime. Placing Weldon in a strip cell and segregating Hague altered the conditions under which they were detained but did not deprive them of any liberty which they had not already lost when initially confined.[64]

[60] An argument implicitly recognized by the Court of Appeal in *R.* v. *Secretary of State for the Home Department, ex parte Doody*, [1993] 1 All ER 151, where it was held that a mandatory lifer is entitled to know the tariff period recommended by the judiciary to the Home Secretary to apply before a release on licence should be sanctioned.

[61] *Bamber* v. *UK*, 59 D. & R. 325.

[62] *Wynne* v. *UK*, judgment of 18 July 1994.

[63] *R.* v. *Secretary of State for the Home Department, ex parte Creamer and Scholey, The Independent*, 23 Oct. 1992. See also *R.* v. *Home Secretary and the Parole Board, ex parte Prem Singh, The Times*, 27 April 1993 (prisoner sentenced to be detained at Her Majesty's Pleasure—equivalent of life sentence for juvenile offender—entitled to see material on which Parole Board ordered his recall after he had already completed 'tariff' part of his sentence).

[64] At 755j.

This seems scarcely compatible with the House's view, in *Raymond* v. *Honey*, that the prisoner retains all rights not expressly or necessarily taken away. His lordship reiterated the availability of remedies in negligence,[65] or public law. A prisoner who suffered injury to his or her health as a result of intolerable conditions could, according to the House, sue in negligence. But the tenor of his remarks suggests a retreat from the bolder approach of the House in *Raymond* v. *Honey*, and a view of prisoners as being at the mercy of the prison authorities who must be left free to govern without constant interference from the judiciary.[66] The European Commission and Court have been as unwilling as the English courts to get trapped in the quagmire of managerial and resource issues, thus leaving it to industrial action, direct action, or official inquiries to point out the unacceptable conditions in which many prisoners are forced to live.[67]

THE IMPACT OF EUROPE ON THE RECOGNITION OF PRISONERS' RIGHTS

While the European Convention provides an enforceable standard by which to measure certain aspects of imprisonment in England and Wales, and which, when invoked, may eventually prompt change, the impact of Europe on how imprisonment is assessed in England and Wales is arguably greater than this. European approaches to imprisonment are the yardstick against which the English system is found wanting.[68] (Even the rioters at Strangeways in 1990 held up a banner stating 'Europe treats prisoners with respect! Why can't British bureaucracy do the same, that's all!!'.)

The Council of Europe's Standard Minimum Rules for the Treatment of Prisoners, which were superseded by the European Prison Rules in 1987, intended as guidelines for the European Convention organs and for national

---

[65] But carelessness by the prison authorities in losing control of confidential information which resulted in a prisoner having to be segregated under r.43 for his own protection was held not to be actionable in negligence by the Court of Appeal in *H* v. *Home Office, The Times*, 7 May 1992. Only if conditions in segregation are 'intolerable' or the prisoner can show malice on the part of the authorities will an action in tort lie in respect of segregation.

[66] For a similar view, see C. Gearty, 'The prisons and the courts' in J. Muncie and R. Sparks, *Imprisonment: European Perspectives* (Hemel Hempstead; Harvester Wheatsheaf 1991). Unfortunately, Gearty's optimism that the courts would emulate the activism of the American judiciary was proved shortlived by the ruling of the House of Lords in *Hague and Weldon*, above.

[67] The Government states that it is committed to raising standards in prisons by, *inter alia*, setting a code of standards, but such a code will not be directly enforceable by prisoners: see 'A code of standards for the Prison Service', discussion document produced by the Code of Standards Steering Group of the Prison Service, March 1992.

[68] See, e.g. NACRO briefings; V. Stern, *Bricks of Shame* (2nd edn., London; Penguin 1989) *passim*; D. Downes, *Contrasts in Tolerance* (Oxford; Oxford University Press 1988)—but note critique by H. Franke, 'Dutch Tolerance: Facts and Fables' (1990) 30 Brit. J. Criminol. 81.

administrations[69] and courts, serve as aspirational standards which seem far away from attainment,[70] as was graphically demonstrated in December 1991. The European Committee for the Prevention of Torture and Inhuman or Degrading Treatment or Punishment found that the cumulative effects of overcrowding, lack of integral sanitation, and the absence of out-of-cell activities in British prisons amount to inhuman and degrading treatment. This was the first occasion when the Committee had made such a finding in relation to a prison system, and it was also the first time a body from outside England and Wales had publicly adjudged prison *conditions* to be, in effect, a breach of Article 3 of the European Convention. We noted above that the English courts and Strasbourg have generally avoided condemning prison conditions. A prisoner relying on the Committee's report, in a complaint to Strasbourg, ought now to expect success, although a remedy will still be wanting at home.

In the Netherlands, the European Convention has directly influenced decisions by the Appeal Committee and the courts. It was, for example, significant or even decisive in decisions on rights of assembly and freedom of expression, although it does not follow that prisoners' complaints have therefore always been upheld. However, foreign prisoners must be given the opportunity to meet others at a remand centre.[71] On the other hand, a claim by prisoners that Article 10 guarantees a right to contact the press was not upheld, although the complaint eventually led to new Ministry rules on contacts between individual prisoners and the media.[72]

As we have seen, Dutch prisoners rarely appeal directly to the European Commission or European Court. But this is not to say that decisions by the European Court have no significance in the field of prisoners' rights. They have, in relation to both substantive and procedural law.[73] Prison disciplinary rules, for example, are governed by the principles of Article 6—the right to a fair hearing—where disciplinary action can, to all intents and purposes, be regarded as criminal proceedings,[74] for example, where a prisoner is placed in isolation because of violence against a prison officer, or having been found in possession of drugs.

---

[69] The Government proposed a code of standards on the provision of services to prisoners, in its White Paper, *Custody, Care and Justice: The Way Ahead for the Prison Service in England and Wales*, above, but did no more than pay lip-service to the European Prison Rules in so doing: see para. 6.14.

[70] See J. Plotnikoff, *Prison Rules: A Working Guide* (London; Prison Reform Trust 1988) and S. Casale and J. Plotnikoff, *Minimum Standards in Prisons: A Programme of Change* (London; NACRO 1989). For a more optimistic evaluation of the potential of the Rules to prompt change, see K. Neale, 'The European Prison Rules: Contextual, Philosophical and Practical Aspects' in Muncie and Sparks, n. 66 above.

[71] BC, 27 December 1984, Series A No. 161, [1985] *Penitentiaire Informatie*, 22.

[72] 14 April 1985, App. 1218/84, [1985] *Penitentiaire Informatie*, 55.

[73] C. Kelk, *Kort begrip van het detentierecht*, 105.	[74] *Campbell and Fell*, above.

CONCLUSIONS

From very different starting-points, the prison systems in England and Wales and the Netherlands are in some ways moving closer together as they wrestle with the common problems of increasing numbers of prisoners, frequently serving longer sentences for serious offences; increasing calls to get tough with crime, and increasing racism and drug abuse within the prisons.

The Dutch system has not been faced with the external scrutiny and criticism to which the English system is regularly subject. This is no doubt due first and foremost to the fact that the Dutch system has been a much more civilized one than the English, and prisoners have had less to complain about. Secondly, a willingness and ability at the national level to ensure conformity of rules and decisions with international obligations such as those under the European Convention on Human Rights have obviated the need for prisoners to go to Strasbourg to seek redress. Thirdly, confidence in the merits of one's own system enables ideas for reform to be developed without constant reference to what is happening elsewhere, although it can also lead to an unwillingness to contemplate that someone else might have some answers too.

The English prison system has had no such luxuries. It has faced a barrage of criticism, and a succession of 'crises' for over a decade, with riots and industrial action punctuated by official inquiries into their causes. Throughout this time, prisoners have used the domestic courts and the European Convention organs to seek individual remedies while government and commentators have pondered how the system itself could be improved. Failure to take on board within domestic law the obligations of the European Convention has resulted in much greater international publicity of the failure of the prison system to safeguard prisoners' human rights, but progress has been slow where questions of resources and conditions are concerned. For the meantime, prisoners, prison staff, and prison reformers in England and Wales continue to look longingly across the Channel to what, from this distance and through the mist, appears a much more successful approach to imprisonment as a penal measure at the end of the twentieth century.

18

The Transfer of Prisoners with Special Reference to The Netherlands and the UK

DÉSIRÉE PARIDAENS AND CHRISTOPHER HARDING

INTRODUCTION

One significant aspect of the 'Europeanization'—or, better perhaps, 'internationalization'—of national penal law relates to the possibility in recent years of the movement of convicted prisoners from one country to another in order to complete their sentences. But while this represents an important development in international co-operation in the penal field, the attempts to establish the necessary mechanisms for transfer of sentences have also made clear some of the differences in penal policy between certain countries. A study of the implementation of a policy of prisoner transfers by the Netherlands and Britain is especially interesting in this respect in bringing to light differing assumptions about the role of the penal system and varying attitudes towards the purpose of international co-operation.

The underlying problem centres around the increasing number of foreign offenders dealt with in many countries, as a result of the greater international mobility of individuals, for purposes of work, leisure, or other activities. A measure of the problem is the number of foreign nationals held in a particular country's prisons. For some time this number of foreign prisoners has been considered sufficiently large to cause general concern, which in turn has led to efforts to set up procedures for the repatriation of such prisoners. However, it is difficult to gain an exact idea of the numbers involved or to draw comparisons between different countries. Such statistics as exist are bedevilled by inconsistent definitions and categorizations. 'Foreign prisoner' may not mean simply 'foreign national' but may include any person 'born overseas'.[1] Similarly, 'held in prison' may not just mean sentenced prisoners but could include those held on remand or otherwise detained (for instance, pending deportation), although it is the sentenced prisoner who is the subject of prisoner transfer schemes. Figures are collected for Council of Europe countries and North America,

---

[1] See e.g. European Committee on Crime Problems, *Report of the Select Committee of Experts on Foreign Nationals in Prisons*, 26 September 1979, PC–R–DE (79) 1, 5–6.

but are essentially diplomatic or consular estimates for most other countries. Perhaps the problem of data collection is best summed up by asking:
are we interested in the total number of foreign prisoners or (as one British report put the matter) 'those belonging to another country to which
they might wish, or could reasonably be expected, to return when free to
do so'?[2] Put another way, it may be asked whether the relevant concept is
one of 'foreign nationality' or 'repatriability', especially in view of the fact
that no country is seriously going to contemplate the transfer of a person
held in prison for only a short period. It could also be asked whether
simple population counts of 'foreign prisoners', however defined, are the
best measure of the problem. Since length of stay will also contribute to
what is perceived as the difficult position of the foreign prisoner, daily
average populations for a given period may be a better indication of what
needs to be done.

However, for what it is worth, it has been asserted that the problem is
greater for continental European countries than for the UK. In 1980 a
figure of around 500, about 1·2 per cent of a total daily average prison
population of about 42,000 in England and Wales,[3] was given as a number
who may wish to be repatriated from the UK.[4] A more realistic figure for
repatriation (because it would be legally feasible) is perhaps provided by
the 1983 estimate that there were some 200 nationals of other Council of
Europe states, the USA, and Canada serving sentences of imprisonment in
British prisons.[5] According to the same source, there were some 150 British nationals alone in the prisons of those other countries.[6] Figures for the
Netherlands provide some measure of the difference. In 1979 there were
1,368 convicted foreign prisoners in Dutch prisons, constituting about 20
per cent of the prison population in the Netherlands; the statistics for 1989
show a total of 1,648 foreign prisoners (though not all these were convicted), just over 25 per cent of the total.[7] It has been suggested that the
lower number of foreign prisoners in the British system may be related to
stricter immigration control into the UK, a smaller number of foreign
migrant workers and a policy of deporting less serious offenders.[8] On the

[2] Home Office, *Report of the Interdepartmental Working Party on the Repatriation of Prisoners*, London; HMSO 1980, point 10.
[3] For the UK prison statistics are given separately for England and Wales, Scotland, and Northern Ireland. The figures for England and Wales are quantitatively the most significant and so are often referred to in comparative discussion.
[4] Cf. the figures given by the European Committee on Crime Problems, note 1 above, which could include immigrant prisoners.
[5] Parliamentary Debates, House of Lords (HL), 1983–4, Vol. 446, col. 765.
[6] Ibid.
[7] Netherlands Parliamentary Debates 83/84, 18 129, no. 3, 55 (for the 1979 figures); *The Population of Penitentiary Institutions in 1989*, Netherlands Central Bureau of Statistics 1991, *Recht en statistiek*, no. 9 (for the 1989 figures).
[8] Interdepartmental Working Party, n. 2 above, at point 10.

other hand, an increasing number of European Union nationals in British prisons should perhaps be expected. Nonetheless, the figures, though relatively unreliable and difficult to compare, present a bold contrast: in terms of numbers, the foreign prison population is considerably more significant in the Netherlands.

In relation to foreign prisoners there are two main arguments in favour of repatriating them to their own countries to complete their sentences. First, arguments based on the 'rehabilitation' or 'social resettlement' of offenders may be used to support the implementation of prison sentences in the foreign prisoner's own country. Secondly, there are humanitarian arguments which focus upon the foreign prisoner's estrangement—arising from communication difficulties on account of language barriers, a sense of alienation from the local culture, especially in the confines of a prison, and a heightened feeling of deprivation on account of the absence of family and other close social contacts.[9] These two arguments are to some extent interrelated: rehabilitation and social readjustment are less likely to occur in a context of increased personal deprivation.[10] A subsidiary point is that, for purely administrative reasons, the 'host' prison system may find some advantage in the repatriation of foreign prisoners, since the latter, by their very circumstances, may present special problems of management. Over the last twenty years or so, therefore, a number of states have realized the desirability of effecting a repatriation of foreign prisoners.

PRISONER TRANSFER TREATIES

The movement towards repatriation gained momentum during the 1970s. The USA and Canada were especially active in this field, negotiating their own bilateral treaty and starting negotiations with other countries. Two conferences—one of Commonwealth Law Ministers in 1977, and the other of Council of Europe Ministers of Justice in 1978—endorsed the principle of repatriation. But although repatriation may be provided for on a bilateral treaty basis, and indeed this may be a necessary way forward in some cases, a multilateral effort on the part of a number of like-minded states with shared penal objectives offers the prospect of a relatively quickly-established network of repatriation procedures.

The Council of Europe had been considering this approach from an

---

[9] See Council of Europe, *Explanatory Report on the Convention on the Transfer of Sentenced Persons* (Strasbourg, 1983), para. 9.

[10] See e.g. the view of the Bishop of Bristol in the UK Parliamentary Debates, n. 5 above, cols. 766–7: 'If the aim of imprisonment is both corrective and remedial then to serve a sentence in a foreign gaol will often reduce the remedial possibilities to a minimum or even eliminate them altogether . . . prisoners in those circumstances inevitably develop an animus against the country in which they are imprisoned.'

early date: most importantly, in 1970 the European Convention on the International Validity of Criminal Judgments[11] was opened for signature. This Convention had been able to draw upon initiatives already taken among the five Nordic countries, who had passed parallel legislation for the enforcement of criminal judgments emanating from each others' systems, and the three Benelux countries, which had already drafted a treaty, signed in 1968, with similar aims. The Convention of 1970 was therefore presented for signature with a fair degree of optimism. In summary, it provided for the enforcement of a penal sanction (deprivation of liberty, fines or confiscation, and disqualification) in a foreign offender's own state, if so requested by the sentencing state. The initiative lay wholly with the sentencing state and the consent of the sentenced person was not required. In the event, only a small number of states became party to the Convention (Austria, Cyprus, Denmark, Iceland, Netherlands, Norway, Sweden, and Turkey) and its impact has been limited. This small number of ratifications, and the fact that the procedure laid down does not enable a speedy transfer of prisoners,[12] has rendered the Convention largely ineffective as a means of prisoner transfer. The muted response to the 1970 Convention prompted the Council of Europe to sponsor another multilateral convention, more specifically concerned with the transfer of prisoners and designed to carry out this transfer in a simple and expeditious fashion.

The resulting 1983 Convention on the Transfer of Sentenced Persons[13] is not restricted to Council of Europe countries—both the United States and Canada participated in its drafting and quickly became parties (see Article 18(1)), and other states may be invited by the Committee of Ministers of the Council of Europe to accede to the Convention (Article 19(1)). However, it is likely to remain an instrument for co-operation between 'like-minded' states. Thailand, for instance, has indicated an unwillingness to enter the Convention network, and the experience of negotiating arrangements with a country such as Thailand reveals the extent of policy differences beyond the North Atlantic region. Canada, the United States, and some European countries have found such negotiations to be difficult and protracted. The different approach to penal policy is illustrated by the Thai insistence at one stage that foreign prisoners should serve a minimum of eight years of their sentence in Thailand before any repatriation may take place.[14] In the case of such countries, therefore, bilateral treaties may have to be negotiated and this may take considerable time and effort.

---

[11] [1970] ILM 445; European Treaty Series, No. 70.

[12] See the Council of Europe's *Explanatory Report*, n. 9 above, at para. 8.

[13] [1983] ILM 530; European Treaty Series No. 112. As of September 1992 there were 20 parties, including Canada, the United States, and Bahamas outside Europe.

[14] Keith Best, 'The Problems of Prisoner Transfer', (1992) 18 *Commonwealth Law Bulletin*, 333 at 335.

THE 1983 CONVENTION

The 1983 Convention provides for the transfer of foreign prisoners at the request of either the sentencing state or that of which the prisoner is a national and to which he will be transferred (the administering state). There is no obligation to accede to the request (and therefore no need, as under the 1970 Convention, to provide any exceptional grounds for refusal). Not only must both states agree to the transfer, but the prisoner must also give his consent. The need for the prisoner's consent (under Article 3(1)(d)) is an important distinguishing feature between the 1970 and 1983 Conventions and reflects the underlying policy aim of rehabilitation. This is unlikely to be achieved if the prisoner is, for whatever reason, unwilling to be repatriated.[15] Furthermore, the offence for which the prisoner has been sentenced must be a crime under the law of the administering state (Article 3(1)(e)). This requirement of double or dual criminality is unsurprising, since there would naturally be a moral reluctance to administer a sanction in respect of conduct not in itself penalized under the law of the offender's own country. However, although the imposition of a penalty in those circumstances would be strange, it will be seen later that the UK has stated its readiness to waive the requirement of dual criminality in certain cases (outside the Convention arrangements), for reasons which reveal a different emphasis in approaching the issue of repatriation.

Certain aspects of the process laid down in the Convention ought to be emphasized. The provision for consent is detailed in Article 7, which requires the sentencing state to ensure that the prisoner's consent is given voluntarily and in full knowledge of the legal consequences of repatriation, and that the administering state should be able to verify the validity of this consent. Although a prisoner cannot himself formally request a transfer to be made, he must be informed of the Convention's applicability to his situation and may communicate an interest to either the sentencing or the administering state in being transferred.

A second aspect of the Convention procedure to be particularly noted concerns the choice given to the administering state in respect of the enforcement of the sanction. Article 9(1) allows the administering state either to *continue* the enforcement of the custodial sanction or to *convert* the sentence (a procedure commonly referred to as '*exequatur*') by substituting a sanction (though not a fine) provided for under its own law. If the sentence is 'continued', the administering state is bound in principle to enforce the sentence decided upon by the other state, but a certain amount of adaptation is possible: for example, the continued enforcement must

---

[15] *Explanatory Report*, n. 9 above, at para. 23.

not exceed the maximum term laid down under the law of the administering state, and the rules of the latter concerning early release will apply (Article 10). 'Conversion' of the sentence, provided for in more detail in Article 11, should take into account the amount of the sentence already completed by the time of transfer and must not aggravate the nature of the sentence. However, this choice of enforcement also means that the sentencing state loses some control over the carrying-out of the sentence and may in some cases then be reluctant to agree to repatriation if it feels that the administering state would opt for conversion to an extent or in circumstances it would not itself so readily approve. Some differences in penal policy certainly remain possible among the Council of Europe states, and this was borne out by an earlier British reluctance to repatriate Dutch offenders in view of the Netherlands' strong preference for conversion (discussed further below).

THE UNITED KINGDOM LAW

As far as the United Kingdom is concerned, enabling legislation, the Repatriation of Prisoners Act, was passed in 1984 and Britain became a party to the 1983 Convention in 1985—an uncharacteristically speedy participation in international penal co-operation for the United Kingdom! This legislation was intended partly to enable Britain to participate in the Convention system of transfers, but also to enter into bilateral treaties with states outside the Convention network. There had been in fact a fair measure of support within the UK for prisoner transfers, as distinct from other forms of co-operation in penal matters—evidenced for instance by strong concern for the plight of British prisoners abroad expressed in Parliamentary debates—and British participation in transfer arrangements had been recommended internally by a report in 1980 from an Interdepartmental Working Party on the Repatriation of Prisoners.[16]

The legal authority for transfers into or from the United Kingdom is laid down in Article 1(1) of the Act, which stipulates three main conditions for the issue of a warrant providing for the transfer of a prisoner. Firstly, the United Kingdom should be party to an international arrangement providing for prisoner transfers, such as the 1983 Convention or a bilateral treaty. Secondly, the authorities of the United Kingdom and the other state concerned must have agreed to the transfer of the particular prisoner (the number of refusals is discussed below). And thirdly, the prisoner must have consented to the transfer. The transfer is in relation to any person

---

[16] UK Parliamentary Debates, House of Lords, 1983–4, vol. 446, col. 762 *et seq.*, especially the speech by Lord Avebury; *Interdepartmental Working Party Report*, n. 2 above.

'required to be detained in a prison, a hospital or any other institution . . . by virtue of an order made in the course of the exercise by a court or tribunal . . . of its criminal jurisdiction' (section 1(7)). 'Prisoner' need not therefore be interpreted literally, and the procedure could apply, for example, to a convicted person detained in a psychiatric hospital in the United Kingdom under a hospital order.

There is no requirement of dual criminality as far as the United Kingdom is concerned. As will be discussed later, this reveals in some respects an important difference in emphasis as between the United Kingdom and other countries engaged in repatriation of prisoners, such as the Netherlands.

DUTCH LAW

Legislation in the Netherlands to give effect to the procedure of the 1983 Convention was later than in Britain, enacted in 1986 and in force at the start of 1988. The late appearance of that legislation, the Act on the Transfer of Enforcement of Criminal Judgments, arises from its more wide-ranging scope, since it deals with the implementation of different kinds of foreign criminal judgments, including non-custodial and non-punitive measures (section 1(1)). In fact, the Act gives effect to a number of international treaties in addition to the 1983 Convention—for example, the Benelux Treaty of 1968 (although this Treaty is not yet in force); the 1970 Convention mentioned above; and also the 1964 European Convention on the Supervision of Conditionally Sentenced or Conditionally Released Offenders. It is therefore in the nature of consolidating legislation.

In so far as the Dutch law is concerned with the transfer of prisoners, certain differences may be noted as between the Dutch and British approaches as laid down in the respective legislation of the two countries. The principle of dual criminality is a basic prerequisite of any Dutch enforcement of a foreign sentence (section 3(1)(c)). Moreover, the Dutch law is explicit in barring the enforcement of a sentence which, in the view of the Dutch authorities, had originally been imposed for reasons of 'race, religion, nationality or political opinions of the sentenced person' (section 5). Under the British legislation this is implicitly a matter within the discretion of the UK authorities and it is conceivable that they would allow such a sentence to be transferred to Britain for 'humanitarian' reasons. The consent of the prisoner to be transferred may or may not be necessary under Dutch law, depending on the treaty basis for the transfer: it will be required if carried out under the 1983 Convention (for instance, if the transfer was to or from Britain), but not if it is under the 1970 Convention (for instance, if the transfer was to or from Norway).

But, most importantly for practical purposes, for any foreign sanction to be implemented *within* the Netherlands, the procedure is different from that used in the UK, since it may require either a court order to give effect to the 'transfer' under Part C of the Act, or at least the court to be consulted before the transfer is made (Article 43(3)). Under the British legislation, on the other hand, a government warrant is used to effect a prisoner's transfer into or from the UK. As was stated in the House of Lords in the debate on the Repatriation of Prisoners Bill, 'the authorization of enforcement in the UK of a sentence imposed in another country is essentially an administrative rather than a judicial function and need not involve the criminal courts'.[17] In the case of a transfer *into* the UK the warrant will authorize 'the detention of the prisoner . . . in accordance with such provisions contained in the warrant, being provisions appearing to the Secretary of State to be appropriate for giving effect to the international arrangements in accordance with which the prisoner is transferred (section 3(1)(c) of the 1984 Act). In short, while Britain provides only for a transfer of custody, the Netherlands provides also for a review of the sentence.

POINTS OF DIVERGENCE

A comparison of the British and Dutch legal provision for the transfer of prisoners reveals—as might be expected—a number of substantive and procedural differences. Space does not permit an exhaustive discussion of these points of difference, but something may be said about those which suggest a significantly different underlying view of the question of prisoner transfers as between the two systems. If such a difference of view does exist, the question then arises how this affects the practical possibility of transfer into or out of both countries.

The Treaty Basis for Prisoner Transfers

The transfer of prisoners into or out of the United Kingdom must be provided for in the first place by a treaty provision.[18] In the debates on the Repatriation of Prisoners Bill, Lord Elton, speaking for the Government, said that 'these arrangements may be a multilateral agreement like the Council of Europe Convention, a bilateral treaty, or an *ad hoc* agreement relating to a particular prisoner or group of prisoners where a permanent agreement is not possible or may not be desirable'.[19] Although up to the present time transfers have only taken place on the basis of the 1983

---

[17] UK Parliamentary Debates, House of Lords, n. 5 above, col. 753.
[18] Repatriation of Prisoners Act, s. 1(1).
[19] UK Parliamentary Debates, House of Lords, n. 5 above, col. 753.

Convention and have therefore been limited to Council of Europe countries and the United States and Canada, the British Government is willing to negotiate bilateral treaties with countries that for some reason cannot accede to the Convention. A bilateral treaty between the UK and Thailand came into force in February 1991 and negotiations have been taking place with both Egypt and Peru for some years;[20] but it may be that in some cases *ad hoc* arrangements will prove to be more feasible than a treaty as such.

The British willingness to conclude bilateral treaties seems to be largely inspired by humanitarian considerations. Although the Interdepartmental Working Party advised in its 1980 report that it would be sensible, at least in the first instance, to deal with countries with a comparable judicial system and standard of justice,[21] doubtful standards of justice in the other country need not prove fatal to transfer negotiations. In this respect, repatriation is viewed differently from extradition since the policy of successive British governments has been to enter into extradition treaties only with those states whose standards of justice and penal administration are acceptable to the UK.[22] But this willingness to discuss repatriation with countries whose standards of justice are in doubt is really confined to the negotiation of bilateral treaties and *ad hoc* arrangements designed primarily to recover British prisoners from intolerable prison conditions abroad; a provision for consent could safeguard prisoners in Britain from repatriation in the other direction. The Interdepartmental Working Party specifically contemplated the conclusion of non-reciprocal *ad hoc* arrangments for this purpose.[23]

On the other hand, the Dutch legislation only requires a treaty basis for the execution of foreign criminal judgments in the Netherlands (section 2). A transfer out of the Netherlands can be made without an international agreement. The principal reason for the treaty basis for transfers into the Netherlands is a requirement of faith in the quality of the legal system of the state of conviction.[24] Here the Dutch approach differs from that of Britain, in being unwilling to execute foreign sentences if fundamental legal principles have been violated in the state of conviction. The Dutch Government had argued that in such circumstances the Netherlands could be held responsible at both a national and an international level—

---

[20] Under the treaty with Thailand, drug offenders in Thai prisons must serve a minimum term of four years before becoming eligible for transfer: see Best, 'The Problems of Prisoner Transfer', n. 14 above, at 334.

[21] Interdepartmental Working Party, n. 2 above, point 79 of Report.

[22] Home Office, *A Review of the Law and Practice of Extradition in the United Kingdom*, Report of an Interdepartmental Working Party, Criminal Justice Department (London, 1982), 5; Interdepartmental Report on Repatriation of Prisoners, point 35.

[23] *Interdepartmental Working Party Report*, n. 2 above, point 35.

[24] Bijl. Hand. II 83/84, 18 129, no. 3, 50. See also (1986) 17 *Netherlands Yearbook of International Law*, 157.

for instance under the European Convention on Human Rights—for the execution of such sentences, even if the transfer had been with the consent of the prisoner.[25] Since a refusal to agree to a repatriation in such a case might prove diplomatically sensitive, it was considered provident to rule it out in the first place by means of a treaty provision. The outcome therefore is that a Dutch national could not be transferred back to the Netherlands from a Thai prison, whereas repatriation from Thailand would be possible for a British prisoner.

It was objected in the Parliamentary debates on the Dutch law that this safeguard would not necessarily be effective in the case of a multilateral treaty. The humanitarian consideration that has swayed the British Government was also strongly put forward, stressing the plight of Dutch prisoners incarcerated abroad under doubtful standards of justice. The Government replied that humanitarian considerations cannot prevail over respect for fundamental legal principles[26] but conceded that *ad hoc* arrangements of limited duration could be considered to deal with this problem.[27] Thus the principle of confidence in the other state's criminal law could be compromised in the context of both multinational and *ad hoc* arrangements.

Double Criminality

According to section 3(c) and (d) of the Dutch legislation a sanction imposed in another state may be executed in the Netherlands only if it was based on a judicial decision in respect of an offence also punishable under Dutch law and where, if convicted, the offender would also have been punished under Dutch law. This principle of double criminality is also laid down under the 1983 Convention. The British Act, however, does not require double criminality, although this was recommended in principle by the Interdepartmental Working Party.[28] In the Parliamentary debates Lord Elton stated that a repatriation may be desirable in the absence of double criminality, for instance in relation to a custodial sentence imposed for an alcohol offence in a Moslem country: 'Given that we should otherwise not be able to get such prisoners back to the United Kingdom, we would need

---

[25] Bijl. Hand. 11 84/85, 18 129, no. 6, 5. The application of the Convention to prisoner transfers was discussed by the European Commission on Human Rights in App. 10487/83, *X* v. *Sweden* (unpublished). The Commission considered that the transfer of a prisoner from a country where close members of his family are living may amount to a breach of Art. 8 of the Convention, which guarantees the right to family life.

[26] See e.g. Bijl. Hand. II 83/84, 18 129, no. 3, 27. See also (1986) 17 *Netherlands Yearbook of International Law*, 158.

[27] Bijl. Hand. 85/86, 18 129, no. 8, 4.

[28] Parliamentary Debates, House of Lords, n. 5 above, col. 759; *Interdepartmental Working Party Report*, n. 2 above, points 50–2.

to be prepared to honour the sentence imposed in such a country, even if the act had not been an imprisonable offence, or a crime at all, in this country.'[29] A number of arguments were put forward to justify this position.[30] Firstly, in practice there would probably be only a small number of cases where either the sentence or the offence would be out of line with the legal position in the UK. Furthermore, the period of detention subsequently served in a British prison would be subject to the English law on early release. These practical points were supplemented by an appeal to humanitarian considerations and finally by pointing also to the safeguard of the prisoner's own consent.

Procedural Questions

In relation to the transfer of a prisoner into the Netherlands, the Dutch law provides for two different procedures: conversion and continued enforcement. Conversion is required when the transfer is based upon the 1970 Convention, whereas the 1983 Convention allows a choice between the two procedures. The Dutch Government has stated that it has a strong preference for using conversion, and in a report submitted to the fifteenth Conference of the European Ministers of Justice in 1986 it was stated by the Dutch delegation that 'states which impose comparatively mild sanctions are justified in not wishing to see this policy disrupted by the need to carry out the decisions of foreign courts and thereby to be confronted by insuperable problems in their prison system'.[31] During the parliamentary debates, the Dutch Government argued that, since prison sentences in the Netherlands were on average shorter than those in other countries, the conversion procedure could diminish such differences or remove them altogether.[32]

The United Kingdom, on the other hand, has declared under Article 3(3) of the 1983 Convention that it intends to exclude the application of the conversion procedure when a prisoner is being repatriated to the UK. The Interdepartmental Working Party had foreseen considerable difficulty in using a power to resentence prisoners repatriated to Britain: 'It would be difficult to provide the courts responsible for resentencing with relevant and adequate evidence to enable a valid sentencing decision to be taken; yet the fact of conviction alone would hardly be sufficient information on which to determine sentence. Both the obtaining of necessary evidence and the process of resentencing itself would be a time-consuming and expensive operation, and it is questionable whether the resources of our criminal justice system should be used for this purpose. In addition, despite

---

[29] Parliamentary Debates, House of Lords, n. 5 above, col. 755.   [30] Ibid.
[31] 1988 *Netherlands Yearbook of International Law*, 298–308.
[32] Bijl. Hand. II 83/84, 18 129, no. 3, 56.

the precedent of the European Convention, the sending state might not be willing to agree to repatriation if its sentence were subject, in effect, to review by the receiving state . . .'.[33] Not only is the United Kingdom unwilling to contemplate the possibility of conversion, but it would also be prepared to enforce longer sentences than would be passed by British sentencers. In the Parliamentary debates, Lord Elton stated that this may be necessary to achieve repatriation from some countries,[34] a position endorsed by Lord Avebury as a lesser of two evils.[35] Therefore the Repatriation of Offenders Act does not prohibit detention for a period exceeding that which would have been passed by a British court.[36]

As regards transfers out of the Netherlands, the Dutch authorities follow in principle an open-minded approach, allowing the receiving state to choose between conversion or continued enforcement. The British attitude has been quite different, refusing for some time to allow transfers from the UK when the receiving state had indicated that it would use the conversion procedure. This has been particularly true in relation to the possible transfer of Dutch prisoners to the Netherlands—originally transfers were refused if the Netherlands proposed to convert the sentences. However, after April 1991 some transfers were agreed to by Britain on a trial basis, to see how the conversion would work. Four prisoners were transferred to the Netherlands, three of them convicted of hard drug offences, but the British authorities were not happy with the outcome of the conversion procedure, so that the 'experiment' has been stopped for the present.[37] There appears to be some unease on the part of the UK that the punitive and deterrent impact of sentences passed there would be undermined by conversion in the 'milder' penal climate of the Netherlands.

EVALUATION

What is the practical outcome of these transfer arrangements? The extent to which the United Kingdom and the Netherlands have been involved in prisoner transfers since their respective legislation came into force can be seen from the figures in Tables 1 and 2. Nearly all the transfers included there were effected under the 1983 Convention. The 1970 Convention was used in only two cases, relating to transfers from the Netherlands to Austria

---

[33] *Interdepartmental Working Party Report*, n. 2 above, point 54.
[34] Parliamentary Debates, House of Lords, n. 5 above, col. 756.   [35] Ibid., col. 764.
[36] For criticism of this, see Gillian Douglas, [1985] *MLR* 182 at 187–8. The point is made there that the tougher sentencing policy of some Third World countries in relation to drug offences has partly come about as a result of pressure from Western countries who 'are now taking fright when their own citizens fall foul of such laws and have to undergo the rigours of paying the penalty'.
[37] Source: Netherlands Ministry of Justice.

TABLE 1:   Transfers into and out of the United Kingdom (1986–1990)

Country	Repatriations to United Kingdom			Repatriations to foreign jurisdictions		
	Requests	Refusals	Transfers	Requests	Refusals	Transfers
Austria	—	—	—	4	—	2
Canada	2	—	—	6	—	1
Cyprus	1	1	—	9	3	—
Denmark	3	—	1	7	1	3
Finland	1	—	—	3	—	1
France	7	2	1	10	2	—
Greece	1	—	—	2	—	1
Luxembourg	—	—	—	—	—	—
Netherlands	2	—	—	92	29	10
Spain	7	—	3	11	—	2
Sweden	4	—	5	1	—	1
Switzerland	—	—	—	—	—	—
Turkey	1	—	1	5	—	—
USA	12	3	4	59	10	27
Italy	—	—	—	20	—	—
Others	—	—	—	—	—	—
Total	41	6	15	229	45	48

Source: UK Prison Department.

(used probably because the sentenced persons did not give their consent to the transfer).

The figures detail the number of requests, refusals, and transfers. Caution should be used in comparing the totals since the British total relates to a five-year period (1986 to 1990) while the Dutch total covers only a three-year period (1988 to 1990). It is noticeable, however, that transfers to the UK have been relatively few (fifteen by 1990), while the Netherlands has received back a much larger number (eighty-six) within a shorter period.[38] Mainly for the reasons already mentioned, the number of transfers from the UK to the Netherlands has represented a small proportion of the total number of requests, and there is a discrepancy in the latter figure as supplied by the UK (ninety-two) and the Netherlands (forty-four). There may be two, not necessarily mutually exclusive, explanations for this last difference. First, the ninety-two requests may be from Dutch prisoners themselves as distinct from formal requests from the British authorities (some

---

[38] A further 53 Dutch prisoners were repatriated during 1991, and another 85 during 1992, bringing the total to 224 since 1988.

TABLE 2:   Transfers into and out of the Netherlands (1988–1990)

Country	Repatriations to the Netherlands			Repatriations to foreign jurisdictions		
	Requests	Refusals	Transfers	Requests	Refusals	Transfers
Austria	7	2	5	2	—	2
Canada	1	—	1	—	—	—
Cyprus	—	—	—	—	—	—
Denmark	28	1	22	—	—	—
Finland	—	—	—	—	—	—
France	13	7	3	—	—	—
Greece	3	1	1	—	—	—
Hong Kong	2	—	—	—	—	—
Luxembourg	4	1	1	—	—	—
Spain	46	3	22	15	3	7
Sweden	19	3	13	—	—	—
Switzerland	10	1	8	1	1	—
Turkey	—	—	—	32	7	4
United Kingdom	44	19	9	4	—	1
USA	6	2	1	2	—	1
Italy	1	—	—	10	2	—
Others	—	—	—	19	13	—
Total	184	40	86	85	26	15

Source: M. H. F. Knaapen and S. M. van der Kallen, *Evaluatie van drie Jaren Wet overdracht Tenuitvoerlegging Strafvonnissen: 1988, 1989, 1990*, report published by the Ministerie van Justitie ('s-Gravenhage 1991).

requests from prisoners may not be forwarded by the British authorities, for instance if the treaty conditions have not been met). Secondly, it may be that some of the requests in the larger total had not been officially transmitted to the Dutch authorities.

It should be borne in mind that not all requests from states or from sentenced individuals need lead either to a refusal or a transfer. In some cases the sentenced person will have withdrawn his consent, and in others will have been released before the transfer could be effected. According to Dutch sources,[39] proceedings for transfers from the Netherlands to the UK have taken on average six months. On the other hand, proceedings for transfers in the opposite direction have taken on average approximately fifteen months, which may be considered far too long. In the interests of sentenced persons and in order to render the transfer procedure effective,

[39] M. H. F. Knaapen and S. M. van der Kallen, *Evaluatie van drie Jaren Wet overdracht Tenuitvoerlegging Strafvonnissen: 1988, 1989, 1990*, report published by the Ministerie van Justitie ('s-Gravenhage 1991), 7.

there needs to be a quicker provision of necessary information so as to speed up the decision-making process.

It is impossible to say exactly why some transfers have been refused, since states are not obliged under the 1983 Convention to give reasons for their refusal. The 1991 Evaluation Report on the working of the Dutch legislation,[40] however, mentions a number of reasons for the refusal on the part of the British authorities to transfer Dutch prisoners. The Dutch preference for the conversion procedure was listed as one problem. When this was indicated as the outcome of a transfer, the UK refused to proceed, at least until the change of policy in 1991, referred to above. Another problem is that most Dutch prisoners in the UK have been convicted of drug-related offences. Since the maximum penalty for soft-drug offences in the Netherlands is lower than in Britain, a transfer might well, irrespective of whether conversion or continued enforcement is used, imply a reduction of the British sentence. However, when hard drugs are involved, conversion would not necessarily entail a reduction of the sentence, the penalty for offences involving hard drugs under Dutch law being more severe than for soft-drug offences. Moreover, the Dutch Supreme Court has ruled that the judge deciding on conversion of a foreign sentence may take into account the sentencing policy of the state of conviction.[41] In fact, there have been several cases involving hard-drug offences in which use of conversion did not lead to a reduction of the sentence imposed abroad.

The experience of prisoner transfers as between Britain and the Netherlands reveals some striking differences in penal policy and demonstrates a different attitude towards the wider question of international co-operation in penal matters. What emerges in particular is a bifurcated policy on the part of the UK, pragmatic when the repatriation of British prisoners from overseas is at issue, but dogmatic when it is a question of transferring prisoners from the UK. It has been seen that the British legislation neither requires double criminality, nor prohibits a completion of sentence in a British prison for a period exceeding the maximum sentence which could be passed by a British court for the offence in question. It was clear in the British Parliamentary debates that the emphasis in this respect is humanitarian, in the sense of recovering the prisoner, if necessary at the cost of legal principle. In relation to transfers out of the UK, this attitude translates into an insistence that the underlying objectives of British sentencing practice be respected by the administering country, if necessary at the expense of the latter's own penal philosophy. The Dutch approach, in contrast, is to view the transfer of prisoners as just one component of a wider network of co-operative procedures which are ultimately concerned to ensure that the existence of international frontiers is not an obstacle to a fair

---

[40] Ibid., 16.   [41] Ibid.

administration of justice. In this approach, participation in co-operative procedures is conditional upon confidence in the other country's system of criminal law. Once that confidence has been established, the Netherlands is unlikely to want to interfere with the administration of a sentence after a transfer of its execution. Yet at the same time the Netherlands may not be willing to deal at all in the first place if that confidence is lacking, especially if to do so would in effect amount to becoming party to a violation of basic rights. It is probable that the incorporation of the European Convention on Human Rights into the Dutch legal system has had at least a psychological effect on Dutch policy in this respect, whereas the relatively weaker impact of that Convention on law and practice within the UK has enabled the latter country to contemplate the continuation of an unjust sentence with a pragmatic shrug of the shoulders. But there may also be more practical considerations at work. The number of foreign prisoners in British prisons is not such a pressing problem, whereas the plight of British prisoners abroad excites public concern. In the UK legal system, *repatriation of prisoners* is a specific issue with a particular emphasis. In the Netherlands, the issue is one of *execution of foreign criminal judgments* and is part of a wider policy of international co-operation and legal protection. It is clear that while such different attitudes exist the effectiveness of procedures such as the transfer of prisoners is itself put under question.

19

Conclusion: Europeanization and Convergence: The Lessons of Comparative Study

CHRISTOPHER HARDING, BERT SWART, NICO JÖRG,
AND PHIL FENNELL

It will have been clear to readers of this book that two principal approaches have been taken in discussing these different areas of criminal justice: in the great majority of contributions the format has comprised a comparison of British and Dutch experience, while at the same time a good number of the chapters have been preoccupied with the impact of European developments and initiatives or, as it may be termed, the process of 'Europeanization'. These two analytical approaches have been undertaken in order to assess what may be perceived as an important potential tendency in the development of criminal justice in western Europe: the convergence of different systems, either as a response to external forces such as 'Europeanization' or for other reasons associated with the internal dynamic of individual systems.

EUROPEANIZATION

A number of the chapters represent an attempt to assess the impact of European legal developments on the criminal justice systems of two West European countries. Two significant points emerge clearly from this collective study. First, the impact of such developments—or, it may be said, the extent of Europeanization—is variable according to which area of criminal justice is under discussion. And secondly, the national reaction to European initiatives and international convergence differs in some important respects as between the Dutch and British systems, reflecting differences both in policy and in legal tradition and organization. Ultimately, a study of this kind provokes a basic question: what objectives drive the Europeanization of criminal justice and how well do such objectives accord (or do they conflict) with national aspirations in this field? Comparative research between European countries, moreover, may also be of more immediate significance in that it provides a better insight into the problems that are involved in achieving further integration of national criminal justice systems in Europe.

It may be seen from some of the discussion in the earlier chapters that Europeanization can be interpreted to mean a number of tendencies, most notably co-operation in criminal procedure (Chap. 5), the development of a regional system of protection of human rights (Chap. 4), and the centipetal and harmonizing drive associated with the establishment of the Single Market of the European Community (Chaps. 5, 6). It might also be seen, in a looser sense, as the coming together of national systems, inspired as much by an internal drive towards reform and improvement as by the exigencies of international or European policies. Yet the very nature of this list should serve notice of the potential tensions and irreconcilable forces within this conglomerate concept of Europeanization. On the one hand there is the obvious tussle between national autonomy and international direction and supervision, which begs awkward questions about competing values: in the 'post-Maastricht' climate of the mid-1990s, with its emphasis upon subsidiarity, insistence upon national approaches may appear more politically acceptable. But there is also on the other hand the problem of reconciling different strands of European policy: harmonization is designed to serve the Community interest; co-operation procedures are conceived to help the national agencies of enforcement; human rights guarantees are there (in this context) largely for the benefit of vulnerable defendants in the system. Such analysis is as likely to point to the potential mess which may result from Europeanization as to confirm any sense of progress or consistent achievement.

A number of the chapters convey such a sense of a mix of objectives which may pull the practical working of the criminal justice system in different directions, or of policies which may be single-minded in one direction while throwing up problems in another. Programmes which are concerned with the position of victims of crime (Chap. 15) inevitably impinge upon the rights of offenders and also compromise the traditional role of the state in criminal justice, while at the same time enabling the state to 'privatize' its responsibilities in this field. Policies of diversion (Chaps. 7, 9, 10) wed a pragmatic appeal (the more 'rational' use of resources) to an ideological distrust of formal state power, yet beget further problems concerning lower visibility in criminal justice and differential treatment as the result of using more diffuse mechanisms of social control. These are, of course, examples of national policy dilemmas as much as international entanglement; but it may be asked whether the increasingly incursive European dimension in criminal justice is likely to clear the minds of national policy-makers and agencies on these issues. Any response to any form of Europeanization should therefore be based on the question: is it clear what this policy is intended to achieve and what are likely to be the consequences, and for whom, at the national level? In that way, the desirable limits of national autonomy may more clearly be identified. Nor, on the other hand, is it sufficient to make emotive appeals concerning the possible disappearance of national law and procedure. There is a good deal of argument, presented at both the political and the academic level, critical of a prospective reduction of national sovereignty in certain areas of criminal justice and suggesting that in itself such a tendency represents a dangerous path (see the concluding comments in Chap. 5). But it must be asked more precisely: dangerous for whom? The imperatives of maintaining a national approach must be evaluated and convincingly explained and *then* balanced against the *agreed* goals of international and European intervention. The first part of such an exercise may be aided by comparative studies of particular areas of criminal justice.

COMPARATIVE EVALUATION

The other main analytical approach in this book—the bilateral comparison of British and Dutch criminal justice—may therefore have some useful bearing on these questions of Europeanization. But it may be helpful at this stage to say something about the comparability of these two national systems. Firstly, it may be noted that in terms of general political and economic structure, and in their general experience of crime (the significance of terrorism apart), the two countries are not too far removed from each other (Chaps. 1, 2, 8). Indeed, in this respect, comparisons across western Europe may be seen as more appropriate and more useful than, for instance, comparisons between Britain and the United States, which formed the basis of a good deal of earlier comparative work in the criminal justice field.

In the second place, and on the other hand, there are variables of potential explanatory force, not only as regards an understanding of different approaches as between national systems, but also perhaps in appreciating some of the resistance to processes of Europeanization and convergence. There are significantly different legal traditions ('common law' as opposed to 'civil law'); different emphases on adversarial and inquisitorial modes of criminal procedure (see, in particular, Chap. 3); and sometimes completely different institutions and personnel. For instance, the respective systems of prosecution have a very different history and experience (Chaps. 7, 11) and the Dutch do not agonize in the British way over 'miscarriages of justice'. Also, there are different types of informal phenomena of criminal justice, such as the English (though not the Scottish) 'plea-bargaining' and the Dutch '*transactie*' (Chap. 7). Sentencers in the two systems have different backgrounds and training (Chap. 16). Serious offences are dealt with by jury trial in Britain (with the exception of the 'Diplock courts'), but not in the Netherlands. Such differences in legal structure and method at the very least merit exposition. They may also, in an analytical fashion, inform assessment.

But there are as well, and thirdly, differences in penological tradition. To be sure, it is possible to identify a broadly similar range of custodial and non-custodial measures and a broadly similar concern with rising crime figures and (at least until very recently in the UK) rising prison numbers. However, a number of commentators have detected a significant difference of penological attitude: the celebrated Dutch 'tolerance', as compared to the more nakedly penal approach of the British. While the Dutch steadfastly refuse to countenance the sharing of prison cells, the British faith in imprisonment sometimes seems impervious to the attrition of recognized crises in the prison system, flirting periodically with 'short, sharp shocks' on the one hand and being drawn increasingly to the use of long prison terms on the other hand (Chap. 2). It is difficult to resist the perception that those involved in the working of the two penal systems start out with rather different beliefs and assumptions. Whether this is in actuality a question of different levels of tolerance is perhaps a matter for debate or is at least an argument which should be treated with care. It may be asked, for instance, whether it is not, at least in some cases, more a matter of Dutch willingness to question openly the use of criminal sanctions, and in particular incarceration, in situations where British policy may not differ so much in the end result but be implemented more furtively, for instance through informal measures (the important reliance on Home Office circulars is a notable example), rather than via clear legislation. In that case, the relevant distinction may be one between official tolerance and the tolerance of public opinion. Related to this is a somewhat different view of state power within the two systems. British literature in the criminal justice field is notoriously suspicious of the role of the state, whereas the Dutch do not appear to share that degree of doubt (see the conclusions to Chap. 3).

Such differences of attitude are of course the meat of comparative study; but this is also a point at which such comparative evaluation touches upon the theme of Europeanization, when attention is focused on the respective responses of the two systems to European and international initiatives. Here the British (state) response tends to be more guarded. The Netherlands has incorporated the European Convention on Human Rights into domestic law while the UK is unwilling to do so. This fact is of great significance for some areas of criminal justice (see Chap. 4), as is shown quite dramatically by the *Brogan* judgment of the Court of Human Rights, addressed to Britain but taken very seriously in the Netherlands (see Chap. 12). In matters of international co-operation in relation to criminal proceedings, the Dutch are apparently more willing to relinquish control to another country, in particular, to transfer criminal proceedings rather than to insist on territorial imperatives (Chap. 5) or to contemplate conversion of a sentence (Chap. 18). In this respect, the Netherlands would appear to have a lower threshold of national autonomy, at least in favour of securing the protection of individual rights and the more effective resocialization of offenders.

Comparative evaluation may therefore serve two purposes in the context of this kind of study. It provides insight into the development of national systems and important evidence of either divergence or convergence; and the evidence from the collection of studies gathered together here points broadly to a process of convergence, even if in a context of some resilient national traditions. But it also informs the examination of national responses to external pressures, such as those being here considered under the umbrella concept of 'Europeanization'.

THE IMPACT OF EUROPEANIZATION

What does the comparative study of the British and Dutch systems reveal about the progress of Europeanization?

It is clear that Europeanization in its narrower sense has a selective impact on the criminal justice field. The Convention on Human Rights (Chap. 4) has repercussions in two main areas: formal criminal procedure (pre-trial and during trial), and as regards the character of penal measures, especially imprisonment. Articles 5 and 6 of the Convention have been invoked in relation to pre-trial detention (Chap. 12), aspects of the trial process (for instance, in relation to witnesses (Chap. 14), the use of expert evidence (Chap. 13), and the procedures used to deal with mentally disordered offenders (Chap. 9). Yet, important though some of these developments must be considered to be, it must be admitted that an instrument such as the Convention is not designed to deal with the less formal and less visible aspects of criminal justice, which are of increasing practical importance, yet by their very nature are less susceptible to legal scrutiny. Similarly, the Convention has been used to assess the procedural aspects of prison discipline and to a lesser extent the conditions and nature of some kinds of detention and penalty (Articles 3 and 8 are most relevant: see Chap. 17), but its general emphasis on formal legal process means that some crucial aspects of criminal justice decision-making may be beyond its terms of reference. This raises the underlying question of how administrative and informal processes may be most effectively subjected to legal scrutiny, and also the feasibility of devising uniform and objective criteria for the evaluation of such processes. Tied to this question is that of the choice between adversarial and inquisitorial modes of procedure, and a number of the chapters (see Chaps. 3, 7) test the reality of that theoretical dichotomy and compare the attempts in the UK and the Netherlands to reconcile the quest for evidence with the demands of procedural justice. It appears from a number of the contributions here that the Convention does not make a choice between inquisitorial and adversarial modes of procedure. Rather, its role, as developed by the European Commission and Court of Human Rights, has been to confirm and develop further existing fundamental notions of fairness which have to be respected by both common law and civil law systems. General legal principles—the impartiality of decision-makers, the individual's right to be heard, the provision of legal assistance, and concepts of legal security and the control of executive action—are seen as imperative for all legal systems, irrespective of their tradition and methods. Without forcing individual national systems to conform to an absolutely uniform pattern, the insistence on such fundamental principles nevertheless acts to harmonize notions of fairness to an increasing extent. The significant impact of the Human Rights Convention may be seen, then, in its reinforcement of a common heritage of ideas about justice, without requiring uniformity at a more superficial level (see Chap. 4).

The other European conventions have also, for the most part, been concerned with aspects of criminal procedure across frontiers: the facilitation of the criminal law process, and the transfer of proceedings and the enforcement of sentences (Chaps. 5, 18). Here progress has been limited by a lack of political will and also by divergence of policy, which may be tied to the existence of differing legal traditions. To talk in terms of British pragmatism and Dutch adherence to principle may suggest too much of a caricature, but it is at least pertinent to point out the Dutch preference for establishing such international co-operation as a coherent package of measures as compared with the British desire to pick and choose. But of general importance, it may be asserted, is the need to link such developments with concomitant guarantees for those subject to procedures of co-operation: it may be asked, for instance, whether the relation between co-operation treaties and international measures of legal protection, as typified by the Human Rights Convention, should not be made more explicit (see Chap. 5).

European Community developments have forced the pace very much in the field of investigations and police co-operation, reflecting a concern with particular forms of criminality, such as drug-trafficking, terrorism, and illegal immigration (which are customarily addressed in part by border controls), but also fraud and other forms of economic crime, which thrive on the existence of borders, external as well as internal. In short, the Single European Market has added to the problems of criminal justice and this now raises what are for some the spectres of harmonization and supranational control—different approaches, but both impinging upon national autonomy. Council of Europe states may be selective in their adherence to European conventions; but Community measures, being by their nature integrationist, are likely to operate more insidiously on the borders of national autonomy. It may be anticipated, however, that there will be extreme wariness in some quarters about developing further the presently sketchy provisions of Article K of the Union Treaty. More fundamentally, a set of interrelated basic questions remains as yet unanswered: should further developments take place at the Community/Union level or intergovernmentally; what should be the balance between the need for further co-ordination in the field of criminal justice and a necessary measure of autonomy; and how are democratic accountability and control best achieved?

The foregoing summary suggests that the impact of Council of Europe and Community-based developments has been and will remain uneven throughout the whole spectrum of criminal justice. Moreover, the impact may be different as between European states, on the basis of some examination of British and Dutch responses. Even in the context of Community measures, in relation to which there is an obligation of full (and therefore uniform) enforcement, based upon Article 5 of the EC Treaty, it should not readily be supposed (without the benefit of further research) that actual enforcement of criminal law giving effect to Community policies will be equally vigorous as between countries such as the UK and the Netherlands (see Chap. 6). While, therefore, it has to be admitted that Europeanization has made significant inroads in the area of criminal justice, these incursions cover only part of the field and are of uncertain—or, in some respects, clearly uneven—consistency.

THE EXTENT OF CONVERGENCE

Alongside the impact of Europeanization in the narrower sense, it is possible to detect some convergence between national systems such as the British and the Dutch. But care should be taken not to mistake what may be expected coincidence for conscious convergence (can the increasing concern for victims of crime, the resort to informal procedures, even of different kinds, or the outreach to non-custodial measures confidently be identified as one or other of these?). Current British interest in inquisitorial methods (Chaps. 7, 11) and the gradual acceptance of minimum standards in relation to imprisonment (Chap. 17) may more persuasively be pointed out as evidence of convergence, but ultimately it must be remembered that a broad consensus on objectives need not imply an agreement as to means. The discussion of sentencing discretion (Chap. 16) suggests that the different outlook and background of sentencers in Britain and in the Netherlands will produce different lines of development in sentencing practice. Similarly, much of the material on informal procedures suggests that diversity of method will continue to be employed in the quest for not dissimilar results.

Indeed, herein may lie some indication of the appropriate limits of national autonomy. To seek uniformity for its own sake may be both undesirable and dangerous. A number of the contributions to this book have emphasized the deep-rooted nature of certain national concepts, procedures, and institutions, and consequently there may be dangers in transposing the approach of other systems without taking into account the depth of national tradition and outlook. On the contrary, to allow for a sensitive and mutually-understood local diversity, regulated ultimately by shared policy objectives in the relevant field of activity and by the protective mechanisms of the Human Rights Convention, may be put forward as a key element in any considered policy of regional development. European-ization of criminal justice need not and should not imply the complete demise of national autonomy and the debate in this area during the com-ing years will surely be concerned with discovering the optimum extent of such autonomy.

Glossary of Dutch technical terms and their British equivalents/synonyms

Aanhouding	Arrest. In the Netherlands this includes a detention period of 6 hours for interrogation by the police
Delikt en Delinkwent (D en D)	Offence and offender (criminal law review, monthly)
Dwangmiddelen	Coercive measures, police powers, legal powers, powers of R-C,
Gerechtelijk vooronderzoek (*gvo*)	Preliminary judicial investigation, pre-trial investigation by R-C judicial inquest, instruction
Gerechtshof (*Hof*)	Court of Appeal
Hoge Raad (*HR*)	Supreme Court of the Netherlands
Nederlandse Jurisprudentie (NJ)	Dutch Case Law Reporter (weekly)
Nederlands Juristenblad (NJB)	Dutch legal professional journal (weekly)
Rechter-Commissaris (R-C)	Investigating judge
Rechterlijke Organisatie (*RO*)	Act on Judicial Organization
Richtlijnen	Guidance, circulars
Staatsblad (Stb)	Bulletin of Acts and Royal Decrees
Tenlastelegging	Charge (after custody), information (without prior custody)
Transactie	Pre-trial financial settlement between the police or prosecution and the suspect, guaranteeing non-prosecution
Wet	Act
Wetboek van Strafrecht (*Wvs*) (*Sr*)	Criminal Code (CC)
Wetboek van Strafvordering (*WvSv*) (*Sv*)	Code of Criminal Procedure (CCP)

Index

Abu Daoud 90
accountability:
  and the State 44–6
  see also discretion
Ackner, Lord 286 n.
ACPO, *see* Association of chief police officers
admissibility of confession evidence 173–4
adversarial, *see* inquisitorial and adversarial
Advisory Board on Restricted Patients 185
Advisory Committee on Alternative Sanctions 15, 19
Advisory Council on the Misuse of Drugs (1979) 153 & n.
AIDS 20, 157, 166, 168
Alkema, E. A. 325 n.
Alldridge, P. ix, xviii, 174, 227–49, 265–82
Allen, R. 211 n.
Alschuler, A. W. 321 n.
Andenaes, J. 321 n.
Anderson, T. 278 n.
anonymity 292–6
Antilla, I. 321 n.
appeal 25 n.
  Committee 344, 346, 347
  see also Court of Appeal; Criminal Appeal Act
Ashworth, A. 128 n., 132 n., 206 & n., 231 n., 315 & n., 333 n., 335 n., 338 n.
Ashworth, P. 357 n.
Association of chief police officers (ACPO) 160, 169
Australia 27 & n., 168
Austria 366, 374, 375, 376
Avebury, Lord 368 n., 374
aviation safety 89–90
Aye Maung, N. 21 n.

Baan 1
Baauw, P. ix, xviii, 251–64
Baldwin, J. 147 n., 230 n.
Ball, C. 212 n., 213 n., 224 n.
Barclay 313 n.
Barneveld, P. D. 176 n.
Beccaria 2, 324 n.
Beeling, H. W. R. 328 n.
Beginselenwet Gevangeniswezen, *see* Principles Act for the Prison System
Beijing Rules 223, 224
Belgium 109, 137 n.

Benelux countries 95, 97, 281, 366, 369
Bennett, T. 139 n., 205 n., 317 n.
Benyon, J. 96 n.
Berghuis, A. C. 228 n., 324 n.
Bergsma, R. L. 228 n.
Berkhout-van Poelgeest, A. M. 257 n., 261 n.
Bernhardt, Judge 193 n.
Best, K. 366 n.
Bevan, V. 173 n., 231 n.
Beyer, A. ix, xix, 283–300
Biggs, R. 27
Biles, D. 27 n.
Bill to Revise Juvenile Criminal Law 215, 217, 218, 225
Bingham, T. 60 n.
Birch, D. 306 n.
Birmingham Pub Bombings (1974) 38
Birmingham Six 71 n., 248 n., 252 n.
Blad, J. R. 129 n.
Blake, G. 27
Blankenburg, E. 6 n., 7 n.
Blom-Cooper, L. 25 n.
body samples 273–8
Bol, M. W. 292 n.
Bonner, D. 39 n.
Booth, T. 208 n.
BOPZ (Psychiatric Hospital Formal Admissions Act) 179 n.
Bosman, J. J. 328 n.
Bot, P. L. 165 n.
Bottomley, A. 208 n.
Bottomley, K. 172 n., 232 n.
Bottoms, A. 206 & n.
Bradley, A. W. 82 n.
Brake, M. 35 n.
Brants, C. H. ix, xvii, xviii, 41–56, 127–48, 214, 237 n., 243 n., 247 n.
Brants, K. L. K. 144 n.
Brearley, N. 231 n.
Brett, P. 266 n.
Bridge, J. W. 107 n.
Bridge, Lord 354
Bridges, L. 232 n., 233 n.
British Crime Survey 21
Broadcasting Act 62 n.
Brown, A. 141 n.
Brown, P. 206 n.
Browne-Wilkinson, N. 60 n.
Bruins, J. ix, xviii, 199–226

Bruinsma, F. 6 n., 7 n.
Bulger, J. 224 n.
Bunt, H. G. van de 144 n.
bureaucracy 6–8
Busch, H. 104 n.
Butler Committee 181 n., 190
Butler Education Act (1944) 23

camera hearings 290, 291–2
Canada 90, 93, 168, 301, 321 n.
  prisoner transfer 364, 365, 366, 371, 375,
    376
Carlebach, J. 199 n.
Casale, S. 360 n.
cautioning 207–11
CCP, *see* Code of Criminal Procedure
CELAD, *see* European Committee to
    Combat Drugs
Central Council for Criminal Justice 11–12
Central Council for the Enforcement of
    Criminal Law 344, 347
Central European Investigation Office 96
Champion, D. J. 321 n.
Cherif Bassiouni, M. 87 n.
Child Welfare Council 216, 225
child witnesses protection 296–7
Children Act (1989) 212
children and young persons 202–3, 214–15,
    223, 224 & n.
  Act 204, 290 n.
  see also juvenile
China 149
Chorus, J. M. J. 134 n., 238 n.
Christian Democrat Employers' Federation
    18
Christie, N. 314 & n.
Churchill, R. 77 n., 80 n.
CICB 312, 317
circulars (59/90 and 18/94) 207–11
Civil Liability for Damage caused by
    Waste 125 n.
civil rights 84, 347
CJA, *see* Criminal Justice Act
Clare, I. 172 n.
Clarke, R. 201 n.
Clegg, J. 273 n.
Co-ordinating Committee 100
Cobley, C. ix, xix, 283–300
Code of Criminal Procedure 183 n., 194,
    239
  control of police investigations 240,
    241 n.
  DNA profiling 267 n., 269 n., 270 n., 273
  European Convention on Human Rights
    (ECHR) 68, 75
  mentally disordered offender 173, 174,
    177, 180, 184

Netherlands 10, 50
  police detention 257–8, 261
  prosecution discretion and accountability
    136, 146
  sentencing practice, policy and discretion
    327
  victim protection and compensation 310
  witness evidence 296
Code for Crown Prosecutors 175 & n., 209,
    309
Cohen, L. J. 267 n.
Cohen, P. 170 n.
Cohen, S. 17 & n.
Coleman, C. 232 n., 257 n.
Collins 195 n.
Commen-van Alphen, L. M. S. 177 n.
Commission for Racial Equality 208
Committee of Ministers 219, 220, 221
Commonwealth Law Ministers 365
Community Council 101
community law, evaluation and
    enforcement of 119–21
compensation 301, 310–12, 313
  see also protection of and compensation
Complaints Committee 345
confession, *see* admissibility
Conlon, G. 252 n.
Connick, E. 314 n.
Conroy, S. 305 n.
Consultation Paper 351
Convention:
  Against the Taking of Hostages 90
  on the Compensation for Victims of
    Violent Crime 301, 312
  on the Control of the Acquisition and
    Possession of Firearms 92
  on Extradition 94
  on Illicit Trade in Drugs and
    Psychotropic Substances 90, 150, 166,
    168 n.
  on the International Validity of Criminal
    Judgments 91, 94, 95, 332, 366
  on Laundering, Search, Seizure, and
    Confiscation of the Proceeds from
    Crime 90–1
  on Mutual Assistance in Criminal
    Matters 91, 92, 94
  (1970) 373, 374
  (1983) 367–8, 372, 373, 374, 377
  on Offences Relating to Cultural
    Property 92
  on the Physical Protection of Nuclear
    Material 90
  on Political Rights and Freedoms 325
  on the Prevention and Punishment of
    Crimes Against Internationally
    Protected Persons 90

on the Prevention of Torture and
Inhuman or Degrading Treatment or
Punishment 92
on the Protection of Individuals with
Regard to Automatic Processing of
Data 279, 281
on the Punishment of Road Traffic
Offenders 91
on Spectator Violence and Misbehaviour
at Sports Events 92
on the Supervision of Conditionally
Sentenced or Conditionally Released
Offenders 91, 369
on the Suppression of Terrorism 91,
93
on the Transfer of Criminal Proceedings
94
on the Transfer of Execution of
Criminal Judgments 95
on the Transfer of Proceedings 91, 95
on the Transfer of Sentenced Persons
91, 93, 95, 366
see also European; Geneva; Hague;
IMO; Single; United Nations
convergence, *see* Europeanization
Corbett, C. 231 n., 303 n., 304 n.
corporal punishment 78
correspondence 76–8
Council of Europe xvi, 221
diversion in juvenile justice 219
DNA profiling 268 & n., 269 n., 277,
279 & n., 280 n., 281
drug problem management 164, 167 n.
European Convention on Human Rights
(ECHR) 65
Europeanization and convergence 385
intergovernmental co-operation 88, 89,
90–5, 98, 100, 101
Netherlands 16
police detention 260
prisoner transfer 364, 365 & n., 366 & n.,
370, 371
prisoners' rights 348
sentencing practice, policy and discretion
320, 323 n., 335 n.
Standard Minimum Rules for the
Treatment of Prisoners 359
victim protection and compensation
301 & n., 305
Council for Juvenile Policy 16
Council of Ministers 281
Council on Tribunals 195
Court, access to 67
Court of Appeal:
control of police investigations 244
DNA profiling 274
drug problem management 158

European Convention on Human Rights
(ECHR) 71
mentally disordered offender 173, 184,
188, 193, 196, 197
Netherlands 17
prisoners' rights 355 n., 358 n., 359 n.,
360
prosecution discretion and accountability
146
sentencing practice, policy and discretion
322, 333, 334, 335, 337
United Kingdom criminal justice policy
39
victim protection and compensation 309
witness evidence 291
Courts, *see* criminal; European; High;
Supreme
Crawford, P. 154 n., 164 n.
crimes or felonies (*misdrijven*) 134, 135,
137, 138
crimes, reported 22
Criminal Appeal Act (1907) 25 n.
Criminal Code 2, 179 & n., 180, 183 n., 324,
325, 326 & n.
diversion in juvenile justice 214, 217
mentally disordered offender 184, 188
Netherlands 13, 14
criminal Courts, powers of 182 n.
Criminal Evidence (Northern Ireland)
Order (1988) 38 n.
Criminal Injuries Compensation Fund 313
Criminal Investigation Department (CID)
233
criminal judgments 91, 94, 95, 332, 366
Criminal Justice Act 23–4 & n., 27–33
diversion in juvenile justice 200, 204,
207 n., 211, 213
DNA profiling 275 n., 279 n.
mentally disordered offender 176, 187 n.,
188
prisoners' rights 349 n., 353, 356, 357
sentencing practice, policy and discretion
336 & n., 337 & n., 338 & n.
victim protection and compensation
306 n., 311 & n., 312 & n.
witness evidence 284 n., 286, 291 & n.,
297 & n., 298
see also Scottish
Criminal Justice (International
Co-operation) Act (1990) 298
criminal justice reorganization 25–6
criminal law:
enforcement 344, 347
substantive 13–14
criminal procedure 14–15, 41–4, 228, 260
Criminal Procedure (Attendance of
Witnesses) Act (1965) 308 n.

Criminal Procedure (Insanity) Act (1964) 178 n., 181 n.
Criminal Procedure (Insanity and Unfitness to Plead) Act (1991) 178 & n., 181 & n.
criminal proceedings, transfer of 94
Criminal Statistics 22
Crombag, H. F. M. 238 n.
Cross, R. 24 n.
Crown Court 178, 181, 182, 267, 348
Crown Prosecution Service 30, 31
  control of police investigations 237, 243, 244
  diversion in juvenile justice 200 & n., 203, 206, 209, 213, 225
  inquisitorial and adversarial systems 46, 54
  legal position 140–3
  prosecution discretion and accountability 131 & n., 133 & n., 143, 147
  victim protection and compensation 308, 309, 315
  see also Code for Crown Prosecutors
Crozier, G. 232 n.
cultural property offences 92
Curios Act (1865) 149
custody, see diversion from
Customs and Excise Management Act (1979) 154
Cyprus 366, 375, 376

damages paid by offenders 310–12
Damaska, M. 43 & n., 44, 265 n., 299 n.
Dangerous Dogs Act (1991) 33
Dart, A. 208 n.
data 279, 281
Data Protection Convention 279
databases and DNA profiling 278–82
DAVA, see Dutch Association for Victim Assistance
Davenport, A. ix–x, xvii, xviii, 21–39, 251–64
Davenport Hill, M. 24
Davies, P. 96 n.
Davis, R. C. 314 n.
Dawson, S. 273 n.
De Beaufort Commission 305 n.
DEA (US Federal Drugs Enforcement Administration) 167
death penalty abolition 25
Deb, H. C. 251 n.
Declaration of Basic Principles of Justice for Victims of Crime 305
Declaration on Police Co-operation 101, 102
defence and pre-trial process 46–50
Defence of the Realm Act (1914) 149

defendants 290–1, 292
degrading treatment 92
Denmark 98, 118, 165, 366, 375, 376
  see also Scandinavia
Denning, Lord 290
deprivation of liberty 73–6
detention 73–4, 75–6, 183–6, 192–7
Detention of Terrorists (Northern Ireland) Order (1972) 34 n.
Devlin, P. 332 n.
Dijk, J. van 204 n.
Dine, J. 107 n.
Dingwall, G. S. x, xvii, 21–39
Diplock Courts 36, 382
Director of Public Prosecutions (DPP) 52, 141, 308, 309
disciplinary penalties and complaints 344–5
disciplinary system complaints 352–5
disclosure of evidence 70–1
discretion and accountability in prosecution 127–48
  diversion and due process 139–43
  diversion and Dutch prosecutor role 143–7
  diversion mechanisms in Netherlands 134–8
  diversion mechanisms in United Kingdom 130–1, 143–7
  expanding diversion 131–3
Ditchfield, J. 203 n., 205 n.
Ditton, J. 29 n.
diversion:
  and due process 139–43
  in England and Wales and Netherlands 143–7, 199–226; cautioning and circulars (59/90 and 18/94) 207–11; children and young people 202–3, 214–15; human rights 220–3; integrated analysis 224–6; policy and practice 203–7, 215–19
  expansion 131–3
  from custody 174–89; detention extension 183–6; mental state relevance at trial 177–9; mental state relevance to sentencing 179–83; personality-disordered offenders, treatment of 186–8; pre-trial 175–7; sentenced prisoners and transfer to hospital 188–9
  mechanisms 137–8; in Netherlands 134–8; public prosecutor 136–7; in United Kingdom 130–1
Diversion of Mentally-Disordered Offenders from Custody Circular 171
Dixon, D. 232 n., 233 n., 257 n.

DNA profiling 265–82
  body samples 273–8
  databases 278–82
  expert evidence 270–1
  forensic scientist, payment for 273
  human rights and scientific evidence
    271–2
  nature 269–70
  procedural regulation of: laboratories by
    exclusionary rules of evidence 268–9
  systems of evidence 267
DNA samples 38
DNA testing 14
Doorn, A. J. van 165 n.
Doran, S. 36 n.
dossier 47, 48, 50–3, 234–40, 245, 287, 300
double criminality 372–3
Douglas, G. x, xix, 341–61, 374 n.
Downes, D. 3 n., 154 n., 161 n., 190 n.,
    359 n.
DPP, *see* Director of Public Prosecutions
Drost, T. R. 184 n.
Drug Policy Foundation 162
drug problem 90, 149–70, 150, 162, 167,
    168 n.
  criminal justice approach 162–4
  dependence 161
  European drug policy 164–9
  historical and international background
    149–51
  illicit trade 166
  law 151–4
  misuse 152, 153 & n.
  Netherlands 152, 154, 156–7
  penalties in England and Wales 153, 155
  policy guidelines 154–61; England and
    Wales 158–61; Netherlands 154,
    156–7
  and prisoners 347
  see also Opium Act
Drug Trafficking Offences Act (1986) 154,
    158
drunken offenders 29
due process 139–43
Duff, P. 304 n., 315 & n.
Duffy, J. 29 n.
Duffy, P. 303 n.
Dunkel, F. 224 n.
Dutch:
  Association for Victim Assistance
    (DAVA) 304
  Code of Criminal Procedure 228, 260
  Prosecution Service 143–4, 237, 244,
    331
  Supreme Court 239, 261, 272, 274, 298,
    300, 377
Dyer, C. 333 n.

ECHR, *see* European Convention on
  Human Rights
ECSC, *see* European Coal and Steel
  Community
Edwards, G. 161 n.
Eliaerts, C. 5 n.
Elias, R. 315 n., 316 n.
Elliman, S. 131 n.
Elton, Lord 370, 372, 374
emergency powers in United Kingdom
    34–9
Emmerik, J. L. van 184 n.
enforcement, alternative approaches of
    121–5
Engelsman, E. L. 157 n.
England and Wales xv, xvi, xvii, xviii, xix,
    308
  child witnesses protection 296–7
  control of police investigations 235 n.,
    238, 240, 247 & n., 248, 249;
    interrogation 227, 228; investigation
    234
  detention extension 185–6
  diversion and due process 139–43
  diversion from custody 175–6
  diversion in juvenile justice 199, 220,
    221, 225
  DNA profiling 266, 267, 268, 272, 273,
    282; body samples 274, 275 & n.,
    277 & n.; databases 279, 280
  drug problem 153, 155, 158–61
  European Convention on Human Rights
    (ECHR) 80 n.
  hospital transfer of sentenced prisoners
    188–9
  inquisitorial and adversarial systems 42,
    43, 44, 46, 53, 54
  interrogation process 230–3
  legal safeguards for patients 194–7
  mental state relevance at trial 178–9
  mental state relevance to sentencing
    180–3
  mentally disordered offender 171, 193,
    198
  personality-disordered offenders,
    treatment of 186, 187
  police detention 251–7
  prisoners' rights 348–59, 360, 361
  prosecution discretion and accountability
    147
  prosecutors and monitoring 243–4
  protection of witnesses 290–1
  psychiatric institutions 190–1
  sentencing practice, policy and discretion
    319, 320, 322, 332–8, 338
  victim protection and compensation 301,
    304, 305, 306, 308, 311

England and Wales (*cont.*):
    witness evidence 289, 298, 299, 300
    witnesses and open justice principle
        284–6
    see also diversion
Enschede, Ch. J. 19 n., 104 n., 328 & n.
equality of arms 69
Europe, *see* Council; European
European Atomic Energy Community
    (Euratom) 107
European Coal and Steel Community
    (ECSC) 107
European Commission on Human Rights
    57, 65, 167, 235 n., 384
    mentally disordered offender 193, 195,
        197
    police detention 252, 254, 259, 260, 262,
        263, 264
    prisoners' rights 356, 358, 359
    witness evidence 287, 288
European Committee:
    on Crime Problems 320
    for the Prevention of Torture and
        Inhuman or Degrading Treatment or
        Punishment 360
    to Combat Drugs (CELAD) 167, 168
European Communities Act (1972) 59
European Community xvi, 380
    co-operation 96–103; European Union
        Treaty 99–103; Single European Act
        and Schengen 97–9; Trevi 96–7
    and criminal law 107–26; diversion
        mechanisms in United Kingdom
        130–1; enforcement 119–21, 121–5;
        individuals' duties 111–15; Member
        States and negative obligations
        108–11; Member States and positive
        obligations 115–19
    drug problem management 166
    inquisitorial and adversarial systems
        41
    intergovernmental co-operation 97, 102
    law 39, 89
    Treaty 109, 110, 111, 112, 117
European Convention on Human Rights
    (ECHR) xvi, xvii, xviii, 98
    Article 6, 8
    control of police investigations 234 n.,
        237 & n., 239, 240
    and criminal justice 57–86; constitutional
        status 58–61; convention in the Courts
        61–5; Strasbourg case law 65–86
    diversion in juvenile justice 202, 219,
        220, 222 n., 223, 226
    DNA profiling 266, 271, 272, 275,
        276 & n., 277
    drug problem management 163, 164

European Community and criminal law
    107
Europeanization and convergence 382,
    383, 384, 386
inquisitorial and adversarial systems 41,
    54, 55
intergovernmental co-operation 89, 99,
    105
mentally disordered offender 172, 184,
    187, 191, 192, 193, 194, 198
police detention 252, 253, 254, 255, 256,
    257, 259–61, 263
prisoner transfer 372, 378
prisoners' rights 341, 347, 348, 352,
    355–9, 360, 361
prosecution discretion and accountability
    137
sentencing practice, policy and discretion
    320, 325
United Kingdom 29
victim protection and compensation 307,
    315 & n.
witness evidence 288
see also witnesses evidence
European Council 96, 166, 167, 168
European Court of Human Rights xvi, xix,
    57, 244
diversion in juvenile justice 223
DNA profiling 272, 273
European Community and criminal law
    122 n.
European Convention on Human Rights
    (ECHR) 66–70, 72, 73, 75, 77, 78, 79,
    81–6
Europeanization and convergence 384
inquisitorial and adversarial systems 41,
    56
mentally disordered offender 192, 196
Netherlands 8, 10 & n.
police detention 254, 255, 259, 260, 263
prisoners' rights 343, 356, 357, 358, 359
prosecution discretion and accountability
    137 n.
sentencing practice, policy and discretion
    320
witness evidence 289
European Court of Justice xvi, 41, 107,
    108, 109, 110, 111
European Community and criminal law
    115, 117, 118, 119, 120, 122
European Economic Community Treaty
    105
European Movement for the Normalization
    of Drug Policy 162
European Parliament 166, 167
European Police Office, *see* Europol
European Political Co-operation 89, 101

European Union xvi, 59, 99, 123, 365
  DNA profiling 281
  drug problem management 164
  intergovernmental co-operation 89
  see also Treaty
Europeanization xvi, xvii, 103, 320, 338,
  363
Europeanization and convergence 379–86
  comparative evaluation 381–3
  extent of convergence 385–6
  impact 383–5
Europol xvii, 101, 102, 103, 105, 166
Evaluation Report (1991) 377
Evans, R. 132 n., 139 n., 140 n., 141 n.,
  205 n., 206 n., 207 n., 208 n., 213 & n.
evidence 26, 268–9, 270–2
  see also disclosure; Police and Criminal
    Evidence Act
examining magistrate intervention 23–4
exclusion 39
expert evidence 270–1
extradition 78–9, 90, 91, 94
Eysenck, S. 128 n.

fair hearing, *see* right to
Farrington, D. 204 n., 205 n.
Fattah, E. 314 n.
Fennell, P. x, xv–xix, 130 n., 171–98,
  379–86
Ferguson, T. 139 n.
Field, S. x, xvii, xviii, 22 n., 41–56, 127–48,
  174, 214, 227–49, 317 n.
Fielding, J. 142 n.
Fielding, N. G. 142 n., 305 n.
Fijnaut C. 5 n., 96 n., 240 n.
file, *see* dossier
Finland 336, 375, 376
  see also Scandinavia
firearms acquisition and possession 92
Fisher, C. J. 139 n., 205 n.
Fisher, Sir H. 248 n.
Fisheries Act (Netherlands) 116 n.
Flin, R. 285 & n.
Foqué, R. 4 n., 322 n.
Forensic Science Service 271 n.
forensic scientist, payment for 273
Forum for Victim Services 302
Fowles, A. J. 351 n., 352 n.
France 76, 90, 165, 375, 376
  control of police investigations 235,
    236 n., 240 & n., 241 n.
  diversion in juvenile justice 221
  inquisitorial and adversarial systems 45
  intergovernmental co-operation 95, 97
  sentencing practice, policy and discretion
    324
Franey, R. 252 n.

Franke, H. 359 n.
Frankfurter Resolution 169
Frazer, A. 160 n.
freedom of speech 79
Frijda, L. 323 n., 327 n., 331 n.
frontier controls abolition 97–9
Fry, E. and M. 23 n.

Gad, N. 139 n.
Galaway, B. 308 n.
Garland, D. 281 n.
Gearty, C. 359 n.
Gelsthorpe, L. x, xviii, 131 n., 141 n.,
  142 n., 199–226
Geneva Convention:
  on Defence for Children International
    224 n.
  (1924) 150
George, M. 160 n.
Germany 77, 81, 165, 236 n.
  European Community and criminal law
    124
  European Convention on Human Rights
    (ECHR) 60
  intergovernmental co-operation 95, 96,
    97, 101
  sentencing practice, policy and discretion
    323
  victim protection and compensation
    302 & n.
  witness evidence 298 n.
Gerver, P. H. M. 238 n.
Gevers, J. K. M. 274 n.
GevM (*Gavangenismaatregel*) 188
Gibson, B. 338 n.
Gill, H. 232 n.
Gill, M. L. 257 n., 303 n.
Giller, H. 131 n., 139 n., 141 n., 142 n.,
  203 n., 204 n., 205 n., 206 n.
Goff, Lord 63
Goldstein, A. 236 n., 238 n., 244 & n., 245,
  246 & n.
Goodpaster, G. 265 & n.
Gossop, M. 161 n.
Gostin, L. 186 n.
Gottfredson, M. 317 n.
Gower, A. 321 n.
Graham, M. H. 289 n.
Greece 97, 117 & n., 118, 119, 375, 376
Gretton, J. 308 n.
Griffiths, J. A. G. 23 n.
Groenhuysen, M. S. 297 n.
Grounds, A. 189 n.
Grubin, D. H. 178 n.
Gudjonsson, G. 172 n.
Guidelines for Experiments with
  Alternative Sanctions 217, 218

Guildford Four 248 n., 252 n.
Guldenmund, R. x, xvii, 107–26

Haan, W. de 3 n.
Haffmans, C. H. 204 n., 239 n.
Hague Convention:
(1912) 150
on Unlawful Seizure of Aircraft (1970)
89–90
Hale, C. 35 n., 208 n.
Hall Williams, J. E. 135 & n., 228 n.,
238 n., 242 n., 245 n., 247 n., 248
HALT projects 214, 216 & n.–17, 219, 221,
222
Hammersley, R. 170 n.
Hand, B. 371 n., 372 n., 373 n.
Harding, C. x–xi, xv–xix, 87–106, 107–26,
130 n., 320 n., 332 n., 334 n., 363–78,
379–86
harmonization 104, 105
Harteveld, A. E. 240 n.
Hartl, D. L. 270 n.
Hartog, J. den 222 & n.
Heany, G. W. 330 n.
hearing 68–9, 71–2, 292
see also right to
Hellerstein, D. 315 n.
Henley, J. 344 n.
Henman, R. J. 321 n.
Hewitt, P. 251 n.
High Court 67, 194, 196
Hill, P. 252 n.
Hirsch, A. von 5 n., 321 n., 330 n., 336 n.
Hobbs, R. 231 n.
Hogarth, J. 327 n.
Hokstra Commission 344
Home Affairs Select Committee 132, 133,
134, 158 & n.
home life 76–8
Home Office 130, 132, 133, 139, 204 n.
control of police investigations 232
diversion in juvenile justice 200 & n.,
202–3, 205 & n., 207
DNA profiling 271 n.
drug problem management 149, 163
Europeanization and convergence 382
mentally disordered offender 175, 185,
186, 189, 198
prisoners' rights 349
sentencing practice, policy and discretion
334
victim protection and compensation 306
Young Offender Psychology Unit 30
Homicide Act (1957) 181 n.
Hondius, E. H. 238 n.
Hong Kong 376
HONLEA 168 & n.

Hood, R. 206 n.
Hope, T. 317 n.
hospitals 179 n., 188–9, 191, 192
hostages, taking of 90
House of Commons 158
Home Affairs Select Committee 132,
133, 134, 158 & n.
House of Lords 354
Howard, J. 1 n.
Hudson, B. 206 n., 321 n.
Hudson, P. S. 314 n.
Hulsman, L. H. C. 3, 4 n., 129 n., 238 n.,
328 & n.
human rights 220–3, 271–2
see also Commission; Convention; Court

identity concealment from defendants
290–1
Immigration Act (1971) 110 n.
IMO Convention for the Suppression of
Unlawful Acts Against the Safety of
Maritime Navigation (1988) 90
imprisonment, movement away from 27–9
imprisonment as punishment 343–4, 350–1
India 150
individuals' duties under community law
111–15
infringement of rights and prisoners 346
inhuman treatment 92
innocence, presumption of 69
inquisitorial and adversarial systems 41–56
authority, accountability, assumptions
and aims 44–6
criminal procedure and legitimacy 41–4
pre-trial process 46–50
trial stage 50–3
insanity, *see* Criminal Procedure (Insanity)
Act; mental; mentally
Institute for the Study of Drug
Dependence 161
instruction 240 & n., 241, 242
instrumentalism 18–20
Interdepartmental Working Party 371, 372,
373
intergovernmental co-operation and
criminal law 87–106
Council of Europe sponsored
co-operation 90–5
European Community co-operation
96–103
International Covenant on Civil and
Political Rights 84, 347
international role law and prisoners 347–8
internationally protected persons 90
internment 34–5
Interpol 168 & n.
interpreters 72–3

interrogation process 227–33
investigative process 233–4
Ireland 98, 118 n.
Irish Republican Army (IRA) 251
Irvine, B. 172 n., 227 n.
Isle of Man 78
Italy 84 n., 97, 236 n., 375, 376

Jackson, J. 36 n., 38 n.
Janse de Jonge, J. A. 319 n., 331 n.
Japan 168
Jareborg, N. 321 n., 336 n.
Jefferson, T. 212 n.
Jeroen, H. T. 134 n.
Johns, A. 161 n.
Jones, H. 353 n.
Jones, P. 257 n.
Jongman, R. W. 5 n., 328 & n.
Jörg, N. xi, xv–xix, 41–56, 174, 227–49,
    379–86
Jowitt, Lord 58, 80
judge, appearance before or other officer
    authorized by law 74–5
Judge, T. 159 n.
judicial monitoring 244–7
judiciary 9–10
Jung, H. 87 n.
Junger-Tas, J. 201 n., 220 n.
'juridification' 3–4
juvenile:
    criminal law 215, 217, 218, 225
    delinquency prevention 224 & n.
    justice administration 223, 224 & n.
    policy 16

Kallen, S. M. van der 376 & n.
Kee, R. 248 n., 252 n.
Keisel 315 n.
Kelk, C. xi, xvii, xix, 1–20, 191 & n.,
    319–39, 343 n., 346, 347 n., 360 n.
Kelly, D. 315 n.
Kempe 1, 2
Kinsey, R. 29 & n.
Klip, A. ix, xix, 283–300
Knaapen, M. H. F. 376 & n.
Knapp, K. 321 n.
Koekkoek, A. K. 238 n.
Koenraadt, F. xi, xviii, 171–98
Koffman, L. xi, xix, 130 n., 257 n., 319–39
Kolthoff, E. 240 n.
Kruissink, M. 217 n., 220 n.
Kuhn, T. 266 n.
Kuile, L. F. D. ter 324 n.
Kumeuther, F. 314 n.

Laan, P. van der 218 n., 220 n.
Landau, S. F. 139 n., 205 & n.

Lane, Chief Justice 158
Langbein, J. H. 235 n.
Langemeijer, G. E. 3 n.
Law Society 25, 195
lawfulness of detention review 75–6, 192–7
Laws, J. 60 n.
League of Nations 150
Legal Aid and Advice Act (1949) 24–5 n.
Legal Aid Fund 25
legal assistance 70
Legemaate, J. 191 & n.
legislation, reforming 23–5
legitimacy 41–4
Leigh, L. H. 80 n., 135 & n., 228 n., 238 n.,
    242 n., 245 n., 247 n., 248
Leng, R. 131 n., 206 n., 227 n., 232 n.,
    235 n., 245 n.
Lensing, J. A. W. 330 n.
Lester 58 n.
Leuw, E. 307 n.
Levi, M. 317 n.
Lewontin, R. C. 270 n.
liberty, *see* deprivation
Lidstone, K. 173 n., 231 n.
Livingstone, S. 349 n.
Loo, K. J. M. van de 184 n.
Lurigio, A. J. 315 n., 316 n.
Lustgarten, L. 26 n.
Luxembourg 375, 376

Maastricht 99, 106, 108, 123, 164, 281
McBarnet, D. 243 n.
McClean, D. 87 & n.
McConville, M. 131 & n., 139, 141 & n.,
    142 & n., 147 n., 206 n., 227 n., 230 n.,
    232 n., 235 n., 245 n.
McEwan, J. 230 n.
McIsaac, M. 199 n.
Mackay, R. D. 181 n.
McKee, G. 252 n.
MacKenzie, I. 172 n.
McKittrick, N. 128 n.
Macmillan, J. 208 n.
McWilliams, B. and W. 206 n.
Magistrates Court 182
Maguire, M. 204 n., 231 n., 232 n., 233 n.,
    303 n., 304 n., 307 n., 308 n., 312 n.,
    313 n., 314 n.
Marcus, M. 236 n., 238 n., 244 & n., 245,
    246 & n.
maritime navigation safety 90
Marks, Dr J. 161
Matthews, H. 141 n.
Mawby, R. I. 139 n., 205 n., 303 n.
Mayhew, P. 21 n.
Maynard, A. 158 n., 162 n.
mediation 307–10

Megaw, L. J. 353
Melai 323 & n.
Member States xvi
  drug problem management 164, 165,
    166, 167, 168
  European Community and criminal law
    107, 108, 113, 114, 119–26
  intergovernmental co-operation 89, 97,
    99, 100, 101, 102, 105
  mentally disordered offender 198
  negative obligations 108–11
  positive obligations 115–19
mental health 191
Mental Health Act 171 n., 176, 181 n.,
  182 n., 185, 189 & n., 194, 196
Mental Health Review Tribunal 75, 183,
  185, 186, 194, 195 & n.
mental state relevance:
  at trial 177–9
  to sentencing 179–83
mentally disordered offender 171–98
  diversion from custody 174–89
  legal safeguards for patients 191–7
  psychiatric institutions 189–91
  vulnerable suspects protection 172–4
Mentally Ill Persons Act (1884) 192
Merry, S. 306 n., 312 n.
Miers, D. 301 n., 312 n., 315 n., 317 n.
MIND (National Association of Mental
  Health) 191
Ministerial Commission 261
Ministry of Health 166
Ministry of Justice:
  inquisitorial and adversarial systems
    44
  mentally disordered offender 176, 183,
    188, 193
  Netherlands 3, 6, 7, 9 n., 10–13, 15, 17,
    18, 19
  police detention 261, 262
  prisoner transfer 374 n.
  prisoners' rights 343, 344, 346
  victim protection and compensation
    304
misdemeanours (*overtredingen*) 134, 135,
  214
misdrijven, see crimes or felonies
Misuse of Drugs Act (1971) 152, 153
Moerings, M. xi–xii, xix, 341–61
Monahan, J. 240 n.
Monetary Sanctions Act (1983) 8
Montesquieu 177
Montreal Convention for the Suppression
  of Unlawful Acts Against the Safety
  of Civil Aviation (1971) 90
Mooij, A. W. M. 177 n.
Morgan, J. xii, xix, 301–18

Morgan, R. 204 n., 353 n.
Morris, A. 199 n., 203 n., 204 n., 205 n.
Mott, J. 128 n.
Mountbatten, Earl 27, 28
Mullin, C. 248 n., 251 n., 252 n.
Mulvaney, A. 232 n.
Muncie, J. 359 n.
Murder (Abolition of the Death Penalty)
  Act (1965) 25
Mustill, L. J. 182
Myjer, E. 262 n.

Naeyé 228 n.
Nathan, G. 205 & n.
National Association for the Care and
  Resettlement of Offenders 133
National Standards 210
Neale, N. 360 n.
Nelken, D. 114 n.
Nellis, M. xii, xviii, 199–226
Netherlands xv, xvi, xvii, xviii, xix
  child witnesses protection 297
  control of police investigations 230,
    232 n., 245, 246, 247, 248
  Council of Europe sponsored
    co-operation 93–5
  criminal justice 1–20; bureaucracy 6–8;
    instrumentalism 18–20; judiciary 9–10;
    Ministry of Justice 10–13; new realism
    5–6; penal law 13–17; Public
    Prosecution Service 8–9;
    resocialization 1–3; social control
    increase 17–18; welfare and
    'juridification' 3–4
  detention extension 183–5
  diversion from custody 176–7
  diversion in juvenile justice 211, 220,
    221, 222, 223, 225
  diversion mechanisms 134–8
  DNA profiling 266, 267, 269, 270 n.,
    272–80, 282
  drug problem 149, 150, 151, 152 & n.,
    162, 163, 164, 170; European drug
    policy 165, 168, 169; policy guidelines
    154, 156–7, 160, 161
  European Community and criminal law
    116, 118 n.
  European Convention on Human Rights
    (ECHR) 57, 58, 60–1, 63–5, 82, 83, 84,
    86 n.
  Europeanization and convergence 379,
    381–6
  hospital transfer of sentenced prisoners
    188–9
  inquisitorial and adversarial systems
    42–6, 48, 50, 53, 54, 55
  intergovernmental co-operation 92, 104

interrogation process 227–9
investigative process 233–4
Kostovski judgment 295–6
legal safeguards for patients 192–4
mental state relevance at trial 177–8
mental state relevance to sentencing
179–80
mentally disordered offender 171, 173,
174, 186, 191, 197, 198
personality-disordered offenders,
treatment of 187
police detention 252, 257–63, 264
prisoner transfer 366, 369–78
prisoners' rights 342–8, 360, 361
prosecution discretion and accountability
127–30, 139, 140, 142, 147, 148
prosecutor role 143–7
psychiatric institutions 189–90
sentencing practice, policy and discretion
319, 321 n., 322, 323 & n., 324–32
serious case monitoring 240–3
victim protection and compensation
301–10, 313
witnesses 284, 286–8, 290, 291–4,
298 & n., 299, 300
see also diversion; Dutch; Strasbourg
Neto, V. V. 315 n.
new realism 5–6
Newburn, T. 306 n., 312 n.
Nijboer, F. 238 n.
Noaks, L. 231 n.
non-terrorist suspects, detention of 255–7
Norris, C. 232 n., 233 n.
North America 301
Northern Ireland 34, 38, 39, 76, 275 n.,
341 n., 364 n.
police detention 252, 253, 254, 263
see also United Kingdom
Northern Ireland (Emergency Provisions)
Act 34 n., 35, 36, 37
Norway 366, 369
nuclear material 90

offenders 29, 91, 133, 310–12, 369, 374
Official Secrets Act (1920) 290 n.
O'Keefe, D. 99 n., 104 n.
O'Neill, T. P. 302 n.
Oomen, C. P. Chr 328 n.
open justice principle, *see* witnesses
evidence
Opium Act (*Opiumwet*) (1928) 13, 151,
152, 154, 156
oral contest 50–3
Osborn, C. 289 n.
overtredingen, see misdemeanours
Owen, T. 349 n.
Öztürk judgment 8

PACE, *see* Police and Criminal Evidence
Act
Paridaens, D. xii, xix, 363–78
Paris Convention on Extradition (1957) 90,
91
Parliamentary Select Committee 209
Parole Board 27, 32, 187, 188, 357, 358 n.
Passas, N. 114 n.
patients 185, 191–7
Peane, J. 172 n.
penal crisis 21–34
criminal justice reorganization 25–6
imprisonment, movement away from
27–9
policy evolution 33–4
political awareness of criminal justice
29–32
reforming legislation 23–5
penal law 13–17
Penders, L. 306 n.
personality-disordered offenders, treatment
of 186–8
Peter, A. A. G. 2 n., 4
Peters, A. 204 n.
Peyster, C. N. 228 n.
Pharmacy Act (1868) 149 n.
Pithouse, S. 317 n.
Pitts, J. 207 n.
Plotnikoff, J. 360 n.
Pointing, J. 314 n.
police 160, 169
Act (1964) 26
co-operation 101, 102
detention: England and Wales 251–7;
Netherlands 252, 257–63, 264
and diversion mechanisms 135–6
investigations, control of 227–49; *dossier*
importance 234–40; interrogation
process 227–33; investigative process
233–4; judicial monitoring 244–7;
prosecutors and monitoring 243–4;
serious case monitoring 240–3
methods 78
and pre-trial process 46–50
station and vulnerable suspects
protection 172–3
treatment and victim compensation and
protection 304–7
see also Police and Criminal Evidence
Act (PACE) *below*
Police and Criminal Evidence Act (PACE)
30, 37 n.
control of police investigations 227, 228,
230, 231 & n., 232, 233
DNA profiling 268, 274 n., 275 n., 279
inquisitorial and adversarial systems 49,
54

Police and Criminal Evidence Act (PACE) (*cont.*):
mentally disordered offender 172, 173, 174
police detention 251, 253, 255, 256, 257, 263
Police and Criminal Evidence (Northern Ireland) Order (1989) 275 n.
policy evolution 33–4
political:
awareness of criminal justice 29–32
rights and freedoms 84, 325, 347
Pompe, W. P. J. xv, 1, 187, 228 n., 330 n.
Pompidou Group 167 & n.
Poor Prisoners' Defence Act (1930) 25 n.
Portugal 97
powers of arrest 37–8
Powers of the Criminal Courts Act (1973) 182 n.
Prakken, T. 14
Pratt, J. 200 n.
pre-trial 46–50, 76–7, 175–7
presumption of innocence 69
Prevention of Terrorism Act (PTA) 37, 38, 39, 251–7
Principles Act for the Prison System 342, 344, 346
Prior Committee 353 & n.
Prison:
Act 2, 25 & n.–6, 349
(Amendment) Rules (1989) 352 n.
population 342, 348–9
Rules 352, 354, 359
Service 10–12, 19, 349, 350, 351, 353, 355, 359 n.
system 342–3, 344, 346, 349–50
see also prisoners
prisoners:
complaints 344–6, 351–5
repatriation 95, 368, 370 & n.
sentenced 188–9
social contacts outside 345–6, 355
treatment 359
see also prisoners' rights; transfer
prisoners' rights 77, 341–61
England and Wales 348–59
Netherlands 342–8
recognition 359–60
private conduct, criminalization of 76
private life, home and correspondence 76–8
Probation Services 12–13, 131, 203
procedural regulation of laboratories by exclusionary rules of evidence 268–9
proceedings instigation 307–10
proceedings, transfer of 91, 95
proceeds from crime 90–1

prosecution:
monitoring 243–4
victim compensation and protection 304–7
see also Crown Prosecution Service; Director; Dutch; discretion and accountability; public
Prosecution of Offences Act 69, 140, 308
Prosecution Service 146
protection:
child witnesses 296–7
and compensation for victims 301–18; damages and compensation by offenders 310–12; mediation and victim's power to instigate proceedings 307–10; state compensation 312–13; treatment by police, prosecution, and Courts 304–7; welfare services provision 303–4
witnesses 289–94
psychiatric hospital admission and commitment 179 n., 192
PTA, *see* Prevention of Terrorism Act
Public Prosecution Service 8–9, 127, 144, 145 n., 216, 328
Netherlands 7, 8–9 n., 15, 16, 18
see also Dutch
punishment, inhuman and degrading 78–9

racial equality 208
Rassaby, E. 186 n.
Rechter-Commissaris (investigating judge) 234, 239, 240, 241 & n., 242, 243
Recommendation Regulating the Use of Personal Data in the Police Sector 281
Recommendations on the Position of the Victim in the Framework of Criminal Law and Procedure 301
Reed Committee 190
reforming legislation 23–5
Regional Health Authority 182
Reiner, R. 142 n., 204 n.
Remmelink, J. 228 n.
Repatriation of Offenders Act 374
Repatriation of Prisoners Act 95, 368, 370 & n.
Republic of Ireland 98, 224
Research and Planning Unit 162
resocialization 1–3
Richardson, G. 354 n., 357 n.
Richardson, N. 205 n.
right to examine witnesses 288–9, 298–9
right to a fair hearing 65–73
Court, access to 67
criminal charge determination 65–6
disclosure of evidence 70–1
equality of arms 69

hearing within reasonable time 68–9
hearing of witnesses 71–2
independent and impartial tribunal 67–8
interpreters 72–3
legal assistance 70
presumption of innocence 69
right to silence 38
Rijn, A. aan de 327 n.
Riyadh Rules 224 & n.
Road Accident Victims Compensation
    Fund 313
Road Traffic Act (1988) 277 n.
road traffic offenders 91
Roberts, P. 266 n., 272 n.
Robertson, B. 270 n.
Rock, P. 303 n.
Rood-Pijpers, E. 6 n.
Rose, D. 248 n.
Rosett, A. 228 n., 241 n.
Royal Commission 49, 54, 59, 150, 215,
    231 n.
    on Criminal Justice 271, 282 & n.
    DNA profiling 268, 273, 277 n.
Rupprecht, R. 104 n.
Ruter, C. F. 204 n., 239 n.
Rutherford, A. 31 n., 207 n.
Rütter, C. F. 105 n.
Rutter, S. 172 n.

Sagel-Grande, H. I. 324 n.
sanctions 15–17, 19
    alternative 15, 19, 217, 218
    monetary 8
Sanders, A. 131, 132 n., 133, 139, 140 & n.,
    141 & n., 147 n., 148 n., 206 n., 227 n.,
    232 n., 233 n., 235 n., 245 n.
Sanders, L. 128 n.
Scandinavia 90, 321 n.
Scarabrook, J. 141 n.
Scarman, Lord 290
Schaaf, R. W. 301 n., 305 n.
Schengen Agreement xvii, 97–9, 104, 105,
    164, 165, 169, 281
Schutte, J. 204 n.
Schwartz, L. B. 104 n.
Scorer, C. 251 n.
Scotland 69, 275 n., 341 n., 364 n.
Scottish Criminal Justice Act 243 n.
Security Service Act 81
sentenced persons, transfer of 91, 93, 95,
    366
sentenced prisoners and transfer to
    hospital 188–9
sentencing practice, policy and discretion
    319–39
    England and Wales 332–8
    Netherlands 324–32

serious case monitoring 240–3
Sevenster, H. G. 107 n.
Sexual Offences (Amendment) Act (1976)
    22 n.
Shanghai Agreement 150
Shapland, J. 212 n., 304 n., 307 n., 312 n.,
    313 n., 314 & n.
Sharpe, J. A. 27 n., 30 n.
Sherlock, A. xii, xvii, 107–26
silence, *see* right to
Silvis, J. xii, xviii, xix, 129 n., 149–70,
    319–39
Single Convention on Narcotic Drugs
    (1961) 150
Single European Act 96, 97–9
Single European Market 380, 384
Smit, N. W. de 184 n.
Smith, L. J. F. 305 n.
social control increase 17–18
Social Services 203
Spain 97, 375, 376
Sparks, R. 359 n.
Special Hospital Services Authority 191
Special Powers Regulations 34 & n.
spectator violence 92
Spencer, J. R. 266 n., 271 n., 285 & n.
Spencer, S. 251 n.
Spierenburg, P. 5 n.
Spjut, R. J. 35 n.
Standard Minimum Rules for the
    Treatment of Prisoners 359
state compensation 312–13
State Party to the Convention 57
Steenstra, S. 184 n.
Steer 139
Stephen, J. F. 268 n.
Stern, V. 335 n., 350 n., 359 n.
Steventon, B. 271 n.
Stolwijk, S. 204 n.
Straelen, F. W. M. van 328 n.
Strasbourg case law 196
    deprivation of liberty 73–6
    European Convention on Human Rights
    (ECHR) 80, 81
    freedom of speech 79
    mentally disordered offender 191
    in Netherlands and United Kingdom
    65–86; right to a fair hearing
    65–73
    private life, home and correspondence
    76–8
    torture, inhuman and degrading
    punishment 78–9
    see also European Court of Human
    Rights
Strikwerde, J. 328 n.
substantive criminal law 13–14

Summary Jurisdiction (Appeals) Act (1933) 25 n.
Supreme Court:
  control of police investigations 229, 232 n., 239 & n., 246 n.
  drug problem management 163
  European Convention on Human Rights (ECHR) 63, 64, 66, 78
  inquisitorial and adversarial systems 44, 50
  mentally disordered offender 178, 187
  Netherlands 10, 14, 68, 69, 73, 82
  police detention 259 n.
  prisoners' rights 348
  prosecution discretion and accountability 136, 146
  sentencing practice, policy and discretion 323 n., 326, 327 n., 329 n.
  witness evidence 286, 287, 292 n., 296
  see also Dutch
suspected terrorists, detention of 251–5
suspects, vulnerable 172–4
Swart, A. H. J. 63 n., 86 n., 99 n., 296 n., 331 n.
Swart, B. xii, xv–xix, 57–86, 87–106, 220, 235 n., 379–86
Sweden 83, 168, 260, 321, 336, 366, 375, 376
  see also Scandinavia
Switzerland 84 n., 224 & n., 323, 375, 376
Symmons, C. 81 n.

't Hart, A. C. 4 n., 322 n., 324 n.
TAC, see total allowable catches
Tapper, C. 268 n.
Taylor, Lord C. J. 173
Taylor, P. 252 n.
Taylor, R. 336 n., 357 n.
TBS (Terbeschikkingstelling) 17, 197, 198
  mentally disordered offender 179, 180, 183, 184, 186, 191, 193–4
Temkin, J. 306 n.
terrorism 34 n., 91, 93
  suspected 251–5
  see also Prevention of Terrorism Act
Thailand 366, 371 & n., 372
Thomas, D. A. 323 n., 338 n.
'Thurso Boy' incident 26
Tigges, L. C. M. 228 n.
Timmerman, H. 328 n.
Tokyo Rules 223
Tonry, M. 321 n.
torture 78–9, 92
total allowable catches (TAC) 114
Tottenham Three 248 n.

transactie 156 & n., 214, 218, 247, 309 & n., 310, 325, 381
  discretion and accountability in prosecution 135, 136 & n., 137 & n., 138 & n., 143, 146
Transfer of Enforcement of Criminal Judgments Act 369
transfer of prisoners 363–78
  double criminality 372–3
  evaluation 374–8
  Netherlands 369–70, 376
  1983 convention 367–8
  procedural questions 373–4
  treaties 365–6, 370–2
  'United Kingdom 368–9, 375
treaties 41, 365–6, 370–2
  see also Treaty; Union
Treaty on European Union xvi, 97, 99–103, 108, 117, 166
Treaty of Rome xvi, 165
Treverton-Jones, G. 353 n., 356
Trevi 89, 96–7, 101, 167 & n.
trial stage 50–3
trial without jury 36
tribunal, independent and impartial 67–8
Tribunals of Inquiry (Evidence) Act (1921) 26
truth 41–4
Tunstill, J. 305 n.
Turkey 366, 375, 376
Tutt, N. 139 n., 205 n.
Twining, W. 278 n.

Uglow, S. 208 n.
unfitness to plead 177–9, 181 & n.
uniformity of justice 261
Union Treaty 89, 96, 103, 385
United Kingdom:
  control of police investigations 235
  Council of Europe sponsored co-operation 93–5
  criminal justice evolution 21–39; emergency powers 34–9; policy as response to penal crisis 21–34; reported crimes 22
  diversion 130–3, 218, 223
  DNA profiling 271 n., 281 n.
  drug problem management 149–52, 161–5, 168–70
  European Community and criminal law 108, 109, 110 n., 116, 118 n.
  European Convention on Human Rights (ECHR) 57, 58–63, 80, 81, 82, 83, 84
  Europeanization and convergence 379, 381, 382, 383, 384, 385, 386
  inquisitorial and adversarial systems 41, 55

intergovernmental co-operation 92, 97, 98, 104
mentally disordered offender 177, 183, 191, 197
police detention 263
prisoner transfer 368–9, 370–7
prisoners' rights 347, 350
prosecution discretion and accountability 127, 128 & n., 129, 138, 146
sentencing practice, policy and discretion 321 & n.
Strasbourg case law 65–86
victim protection and compensation 302 & n., 303, 309, 310, 312, 315, 317
see also England and Wales; Northern Ireland; Scotland
United Nations 150, 167, 212 n., 221 n., 223 n., 301
Children's Fund 224 n.
Convention Against Illicit Traffic in Narcotic and Psychotropic Drugs (1988) 90, 166
Convention on the Rights of the Child 223, 224 & n.
Declaration of Basic Principles of Justice for Victims of Crime 305
Standard Minimum Rule for the Administration of Juvenile Justice (Beijing Rules) 223, 224 & n.
Standard Minimum Rule on the Prevention of Juvenile Delinquency (Riyadh Rules) 224 & n.
Standard Minimum Rules for Non-Custodial Measures (Tokyo Rules) 223
United States of America 5, 6, 21, 146, 298 n., 301, 381
diversion in juvenile justice 199, 224
DNA profiling 279
drug problem management 168, 169
and European Convention on Human Rights (ECHR) 60, 78, 79, 84
intergovernmental co-operation 93, 103
prisoner transfer 364, 365, 366, 371, 375, 376
prisoners' rights 352
sentencing practice, policy and discretion 321 & n., 322, 330, 331
victim protection and compensation 301, 315 n., 316
Utrecht School 1, 2, 3, 4 & n.

Vaillant Commission 306
Van Bemmelen 1 n.
Van de Bunt, H. G. 236 & n., 245, 246 n., 247 n., 321 n., 322 n.

Van de Pol, U. 292 n.
Van de Wijngaart, G. F. 157
Van der Werff 292 n.
Van Koppen, P. J. 238 n.
van Poelgeest, S. B. ix, xviii, 265–82
Verhey, L. F. M. 281 n.
Versailles Peace Settlement 150
Vervaele, J. A. E. 114 n.
Verwers, C. 217 n.
Victim Support Scheme 303, 304
Victim's Charter 209, 306
victims of crime 302, 304–7
Vienna Convention against Illicit Traffic in Narcotic Drugs and Psychotropic Substances (1988) 150, 168 n.
Vignaux, G. A. 270 n.
Villmoare, E. 315 n.
Vliet, A. van xii–xiii, xviii, 199–226
Vrij 1 n.
vulnerable suspects protection 172–4

Wagenaar, W. A. 238 n.
Wagstaff, A. 158 n., 162 n.
Wales, *see under* England and Wales
Walker, C. 251 n.
Wall, D. 232 n., 257 n.
Waller, L. J. 353, 356 n.
Walsh, D. 252 n.
Walsh, J. J. 270 n.
Wasik, M. 336 n., 357 n.
waste, damage caused by 125 n.
Watkins, L. J. 209
Weijers, I. 2 n.
Weinreb, E. 235 n.
welfare 3–4, 303–4
child 216, 225
Wells, C. 317 n.
Werff, C. van de 328 n.
Westwood, D. 309 n.
Whitaker, B. 159 n.
White Paper 28, 81, 350 n., 351, 353 n.
Crime, Justice, and Protecting the Public 200, 204 n., 212, 336
Custody, Care, and Justice 349 n., 360 n.
White, S. 178 n.
Wigmore, J. H. 285 & n.
Wilberforce, Lord 350
Wilkinson, C. 132 n., 140 n., 205 n., 206 n., 207 n.
Williams, K. S. xiii, xviii, xix, 149–70, 265–82, 301–18
Willis, A. 96 n.
Willmore, C. 266 n., 272 n.
Willmore, J. 304 n.
Wilson, C. 27
Winkel, F. W. xiii, xix, 301–18

witnesses 283–300
  anonymity 292–6, 294–6
  attendance 308 n.
  child witnesses protection 296–7
  hearing of 284–8
  intimidation 289–90
  protection 289–94, 296–7
  right to examine 288–9, 298–9
Woolf, H. 60 n.
Woolf Report 335 n., 349 n., 350 & n.,
  351 & n., 352 n., 353 & n., 354, 355

Working Party on Habitual Drunken
  Offenders (1971) 29
Wright, M. 308 n.

Young, J. xiii, xvii, 34 n., 57–86, 220,
  235 n.
young people, *see* children
Younger, K. 25 & n.

Zander, M. 30 n., 230 n.

Printed in the United Kingdom
by Lightning Source UK Ltd.
124259UK00001B/165/A